W16

*A Directory of
Specialist Crafts
for
Architects and Builders*

A Directory of Specialist Crafts for Architects and Builders

REBECCA J. SMITH

With a Foreword by C. Keith Chapman,
President of the Architects and Surveyors Institute

ROBERT HALE · LONDON

Copyright © Rebecca J. Smith 1990
First published in Great Britain 1990

Robert Hale Limited
Clerkenwell House
Clerkenwell Green
London EC1R 0HT

British Library Cataloguing in Publication Data

Smith, Rebecca
A directory of specialist crafts: for architects and
builders
1. Great Britain. Building restoration industries.
craftsman. Directories
I. Title
338.4'769024

ISBN 0–7090–3934–4

The right of Rebecca J. Smith to be identified as
author of this work has been asserted by her
in accordance with the Copyright, Designs and
Patents Act 1988.

Photoset in Palatino by
Derek Doyle & Associates, Mold, Clwyd
Printed in Great Britain by
St Edmundsbury Press, Bury St Edmunds, Suffolk
Bound by WBC Bookbinders Ltd

Contents

Foreword by C. Keith Chapman — 7
Explanation of Directory — 9
Abbreviations — 13

SKILLS DIRECTORY — 17
DIRECTORY OF FIRMS AND CRAFTSPEOPLE — 127
Associations — 445

Foreword

An important part of the character of Britain is its vast heritage of period buildings and their contents. Magnificently ornate, or beautiful in their simplicity, such buildings may be awe-inspiring or amusingly eccentric, but each is unique, and there must be few of us who have not admired them, and wondered at the work of our forefathers.

As the years pass, and time takes its inevitable toll, more and more of these great buildings need care and attention if they are to survive. As a result this valued heritage is often put at risk through ignorance and bad workmanship. This much-needed directory can do nothing to overcome the latter, but one hopes it might help with the former, for within its pages are listed firms and craftspeople who have spent years learning the time-honoured skills needed to conserve, restore and renovate the irreplaceable.

However, this directory does not deal merely with the heritage of the past: it also hopes to contribute something to the future. In these days of mass-produced goods we should respect artists who have the patience and integrity to create the thoughtfully designed and carefully executed treasures of tomorrow.

With the help of the skilled craftspeople listed in these pages we can preserve the standard of

FOREWORD

workmanship we value so much from the past, and create something new which our children and grandchildren will be able to pause at and admire in the future.

C. Keith Chapman, President of the Architects and Surveyors Institute.

Explanation of Directory

Architects, interior designers and other professionals in the building trade frequently have to employ skilled craftspeople and specialist firms to assist in the conservation and restoration of historic buildings, or to design and construct unique fixtures and fittings. Such firms and craftspeople can be difficult to trace. This Directory lists artists, building professionals, craftspeople and companies experienced in undertaking such work.

The Directory is divided into two sections.

The first section is a directory of SKILLS, which is divided into the main skills and products included in the Directory e.g. Architectural Antiques/Salvage; Carpenters, Joiners and Associated Woodworkers; Ceramic Tiles; Metalworkers.

Each heading is subdivided into more specific skills, and each is allocated a letter e.g.

(a) Conservation
(b) Restoration
(c) Reproduction
(d) Reproduction to match existing
(e) Design to specification/new work

So, if for example you needed to find a craftsperson willing to conserve a piece of cast ironwork, you would look under the heading Metalworkers, find the subheadings Conservation and Cast iron, and note the

EXPLANATION OF DIRECTORY

letters beside each heading (a) and (p). You then search through the list of craftspeople/firms below, and all those with the letters (a) and (p) beside their name/title have stated that they would be willing to consider undertaking such work.

Each craftsperson/firm is listed under their county of origin, with a note of the area within which they are willing to consider working/supplying/fixing, i.e. HC – Home County; HSC – Home and surrounding counties; UK – United Kingdom; EUR – Europe; World – World.

Where a craftsperson has indicated that they would be willing to work in more than one area I have listed the largest area, i.e. if they indicated that they would work throughout their home county, the UK and Europe, I have just noted Europe, as the first two come within that area.

I should point out that although in many cases it is advisable to choose a local firm, in certain categories, such as manufacturers of certain ceramic tiles, it is irrelevant where the company is based, just so long as they produce the work required and will deliver in your area.

When you have selected a craftsperson/firm, turn to the second section, the FIRMS AND CRAFTSPEOPLE, which lists everyone included in the directory in alphabetical order, and work your way through the alphabet until you find the name selected. Each entry is subdivided as follows:

Name/title, Number of trade employees,* Date established*
Description of firm
Address, Telephone number
Apprenticeship, Qualifications, Membership of relevant organizations
Previous commissions which may be of interest*
Any other information which may be relevant

EXPLANATION OF DIRECTORY

Many entries do not include all the above details, simply because not all firms provided full details.

I would like to caution that I can in no way recommend any of the firms included in these pages, and would urge that you take all precautions necessary to ensure that the firm selected produces work that is to your satisfaction.

Everyone's standards of quality are different, and the work produced by a firm can vary depending on experience, the qualifications and amount of supervision, the resources available, and – where larger firms are involved – the experience of their workforce (it has been repeatedly pointed out to me that if a key person retires then the firm's work standards could be affected – for better or worse).

All this should be taken into account before commissioning any work, and it may be wise to check on any subcontractors, where they are employed.

If you are dissatisfied with work done by anyone included in this Directory please get in touch with me; if it is warranted, and if I can confirm that the problem is the craftsperson's/firm's fault, I will omit their details from the next edition of the Directory.

Finally I must thank all the associations, organizations, local authorities and individuals who took the time and trouble to list craftspeople/firms who might wish to be included in the Directory, and gave me many kind words of encouragement; without their help this directory would be half the size, and of far less value. I would especially like to thank A. D. G. Webb, Past Secretary of the former Faculty of Architects and Surveyors, and everyone who gave me support and advice in the Architects and Surveyors Institute.

If you would be interested in being included in subsequent editions of this Directory, or know of anyone who might be interested, please write to the following address, including at least three references from reliable sources.

EXPLANATION OF DIRECTORY

I am particularly interested in hearing from landscape architects experienced in specialist works such as conservation, restoration of historic gardens, Japanese gardens, etc. However I would welcome enquiries from any craftsperson/firm whose work is compatible with the Directory.

    R.J. Smith,
    38 Cedar Walk,
    Acton,
    Sudbury,
    Suffolk CO10 0UW

* Various abbreviations are used throughout the Directory, please see the Abbreviations listed on page 13.

Abbreviations

Authors' Abbreviations

Assoc	Association	CC	County Council
BC	Borough Council	C & Gs	City & Guilds
Brit	British	Co	Company
Cert	Certificate	DC	District Council
Dip	Diploma	inc	including
Empl	Number of trade employees*	Inst	Institute
		M	Member
Eng. Heritage	English Heritage	Nat	National
		Pc	previous commissions
Est	Date established	V & A	Victoria & Albert
Fed	Federation		

* Please note that where a firm/craftsperson has indicated no employees I have entered solo, although the firm may have more than one partner.

Most common abbreviations used for Associations & Organisations

AFGE	Associate Fellow of the Guild of Glass Engravers
AMU	Association of Master Upholsterers
ASI	Architects and Surveyors Institute
BA (Hons)	Batchelor of Arts (Honours)
BABA	British Artist Blacksmiths Association

ABBREVIATIONS

BAFRA	British Antique Furniture Restorers Association
B Arch	Bachelor of Architecture
BDA	British Decorators Association
BEC	Building Employees Confederation
BIM	British Insititute of Management
B Sc	Batchelor of Science
BMGP & BSMGP	British Society of Master Glass Painters
BWPA	British Wood Preservation Association
C Eng	Civil Engineering
CGLI	City and Guilds, London Institute
CIOB	Chartered Institute of Builders
CPA	Craftsmen Potters Association
CSD	Chartered Society of Designers
Dorset MTA	Dorset Master Thatchers Association
DSWA	Dry Stone Walling Association
E Anglian MTA	East Anglian Master Thatchers Association
EASA	Ecclesiastical Architects and Surveyors Association
ECA	Electrical Contractors Association
EIA	Engineering Industries Association
FAS	now ASI
FMB	Federation of Master Builders
GGE & GE	Guild of Glass Engravers
GGF	Glass and Glazing Federation
GMC	Guild of Master Craftsmen
Hants & Wilts MTA	Hampshire and Wiltshire Master Thatchers Assoc
HND	Higher National Diploma
IAAS	Incorporated Association of Architects and Surveyors
IDDA	Interior Decorators and Designers Association
Inst Struct E	Institute of Structural Engineers
LAMS	London Association of Master Stonemasons

ABBREVIATIONS

LAPADA	London and Provincial Antique Dealers Association
LCA	Lead Contractors Association
LDA	Lead Development Association
MTA	Master Thatchers Association
NAFBAE	National Association of Farriers, Blacksmiths and Agricultural Engineers
NCMTA	National Council of Master Thatchers Associations
NFRC	National Federation of Roofing Contractors
NHBF	National House Building Federation
NSMT	National Society of Master Thatchers
Oxon, Berks & Bucks MTA	Oxfordshire, Berkshire and Buckinghamshire Master Thatchers Association
RCA	Royal College of Art
RIAS	Royal Institute of Architects and Surveyors
RIBA	Royal Instititute of British Architects
RICS	Royal Instititute of Chartered Surveyors
RTPI	Royal Town Planners Institute
SD-C	Society of Designer-Craftsmen
SSCR	Scottish Society for Conservation and Restoration
SPAB	Society for the Protection of Ancient Buildings
Suffolk MTA	Suffolk Master Thatchers Association
UKIC	United Kingdom Institute for Conservation
WI	Wood Institute
Wilts & Hants MTA	Wiltshire and Hampshire Master Thatchers Association

Skills

ARCHITECTS

Architects
See PROFESSIONALS

Architectural Antiques/Salvage
See also FIREPLACES; LIGHTING; SANITARY FITTINGS

- (a) Bricks
- (b) Ceramic tiles
- (c) Fireplaces
- (d) Fixtures and fittings
- (e) Flooring materials
- (f) Ironmongery
- (g) Joinery products
- (h) Lighting
- (i) Roofing materials
- (j) Stained glass/general glazing
- (k) Staircases
- (l) Stone ornamentation
- (m) Dismantled Buildings

Avon
'An Englishmans Home' $d f h j k l$ (Local)
Walcot Reclamation Ltd $a b c d e f g h i j k l$ (World)

Clwyd
Main, Michael Ltd $b c d e f g h j k$ (EUR)

Devonshire
Britannia Restoration $d g h m$ (EUR)
Cantabrian Antiques & Architectural Furnishings $d e f j k l m$ (EUR)
Architectural Antiques – André Busek $a b c d e f g h i j k l$ (UK, assist World)

Gloucestershire
Architectural Heritage $e g j l$ (World)
Posterity Architectural Antiques $b c e f j l m$
Stead, Geoffrey $d e g h l m$ (World)

Hampshire
Glover & Stacey Ltd $a b c d e f g h j k l$ (World)

Highland
Old Flame $b c d l m$

SKILLS

Humberside
R & R Reclamation *a c d e f g i j* (UK)

Kent
Frederick's Ltd *b c d e f g h i j k l* (15 mile radius)
Hinsley, T. *i*

London
Chapman, Peter Antiques (LAPADA) *c d h j l* (World)
Hallidays *b c g* (World)
London Architectural Salvage & Supply Co Ltd, The *b c d e f g h j k l m* (World)
Poulter, H. W. & Son *c* (HC)
Townsends *b c d e f g h j k l m*
Whiteway & Waldron Ltd *c d h j k l m* (World)

Lothian
Edinburgh Architectural Salvage *b c d e f g h k l m* (UK)

Merseyside
North-West Architectural Antiques *a b c d e f g h i j k l* (World)

Middlesex
Crowther of Syon Lodge *c f g l*

Northumberland
Railton, Jim *b c d f g h l* (UK)
Smith, John of Alnwick Ltd *g*

Oxfordshire
Hallidays *b c g* (World)
Oxford Architectural Antiques *a b c d e f g h i j k l m* (HC)

Somerset
Crystal Lines *j*
Stuart *c f g h k l*

Surrey
Antique Buildings Ltd *a g i m* (UK)

Sussex
Brighton Architectural Salvage *b c d f h j k m*

ARCHITECTURAL SCULPTURE & CARVING

West Midlands
Conservation Building Products Ltd *a c d e f g i j k l* (World)
Hopkins, Noel Ltd *b e i* (UK)
Reclaimed Building Supplies *a b c d e g i j k l* (World)

Wiltshire
Relic Antiques *b c d f g h j k l m*

Yorkshire, North
Old Oak Beams *c g* (World)
York Handmade Brick Co Ltd, The *a i* (UK)

Yorkshire, West
Bingley Roofing and Stone Centre *a i l* (World)
Thornton, Andy Architectural Antiques & Reproductions *g j*
( ) Lettering in brackets denotes area within which willing to deliver.

Architectural Ceramics, Terracotta & Mouldings
Amberley Chalk Pits
Architectural Antiques
Armitage Brick Ltd
Bridd, Teilsen
Collier, W. H. Ltd
Hathernware Ceramics Ltd
Ibstock Building Products Ltd
Red Bank Manufacturing Co Ltd
Saviac Prototypes
Stonewest Cox
Universal Stone

Architectural Sculpture & Carving
See also ARCHITECTURAL ANTIQUES/SALVAGE; CARPENTERS and JOINERS; CERAMIC ARTISTS; METALWORKERS; MISCELLANEOUS (antique tools); STONE

- (a) Conservation
- (b) Restoration
- (c) Reproduction
- (d) Reproduction to match existing
- (e) Design to client's specification/new work
- (f) Abstract
- (g) Figurative
- (h) Classical
- (i) Carving
- (j) Lettering
- (k) Fountains
- (l) Heraldry
- (m) Plaques
- (n) Statuary
- (o) Brick
- (p) Ceramic
- (q) Cast stone
- (r) GRP/GR gypsum/resins/plaster
- (s) Metal
- (t) Stone
- (u) Wood
- (v) Glass

SKILLS

Avon
Henderson, Michael *i u*
*More, Sarah *b d e j m* (World)

Bedfordshire
*Parker, Keith *b g h j m u*

Buckinghamshire
Davis, Phil & Davis, Mike *a b c d e f g h j m n s* (World)

Cambridgeshire
*Bailey, Keith *e g h i j l o p s t m n* (World)
*Fleuss, Gerald & Gidney, Patricia *j l*
Perkins, Tom *l m* (World)
†Rattee & Kett *a b c d e f g h j k l m n o q t u* (EUR)

Cheshire
Cheshire Reclaimed Building Materials Ltd *a i* (UK)

Clwyd
Jakim Artifacts Ltd *b d e f g h j k n q s* (World)
Roberts, David & Co *a b c d e f g h n s* (supply World)
Winter, S. & J. *b c d e f g h j l m n t* (World)

Cornwall
Prosser, Deborah *e f g j k m p*

Devonshire
Cooper, Harry Associates *d e g m n s* (World)
Read, Herbert Ltd *a b c d e f g h j k l m n p q t u* (World)
Smith, Rodney *b c d e f g h j l m u* (UK, supply World)

Dorset
Bakehouse, The *a b c d e f g h i j k l m n o p q r s t* (World)
Design Sculpture & Crafts *b c d e g h j m n p t* (World)
Saviac Prototypes *j p s* (EUR)
Sells, Jonathan (Jonathan-Living-Stone) *a b c d e f g h j k l m n p t* (World)
Viney, Tony *b d e f g h j k m n t* (World)

Dumfries & Galloway
Solway Studios Ornamental Plasterers *a b c d e g h m n r* (S. W. Scotland, N. E. border)

ARCHITECTURAL SCULPTURE & CARVING

Essex
Authentic Interiors *c d e f g l m r* (World)
Ornamental Stone *c i j k l m n t*

Fife
Regent, Peter *b c d g h i j m n s t u*

Glamorgan, South
Palazzo Ceramics *m n p* (World)

Glamorgan, West
Chatfield, Philip *d e f g h j k l m n t* (UK)

Gloucestershire
Bruno Bronze *a b c d e g h j k m n s*
Fedden, Bryant *f j m o t u* (World)

Hampshire
Morris Singer Foundry Ltd, The *b f g h k n s* (World)
Smith, D. J. *i u* (HC)

Kent
Budd, Kenneth & Budd, Oliver *e f g h j m n r* (World)
Durnan, Nicholas *a b e j m n t* (HC)
Fox, A. E. *b d e g j l m u*
Harrington, Anthony *a b c d e h l m u* (World)
Rust, Michael *b c d e f g h j l u* (World)

Lancashire
McLaughlin, James *b c d g h i j l m t u*

Leicestershire
Tarver, David *a b c d e f g h i k m n s t u* (World)
*Wenham, Martin *c d e f j m u* (supply World)

Lincolnshire
Linley, Beauford D. *b c d e g h l j m n t u* (World)

London
Architectural Ceramics Ltd *b c d e f g h k n p m* (World)
Architectural Sculptors & Lettering *e f g h j l m n o p s t*
Designers Workshop, The *e g l q r s u* (World)
Erskine, Robert Simon *a b c e f g n s t* (World)
HAT Interiors – Veronese *a b c d e g h j l m n r* (World)

SKILLS

*Incisive Letterwork *d e j* (World, outer space!)
Merry-Henriksen, L. *c d f h k m p* (World)
*Nash, John R. *j m t*
Norbury, Jane *e f g h k n p*
Raby, June *e f g h m p* (World)

Lothian
Laing, Charles & Sons Ltd
Munro, Kenny (Environmental Artist) *a b c d e f g h m n r s*

Oxfordshire
†Symm & Co Ltd *a b c d e g h j l m t u*

Norfolk
*Baker, David *g j l m n o p q s t u* (World)
Holgate, David *a b d e f g h j k l m n o r s t u* (World)
Quail, Jane *b g k l m n p t u* (World)

Northumberland
Shaw, John *e j l m t* (World)

Orkney
Pelly, Frances *c d e f g h j m n p t* (World)

Shropshire
†Cunningham, John Patrick *a b c d e f g h i j k l m n o p q r s t* (World)
Woodscape – Frank Triggs *b c d e f g h i m n s u* (EUR)

Somerset
Griffiths, M.E. & S.R. *e m p* (World)
Hayman, Peter *c d e h j l m t* (supply UK, fixing arranged)
Hodgson, John *a b c d e f g j l m n o p q r s t u* (World)
Sloan, Nicholas K. *h j m t* (World)
Smith, Peter E. *a b c d e f g j k l m n s t u* (UK)
Thomason, Philip *b c d e g h n p t* (World)

Strathclyde
Pollock Crafts *b i m u*

Suffolk
Clark, Jean M. *e k p*

Surrey
†Structoplast Contracts Ltd *b n o t* (UK)

ARTISTS, GILDERS, PAINTERS & DECORATORS

Sussex, East
Chatterley, G.E. *b g h i j m n u* (World)
Lewenstein, Eileen *e f p* (UK, possibly world)
*Renton, Michael *e f g j l m n s t u* (UK)

Sussex, West
Skelton, Helen Mary *a b e f g i j m t* (HC)

Tyne & Wear
Albion Ceramics *c h p* (UK)

West Midlands
Crews, Anne *b c d e f g h m n p* (World)
Glass Mountain Studios *b c d e f g h j p* (World)
Majorfax Ltd *a b c d e f g j m n s* (World)

Worcestershire
Weingart, Christel Associates *f g j k v* (World)

Yorkshire, North
Nidd House Antiques *b n s* (EUR)
Reid, Dick *a b c d e g h i j l m n t u* (EUR)

Yorkshire, West
Architectural Sculptors *a b c d e f g h j k l m n q t u* (World)
Robison, J. *e f g h j k m n o p* (World)
*Shield, John *e j l m t* (possibly World)

† Building contractors undertaking all/part such work using their own labour.
* Letter-cutting only.
( ) Lettering in brackets denotes area within which willing to supply/work.

Artists, Gilders, Painters & Decorators
See also FURNITURE – PAINTED: MISCELLANEOUS (antique tools)
- (a) Conservation
- (b) Restoration
- (c) Reproduction to match existing
- (d) Design to client's spec/new work
- (e) Marbling, graining and other broken colour work
- (f) Stencilling
- (g) Trompe l'œil
- (h) Murals
- (i) Fresco
- (j) Water/oil gilding
- (k) Specialist wallcoverings
- (m) High standard signwriting/lettering and/or heraldry

SKILLS

Avon
Chappell, Geoffrey Keith *a b c d e f h* (UK)
Hicks, Anne & Jerry *h* (World)
'Innervisions' *d e f g h k* (EUR)
Moon, Christopher J. *a b c d e f g h j k m* (World)

Buckinghamshire
Hopson, Jock Conservation Service *d j* (UK)

Cambridgeshire
*Rattee & Kett *a b c d e f g j m* (EUR)

Cheshire
Timperley Decorating Co *a b c d e f g h i k m* (EUR)

Devonshire
Grafton/Tilly *c d e f g h i j k m* (UK)
McGarry, M. *b c d e f* (UK)
*Read, Herbert Ltd *a b c d f j m* (World)
Wren Loasby Designs *a b c d f h* (World)

Dorset
Pinhey, Sally *b c g h* (S. England)
Timings, Clare Gilding *a b c j* (HSC)

Essex
Dec-Art *a b c d e f j k* (EUR)
Exclusive Decor *a b c d e f g h i j k m* (HC)
Hare, Peter J. *b c d e f g j k m* (World)
Moore, A. S. *e* (World)
Ornamental Stone *b c d h i j m* (World)

Glamorgan, West
Pease, Steve *b c d e f g h* (World)

Hampshire
Chase Decorating & Artexing *c d e f k* (UK)
Fisher, Graham C. *d e f* (UK)
Galvin, C. T. *a b c d e f j k* (World)

Herefordshire
Richards, Paul & Paule *b c d e f g h* (World)

ARTISTS, GILDERS, PAINTERS & DECORATORS

Hertfordshire
Colour Decor *e f g h i j k*
*Roberts, C. P. Ltd *b c d e f g k* (HC)
Something Special – Sharon Dowie *b c d e f* (UK)

Highland
Roberts, Dr David & Roberts, Marion *b c d e g h j l m* (World)

Humberside
Brown, Dennis *e f g h k* (HC)
Cannons Decorators *b d e i k* (EUR)

Invernesshire
Docherty, Bill *a b c d e f h i k* (World)

Kent
*Cox Brothers *a b c e f j* (UK)
Durtnell, R. & Sons Ltd *a b c d e* (HSC)
Holley & Frost *a b c d e f j k* (World)
*Palmer, A. T. Ltd *a b c d e f g h i j k* (HC, possibly UK)

Lancashire
Hince, David *a b c e k* (World)
*Renofors (UK) Ltd *a b c d e f j k l m* (World)

Leicestershire
Armitage, G. D. (Clock & Belfry Works) Ltd *a b c d j m* (World)

Lincolnshire
Hirst Conservation *a b c f g h i j m* (World)

London
Academy Interiors *a b c d e f g h i j k l m* (World)
Bateman, Jacqueline *c d f g h m*
Binnington, P. & F. *j*
Boulter, Christopher *a b c d g h i* (World)
Brady, Simon *g h i* (World)
Cinalli, Ricardo *h i* (World)
Davies Keeling Trowbridge Ltd *a b c d e f g h i m*
Farlow, Peter *a b c d e f g h i j* (World)
Hampstead Decorative Arts *a b c d e f g h j* (World)
Harding, Pauline *d h* (UK)
Jones, Robert *d e f g h* (World)
Keevil, Maurice E. *a b h* (HC)

SKILLS

Miles, Sally *d g h* (World)
Plant, Timothy *d g h* (World)
Saint George, Amelia *c d f* (World)
Village Decorating Services Ltd *c e f k m* (UK)
Williams, Harold & Sons *c e* (UK)
Wysocka, Sophie *a b h* (World)

Lothian
Harvey, J. T. *a b c d e f g k m* (EUR)
Pryor, Michael McKenzie *c e f g j k m* (World)

Merseyside
Hughes, Harriet Owen *a b h* (World)
Williams, W. R. (PC) Ltd *a b c e f g h k m* (World)

Norfolk
Bateman, Dudley *b c d m* (EUR, possibly World)

Northamptonshire
Decorum *a b c d e f* (EUR)
Jackson, Pat *d f* (World)
Rawlings, Eric *a b c d e f g h i j k m* (World)
Ridgewell, R. B. *e k* (UK)

Northumberland
Bacon & Bacon *a b c h* (World)
Railton, Jim *a b c d e f* (UK)
Shaw, John *j m* (World)

Oxfordshire
Aarran Decorators *c d e f k* (World)
Binyon & MacFarlane Stencils *d f*
*Butler, Arthur Ltd *a b c e f g* (HC)
Heritage Preservation *a b c d e f g h i j k m* (HC)
*Symm & Co Ltd *a b c d e f j k l m* (HC)

Somerset
Garmston, C. *e f k* (HC)
Goldsworthy, Andrew *b c d e h j m* (UK, possibly EUR)
Trenchard, Sara *c d f g h j* (HC)

Staffordshire
Skidmore, D. (Fisher Decorations) *b c d e f j k l* (World)

ARTISTS, GILDERS, PAINTERS & DECORATORS

Strathclyde
Carroll Decorators *b c d e f h i j k m* (UK)
Maclean & Speirs *b d e k m* (EUR)
Miller, John & Sons *c d e f h i j k m* (World)

Suffolk
*Bennett, R. & Snare Ltd *b c e k m* (UK)

Surrey
Masterstroke Interiors (Robert Aldous & Veronica Duggan) *b d e f g h* (UK)
Maybank, L. W. & Sons *e* (UK)

Sussex, East
Optical Illusion Co *c d e f g h j m* (World)

Wiltshire
Designer Decorations (R. W. A. Lever) *a b e f g h k m* (UK)
Taylor, Frederick C. *b c d e f h i j k m* (World)

Worcestershire
Sparrow, Alan Signs *b c d e f h j k m* (UK)

Yorkshire, North
Blades, G. & Sons *a b c e f j k* (UK)
Tabner, Len *d g h* (EUR)

Yorkshire, West
Adamson, Yvonne *a b h i*

* Building contractors undertaking all/part such work using their own labour.
( ) Lettering in brackets denotes area within which willing to work.

Balustrading
See ARCHITECTURAL ANTIQUES/SALVAGE; CARPENTERS & JOINERS; METAL-WORKERS; STONE

Bamboo
See FURNITURE – CANE

Bells
See MISCELLANEOUS (bells)

SKILLS

Bricks – Handmade, Specials, Suitable for Conservation/ Restoration Work and Quality Facings
See also ARCHITECTURAL ANTIQUES/SALVAGE

(a) Reproduced
(b) Reproduced to match existing
(c) Handmade bricks
(d) Embossed bricks
(e) Special moulded feature bricks
(f) Hardwearing bricks for external pavings, paths, etc.
(g) Resistant surface bricks suitable for internal feature work
(h) Period products suitable for restoration/conservation work
(j) Special colours and colour mixes

Cheshire
Station Roofing Supplies Ltd (UK)

Clwyd
Bridd, Teilsen *c d i* (World)

Dorset
Beacon Hill Brick Co Ltd *b c e g j* (UK)
Saviac Prototypes *e i*

Essex
Collier, W. H. Ltd *a b c d e g l* (UK)

Glamorgan, South
Palazzo Ceramics *e g*

Gloucestershire
Coleford Brick & Tile Co Ltd *a b c d e f* (UK)

Hampshire
Michelmersh Brick Co Ltd, The *a b c d e* (UK)

Hertfordshire
Bovingdon Brickworks Ltd *c e* (EUR)

Lancashire
Shaw Hereford Ceramics Group

Leicestershire
Charnwood Forest Brick & Tile Works Ltd *a b c d e*
Hathernware Ceramics Ltd *a b f g h i* (World)
Ibstock Building Products Ltd *a b c d e f h i* (World)

BUILDING CONTRACTORS SPECIALIZING IN CONSERVATION

Shropshire
Blockleys plc *c e f g* (UK)

Staffordshire
Red Bank Manufacturing Co Ltd *a b c d e g h i* (UK)

Suffolk
Bulmer Brick & Tile Co Ltd *b c d e h* (UK)

Sussex, East
Aldershaw Tiles *a b c d e f g h* (World)

Sussex, West
Redland Bricks Ltd *a b c d e f g* (World)

West Midlands
Proctor & Lavender Ltd *b c e f g* (World)

Yorkshire, North
York Handmade Brick Co Ltd, The *c d e f g* (UK)

Yorkshire, West
Armitage Brick Ltd *a b d e f g h* (World)
( ) Lettering in brackets denotes area within which willing to deliver.

Buhl/Boulle work
See FURNITURE RESTORERS

Building Contractors Specializing in Conservation/Restoration Work
See also MISCELLANEOUS (antique tools); SPECIALIST CONTRACTORS
Brickwork
(a) Match to existing
(b) Ornamental
(c) Repairs/restoration
Decorative plasterwork
(d) External
(e) Internal
Ecclesiastical
(f) Interior fittings and finishings
(g) Structure
(h) Carpentry and joinery (high class)

Painting and decorating
(i) General
(j) Specialist finishes
(k) Period timber-framed buildings
Roofing
(l) Clay
(m) Copper
(n) Lead
(o) Slate
(p) Tile
(q) Zinc

SKILLS

Stonework
(r) Clean
(s) Repair/restore

Other
(t) Facade reinstatement/resin injection

Note: letters denote those areas within which the firms are willing to undertake conservation/restoration, general building skills have not been specified.

Avon
Dorothea Restorations Ltd
Poplar Building

Bedfordshire
Endersby, M. E. *a c g h i k l o p* (HC)

Berkshire
Durtnell, R. & Sons *a b c d e f g h i j k l m n o p q r s* (HSC)

Buckinghamshire
Gates Builders Ltd *a b c g h i l o p* (HSC)
RBR Contract Services *c g k s t* (UK)

Cambridgeshire
Coulson & Son Ltd *a b c d e f g h i r s*
Rattee & Kett *a b c f g h i j k m n o p q r s* (EUR)
Sindall Construction Ltd *b c f g h i n o p r s* (UK)
Waymans Ltd *a b c e g h i k l o p s* (HSC)

Cheshire
Dorothea Restorations Ltd
Hopley & Speed *a b c d e h i j l n o p* (UK)
Hughes, William & Son *a b c k o s* (HC)
Mottersheads *f g h k n* (EUR)

Cornwall
Craze, Ken *a b c i l m n o p q r s* (HC)

Devonshire
Dart & Francis *a b c f g h i j k l o p r s* (UK)
Read, Herbert Ltd *c e f h j k r s* (World)

Dorset
Case Construction/Joinery *a f g h* (EUR)
Griffin, A. E. & Son *a b c d e f g h i k n o p r s* (HC)
Saint Blaise Ltd *a b c d e f g h j k l m n o p q r s* (World)

BUILDING CONTRACTORS SPECIALIZING IN CONSERVATION

Essex
Bradford Construction Ltd *a c d e f g h i l n o p* (World)
Willarm Properties Ltd *a b c h k n o p* (HC)

Fife
Watson, W. L. & Sons

Gloucestershire
Jotcham & Kendall Ltd (Glos, Avon, Wilts)

Gwent
Teagle, Alun

Hampshire
Gates Builders Ltd
Kemp, George Stroud & Co Ltd *a b c d e f g h i j k l m n o p q r s* (30 mile radius)
King, Thos. & Sons (Builders) Ltd *a b c e g h i l n o p r s* (HSC)
Moreton & Sons Ltd *a b c d e f g h i j k l m n o p q r s* (HC)
Shering Builders Ltd *a b c f g h i k* (Wilts, Hants, Dorset)

Herefordshire
Capps & Capps Ltd *a b c d e f g h i j l n o p r s*

Hertfordshire
Bickerton & Son Ltd
Roberts, C. P. Special Works Ltd *a b c d e f g h i j m n o p r s* (HC)

Humberside
Quibell & Son (Hull) Ltd *a b c h n o s*

Kent
Babbs, Walter Ltd *a b c d e f g h i l m n o p q r s* (HC)
Barwick, R. J. & Sons *a b c d e f g h i j k l m n o p r s*
Briggs, A. A. & Son *a b c d e g h k* (UK)
Cox Brothers Builders (Kent) Ltd *a c d e h i k n s* (South East)
Crates, J. & Son Ltd *a c f g h i k n o p r s* (HC)
Durling, W. & O. Ltd *a b c i l*
Durtnell, R. & Sons *a b c d e f g h i j k l m n o p q r s* (HSC)
Kier Wallis Ltd
Leighs (Edenbridge) Ltd *a b c d e f g h i k l m n o p* (HC)
Palmer, A. T. Ltd *a b c d e f g h i j k n o p r s* (HC)

SKILLS

Lancashire
Hempstock, J. & Co (Builders) Ltd *a b c d e f g h i l m n o p q r s* (UK)
Renofors UK Ltd *a b c d e g h i j k r s* (World)

Lincolnshire
Bowman, E. & Sons Ltd
Simons Construction Group *a b c d e f g h i j k n r s* (N. Wales and England)

London
Fox, R. & Sons Ltd *c f j r s* (UK)
Grange 81 Ltd
Planned Appearances Ltd *a c e i n* (HC)

Lothian
Campbell & Smith Construction Co Ltd

Norfolk
Anderson, Robin Ltd *a c f g h i*
Bullen, H. & Son Ltd *c h i o p* (N. Norfolk)
Bullock, Malcolm & Son *a c h k o p s* (HC)
Carter, R. G. Harleston *a b c d e f g h i j k l m n o p r s* (HC)
Carter, R. G. Ltd *a b c g h i* (UK)
Mace, William & Bros Ltd *a b c d e f g h i j l m n o p q r s* (HC)

Northamptonshire
Bowman (Oxon) Ltd
Kier Marriott Ltd *a b c d e f g h i j k l m n o p q r s* (HSC)
McCrone, Philip Builders *a b c g h k l n o p r s* (UK)
Wright, K. G. (Builders) Ltd *a b c f g h i k l m n o p r s* (HC)

Northumberland
Coe, E. M. (Builders) *e h n o p r s* (HC)
T K Builders

Nottinghamshire
Fish, Thomas & Sons Ltd *a c f h i* (UK)

Oxfordshire
Alcock, P. R. & Sons Ltd *a c g h i o p s* (HC)
Boshers (Cholsey) Ltd *a b c d e f g h i j k l m n o p q*
Butler, Arthur Ltd *a b c d e f g h i j k l m n o p q r s*
Cherry & Son Ltd *a b c d e f g h i k l m n o p q s* (25 mile radius)
Joslin, J. (Contractors) Ltd

BUILDING CONTRACTORS SPECIALIZING IN CONSERVATION

Symm & Co Ltd *a b c d e f g h i j k m n o p q r s* (possibly UK)

Shropshire
Bridge Farm Renovations *a c e k l n o* (HC)
Cunningham, John Patrick *a b c d e f g h k l m n o p q r s* (World)

Somerset
Knott, R. W. & Sons *c g h i l m n o p r s*
Greens of Wincanton Ltd *a c g h i* (Somerset, Dorset, Wilts)
Webb & Kempf Ltd *a b c d e f g h i j k l m n o p q r s* (World)

Suffolk
Bennett R. & Snare *a b c d e f g i j k l n o p r s* (UK)

Surrey
APA Builders Ltd *c i k*
Planned Appearances Ltd *a c e i n* (HC)
Simms, J. V. (Reigate) Ltd *a c h l* (HC)
Structoplast Contracts Ltd *c g s* (UK)

Sussex, East
Sands, William & Sons *a c g i j k l n o p* (HC)
Paris Construction Ltd *a b c d e f g h i j k l m n o p q r s* (60 mile radius of Brighton)

Sussex, West
Coomber & Son
Fowler Bros (Cowfold Ltd) *a b c f g h k p* (HC)
Longley, James & Co Ltd *a b c d e f g h i k l m n o p q r s* (S. E. England)

Tyne & Wear
Lowry, J. & W. Ltd *a b c d e f g h i j k l m n o p q r s t* (HC)

West Midlands
Beaver Builders *a b c d e k n o p* (UK)
Bird & Hough Ltd
Elvins Construction Co Ltd *a b c f g h k s* (100 mile radius)
Glenwood Ltd *a b c d e f g h i k l m n o p q r s*
Sapcote, William & Sons Ltd *a b c d e f g h i j k l m n o p q r s*

Warwickshire
Parker & Morewood Ltd *h k*

SKILLS

Wiltshire
Butcher, R. & Son
Moulding, R. & Co (Salisbury) *a b c d e f g h i j k l m n o p q r s t* (30 mile radius)
Payne, R. D. Building Services Ltd *a b c d e h i l n o p s* (UK)

Yorkshire, North
Anelay, William Ltd *a b c f g h k m n r s* (UK)
Birch, William & Sons Ltd *a b c d e g k s* (40 mile radius)
Houghton A. E. & Son *a b c f g h k* (World)
( ) Lettering in brackets denotes area within which willing to work.

Cane
See FURNITURE – CANE, RUSH, ETC.

Carpenters, Joiners and Associated Woodworkers Experienced in Conservation/Restoration Work inc. Carvers, Marquetarians and Turners
See also ARCHITECTURAL ANTIQUES; ARCHITECTURAL SCULPTORS; MISCELLANEOUS (tools – antique); STAIRCASES – BESPOKE SPECIALISTS

(a) Design to client's specification/new work
(b) Reproduce to match existing
(c) Will work in situ
(d) Prepare in workshop/install
(e) Period products for restoration/conservation work
(f) Built in fitments to design
(g) Doors
(h) Linenfold panelling
(i) Panelling (general)
(j) Period mouldings
(k) Open timber roofs (e.g. hammer beam trussed)
(l) Other period roofs
(m) Staircases/balustrading
(n) Windows
(o) Carving
(p) Marquetry/inlay
(q) Turning
(r) Ecclesiastical
(s) Simulated wood
(t) Gilding
(u) French Polishing Contractors

Avon
Coles, Robert *a b d g h i j m n o q r* (HC)
Dorothea Restorations Ltd *a b c d f i j k l m n r* (World)
*Henderson, Michael *a b c d o r* (World)
Hosegood, Alan *a b c d f h i j m o p q r* (HC)
Rice & Wallis *b d f g i j m n q* (UK)

Bedfordshire
*Hudson, Thomas *a b d h i o r*
McCalla, G. B. *b c d f g h i m n q* (HC)
*Parker, Keith *a b d o r*

CARPENTERS, JOINERS AND ASSOCIATED WOODWORKERS

Berkshire
Durtnell, R. & Sons *a b c d f g i j k l m n r* (HSC)
Sandleford Woodturning Ltd *a b d j m q*

Buckinghamshire
Preservation Craftsmen Ltd *b c d i j k l m n* (EUR)

Cambridgeshire
†Coulson & Son Ltd *a b c d f g j k m n o q r* (HC)
†Rattee & Kett *a b c d f g h i j k l m n o q r t* (EUR)
†Sindall Joinery *a b c d e f g h i j m n* (UK)

Cheshire
Dorothea Restorations Ltd *a b c d f i j k l m n r* (World)
Mottersheads *a b c d f g h i j k l m n o q r*
Pedley, Nicholas G. *a d f g i n r* (UK)
Riva Design Ltd *a b d f g h i j m n o p q r* (UK)

Clwyd
Morris, Hugh Lloyd *a b c d f g h i j r* (World)

Derbyshire
Hampton, Ralph *a b d f g i n* (EUR, supply USA)

Devonshire
Architectural Woodworkers *a b c d e f g h i j m o p q r*
*Garner, Charles F. *a b d o r* (EUR)
Garvey, William *a c d f g i j m n p q* (World)
Grandisson International *a b g h i j m o r*
*Jewell & Collacott *a b c d e g h i j n o r* (World)
Period Joinery *a b d f h i l m q*
†Read, Herbert Ltd *a b c d e g h i j k l m n o q r* (World)
*Smith, Rodney *a b c d e g h i j k l m o r*

Dorset
Barrington, Michael *a b c d g j n o p q r* (World)
Boyland Joinery Ltd *a b d g i j m n* (Southern & Home Counties)
†Case Construction/Joinery *a b d f g h i j k l m n o q r* (EUR)
†Griffin, A. E. & Son *a b c d f g h i j k l m n o p q r*
Osmington Workshop, The *a b c d f g h i j k l n* (World)
†Saint Blaise Ltd *a b c d f g h i j k l m n o p r* (World)
Truewood Products Ltd *a b g i j m n r* (deliver World)

SKILLS

Dyfed
Bridge, James Ratford *a d f g i j m n* (S. Wales)

Essex
Bradford, H. Construction Ltd *a b d f g i j k l; m n r* (HSC)
*Hilliard, Terence *a b c d h j o* (UK)
J. S. R. Joinery Ltd *a b d g i j m n q* (UK)
McKenzie, W. J. & Son *a b c d f g h i j k l n r*
Mumford & Wood Ltd *n* (UK)
Stock Furniture Restorations Ltd *a b d e f g h i j o p q* (HC)
†Willarm Properties *a b c d f g h i j k l m n* (HC)

Glamorgan, Mid
Jakeway, Kevin Furniture *a b c d e f i m o p q r* (World)

Glamorgan, South
Geometrical Stairbuilding *a b c d f g m n* (World)

Gloucestershire
Clark, Colin *a b c d f g h i j k l m n o q r* (World)
Payne, Geoff & Poole, Robert *q*
Smith & Choyce Ltd *a b d e f g i j k m n q* (HC)

Greater Manchester
Whitehead, John *a b c d h j o q r* (UK)

Gwynedd
*Brown, B. G. *a b g i n o*
Marshall, David *a b c d f g h i j m n o p q r* (EUR)
'One Off Joinery' (M. K. Charlesworth) *a b c d e f g h i j k l m n o q r* (World)

Hampshire
Bagshaw, Guy *a b c d e h i j m o p q r* (EUR)
†Gates Builders Ltd *b c d f g i m n* (HSC)
Kestrel Joinery Co Ltd *a b c d f g h i j k m n o q r* (UK)
†King, Thos & Sons (Builders) Ltd *a b c d f g i j k l m n* (Hants, Wilts, Berks)
Robertson, Gordon E. *a b c d f g h i j k l m n o p q r* (World)
*Smith, D. J. *a b c d n t* (Home Counties)

Herefordshire
†Capps & Capps *a b c d f g i j k l m n o q r* (World)

CARPENTERS, JOINERS AND ASSOCIATED WOODWORKERS

Hertfordshire
†Bickerton, T. A. & Son *b c d f g h i m n* (HC)
†Roberts, C. P. Special Works Ltd *a b c d f g h i j k l m n q r* (HC)

Highland
Beaton, John McW. *a b c d e f g i k l m n o q* (Isle of Skye)

Kent
Ashmore, M. J. *b d g i j m n r* (HC)
†Babbs, Walter Ltd *c d k l r* (HC)
†Cox Brothers *a b c d e g i j k m n q r* (UK)
Durtnell, R. & Sons *a b c d f g i j k l m n r* (HSC)
Fox, A. E. (Woodcarver) *a o r* (UK)
*Harrington, Anthony *a b c d e g h j l m n o r* (World)
*Holman, R. W. *a b d e g h i j o r* (World)
Mounts Hill Woodcraft *a b c d f g h i j k m n o q r* (EUR)
Palmer, A. T. Ltd *a b c d f g h i j k l m n o p q r* (HC)
*Rust, Michael *a b c d e f g h i j k l m n o q r* (World)
Wallis Joinery Ltd *a b d e f g h i j m n o q r* (London & Home Counties)

Lancashire
Jacksons *a b c d e f g i j k m n q r* (World)
†Renofors (UK) Ltd *a b c d f g h i j k l m n q r* (World)
Whittle, D. & Sons (Joiners) Ltd *b c d e f g h i j m n o p q r* (North West)

Leicestershire
Gallier, Paul de *a b c d f g i j k l m n o p q* (EUR)

Lincolnshire
Czajkowski, E. & Son
Hall Marque Designs (W. L. Leggett) *q* (UK)
*Linley, Beauford D. (Sculptor) *a b c d h j o q r* (World)

London
Beadon, J. R. Ltd *u*
Browne Winther & Co Ltd *b j m q*
Constructional Units Ltd *a b c d f g h i j m n o p q r* (UK)
*Griffin & Ashwell *b o*
Hallidays *a b d f i j o* (World)
Hide, W. R. & A. Ltd *b g i j m n o q* (UK)
Higginson, E. A. & Co Ltd *a b d g j m n* (HC)
*K. D. Crafts *a b c j o* (World)
London Door Co, The *a b d g* (HC)
*Ossowski, A. & M. *a b o*

SKILLS

Ott, Max E. Ltd *a b c d e f g h i j n* (World)
*Poole, Phil *a b c d h j o r* (World)
Shield, John *b c d j o r* (World)
*Signmaking Developments (The Lettering Centre) *a b c d o* (EUR)

Lothian
†Campbell & Smith *a b c d f g h i j k l m n p q r* (EUR, possibly World)
Dawson, Ben *a b c d e f g h i j m n o p q r* (World)
*Donaldson, John *a b c d e j n r* (HC)

Middlesex
Grange Restorations *a b c d f h i j o p q r* (HC, consider World)

Norfolk
*Adams, Gerald *b d h o p* (HC)
†Carter, R. G. Ltd *b d f g i j k l m n p q r* (UK)
Dawes, Joe *a b c d f g h i j k m n o p q r* (World)
Smith, Robert *a b c d g m n*
V. & M. Joinery Ltd *a b c d e f g i j m n* (UK)

Northamptonshire
Haynes, Nelson *a b d f i m n* (UK)
Parker, Ron *a b c d e f g h i j m n* (UK)
Thirty-Eight Antiques *i* (World)
†Wright, K. G. (Builders) Ltd *b d f g i j k l m n r* (HC)

Northumberland
*Radcliffe, Louis A. – Bauern Kunst *a b c e h i j m n o r* (EUR)
Railton, Jim *a b c d e f g h i j m n o p q r* (UK)
Smith, John of Alnwick Ltd *a b d e f g h i n o p q* (HC)

Nottinghamshire
†Fish, Thomas & Sons Ltd *a b c d f g i m n r* (UK)
PHI Interiors

Oxfordshire
Hallidays *a b d f i j o* (World)
†Symm & Co Ltd *a b c d f g h i j k l m n o r* (UK & USA)

Shropshire
Ackroyd, D. Ltd *a b c d f g h i j m n o p q r*
†Cunningham, John Patrick *a b c d e g h i j k l m n o p q* (World)
Hazlin of Ludlow Ltd *b d f g i m p r* (World)
*Woodscape (Frank Triggs) *a b c d f g m o q r*

CARPENTERS, JOINERS AND ASSOCIATED WOODWORKERS

Somerset
Gilson, David (Joiner & Turner) *b d f g j n q r* (HC)
Octagon Joinery Ltd *a b c d e f g h i j k l m n o p q r* (World)
Somerset Joinery Ltd *a b d f g i m n r* (UK)
Stuart *a b c d e g h i j k l m n o p q r* (World)
†Webb & Kempf Ltd *a b c e g n o r*

Staffordshire
Linford-Bridgeman Ltd *a b c d e f g h i j k l m n o q r* (UK)
Venables, Henry Ltd *b c d e f g h i j k l m n o r* (EUR)

Strathclyde
Pollock Crafts *n*
Wilson, James & Son (Auchmillan) Ltd *a b c d f g i j l m n q* (30 mile radius)

Suffolk
†Bennett, R. & Snare Ltd *a b c d e f g h i j k l m n o p q r* (UK)
Oak Hall Joinery *a b c d f g h i j k l m n o p q r* (EUR)

Surrey
Glover & Stacey *a b d f g i j m n o q*
Oakwood Joinery *b c d e f g i j m n* (HC)

Sussex, East
Blakeley, Sebastian *a b c d f o q* (World)
*Chatterley, G. E. *o* (World)
E. & I. Furniture Makers *a b c d e g i m p* (UK)
Herriott, M. J. *a b c d e h i j m n o p q r* (World)
Manning, W. J. *b c d h i j o p q r* (HC)

Sussex, West
Amberley Chalk Pits Museum
Bilsham Joinery Works *a b d f g i j m n r* (HC)
*Brown, S. F. & Sons *a b c d f g h i j m o r* (UK)
Castle Crafts/Castle Construction *a b c d f g i j l m n o q* (EUR)
Coomber & Son
†Longley, James Joinery *a b c d e f g h i j m n o p q r* (EUR)
Parker, Geo. (Joinery) Ltd *b d e f g i m* (London & South East)
Richard Joinery Ltd *a b c d f g h i j k l m n o p q* (UK, possibly World)

Tyne & Wear
†Lowry, J. & W. Ltd *a b c d e f g h i j k l m n o q r* (HC)

SKILLS

West Midlands
†Bird & Hough Ltd *b c d f g h i j k l m n o q r* (UK)
†Glenwood Ltd *a b c d f g h i j k l m n r* (UK, possibly World)
Kentel Joinery Ltd *b f g i j n* (UK)

Wiltshire
*Barberton, Nick *o q*
Butcher, R. & Son *b c d e f g h i j k l m n q* (HC)
*Harrison, A. E. & Son *a b c e h i p r*
Knowles, B. J. *a b c d f g i j k l m n o q r* (HC)

Worcestershire
Malvern Studios *a b c d i j o p q r* (UK)
*Tyler, Roger *a b c d e o q* (World)

Yorkshire, North
Dent, Robert & Son Ltd *b c d f g i j l m n r* (EUR)
Freeborn, E. J. & Son *a b c d e g h i n o p q* (UK)
†Houghton, A. E. & Son Ltd *a b c d e f g h i j k l m n o p q r* (World)
Jeffray, Albert *b d g h i o q r*
Old Oak Beams
*Reid, Dick *a b c d f g h i j m o q r* (EUR)
Thompson's, Robert Craftsmen Ltd *a d f g h i m o r* (World)

Yorkshire, South
Dixon, J. (Joinery) Ltd *a b n* (UK)

Yorkshire, West
Brunavs, L. & Son *b h m o q*
Conroy & Booth Group *a b c d f g i j m n* (UK)
Oakleaf Reproductions *a b h i j k s*
Ryan, John (J. & J. Manufacturing) *a b c d f g h i j k l m n o q r* (World)
Taylor, J. W. Ltd *a b c d f g i j k l m n r* (HC)
Vickerman, E. W. & Sons *a b c d e f g h i j o p q r* (HC)
†Building contractors undertaking this work using all or part of their own labour force.
* Only undertake carving or marquetry/inlay work.
( ) Lettering in brackets denotes area within which willing to work.

Carpets
See FLOORCOVERINGS

Carvers
See CARPENTERS, JOINERS AND ASSOCIATED WOODWORKERS

CERAMIC TILES

Castings
See ARCHITECTURAL SCULPTURE; METALWORKERS

Ceramic Artists
WILLING TO MAKE ALMOST ANYTHING IN THIS MEDIA
Palazzo Ceramics
Saviac Prototypes
Joslin, Tony

Ceramic Tiles
CONSERVED/RESTORED AND PRODUCED TO SPECIFICATION INC. MODERN WORK
See also ARCHITECTURAL ANTIQUES/SALVAGE; CERAMIC ARTISTS

(a) Conservation
(b) Restoration
(c) Reproduction to match existing
(d) General reproduction
(e) Holds stocks of original tiles
(f) Design to client's specification/new work
(g) Coloured to specification
(h) Hand-painted
(i) Hand-printed
(j) Silk-screened
(k) Airbrushed
(l) Embossed tiles
(m) Encaustic tiles
(n) Majolica
(o) Terracotta
(p) Tile murals
(q) Lustreware/enamelled
(r) Mathematical tiles
(s) Delft tiles

Avon
Tahla Designs *d e f g i j o*

Berkshire
Simanyi Ceramics *f h l n o* (supply World)

Buckinghamshire
'Basia' *e f h p* (World)

Central
Delftfield Co & Onslow Services *a b c d e f g h l m n o p r s* (supply World)

Clwyd
Bridd, Teilsen *d f g h i l m n o* (supply World)

Cornwall
Godfrey, Joan *e f g h l n o* (HC)
Prosser, Deborah *e f g h l n o* (supply World)

SKILLS

Cumbria
Berkowitz, Maggie Angus Tiles *e f g h n o* (World)

Devonshire
Brown, Sandy *h*

Dorset
Bakehouse, The *a b c h l m n o p* (World)
Saviac Prototypes – David Ballantyne *c d f g h l m n o* (supply EUR)

Dumfries and Galloway
Kirkland Tiles *a b c d e f g h n* (EUR)

Fife
Fraser, Ian *d f* (supply UK)

Glamorgan, South
Palazzo Ceramics – Nancy Pickard *d e f g h i j l m n o p* (World)

Gloucestershire
Prestbury Pottery *c e f h i l m n o* (World)
Zschock, Kerry von *h n*

Gwent
Hamer, Frank *f* (UK)

Kent
Robus, Clive & Rosemary – Acrise Pottery *a f h n o p* (UK)

Lancashire
Majolica Works *h n p*
Shaw Hereford Ceramics Group *a b c d f g h i j l n o* (supply World)

Lincolnshire
Hirst Conservation *a b* (World)

London
Ceramique Internationale Ltd *c d h l m n o* (supply World)
Greeves, Eleanor *f i j* (supply UK)
Harding Restoration *b c g h k n*
Hillfield Studios Ltd *d f g h* (World)
Langley London Ltd *e f h j p* (supply World)
Moore, Jane *c d f g j n p* (World)
Paris Ceramics *b c f h m n o*
Purbeck Decorative Tile Co *b c d f g h i j k l n o* (supply World)
Raymond, Ginny *c d f g h j*

CERAMIC TILES

Rosenthal, Maria *d e f g h l o* (World)
Simpson, W. B. & Sons Ltd *a b c d f j l m n o p* (HC)
World's End Tiles *f g h i j o* (supply UK)

Lothian
Averbuch, Shaeron *f g h k l n o* (World)
Edinburgh Ceramics *c d f g h i j k l m n o p* (supply World)

Northamptonshire
Mabelson, Gus *c d f h j l o* (UK)

Oxfordshire
Fired Earth *h m o* (supply UK)

Shropshire
Burgess, John & Co *c d f g h i j k l m n o* (supply World)
Decorative Tile Works, The *a b c d e f g h i j l n* (UK)
Heritage Tile Conservation Ltd *a b c d e f g h i j k l m n o*

Somerset
Hodgson, John *a b c l m o p* (World)
Threlfall, Philippa & Collins, Kennedy *f l o* (World)
Stuart *d*

Staffordshire
Griffiths, M. E. & S. R. *o* (supply World)
Johnson, H. & R. Tiles Ltd *b c d f g h i j l m n* (supply World)
Smith, H. & E. Ltd *b c d e f g h i j l n o* (supply World)

Sussex, East
Aldershaw Tiles *b c d f g o r* (supply World)
Angus Designs – Diana Hall *f i j m* (supply World)
Brandis, Marion *c d f g h i j n o p*
Rye Tiles/Rye Pottery *e f g h i j k n* (supply World)

Sussex, West
Southwell, Sheila Studios *b c d f h* (World)

Tyne & Wear
Albion Ceramics *d f g h i l n o p* (supply UK)

West Midlands
Crews, Anne *b c d f g h i j l n o p* (World)
Glass Mountain Studios *a b c d f g h j p* (World)

Yorkshire, North
Roberts, R. E. & N. M. *b c d h i j l n* (World)

SKILLS

York Handmade Brick Co Ltd, The *o*

Yorkshire, West
Taylor, Sutton Ceramics *f h i j k q* (supply World)
( ) Lettering in brackets denotes area within which willing to fix/supply unless otherwise specified, i.e. (supply World) indicates they are unwilling to fix throughout the world.

Chandeliers
See LIGHTING

China, Porcelain and Pottery Ornaments
See MISCELLANEOUS (china...)

Clock Restoration (Not Public or Turret)
See MISCELLANEOUS (clock restoration...)

Clocks – Public, Turret, Etc
See TURRET CLOCKS/AUTOMATIA

Conservatories – Made to Specification
See MISCELLANEOUS (conservatories...)

Curtains, Drapes and Tails, Pelmets and Swags
See MISCELLANEOUS (curtains)

Damp Proofing
See SPECIALIST CONTRACTORS

Decorators
See ARTISTS

Delft Tiles
See ARCHITECTURAL ANTIQUES/SALVAGE; CERAMIC TILES

Dismantled Buildings
See ARCHITECTURAL ANTIQUES/SALVAGE

Door Furniture – Period
See ARCHITECTURAL ANTIQUES/SALVAGE; CARPENTERS, JOINERS; CERAMIC ARTISTS; METALWORKERS; MISCELLANEOUS (door furniture...)

Doors
See ARCHITECTURAL ANTIQUES/SALVAGE; CARPENTERS, JOINERS

FABRIC AND SOFT FURNISHINGS

Dry Stone Walling
See STONE

Electrical Switches – Period
See MISCELLANEOUS (electrical switches)

Enamelled Glass
See GLASS – DECORATIVE FINISHES

Encaustic Tiles
See ARCHITECTURAL ANTIQUES/SALVAGE; CERAMIC TILES

Engraved Glass
See GLASS – DECORATIVE FINISHES

Etched Glass
See GLASS – DECORATIVE FINISHES

Fabric and Soft Furnishings Conserved, Restored, Designer-Makers
See also WALLHANGINGS/TAPESTRIES; FLOORCOVERINGS; MISCELLANEOUS (curtains, drapes; petit point seating; trimmings; yarns)

- *(a)* Conservation
- *(b)* Restoration
- *(c)* Reproduction to match existing
- *(d)* General reproduction
- *(e)* Design to client's specification/new work
- *(f)* Hand-painted
- *(g)* Hand-printed
- *(h)* Hand-woven
- *(i)* Silk
- *(j)* Cotton
- *(k)* Linen
- *(l)* Wool
- *(m)* Synthetics
- *(n)* Mixed fibres

Cleveland
Carr, Myrna *e f g h i j k l m n* (World)

Derbyshire
Hodgson, Sally *e g h i j l m n o* (World)

Devonshire
Johns, Pat *e h i l n* (World)
Vivian, Sarah *e f h i j k l n*
Wren Loasby Designs *a b c d e f i j k m n* (World)

Dorset
Sue's Sews *c d e f i j k n* (World)

SKILLS

Durham
Picktree Upholstery Fabrics *c d e h i j k l m n* (EUR)

Dyfed
Griffiths, H. & Son (Melin Tregwynt) *e l* (World)
Weatherhead, Martin & Nina *c d e h i j k l n* (World)

Essex
Marbling Inc *c e f g i j k n* (World)

Gloucestershire
Campion, Pam *a b i j k l* (HC)
Lippiatt, Liz *g i j k l* (UK)

Greater Manchester
Brown, John Armstrong Ltd *c d e g i j* (World)

Hampshire
K. A. B. Textile Designs *c e g h i l* (World)

Lincolnshire
Timberland Art & Design

London
Bentley & Spens *c e f g i j k l* (World)
Edwards, Jay *e h i j k l n* (HC)
Greaves-Lord, Sally *f g i* (UK)
Jowitt, Janet *a b* (World)
Nix, Annette *g* (World)
Percheron, H. A. Ltd *c d e h i j k l m n* (UK)
Raymond, Ginny *e* (HC)
Saint George, Amelia *c e f g h i j k l m n* (World)
Stride, Christina *e f g i j k l m* (World)
Szell, Michael Ltd *c e g i j n* (World)
Textile Conservation Studio/Ksynia Marko *a* (World)

Middlesex
Custom Designed Prints *e g i j k* (EUR & USA)

Norfolk
Grace, Carole *e h i j k l m n* (UK)

Northamptonshire
Jackson, Pat Stencil Interiors *c d e i j k*

FIREPLACES, PERIOD – REPRODUCTION AND ANTIQUE

Somerset
Stuart *c d e i j k l n* (World)

Yorkshire, West
Cooks Mills (Bradford) Ltd *c d e i j k l m n* (World)
( ) Lettering in brackets denotes area within which willing to deliver.

Fanlights
See MISCELLANEOUS (fanlights)

Fibrous Plasterwork
See PLASTERWORK

Fireplaces, Period – Reproduction and Antique
See also ARCHITECTURAL ANTIQUES/SALVAGE; STONE; CARPENTERS AND JOINERS; CERAMIC ARTISTS; CERAMIC TILES (for inserts); METAL

- (*a*) Conservation
- (*b*) Restoration
- (*c*) Reproduction
- (*d*) Willing to work in situ
- (*e*) Inglenook
- (*f*) Pre 16th century
- (*g*) 17th century
- (*h*) 18th century
- (*i*) 19th century
- (*j*) 20th century
- (*k*) Adam or similar style work
- (*l*) Marble
- (*m*) Stone
- (*n*) Brick
- (*o*) Terrazzo/mosaic
- (*p*) Ceramic/terracotta/porcelain, etc.
- (*q*) Wood
- (*r*) Ornamental plaster
- (*s*) Metal/cast iron
- (*t*) Consultancy firm
- (*u*) Scagliola
- (*v*) Inlays for period reproduction surrounds

Berkshire
Fireplace (Hungerford) Ltd, The *b c e h i j k l m*

Devonshire
Architectural Woodworkers *b c g h i j k l m p q* (HC arrange World)
Exeter Marble & Slate Co *b c k l* (World)
Taylor, Brian Antiques & Fireplace Centre *h i j k*

Dorset
Viney, Tony *b c d e h i j l m* (World)

Essex
Firestyle *a b c d e f g h i j k l m n q* (World)
MW Mouldings (London) Ltd *k r* (HC)

SKILLS

Gloucestershire
Architectural Mouldings Ltd *r*

Grampian
Moray Stone Cutters *a b c k m* (UK)

Highland
Old Flame (World)

Leicestershire
Britain's Heritage *b c f i j k l q t*

London
Acquisitions (Fireplaces) Ltd *c f i j k l p q*
Architectural Antiques *a b c d f i j k l m r* (UK)
Capital Marble *s*
Fairfax *a b c e f g h i j m q s* (Locally)
Grate Expectations *a b c g h i j k l q s* (UK)
Kerley, Richard *b c f g h i j k q* (Painted and Gilded)
Knights of London *b d e f g h i k l m n q* (World)
Poulter, H. W. & Son *b h i l q* (HC)
Scallywag *b c h i j q* (World)
Townsends *b c d*

Lothian
Edinburgh Architectural Salvage *h i j l p q* (HC)
Merriman, R. T. *a b c d j k q* (UK)
Pritchard, Hugh (Stonemasons) Ltd *l m* (HC)

Merseyside
Phoenix Fireplaces *b c d i j k q s* (North West)

Northamptonshire
Thirty-Eight Antiques *k l* (World)

Northumberland
Railton, Jim *a b c d e f g h i j k l m q* (UK)

Oxfordshire
Hallidays *c h i k l p q* (World)
*Symm & Co Ltd *a b c d f g h i j k n q* (HC, supply World)

Somerset
Poirrier, Bill

50

FLOORCOVERINGS

Staffordshire
Heritage Furniture Ltd *c h i j k l q*

Strathclyde
Gibson & Goold Ltd *b l m q* (HC)

Sussex, East
Chatterley, G. E. *b r* (World)
Herriott, M. J. *a b c d h k q*
Ripley, Mark *c* (firebacks, etc.)

Sussex, West
Brown, S. F. & Son (Architectural Woodcarvers) *b c h i j k l r* (UK)

Tyne & Wear
Albion Ceramics *c i j k p* (UK)

West Midlands
Allied Guilds *a b c d f g h i j k r* (UK)

Yorkshire, North
Aagaad, Robert Ltd *a b c d f h i j k l q r* (EUR)
Nidd House Antiques *a b c d e f g h i j l m o q s* (EUR)
Roberts, R. E. & N. M. *b c d e h i j k l n p q* (World)

Yorkshire, West
Scagliola Studio (Michael Koumbouzis) *a b c d f g h i j k l o* (World)

Wiltshire
Fairfax *a b c e f g h i j m q s* (Locally)

Worcestershire
Tyler, Roger *v*
* Building contractor.
( ) Lettering in brackets denotes area within which willing to deliver.

Floorcoverings
- (a) Conservation
- (b) Restoration
- (c) Design to client's specification/new work
- (d) Hand-woven
- (e) Hand-tufted
- (f) Tapestry/needlepoint
- (g) Coloured to client's specification
- (h) Vinyl
- (i) Rush, seagrass, sisal, etc.
- (j) Willing to install
- (k) Rugs only
- (m) Oriental
- (n) Cleaning
- (o) Reproducion
- (p) Linoleum
- (q) Carpet broker

SKILLS

Cheshire
'Cheshire Wallhangings' *c d e f g k* (World)

Cornwall
Beswick, Thelma *d f j*

Cumbria
Foster, Susan *d g k* (World)
Steinbugler, C. J. *b g*

Devonshire
Underfoot Rugs *c e g j k*

Dorset
Green, Dr Toby *a b d e* (World)

Dyfed
Weatherhead, Martin & Nina *c d g j k* (World)

Essex
Collingwood, Peter *c d g j k* (World)

Gloucestershire
Pride, Eric *b d f k*

Herefordshire
Oates, Roger Design Associates *c d e g j* (supply World)

Kent
Pantiles Oriental Carpets *a b d e f m* (HC)

Lancashire
Acorn Mills *c g j o* (UK)
Burgoyne, Elizabeth *c e g j k* (World)

Lincolnshire
Timberland Art & Design *c d e f g j k* (World)

London
Anglo Persian Carpet Co *a b d e f j m n* (World)
Behar Profix Ltd *a b c d e f j* (UK)
Bohun & Busbridge *a b c d e f g j k*
Bosly, Caroline *b j k m q*
Crucial Trading Ltd *i*
Edwards, Jay *c d g k* (HC)

FLOORCOVERINGS

Harrington, Celia *c e g k* (World)
Jowitt, Janet *a b* (World)
Moncur, Jennie *c e g h j p* (World)
Nix, Annette *c e g j* (World)
Preston, V. *c e g j* (World)
Saint George, Amelia *c f g* (World)
Talar Carpet Repairs (Oriental) *b f m* (World)
Textile Conservation Studio/Ksynia Marko *a*

Lothian
Edinburgh Tapestry Co Ltd *c e* (World)
Martin & Frost *a b c d g h j* (UK)

Merseyside
North of England Carpet Cleaning Co Ltd *a b n* (UK)

Northumberland
Hind, Don *c e g j* (EUR)

Oxfordshire
Steeles Carpets *g* (supply World)

Somerset
Lewis, Michael & Amanda *a b d k* (World)
Osborne, Angela *a b c d e f m* (UK)

Staffordshire
Criss Cross Textiles (Mrs Joanne K. Weeks) *d* (World)

Suffolk
Hopkins, Jan *c d k* (World)
Toulson, Mary Jane *c d e g j k* (World)
Waveney Apple Growers Ltd *i* (World)

Sussex, East
Fell, Anita – A. F. Designs *c g k* (UK)

Tayside
Robertson & Cox *a b k* (HC)

Warwickshire
Wright, Susan *c d g* (UK)

West Midlands
Pearson, Cynthia *c f g j k* (World)

SKILLS

Yorkshire, South
Franklin, W. E. (Sheffield) Ltd *a b c d e* (UK)

Yorkshire, West
Atelier Interiors *c d e g j* (World)
Avena Carpets Ltd *c g*
Beddows, Terry *c d e f g j* (World)
Dorrien, Lynne *c e g j* (World)
( ) Lettering in brackets denotes area within which willing to work/deliver.

Fountains
See ARCHITECTURAL ANTIQUES/SALVAGE; ARCHITECTURAL SCULPTURE; CERAMIC ARTISTS; METALWORKERS; STONE

Frame Restoration/Gilding
See MISCELLANEOUS (frame restoration/gilding)

Fresco Artists, Conservators and Restorers
See ARTISTS

Furniture – Cane, Rush, Etc
See also ASSOCIATIONS (THE BASKETMAKERS ASSOCIATION)

- (a) Cane
- (b) Rush
- (c) Willow/willow skeined seating
- (d) Ratten
- (e) Seagrass
- (f) Bamboo
- (g) Bergere
- (h) Fibre/synthetic rush
- (i) Cord/thong/string, etc.
- (k) Restoration of frames, etc.

Berkshire
Pilkington, Sheelagh *a g*

Buckinghamshire
Urch, Colin J. *a b e*
Wycombe Cane & Rush Works *a b c d e g k*

Cambridgeshire
Cladgild Ltd *a b c d e f g*
Doddington House Antiques (B. A. & L. Frankland) *a b e*

Derbyshire
Gilbert, Joan *a b d e g*

FURNITURE – CANE, RUSH, ETC

Devonshire
Cane Corner (Brigette L. Stone) *a b d e g*
Grandisson International *d g*
Homewood, Joan *a b g*

Dorset
Broadwindsor Chairs & Crafts *a b e f*
Design in Cane *a b c d e f g*

Gloucestershire
Bawden, Keith *a b*
Payne, Geoff & Poole, Robert *b*
Spriggs, Paul *b e*
Stewart, Angus *a*

Grampian
Homecraft Dyce *a b c d e f*

Greater Manchester
Whitehead, John *a b*

Hertfordshire
Cane Smiths, The *a e g*
Sherman, Jackie *a b c d e f g i*

Humberside
Dunn, Martin H. *a*

Kent
Arbus, David *d*
Holdstock, Ricky *a b d e g i*

Leicestershire
Littlewood, Margaret *a b*

Lincolnshire
Cane & Rush (Harriet Bisson) *a b c d e g h i*

London
Ballybeg Restorations *a b*
Moore, E. T. *a b g*
Pritchard, I. & P. *a b d e g i*

SKILLS

Lothian
Trist, William & McBain, Andrew *a b*

Merseyside
Seralian, H. N. *a b e g k*

Norfolk
Leckie, Mona *a b c d e g*

Nottinghamshire
Barrows, T. S. & Son *a b*

Oxfordshire
Chairperson, The (Mr Hilary B. Melling) *a b*
Country Chairmen *a b e g k*

Somerset
Baker, M. E. *a*
Geers, Philip *a b d e g i k*
Vowles, Mrs N. *a g*

Staffordshire
Stoke on Trent Workshops for the Blind *a b*

Suffolk
Usher, Jean *a e g*
Trayler, K. J. *a b e g*

Surrey
Dodd, P. *a b d e g h*

Wiltshire
Chairpersons of Marshfield *a b c d e f g i k*
Restorations Unlimited *a b*

Furniture – Painted, Lacquered, Marbled, Gilded, etc.
See also ARTISTS
- *(a)* Conservation
- *(b)* Restoration
- *(c)* Reproduction to match existing
- *(d)* General reproduction
- *(e)* Will design to client's specification
- *(f)* Marbling
- *(g)* Graining
- *(h)* Gilding
- *(i)* Stencilling
- *(j)* Lacquerwork
- *(k)* Painted to client's specification
- *(l)* Japanning
- *(m)* Scagliola

FURNITURE – PAINTED, LACQUERED, ETC

Buckinghamshire
Hopson, Jock Conservation Service *a b c e h* (also carving)

Cheshire
Riva Design Ltd *m* (UK)

Devonshire
Cobb, Clive & Lesley *b c e j*
Coldrey Furniture *e f*
Grafton/Tilly Fine Antique Restoration *a b c e f g h i j*
Hunter, Lavinia *a b c d e h*
Wren Loasby Designs *a b c d e i*

Dorset
Barrington, Michael *b h j*

Essex
Forge Studio Workshops *b j*

Gloucestershire
GMS Restorations *a b c e h*
Harper, Paul (World)

Herefordshire
Richards, Paul & Paule Decorative Painters *b e j*

Kent
Caudell Restorations *j*

London
Academy Interiors
Binnington, P. & F. *a b c e f g h i j l*
Jones, Robert *e f i*
Kerley, Richard *a b c h*

Middlesex
Dudman, Reginald W. *a b f g h j*
Grange Restorations (Michael Nickson) *a b c d h j*

Northamptonshire
Jackson, Pat *c d e i*
Thirty-Eight Antiques Ltd *k*

SKILLS

Northumberland
Railton, Jim *a b c d e f g h i*

Oxfordshire
Binyon & MacFarlane *e i*

Somerset
Trenchard, Sara *a b c h i j*

Suffolk
Usher, Jean *b h*

Surrey
Hearn-Cooper Ltd *a b j*

Wiltshire
Factory *c e j*
Taylor, Frederick *c*

Yorkshire, West
Scagliola Studio (Michael Koumbouzis) *m* (World)

Furniture Restoration Materials
See MISCELLANEOUS (furniture restoration materials)

Furniture Restorers and Bespoke Furniture Designer/Makers
See also CARPENTERS, JOINERS (built in furniture, marquetry, carving), FURNITURE – CANE, RUSH ETC.; FURNITURE – PAINTED; METALWORKERS; MISCELLANEOUS (antique tools); STONE

(a) Conservation
(b) Restoration
(c) Reproduction to match existing
(d) General reproduction
(e) Design to client's specification/new work
(f) Ecclesiastical
(g) Upholstery
(gg) Handmade upholstery
(h) Marquetry/inlaid work
(i) Buhl/Boulle work
(j) General brass inlay
(k) Carving
(l) Turning
(m) French polishing
(n) Leather lining
(o) Gilding
(p) Contemporary
(q) Hardwoods
(r) Softwoods
(t) Metal
(u) Plastic
(v) Glass
(w) Leather upholstery, coloured

Avon
Abbott, Mike *b c d e l q* (EUR)

FURNITURE RESTORERS, DESIGNER/MAKERS

Bastex *b d g gg* (HC)
Coles, Robert *a e f l p q s*
Dewey, Timothy H. *b g h j k l m*
Henderson, Michael *a b c e f k p q r* (World)
Hosegood, Alan *a b c e f h i j k l m n p q r s*
Jefferies, Michael *g gg*
Ross, Alan *b c e l m q r s* (HC)
Starling, R. & R. *c d e f h q s* (UK)
Sutton, Hazel *b gg*

Bedfordshire
*Elegance Restored *a b c d e f g* (UK)
Hudson, Thomas *a b c e f k p q*
Urch, Colin J. *a b c d e f g h j k l m n p q r s t* (EUR)

Berkshire
Ashley Antiques/Furniture *b c d e f h i j k l m n q r* (World)
Havers, Hamilton *a b h i j m s* (arrange World)

Buckinghamshire
Browns of West Wycombe *b c e g h i j k l m n o p q r s* (World)
Christmas, Jack *e f l p q s t v* (UK)
Williamson, Rupert *e f g h l p q r s*
Wycombe Cane & Rush Works *b gg m* (HC)

Cambridgeshire
Barnes, Graham *a b c d e f g h i j k l m n o q r s* (HC)
Euroom International (UK) Ltd *a b c d e f g h k l m n o q r s* (World)

Channel Islands
Guernsey Woodcarvers *b c e f h k l m q r s* (World)

Cheshire
Archer, Roy *b e f p q s* (World)
Old Bakery Antique Restoration Co, The *a b c q r s* (World)
Olson, Garry & Bell, David *e f h j l m p q* (UK)
Pedley, Nicholas G. *b c d e f p q r* (World)
Riva Design Ltd *b c d e f h j k l m o p q r s v* (UK)
Robertson, Iain *e p q r* (HC)
Syson, Leslie *b e f h j l m q s* (arrange World)

Cornwall
†Eke, Roger & Son *b c k o* (World)
Stanton, Peter *a b c f g h j k l m n q r s t* (EUR)

SKILLS

Tudor Rose Restorations *b c d e g h j k l m n o q r s*

Cumbria
Hall, Peter & Son *a b c d e f g h i j k l m n o p q s*
Laval, Ian *d e f p q s* (World)

Derbyshire
Hampton, Ralph *c d e f q r* (EUR)
Lawton Andrew *e f h p q r v* (World)

Devonshire
Ashburton Upholstery *a b c d e f g gg l m n p q r t u* (World)
Bellchambers, James *a b c f h i k l m n p q r s t* (HC)
Coldrey Furniture *e f j n p q s t v* (World)
Garvey, William *e h i j l p q r s v* (UK)
Grafton/Tilly Fine Antique Restoration *b e f h i j k l m n o q r s t* (arrange World)
Grandisson International *d e k q* (World)
Hunter, Lavinia *a b c d e f o* (UK)
Jewell & Collacott Woodcarvers *f k*
Moore, Gordon *d e f l p q r t* (UK)
Peters, Alan *e f p q s* (World)
Savage, David *e f g h i j k l m n p q s u v* (World)
Towsey, P. – Towsey Furniture *g gg* (HC)
Vernon, Tony *a b c d e f g h i j k l m n o p q r s t u v* (arrange World)

Dorset
Bagnell, R. C. *b c e h i j l m n q r s* (UK)
Barrington, Michael *a b c e f g gg h i j k l m n o p q r s t* (World)
Chell, A. M. *b c d e h p q r s* (UK)
Hussey, Alan *e f k p q s*
Matthews, G. A. *b c e f h m o q s* (World)

Dumfries & Galloway
Clowe, Ian F. *b g m* (20 mile radius)
Spence, Robert & Co *c f k l* (HC)

Dyfed
Dafydd, Dodrefn *c d e k l m q r* (UK)

Essex
Forge Studio Workshop *a b c e f h i j k l m q r s*
Sabine Antiques & Restoration Services *b c d e g m* (UK)
Stock Furniture Restorations Ltd *a b c d e g h i j k l m n o p q r s t v* (World)

FURNITURE RESTORERS, DESIGNER/MAKERS

Swan Upholstery *g gg m n* (HC)

Fife
Craft, Alexander *c d e k l q r* (HC)
Livingston, Judith A. *a b c e f g gg h k l m n q r s* (UK)

Glamorgan, Mid
Jakeway, Kevin *a b c e f g h j k l m p q s* (World)

Gloucestershire
Antique Furniture Restoration *b c e g h i j k l m n* (World)
Atelier Damien Dewing *c e f q* (World)
Bawden, Keith *a b c e f g h i j k l m n o q s t* (UK, arrange World)
Clark, Colin *a b c e f g k l m q r* (World)
GMS Restorations *a b c d e g h k l m n o p q r s* (World)
Harper, Paul *c e f p q r s t* (World)
Ponsford, A. J. *a b c d e g h j k l m n o q r s* (World)
Pyke, Andrew J. *b c e f p q r s t v* (HC)
Spriggs, Paul *e f k l p q* (HC)
Stewart, Angus *a b c e f g h i j k l m n o p q r s* (UK)
Uedelhoven & Campion *a b c h i j l m n q s* (EUR)

Greater Manchester
Gavin David *g gg* (UK)
Whitehead, John *b c e f g k l n p q r s t v* (UK)

Gwent
Herbert, Stuart *b c e f h k l q s v* (World)

Gwynedd
'One Off Joinery' (M. K. Charlesworthy) *a b c d e f k l p q r* (World)

Hampshire
Bagshaw, Guy F. *a b c d e f g h i j k l m n o q r s t* (EUR)
Barnsley, Edward Educational Trust Workshop Ltd, The *e f p q s v* (World)
Design, F. B. *b c e f h l p q s t u v* (HC)
Gaylords Antiques *a b c e f g h i j k l m n o q r s* (UK, ship World)
Morgan Furniture Ltd *d g gg l q* (World)
Newman, A. T. *a b c h k l q r s* (HC)
Robertson, Gordon E. *a b c d e f h k l p q r s*
Routh, Hugh & Hartley, John *a b c e f g h i j k l m o p q r s t* (World)
Sholing Re-upholstery Services *b c d e g gg p* (HC)

SKILLS

Hertfordshire
Burgin, Angela *a b c e g gg k l m n o* (World)

Highland
Beaton, John McW *a b c d e f g h j k m n o p q r s t*

Humberside
Black, Adrian J. *a b c d e f h j k l m n o p q r s t* (World)
†Doak, James *b h* (HC)
Dunn, Martin H. *a b c d e f g h k l m n p q r s* (UK)

Kent
Caudell Restorations *b c d e h k m q r s* (HC)
Long, Timothy *b gg h i j l m n* (HC)
Mounts Hill Woodcraft *c d e p q*

Lancashire
Casements The Cabinet Makers *a b c e f h l m n o p q r s* (World)
Tomorrow's Antiques *a b c e f h m q r s* (UK)
Grice, Alan *b g m* (HC)

Leicestershire
Cross, A. *b d*
Gallier, Paul de *a b c d e f h j k l m n p q r s* (EUR)
Lowe, Charles *a b c d g k l m n o q s* (UK)

Lincolnshire
Carter, Roger Period Furnishings *b c d e g h k l m n q r s* (World)
Czjkowski, E. & Son *a b c d e f h i j k l m o p q s* (UK, arrange World)
Hall Marque Designs (W. B. Leggett) *b d e l p q r s* (UK)
Thimbleby, E.J. & Son Ltd *b c d e f g h m p q r s* (World)

London
Antique Leathers *b c g gg n* (HC)
Ashley Furniture Workshops *c d e g gg n w* (World)
Ballybeg Restorations *a b c g h j k l m n o q r s* (HC, arrange World)
Bass, Percy Ltd *b e g gg* (UK)
Beadon, J. R. Ltd *b m*
Binnington, P. & F. *a b c e f g gg h i j k l m n o p q r s t v* (World)
Cathedra Ltd *e f h p q r* (World)
Chapman, Albert E. Ltd *a b c e g gg*
Chapman, Peter *a b g h k l m n o w* (World)
Christian Reproductions *c d e l q r*
Collins, Matthew *c d e f g k l m p q r s v* (World)

FURNITURE RESTORERS, DESIGNER/MAKERS

Connell, Paul *e p q s t* (UK)
Crawford, Matthew *a b c d e g gg h i j k l m n o q r s* (HC)
Deans, Tim *b e fh j n o p q s t* (World)
Designer Workshop, The *e*
Dudgeon, Peter Ltd *b c e g gg* (UK)
Eight by Four Ltd *c e k l p q s t v* (UK)
Harris, James *b c e g gg m* (HC)
Howard Chairs Ltd *e g gg*
Inventive Design *e h l p q r s t v* (World)
Jacquard (London) Ltd *b c d e g gg p* (World)
K. D. Crafts *b c d e k o q r s v*
Kerley, Richard *a b c gg h i j k l m o*
Kindler, Andrew Ltd *e f g h j k m n p q r s t u v* (World)
Modulus Designs Ltd *e h p q r s* (HC)
Moore, E. T. *b c d e g k m n* (World)
Morley Upholstery Ltd *b c d e g gg* (EUR)
Original Furniture Craft Ltd *b c m n q r s*
Ott, Max E. Ltd *a b c d e h i j m p q r s t* (World)
Treske Shop, The *c e f l p q*
Webb, Andrew *e p q r t u v* (World)
White, Andrew *b c e f g gg m p q r s t u v w* (World)

Lothian
Dawson, Ben
Essex, A. & Co *b g h j l m o q s*
Fraser, Anselm *a b f h i j k l m n o q r s t v* (HC)
Martin Reproductions *b c d e f l m p q r* (World)
Trist, William & McBain, Andrew *a b c d e f g gg h i j k l m n o p q s* (World)

Middlesex
Dudman, Reginald W. *a b k o*
Grange Restorations (Michael Nickson) *a b c e h i j k l m n o q r s t*
Melson, Sinclair Designs Ltd *c d e g p* (UK)
Morgan, R. V. & Co of London *b c g gg h i j k l m n o q r s* (HC)

Norfolk
Bates, Eric & Sons *b c d e g k l m n q r s v* (World)
Corbett, Rob *a b e p q* (UK)
Dalton, P. *a b c d e f k l p q r s t u* (World)
Flower, Nigel *e f p q* (UK)
Gregson, David *e f p q s* (World)
Lain-Rogers, Lorie *a b c e f h j k l m q r s* (UK)
Palfrey, M. & L. E. *b g gg m*

SKILLS

Read, Stephen & Co *b c e f h l m q r s* (UK)
Wiles, Steve Furniture *e p q* (EUR)
Winteringham, Toby *e f h p q s* (HC)
Woolsey, Roy *a b c d e h i j k l m q r s t*

Northamptonshire
Classic Upholstery *a b c d e f g gg p q r t* (UK)
Collins, R. G. Partnership, The *g gg* (UK)
Goff, Leonard *c e f k q s*
Parker, Ron *c d e f q r*
Thirty-Eight Antiques *e*

Northumberland
Put Your Feet Up *g gg* (HC)
Railton, Jim *a b c d e f g h k l m n o p q r s t* (UK)

Nottinghamshire
Artistic Upholstery Ltd *c g gg* (World)
Barrows, T. S. & Son *a b c d e f g h i j k l m n p q r s t v* (UK)
PHI Interiors *b c d e*
Railton, Jim *a b c d e f g h k l m n o p q r s t* (UK)
Sinclair, Lee *e f g p q r s t r u v* (World)

Oxfordshire
Boulting, Rupert *a b c d e h k l m o* (UK, possibly World)
Crowdys Wood Products Ltd *e p q* (UK)
Desk Shop *b c d e g h j k l m n q r s t* (World)
Leech, Lucinda *e f p q* (World)
Symm & Co Ltd *c d f k m p q r s*
Waywood *e f h p q r s v* (UK)
Weaves & Waxes *a b g h l m n o q r s*
Wickham, Charles *e f h k l p q r s* (EUR)
Witney Restorations Ltd *a b c f h i j k l n o q r s t* (arrange World)

Powys
Caenwood Furniture *b c d e f h k l m p q r s* (UK, arrange World)

Shropshire
Ackroyd, David Ltd *a b c d e f g gg h i j k l m n o p q r s* (World)
Lowcross *c d g gg* (UK)
Wakeman, D. J. & Co Ltd *b c d e h k l m q r s* (HC)

Somerset
Applegate, David *b c d e f j k l m n p q r s t u* (UK)

FURNITURE RESTORERS, DESIGNER/MAKERS

Cherry's Furniture *c e k l m q* (UK)
Stuart *a b c d e f g h k l m q t v* (World)
Venn, Edward *a b c e f g h i j k l m n o q r s* (UK)

Strathclyde
Golightly Antique Restorations *a b c g h k l m n q r s* (HC)
Muirhead Moffat & Co *a b c h l m q r s*
Old Curiosity Shop, The *b c d e g gg h j l m n p q r s* (HC)

Suffolk
Antique Renovations Ltd *a b c d e f g gg h i j k l m n o p q r s t u v* (World)
Denton-Cardew, Andrew *b c d e f g gg k l m n q r* (HC)
Finewood (Albert J. Lain) *b c d e f h l m p q r s t u* (EUR)
Jonmar *b c g gg h i l m o q r s* (UK)
Mulley, Peter *b e f l o p q r* (HC)
Turner, Edwin *b c d e g h j k l m n p q s* (World)
Yoxford Carriageworks Ltd *c e f h k l n o p q r s t v* (World)

Surrey
Fitzgerald, Sean *b f g h j k l m n o p q s*
Hedgecoe, Michael *a b c g h i j k l m n o q r s t* (UK, arrange World)
Senior, Rupert & Wheeler-Carmichael, Charles *e h k p q s*

Sussex, East
Blakeley, Sebastian *e k l p q s t v* (EUR)
E. & T. Furniture Makers *a b c e l p q r* (UK)
Fowler & Brace *e f p q s* (World)
Hedgehog Design *e p q r t u* (World)
Horey Woodcraft (Eric Beckmann) *c d e l q r* (UK)
Old Bakery Furnishing Co, The *b c g gg* (UK)
Reading, A. J. *b c d e q r s* (World)
Redman, F. & Sons *a b c d e g h j k l m q s* (UK)
Wyndham, John Designs *e p q r t u v* (World)

Sussex, West
Amberley Chalk Pits Museum
British Antique Exporters Ltd *b c d e g h k l m n q r s*
†Brown, S. F. & Son *b c e d k q r* (World)
MRM Designs *e p q r s t u v* (UK)
Sladden, Humphrey *a b h j l m n s t*
Smith, Roger E. *c e f p q r s* (HC)

SKILLS

Warwickshire
Pumfrey, Bernard *a b d e f l m p q r s* (UK)
R. D. S. Furniture Contracts Ltd *c d e f g h j k l m n o p* (World)

Wiltshire
Barberton, Nick *e f k l p q r*
Black Lane Pots Workshops *a b c d e f h j k l p q r s t u v* (UK)
Englefield, Alan R. *e f h k l m n p q s* (World)
Factory *e p q r s t u v* (World)
Henderson, Michael *a b c e f k p q r* (World)
Miles, Ian Upholstery *a b g gg* (100 mile radius)
Restorations Unlimited *a b c d e f g h i j k l m n o p q r s*

Worcestershire
L. G. M. Ltd *g gg m* (HC)
Malvern Studios *a b c d e f g h i j k l m n o q r s* (arrange World)
†Tyler, Roger *a b c d e f h p s* (HC)

Yorkshire, East
Norton, Peter *b c d e f k l q r* (UK)

Yorkshire, North
Freeborn, E. J. & Son *b c d e f h i j k l p q s* (UK)
Jackson, Adam *b c d e f h j l m p q r s t* (World)
Jeffray, Albert *b c f g k l q r* (UK)
Preston, Donald *b c d e g h i j l m n o q r s t u* (EUR)
†Reid, Dick *a b c d e f k l q r* (EUR)
Thompson's Robert Craftsmen Ltd (World)
Wilkinson, K. A. *a b c d e f g l p q r s t* (World)
Woodpohl Ltd *c d e f l p q r* (World)

Yorkshire, West
Beal, Robert Furniture *b c d e f g h l m p q r s t u v* (World)
Design Workshop (Shelley) Ltd *a b c d e f g p q r s t u v* (World)
Designer Maker Furniture Ltd *a b c d e f h l p q r s* (World)
Dobbins, Philip *b c d e f g h j k l m p q r s t u v* (UK)
Fisher, Tom *e p q r s t u v* (World)
Vickerman, E. V. & Sons *a b c d e f g h i j o p q r* (HC)
Welsh, Ewan Furniture *e* (UK)
* Only undertakes petit point.
† Only undertakes carving or marquetry/inlay work.
( ) Lettering in brackets denotes area within which willing to deliver.

GLASS – DECORATIVE FINISHES

Gates
See CARPENTERS, JOINERS; METAL

Gilding
See ARTISTS; FURNITURE – PAINTED; GLASS – DECORATIVE FINISHES; MISCELLANEOUS (frame restoration/gilding)

Glass – Decorative Finishes other than Stained/Painted, Leaded
See also ARCHITECTURAL ANTIQUES/SALVAGE

- (a) Conservation
- (b) Restoration
- (c) Reproduction to match existing
- (d) Design to client's specification/new work
- (e) Will work in situ
- (f) Abstract designs
- (g) Figurative designs
- (h) Classical designs
- (i) Lettering
- (j) Heraldry
- (k) Engraving
- (l) Etching
- (m) Sandblasting
- (n) Stencilling
- (o) Enamelling
- (p) Glass fusing/kilnwork
- (q) Bending (shaping) glass
- (r) Verre eglomise (gilding on glass)

Bedfordshire
Whitworth, John *d f g h i k* (World)

Cambridgeshire
Peace, David *e g i j k* (UK)
Phillippo, Roger *a b c d e f g h i j k*

Cornwall
Nisbet, Tim *c d h i j* (Western Counties)
Thorpe, Lavinia *h i j o*

Cumbria
Yates, Neil *c d f g h i j m*

Devonshire
Beard, John Wales *c d e g h i j k*
McLaren Glass *m*

Dumfries & Galloway
Border Glass & Glazing Co Ltd *a b c d f g h i j l m* (UK)
Scott, Sonia *b c d e f g h j* (UK)

Dyfed
Whistler, Laurence K. *k*

SKILLS

Essex
Conway, Jennifer *c d e g h i j* (World)

Glamorgan, West
Mangold, Deanne *c d f g h i m* (World)

Gloucestershire
Fedden, Bryant *e f g i k* (World)

Gwent
Smith, Jonathan R. H. *b c d f g h i j k*

Hampshire
Gilliam, Tony *b c d e f g h i j k m* (World)
Hill-Norton, Jenny *d e g i j k* (World)

Kent
Clark, Jenny *b c d e f g i j k* (depends on work load)

London
Allwood, Jacqueline *d e f g h i j k*
Binnington Peter & Francis *r*
Lawson Johnston, Philip *d e f g i j*
Radford & Ball Partnership *b c d f g h i l m* (World)
Whistler, Simon *g i j k* (World)

Northamptonshire
Jackson, Pat *n*

Oxfordshire
Cox, Gillian *c d e f g h i j k*
Quartley, Freddie *e h i j k* (HC)

Strathclyde
McKee, A. *l m*

Suffolk
Oliver, Stefan *c d e g h i j* (World)
Palmer, Stuart & Shirley *d e f g i j k* (World)
Wilde, Linda *b c d e f g i j k m*

Surrey
Broadhead, Sarah *d f p* (EUR)
Mocatta, Charmian *d e i j k* (World)

GLASS – STAINED, PAINTED AND LEADED LIGHTS

Ridley, Annabel *c d h i j k* (World)

Sussex, West
Majella, Josephine *a b c d e f g h i j k l* (World)
Opus Stained Glass *b c d e f g h l m q* (World)
Ruijterman, Jacques *a b c d f g h i j*

Midlands West
Allied Artists *b c d e f g h i j k m* (World)
Rigg, Donal *c h i j* (HC)

Wiltshire
Pullan, Peter *d g i j k* (UK)

Worcestershire
Weingart, Christel Associates *m p* (World)

Yorkshire, West
Thornton, Andy Architectural Antiques & Reproductions *d f g h i l*

Glass – Stained, Painted and Leaded Lights
See also ARCHITECTURAL ANTIQUES/SALVAGE
- (a) Conservation
- (b) Restoration
- (c) Reproduction to match existing
- (d) Design to client's specification/new work
- (e) Will work in situ
- (f) Abstract designs
- (g) Figurative designs
- (h) Classical designs
- (i) Lettering
- (j) Heraldry
- (k) Specialist glass cleaning
- (l) Will undertake protective measures

Avon
*Angus, Mark *f g* (World)
Bath Architectural Glass *a b c d e f g h i j*
*Coomber, Roy *a b c d e f g h i j k l* (World)
Creative Glass *a b c d e f g h i j k l*
*Gale, Keith *b d f* (World)
Godden, J. & P. Glass Design *a b c d e f g h i j k l*
H. M. G. of Bristol *a b c d e f g h k l* (World, Venus & Mars)
*Lassen, Michael G. Stained Glass *a b c d e f g h i j k l*
Masonry Associates Ltd *a b c d e f g h k l* (World)
*Robinson, Jeffrey A. K. *a b c d f g i j k l* (UK)
Solaglas Stained Glass *a b c d e f g h i j l* (UK)
Stanton Leaded Light Windows *a b c d e f g h i j k l* (World)

SKILLS

Bedfordshire
Glass Works, The *b c d e f g h i j l*

Berkshire
Balson, J. L. *a b c d e f g h i j k l* (EUR)
Jones, Ceri Lead Lights *b c d e f g l* (EUR)

Buckinghamshire
The Glass Market *b c d e f g h i j k l* (World)
Jackson Glasscraft *a b c d e f g h i j k* (World)
*Nuttgens, Joseph *b c d f g h i j l* (World)
*Wasley, David *a b c d e g h i j k l* (World)

Cambridgeshire
Artists in Stained Glass *b c d e f g h j* (World)
Cambridge Stained Glass (Dean Cullum) *a b c d e f g h i j* (EUR)
Fine Lines *d e f g h i j*

Central
Aurora Glass *a b c d e f g h i j k l* (World)

Cheshire
Bell, K. G. *a b c d e f g h i j k l* (UK)
Crafty Glass House *d f g h i* (UK)
Illumin Glass Studio *a b c d e f g h i j l* (20 mile radius)

Cleveland
Kyme's Stained Glass *a b c d e f g h i* (HC)

Clwyd
Ancient & Modern Glass *a b c d e f g h i j*
Bird-Jones, Chris *a b c d e f g h i j k l* (World)
LGS *a b c d f g h i j k l*

Cornwall
Upton, Phillip *b c d e f g h i l* (EUR)

Devonshire
Ayles, Roberta *b c d f g h i j*
Bright Designs
Edwardes, Paul *a b d e f g h i j k* (UK)
Gubbin, David *a b c d e f g h i j k l*
McLaren Glass *b c d e f g h i j l* (World)
MacKenzie Glass Ltd *b c d e g h* (HC)

GLASS – STAINED, PAINTED AND LEADED LIGHTS

Dorset
ADA Partnership *a b c d e f g h i j l* (World)
Callan, Jon *a b c d e f g h i j k l*
Powell, Hugh *a b d c e f g h i j* (UK)

Dumfries & Galloway
Border Glass & Glazing *a b c d e f g h i j k l* (UK)

Dyfed
Shaw, Lilian *b c d e f g h i j* (World)

Essex
Lacey, Amanda Dawn *a b c d f g h i j k l*
Mission Glass *a b c d e f g h i k l* (World)
Widdington Stained Glass *c d f g h j* (World)

Glamorgan, Mid
Winfield Stained Glass *a b c d e f g h i j k l* (World)

Glamorgan, West
Celtic Studios Ltd (H. P. Thomas) *a b c d f g h i j k l*
Designer Glass *d f g*
Glantawe Studios *a b c d e f g h i j k l*
Glasslight Studios Ltd *b c d e f g h i j*
Hiscott, Amber & Pearl, David *f g h* (World)
Jones, Catrin *e f g* (World)
Mangold, Deanne *c d e f g h i l* (World)
Toft, C. G. (Leaded Lights) Ltd *a b c d e f g h i l*

Gloucestershire
Dowding, Graham *b c d e f g h i j k l* (UK)
Friend, Rodrick *b d f g h i j* (World)

Grampian
Arcadia Stained Glass Studio *a b c d e f g h i j k l*
Farrelly, Martin N. *a b f g j*
Jennifer-Jane Stained Glass *a b c d e f g h i j k l* (EUR)

Greater Manchester
Design Lights *a b c d e f g h i j l*
Lightfoot, Charles Ltd *a b c d e f g h i j k l*

Gwent
Petts, John *d e f g i k* (World)

SKILLS

Hampshire
Inside Art & Design Ltd c d e f g h i j l (World)
Knight, Simon b c e f g i l (World)
Moreton & Sons Ltd
'Rainbow Glass' – V. N. Voysey a b c d e f g h i j
Sunrise Stained Glass a b c d e f g h i j (World)

Hertfordshire
*Chapel Studio (A. Fisher, P. Archer, R. J. Holloway) a b c d e f g h i j k l
Coffey, Graham a b c d e f (World)
Renninson, Gill a b c d f g h i (50 mile radius)
*Skeat, Francis b c d f g h j l (EUR)

Kent
Arena Glass Studio a b c d e f g h
*Hayward, John a b c d f g h i j k (EUR)
*Hill, Keith & Judy a b c d e f g h i j k l (World)
*Lawrence & Co b d g k l (UK)

Lancashire
*Brown, David J. a b c d e f g h i j l
Courtney, Alan b c d g h i j
Eckersley, D. a b c d e f g h i j k l
Leyland Stained Glass a b c d e f g h i l (UK)
Pendle Stained Glass a b c d e f g h i j k l
Twibill, Geoff & Sons a b c d e f g h i j k l

Leicestershire
Limelight Studios a b c d e f g h i j k l (World)
Norman & Underwood a b c d e f g h i j k l (World)

Lincolnshire
*Hollaway, Anthony a b c e f i j (World)

London
Amery, Leo b d f g h i j l
Artful Glass Co Ltd c d f g h i j l
Becker, Bernard
Bender, Rodney a b d f g h i j
Bradley, Ray a b c d e f g h i j (World)
Conti, Anna a b c d e f g h i l
Corrin, Adelle a b c d f g h i j k l (World)
Fuller, Kate Baden a b c d e f g j k (World)
'Juelle' Stained Glass (June Standing) a b c d e f g h i (World)

GLASS – STAINED, PAINTED AND LEADED LIGHTS

*Kantorowicz, Nicola *a b c d f h i j l* (UK)
Lloyd, Matthew *a b c d e f g h i j k l*
London Door Co, The *c d f g h i j* (HC)
McClafferty, Maria Designs Ltd *a b c d e f g h l* (World)
Moor, Andrew Associates *a b c d e f g h i j k l* (World)
Neave, Penelope *c d f g h i j*
New, Keith *d f g h j*
*Preece, James *c d f g h i j*
Prisms Stained Glass Design *b c d e f g h i j* (EUR)
Shades of Light *a b c d e f g h i j l* (World)
Sklovsky, Anna *d f g h* (World)
Tomkinson's *a b c d e f g h i j l* (EUR)
Townsends *b c d e f g h*
Whiteway & Waldron *a b c d f g h i j* (World)
*Younger, Alan *a b c d e f g h i j k l* (World)

Lothian
Mitton, Roland *b c d f g h i j*
Shaw, Christian *a b c d e f g h i j k l*

Merseyside
Davies, William *a b c d e f g h i j k l* (UK)

Middlesex
Kendall, Barry *b c d f g h i j* (EUR)

Norfolk
Ashton & Co *a b c d e f g h i j k l* (World)
Church Lane *a b c d e f g h i j l* (World)
*Quail, Paul *a b c d e f g h i j*
Stained Glass Overlay UK Ltd *c d e f g h i j* (UK)

Northamptonshire
MacRae, Anthony *b c d e f g h i j*
*Pentelow, Graham *a b c d e f g h i j k l* (UK)

Northumberland
Iona Art Glass *a b c d* (EUR)
Richardson, Sarah *d f g l* (World)

Nottinghamshire
Lenton Lamp Studios *c d f g h* (HC)
Stokes, Michael *a b c d e f g h i j k l* (World)

SKILLS

Oxfordshire
*Casciani, Paul San Glass Activities *b c d f g h i j*
Swingler, E. J. & S. Kennedy Associates *a b c e i j k l* (EUR)

Powys
Empress Stained Glass – Robert Mullen *b c d e f* (UK)

Somerset
Chinks Vere Grylls *a b c d e f g h i j k l*
Crystal Lines *a b c d e f g h j*
Rainbow Glass *a c d f g h i j l*
Unicorn Glass Workshop *c d f g h i j* (World)

Shropshire
Chaplin, G. *a b c d e f g h i j k l*
†Cunningham, John Patrick *a b c d e f g h i j k*
*Gray, Jane *d g h i j* (UK)

Strathclyde
Blue Sun *a b c d e f g h j* (World)
Galaxy Glass Glasgow *a b c d e f g h i j k l* (World)
GB Glazing *b c j k* (HC)
Glashaus – Architectural/Interior Glass *a b c d e f g h i j l* (World)
McCartney, Crear *e f g i j* (World)
McKee, A. *a b c d e f g h i j k l*
Speirs, Artur *c d e f g h i j k* (EUR)
Stained Glass Design Partnership *a b f g i j k* (UK)
Wee Glass Works, The *a b c d e f g h i j l* (World)

Suffolk
The Chapel Studio *c d f g h i j* (UK)

Surrey
*Caine, Osmund *d f g* (World)

Sussex, East
Cox & Barnard (Hove) Ltd *a b c d e f g h i j k l* (World)

Sussex, West
Amberley Chalk Pits Museum
Durant, Cliff (Glimmer Glass) *a b c d e f g h i j k l* (World)
Majella, Josephine *a b c d e f g h i j* (World)
Opus *b c d e f g h* (World)

74

GLASS – SUPPLIERS OF ANTIQUE GLASS

Tyne & Wear
Vitrail Studios – P. M. Crook *a b c d f g h i j* (UK)

West Midlands
Allied Artists *b c d e f g h i j* (UK)
Bayliss & Williams *a b c d e f g h i j k*
*Glass Mountain Studios *a b c d e f g h i j k l* (World)
Hardman, John Studios *a b c d e f g h i j k l* (World)
Stourbridge *a b c d e f g h i k l*

Wiltshire
Leatherhead, Pamela *d e f g*
Ward, Sasha *d f g h i* (UK)

Worcestershire
Heron Glass Studio Ltd *a b c d e f g h l* (World)
Norgrove Studios Partnership *a b c d e f g h i j k l*
Smith, Gail Designs *a b c d f g h* (EUR)
Weingart, Christel Associates *a b c d f g h i* (World)

Yorkshire, North
Belvedere Glass *a b c d e f g h i j k l* (World)
Bruce, R. R. *a b c d e f g h i j*
Lazenby, Alan *a b c d e f g h i j l*
Stained Glass Design by Valerie Green *a b c d e f g h i j l*
*Waugh, Sep *b c d e f g h i j k l*

Yorkshire, South
Finch, John A. Ltd *a b c d e k l* (HC)

Yorkshire, West
Archive Stained Glass Design *a b c d e f g h i j l*
Art Glass Ltd *a b c d e f g h i j k l* (UK)
Beaumont R. G. *a b c d e f g h i j k l* (World)
Elliff, P. & Sons *a b c d e g h i j l* (HC)
Odyssey Glass Ltd *a b c d e f g h i j k l* (World)
Smith, R. A. *b c d e f g h i j l* (World)
Thornton, Andy Architectural Antiques & Reproductions *d f g h i*
Wetherby Stained Glass & Glass Merchants *a b c d e f g h i j k l* (World)
† Building contractor.
* These glass painters/artists are approved by the British Society of Master Glass Painters (See Associations).

Glass – Suppliers of Antique and other Specialist Glass
See MISCELLANEOUS (glass...)

SKILLS

Graining
See ARTISTS...

Guttering
See MISCELLANEOUS (rainwater goods...)

Gypsum
See PLASTERWORK

Handles
See ARCHITECTURAL ANTIQUES/SALVAGE; CARPENTERS, JOINERS; CERAMIC ARTISTS; METAL; MISCELLANEOUS (handles)

Heraldry
See ARCHITECTURAL SCULPTURE; ARTISTS; GLASS – DECORATIVE FINISHES; GLASS – STAINED...; MOSAIC/TERRAZO

Inlays
See CARPENTERS, JOINERS; FURNITURE RESTORERS

Interior Designers
See PROFESSIONALS

Ironmongery
See ARCHITECTURAL ANTIQUES/SALVAGE; LOCKSMITHS; METAL; MISCELLANEOUS (ironmongery)

Lampshades
See ARCHITECTURAL ANTIQUES/SALVAGE; GLASS – DECORATIVE FINISHES; GLASS – STAINED; LIGHTING

Landscape Architects
See PROFESSIONALS

Leaded Lights
See ARCHITECTURAL ANTIQUES/SALVAGE; GLASS – STAINED

Lead Sash Window Weights
See MISCELLANEOUS (lead sash window weights manufacturers)

Lettering
See ARCHITECTURAL SCULPTURE; ARTISTS...; GLASS – DECORATIVE FINISHES; GLASS – STAINED...

LIGHTING

Library Joinery
See CARPENTERS, JOINERS; MISCELLANEOUS (library joinery)

Lighting – Conservation, Restoration, Antique, Designed to Specification (Period and Contemporary)
See ARCHITECTURAL ANTIQUES/SALVAGE; CARPENTERS, JOINERS; CERAMIC ARTISTS; FURNITURE – PAINTED; GLASS – DECORATIVE FINISHES; GLASS – STAINED; METAL

- (a) Classical
- (b) Conservation/restoration
- (c) Chandeliers/cut glass
- (d) Tiffany
- (e) Metal/wood
- (f) Brass/bronze
- (g) Gilding
- (h) Gold and silver plating
- (i) Reproduction to match existing
- (j) External light fittings
- (k) Replacement parts
- (l) Contempory
- (m) Design to client's specification/new work
- (n) Neon
- (o) Painted
- (p) Plastic
- (q) Lampshades
- (r) Bases
- (s) Wall lights
- (t) Bending (shaping) glass
- (u) Terracotta/porcelain/stoneware/raku

Buckinghamshire
Temple Lighting *e f* (supply World)

Cheshire
Crafty Glass House *d m q s*
Illumin, Glass Studio *b d i m* (20 mile radius)
Riva Design Ltd

Cumbria
Dennison Drake Designs *a b d e f g h i j k l m n o q r* (World)

Derbyshire
Kingswood Services Ltd *a b j m*

Devon
Lantern Shop, The *b d f h k q r*

Dorset
Barrington, Michael *a b e f g i j k m* (UK)

Essex
Widdington Stained Glass *d m*

SKILLS

Hampshire
Inside Art & Design Ltd *d*

Hertfordshire
Rennison, Gill *a b d i j l m q* (50 mile radius)
Windsor, D. W. Ltd *a b e f h i j k m o r* (supply World)

Kent
Arena Glass Studio *a d i l m q* (World)

Leicestershire
The Copper Lamp Co Ltd *b i j m* (World)

London
Clare House Ltd *a b e f g h i k m o q r* (World)
Crystal Lite Chandeliers *a b c e f g h i k m* (World)
Designers Workshop, The *m*
Eisl, Thomas *j l m* (World)
*Fox, R. & Sons *a b c d e f g h i j k l m n o p q r* (UK)
Hamilton-Hill, Maureen *m q* (HC)
Haywood, Thomas & Sons Ltd *a e f i j m o* (World)
Jones Original Antique Lighting 1860-1960 *d k q r*
Lead & Light *d l m*
Lloyd, Matthew *a b d i l m o q* (World)
Metalcrafts B. C. Ltd *a b c f g h r* (World)
Period Brass Lights *a b c d e f g h i j k l m o p q r* (W. London, supply World)
Preece, James Stained Glass *a b d i l m o q r* (UK, supply World)
Prisms Stained Glass Design *a b d i j l m q* (EUR)
Sitch, W. & Co Ltd *a c e f g h i j k m* (World, supply only)
Turn On Lighting *c q* (UK)
Wilkinson, R. & Son *a b c d e f g h i j k l m o q r* (World)
Wrays, Christopher Lighting Emporium *b d e f i j k m o q r*

Lothian
Lonsdale & Dutch *b e f i* (World)
Shaw, Christian Stained Glass *b d e f g h i l m q* (EUR)

Middlesex
Kendall, Barry *d l m q*
Starlite Chandeliers Ltd *a b c e f g h i j l m r* (World)

Nottinghamshire
Lenton Lamp Studios *a d i j l m q* (supply UK)

LIGHTING

Powys
Eickhoff, Angus *c e f j l m n* (World)

Shropshire
Hughes, Martin Design *a b g i k l m o p q s* (World except USA & Canada)
Ragdon Art *a b e f i j k l m* (World)

Somerset
Crystal Lines *a b d i l m o q*
Poirrier, Bill
Stuart *c e m*

Strathclyde
Wee Glass Works, The *a b d i q r* (World)

Suffolk
Brookes Forge Flempton *a b c e f g h i j k m r* (World)

Surrey
Smithbrook Barn *e f i j m* (supply UK)

Sussex, West
Opus Stained Glass *o q t*
Sugg Lighting Ltd *a b d e f i j k l m o* (supply World)

Tyne & Wear
Albion Ceramics *a r u* (UK)

Warwickshire
Hunt, David Lighting Ltd *a b c e f i j k l m o* (World)

West Midlands
Best & Lloyd Ltd *a b e f h i m* (supply World)

Worcestershire
Weingart, Christel Associates *a d e f h l m q r* (World)

Yorkshire, North
Stained Glass Design by Valerie Green *d m* (UK)

Yorkshire, West
Beaumont, R.J. *d i m o q* (World)
Thornton, Andy Architectural Antiques & Reproductions *a m q s*

SKILLS

Wetherby Stained Glass & Glass Merchants *d i m o q* (World)
* Building contractor.

Lime
See PLASTERWORK; SPECIALIST PRODUCTS

Linoleum
See FLOORCOVERINGS

Locks
See ARCHITECTURAL ANTIQUES/SALVAGE; LOCKSMITHS; METALWORKERS

Locksmiths Experienced in Work on Period Locks
See also METALWORKERS

- (a) Conservation
- (b) Restoration
- (c) Reproduced
- (d) Reproduced to match existing
- (e) Will make to specification
- (f) Keycutting
- (g) Replacement parts
- (h) Brass
- (i) Iron
- (j) Steel

Bedfordshire
Antique Lock Services *b c d e f g h i j* (UK)

Cambridgeshire
Citylocks *b e f g h i j* (UK)

London
Locks & Handles (Architectural Components) Ltd
Tower Key Co (Homeguard Ltd) *b c d f g h i j* (UK)

Nottinghamshire
Cookson's Master Locksmiths & Safe Engineers *a b c d e f g h i j* (World)
Keyhole, The *b c d f g* (World)

Suffolk
Brookes Forge Flempton *a b c d e f g h i j* (supply World)

Sussex, East
Blakeley, Giles Creative Blacksmith *b c d e f g h i j* (HC)

Yorkshire, South
Wood, Charles H. (Security) Ltd *b c d f g h i j* (UK, supply World)

METALWORKERS

Majolica Tiles
See CERAMIC TILES

Marbling
See ARTISTS...

Marquetry
See ARCHITECTURAL ANTIQUES/SALVAGE; CARPENTERS, JOINERS; FURNITURE RESTORERS

Mathematical Tiles
See CERAMIC TILES

Mechanical Antiquities
See TURRET CLOCKS; MISCELLANEOUS (steam engines)

Metalworkers Experienced in Conservation/Restoration Work
See also ARCHITECTURAL ANTIQUES/SALVAGE

- (a) Conservation
- (b) Restoration
- (c) Reproduction
- (d) Reproduction to match existing
- (e) Designed to client's specification
- (f) Period products for conservation/restoration work
- (g) Specialist castings/ironmongery
- (h) Aluminium
- (i) Brass
- (j) Bronze
- (k) Copper
- (l) Gold plated/gold leaf
- (m) Lead
- (n) Silver plated
- (o) Steel
- (p) Wrought/cast iron
- (q) Door/window furniture
- (r) Gates
- (s) Railings
- (t) Staircase/balustrading
- (u) Sanitary fittings (taps etc.)
- (w) Special doors/windows

Avon
Almondsbury Forge Works Ltd *b c d o p r s t* (supply UK, fix Bristol area)
Dorothea Restorations Ltd *a b c d e g h i j k m o q r s t* (World)
Morrisey, Patrick *b c d e k o p r s t* (World)

Central
Agar & Son *a b c d e f g h i j k l m n o p q r s t u v* (World)
Grahamston Iron Co Ltd *p*
Longbotham, John (Ironfounders) Ltd *a c d f g h p s t* (UK)
Machan Engineering Ltd *b c d e g h o p r s t* (UK)

SKILLS

Cheshire
Broadbent, D. C. *a b c d e f o p r s t* (UK)
Broxap & Corby Ltd *d e f g h i o p r s* (World)
Dorothea Restorations Ltd *a b c d e g h i j k m o q r s t* (World)

Cleveland
Oberon, Peat *b d e i j k n o p q r s* (UK)

Clwyd
Jakim Artifacts *b d e f g j* (World)
Roberts, David & Co *a b c d e f g m* (supply World)

Cornwall
Davey & Jordan *a c d e f h i o p q r s t*
*Hodgetts, Graham *a b c d e f g i j k l m n o p q r s t u*
Railway Forge *a b c d e f h o p q r s t* (World)

Cumbria
Shepley Dawson Architectural Engineers Ltd *a b c d e f g h i j k l n o p q r s t* (World)

Derbyshire
Dorothea Ltd *b c d e f g h i j o p r s t*
Pearson, Cameroon *d h i j*
Wilgran

Devonshire
Hawkins, Neil *b c d e f k o p q r s* (EUR)

Dorset
Barrington, Michael *b c d e i j k o*
Fortune, Tim *a b c d e f g k l o p q r s t* (World)
Malleson, Michael *b c d o p q r s t* (UK)
Ring, I. J. *b c d e f g o p r s t* (World)
Saviac Prototypes *c q*
Wing & Staples *a b c d e f g o p q r s t*

Dumfries & Galloway
Armstrong Ironwork *a b c d e g o p q r s t u* (100 mile radius, consider UK)
Martin, Edward *b c d e o p q r s t* (UK)

Durham
Russell, Brian *a b c d e f i j o p q r s t* (UK, supply World)

METALWORKERS

Essex
Carford, Geo. Ltd *b d e o p q r s t*
Crittall Windows Ltd *o w* (UK)

Fife
Henderson the Blacksmith *a b c d e f g h i j k o p q r s t v* (UK)

Glamorgan, Mid
Grunewald, Theo *b c d e f i j k o q r s t*

Gloucestershire
Bruno Bronze (Andy Mitchell) *a b c d e f g h i j k l* (World)
Eaton, Les *a b d*

Grampian
Newmill Castings Ltd *b c d e f g i j m p r s t* (UK)

Hampshire
Britannia Architectural Metalwork Ltd *a b c d e f g h i j o p r s t* (World)
Forge, The (Peter Clutterbuck) *a b c d e f g o p q r s t* (100 mile radius)
Morris Singer Foundry, The *b e g j m s t* (World)
Ornate Ironworkings *e r s t* (HC)
Smith, Robert *b c d e f g o p q r s* (HC)
Waight, David *b c d j p q r s t* (HC)
Wessex Ironcraft *a b c d e f g o p q r s t* (World)
West, Anthony *a b c d e f i j k o p q r s t* (UK)

Hertfordshire
Enfield Foundry Co Ltd *c d e g h i j k p q r s t*
Ironcrafts (Stofold) Ltd *b e o p r s t* (UK)
Issac, Henry *d g p r s t* (HC supply UK)
†Roberts, C. P. Special Works Ltd *d e g i o p r s t* (HC)

Highland
Crummy, Mike *a b c d e f g i j k l m n o p q r s t* (UK)

Kent
Barwick, R. J. (Building) Ltd *g m* (Kent only)
Cole, W. & D. Ltd – Kentish Ironcraft Ltd *b c d e f g o p r s t*
Culverden Metalworks Ltd *a b c d e p r s t* (HC)
Dartford Metalcrafts Ltd *a b c d e f g o p r s t* (HC)
Henwood Decorative Metal Studios Ltd *b c d e f i j k l n* (supply World)
Hutton, Len *a b c d e o p q r s t* (EUR)

SKILLS

Medway Brass Restoration *b d i q u* (HC)
Metalock (Britain) Ltd *b p r s t* (HC)

Lancashire
Varley, John (Ironfounders) Ltd *b c d e g p r s t* (UK)

Leicestershire
Spence, J. F. & Son *b c d e f g i o p r s t* (HSC)

London
A. & H. Brass *b d e i j l n*
Bleasdale, R. (Weldings) *d e f g h i j o p r s t* (World)
Brass Tacks Hardware Ltd *c d e f g i j l n q t* (World)
Capricorn Architectural Ironwork Ltd *a b c d e f g k o p q r s t* (World)
Comyn Ching Ltd *c p q* (fix World)
Foulger & Son *b h i j k o p q r s t u* (World)
†Fox, R. & Sons *a b h i j k l m n o v* (UK, supply World)
Porter, J. H. & Son Ltd *a b c d e f g o p q r s t* (London)
Signmaking Developments *c d e h i j k l m n o s* (EUR)
Southwell Stockwell Ltd *a b c d e f g h o p r s t* (HC)
Steel Arts *b c d e g h i j o p r s t* (HC)
Turner & Ross Ltd *b f g h o p r s t* (Gtr London)
Verdigris *a b c d g i j k l m n q t*

Lothian
Ballantine Boness Iron Co Ltd *b c d e g p q r s t* (World)
Henshaw, Charles & Sons Ltd *a b c d e g h i j k l n o q r s t* (UK)
Johnson, Phil *a b d e h i j o p q r s t* (World)
Laing, Charles & Sons Ltd *e g h i j m p s t* (supply World)
Munro, Kenny *a b e f g i j o*

Norfolk
Cordaroy, Bill *a b c d e f h i j k m o p q r s t* (World)
Skipper, Jonathan *a b c d e f p q r s t* (World)
Thurton Foundries Ltd *a b c d e f g h i j m p q r s t*
Veetrac Engineering Ltd *o r s t* (World)

Northamptonshire
Bassett & Findley Ltd *b d e h i j k l q r s t* (UK)
Long, Maurice *b d e f o p r s t* (EUR)

Northumberland
Lunn, J. S. & Sons *b c d e f g h i j k o p r s* (World)

METALWORKERS

Nottinghamshire
Universal Railing Co Ltd *a b c d e f g l p r s t* (UK)

Powys
Dennis, Paul & Sons *b c d j k o p q r s t* (World)
Eickhoff, Angus *c d e o q r s t* (World)
Smith, P. J. I. *a b c d e f g i j k m o p q r s t*

Shropshire
Glynwed Foundries *d e g o p s* (World)
Ironbridge Gorge Museum *d p* (World)

Somerset
Poirrier, Bill *c d e o q r s t* (UK)
Stuart *c d e i p q r t*
Waterslade Forge *b c d e f l o p q r s t* (World)
Webb & Kempf Ltd *a b c d e g*

Suffolk
Brookes Forge Flempton *a b c d e f g h i j k l m n o p q r s* (supply World)
Gedding Mill Forge *a b c d e f o p q r s t* (HC)

Surrey
Clark, Terrence *a b c d e f g h i j k l m n o p q r s t u* (World)
Clement Brothers Haslemere Ltd *a b c d e f g o w* (supply World)
Owens, D. R. *a b c d e f i k o q r s t* (World)
Quinnell, Richard Ltd *a b c d e f g h i j k l m n o p q r s t u* (World)

Sussex, East
Blakeley, Giles *a b c d e f h i k o p q r s t* (UK)
Day, G. W. & Co *a b c d e f k o p q r s t* (London & Home Counties, supply World)
Ironcrafts Ltd *b d e f g o p r s t* (UK)
Squires Irondesigns (Steel Erections) Ltd *c d e o q r s t*

Sussex, West
Breese, Andrew *b c d e o p q r s t* (HC)

Warwickshire
Ball Bros (Engineers) Ltd *b d e g h j p r s* (UK)

West Midlands
Cradley Castings Ltd *g h p s t* (UK)
Majorfax Ltd *a b c d e g p r s* (World)

SKILLS

Shenton, James W. *c d g p r s t*
Tipper, Joseph Ltd *g p*

Wiltshire
Cole, Hector Ironwork *a b c d e f o p q r s* (supply World)

Worcestershire
Crownshaw, Peter *a b c d e f g h i j k m o p q r s t* (UK)
Dereford of Badsey Hall *b c d e i j k l o p r s* (World)
Knight, Alan *a b c d e i j k o p q r s t* (UK)

Yorkshire, North
Barker, Don *a b c d e f g h i j k o p q r s t* (World)
Cassell, Joseph *a b c d e f h i k o p r s t* (UK)
Nidd House Antiques *a b d e i j k m o p q* (EUR)

Yorkshire, South
O'Dwyer, Michael *b c d e f g o p q r s t*
Smith Widdowson & Eadem Ltd *b c d e f g h i j k l n p q* (UK, supply World)

Yorkshire, West
Craven Forge Wrought Iron *a b c d e f g o p q r s t* (HC)
Leggott, W. & R. Ltd *b c d e g h i j k l q r s t* (World)
Porritt, Don *a b e h i j k l n o* (EUR)
Thornton, Andy Architectural Antiques & Reproductions *c e h i s t*
† Building contractor.
* Consultant/advisor in all categories.

Miscellaneous

Bells
Armitage, G. D. (Clock & Belfry Work) Ltd
Munro, Kenny (Environmental Artist)
Taylor, John & Co (Bellfounders) Ltd

Bending (shaping) glass
Opus Stained Glass

China, porcelain and pottery ornaments
Ashton-Bostock, David
Bawden, Keith
Restorations Unlimited

MISCELLANEOUS

Clock restoration (not public or turret)
Bawden, Keith
Cobb, Clive & Lesley (painted dial and lacquer)
Lowe, Charles
Newcombe & Son
Nidd House Antiques
Restorations Unlimited
Stewart, Angus
Tomorrow's Antiques
Venn, Edward Antique Restorations

Conservatories – made to specification
Cowie & Roberts
Kidby, M. D. Buildings Ltd
Marston & Langinger Ltd
Viceroy Buildings Ltd

Curtains, drapes and tails, pelmets and swags, etc.
Gavin, David Furnishings
Jacquard (London) Ltd (also upholstered walls and tented ceilings)
Jonmar (handmade)
Moore, E. T. (also upholstered walls and tented ceilings, carpets)

Door furniture – period
Locks & Handles (Architectural Components Ltd)

Electrical switches, etc. – period
Hamilton, R. & Co Ltd

Fanlight maker
Period Joinery
Sambrook, John

Frame restoration/gilding
Binnington, P. & F.
Eke, Roger & Son
Hopson, Jock Conservation Service
Ponsford, A. J. Antique Restoration

Furniture restoration materials
Weaves & Waxes

Glass – suppliers of 'antique' and other specialist glass
Hetley, James & Co

SKILLS

Handles, mounts, locks and keys, etc. for furniture
Ballybeg Restorations
Bawden, Keith
Sladden, Humphrey Fine Furniture Restoration
Stewart, Angus

Ivory, mother of pearl, tortoise-shell
Bawden, Keith
Grange Restorations (Michael Nickson)
Havers, Hamilton

Lead sash window weight manufacturers
Forbes, Don

Library joinery
Thirty-Eight Antiques
Thistle Joinery Ltd

Musical instruments made and/or restored and conserved
Binnington, P. & F. (keyboard & harp restoration)

Objet d'art – restoration
Harding Restoration

Oil paintings, water colours, etc.
Bawden, Keith
Hirst Conservation
Keevil, Maurice E.
Ponsford, A. J.
Tabner, Len

Petit point seating, etc.
Elegance Restored by Tony Churcher

Planters
Clark, Jean M.
Griffiths, M. E. & S. R. Garden Pots
Terracopia Ltd

Rainwater goods, gutters, fittings – cast iron
Glynwed Foundries

Rainwater goods, gutters, fittings – lead
Dennision, Frederick Ltd
Dyson, Ion (Plumbing) Ltd
Fillary, Terry & Paul (Fillarys Ltd)

MOSAIC/TERRAZZO

Hempstock, J. & Co (Builders) Ltd
Norfolk Sheet Lead Ltd
Roberts, David & Co
Sheldon, H. T. W.
Tuxord-Williams of Wales

Rocking horse restoration
Livingston, Judith A.

Scale models
Beaton, John McW.

Steam engines built and restored – model and small stationary
Barrington, Michael

Timber resin repairs
Briggs, A. A. & Son

Tools – antique
Bristol Design Tools
Weaves & Waxes

Trimmings – custom made and reproduced
Percheron, H. A. Ltd

Upholstery – specialist supplier
Forster, D. L. Ltd

Verre eglomise (gilding on glass)
Binnington, Peter & Francis

Weather-vanes
Sunrays (Graham Smith)
Universal Railing Co Ltd

Yarns for restoration of ancient and old textiles
'Farm Spinners' – Penny Walsh

Mosaic/Terrazzo
(a) Conservation
(b) Restoration
(c) Design to client's specification/new work
(d) Pre-cast
(e) Willing to fix on site
(f) Glass mosaic
(g) Marble
(h) Ceramic/terracotta
(i) Glass fibre
(j) Resin
(k) Stone

SKILLS

Avon
Wessex Mosaic Studios Ltd *c d e* (World)

Buckinghamshire
Muir, Jane *c d e f g k* (UK)

Devonshire
Read, Herbert *a b e g i* (World)

Kent
Budd, Kenneth & Budd, Oliver *c d e i j* (World)

Lincolnshire
A. H. Associates Ltd *a b d e f g h* (World)
Hirst Conservation *a* (World)

London
Caley, Trevor (Caley Mosaic) *b c e g h*
Fox, R. & Sons Ltd *b e f g h k* (UK)
Langley London Ltd
Mosaic Arts *c d f h* (World)
Mosaic Studio, The *c* (UK)
Simpson, W. B. & Sons Ltd *a b c d e g h* (HC)
Wyner, Anna *c d e f h* (World)

Somerset
Wates, Rosalind *c e f* (World)

West Midlands
Glass Mountain Studio *a b c e f* (World)

Worcestershire
Dereford of Badsey Hall *b c e f h* (World)

Mouldings
See CARPENTERS, JOINERS; PLASTERWORK

Mural Artists other than Painters
- (a) Design to client's specification/new work
- (b) Abstract
- (c) Figurative
- (d) Classical
- (e) Ceramic/terracotta
- (f) Fibreboard
- (g) Fibrous Plaster
- (h) Mellamine
- (i) Metal
- (j) Wood
- (k) Vitreous enamel

PETIT POINT SEATING

Hampshire
Frith, Francis Collection, The *a h* (UK)
Morris Singer Foundry, The *b c d i*

London
Designers Workshop, The *a*
HAT Interiors – Veronese *a g* (World)
Merry-Henriksen, L. *a d e*
Raby, June *a e*

Lothian
Munro, Kenny *a b c d i k*

Northamptonshire
Escol Panels (S & G) Ltd *b c d k* (World)

Somerset
Threlfall, Philippa & Collings, Kennedy *a e* (World)

West Midlands
Allied Artists *a b c d f h i j* (World)
Glass Mountain Studios *a b c d e k* (World)

Yorkshire, West
HAT Interiors – Phillips *g*

Musical Instruments
See MISCELLANEOUS (musical instruments)

Objet d'art
See MISCELLANEOUS (objet d'art)

Oriental Rugs
See FLOORCOVERINGS; WALLHANGINGS

Painters
See ARTISTS

Pargetting
See PLASTERWORK

Petit Point Seating
See FURNITURE RESTORERS; MISCELLANEOUS (petit point seating)

SKILLS

Plaques
See ARCHITECTURAL CERAMICS, TERRACOTTA; ARCHITECTURAL SCULPTURE (inc. lettercutters); CARPENTERS, JOINERS; CERAMIC ARTISTS; METALWORKERS; PLASTERWORK; STONE

Plasterwork
See also SPECIALIST PRODUCTS (lime plasters & mortars, wattle, daubs, etc.)

- (a) Conservation
- (b) Restoration
- (c) Reproduction to match existing
- (d) Fibrous
- (e) Gypsum
- (f) Stucco-work
- (g) Scagliola
- (h) Hair plaster
- (i) Wattle and daub
- (j) Pargetting (decorative finishes)
- (k) Renewal of supporting beams
- (l) Lime
- (m) Analysis

Avon
Artistic Plastercraft *a b c d e f g* (World)
Hayles & Howe Ornamental Plasterers *a b c d e f g h* (World)
Wheatley Ornamental Plasterers Ltd *a b c d* (UK)

Borders
Grandisson, L. & Son *a b c d e h* (Scotland & N. England)

Buckinghamshire
Chess Interiors Ltd *b c d* (UK)

Cheshire
Riva Design Ltd *g*

Derbyshire
Hodkin & Jones Ltd *b c d*

Devonshire
Crocker, F. H. & Co *a b c d e f g h i j k* (World)
Paul, Alistair & Co *a b c d e f h i j k* (World)
Read, Herbert Ltd *a b k* (World)
Schofield, Jane *a h i k* (S. W. England)

Dorset
Bakehouse, The *a b c d e f g h i j k* (World)
Neo Designs *b c d* (World)
Saint Blaise Ltd *a b c e f g h i j k*
Teychenne, G. C. *b c* (EUR)

PLASTERWORK

Dumfries & Galloway
Solway Studios *a b c d e f g h k* (S. W. Scotland, N. E. border)

Essex
Anthony, J. R. *b c d e f* (HC)
MW Mouldings (London) Co Ltd *b c d* (HC)

Gloucestershire
Architectural Mouldings Ltd *a b c d e*
Young, Rory *a b c d e f h* (World)

Grampian
Brodie, J. & Son *a b c d e f g h i j* (World)

Gwent
Teagle, Alun Building Restoration *m*

Hampshire
D. G. O. Restoration *b c d*
Honey Allaway (Building Conservation) Ltd *f* (EUR)
Young, R. J. & Son *b c d e f* (EUR)

Herefordshire
*Capps & Capps Ltd *a b c d e f h i k l* (World)

Hertfordshire
†Roberts, C. P. Special Works Ltd *b c d e f* (HC)

Kent
*Babbs, Walter Ltd *a b c d e f g h i j k* (S. E. London)
*Cox Brothers
*Kier Wallis Ltd
Palmer, A. T. Ltd *a b c d e f g h i j k* (HC)
Plasterite Ltd *a b c d* (UK)

Lancashire
*Renofors (UK) Ltd *a b c f g h i j k* (World)

Lincolnshire
Hirst Conservation *a b c d e h i m* (World)

London
HAT Interiors Veronese *a b c d* (World)
Badcock, H. & F. (Fibrous Mouldings) Ltd *a b c d e f h* (UK)

SKILLS

Butcher Plastering Specialists Ltd *a b c d* (World)
Eaton-Gaze Ltd *b c d*
Honey Allaway (Building Conservation) Ltd *f* (EUR)
O'Reilly, H. F. *b c f* (HC)
Plaster Decoration Co Ltd, The *a b c d e f h* (World)
Thomas & Wilson (Plastering) Ltd *a b c d e f* (World)

Middlesex
Arkwright Decorative Plastering *a b c d e f h i j* (World)
New Stone & Restoration Ltd *b c f* (HC)

Norfolk
Stevensons of Norwich Ltd *a b c d*

Oxfordshire
*Butler, Arthur Ltd *a b c d e* (HC)
*Symm & Co Ltd *a b c d e f h* (HC)

Somerset
†Webb & Kempf *a b c d f g h i k* (World)

Staffordshire
Prototype Productions *b c e f* (UK)

Strathclyde
Rome, George (Ornamental Plasterwork) Ltd *a b c d e f* (UK)

Suffolk
Crotch, W. G. Ltd *a b c d e f h i j* (World)

Surrey
Architectural & Industrial GRP *a b c* (EUR)
Master Arts Plastering Co *b c d i*
Stonewest Cox Ltd *f*

Tyne & Wear
Decorative Plaster Co (Newcastle) Ltd *a b c d* (Northern region)
Smiles, J. B. *a b c d e f g h i* (UK)

West Midlands
Allied Guilds *a b c d* (UK)
Cartwright, Harry *a b c d e f h i j k* (Midland Counties & Cotswolds)
Classic Renaissance *a b c d f* (World)
*Glenwood Ltd *a b c d e i k* (UK, possibly World)

PROFESSIONALS IN CONSTRUCTION

Yorkshire, South
Antiquity *a b c d e* (World)

Yorkshire, West
Adamson, Yvonne J. *m* (all forms of historic plasterwork)
Architectural Sculptors *a b c d e f j* (World)
Darwent, R. & D. E. Fibrous Plasterers *b c d* (HC)
HAT Interiors – Phillips *a b c d g* (UK)
Scagliola Studio (Michael Koumbouzis) *a b c d e f g h j* (World)
* Building Contractor.

Professionals in Construction Specializing in Conservation/Restoration, also Consultants

- *(a)* Conservation
- *(b)* Restoration
- *(c)* Architecture
- *(d)* Engineering
- *(e)* Interior design
- *(f)* Surveying
- *(g)* 16th century or earlier
- *(h)* 17th century
- *(i)* 18th century
- *(j)* 19th century
- *(k)* 20th century
- *(l)* Ecclesiastical
- *(m)* Computerise/digitise record plans/maps
- *(n)* Specialist landscaping
- *(o)* Consultants
- *(p)* Quantity surveyors (letters denote areas covered)

Avon
Burrough & Hannam Group Practice *a b c g h i j k l* (HC)
Coffin, Jones & Roden *a b c e f g h i j k l* (HC)
Dorothea Restorations *o* (consultancy/surveys of decorative/structural ironwork)
Goodchild Designs *b e* (period design work undertaken, World)
Pedlar, Richard *a b c f g h i j k l*

Bedfordshire
Farrar, Victor Partnership, The *a b c f g h i j k l* (50 mile radius)

Berkshire
Solway Brown Partnership, The *a b c e g h i j k l* (UK)

Borders
Mylne, David *a b c g h i j k* (UK)
Rodwell, Dennis G. – Architect *a b c e f g h i j k l* (World)

Buckinghamshire
Martindale, C. B. *a b c g h i j k l* (World)
Sadler, Jane *e g h i j k* (Oxford area)

SKILLS

Cambridgeshire
Cowper Griffiths Associates *a b c e f g h i j k* (UK)
Pepper, William F. R. *o* (consultant and advisor on straw/reed thatching)
Steen, Ian Architects *a b c e f g h i j k l* (UK)

Central
Bracewell, Stirling Partnership *a b c f*

Cheshire
Buttress Fuller Geoffrey Alsop Practice, The *a b c d e f g h i j k l* (UK)
Dorothea Restorations *o* (consultancy/surveys of decorative/structural ironwork)
Holland, Graham D. *a b c e f g h i j k l* (UK)
Hurd Rolland Partnership
Rank, Nicholas Associates *a b c e f g h i j k l* (EUR)

Cornwall
Clift, Nicholas & Associates Chartered Architects *a b c e f g h i j k* (HC)
Hodgetts, Graham *o* (technical advisor/lecturer on metalwork)
Toy, R. J. & Associates *a c* (HC)

Cumbria
Johnston & Wright, Chartered Architects *a b c e f g h i j k l* (UK)

Derbyshire
Hill, J. *o* (all types of dry stone work)

Devonshire
Gibbs, Christopher *c f g h i j k* (UK)
Howard, A. M. *o* (cob consultant)

Dorset
Design Group, The *a b c e f g h i j k l*
Mitchell Harvey Partnership
Stark, John & Partners *a b c e g h i j k l* (UK)

Dyfed
Pembroke Design Ltd *a b c d e f g h i j k l* (UK)

Essex
Authentic Interiors Ltd *o* (period details design work)
Iffland & Associates *a b d f g h i j k l m* (World)
MacMillan, Carol *a b e* (UK)
Tooley & Foster Partnership, The *a b c d e f h i j k l*

PROFESSIONALS IN CONSTRUCTION

Fife
Fisher, Jack Partnership *a b c f g h i j k l* (UK)
Hurd Rolland Partnership *a b c d e f g h i j k l* (World)
Moir, David – Architect *a b c e f* (UK)

Glamorgan, West
Pembroke Design Ltd

Gloucestershire
Astam Design Partnership *a b c g h i j l* (UK)

Grampian
Alexander-Forsyth, B. Design Group, The *a e g h i j k l* (World)
Forrest, Douglas T. Architects *a b c g h i j k* (Scotland)
Hurd Rolland Partnership
Kennedy, Messrs GRM & Partners *a b c d e g h i j k l* (EUR)
MacKie, Ramsey & Taylor *a b c j k l* (HC)
Meldrum & Mantell *a b c f l* (HC)

Gwynedd
Price, Gruffydd *a b c g h i j k l* (UK)
Voelcker, Adam & Frances Architects *a b c f g h i j k l* (UK)

Herefordshire
Nature's Way *a n* (EUR)

Highland
Goulder, Dave *o* (dry stone walling)
Hurd Rolland Partnership
Munro, Thomas & Co *a b c d f h i j k l* (UK)

Humberside
Blackmore, Antony *a b c f g h i j k l* (UK)
Johnson, Francis F. & Partners *a b c h i j k l* (UK)

Kent
Clague *a b c e g h i j k l* (UK)
Ford, Thomas & Partners *a b c e f g h i j k l* (World)

Lancashire
Harrison & Pitt Chartered Architects & Surveyors *a b c f g h i j k l* (UK)

Leicestershire
Curl, Professor James Stevens *a b c e g h i j k l* (EUR)

SKILLS

Drew-Edwards Keene *a b c d e f g h i j k l* (Midlands & E. Anglia)

Lincolnshire
Hirst Conservation *a b l o* (monitoring of historic buildings)
Rowe, David N. *d f g h i j k l* (UK)

London
Andrews Downie & Partners *a b c e f g h i j k l* (EUR)
Ashton-Bostock *a b e g h i j k l* (World)
Bowyer, Gordon & Partners *a b c e g h i j k l* (World)
Burn, Frederick Bennet Cook Architects *a b c d e g h i j k l* (World)
Caroe & Martin *a b c f g h i j k l* (UK)
Frizzell, F. G. & Partners *a b c e g h i j k l* (World)
Gibberd, Vernon *b c g h i j k l* (EUR)
Gordon, Alex Partnership *a b c e g h i j k* (EUR)
Hamilton, Rosemary O. de C. *e j k* (World)
Hunter & Partners *a b c f i j k l* (UK)
Hurd Rolland Partnership
Inventive Designs *o* (design work undertaken for furniture)
Knights of London *o* (independent fireplace consultancy)
MacKenzie Wheeler (Architects) *c e f g h i j k* (World)
Mears, Roger Architects *a b c h i j k l* (UK)
Parsons, Julie Interiors *e* (EUR)
Pountney, John Architect *a b c j k* (HC)
Summers, Royston & Associates, Architects & Designers *a b c e g h i j k l* (World)
Scarisbrick & Bate Ltd *a b e g h i j k* (World)
Scarlett Burkett Griffiths (Architects) *a b c g h i j l* (EUR)
Schemes *b e h i j k* (World)
Simmons, Roger S. – Architect *a b c g h i j l* (UK)

Lothian
Anderson, Bob Architect *b c j k l* (Scotland)
Begg, Ian Architect *a b c e g h i l* (World)
Cadell, William A. Architects *a b c e f g h i j k l* (Scotland)
Cannongate Building Consultants *a b c f g h i j k l o* (building defects, World)
Cuthbertson, Robert H. & Partners *a b d f g h i j k l* (UK)
Johnston Erdal Architects *a b c f g h i j k l* (UK)
Hurd Rolland Partnership
Kennedy, Messrs GRM & Partners *a b c d e g h i j k l* (EUR)
Laird, Michael & Partners *a b c e g h i j k* (Scotland)
Peddie, Dick & McKay *c e f g h i j k* (UK)
Rodwell, Dennis G. – Architect *a b c e f g h i j k l* (World)

PROFESSIONALS IN CONSTRUCTION

White, Thomas Associates *a b c e*

Merseyside
Norman Jones Sons & Rigby – Chartered Architects *a b c e f g h i j k l* (UK)

Norfolk
Drew-Edwards Keene
Feilden & Mawson *a b c d e f g h i j k l* (World)
Mace Interiors *e* (Home & Eastern Counties)

Northamptonshire
Gotch Pearson *a b c f g h i j k l* (UK)
Scott, J. M. I. *a b c g h i j k l* (UK)

Northumberland
Railton, Jim *a b c e f g h i j k l* (UK)
Wilbie, D. Wilbie-Chalk & Associates *a b c e h i j k l* (UK)

Nottinghamshire
Fish, William Design *e*

Somerset
Caroe & Martin *a b c f g h i j k l* (UK)
Mitchell Harvey Partnership *a b c f g h i j k l* (UK)
Stuart *a b c e g h*

Staffordshire
Wood Goldstraw & Yorath *a b c e f g h i j k l* (EUR)

Strathclyde
Assist Architects *a b c* (UK)
Bercott, Baron & Associates *a b c f g h i j k l* (EUR)
Boswell Mitchell & Johnston *a b c e f g h i j k l* (Scotland)
Cuthbertson, James G. *a b c e f g h i j k l* (UK)
Forrest, Douglas T. Architects *a b c g h i j k* (Scotland)
Frew, Jim *c f* (HC)
Houston Boyce Partnership *a b c e f* (UK)
Kennedy, Messrs GRM & Partners *a b c d e g h i j k l* (EUR)
Houston Boyce Partnership *a b c e f* (UK)
Lane, Bremner & Garnett *c e f* (UK)
Macpherson, Donald H. *a b c f l* (UK)
Munro, W. I. Chartered Architect *a b c e f h i j k l* (UK)
Robertson, Charles Partnership, The *a b c e f h i j k l* (World)

SKILLS

Suffolk
Drew-Edwards Keene
Whitworth Co-Partnership, The *a b c e f g h i j k l* (UK)

Surrey
Antique Buildings Ltd *a b c g h i* (UK)
Beechwood Services (B. W. Rogers) *a b n* (UK)
Booking, Charles *o* (the history/development of period features, UK)
Davey, Norman *b c e g h i j k l* (HC)
Hutton & Rostron Environmental Investigations *o* (investigation of building defects)
Northover Interiors Ltd *e g i j k* (EUR)

Sussex, West
Clague, Betts Hanbury
Warren, John *a b c e f g h i j k l* (EUR & Moslem world)

Tayside
Allen, Gordon & Co *d f* (UK)
Ritchie Dagan & Allan *a b c d e f g h i j k l*
Roger, A. B. & Young – Architects *a b c f g h i j k l* (HC)
Smoor, Franc Architect (Country Life Homes) *a b c d e f g h i j k l* (Scotland)

Tyne & Wear
Spence & Dower *a b c f g h i j l* (UK)

Warwickshire
Kenneth-Duncan *a b d f l* (EUR)
RDS Furniture Contracts Ltd *o* (resources/contracting - original/replica furniture)
Reardon, Michael & Associates *a b c e g h i j l*

Western Isles
Bagshaw, Stuart & Associates *a b c e f g h i j k l* (World)

West Midlands
Cordin, Ronald Associates *a b c g h i j k l* (UK)

Wiltshire
Bare Leaning & Bare *a b c d e f g h i j k l p* (UK)
Sarum Partnership, The *a b c f g h i j k l* (EUR)

ROOFING CONTRACTORS

Worcestershire
Hinchcliffe, Lawrence & Wynn *a b c e f g h i j k l* (UK)
Joyce, Nick Architect *a b c f g h i j k l* (World)

Yorkshire, North
Gordon, Alex Partnership *a b c e g h i j k* (EUR)
Ashton-Bostock *a b e g h i j k l* (World)
Stancliffe, Martin *a b c e f g h i j k l* (EUR)

Yorkshire, West
Adamson, Y. J. *o* (conservation of sculpture/decorative details, plaster/cement)
Fisher, Tom *o* (design work undertaken for manufacturers of furniture, world)

Railings
See ARCHITECTURAL ANTIQUES/SALVAGE; CARPENTERS, JOINERS; METAL

Roofing Contractors Experienced in Conservation/Restoration of Historic Buildings
See also CARPENTERS, JOINERS (roof timbers, open truss)

- (a) Conservation
- (b) Restoration
- (c) Reproduction
- (d) Reproduced to match existing
- (e) Aluminium
- (f) Copper
- (g) Lead
- (h) Steel
- (i) Zinc
- (j) Coated metals
- (k) Clay
- (l) Peg tiles
- (m) Slate
- (n) Stone slates (Collyweston, Purbeck, etc.)
- (o) Timbers repaired/replaced
- (p) Renovation of slate using bonding material obviating nail fixing
- (q) Natural stone tiling
- (r) Period/ornamental guttering

Cheshire
*Mottersheads *b c d g o* (EUR)

Derbyshire
Shelton, H. T. W. *g r*

Devonshire
*Read, Herbert Ltd *a b c d o*
UK Coatings Ltd *m o*

SKILLS

Dorset
*Griffin, A. E. & Son *a b c d g h l m n* (HC)
*Saint Blaise Ltd *a b c d e f g h i j k l m n o r*

Durham
Dennison, Frederick Ltd *c f g* (100 mile radius)

Essex
T. & P. Lead Roofing Ltd *e f g i j* (EUR)

Gloucestershire
*Jotcham & Kendall Ltd *a b l q r* (Glos, Avon, Wilts)

Gwynedd
Furlong & Davies *a b c d g* (UK)
Tuxford-Williams of Wales *a b c d f g k l m n o r* (World)

Humberside
Dryden & Kennedy

Kent
Babbs, Walter Ltd *a b g i k l m o* (S. E. London)
Barwick, R. J. & Sons *b c d e f g* (Kent only)
Byard, D. J. Ltd *b g* (HC)
Coma Roofing Ltd *a b d f g* (EUR)

Lancashire
Hempstock & Co Ltd *a b c d e f g i k l m o* (UK)
*Palmer, A. T. Ltd *a b c d g k l m o r* (HC)

Lincolnshire
Spall, R. J. *a b d l m n o r* (EUR)

London
Braby Carter Ltd *e f g i j* (World)
Maintracts Ltd *g* (HC)

Lothian
Alexander & Roberts (Plumbers) Ltd *a b c e f g h i j r* (UK)
Blake, D. & Co Ltd *a b c f g* (UK)
*Campbell & Smith Construction Co Ltd *a b c d f g i k m*

Middlesex
Permanent Roofs Ltd *a b d e f g h i j k l m n o p q* (UK)

ROOFING MATERIALS

Richardson Roofing Co Ltd *b e f g* (UK)

Norfolk
Anglia Lead Roofing Co *b g* (HC)
Aqua Plumbing & Leadwork Specialist *g* (HC)
Norfolk Sheet Lead Ltd & BKF Industrial & Domestic Plumbing Ltd *f g i r* (EUR)

Oxfordshire
*Boshers (Cholsey) Ltd *a b c d l g i k m o r* (25 mile radius)
Butler, Arthur Ltd *a b c d g k l m o r*
Sharp & Howse Ltd *g* (60 mile radius)

Strathclyde
Alexander & Roberts (Plumbers) Ltd *a b c e f g h i j r*

Suffolk
*Bennett, R. & Snare Ltd *b d g k l m o r*

Yorkshire, East
Clubley, D. & Sons Roofing Co *a g k m r* (HC)

Yorkshire, North
Hardgrave, Joseph Ltd *m* (HC)
Neal, Geoff (Roofing) *a b c d g k l m o q* (HC)
Shouksmith, J. H. & Sons Ltd *g* (UK)

Yorkshire, West
Dyson, Ion (Plumbing) Ltd *a b c d f g*

Wiltshire
WW Roofing *d f g* (World)

* Building contractor undertaking such work using all/part own labour.
( ) Letters in brackets denote area within which willing to work/fix.

Roofing materials
See also ARCHITECTURAL ANTIQUES/SALVAGE
- *(a)* Reproduction
- *(b)* Reproduction to match existing

Clay
- *(c)* Plain
- *(d)* Pantile
- *(e)* Roman
- *(f)* Peg tiles
- *(h)* Natural stone/slate

Other roofing materials
- *(i)* Riven lathes
- *(j)* Thatching spars and combed wheat reed
- *(k)* Concrete/reconstructed stone

SKILLS

Avon
Abbot, Mike *i*

Cheshire
Station Roofing Supplies Ltd (UK)

Cumbria
Burlington Slate

Humberside
Blyth, William *c d e* (supply World)

Kent
Hinsley, T. (Tiles) *e*
Marley Roof Tiles *k*
Robus, Clive & Rosemary *a b f*

Oxfordshire
ARC Conbloc *b k* (HC, most of UK)

Somerset
Manor Mortars *i*

Sussex, East
Aldershaw Tiles *a b c f* (supply World)

Sussex, West
Keymer Hand Made Clay Tiles *b c e f* (supply World)
Weald & Downland Open Air Museum *i j*

West Midlands
Hinton Perry & Davenhill Ltd *c* (EUR)

Yorkshire, West
Pickard, Percy (Sales) Ltd *h* (Eng, Scot, Wales)
( ) Letters in brackets denote area within which willing to supply/fix.

Rugs
See FLOORCOVERINGS

Rush Work
See FLOORCOVERINGS; FURNITURE – CANE, RUSH ETC.

Salvage
See ARCHITECTURAL ANTIQUES/SALVAGE

SCULPTURE

Sanitary Fittings
See also ARCHITECTURAL ANTIQUES/SALVAGE; CERAMIC ARTISTS; METAL (sanitary fittings, taps, etc.)

- (a) Reproduction
- (b) Reproduced to match existing
- (c) Design to client's specification/new work
- (d) Period products suitable for refurbishment
- (e) Basins/sinks
- (f) Baths
- (g) Fittings
- (h) WCs
- (i) Brass
- (j) Silver plated
- (k) Gold plated
- (l) Ceramic
- (m) Willing to re-enamel, resurface
- (n) Painted
- (o) Plastic/glass fibre/GRP

Cheshire
Bath Re-enamelling *f g i m* (UK)

Cornwall
Prosser, Deborah *c e l*

Gloucestershire
Hillhouse Interiors *a e f g h i l* (UK)

London
Bonsack Baths (London) Ltd *c e f g h i k l m* (World)
Czech & Speake Ltd *g*
Renubath Services (London) *e f h m* (HC)

Norfolk
Complete Bathroom, The *a b c d e f g h i j k l n o* (UK)

Surrey
Architectural & Industrial GRP *a b c d e g n* (World)

Wiltshire
Restorations Unlimited *e f h*
( ) Letters in brackets denote area within which willing to deliver.

Scagliola
See ARCHITECTURAL ANTIQUES; PLASTER; STONE

Sculpture
See ARCHITECTURAL ANTIQUES/SALVAGE; ARCHITECTURAL SCULPTURE; CARPENTERS, JOINERS; CERAMIC ARTISTS; METAL; PLASTER; STONE

SKILLS

Seagrass
See FLOORCOVERINGS; FURNITURE – CANE, RUSH, ETC.

Signwriting
See ARTISTS

Soft Furnishings
See FABRIC; FLOORCOVERINGS; WALLHANGINGS

Specialist Contractors Experienced in the Restoration/Conservation of Historic Buildings
See also BUILDING CONTRACTORS

- (a) Conservation
- (b) Restoration
- (c) Underpinning
- (d) Damp proofing/rising damp removal
- (e) Waterproofing/tanking
- (f) Timber preservation/replacements

Buckinghamshire
Preservation Craftsmen Ltd *a b d e f* (UK)

Cheshire
Mottersheads *a b f* (EUR)

Devonshire
UK Coatings Ltd *b d e f* (UK)

Dorset
Hydrotek Wessex *d* (UK)

Essex
Frintongate *a b d* (UK)
Hydrotek *d* (E. Anglia, Kent, London)

Northumberland
Coe, E. M. (Builders) *d*

Oxfordshire
Symm & Co Ltd *a b c d f* (HC)

Surrey
Cox, Peter Preservation *a d e f* (UK)
Structoplast Contracts Ltd *b d e*

SPECIALIST PRODUCTS

Wiltshire
Wayne, R. D. Building Services Ltd *c*

Yorkshire, North
Birch, William & Sons Ltd *c*
( ) Letters in brackets denote area within which willing to work/fix.

Specialist Products for use on Historic Buildings
Coatings for weather resistance
- (a) Clear
- (b) Pigmented
- (c) Silane
- (d) Epoxy
- (e) Acrylic
- (f) Decorative finishes

Repair materials
- (g) Cementitious
- (h) Epoxy
- (i) Polyester

Traditional mortars
- (j) Clay
- (k) Lime
- (l) Harl or roughcast

Traditional finishes
- (m) Parget, daub and torch
- (n) Limewashes
- (o) Lead paints

Timber
- (p) Pre-treatments
- (q) Woodworm treatments
- (r) Dry rot treatments
- (s) Preservative treatments
- (t) Micro-porous decorative finishes
- (u) Decorative finishes – paint
- (v) Decorative finishes – stain
- (w) Decorative finishes – varnishes

Berkshire
Tretol Ltd *a b c d e f g h* (World)

Buckinghamshire
Cementone Beaver Ltd *p q r s u*
Langlow Products Ltd

Cambridgeshire
Sadolin (UK) Ltd *s t u v w* (UK)

SKILLS

Devonshire
UK Coatings Ltd *a b c d e f g h i* (World)

Gloucestershire
Young, Rory *k l n* (World)

Northamptonshire
Rose of Jericho *j k l m n o*

Somerset
Manor Mortars (Hempway Ltd) *j k l m n o* (World)

Surrey
Protective Materials Ltd *g h i* (World)

Yorkshire, West
Hickson Timber Products Ltd (World)
( ) Letters in brackets denote area within which willing to supply.

Stained Glass
See ARCHITECTURAL ANTIQUES/SALVAGE; GLASS – STAINED...

Staircases – Bespoke Specialists
See also ARCHITECTURAL ANTIQUES/SALVAGE; CARPENTERS, JOINERS; METALWORKERS; STONE

- (a) Conservation
- (b) Restoration
- (c) Modern
- (d) Reproduction
- (e) Reproduction to match existing
- (f) Will design to client's specification
- (g) Willing to fix on site
- (j) Georgian
- (k) Provincial
- (l) Victorian
- (m) Colonial
- (n) Regency
- (o) Aluminium
- (p) Cast iron
- (q) Concrete
- (r) Steel
- (s) Stone
- (t) Wood
- (u) Brass

Cornwall
Cornish Stairways Ltd *c e f o p q r s u* (World)

Derbyshire
Cottage Craft Spirals Ltd *d f o t* (World)

STONE

Essex
Bamber, H. H. *e r* (HC)

Glamorgan, South
Geometrical Stairbuilding

London
Higginson, E. A. & Co Ltd *a b c e f g j t* (HC)

Northamptonshire
Parker, Ron

Shropshire
Burbridge, Richard Ltd *b g j k l m n t* (EUR)

Somerset
Malden Joinery *b c d e f t* (HC)
( ) Letters in brackets denote area within which willing to supply/fix.

Statuary
See ARCHITECTURAL ANTIQUES/SALVAGE; ARCHITECTURAL SCULPTURE

Stencilling
See ARTISTS; FABRICS; FURNITURE – PAINTED; GLASS – DECORATIVE FINISHES; WALLPAPER

Stone
See ARCHITECTURAL ANTIQUES/SALVAGE; MISCELLANEOUS (antique tools)

- *(a)* Conservation
- *(b)* Restoration
- *(c)* Reproduction to match existing
- *(d)* Will design to client's specification
- *(e)* Reconstructed, cast stone, scagliola and other forms of artificial stone
- *(f)* Specialist cleaning (mist sprays/miniature air abrasives)
- *(g)* Dry walling
- *(h)* Marble
- *(i)* Natural stone
- *(j)* Slate
- *(k)* Granite
- *(m)* Repellency treatment

Avon
*English Elm Landscapes *b c d g i* (World)
Masonry Associates Ltd *a b c d g i j* (World)
†Poplar Building *a b c e i* (UK)

SKILLS

Borders
Arres, Thomas & Son *g i* (World)
*Grieve, Thomas *b c d g i*

Buckinghamshire
†RBR. Contract Services *b c f i* (UK)

Cambridgeshire
†Coulson & Son Ltd *a b c d e f i j* (HC)
†Rattee & Kett *a b c d e f h i j* (EUR)

Cleveland
Rowney, Eddie *a b g*
*Wheatley, Ray Drystone Walling Contractor *a b c d g i* (World)

Clwyd
Jakim Artifacts *e* (World)
Salter, Cedric Emrys *a b c d e g i j* (World)
Walling, L. J. Stone Masonry Contractors Ltd *a b c d h i j* (HSC)

Derbyshire
*Hill, Joe *g* (consultant)

Devonshire
Connaught Southern Ltd *a b c d f* (UK)
Exeter Marble & Slate Co *b d h j* (World)
*Mold, Peter *g* (World)
†Read, Herbert Ltd *a b c d f h i j* (World)

Dorset
†Griffin, A. E. & Son *a b c h i j* (HC)
†Saint Blaise Ltd *a b c d f g h i j* (World)
Sells, Jonathan (Jonathan-Living-Stone) *a b c d g h i j*
Teychenne, G. C. *a c* (EUR)
Viney, Tony *b c d g h i* (World)

Dumfries & Galloway
Prestige Stonework *a b c d g i j* (UK)
*Tufnell, R. N. *a b c d g i j*

Durham
Allison, Wm. & Sons Ltd *b c d g i k* (UK)

STONE

Dyfed
*Davies & Haddock *a b c g i j* (HC)

Essex
†Frintongate Ltd *b c d i* (UK)
Ornamental Stone *b c d h i j*

Fife
†Watson, W. L. & Sons *a b h i* (Scotland)

Grampian
Moray Stone Cutters *a b c d f i j* (HC, supply World)
Urquhart, Alistair G. *a b c i* (Scotland)

Gwent
†Teagle, Alun Building Conservation *a b c e f g h i j*

Gwynedd
*Jones, Alan *g* (UK)

Hampshire
Honey Alloway (Building Restoration) Ltd *b d f g h i j* (EUR)

Herefordshire
†Capps & Capps Ltd *a b c d f g h i j* (World)

Humberside
Quibell & Son (Hull) Ltd *a b c d f g i* (HC)

Kent
Chilstone Architectural Ornaments *b c d e*
†Cox Brothers *b c g* (UK)
Durnan, Nicholas *a b e f h i j* (HC)
Heritage Stone Restoration Co Ltd *a b e f i* (HC)
Lonsdale, Stephen Ltd *a b c d f g h i j* (World)
†Palmer, A. T. Ltd

Lancashire
*Greenwood, Eric *a b g i* (local)
†Renofors (UK) Ltd *a b c d e f g h i j* (World)
Stoneguard *a b c d e f g h i* (UK)

Lincolnshire
Bullard, Simon *b c d h i* (World)

SKILLS

Linley, Beauford D. (Sculptor) *b c d h i j* (UK)

London
Bysouth, J. Ltd *a b c d f i* (UK)
Capital Marble Ltd *a b c d f h i* (EUR)
Cox, Nigel Ltd *a b c d e f h i* (HC)
†Fox, R. & Sons *f h i j m* (UK, World by arrangement)
Harding Restoration *b c e f h i j*
Honey Alloway (Building Restoration) Ltd *b d f g h i j* (EUR)
Miccoli, G. & Sons Ltd *b e h i* (HC)
Poulter, H. W. *b h* (HC)
Shield, John *b c i j* (World)
Signmaking Developments (The Lettering Centre) *a b c d h i j k* (EUR)
Universal Stone Ltd *a b c f h i j* (HC)

Lothian
Campbell & Smith Construction Co Ltd *a b c d e f i j* (World)
Pritchard, Hugh (Stonemasons) Ltd *a b c d e f h i j k* (HC)
Stoneguard

Merseyside
Burleigh Stone Cleaning & Restoration *a b c d e f g h i* (UK)

Middlesex
New Stone & Restoration Ltd (HC)
Stoneguard

Norfolk
Holgate, David *a b c d h i j* (World)

Northamptonshire
Boden & Ward Stonemasons *a b c d i* (Midlands)
†Bowman (Oxon) Ltd *a b c d f i j* (HC)
Coles, E. *a b c i*
Haddonstone Ltd *b c d e*
Heritage Stone *d e* (supply World)
†McCrone, Philip Builder *a b c d g i j* (UK, supply World)
Weldon Stone Enterprises Ltd *a b c i* (London & adjoining counties)
†Wright, K. G. (Builders) Ltd *a b c g i* (HC)

STONE

Nottinghamshire
Jowett, H. & Co Ltd *a b c d f h i j* (Midlands)
Natural Stone Products Ltd *a b c d g h i k* (supply World)

Oxfordshire
Axtell Perry Symm Masonry Ltd *b c d f i k* (60 mile radius)
†Joslin (Contractors) Ltd *a b c d f g h i j* (HC)

Powys
Wincilate Ltd *a b c d j*

Shropshire
†Cunningham, John Patrick *a b c d e f g h i j* (World)
*Liebscher, Karl *g* (HC)

Somerset
Octagon Joinery Ltd *a b c d i* (World)
Smith, Peter E. – The Stonecarving Workshop *a b c d h i j* (UK)
†Webb & Kempf Ltd *a b c d e f h i* (World)

Staffordshire
Linford-Bridgeman Ltd *a b c d i j* (UK)
Macc Stone Co *a b c d e g i j* (UK)

Strathclyde
Pritchard, Hugh (Stonemasons) Ltd *a b c d e f h i j* (HC)
Stoneguard

Suffolk
†Bennett, R. & Snare Ltd *b c e f g h j* (UK)

Surrey
*Beechwood Services (B. W. Rogers) *a b c g i* (UK)
Stonewest Cox Ltd *b c d e f i* (UK)

Sussex, West
Cathedral Works Organisation (Chichester) Ltd *a b c d f i j* (UK)
Skelton, Helen Mary *a b d i j* (HC)

Tayside
Rowan, Colin *a b c d i*
*Tirlin Pin Dykers/Norman Haddow *a d g* (World)

SKILLS

Tyne & Wear
†Lowry, J. & W. Ltd *a b c d f h i j* (HC)
Smiles, J. B. *b c d* (UK)

Wiltshire
Bloomfield Stonecraft *a b c i* (wherever limestone used)
Lloyd of Bedwyn *c d h i j k* (EUR)

Yorkshire, South
Dry Stone Walling *g*

Yorkshire, North
Eskdale Stone Supplies – T. H. Atkinson *a b c d i* (HC)
*Fletcher, Gordon (Dry Stone Walling & Flagging) *a b d g i* (UK)
Reid, Dick *a b c d h i j* (EUR)

Yorkshire, West
Architectural Sculptors *e* (World)
*Hallam, Paul *b g i* (HC)
Walker, Stuart *g* (HC)
* Dry stone walling only.
† Building contractors undertaking all/part such work using their own labour.
( ) Letters in brackets denote area within which willing to work/fix.

Stucco-work
See ARCHITECTURAL ANTIQUES/SALVAGE; PLASTER

Surveyors
See PROFESSIONALS

Tanking
See SPECIALIST CONTRACTORS

Thatchers
(a) Re-timbering undertaken
(b) Re-timbering undertaken without removal of roof
(c) Water reed
(d) Wheat reed
(e) Long straw
(f) Others (see alphabetical index for details)

Bedfordshire
Wilmott, M. *c d* (HC)

THATCHERS

Berkshire
Bardsley, M. D. *a b c d*
East, George *a c* (Wessex)
Sharp, E. E. & Son *a b c d e* (World)
Thatching Advisory Service *a b c d e* (World)

Buckinghamshire
Cotswold & Chiltern Master Thatchers Ltd *c* (UK)
Craker, Malcolm *d*
Underwood, David *a b c d e* (40 mile radius)

Cambridgeshire
Dodson, Clive *c e* (HSC)
Mizon, P. & B. *b c d e* (HSC)
Pepper, William F. R. *c d e* (World)

Cheshire
Brugge, Peter *a b c* (World)
Burke, J. & Son *a c d e*

Devonshire
Bovey, Christopher *a c d* (HC)
Dray, G. R. & Son *a b c d* (World)
Gard, Nigel *a b c d*
Hallworth, Simon *a b c d*
Harz, Anthony John *a b c d*
Hayman, G. H. *a b c d*
Jones, J. H. *a b c d* (HC)
Kirby, Michael *a c d* (World)
Prince, Alan *a b c d* (HC)
Thatching Supplies Ltd *a b c*
Trezise, David *a b c d* (World)

Dorset
Banwell, Andrew *a b c d* (anywhere interesting)
Bulgin, D. A. *c* (Dorset & Somerset)
Fletcher, Jon *a b c d e* (World)
Symonds, D. S. *a c d*

Essex
Letch, Stephen J. *a b c d e* (World)
Osborne, A. H. & Son *a c e* (World)

SKILLS

Gloucestershire
Lyons, J. *a b c d* (World)
White, David *d* (Glos, Worc, Heref)

Greater Manchester
Towey, Michael *a b c d*

Hampshire
Crouch, Simon M. F. *a c d* (World)
Cleeve, Stephen *c d e* (World)
Gates, Geoff *a b c d e* (UK)
G. B. Properties *a c d*
Hall, Adrian Wessex Thatchers *c d* (HC, World)
Sinkinson, Simon *a b c d e* (HC, World)

Lancashire
Milne, B. D. *a b c* (World)

Leicestershire
Raffle, Andrew V. *a c d* (EUR)

Lincolnshire
Franklin, Michael *a b c d e* (UK)

Norfolk
Dunthorne, Keith *a b c d e* (World)

Northamptonshire
Pinfold, J. H. *a b c d*
Scanlan, Roger *a c d* (World)
Watts, B. J. *a c d e* (UK)
Wood, Leo *a b c d* (World)

Oxfordshire
Lisi, F. & Son *a c d*
Pinfold, G. F. *a b c d* (World)

Shropshire
Cosy Thatch Ltd *a b c d e f* (World)
Jones, Roy *c f* (HC)

Somerset
Brown, Clive *a b c d* (World)
Fryer, Richard A. *a b c* (World)

TRAINING, TEACHING, LECTURING

Griffiths, T. J. *b c d* (EUR)
Hindle, E. P. *a b c d* (HC)
Lewis, Jack *c d* (World)
Parks, E. H. & Co *a b c d* (UK)
Parr, Jerry *a b c d* (World)
Reedways Ltd *a b c d* (World)
Rodger, Paul *a b c d* (HSC, possibly World)

Suffolk
Davies, Peter *a b c e* (World)
Mansell, Terry *a b c d* (World)
Shannan, Paul *b c e* (HC)
Yates, Roger *a b c d* (World)

Surrey
Anderson Thatching Ltd *c* (World)

Warwickshire
Raison, J. D. & Partners *a c d* (EUR, possibly World)
Thatchers *a c d f* (World)
Warner, S. *a b c d e f* (World)

Wiltshire
Blake, S. G. *a b c d* (World)
Chisbury Thatchers *d* (HSC)
Foster, L. C. & Sons *a b c d* (HSC)
Giddings, Christopher John *b e*

Worcestershire
Barnard, Robin *a c d e* (World)

Yorkshire, North
Ryedale Thatchers *a b c d e* (World)
( ) Letters in brackets denote area within which willing to work.

Tiffany Lights
See ARCHITECTURAL ANTIQUES/SALVAGE; LIGHTING

Training, Teaching and Lecturing on Specialist Craft/Conservation Subjects

Binnington. P. & F.
Run 2 wk courses in water, oil, glass gilding and restoration.

SKILLS

Fraser, Anselm Antique Furniture Restorer
Offers 1 yr intensive course on all aspects of antique furniture restoration to students of all ages.

Goulder, Dave
Instruction on dry stone walling projects.

Hodgetts, Graham
Consultant technical advisor and lecturer on all categories of metalwork.

Pryor, Michael McKenzie
Teacher of marbling, graining, and other broken colour work.

Rowney, Eddie
Instruction, talks and lectures given in dry stone walling.

Simons Construction Group Ltd
Runs courses in building crafts.

Sladden, Humphrey
Senior tutor of furniture, West Dean College (BADA course).

Teychenné, G. C.
Course tutor – conservation of architectural stonework, Weymouth College.

Trompe l'œil
See ARTISTS

Turning
See CARPENTERS, JOINERS

Turret Clocks/Mechanical Antiquities
- (a) Public clocks
- (b) Windmills
- (c) Water mills
- (d) Conservation
- (e) Restoration
- (f) Design to client's specification/new work
- (g) Will maintain
- (h) Electrification
- (i) Replacement parts produced
- (j) Sundials

Berkshire
Pawley, David *a d e f g h i j* (UK)

Central
Agar & Son (mechanisms)

VENEERS

Derby
Smith John & Sons *a d e f g h i* (World)

Dorset
Booth, G. W. & Booth, C. J. W. *a d e f g h i* (EUR)

Hertfordshire
Blaxill, P. M. *a b e f g h i* (World)

Leicestershire
Armitage, G. D. (Clock & Belfry Works) Ltd *a d e f g h i* (World)

Lincolnshire
Czjkowski, E. & Son

Northamptonshire
Veetrac Engineering Ltd *b c e*

Oxfordshire
Meecham, P. A. *a d e g h i* (HC)

Surrey
Gillett & Johnston (Croydon) Ltd *a e f g* (World)

Sussex, East
South East Time Service *a d e f g h i* (UK)

Sussex, West
Stenning, P. R. Millwrights Co *b c d e f g i* (World)
( ) Letters in brackets denote area within which willing to work.

Underpinning
See SPECIALIST CONTRACTORS

Upholstery
See FURNITURE RESTORERS

Veneers
See also CARPENTERS, JOINERS; FURNITURE RESTORERS
- (a) Restoration
- (b) Reproduced
- (c) Reproduced to match existing
- (d) Inlays
- (e) Doors
- (f) Furniture
- (g) Panelling
- (h) Banding
- (i) Marquetry
- (j) Security panels

SKILLS

Buckinghamshire
Wooster-Williams Ltd *e f*

Hertfordshire
Silverman, S. & Son (Importers) Ltd *e g j* (UK)

London
Aaronson, R. (Veneers) Ltd *d g h i*
Griffiths, A. D. (Veneers) Ltd *a b c d e f g*

Shropshire
Hazlin of Ludlow Ltd *e g* (World)

West Midlands
Midland Veneers Ltd e g (EUR)

Wallhangings/Tapestries
See also FLOORCOVERINGS (rugs)

- *(a)* Conservation
- *(b)* Restoration
- *(c)* Design to client's specification/new work
- *(d)* Hand-woven
- *(e)* Hand-tufted
- *(f)* Hand-painted
- *(g)* Hand-printed
- *(h)* Abstract
- *(i)* Figurative
- *(j)* Classical
- *(k)* Batik
- *(l)* Embroidered
- *(n)* Oriental
- *(o)* Hand cleaning

Buckinghamshire
Pearce, Barbara *c d e h l* (World)

Cambridgeshire
Lichterman, Heidi *c d h* (World)

Cheshire
'Cheshire Wallhangings' *c d e h i j l* (World)

Cornwall
Beswick, Thelma *c d h i (supply World)*

Cumbria
Nicholson, Maddi *c f g h i j k l* (World)

Devonshire
Benedikte, Maya S. *c i* (World)

WALLHANGINGS/TAPESTRIES

Cook, Jenny *c d i* (World)
Cox, Bobbie *d h j* (World)
Erickson, Grace *d f h i l* (World)
Vivian, Sarah *c d f l*

Dorset
Sues Sews *e f* (World)

Durham
Crompton, Michael *c d h* (World)
Rosengarten, Baruch *c d e h i j l* (World)

Dyfed
Weatherhead, Martin & Nina *c d h i j* (World)

Essex
Clucas, Joy *c l* (World)
Collingwood, Peter *c d h* (World)

Gloucestershire
Lauder, Sylvia *d*

Hampshire
Bailey, Ro *c d e h i* (UK)
Kettle, Alice *c h i j l* (World)

Kent
Pantiles Oriental Carpets *a b d e h i j l* (HC)
Springall, Diana *c e h i l*
Stinson, Dilys *c d h* (World)

Lancashire
Booth, Caroline J. *a b d f l* (UK)
Burgoyne, Elizabeth *c e* (World)
Yorke, Sandra C. *b h i j* (World)

Lincolnshire
Timberland Art & Design *c d e h i j* (World)

London
Anglo Persian Carpet Co *a b d e i j l n o* (World)
Behar Profix Ltd *a b c e l* (UK)
Benardout, Raymond *a c* (World)
Bohun & Busbridge *a b c f g h i j l*
Cato, Laura *c d f h i j l* (World)

SKILLS

Culbert, Pip *c h* (World)
Day, Lucienne *c h i*
Edelstein, Livia *c d e h i* (World)
Edwards, Jay *c d f* (HC)
Etemadzadeh, Doulat *f g h j k* (EUR)
Evans, Joyce Conwy *c l*
Hamilton-Hill, Maureen
Kinley, Susan *c f h i j* (World)
Moncur, Jennie *c d e f h j* (World)
Nix, Annette *c e h i j* (World)
Pincus, Helen *c h i l* (World)
Preston, V. *d* (World)
Rogoyska, Marta *c d h j* (World)
Saint George, Amelia *c d e f g h i j k l* (World)
Silkroot (Brian Lorentz) *a b c f g h i j k* (World)
Stride, Christina *c f g h i j k l* (World)
Talar Carpet Repairs (Oriental) *d e l n* (World)
Textile Conservation Studio/Ksynia Marko *a* (World)

Lothian
Edinburgh Tapestry Co Ltd *a b c d* (World)

Middlesex
Norton, Maggi Jo *c h i l* (supply World)

Norfolk
Barrow, Margot *c d* (World)
Durrant, Jeanette *a c h i l* (World)
Grace, Carole *c d h* (UK)

Northamptonshire
Atelier, John French *c d e f h i k l* (World)

Northumberland
Hind, Don Rugs *c e g j* (EUR)

Nottinghamshire
Baxter, Joan *c d h i* (World)
Usha *f g* (World)

Shropshire
Maund, Heather *c d f h i l*

Somerset
Falk, Gabriella *c d h i* (World)

WALLPAPER

Osborne, Angela *a b c d e f k l m* (UK)

Staffordshire
Criss Cross Textiles (Mrs Joanne K. Weeks) *d* (World)

Strathclyde
Fleming, Gail A. *c f g l* (UK)

Suffolk
Budd, Jo *c h i k l* (UK)
Hopkins, Jan *c d e h i j* (World)
Toulson, Mary Jane *c d e h i* (World)

Sussex, East
Fell, Anita – A. F. Designs *c h i j* (UK)
Potter, Mary *c k* (UK)

Sussex, West
McQuoid, Rebecca *c d h i*

Warwickshire
Wright, Susan *c d h* (World)

West Midlands
Pearson, Cynthia *c h i l* (World)

Wiltshire
Short, Mrs Elaine F. *c d e h i* (World)

Yorkshire, North
Lewis, Elain *c f g h i j k* (World)

Yorkshire, West
Beddows, Terry *c d b e h i* (World)
Dorrien, Lynne *c e h* (World)
( ) Letters denote area within which willing to work.

Wallpaper
- (a) Conservation
- (b) Restoration
- (c) Reproduced to match existing
- (d) Will design to client's specification
- (e) Special coverings, e.g. silk
- (f) Stencilled
- (g) Hand-printed
- (h) Hand-painted
- (i) Airbrushed
- (j) Coloured to specification
- (k) Analysis
- (l) General reproductions of historic wallpapers

SKILLS

Avon
Muraspec Ltd *c d e j* (World)

Cheshire
Muraspec Ltd *c d e j* (World)

Durham
McDermott, Allyson International Conservation Consultants *a c d f g h k* (World)

Gloucestershire
Beauchamp, Alexander *c d l g j* (World)

London
Armitage, Marth Wallpapers *d e g j* (UK)
Gournay, de Designs *a b c d h j l* (World)
McCaw, Norma Conservation *a b* (World)
Muraspec Ltd *c d e j* (World)
Raymond, Ginny (Polychrome Ceramics) *d j* (HC)
Sanderson, Arthur & Sons Ltd *b c d l e g j* (World)
Toynbee-Clarke Interiors Ltd *e j* (World)
Watts & Co Furnishings Ltd *c d g j l* (World)

Strathclyde
Muraspec Ltd *c d e j* (World)

Surrey
Hamilton Weston Wallpapers Ltd *c d g h j* (World)

West Midlands
Muraspec Ltd *c d e j* (World)

Yorkshire, West
Muraspec Ltd *c d e j* (World)
( ) Letters denote area within which willing to supply/work.

Water Mills
See TURRET CLOCKS/MECHANICAL ANTIQUITIES

Waterproofing
See SPECIALIST CONTRACTORS

Wind Mills
See TURRET CLOCKS/MECHANICAL ANTIQUITIES

WINDOWS

Windows
See ARCHITECTURAL ANTIQUES/SALVAGE; CARPENTERS, JOINERS; GLASS – DECORATIVE; GLASS – STAINED; METAL; STONE

Firms and Craftspeople

AAGAAD, ROBERT LTD (Est: 1961)
Period Fireplaces
Frogmire House, Stockwell Rd, Knaresborough, N. Yorks HG5 0JP.
0423-864 805.
GMC; NAMM.
Pc Burton Agnes Hall. Grand Hotel, Brighton. Devonshire Hall.
Brochure.

AARONSON, R. (VENEERS) LTD (Est: 1963)
45 Redchurch St, London E2 7DJ. 071-739 3107.
Veneers – banding and marquetry panels a speciality.

AARRAN DECORATORS (Empl: one; Est: 1977)
Windrush Cottage, Hinton Waldrist, Nr Faringdon, Oxon SN7 8RS.
0865-821 088.
Chairman Oxford & District Branch of BDA.
Also undertakes carpentry, tiling and general repairs.

ABBOTT, MIKE (Empl: solo; Est: 1985)
Windsor & Spindleback Chairmaker
159 Cotswold Rd, Windmill Hill, Bristol, Avon BS3 4PH. 0272-636 244.
BSc Combined Science; Dip Management Studies; Cert in Arboriculture; M Somerset Guild of Craftsmen.
Pc Made cleft ceiling laths for restoration contract – S. Wales.
Will consider any projects involving green (unseasoned) wood.

ACADEMY INTERIORS LTD (Empl: 6; Est: 1985)
Fine Art Decorators
3 Ridgmount Place, London WC1E 7AG. 071-631 4270.
Former fully bound apprentices trained to C & Gs and Advanced C & Gs standard.
Pc Adam ceiling – Institute of Psychoanalysis, New Cavendish St, London, W1. Marbling works – Hyde Park Hotel, Knightsbridge. Specialist decoration – the Dorchester, Park Lane. Various palace and royal standard projects in the Middle East.
   Aims to maintain the highest standard of workmanship from basic finishes to specialized fine-art decoration.

FIRMS AND CRAFTSPEOPLE

ACKROYD, DAVID LTD (Empl: 8; Est: 1973)
Cabinet Makers & Antique Restorers
Bleathwood Manor Farm, Bleathwood, Ludlow, Shropshire SY8 4LT. 0584-810 726.
Employees trained at furniture colleges (Ryecotwood/Shrewsbury Tech) or apprenticed.
Pc Cuban mahogany bookshelves, based on bookcase designed by Adam formerly at Crome Court (now in V & A) made by Vile & Cobb (1762), for a library in Australia. Replacement cupola to house the bell of a stable clock – local county house.

ACORN MILL CO LTD (Empl: 40; Est: 1958)
Bespoke Carpet Weavers
Mellor St, Lees, Oldham, Lancs OL4 3DA. 061-624 4259.
Pc Bolton Metro College, St John's Wood Synagogue. York House, Ashton. Red Mogreggor, Aviemore. Baslow Hall, Bakewell. Lym Royal British Legion. Shelton Hall, Shrewsbury. Cumberland Hotel, Kensington, London.
Heavy contract carpets (80% wool/20% nylon) woven to client's design and colour specification inc. copying and incorporating logos if desired; quotations made from blueprints; a wide selection of their own designs. Brochure.

ACQUISITIONS (FIREPLACES) LTD
8 Laxcon Close, Drury Way, Brent Park, Neasden, London NW10 0TG. 081-459 5500. London Showroom: 269 Camden High St, London NW1 7BX. 071-485 4955.
Original and reproduction Victorian/Edwardian fireplaces, tiles, accessories, mantelpieces, hand-painted tile inserts; gas-coal or log effect fires. Apply to head office for details of your nearest supplier. Brochure.

ACRISE POTTERY & TILES
See ROBUS, CLIVE & ROSEMARY

ADA (APPLIED DECORATIVE ARTS) PARTNERSHIP (Est: 1985)
Painters & Decorators
Lower Farm, Longford Rd, Thornford, Nr Sherborne, Dorset DT9 6QQ. 0935-873 210.
Higher Dip in Art & Design.

ADAMS, GERALD (Empl: one; Est: 1979)
Maker & Restorer of Fine Furniture, Wood Carving & Gilding
3 Hall Farm Buildings, Morningthorpe, Norwich, Norfolk NR15 2LJ. 050 842-8144.

BA (Hons) Fine Art; C & Gs Advanced Craft, Carving & Gilding (Distinction).

ADAMSON, YVONNE J.
Consultant – Historic Plasterwork & Cements
7 Newport View, Headingley, Leeds LS6 3BX. 0532-751 884 & 686 715.
BA; PGCE; MA (Conservation).
Pc Currently working on Jacobean overmantel and fireplace – Little Moreton Hall.
Consultant in historic materials and analysis, specializing in plasters and cements, inc. colour analysis. May undertake restoration work on plaster and painted surfaces (i.e. fresco, or murals) and any cast or modelled forms in cements or GRP.

AGAR & SON (Empl: 3; Est: 1976)
Wrought-iron Worker
Cadgers Loan, Lochgreen Rd, Bonnybridge, Stirlingshire FK4 2EU. 0324-812 833.
C Eng; CCM; DA Silversmithing Product Design (post grad).
Pc Clan Donald Centre, Skye. Chatelherault High Parks. Linniclate Centre, Benbecula. Drumpellier Peace Park. Restoration of Dunkeld Cathedral; Wallace Monument; Mugdock Castle; South Church, Stirling. SDA Commissions – Mark Phillips Equestrian Centre; Gleneagles Hotel; Saltgreens Home, Eyemouth; Alloa town centre sculpture.
Willing to undertake pattern making; armorial works; design; prototyping; conceptual and production artwork. Also experienced in precious metals. Brochure.

A. H. ASSOCIATES LTD (Empl: varies; Est: 1959)
Home Farm House, Bottesford Rd, Allington, Grantham, Lincs NG32 2DH. 0400-81754.
ARCA; ATD; FRSA; FCSD.
Pc Mosaic (35 ft × 5 ft) – Lloyds Bank Overseas Banking headquarters, Gracechurch St, City of London. Lloyds Development Gravesend Mosaic. Numerous mosaic murals for the London County Council Housing Division and for Liverpool City Architects.
Colour prints and transparencies available on request.

A. & H. BRASS (Empl: 4; Est: 7 yrs)
Metalworkers
201–203 Edgware Rd, London W2 1ES. 071-402 1854.

ALBION CERAMICS (Empl: 6; Est: 1987)
3 St Oswins Avenue, Cullercoats, Witney Bay, Tyne & Wear.

FIRMS AND CRAFTSPEOPLE

Architectural and garden ceramics sold through various heritage centres, interior design houses and garden centres; various terracotta, porcelain, stoneware and earthenware fireplaces and overmantels; table lamps and uplights.

ALCOCK, P. R. & SONS LTD (Empl: 25; Est: 1925)
Building Contractors
Castle St, Banbury, Oxon OX16 8NX. 0295-62321.
BEC; NHBC. Approved: Oxfordshire CC and Health Authority; Northampton CC; Cheewell DC.
Pc External masonry restoration – Broughton Castle. Brickwork and masonry repairs – Sulgrave Manor, Compton Wynyates. New roof – Upton House. Several churches within 20 mile radius of Banbury.
Also willing to undertake Stonesfield slating.

ALDERSHAW TILES (Empl: 6; Est: 1984)
Handmade Bricks & Tiles
Kent St, Sedlescombe, Battle, E. Sussex TN33 0SD. 0424-754 192.
Pc Handmade peg tiles – Staunton Museum, Virginia, USA (Eng. buildings of historic interest re-erected in USA). Open Air Museum, Singleton, W. Sussex. 9,000 mathematical tiles finished to appear antique – The Royal Star Arcade, Maidstone, Kent. Repair work matched for Eng. Heritage, National Trust, etc.
Brick specials and tiles made to almost any specification for any size of order, inc. mathematical tiles; oast tiles; peg tiles; scallop tiles; fishtail tiles; bullnose tiles, plain and patterned terracotta floor tiles and paviors; Victorian garden tiles; glazed bricks to match existing. Brochure.

ALEXANDER-FORSYTH, B. DESIGN GROUP, THE (Est: 1984)
Interior Designer
51 Mayne Rd, Elgin, Moray IV30 1PF. 0343-49313.
RIBA (INTER); MA (Hons).
Pc Distillery centres. Castle refurbishment, etc. Antiques suppliers.

ALEXANDER & ROBERTS (Empl: 30; Est: 1969)
Specialist Roofing Contractors
240 Crownpoint Rd, Glasgow G40 2UJ. 041 554-6069 & 551 8050.
Scottish & N Ireland Plumbing Employers' Fed; LDA; MRCA.
Pc Renovation lead roofing, flashings and gutter repairs – Motherwell Cathedral. Replacement of lead roofing – Clydesdale Bank head office, Glasgow. Zinc roofing – Newton Aycliffe Magistrates Court. Longstrip and aluminium roofing/cladding – The Gantock Hotel, Gourock.

ALLWOOD, JACQUELINE

ALLEN, GORDON & CO (Est: 1971)
Structural & Civil Engineering
1 Charlotte St, Perth PH1 5LW. 0730-39881.
M Assoc Consulting Engineers. Staff – M's and/or Fellows ICE; I Struct E; IWEM.
Pc Floor strengthening and stable block repairs – Brodie Castle for National Trust. Restoration – Lower City Mills for Perth & Kinross District Council. Restoration of masonry canal aqueduct – Almond Aqueduct for British Waterways Board.

ALLIED ARTISTS (Empl: 7; Est: 1936)
Glass Craftsmen
Upper Marshall St, Lee Bank, Birmingham, W. Midlands B1 1LA. 021-643 6927. FAX 021-643 9059. TELEX 336544.
Pc TGI Fridays. Cabthorne Hotels. Thistle Hotels. J. C. Bamford. All major breweries. GKN Steelstock, Wombourne, West Midlands. Sandblast engraved window – The Manor Tavern, Aston. Deeply engraved mirror wall – Thursdays Night Club, Birmingham. Engraved coat-of-arms – Midland Bank.
Entablatures in glass, marble and slate; glass etching, sandblasting, etc; low-relief glass sculptures; sculpture in fibreglass or welded metal; fibre board and melamine murals.

ALLIED GUILDS (Empl: 15; Est: 1920)
Ornamental Plasterwork
Unit 19, Reddicap Trading Estate, Coleshill Rd, Sutton Coldfield B75 7BU. 021-3292 874.
Pc Stoneleigh Abbey – Kenilworth. Café Royal – Regent St, London. Music Room – Lancaster. Hippodrome Theatre – Birmingham. Chateau Impney – Droitwich.
Class 'O' fire rating. Handmade using traditional ingredients. Brochure.

ALLISON, Wm. & SONS LTD (Empl: 19; Est: 1870)
Stone Merchants & Masonry Contractors
7 South Church Rd, Bishop Auckland, Durham DL14 7LB. 0388-603 245 & 602 322, 607 876, 607 877.
In-house apprenticeship; Stone Fed; BEC.
Pc Kirkleatham Old Hall. Strawton Parish Church, Cleveland.
Suppliers and carvers of stone, marble, granite and slate; rubble walling; stone cleaning; monumental restoration work. Brochure.

ALLWOOD, JACQUELINE (Empl: solo; Est: 1978)
Glass Engraver
163 Charlton Church Lane, Charlton, London SE7 7AA. 081-858 3929.
Dip AD at Goldsmiths College; AFGE; Soc of Botanical Artists.

FIRMS AND CRAFTSPEOPLE

Pc Various work in private collections.

ALMONDSBURY FORGE WORKS LTD (Empl: 12; Est: 1950, incorp 1970)
Blacksmiths/Fabricators in Iron & Steel
Sundays Hill, Almondsbury, Bristol BS12 4DS. 0454-613 315.
Pc Restoration work – Bristol Cathedral; St Mary's Redcliffe; Roman baths and pump room, Bath; St Endellion Church, Cornwall.

AMBERLEY CHALK PITS MUSEUM
Houghton Bridge, Amberley, Arundel, W. Sussex BN18 9LT. 0798-831 370.
This working museum has several craftspeople working on the site inc. Andrew Breese who makes and restores ornamental ironwork; Don Harmer, a maker of high-quality furniture to his own or client's designs, willing to undertake restoration work; Michael Ray who deals with handmade earthenware especially suited to architectural application; Anne Goodman who restores and makes stained glass. Open spring and summer.

AMERY, LEO STAINED GLASS (Est: 1974)
Kingsgate Workshops, 110–116 Kingsgate Rd, London NW6. 071-624 3240.
SAS Stained Glass of Central School of Art & Design; M BSMGP; The Worshipful Co of Glaziers & Painters of Glass.

ANCIENT & MODERN GLASS (Empl: one; Est: 1987)
Stained Glass Artist
Unit 3, The Plassey, Eyton, Bangor-on-Dee, Wrexham, Clwyd LL13 0SP. 0978-780 931(day) & 759 331(night).
HND Design Crafts (Architectural Glass).
Pc Four 10 ft panels depicting Clwyd countryside inc. activities, flora and fauna – Loggerheads Countryside Centre, Loggerheads, Mold, Clwyd.
Principal business is designing and building one-off panels for domestic dwellings – front doors and internal panels.

ANDERSON, BOB (Est: 1984)
Architect
16 Rutland Square, Edinburgh EH9 3AD. 031-229 4675.
B Arch, Liverpool; Dip Bldg Sc – Liverpool; ARIBA; ARIAS.
Pc Consultant to Stephen & Maxwell – Glenborrodale Castle Hotel. Repairs and improvements – 4–10 Jeffrey St, Edinburgh.

ANDERSON, ROBIN LTD (Empl: 10; Est: 1928)
Building Contractors
Park Lane, Norwich, Norfolk NR2 3EL. 0603-620 058.

FMB.
Pc Staircase – Bigod Tower. Castle Museum, Norwich.

ANDERSON THATCHING LTD (Empl: 2; Est: 1975)
Flat 4, Leith House, Station Rd, Leatherhead, Surrey. 0372-386 835.
G. Magraw, 6 Shawley Crescent, Epsom Downs, Surrey. 0737-50277.
Fed of Master Thatchers.
Pc Queen Charlotte's Cottage, Kew Gardens. Queen Mother's House, Royal Lodge, Windsor. Angus Ogilvy, Richmond Park.

ANDREWS DOWNIE & PARTNERS (Est: 1963)
Chartered Architects & Planners
6 Addison Avenue, London W11 4QR. 071-602 7701.
Raymond Andrews – MBE; M Arch; RIBA   Donald Downie – M Sc; M Arch; RIBA   Pierre La Gesse – Dip Arch; MA; RIBA   Charles Dorin – Dip Arch; MA; RIBA.
Pc Restoration of Grade I buildings inc. Moor Park, Herts; Salisbury Hall; Brochet Hall, Herts. Grade II – The Grange, Wembley; Kensington Close; The Grange, Chalbury; many houses in London; 2 tythe barns. Work for National Trust, Eng. Heritage.

ANELAY, WILLIAM LTD (Empl: 40; Est: 1740)
Building Contractors
Murton Way, Osbaldwick, York YO1 3UW. 0904-412 624.
Run own apprenticeships. Management M – CIOB; RIC. Firm M – BEC & LCA. Approved: Eng. Heritage; several local authorities; regular Diocesan and National Trust contracts.
Pc Dry rot and roofing repairs – Nostell Priory for NT/Martin Stancliffe. Stone repairs – Chapterhouse staircase, Howden Minster for Eng. Heritage/Alex Gordon. Brethane treatment – Asheton Chapel. Repairs – St Magnus Cathedral, Orkney; St Luke's Church, Chelsea. Cawood Castle gatehouse. Structural repairs – Stank Hall Barn.
Employ all basic trades and so can manage large and complex projects. Fully equipped stonemasons' shop. Also undertakes woodworm and dry rot treatment.

'AN ENGLISHMANS HOME'
Architectural Antiques
56 Stokes Croft, Bristol, Avon BS1 3QU. 0272-424 257.

ANGLIA LEAD LTD (Empl: 20; Est: 1961)
Roofing Contractors & Cast Lead Manufacturers
49 Barker St, Norwich, Norfolk NR2 4TN. 0603-630 979 & 626 856.

FIRMS AND CRAFTSPEOPLE

Pc Received awards for leadwork – Bigod Tower, Norwich Castle Museum; Church of St Peter, Mancroft, Norwich; Heveningham Hall, Suffolk. Engaged at Cathedrals inc. St Paul's; Lincoln; Norwich; Salisbury. Re-roofing – Caernarvon Castle; Houses of Parliament; Westminster Hall; Royal Academy; Blickling Hall.
Brochure.

ANGLO PERSIAN CARPET CO (Empl: 3; Est: 1910)
South Kensington Station Arcade, London SW7 2NA. 071-589 5457.
M BADA.
Hand cleaning and repairing specialists of rare old and antique Oriental carpets, etc. Contact Nash Dan, Manager.

ANGUS DESIGNS – DIANA HALL (Empl: 2; Est: 1978)
Designer & Producer of Ceramic Tiles
1 Thatched Cottage, Iford, Nr Lewes, Sussex BN7 3EW. 0273-478 686.
Guild of Sussex Craftsmen.
Pc Floor – Football Pavilion, Milton Keynes Development Corporation. Restoration of floor – Beaulieu Motor Museum, and also Law Courts, London.
Unglazed, non-slip, hand-printed ceramic floor tiles and also medieval and Victorian encaustic tiles made using traditional methods. Brochure.

ANGUS, MARK (Empl: 2)
Stained Glass Artist/Painter
144 North Rd, Combe Down, Bath, Avon BA2 5DL. 0225-834 530.
F BSMGP; Dip Architectural Glass, Swansea School of Art.
Pc Durham & Guildford Cathedrals. Churches, private houses, restaurants, etc.
This artist/craftsman mixes both the abstract and the figurative in his designs. Author of Modern Stained Glass in British Churches *(Mowbrays 1984).*

ANTHONY, J. R. (Empl: 4; Est: 1970)
Ornamental Plasterwork
28 Kingshill Avenue, Collier Row, Romford, Essex RM5 2SD. 0708-23370.
Partners – Full Technological Certificates (2nd) 1959.
Brochure.

ANTIQUE BUILDINGS LTD (Est: 1975)
Architectural Practice/Architectural Antiques
Hunterswood Farm, Dunsfold, Surrey GU8 4NP. 048 649-477.
Directors – ARICS; ARIBA; MSc (Civ Eng); ACI Arb. Recipients of 4 awards for conservation and design work.
Specialists in ancient timber-framed buildings inc. re-locating redundant

APA BUILDERS LTD

buildings. Stock ancient dismantled timber-framed buildings for re-erection; reclaimed handmade bricks; roof tiles and a stock of old oak beams 'second to none'.

ANTIQUE FURNITURE RESTORATION (Empl: 32; Est: 1945)
Antique Centre, 1 Severn Rd, Gloucester GL1 2LE. 0452-29716.
Pc Restoration work on contents of British Embassy in Europe through DOE.

ANTIQUE LEATHERS (Empl: 2 + 2 partners; Est: 1961)
4 Park End, South Hill Park, London NW3 2SE. 071-435 8582 & 7799.
One apprentice for upholstery; LAPADA; AMU.
Pc Work for Mallett – Bourdon House. Colefax & Fowler Designs.
Gilding is undertaken on leather only.

ANTIQUE LOCK SERVICES (Empl: 2; Est: 1986)
48 Arthur St, Luton, Beds LU1 3SG. 0582-34453.
Brochure.

ANTIQUE RENOVATIONS LTD
Antique Furniture Restorations
Unit 1, Lavenham Craft Units, Brent Eleigh Rd, Lavenham, Suffolk CO10 9PE. 0787-248 511.
Pc Ickworth House. Kentwell Hall. Melford Hall.
Brochure.

ANTIQUITY (Empl: 26; Est: 1981)
Fibrous Plasterers
River Works, Grange Lane, Sheffield S5 9JS. 0742-463 636.
GMC.
Brochure.

APA BUILDERS LTD (Empl: 4 + assorted tradesman; Est: 1974)
30 Monument Rd, Woking, Surrey GU21 5LT. 048-62373 & 68704.
4 yrs apprenticeship; C & Gs Second, Weybridge Tech College; C & Gs Second all finals; AM IACM; Corporate M GMC. Approved: Woking Borough Council.
Pc Grade I buildings inc. 17th-century cottages – Old Woking High St; row of 17th-century cottages and flint and stone barn – Bingham, Norfolk; flint cottage – Norfolk; French ceiling – Hove, Brighton.
Will rebuild as period, and undertake flint and stone work (mainly in Norfolk).

FIRMS AND CRAFTSPEOPLE

APPLEGATE, DAVID (Empl: 3; Est: 1982)
Furniture Designer & Maker
Cedarwood, Stoke Rd, N. Curry, Taunton, Somerset TA3 6HN. 0823-490 408.
David Applegate, owner/manager (now in mid 50s) – served apprenticeship as toolmaker and patternmaker.
Pc Extending mahogany dining table featured in *Woodworker* magazine June '86. Segmented circular oak dining table in *Woodworker* Mar '88. 10 'Kew benches' to be made from storm felled Kew trees to be sold at Kew early 1990.
Restoration work also undertaken, but with reservations. Leather lining only applied as an integral part of design. Limited experience of brass inlay, carving, veneers, and plastic. Brochure.

AQUA PLUMBING & LEADWORK SPECIALIST (Empl: 4; Est: 1985)
'Brackenfield', The Street, Billingford, Dereham, Norfolk NR20 4RF. 036 281-8857.
M Inst Plumbing; M LCA.
Pc Lead roofing (500 sq m), casting of lead hopper and rainwater pipes – Dogmersfield Park.

ARBUS, DAVID (Empl: 3; Est: 1976)
Ratten Furniture – Designer & Maker
The Granary, Railway Hill, Barham, Nr Canterbury Kent. 0227-831 540 & 456 413.
Brochure.

ARCADIA STAINED GLASS STUDIO (Empl: 4; Est: 1987)
9 Bridgefield, Stonehaven, Kincardine & Deeside District AB3 2JE. 0569-66274.
Stained/leaded glass apprenticeship, Glasgow; M BSGP; training in Aberdeen inc. Dip Art, Gray's School of Art; Dip Art & Design; Dip Spatial Design; RICS Part 1 & 2.
Pc Main altar window – South Esk Church, Brechin. Royal Arch Bar, Broughly Ferry, Dundee.
Traditionally constructed Art Nouveau style leaded glass.

ARC CONBLOC
PO Box 14, Appleford Rd, Sutton Courtenay, Abingdon, Oxon OX14 4UB. 0235-848 877. Whaleford Rd, Fairford, Glos. 0285-712 128.

ARCHER, ROY – FURNITURE (Empl: one; Est: 1983)
Oak Farm, Chester Rd, Aldford, Cheshire CH3 6HJ. 0244-65371.
Teachers Cert, University of London; C & Gs Cabinet Making (1st class).

ARCHITECTURAL MOULDINGS LTD

Pc Lectern for conferences – Professional Assoc of Teachers. Circular table – managing directors office, Reed Corrugated Cases.

ARCHITECTURAL ANTIQUES (Est: 1983)
Antique Mantelpieces
351 King St, London W6 9NH. 081-741 7883.
Brochure.

ARCHITECTURAL ANTIQUES – ANDRÉ BUSEK
Savoy Showroom, New Rd, S. Molton, Devon EX36 4BH. 07695-3342.
Spiral staircases; Art Nouveau tiles; Victorian fireplaces and marble surrounds; bathroom fittings; doors; panelling; pub fittings; pulpits. Complete schemes for restaurants, wine bars and public houses undertaken at Ley Farm workshops. Willing to assist with export documentation and shipping.

ARCHITECTURAL CERAMICS LTD (Empl: 4; Est: 1986)
Unit 120, Building A, 3–12 Creekside, London SE8 4PJ. 081-692 7237.
Angela Lewis Dip AD, Sarah Shirley and Jeremy Newland – all have BA (Hons) Ceramics. John Shirley has a BA (Hons) History.
Pc Architectural detail for Noah's Ark (designed and built by Branson Coates Architecture) – Sapporo, Japan. 2 Egyptian style bas reliefs – Deep Pan Pizza Co. 5 ft long terracotta sphinx – Sainsbury's Homebase, London, W14.
Terracotta and faience produced to client's design, with emphasis on interpreting the classical. Limited stock of own designs available.

ARCHITECTURAL HERITAGE LTD
Architectural Antiques
Taddington Manor, Taddington, Nr Cutsdean, Cheltenham, Glos GL54 5RY. 038-673 414.
Stone marble and wood fireplaces; period oak flooring; statuary; seats; well heads; gazebos; panelling and pub fitments.

ARCHITECTURAL & INDUSTRIAL GRP (Empl: 5; Est: 1982)
Glassfibre Mouldings, Exterior Cornices, Exclusive Bathrooms
400 Ewell Rd, Tolworth, Surrey KT6 7HF. 081-399 3004.
Pc Custom built bathrooms for large houses in London. Cornices and columns to form Plant Room, Kensington Palace Gardens, London. Cornice – new flats, Mile End Rd. Columns – Shopping Centre, Maidstone, Kent.

ARCHITECTURAL MOULDINGS LTD (Empl: 10; Est: 1987)
City Business Centre, Hemmingsdale Rd, Gloucester GL2 6HN. 0452-300 071.

FIRMS AND CRAFTSPEOPLE

5 yr apprenticeship; C & Gs Plastering Craft Cert; Plastering Advanced Craft Cert – London Institute.
Pc Midland Bank, Cullompton and Cheltenham. Cheltenham & Gloucester Estate Agency. Guru Nanak Sikh Temple, Wolverhampton. BBC Radio Gloucester Building. Restoration of large town houses, manor houses and hotels inc. Hygrove House, Minsterworth, Glos; Fownes Hotel, Worcs; Tewkesbury Hall Hotel, Tewkesbury, Glos.
Fibrous plaster mouldings; GRP; GRC; fireplaces. Brochure.

ARCHITECTURAL & PLANNING PARTNERSHIP
See WARREN, JOHN

ARCHITECTURAL SCULPTORS (Empl: 2; Est: 1986)
Holroyd Mill, Beck Rd, Micklethwaite, Bingley, Bradford, W. Yorks BD16 3JN. 0274-551 082.
Managing Director – BA (Hons) Fine Art Sculpture. Apprentice trained employee in ornamental and fibrous plaster. Sub contractors apprentice trained as needed.
Pc Matching ornamental plaster mouldings to existing – Wayne Sleep Dance Studio, 17 Queensbury Mews West, London. Supply to Dykes Bros Lakes Ltd – new offices, Derby Sq, Windermere, Cumbria and refurbishment of listed buildings.
Also undertakes decorative internal and external fibreglass mouldings. Will match stone to existing.

ARCHITECTURAL SCULPTORS & LETTERING (Empl: 2; Est: 1970)
40 Cardigan Street, London SE11 5PF. 071-735 9374.
Apprenticed to David Kindersley; Cambridge School of Art.
Pc Sculpture for British Telecom; Lloyds Register of Shipping; Exeter University; Westminster Abbey; etc.
Also willing to undertake graphics. Brochure.

ARCHITECTURAL WOODWORKERS (Empl: 4; Est: 1976)
6a Station Rd, Bovey Tracey, Newton Abbot, Devon TQ13 9AL. 0626-833134.
GMC.
Pc 35 ft panelling and bookcase – Devon Longhouse. Room panelling and carved pulpit for USA. Numerous carved fireplaces to individual design in knot-free Russian or Scandinavian pine.
Only marble and stone inserts undertaken. Further information on request.

ARCHIVE STAINED GLASS DESIGN (Empl: 3; Est: 1983)
'Denehurt', 62 Denton Avenue, Leeds 8, Yorks LS8 1LE. 0532-696 334.

ARMSTRONG IRONWORK

ARENA GLASS STUDIO (Empl: 3; Est: 1981)
Stained Glass Artist
110 The Broadway, Sheerness, Kent ME12 1TS. 0795-661 975.
Pc Roof domes; sky lights; picture windows; tiffany lamps; screens; etc.

ARKWRIGHT DECORATIVE PLASTERING (Empl: 5; Est: 1982)
Unit 3, New Rd, Hounslow, Middx TW3 2AN. 081-570 0464.
All employees have C & Gs qualifications (Craft and Advanced); M GMC.
Pc Supplied and installed all plasterwork to 3 restored flats – 33 Eaton Avenue, London, NW3 (photographs and references can be supplied).
Brochure.

ARMITAGE BRICK LTD (Empl: 400; Est: 1824)
Robin Hood, Wakefield, W. Yorkshire WF3 3BP. 0532-822 141.
Produce terracotta and mouldings, 73 mm and 80 mm bricks for matching up to 3 inch brickwork. No minimum quantity. Brochure.

ARMITAGE, G. D. (CLOCK & BELFRY WORK) LTD (Empl: 2, hope to train more; Est: 1979)
Turret Clock & Belfry Specialists & Gilding of Architectural Features
31–33 High St, Husbands Bosworth, Lutterworth, Leics LE17 6LJ. 0858-880 066.
Worked Wm. Potts of Leeds, tower clock specialists; BA (open) technology and music; M Brit Horological Instit; M GMC. Approved: Eng. Heritage; Conservation Unit; Council for the Care of Churches.
Pc Repair, restoration, painting and gilding – 23 bell carillon, 24 Old Bond St, London. Restoration, gilding, replacement clock – All Saints Church, Leighton Buzzard. Overhaul and repair of mechanism – Rotherley Parish Church. Rebuild R C Cathedral, Armagh, N. Ireland. Gilding and painting – Royal Coats of Charles II, Ancient House, Buttermarket, Ipswich.

ARMITAGE, MARTH WALLPAPERS
1 Strand on the Green, London W4 3PQ. 081-994 0160.
Art Workers Guild; Wallpaper History Society.

ARMSTRONG IRONWORK (Empl: 6; Est: 1986)
Artist Blacksmith
Drumsleet Old School, Cargenbridge, Dumfries DG1 1RG. 0387-51984.
16 yrs experience; M BABA.

FIRMS AND CRAFTSPEOPLE

ARRES, THOMAS & SON (Empl: 2–3; Est: 1966)
Dry Stone Walling
23 Barony Park, Kelso, Roxburghshire TD5 8DJ. 0573-24836.
All time served stone dykers.
Pc Drystone dyke round extension to kirk yard at Hownam. Wishing Well – Jedburgh.
Willing to undertake ornamental stonework.

ARTFUL GLASS CO LTD (Empl: 3; Est: 1988)
Unit 106, Brune Street Workshops, Brune Street, London E1. 071-247 9777.
Pc Breweries Whitbread and Carringtons. Private residential commissions.

ART GLASS LTD (Empl: 30; Est: 1929)
Stained Glass Artist
Providence Street, Westgate, Bradford, W. Yorkshire BD1 2PW. 0274-732 735/6.
M GGF.
Pc Repairs – Bradford Cathedral. Repairs and new windows City Hall, Bradford.

ARTISTIC PLASTERCRAFT (Empl: 12; Est: 1985)
Ornamental Plasterers
Lyndhurst Studios, 16–18 Lyndhurst Rd, Oldfield Park, Bath, Avon BA2 3JH. 0225-315 404.
Craftsman M Fed of Crafts & Commerce; C & Gs Plastering.
Pc New ceiling – Swansea Grand Theatre. Restoration of c. 1620 ceiling and frieze, Heytesbury.
Brochure.

ARTISTIC UPHOLSTERY LTD (Empl: 30; Est: 1952)
Bridge St, Long Eaton, Nottingham NG10 4QQ. 0602-734 481. FAX 0602-461 032.
Brochure.

ARTISTS IN STAINED GLASS (Empl: 2; Est: 1983)
81 Bradwell Rd, Netherton, Peterborough, Cambs PE3 6QL. 0733-262 178.
M CSD; Dip Industrial Design.
Pc Public houses; night clubs; hotels; private residences.

ASHBURTON UPHOLSTERY (Empl: 5; Est: 1970)
Unit 1. 31a East St, Ashburton, Devon TQ13 7AQ. 0364-52040. FAX 0364-53535.

ASSIST ARCHITECTS

AMU.
Pc National Trust. Lord and Lady O'Hagen Dowager Bastarde. Dartmoor National Park.
Specialists in the office refurbishment of leather. Brochure.

ASHLEY ANTIQUES/FURNITURE (Empl: variable; Est: 1974)
129 High St, Hungerford, Berks RG17 0DL. 0488-82771.
Furniture/fittings made to requirements (inc. kitchens) and antiques restored. Brochure.

ASHLEY FURNITURE WORKSHOPS (Est: 1968)
3a Dawson Place, London W2 4TD. 071-229 6013.
Specialists in hand-dyed and antiqued leather, this firm makes and renovates classical hand-polished, deep-buttoned leather furniture.

ASHMORE, M. J. JOINERY SPECIALIST (Empl: one)
Unit B, Manston Green Industries, Preston Rd, Manston, Nr Ramsgate, Kent. 0843-823 624.
C & Gs in Carpentry & Joinery; M GMC.
Pc Joinery for old barn and oast house conversions and for listed buildings.

ASHTON & CO STAINED GLASS (Empl: 4; Est: 1987)
28 St Mary's Works, Duke St, Norwich, NR3 1QA. 0603-760 464.
M BSMGP.
PC TGI Fridays – Covent Garden. Felbrigg Hall – National Trust.
Will also reproduce brass work (i.e. missing handles, stays, etc.) to match existing. Wholesalers for materials for the area.

ASHTON-BOSTOCK, DAVID (Est: 1963)
Interior Designer
21 Charlwood St, London SW1V 2EA. 071-828 3656.
M IDDA.
Pc Restoration, decoration and design – Avebury Manor (Grade I), N Marlborough and Dominican Convent, Co Wicklow, Ireland.
Also have a well established china repair business, which has undertaken work for HM The Queen, galleries, museums and stately homes.

ASKELL, L.
See BLACK LANE POTS WORKSHOPS

ASSIST ARCHITECTS
6 Dixon St, Glasgow, Strathclyde G1 4AX. 041-221 0505.
Pc Martyrs School restoration and conversion of C. R. Mackintosh

building (Grade I). Glasgow Fishmarket restoration and conversion (Grade II).
A large practice incorporating 12 architects.

ASTAM DESIGN PARTNERSHIP (Est: 1847)
Architects, Quantity Surveyors & Planning Consultants
St Nicholas House, 47 London Rd, Gloucester GL1 3HF. 0452-308 500.
Thomas Street House, Cirencester, Glos GL7 2AY. 0285-652 106.
RIBA; RICS.
Pc Nat Trust; DOE (listed buildings re-survey); The Marquis of Bath; Lord Farringdon. Gloucester Cathedral; Worcester Cathedral; Kings School, Gloucester; Westonbirt School; Hathdrop Castle School; Prinknash Abbey.

ATELIER DAMIEN DEWING (Empl: 5; Est: 1979)
Designers & Makers of Furniture and Vernacular Structures
Showroom, Glenholm, George St, Nailsworth, Glos GL6 0BT. Workshop, Unit 10, Nailsworth Mills Estate, Glos GL6 0BT. 045 383-4100.
Furniture made using naturally sculptured materials from old derelict oak barns, windswept seashores, etc. The shape of each piece of material dictating its place and function.

ATELIER INTERIORS (Empl: 5; Est: 1987)
Hand-woven, Hand-tufted Floorcoverings
Windsor Mill, Hanson Lane, Halifax, W. Yorks HX1 4SD. 0422-330 134.
Yvonne Hughes – MA   John French – NDD; ATC   Andy Warburton – BA (Hons).
Pc Debenhams. Horseguards Hotel. Fenwicks. Reiss Menswear. Washouse Modes. Scottish Gallery. Private client's in UK, Europe, Middle East and USA.
Brochure.

ATELIER, JOHN FRENCH
Hand Woven, Hand Tufted Wallhangings
Peartree Cottage, Moreton Pinkney, Northants NN11 6SG. 0295-76343.
See ATELIER INTERIORS for qualifications, etc.
Pc P & O Royal Princess. Bank of Ireland. Scandinavian Bank. Shaq Industries, Saudi Arabia. Rickett & Coleman Bank. Julius Baer.

AXTELL PERRY SYMM MASONRY LTD

AURORA GLASS (Empl: 2; Est: 1984)
Stained Glass Artist/Painter
Unit Block D, Castle Street Ind. Estate, Riverbank, Alloa, Clackmannanshire FK10 1EU. 0259-216 487 (24 hr) & 217 510 (night).
BA (Hons) Design & Crafts, Edinburgh; Scottish Glass Soc; Soc of Master Craftsmen; Central Arts; Scottish Council Development & Industry; Master Glass Painters.
Pc Restoration of Cottier windows – St Machar's Cathedral, Aberdeen. Windows restored and designed – Rhu & Shandon Parish Church, Helensburgh. Various other Scottish churches and private clients. Corporate clients inc. Britoil; British Gas; Scott-Stern; Tayburn; Tennets Caledonian; Maclays; Scottish & Newcastle Breweries; Filion Ass, Canada.

AUTHENTIC INTERIORS LTD (Empl: 8; Est: 1974)
Design Construction Furnishing Consortium
Queens House, Queens Rd, Buckhurst Hill, Essex IG9 5BX. 081-506 1577.
Staff are members of professional institutions.
Pc Design of period interiors and fitments for public and private clients. Details can be forwarded to serious enquirers.
This firm can obtain original items and can also reproduce mouldings in GRP for replacement of damaged areas. Brochure.

AVENA CARPETS LTD (Empl: 30; Est: 1976)
Bankfield Mill, Haley Hill, Halifax, W. Yorks HX3 6ED. 0422-330 261.
Pc Copied 1830 carpets for Swedish Royal collections. Reweaving designs from 19th century for National Trust Properties.
Specialists in Brussels and Wilton weaving.

AVERBUCH, SHAERON CERAMIC DESIGNS (Empl: solo)
7 James St, Portobello, Edinburgh EH15 2DS. 031-6693 082.
BA (Hons) Degree Art & Design, specializing in Ceramics & Textile Design.
Pc Terracotta tiles for Garden Festival '88, Glasgow.
Highly decorative relief tiles – floral, fish and birds being the main subject matter, although also utilizes texture and unusual outer tile shapes.

AXTELL PERRY SYMM MASONRY LTD (Empl: 30; Est: 1827)
Osney Mead, Oxford OX2 0EQ. 0865-246 677. FAX 0865-790 070.
BEC; Stone Fed; London Assoc of Master Stonemasons. On the Diocesan, Eng. Heritage, Local Authority, Property Services Agency list of approved contractors.
Pc New College, Oxford. Exeter College, Oxford. Great Missenden Abbey. Englefield House, Theale.

FIRMS AND CRAFTSPEOPLE

AYLES, ROBERTA (Empl: solo; Est: 1977)
Stained Glass Artist
Glass-works, 21 Leechwell St, Totnes, Devon TQ9 5SX. 0803-863 505.
BA (Hons) Art – Aberystwyth; apprenticeship with Peter Tysoe; Devon Guild of Craftsmen.
Pc Aztec style panels – The Mission Nightclub, Union St, Plymouth. Victorian style panels – The Waterman's Arms, Bow Bridge, Tuckenhay, Devon. Japanese style screens – D. H. Evans, London.
Also works with fused glass which has potential for use as tiles and mosaic. Interested in collaborating with a mosaicist.

BABBS, WALTER LTD (Empl: approx 50; Est: 1922)
Building Contractors
4/6 Star Lane, St. Mary Cray, Orpington, Kent BR5 3LT. 0689-21132 & 77607.
BEC; FMB. Approved: Diocese of Rochester; Eng. Heritage; Kent CC; London Borough of Bromley & Bexley; MOD; PSA; British Rail, and many others.

BACON & BACON (Est: 1972)
Conservation of Paintings & Historic Interiors
Sunniside Lodge, Painshawfield Rd, Stocksfield, Northumberland NE43 7EA. 0661-842 368.
Mrs A. F. Bacon – Dip AD; Dip Conservation of Paintings; IIC; UKIC; SSCR. Mr C. D. Bacon: BA; M Phil.
Pc Restoration – 18th-century painted room by Barrett, Gilpin, Cipriani, Mickleham, Surrey. Restoration – large painting by Pietro Da Cortona, Oxford Town Hall and also one by Greiffenhagen, Langside Library, Glasgow. Paint sample analysis – Old Executive Office Building, 1700 Pensylvania Ave, Washington DC, USA.

BADCOCK, H. & F. (FIBROUS MOULDINGS) LTD (Empl: 15; Est: 1876)
Unit 9, 57 Sandgate St, Old Kent Rd, Peckham, London SF15 1LE. 071-639 0304.
GMC; FMB.
Pc Refurbishment and renewal of Queens Colonnade, Royal Naval College, Greenwich and also the Foreign Office, SW1 (fibrous plaster work). Fitting out of Palace – Oman, Middle East.
Will design anything to commission and also match to existing, inc. aging. Hold extensive stock of 40 designs of cornice. Brochure.

BAGNELL, R. C. (Empl: solo; Est: 1978)
Antique Furniture Restorer & Cabinet Maker
Stables Farm, Bradford Peverell, Dorchester, Dorset DT2 9SE. 0305-88312 & 889312.
Trained on BADA Restoration Course, W. Dean College.

BAGSHAW, GUY F. (Empl: 3; Est: 1975)
Period Cabinet Maker & Furniture Restorer
Park Cottage, Farringdon, Alton, Hants GU34 3HA. 0420-58362.
BAFRA.
Pc 20 ft dining table and 24 chairs. Altar canopy – Winchester Cathedral. Panelled rooms – Berkeley Square, London.
Only a limited amount of turning is undertaken. Brochure.

BAGSHAW, STUART & ASSOCIATES (Est: 1982)
Architects & Designers
Laxdale, Stornoway, Western Isles PA86 0DS. 0851-4889.
Dip Arch (Leics); MRIBA; MRICS; registered architect with ARCUK.
Pc Survey, partial restoration – Kissimul Castle, Isle of Barra. Restoration of thatched houses (Grade I).
Interested in the restoration of old buildings, together with finding alternative uses when original function no longer exists.

BAILEY, J. A. & SONS (BUILDERS) LTD (Empl: 15; Est: 1954)
25 Tape St, Cheadle, Stoke-on-Trent, Staffs ST10 1BG. 0538-752 115 & 753 410.
M FMB; NHBC.
Pc Restoration of conservatories and Banqueting Hall – Alton Towers, Staffs.

BAILEY, KEITH (Empl: solo; Est: 1975)
Architectural Sculptor
63 Eden St, Cambridge CB1 1EL. 0223-311 870.
Fellow SD-C; M Art Workers Guild.
Pc Opening plaque (by HM the Queen) – New Chapter House, St Albans. Thaxted War Memorial. Civic and memorial lettering and heraldic carving in UK and abroad. Sculpture in various private collections.

BAILEY, RO (Est: 1982)
Tapestry Weaver
44 Thornbury Avenue, Shirley, Southampton. Hants SO1 5DA. 0703-221 876.
M Local Crafts of Wessex; Guild of Spinners, Weavers and Dyers.

FIRMS AND CRAFTSPEOPLE

Pc Tapestry of Portchester Castle for local estate agent.
Photographs of previous work can be supplied.

BAKEHOUSE, THE (Est: 1987)
Restoration, Conservation & Reproduction of Ceramic Objects
Horsecastles (Corner with Acreman St), Sherborne, Dorset. Postal address, 1 Acreman St, Sherborne, Dorset DT9 3NU. 0935-813 128.
Dip Art & Design, 3d Design course, Epsom School of Art & Design; M Brit China & Porcelain Artists Assoc; F RCA; M UKIC, Ceramic, Glass & Conservation Group; M GMC.
Pc Restoration carried out for private collectors inc. some items among the Digby Collection of Ceramics in Sherborne Castle. Also work done for the antique trade, and for National Auction Houses, throughout the UK.
Also undertakes small amounts of fibrous plasterwork, gypsum, pargetting and scagliola. Photography arranged for records. Cataloguing of ceramic collections undertaken.

BAKER, DAVID – LETTERCUTTER (Empl: one; Est: 1979)
The Workshop at Ford Cottage, Low Rd, West Acre, King's Lynn, Norfolk PE32 1TR. 0760-755 626.
Central School of Arts & Crafts – Goldsmiths College; M Letter Exchange.
Pc Lettering on Lady Chapel windows – Ely Cathedral. Plaques for opening ceremonies at many buildings throughout UK.
Brochure.

BAKER, M. E. (Empl: solo; Est: 1975)
Canework
46 Bishopston, Montacute, Somerset TA15 6UU. 0935-822 172.
Apprenticed.
All types of chairs caned. Free estimates given.

BALLANTINE BONESS IRON CO LTD (Empl: 150; Est: 1853)
Links Rd, Bo'ness, W. Lothian EH51 9PW. 0506-822 721 & 822 281.
BSI Registered Firm.
Pc Gates and railings – Jeddah Royal Palace; Kuwait; Athens; Waverley Market, Princess St, Edinburgh.
Brochure.

BALLANTYNE, DAVID
See SAVIAC PROTOTYPES

BALL BROS (ENGINEERS) LTD (Empl: 60; Est: 1870)
Metalworkers
Arden St, Stratford-upon-Avon, Warwick CV37 6NS. 0789-292 268.
Various qualifications in welding; moulding; patternmaking; machining.
Pc Railing castings in alum and iron. Plaques and statues in gunmetal.

BALLYBEG RESTORATIONS (Empl: 2; Est: 1980)
Furniture Restorer
51 Cross St, Islington, London N1. 071-226 3465. 101 Kingsway, Mildenhall, Suffolk IP28 7HS. 0683-712 378.
Dip London College of Furniture.
Pc Commissions inc. large items such as bookcases, tables and settees, down to the smallest items, such as lock repair for writing slope. References available.

BALSON, J. L. (Empl: one; Est: 1985)
Stained Glass Artist, Designer, Restoration, Surveys, Consultancy
11 Butchers Lane, Shottesbrooke, Nr Maidenhead, Berks SL6 B5O.
Courses at the 'Glass Market', but largely self taught; M of *Art of Living* Directory; accepted by the GMC.
Pc Window of St Edmund Campion – RC Church, Maidenhead. 17th-century windows – Nowkes Hill Cottage, Ashampstead, Reading. Stained and painted bathroom window of moon – Addys Cottage, Shottesbrooke, Berks.

BAMBER, H. H. (Empl: 3; Est: 1934)
Metalworker
Clayton & Bamber Ltd, 51/52 Cartersfield Rd, Waltham Abbey, Essex EH9 1JD. 0992-712 929.
C Eng; all have practical qualifications.
Pc Period restoration work in staircases and balustrading.

BANWELL, ANDREW (Empl: 3; Est: 1982)
Master Thatcher
Wynchard, 32a Durweston, Blandford Forum, Dorset DT11 0QA.
Apprentice training with CoSIRA M Dorset MTA.

BARBERTON, NICK (Est: 1983)
Furniture Designer & Maker
'Windrift', Highfield Lane, Woodfalls, Salisbury, Wilts SP5 2NG. 0725-20364.
Dip in Industrial Design; M Dorset Craft Guild.
Pc Stations of the Cross, St Martin's, Salisbury.

FIRMS AND CRAFTSPEOPLE

Also undertakes architectural carving and turning.

BARDSLEY, M. D. (Empl: one; Est: 1980)
Master Thatcher
1 Marlston Cottages, Marlston, Newbury, Berks RG16 9UN. 0635-201 546.
4 yr apprenticeship; M Oxon, Berks & Bucks MTA; M NCMTA.

BARE LEANING & BARE (Est: 1904)
Chartered Quantity Surveyors
Clifton House, Lethbridge Rd, Swindon, Wilts SN1 4BY. 0793-21337/8.
All partners are Fellows or Associates RICS.
Pc Many restoration and refurbishment projects for National Trust; Landmark Trust; local authorities; national companies; well-known organizations and private individuals. Work ranges from small schemes to ones costing millions of pounds.

BARKER, DON – ARCHITECTURAL & DESIGN BLACKSMITH
Bracken Edge Forge, Plainville, Wigginton, Yorks YO3 8RG. 0904-769 843.
Qualified Design Engineer; Council Member of BABA.
Pc Modern ironwork – McLean Holmes project. Restoration and lighting – Mount Grace Priory, N. Yorks for Eng. Heritage. Plantation gates for Nevis Island, W Indies. Railings, lightings, hanging pyx – Christ Church Lady Chapel, Oxford.
Brochure.

BARNARD, ROBIN (MASTER THATCHER) (Empl: one; Est: 1985)
Jessamine House, 49 Main St, Bretforton, Evesham, Worcs WR11 5JH. 0386-830 873.
4 yr apprenticeship; M Glos, Heref, Warwicks & Worcs MTA; M NCMTA.
Pc Stags Head Public House, Offchurch, Warwicks.

BARNES, GRAHAM (Empl: solo; Est: 1979)
Antique Furniture Restoration & Conservation
14 St Mary's St, Ely, Cambs CB7 4ES. 0353-665 218.
Trained West Dean College; founder M BAFRA.
Pc Ely Cathedral. Cambridge University. Very varied encompassing both private and trade.

BARNSLEY, EDWARD EDUCATIONAL TRUST FURNITURE WORKSHOP LTD, THE (Empl: 3 senior craftsmen; Est: 1923)
Cockshott Lane, Froxfield, Petersfield, Hants GU32 1BB. 073 084-233 & 329.
Pc Archbishop's throne and prie-dieu – Canterbury Cathedral. Boardroom and dining room – Courtaulds head office. Complete furnishing of private houses.
Brochure.

BARON BERCOTT & ASSOCIATES (Est: 1951)
Chartered Architects & Planning Consultants
1 Park Terrace, Glasgow G3 6BZ. 041 332-8221.
Mr Bercott – B Arch; Dip CD; ARIBA; AMTPI Mr Hill – ARIBA; ARIAS Mr Feruson – ARIBA; ARIAS.
Pc Albany Chapel, Albany St, Edinburgh. Stock Exchange Building, St George's Place, Glasgow. Ardkinglas House, Cairndow, Argyll.

BARRINGTON, MICHAEL RESTORER (Empl: 2; Est: 1978)
The Old Rectory, Warmwell, Dorchester, Dorset DT2 8HQ. 0305-852 104.
M BAFRA; GMC.
Pc Pipe organ casing (18thcentury) – Lulworth Castle Chapel, Dorset. Masters Chair – Stationers' Hall, London. Conservation of icons. Large amount of 17th, 18th and 19th-century furniture for trade and private clients.
Although principally antique furniture restorers, also undertake restoration and repairs to lanterns; iron hearths; fire irons; iron gates; papier maché work; picture frames. Steam engines (model and small stationary) built and repaired.

BARROW, MARGOT (Est: 1986)
Hand-woven Tapestries
43 Mount Pleasant, Norwich, Norfolk NR2 2DH. 0603-501 374.
MA RCA; Member and Gallery Artist Contemporary Applied Arts, Covent Garden. Tapestry, Thumbe Gallery, 38 Lexington St, W1.
Pc Collages (handmade and dyed paper) – Newcrane Wharf Show Flat, Wapping, London. Art work and tapestries – new 400 bed hotel opening Heathrow, 1990.
Has exhibited in Foyles Gallery, London; Tattershall Castle, London; Castle Museum, Norwich, and many other such venues. Slides and details on request.

FIRMS AND CRAFTSPEOPLE

BARROWS, T. S. & SON (Empl: 3; Est: 1935)
Cabinet Maker & Restorer
Hamlyn Lodge, Station Rd, Ollerton, Newark, Notts NG22 9BN. 0623-823 600.

BARWICK, R. J. & SONS (Empl: approx 180; Est: over 100 yrs)
Building Contractors
Coombe Valley Rd, Dover, Kent CT17 0UJ. 0304-023 716. Tennyson Rd, Ashford, Kent. 0233-627 963.
ECA; NECEIC; LCA; BEC.
Pc Many historic buildings throughout Kent.
Only undertakes castings in lead.

'BASIA' (Est: 1978)
Hand-Painted China & Porcelain
Squirrel Court Studio, Hare Lane, Little Kingshill, Gt Missenden, Bucks HP16 0EF.
BA (Hons); Soc of Women Artists; International Porcelain Artists (USA); Confraternity of Polish Artists.
Pc A great range, from antique to modern, inexpensive to £10,000 per piece, depending on techniques and material used. Currently working on tiles for church in Australia incorporating 20 designs.
Commissions cover a wide spectrum of subjects from icons and miniatures to naturalistic and historial pieces; often incorporating specially developed lustres and precious metals.

BASS, PERCY LTD (Empl: 18; Est: 1930)
Bespoke Upholsterers.
184–188 Walton St, London SW3 2JL. 071-589 4853.

BASSETT & FINDLEY LTD (Empl: 71; Est: 1914)
Architectural Metal Craftsmen & Specialist Shop Fitters
Talbot Road North, Wellingborough, Northants NN8 1QS. 0933-224898.
NAS; ASSM; ISO; WI; SSFA.
Pc Stainless steel balustrading – Heathrow Terminal 4. Stainless steel canopies and sashes – Standard Chartered Bank, Park Lane, London. Aluminium screen for segregation, Gatwick North Terminal. Brass balustrading – Poultney Hill, London, EC3.
Also undertakes metal gilding. Brochure.

BASTEX (Empl: 6; Est: 1974)
Upholsterers & Curtain Makers
Unit 22, Southfield Trading Estate, Nailsea, Bristol BS19 1JE. 0272-810 135.

GMC.
Pc Drapes, swags and tails, pelmets, bedspreads, etc. – Hyatt Carlton Tower Hotel and also Holiday Inns in London; Slough; Plymouth; Cardiff; Bristol (inc. re-upholstery and re-polishing work). Similar work – Duke of Richmond Hotel.
Brochure.

BATEMAN, DUDLEY HERALDIC ARTIST (Empl: one; Est: 1982)
'Revonah', Bourne Close, S Wooton, King's Lynn, Norfolk PE30 3LZ. 0553-672 381.
M Norfolk Rural Craftsmans Guild.
Pc All types of heraldic work.
Makes heraldic plaques, shields, etc.

BATEMAN, JACQUELINE MURALS (Empl: solo; Est: 1976)
Mural Painting & Stencilling
7 Rylett Crescent, London W12 9RP. 081-749 3596.
Art school and 22 yrs experience; 2 solo art exhibitions and many mixed shows.
Pc ICI; Business Design Centre, Islington; French Institute, Kensington; property companies; hotels; restaurants; and private clients.

BATES, ERIC & SONS (Empl: 20)
Furniture Designers, Makers & Restorers
Melbourne House, Bacton Rd, N Walsham, Norfolk NR28 0RA. 0692-403 221. Showroom: High Street, Cottishall. 0603-738716.
M GMC; M LAPADA.

BATH ARCHITECTURAL GLASS (Empl: one; Est: 1981)
Stained Glass Artist
108 Walcot St, Bath, Avon BA1 5BG. 0225-444 404.
HND Architectural Stained Glass, Swansea.
Mostly secular work and 'modern' designs to complement the situation, or to client's request, although has produced new work of medieval character. Will undertake restoration of older glass and has 'successfully restored panels of all descriptions and age'.

BATH RE-ENAMELLING CO (Empl: 6; Est: 1976)
Victoria Works, Pall Mall, Nantwich CW5 5BN. 0270-626 554.
Pc QE2 baths (whilst on re-fit). Royal residences.
Original baths re-enamelled and supplied re-furbished. Brass taps and mixes also available. Brochure.

FIRMS AND CRAFTSPEOPLE

BAWDEN, KEITH (Empl: solo; Est: 1970)
Cabinet Maker & Restorer
Mews Workshops, Montpellier Retreat, Cheltenham, Glos GL50 2XG. 0242-230 320.
5 yr apprenticeship; M BAFRA.
Pc Regular work for the antique trade; private clients; National Trust; DOE; Landmark Trust. Has been commissioned from abroad to work on period furniture on various occasions.
Also willing to deal with woodworm; supply brass handles, mounts, etc.; undertake work on ivory; mother of pearl; clocks; oil paintings; water colours; textiles; porcelain; pottery and Oriental carpets.

BAXTER, JOAN (Empl: solo; Est: 1988)
Tapestry Weaver
6 West Workshops, Tan Gallop, Welbeck, Nr Worksop, Notts S80 3LW. 0623-843 384 (nights).
DA Edinburgh College of Art; post grad study in Edinburgh and Warsaw; worked as professional weaver at West Dean Tapestry Studio and also Victorian Tapestry Workshop, Australia.
Pc Many large commissions during past 9 yrs inc. work for Henry Moore; Howard Hodgkin; John Piper.
Brochure.

BAYLISS & WILLIAMS (Empl: 7; Est: 1986)
Stained Glass Artists/Painters
17–19 Spencer St, Hockley, Birmingham B18 6DD. 021-233 1985.
M BSMGP; GMC.
Pc Memorial window – Hammerwich Parish Church. 'Three Kings' window – Horninglow Parish Church, Burton-on-Trent. Two abstract windows – Royal Orthopaedic Hospital, Birmingham. Restoration, conservation and new work – Hunting Lodge, Warwick Castle.

BEACON HILL BRICK CO LTD (Empl: 25; Est: 1937)
Corfe Mullen, Wimborne, Dorset BH21 3RX. 0202-697 633 & 697 851.
M Brick Development Assoc; Founder M Calcium Silicate Brick Assoc.
Pc Wide range of shapes and colours of brick, particularly 'special specials', often to architect's own design. Reference sites can be provided on request.
Brochure

BEADON, J. R. LTD (Empl: 30; Est: 1947)
French Polishing Contractors
366 City Rd, London, EC1V 2PY. 071-278 6803/4/5.

BEAUMONT, R.J.

FMB.
Pc Hampton Court Palace following extensive fire damage.

BEAL, ROBERT FURNITURE (Empl: 2; Est: 1980)
Commercial Mill, Savile St, Milnsbridge, Huddersfield, Yorks HD3 4PG. 0484-658 344 & 460 126.
Apprentice trained engineer turned to cabinet making.
Pc Screens – Preston Art Gallery. Pair of children's hobby horse chairs – Saudi Arabia.

BEARD, JOHN WALES (Est: 1976)
Glass Engraver
South Yeo, Yeo Vale, Bideford, Devon EX39 5ES. 023-75218.
AF GGE.
Pc Many commissions large and small, home and abroad.
Perceiving glass as a pictorial medium, rather than for abstract decoration, Mr Beard favours marine subjects, although portraiture has been a subject of growing interest.

BEATON, JOHN McW. (Est: 1972)
Woodcarver & Furniture Restorer
11 Peinchorran, Braes, Isle of Skye IV51 9LL.
Worked with D. Gilbert, sculptor (mainly wood). M SSCR.
Pc Details on application.
Although willing to undertake work on staircases/balustrading, will not undertake curved hand rails. Will also make scale models. Photographs available.

BEAUCHAMP, ALEXANDER – HAND-PRINTED WALLPAPER (Empl: 6; Est: 1982)
Griffin Mill, Thrupp, Stroud, Glos GL5 2AZ. 0453-884 537.
Pc Majority of work is carried out as special commissions for the restoration of historical buildings. Exciting projects completed inc. work for Eng. Heritage, Australian National Trust and the British Interior Design Exhibition.
All wallpapers are printed to specification inc. reproduction of historical designs and colourings. This firm has a large archive of French and English wallpapers, dados, friezes and borders. Pattern books can be obtained on application.

BEAUMONT, R. J.
See WETHERBY STAINED GLASS & GLASS MERCHANTS

FIRMS AND CRAFTSPEOPLE

BEAVER BUILDERS (Est: 1982)
13 Belmonnt Rd, Penn, Wolverhampton, W. Midlands WV4 5UD.
0902-341 990.
FMB.
Also hold stocks of timber; beams; roof tiles; stone; wrought-iron, and other architectural antiques.

BECKER, BERNARD & PARTNERS STAINED GLASS STUDIO (Empl: 2; Est: 1987)
13 Hague St, London E2 6HN. 071-739 7534.
Technical advice; preparation of existing frames; design and supply of new frames; insulating and protective glazing; a specialist stained glass installation service to artists and designers.

BEDDOWS, TERRY (WOVEN TEXTILES) (Empl: solo; Est: 1984)
6 Moorland Gardens, Moortown, Leeds 17, Yorks LS17 6JT. 0532-688 231.
BA Fine Art, Birmingham; C & Gs Textiles, Leeds; DATEC Surface Pattern Design, Leeds.
Pc 30 individual rug commissions. 10 ft × 10 ft square Tibetan style rug. Several abstract wallhangings for private clients.
Decorative wallhangings and rugs for the home, offices, hotel foyers, hospitals. Can incorporate company logo if desired. Brochure.

BEECHWOOD SERVICES (B. W. ROGERS) (Empl: solo; Est: 1985)
Dry Stone Walling & Landscape Conservation
8 Gordon Avenue, Sanderstead, Surrey CR2 0QN. 081-660 7548.
GMC; FMB; Soc of Wood Craftsmen; DSWA; Associate M Arboricultural Assoc.
Pc Current environmental project being carried out in school grounds at Christ Church School, Purley, Surrey.
Conservation/restoration landscaping inc. historical gardens; specialist water features; hedgelaying; ornamental features (i.e. lych gates, dove cotes).

BEGG, IAN ARCHITECT (Est: 1984)
4a Howe St, Edinburgh EH3 6TD. 031-225 1781. FAX 031-226 2214.
Ian Begg – DA (Edin); FRIAS; FSA Scot   Raymond Muszynski.
Pc Replacement of part of ornate 18th-century ceiling of decorative plaster which collapsed, and exterior re-decoration of castle – Blair Castle, Blair Atholl. Reconstruction, conservation and restoration – Couston Castle, Leven Castle and Low Castle. Restoration and substantial rebuilding in traditional Scottish style – The Royal Mile, Edinburgh. Visitors Centre – Glasgow Cathedral Square.

BEHAR PROFIX LTD (Empl: 7; Est: 1917)
Cleaners, Conservators, Valuers of Historic Tapestries & Oriental Rugs
The Alban Building, St. Albans Place, Upper St, London N1 0NX.
071-226 0144.
GMC. UKIC.
Pc Lord Brownlow, Channel Islands. Inst of Secretaries. Bank of England. Inst of Chartered Accounts. Drapers Co. Floors Castle. Merchant Taylors Co. Chavenage.
Small family firm working in this field for 70 yrs, and proud of their standards of service, quality and professionalism. Brochure.

BELL, K. G. (Empl: 4; Est: 1979)
Stained Glass Artist
Works: 4B Bridge St, Neston, South Wirral, Cheshire L64 9UJ. 051-336 6020. Home: 51 Moorside Avenue, Parkgate, South Wirral L64 6QS. 051-336 1065.
GMC.
Pc Private Chapel – Liverpool Cathedral.

BELL, JOSEPH & SON
See ROBINSON, GEOFFREY A. K.

BELLCHAMBERS, JAMES (Est: 1980)
Repair & Restoration of Woodwork, Furniture, Fittings & Furnishings
Hayhill Coach House, Plymouth Rd, Devon TQ9 5LH. 0803-863 465.
BADA Dip, West Dean College.
Pc Numerous items in National Trust houses throughout Devon and Cornwall.

BELVEDERE GLASS
Stained Glass Artist/Painter
39 St Georges Rd, Harrogate, N. Yorks HG2 9BP. 0423-509152.
M BSMGP; M GMC.
Pc Domestic, church, public houses, theatres, etc. *Free estimates within 15 miles radius. Stained glass mirrors and clocks also a speciality.*

BENARDOUT, RAYMOND (Empl: 6; Est: 1961)
Textile Conservation/Restoration
4 William St, Knightsbridge, London SW1X 9HL. 071-235 3360 & 071-235 9588.
BADA.

FIRMS AND CRAFTSPEOPLE

BENDER, RODNEY (Empl: solo; Est: 1984)
Stained Glass Artist
10 Rookfield Close, London N10 3TR. 081-444 8536.
Studio trained in Australia and Britain; BTEC HND, Architectural Stained Glass, Swansea; CNAA; Master of Philosophy.
Pc 2 memorial windows commemorating the Welsh Guards lost in the Falklands – Collegiate Parish Church of Swansea, St Mary's.
Only sandblasting work undertaken in situ.

BENEDIKTE, MAYA S. (Est: 1982)
Needlepoint Designer
The Flat, Meleta, 4 Seymour Terrace, Bridgetown, Totnes, Devon TQ9 5AQ. 0803-864 823.
No official qualifications, but years of interest and practice. Also 3 yrs as an exhibiting M of Devon Guild of Craftsmen.
Individual needlepoints designed on commission – 23 needlepoint stitches per inch. Brochure.

BENNETT, R. & SNARE LTD (Empl: 42; Est: 1846)
Building Contractors
Richmond House, PO Box 21, Sproughton Rd, Ipswich, Suffolk IP1 5AW. 0473-47287.
BEC; FMB.
Pc Restoration – St Pancras Church, Ipswich. Refurbishment – Surrey Horse Mews. Rebuilding Orangery, Coddenham, etc.
Brochure.

BENTLEY & SPENS (Empl: 2, print work sub-contracted; Est: 1981)
Textile Designers
Studio 25, 90 Lots Rd, London SW10 0QD. 071-352 5685.
BA (Hons) Textiles/Fine Art University of London and Goldsmiths College.
Pc Fabric for tented ceiling – Armitage Silver display, Grosvenor Antiques Fair. Many private commissions for furnishing fabric to compliment the interior scheme.
Specialists in batiked and painted natural fabrics, ordered by the metre or as finished interior products, i.e. curtains; pelmets; swags and tails; blinds; sheers; upholstery; bed linen. Willing to supply any quantity. Brochure.

BERKOWITZ, MAGGIE ANGUS – TILES
21/23 Park Rd, Milnthorpe, Cumbria LA7 7AD. 044 82 3970.
NDD; ATD; Full M CPA; Director Art & Architecture; Craft North; Northern Potters.
Pc Murals – Landale Estate Timeshare, Great Ormond St Hospital.

Burlington slate, Many domestic installations – swimming pools, kitchens, bathrooms, conservatories and gardens.
Tile designed to commission inc. frostproof, waterproof ironstone and quarry tiles. Colours are permanent. Holds stocks of original tile panels. Brochure.

BEST & LLOYD LTD (Empl: 27; Est: 1840)
Lighting Designers & Manufacturers
William Street West, Smethwick, Warley, W. Midlands B66 2NX. 021-558 1191.
British Contract Furnishing Assoc; Design and Industries Assoc.
Pc Restoration after a serious fire – Albert Hall, Bolton. Restoration – The National Mutual Building, Melbourne. Refurbishment – Crowne Plaza, Midland Hotel, Manchester. New light fittings ('We made the originals in approx 1870') – Great Western Arcade, Birmingham.
Brochure.

BESWICK, THELMA (Empl: solo; Est: 1970)
Wallhangings and Tapestries using Woven Techniques
1 Diddies House, Diddies, Stratton, Bude, Cornwall EX23 9NE. 0288-2558.
5 yrs at Art Schools, Manchester Regional College of Art, Bath Academy of Art, Corsham. Lectured in Colour and Design at Plymouth College of Art.
Pc 9 ft long woven tapestry seascape tripych for Derriford Hospital, Plymouth which attracted a grant from a murals fund administered by the Royal Academy.
Worsted wool semi-abstract and figurative wallhangings using designs based on landscapes.

BICKERTON, T. A. & SON LTD (Empl: 50; Est: 1930)
Building Contractors
Oak Yard, Waverley Rd, St Albans, Herts AL3 5PL. 0727-50851.
BEC.
Pc Restoration works inc. Court Room, St Albans Town Hall; Salisbury Hall, London Colney, Herts; Stable Block, Pawshanger House, Herts.
Brochure.

BILSHAM JOINERY WORKS (Empl: 56; Est: 1964)
Bilsham Rd, Yapton, Arundel, W. Sussex BN18 0JN. 0243-551233.
GMC; BEC; Fed of Sussex Industries; on approved list of Eng. Heritage.

FIRMS AND CRAFTSPEOPLE

BINGLEY ROOFING & STONE CENTRE
Specialists in Demolishing Old Buildings & Reclaiming the Materials
Cullingworth Mills, Cullingworth, Bradford, W. Yorks BD13 5DG.
0535-273 813. FAX 0535-273 194.
Reclaimed stone; flags; crazy paving; oak; etc.

BINNINGTON, P. & F. (Empl: 5; Est: 1978)
Specialist Painters and Gilders
65 St John's Hill, London SW11 1SX. 071-223 9192.
Partners – Dip AD Painting & Sculpture; CGLI Restoration; BADA Cert Restoration; Dip Ed; Dip AD Illustration & Design; M BAFRA; UKIC; ADAS; Soc of Gilders. Staff equally qualified.
Pc Gilded chairs – Mansion House, Corp of London. Restoration – 18th-century commemorative signwritten 'Peal Board', St Martin in the Fields. Extension of suite of vermilion and silver japanned 18th-century chairs. Creation of room of gilt glass panels – Sultan of Brunei. Restoration – State Bed, Speakers House, House of Commons.
Also restore keyboard musical instruments and harps; restore frames; gild architectural enrichments on site. Also specialize in Verre Eglomise (decoration of glass by gilding on reverse, engraving with designs and applying coloured paints and varnishes). Gilding courses arranged.

BINYON & MACFARLANE STENCILS (Est: 1976)
53 Thorncliffe Rd, Oxford OX2 7BA. 0865-56072 & 071-639 9885.
Trade Assoc M IDDA.
Pc Doddington Hall – Lincoln. Tudor House by Smythson Wolley Park. A Wyatt House, Nr Wantage, Berks.
Estimates and initial consultation are free of charge. Brochure.

BIRCH, WILLIAM & SONS LTD (Empl: 50; Est: 1874)
Building Contractors
Foss Islands Rd, York YO3 7UP. 0904-611 611.
Full craft trade apprenticeship for bricklayers and plasterers. Approved: Eng. Heritage; York City Council; Ryedale DC; DOE; York Diocesan Board; York Civic Trust.
Pc Adaption and extension – Helperby Hall, York. Renovation for York Civic Trust – Fairfax House, York. Renovation – Ledston Hall, Castleford. Refurbishment – Duncombe Park Mansion, Helmsley. Largely civil engineering work – Studley Royal, Fountains Abbey for Historic Buildings Commission.

BIRD & HOUGH LTD (Empl: 20; Est: 1947)
Building Contractors
Portland St, Walsall, W. Midlands WS2 8AB. 0922-24381.
FMB; GMC.
Pc Walsall Leather Centre, awarded Heritage Award, 1988. Limehouse, Walsall. Supplied joinery for Guildhall, Walsall.

BIRD-JONES, CHRIS (Empl: self employed/freelance; Est: 1977)
Stained Glass Artist
Bron Haul, Oernant, Llangollen, Clwyd LL20 8DP. 0978-860 177. 64 Vespan Rd, London, W12 9QQ. 081-740 8021.
MA (RCA) Glass.
Pc Windows, screen and glass sculptures for churches, hospitals and private homes.

BLACK, ADRIAN J. (Est: 1968)
Furniture Designer, Maker & Restorer
244 Louth Rd, Scartho, Grimsby DN33 2LF. 36a Freeman St, Grimsby DN32 7AG. 0472-824 823 & 355 668.

BLACK LANE POTS WORKSHOPS (L. ASKELL) (Empl: one; Est: 1979)
Furniture Designer
Black Lane, Hamptworth, Nr Salisbury, Wilts SP5 2DS.
Higher Dip Craft & Design – London College of Furniture; Licentiateship of SD-C; E. W. Goodwin Award for Craftsmanship 1985.
Pc Full size lime wood figure of Christ – Southampton General Hospital.
Carved work to match or replace existing, and general work in solid timber to designs produced in conjunction with client.

BLACKMORE, ANTONY (Est: 1910, A. Blackmore since 1971)
Chartered Architect
Blackmore Son & Co, Blades House, High St, Hull, Humberside HU1 1PZ. 0482-26406.
Church Architect (M EASA) in York & Lincoln Dioceses; MA Cantab; RIBA; panel architect to Nat Assoc of Almshouses.
Pc Restoration of Mary Lowther Hospital, Ackworth, Nr Wakefield; Watton Abbey, Nr Driffield. Consolidation of ruins – Harwood Dale, Lowthorpe, Nunkeeling. Many projects for Eng. Heritage.

BLADES, G. & SONS (Empl: 4; Est: 1836)
Painters & Decorators, Gilders, Stencillers.
The Square, Little Market Place, Masham, Nr Ripon, N. Yorks HG4 4DY. 0765-89251.
6 yr apprenticeship.

FIRMS AND CRAFTSPEOPLE

BLAKE, D. & CO (Empl: 60; Est: 1877)
Roofing Contractors
10 Beaverhall Rd, Edinburgh EH7 4JE. 031 556-9632 & 1744.
LCA; LDA; SNIPEF.
Pc Drumlanrig Castle, Dumfries-shire. Usher Hall, Edinburgh, and many more.
Brochure.

BLAKE, S. G. (Empl: solo; Est: 18 yrs)
Master Thatcher
Oxen Place, Bishopstone, Swindon, Wilts SN6 8PS. 0793-790 443 & 0672-810 494.
Full Master Thatchers apprenticeship; M Hants & Wilts MTA.
Pc Too numerous to mention.
Studied architecture for a period to RIBA level.

BLAKELEY, GILES CREATIVE BLACKSMITH (Est: 1987)
Towsers Lodge Nursery, Brickyards Lane, Mark Cross, E. Sussex. 089 285-3230.
4 yr apprenticeship in General & Ornamental Blacksmithing and Wrought Ironwork.
Pc Restoration of 17th-century locks and lock plates. Reproduction of early locks and plates. Forges keys to match existing locks and furniture.
Also undertakes sword and knife making and restoration.

BLAKELEY, SEBASTIAN
Furniture Designer & Maker
Towsers Lodge Nursery, Brickyards Lane, Mark Cross, E. Sussex. 089 285-3230.
2 yrs with Ralph Lyle/Interspace Design; 2 yrs with Colins & Associates; 1 yr with John Gubbings, restorer; 3½ yrs solo doing restoration, commissioned pieces and kitchens.
Pc Individually designed series of tables and chairs, and unusual commissions.

BLAXILL, P. M.
Clockmaker
13 Oakfields Rd, Knebworth, Herts SG3 6NS. 0438-812 432.
BA (Hons) 3d Design.
Pc Proposed designs for National Theatre, Swindon Town Centre. Clocks made for various private environs.
Silver repairs also undertaken. Portfolio available.

BODEN & WARD STONEMASONS

BLEASDALE, R. (WELDINGS) (Empl: 16; Est: 1966)
Metalworkers
301 Caledonian Rd, London N1 1DW. 125 Kings Cross Rd, London WC1. 071-609 0934 & 071-607 7565. FAX 071-833 4174.
FMB; EIA.
Stock a large number of castings inc. balusters; balconies; panelling; gratings; etc. Brochure.

BLOCKLEYS PLC (Empl: 200; Est: 1890)
Brick Manufacturers
Sommerfield Rd, Trench Lock, Telford, Shropshire TF1 4RY. 0952-251 933.

BLOOMFIELD STONECRAFT (Est: 1983)
6 Home Mill Buildings, Castle St, Trowbridge, Wilts BA14 8BD. 0225-755 314.
Two working partners – apprenticeship training and craft qualifications plus a total of 19 yrs industrial experience prior to establishing own business. Approved: Local Authority and Eng. Heritage.

BLUE SUN STAINED GLASS STUDIO (Empl: solo; Est: 1987)
39 Waverley Gardens, Shawlands, Glasgow G41 2DW. 041-632 7178.
Evening classes in stained glass, Nova Scotia College of Art & Design, Halifax, Canada; experience in installing stained glass with Terry Smith-Lamothe, stained glass artist & instructor of the course. Otherwise self taught and still learning.
Pc 2 contemporary stained glass panels based on development and birth of child – Dr Catherine Follinsbee, Prince St Truro, Nova Scotia, Canada. Abstract panels bearing 'Temple' motif – David Churchley, Minard Rd, Glasgow.
Will undertake stained glass work of any kind but mainly interested in contemporary work of own design and individual style, i.e. windows and panels containing fused glass pieces to create relief and textural effects.

BLYTH, WILLIAM (Empl: 25; Est: 1840)
Roofing Materials
Hoe Hill, Barton-on-Humber, S. Humberside DN18 5ET. 0652-32175.

BODEN & WARD STONEMASONS (Empl: 4; Est: 1983)
Dairy Farm, Gt Brington, Northampton NN7 4JB. 0604-770 879.
Apprenticed and time served stonemasons; C & Gs in stonemasonry. Pc Renewal of carved stonework – Holy Trinity Church – Stratford-upon-Avon. Renewal of tracery windows – St Leodagarius, Ashby St Ledgers. Restoration of main elevation – Delapré Abbey,

FIRMS AND CRAFTSPEOPLE

Northampton. Restoration – Earls Barton Church.

BOHUN & BUSBRIDGE (Empl: one; Est: 1978)
Wallhangings & Floorcoverings
24 Iverna Gardens, Kensington, London W8 6TN. 071-937 9145

BONSACK BATHS (LONDON) LTD (Empl: 35; Est: 1958)
14 Mount St, Mayfair, London W1Y 5RA. Also at Harrods, Knightsbridge. 071-629 9981. FAX 071-629 0743. TELEX 8814034 G.
GMC.
Hand crafted baths, basins and WCs designed and produced to client's specification in any of 1,000 colours, inc. metallic. Taps and fittings available, many inlaid with semi-precious stones, l'aque-de-chine or enamels. Standard range inc. Classical, Art Deco and High Tech styles, designed to give maximum body comfort. A range of classical motifs available to decorate bath furniture, or alternatively order your own designs, inc. crests, heraldry and company logos. Metal can be inlaid into the bath furniture to produce an ormulu effect. Brochure.

BOOTH, CAROLINE J. (Est: 1980)
Textile Conservator
Fold Farm, Higher Eastwood, Todmorden, Lancs OL14 8RP. 0706-816 888.
Dip AD (Hons) Fashion & Design; 4 yrs at V & A Museum, Textile Conservation Dept.

BOOTH, G. W. & BOOTH, C. J. W. (Empl: one; Est: 1974)
Turret Clockmakers
Tower House, Tower Hill, Bere Regis, Dorset BH20 7JA. 0929-471 586.
G. W. Booth – Fellow Brit Horological Inst   C. J. Booth – Craft M Brit Horological Inst.
Photographs available.

BORDER GLASS & GLAZING CO LTD (Empl: 11; Est: 1978)
Stained Glass, Leaded Lights, Glass Engraving & Decorating
12 Howgate St, Dumfries DG2 7AE. 0387-53029.
1 designer; 2 sandblast engravers, acid etchers and embossers; 1 stained glass designer; 1 artist and 1 apprentice; 4 leaded light makers and 1 apprentice.
Stained glass design and production; leaded lights; sandblasting; engraving and acid etching/embossing.

BOSHERS (CHOLSEY) LTD (Empl: 50 +; Est: c. 175 yrs)
Building Contractors
Reading Rd, Cholsey, Wallingford, Oxon OX10 9HN. 0491-651 242.
Train between 12 and 14 apprentices at any one time. Approved: Diocesan Lists; Eng. Heritage; PSA; Berks CC; Oxon CC; S Oxon DC; etc.
Pc Conversion of 5 barns into 6 houses, Sunningwell, Oxfordshire – RIBA Recommendation. The Lamb, Wallingford – The Times/RICS Conservation Award and Civic Trust Award). 35 Flats, Goldsmiths Lane, Wallingford – RIBA Award. Rush Court Nursing Home, Wallingford. The Gainsborough Stud & Harwood Lodge. Rectory Farmhouse, North Stoke. Lead Roofing Ewelme Church. Phyllis Court, Henley. Springs Farm, Purley.

BOSLY, CAROLINE (Empl: 5; Est: 1968)
Persian & Oriental Carpet Wholesalers & Brokers
13 Princess Rd, Regent's Park, London NW1 8JR. 071-722 7608.
Appointed by the Board of Trade to represent UK as supplier of Oriental rugs.
The purchase of Oriental rugs can be bewildering and expensive, which is why C. Bosly decided to act as a broker, enabling customers to avoid the high mark-ups often charged by retail stores by purchasing direct from the warehouse, with expert advice on hand to guide the customer through the vast range and variety of new and antique carpets and rugs. Full valuation service (free, verbal only, valuation if rug taken by appointment to office). Author of Rugs to Riches.

BOSWELL MITCHELL & JOHNSTON (Est: 1911)
Chartered Architects & Planning Consultants
18 Woodlands Terrace, Glasgow G3 6DH. 041-332 9184.
Scott Noble – B Arch; RIBA; MRTPI; RIAS   Donald Gavin – B Arch; RIBA; FRIAS   Malcolm Mclean – B Arch; RIBA; RIAS   Ian Bassy – Dip Arch; RIBA; RIAS.
Pc 18th-century Customs House, William St, Greenock. The Grecian Building (19th century), Sauchiehall St, Glasgow.

BOULTER, CHRISTOPHER (Empl: 2–6; Est: 1976)
Mural Painter & Restorer
43 Goodrich Rd, E Dulwich, London SE22 9EQ. Unit 22, Grand Union Centre, Kensal Rd, London W10 5BX. 081-299 2219 & 081-969 2847 (workshop).

FIRMS AND CRAFTSPEOPLE

BOULTING, RUPERT (Empl: 2; Est: 1973)
Furniture Restorer
34 Newland St, Eynsham, Oxford OX8 1LA. 0865-881 320.
Served apprenticeship.
General restoration of 17th- and 18th-century furniture – all aspects except upholstery.

BOVEY, CHRISTOPHER (THATCHER) (Empl: one; Est: 1987)
17 High St, Silverton, Devon EX5 4JD. 0392-861 111.

BOVINGDON BRICKWORKS LTD (Empl: up to 36 (5/6 hand makers); Est: 1922)
Ley Hill Rd, Pudds Cross, Bovingdon, Nr Hemel Hempstead, Herts HP3 0NW. 0442-833176 & 832 575.
Pc St Albans Chapter House, St Albans Cathedral. Various National Trust and Eng. Heritage projects.
Willing to provide any quantity from standard lines of manufacture (special sizes by discussion with client but possibly 5,000 mimimum). Brochure.

BOWMAN, E. & SONS LTD (Est: 1886)
Building Contractor
Cherryholt Rd, Stamford, Lincs. 0780-51015.
Pc Alterations – Wolthorpe House. Masonry repairs – Withcote Church. Repairs – St Markham Church. Bell tower and roof repairs – West Walton Church. Masonry – Thorpe Hall. Extension – Uppingham School Chapel.

BOWMAN (OXON) LTD (Empl: 6; Est: 1886)
Building Contractors
4 Lumbertubs Lane, Boothville, Northants NN3 1AH. 0604-43936.
NFBTE; Stone Fed.
Pc Masonry restoration and cleaning to entire facade – Northampton Guild Hall. Masonry restoration and cleaning, internal works – St Peter's, Northampton. Stone supply to 4 flying butresses – Harold Church.
Brochure.

BOWYER, GORDON & PARTNERS (Est: 1948)
Chartered Architects & Designers
Russell Chambers, The Piazza, Covent Garden, London WC2E 8RH. 071-836 1452.
Gordon Bowyer – OBE; RIBA; FCSD   Ursula Bowyer – RIBA; FCSD   Iain Langlands – RIBA; FCSD   Stephen Batchelor – RIBA.
Pc National Gallery. National Portrait Gallery. British Museum.

BRADFORD, H. CONSTRUCTION LTD

Science Museum. Hampton Court Palace. Windsor Castle. Cabinet War Rooms Museum. Vanbrugh Castle. Hill Hall, Essex.

BOYLAND JOINERY LTD (Empl: 40; Est: re-registered 1961)
Stony Lane, Christchurch, Dorset BH23 1EZ. 0202-499 499.
M Brit Woodworking Fed (Architectural Section); BEC.
Pc Joinery to match existing and new build work – Buckingham Palace. Reproduction period doors – Wardrobe Dept, BBC. Joinery – The Holy Innocents Church, Orpington (RIBA Award winner). Work for many listed buildings – mainly windows to match existing.

BRABY CARTER LTD (Empl: 24; Est: over 100 yrs)
Roofing Contractors
33 Chase Rd, London NW10 6PU. 081-965 1161. FAX 081-965 1985.
MRCA; LCA.
Pc Liverpool Anglican Cathedral. Lead gutters and main roofs, cast lead rainwater pipes – Royal Naval College, Greenwich. Gilded copper to dome – the London Mosque, Regent's Park.
Specialists in metal roofing, cladding and weatherings inc. stainless steel; aluminium; coated metals; fabrication of cavity gutters, copings, flashings. Work carried out in accordance with BSI codes of practice. Brochure.

BRACEWELL, STIRLING PARTNERSHIP (Est: 1924)
Chartered Architects
38 Walker Terrace, Tillicoultry, Clackmannanshire FK13 6EF. 0259-50301.
Chartered Architects; RIBA; RIAS.
Pc Restoration – Broomhall, By Stirling. Restoration – Old House of Orchill, Perthshire. Conservation works – Blairlogie Village, Stirling; Marine Place, St Andrew's.

BRADFORD, H. CONSTRUCTION LTD (Empl: 6; Est: 1977)
3 Kings Avenue, Buckhurst Hill, Essex IG9 5PL. 081-506 1566. FAX 081-504 6940. TELEX 896874 Call back COFRSA G.
FMB. Approved: ILEA; PSA; Eng. Heritage.
Pc Restoration work inc. Blackwall tunnel entrances and gate house for GLC; clock tower – Avery Hill College, Barking Magistrates Court, GLC. Complete replacement Barry style library in Marble Hill House, overseen by Manning Clamp & Partners for GLC. Period Victorian joinery – Mainz, Germany. Oak framed interior – Norway.
A full detailing service for period construction available; installation and supply service to overseas clients; specialist interior installation of any architectural period; copies of original mouldings in GRP.

FIRMS AND CRAFTSPEOPLE

BRADLEY, RAY (Empl: 2 part-time specialists; Est: 1962)
Glass Decorator
3 Orchard Studios, Brook Green, London W6 7BU. 071-602 1840.
Wimbledon School of Art; NDD Stained Glass; ARCA; A BSMGP; Sir Arthur Evans Travelling Scholarship; F BSMGP; Crafts Council Bursery; Churchill Fellowship.
Pc Countless commissions in this country and abroad for windows and screens for public, private, secular and ecclesiastical situations. See Crafts Council Selected Index, or contact directly for details of previous works.
Although primarily known for new works, he may undertake restoration work and reproduce if original work is of interest and quality.

BRADY, SIMON (Est: 1982)
Mural Artist
31 Okehampton Rd, London NW10 3EE. 081-459 0396.

BRANDIS, MARION (Empl: solo; Est: 1985)
Ceramic Fireplaces, Murals & Garden Ware
9 Bloomsbury Place, Brighton, E. Sussex BN2 1DA. 0273-688 299.
BA (Hons) Design & Crafts (Ceramics), post grad Dip in Ceramics – both at Edinburgh College of Art; Junior Fellow in Ceramics, SGIHE, Faculty of Art & Design, Cardiff.
Pc 2 murals – Cardiff County Hall. Bathroom commissions. Private commissions for fireplaces.
Designer and maker of fireplaces; stoves; basins; garden furniture; clocks; and other such ceramic work. Will reproduce to match existing where possible.

BRASS TACKS HARDWARE (Empl: 30; Est: 1979)
Hardware Manufacturer
50/54 Clerkenwell Rd, London EC1M 5PS. 071-250 1971. FAX 071-251 3473.
M GAI; M GMC.
Pc Produced brass cremone bolts to match existing items in the Ritz Hotel, London.
Brochure.

BREESE, ANDREW (Empl: solo; Est: 1981)
Artist Blacksmith
Chalk Pits Forge, Houghton Bridge, Amberley, Nr Arundel, W. Sussex BN18 9LT. 0798-831 370.
BABA.

Pc 12 reproduction chandeliers to match existing – the Duke of Norfolk at Arundel Castle.
Specialist in finely wrought traditional ironwork. See also AMBERLEY CHALK PITS MUSEUM.

BRIDD, TEILSEN (Est: 1988)
Ceramic Artist
Craig yr Iyrchen, Cerrig y Drudion, Corwen, Clwyd LL21 9TE. 049 082-514.
Dip Architectural Glass, Swansea College of Art; C & Gs Architectural Glass; studied 3d Design in Glass & Ceramics at Stourbridge College of Art.
Will consider anything that has to be made to commission in ceramics inc. tiles; handmade bricks; architectural ceramics. Brochure.

BRIDGE FARM RENOVATIONS (Empl: 5; Est: 1983)
Building Contractors
Mardu, Clun, Shropshire SY7 8QG. 05884-515.
C & Gs; BEC. Approved: Local Authority; South Shropshire DC; Shrewsbury & Atcham BC.
Small company offering BEC guaranteed scheme. References available on request.

BRIDGE, JAMES RATFORD (Empl: 14 + 8 apprentices; Est: 1948)
Specialist Carpenter & Joiner
Dale Rd, Haverfordwest, Pembs, Dyfed SA62 3SA. 0437-765 814 & 763 623.
All C & Gs Craft Carpentry & Joinery; M BEC.

BRIGGS, A. A. & SON (Empl: 2; Est: c. 1974)
Building Contractors
Cherry Tree Cot, Island Rd, Westbere, Nr Canterbury, Kent CT2 0EX. 0227-710 978.
C & Gs Joiner and Carpenter; GMC. Approved: Canterbury City Council.
Pc New Tourist Information Centre – St Margaret's St, Canterbury. Cogan House (oldest town house in Cibury). Restaurant, 74 Whincheap, Cibury, etc. Called in by Canterbury City Council Conservation Dept to ratify previous works to quality required, inc. repair of 7 inglenook fires on one stack, and timber beams.
Will repair a structure which others would demolish, as near as possible to original design. All salvagable material used so as to preserve original rather than create a copy. All work has to satisfy the proprietor, who is very proud of his standards of quality and workmanship. Timber resin repairs undertaken.

FIRMS AND CRAFTSPEOPLE

BRIGHT DESIGNS (Empl: 4; Est: 1987)
Stained Glass Artist
The Studio, Parton & Bobena's Yard, Horsepool St, Brixham, Devon.
0803-883 362 & 550 068.
Pc Prestigious houses. Repairs and installation of windows and panels.

BRIGHTON ARCHITECTURAL SALVAGE
33-34 Gloucester Rd, Brighton, Sussex BN1 4AQ. 3 Kensington Place, Brighton. 0273-681 656.

BRISTOL DESIGN (TOOLS) LTD (Empl: 3; Est: 1980)
14 Perry Rd, Bristol, Avon BS1 5BG. 272-291740.
C. Stirling, director – BSc, Ph D   G. Turner, director – C Eng.
Specialize in the manufacture and supply of second-hand and antique tools in the country, suitable for use by cabinet makers; restoration carpenters and joiners; musical instrument makers; wheelwrights; coach builders; shipwrights; plumbers; clock and watch repairers; bookbinders; etc. Also have limited stocks of items useful to painters & decorators, and stonemasons. Will manufacture to client's specification. Willing to deliver anywhere in the world.

BRITAIN'S HERITAGE
Fireplaces
Shaftesbury Hall, 3 Holy Bones, Leics LE1 4LJ. 0533-519 592.
Mechanical Engineering; C & Gs; M GMC.

BRITANNIA ARCHITECTURAL METALWORK LTD (Empl: 5; Est: 1983)
5 Normandy St, Alton, Hants GU34 1DD. 0420-84427.
One director is a chartered architect specializing in listed buildings. Firm is M GMC.
Pc New metal windows – Royal Pavilion, Brighton. New entrance canopy – Grand Hotel, Brighton. No 1 Bessborough Gardens – The Commonwealth Office. Railings to many listed buildings inc. 26 Hampstead Grove. NW1
Stock one of the largest ranges of standard Victorian and Georgian patterns in the country. Most castings are aluminium, although willing to make in cast iron. A full pattern making service available and also advice on all aspects of metal casting from original patterns. Brochure.

BRITANNIA RESTORATIONS
Old Britannia House, Castle St, Combe Martin, Nr Ilfracombe, N. Devon EX34 0JF. 027 188-2887.
Stock antique and reproduction fireplaces; various fittings and fixtures; fully restored joinery products; various lighting and traditional handmade chairs.

BRODIE, J. & SON

BRITISH ANTIQUE EXPORTERS LTD (Empl: 50; Est: 1963)
Bespoke Furniture to Specification
School Close, Queen Elizabeth Avenue, Burgess Hill, W. Sussex RH15 9RX. 04446-45577.
M LAPADA; GMC.

BROADBENT, D. C. (Empl: 3; Est: 1976)
Artist Blacksmith
Barnshaw Smithy, Pepper St, Mobberley, Knutsford, Cheshire WA16 6JH. 0565-873 743.
Blacksmith apprenticeship; BABA.
Pc Many private commissions. Regular restoration and new work for National Trust. New work for architects, interior designers and brewers. Entrance gates – Birtles Old Hall, Macc. Gates – Overthrow Castle, Brom Gardens.

BROADHEAD, SARAH (Empl: solo; Est: 1985)
Kiln Formed Glass
69 Riverdale, Wrecclesham, Farnham, Surrey GU10 4PJ. 0252-724 395.
BA in Textiles (Tapestry) with supporting study in Glass; post grad Dip in Glass; M Surrey Guild of Craftsmen.
Pc Front door glass, commemorative plates, etc.
Using two or more layers of glass Sarah Broadhead produces a most unusual form of decorative glass. Patterns, mostly abstract, are created by pockets of air trapped between the layers, enamel colours, glass engraving or sandblasting, used in a variety of combinations. As the glass is laminated it is very strong and ideal for use in architecture.

BROADWINDSOR CHAIRS & CRAFTS (Empl: solo; Est: 1983)
Caning, Rush and General Chair Repairs & Restoration
Old Exchange Workshop, Broadwindsor, Dorset DT8 3QL. 0308 68909 & 68784.
Former MI Mech E; Cert Ed; BA; Assoc M Dorset Craft Guild.

BRODIE, J. & SON (Empl: 6; Est: 1879)
Plasterers
274 High St, Elgin, Morayshire IV30 1AG. 0343-3861.
SBEF.
Pc Too many to list, but inc. Logie House; Rothes Glen Hotel; Gordonstoun School; Glenborrodale Castle; Inchmarlo House, Aberdeenshire; Darnaway Castle; Cawdor Castle.

FIRMS AND CRAFTSPEOPLE

BROOKE, DR C. J. (Est: 1982)
Archaeological, Photographic & Remote Sensing Consultancy
3 Woodland View, Halam Rd, Southwell, Notts NG25 0AG. 0636-812 607. c/o Dept of Archaeology, The University, Nottingham NG7 2RD. 0602-484 848 (ex 2564).
1st degree – B Tech Archaeological Sciences, University of Bradford; Ph D Ground-based Remote Sensing (Historic Buildings), University of Nottingham; Full M Inst of Field Archaeologists; Full M Assoc of Archaeological Illustrators and Surveyors.
Pc Various survey and remote sensing work for HMBC; churches; universities; and private individuals. Archaeological survey of standing buildings. Photographic recording of historic buildings, artefacts (photographs and glass plate negatives, etc.) for various clients inc. Notts County Library.
Specializes in the archaeological survey and recording of historic buildings, both to assess the archaeological nature of the fabric and fittings (e.g. during repair or threats, or for research), and to recover and record non-visible information – using a variety of remote sensing methods.

BROOKES FORGE FLEMPTON – BRIAN R. BROOKES (Empl: solo; Est: 1972)
Metalworker
Flempton, Bury St. Edmunds, Suffolk IP28 6EN. 0284-84473. Home: Flint Cottage, Wyverstone, Stowmarket, Suffolk IP14 4SW. 0449-781 376.
Assoc Inst of Medical Laboratory Sciences; Fellowship Royal Soc of Health – now lapsed but he considers the scientific and technical training has been an asset in his work.
Pc Repair and replacement – bronze patinated brass fittings (67 windows), Hengrave Hall. 25+8 Shako helmet plates as original patterns – 2 private regiments. Restoration – main gates, Hengrave Hall and West Stow Rectory. Gates Rougham Estate. Restoration of 10 brass cased locks. Opened 6 latch Spanish sea chest.
Also produces a range of traditional chandeliers, and is willing to restore antiques. Undertakes most kinds of replacement brass fittings patinated to exactly match original patterns inc. decorative cast brass key escutcheons.

BROOKING, CHARLES
See entry under Associations

BROWN, B. G. (Empl: solo)
Wood Carver
Coed Helen, Llanwyndyrs y Ffor, Pwllheli, Gwynedd. 0758-65603.
Full apprenticeship at R. A. Listers of Dursley; lifetime in building trade; carpenter & joiner – contract supervisor on many varied types of contract.

BROWN, S. F. & SON (ARCHITECTURAL WOODCARVERS)

Pc 30 coloured panels depicting Bible story – client in Bucks.
Mr Brown is semi-retired and therefore is only able to undertake those commissions which are of particular interest to him. Portfolio of photographs available.

BROWN, CLIVE (Empl: one; Est: 1979)
Master Thatcher
2 Stephens Cottages, Buckland St. Mary, Chard, Somerset TA20 3SL. 046 034-439.
Pc Thatchers to the National Trust for the last 5 yrs.

BROWN, DAVID J. (Empl: one; Est: 1978)
Stained Glass Artist/Painter
8 St Johns Avenue, Pilling, Nr Preston, Lancs PR3 6HD. 0253-790713.
M BSMGP.
Also incorporates brilliant cutting.

BROWN, DENNIS DECORATORS (Est: approx 10yrs)
105 Rochdale Rd, Scunthorpe, S. Humberside DN16 3JD. 0724-866 968.
Father – 34 yrs experience; previously managing director of 2 companies employing 60 and 160; 'Now content to just handle specialist work which we carry out ourselves knowing that we can guarantee high class and satisfactory results'. Son – C & Gs training.
Willing to fit plaster cornices, moulds and centrepieces.

BROWN, JOHN ARMSTRONG LTD (Empl: 40; Est: 1970)
Fabric Designer
53 Higher Rd, Urmston, Manchester M31 1AP. 061-748 1144 & 747 9919.
M BCFA; AMU
Fabric hand-printed to specified design – no minimum run.

BROWN, SANDY (Est: 1980)
Hand-painted Ceramics
38 East St, South Molton, Devon EX36 3DF. 076 95-2829.
M Craftsmen Potters Assoc; M Crafts Council Slide Index; Contemporary Applied Arts.
Hand-painted, colourful, boldly expressionistic tile murals.

BROWN, S. F. & SON (ARCHITECTURAL WOODCARVERS) (Est: 1946)
19 Buckingham Rd, Worthing, W. Sussex BN11 1TH. 0903-204 758 & 210 607.
L. F. Brown – B Sc; Master Carvers Assoc.

FIRMS AND CRAFTSPEOPLE

Pc Cathedral screen – Ukranian Exchange, London. Chimneypieces.
Cabinet making; church embellishment. Brochure.

BROWNE WINTHER & CO LTD (Empl: 35; Est: 1893)
Woodturning & Machining
Nobel Rd, Angel Rd, Edmonton, London N18 3DX. 081-803 3434.
Dowel & Woodware Importers Assoc; Assoc of Suppliers to the Furniture Trade.
Woodturning and machining to specification, inc. mouldings; dowels; knobs; curtain poles; staircasing; brio; brass; gallery rails; chrome tubing. Brochure.

BROWNS OF WEST WYCOMBE (Empl: 6; Est: chairmakers since 1863)
Cabinet Makers & Restorers
Church Lane, West Wycombe, High Wycombe, Bucks HP14 3AH. 0494-24537.
High Wycombe Furn Makers Assoc.

BROXAP & CORBY LTD (Est: 1976)
Manufacture, Design & Reproduction of Street Furniture.
Walker St, Radcliffe, Manchester M26 9JH. 061-773 7831; FAX 061 766 5343; TELEX 667077 BADGER G.
Also stock a standard range of products. Brochure.

BRUCE, R. R. STAINED GLASS (Empl: solo; Est: 1983)
St. Hilda's, The Ropery, Whitby, N. Yorks YO22 4ET. 0947-600513.
Pc Replacement leaded lights – Bagdale Olde Hall, Whitby (AD 1516). Replacement windows – Nat West Bank, Whitby. Replacement windows and repairs – Ampleforth College, Ampleforth (AD 1570).

BRUGGE, PETER (Empl: 5; Est: 1985)
Thatcher
8 Thorsby Rd, Altrincham, Cheshire WA15 7QP. 061-9411986.
BA (Hons).
Pc Work for building firms inc. Bovis, Milton Keynes and Balfour Beatty.

BRUNAVS, L. & SON (Empl: 4–8; Est: 40 yrs)
Abbey Mills, Abbey Rd, Kirkstall, Leeds LS5 3HP. 0532-759 449.
GMC; Northern Furniture Manufacturers Assoc.

BRUNO BRONZE (ANDY MITCHELL) (Empl: 2; Est: 1984)
Whitehall, Alderley, Wotton-under-Edge, Glos GL12 7QT. 0453-844 253.
Higher Dip Art & Design.

Professional art bronze foundry. Many small and large scale sculptural castings and repairs executed. Specialist welding techniques for bronze, aluminium and cast iron. Repair and restoration of old bronze patinas.

BUDD, JO TEXTILE ARTIST (Empl: solo; Est: 1981)
35 Marine Parade, Lowestoft, Suffolk NR33 0QN. 0502-511 799.
BA (Hons) Fine Art, University of Newcastle-upon-Tyne.
Pc St Oswald's Hospice, Newcastle-upon-Tyne. Bedfordshire County Council Teaching Media Resource Service. Has collaborated on a number of commissions for libraries, teaching hospitals and schools inc. Newcastle-upon-Tyne College of Arts and Technology Library.
Wallhangings inspired by architecture and landscape. Prefers to make large hangings suitable for public buildings and large spaces, although will consider any project from 8 sq in upwards.

BUDD, KENNETH (ARCA) & BUDD, OLIVER BA (Hons) (Est: 1962)
Mosaic Artists
The Old Barn, Betsoms Farm, Pilgrims Way, Westerham, Kent TN16 2DS. 0959-64845 & 62219.
M Art Workers Guild (Oliver on Committee).
Pc Inner Ring Road Mosaics – Birmingham. The Chartist and Old Green murals – Newport, Gwent. Quarter mile long NAB Wall and Halley/Giotto murals – Telford. Full details of commissions listed in *Who's Who in Art* (list sent on request).
Brochure.

BULGIN, D. A. (Empl: solo; Est: 1958)
Master Thatcher
3 Trusthams, Broadwindsor, Beaminster, Dorset DT8 3QB.
Apprenticed to W. Grundy for 5 yrs; qualified Master Thatchers Cert; Thatchers Assoc.
Willing to undertake re-timbering if the project is not too large.

BULLARD, SIMON STONEMASON (Empl: solo; Est: 1989)
16 Conduit Rd, Stamford, Lincs PE9 1QQ. 0780-52989.
C & Gs Stonemason; Cert for Restoration & Preservation of Old Buildings (course held in Venice).
Mr Bullard has just completed 9 yrs as fixer mason for J. Bysouth, Tottenham (see entry under BYSOUTH, J. LTD).

BULLEN, H. & SON LTD (Empl: 120; Est: 1896)
Building Contractors
Central Rd, Cromer, Norfolk NR27 9BW. 0263-511 264.

FIRMS AND CRAFTSPEOPLE

M BEC. Approved: Norwich Diocesan; Eng. Heritage; North Norfolk D C; Norfolk C C; E Anglia Regional Hospital Board.
Pc National Trust, Felbrigg Hall – Messrs Purcell, Miller, Tritton & Partners, Architects, Bethel St, Norwich. East Ruston Church – Messrs Freeland, Rees & Roberts, Architects, 25 City Rd, Cambridge.

BULLOCK, MALCOLM & SON (Empl: 24; Est: 1982)
Building Contractors
Enterprise Business Centre, St. Anne's Fort, Kings Lynn, Norfolk PE30 1QS. 0553-760 384.
NHBC; GMC; Civic Trust Award winner. Approved: Norfolk CC; Breckland DC; BC of Kings Lynn & W Norfolk; Kings Lynn Preservation Trust.
Pc Restoration and alterations – 23/25 & 40/42 King St, Kings Lynn for Robert Freakley Assocs. New extension – Reffley C P School for Norfolk CC. Alterations and new building – Docking Rural Workshops for Eng. Estates.
Also will sympathetically convert barns.

BULMER BRICK & TILE CO LTD (Empl: 10)
The Brickfields, Bulmer, Nr Sudbury, Suffolk CO10 7EF. 0787-29232.
Pc Hampton Court Palace. Feering Church. Oxborough Hall. St Osyth Priory. Castle Bromwich House. Compton Wynyates. Layer Marney Towers. St John's College, Cambridge. St Saviours Church.
Bricks made from seams of London bed clay dug since early Tudor times, producing the traditional mellow reds with a coarse sand-veined or fine sand-finish in a range of sizes from $1^7/_8$ in–$2^7/_8$ in. Purpose-made specials produced to match individual requirements of each building available.

BURBRIDGE, RICHARD LTD
Staircase Manufacturers
Whittington Rd, Oswestry, Shropshire SY11 1HZ.

BURGESS, JOHN & CO (Empl: 4; Est: 1984)
Reproduction Ceramic Tiles
Unit B25, Maws Craft Centre, Jackfield, Telford, Shropshire TF8 7LS. 0952-884 094.
BA (Hons) Fine Art; John Moores Fellow, Liverpool Poly.
Pc Re-manufacture of tiles for V & A Museum and Frogmore Dairy, Windsor. Floor tiles – Foreign Office, Whitehall.
Hand-painted embossed ceramic tiles. Brochure.

BURGIN, ANGELA TRADITIONAL UPHOLSTERY (Empl: 5; Est: 1968)
The Long Barn, 50 High St, Tring, Herts HP23 5AG. 044 282 3151.
AMU; GMC.

Pc Stately homes throughout England and abroad. Executive yachts.
Also handmade curtains, drapery and an interior design service. Brochure.

BURGOYNE, ELISABETH (Est: 1983)
Hand-tufted Rugs & Wallpieces
84 Waverley St, Oldham, Lancs OL1 4HF. 061 652-3663.
BA (Hons) Carpet Design & Related Textiles.

BURKE, JOHN & SON (Empl: 9; Est: 1946)
Thatcher
Delaheys Farm, Green Lane, Timperley, Cheshire WA15 8QP. 061-980 5735.

BURLEIGH STONE CLEANING & RESTORATION CO (Empl: 12; Est: 1976)
PO Box 132, Liverpool L69 8BR. 051 708-6107. FAX 051 708-6924.
Stone Fed; BEC; Brit Inst of Cleaning Science.
Pc Refurbishment of ornate door entrance and roof – Magistrates Courts. Restoration and replacement to Portland Stone – Lady Lever Art Gallery. Dismantling/rebuilding facade inc. major replacement in reconstituted stone – Clayton Square II. Stonework, brickwork, plasterwork – Canning St. Cleaning and repointing stone, replacing lettering, and cleaning and renewing bronze castings – Port Sunlight Village.
Brochure.

BURLINGTON SLATE LTD
Cavendish House, Kirby-in-Furness, Cumbria LA17 7UN. 022-989 661/6.
Suppliers of green and blue slate for all architectural and restoration purposes inc. roofing slates; name plaques; headstones; cladding; paving; cills; walling stone; crazy paving.

BURN, FREDERICK BENNETT COOK ARCHITECTS (Est: 1958)
Formerly Frederick Burn Smith & Partners
114 Great Portland St, London W1N 6EP. 071-636 8868.
Frederick Burn – FRIBA; experience; lecturer on the conservation, restoration and conversion of historic buildings and structures to the SPAB and also on BBC Radio.
Pc Architects to Country Houses Assoc Ltd for over 30 yrs, for the continuing specialist conservation and restoration of 9 country houses. Rescue of Charlton Park, Wilts for DOE. Conservation – St Albans Church tower, London EC2.
Will take on engineering only as co-ordinating and supervising consultants.

FIRMS AND CRAFTSPEOPLE

BURROUGH & HANNAM GROUP PRACTICE (Est:1946)
Architects
Bedford House, 23 Richmond Hill, Bristol BS8 1BE. 0272-730 217.
Maurice A. Chapman – ARIBA   Julian F. Hannam – Dip Arch; (RWA) Hons; ARIBA   Stephen P. Chapman – M Sc; BA; Dip Arch; RIBA.
Pc Repairs – Montacute House for National Trust. Almhouse restorations for trustees. Conversion and extensions in conservation areas.

BUTCHER PLASTERING SPECIALISTS LTD (Empl: 25; Est: 1966)
8 Fitzroy Rd, Primrose Hill, London NW1 8TX. 071-722 9771/2.
FMB.
Brochure.

BUTCHER, R. & SON (Empl: 138; Est: 1800)
Building Contractors
39 George St, Warminster, Wilts BA12 8PU.
Partners – Corp M of CIOB. Craftsmen – apprenticeship served.
Pc Re-roofing and restoration – Marston House, Frome. Restoration – Scaplen's Court, Poole for Poole Borough Council (recently won a Civic Award). Conversion of old 6-storey grain mill to maritime museum – The Waterfront, Poole for Poole Borough Council.
Brochure.

BUTLER, ARTHUR LTD (Empl: 25; Est: 1850)
Building Contractors
Blounts Court Rd, Peppard Common, Nr Henley on Thames, Oxon RG9 5EU. 0734-722 232. FAX 0734-722 410.
BEC.
Pc Prefers not to publically disclose contracts that have been carried out for private clients, etc. However, should an enquiry be forthcoming they will happily provide a list and take prospective clients around.
Contracts are usually kept within the £100,000–£1,000,000 cost bracket.

BUTTRESS FULLER GEOFFREY ALSOP PRACTICE, THE
Chartered Architects & Historic Building Consultants
176 Oxford Rd, Manchester M13 9QQ. 061-273 5405.
Pc Restoration works – Westminster Abbey; Palace of Westminster; Chichester, Llandaff, Sheffield, Bangor and Leeds (RC) Cathedrals; Penrhyn Castle; All Souls, Havey Hill, Halifax; country houses; conversion of chapel to concert hall, Worcester.
Engineering is only undertaken in liaison with structural engineers or specialists.

BYARD, D. J. LTD (Empl: 10; Est: 1983)
Plumbing & Leadwork
138 Birchwood Rd, Wilmington, Kent DA2 7HG. 0332-66474.
M LCA.
Pc Restoration of numerous church lead roofs.

BYSOUTH, J. LTD (Empl: 45 approx; Est: 1873)
Stonemasons
Dorset Rd, Tottenham, London N15 5AL. 081-800 3404. FAX 081-802 6312.
BEC; Stone Fed; London Assoc of Master Stonemasons.
Pc Various works throughout the country for National Trust, Eng. Heritage, DOE, etc. inc. Roman Wall, London; Wells Cathedral; Felbrigg Hall; Houses of Parliament; St James's Palace; Buckingham Palace; Brighton Royal Pavilion; Somerset House; Woburn Abbey; Guildford Cathedral; Winchester Cathedral; numerous less well known properties and churches.
A long established family concern with particular expertise in the fields of repair, restoration and conservation, although they will also undertake new work. Brochure.

CADELL, WILLIAM A. ARCHITECTS (Est: 1973)
Grange West, Linlithgow, W. Lothian EH49 7RH. 0506-84729.
William A. Cadell, partner – MA (Cantab); Dip Arch (The Polytechnic) RIBA; FRIAS   Thomas A. J. Pollock, partner – B Arch (Edin); RIBA; ARIAS.
Pc Restoration – keep (c. 1500), Niddry Castle, Winchburgh. New terrace adjacent to Brigeness tower, Harbour Rd, Bo'ness. Conservation of 14th-century tower (Grade I), restoration of stables block – Mugdock Castle and Country Park. Maintenance – 13/14th century St Michael's Church, Linlithgow. Conversion of stables to 13 holiday homes and Clan centre – Hunterston Castle, Ayrshire.
Also experienced in preparation of conservation reports; work in conservation areas and infill of gap sites; the establishment of a Town Trust.

CAENWOOD FURNITURE – MARTIN BOWN (Empl: self + sub-contractors; Est: 1985)
Designer & Cabinet Maker
Slough Rd, Presteigne, Powys LD8 2NH. 0544-260 040.
Ex Craft Design & Technology Teacher.
Pc Chess boards and boxes for bronze pieces by Michael Ayrton, sculptor. Pieces of furniture sold in London and N. York, and exported to places as disparate as Nairobi and the Falkland Isles.
Brochure.

FIRMS AND CRAFTSPEOPLE

CAINE, OSMUND (Empl: solo; Est: 1950)
Stained Glass Artist/Painter
Bedford House, 25 Kingston Hill, Kingston-on-Thames, Surrey KT2 7PW. 081-546 3713.
Studied at the Birmingham College of Art; BA Hons; M SIA; A BSMGP; MDCS.
Pc Stained glass windows inc. south and north aisle – All Saints' Church, Four Oaks, Sutton Coldfield; south aisle – All Saints' Church, Stechford, Birmingham; north aisle St Keyne's Church, St Keyne, Liskard, Cornwall.

CALEY, TREVOR (CALEY MOSAIC)
70 Gipsy Hill, London SE19 1PD. 081-670 8068.
National Dip Design (Mural Design); M Assoc for the Study & Preservation of Roman Mosaic.
Pc Mosaics murals – London Underground Stations, Tottenham Court Rd, Oxford Circus, Finsbury Park. Travelcard posters. Mosaics – head offices of Lloyds; Prudential Assurance; Barclays Bank. Mosaic mural – Westminster Cathedral. Mosaic floors, etc. – Whitbreads Henry's Café Bars. Also small private commissions.
Experienced in a variety of styles (classical and abstract); perspectives and reconstruction illustration; general environmental design. Brochure.

CALLAN, JOHN STAINED GLASS & LEADED LIGHTS (Empl: 2; Est: 1980)
19 Edwards Rd, Dorchester, Dorset DT1 2HL. 0305-69113.
Trained at Swansea School of Art.
Pc New church windows – St Andrew's, Portland; St Francis of Assisi, Littlemoor, Weymouth; St Aldhelm's, Radipole, Weymouth. Restorations – Woodsford Manor, Dorset; Waterson Manor, Dorset; Cruxton Manor, Dorset; Brownsea Island Parish Church. Commercial work for Eldridge Pope Brewers; International Leisure.

CAMBRIDGE STAINED GLASS (DEAN CULLUM) (Est: 1980)
8 George St, Willingham, Cambridge CB4 5LJ. 0954-60301.

CAMPBELL & SMITH CONSTRUCTION CO LTD
General Building Contractors
Old Sawmill, Ormiston, E. Lothian EH35 5NQ. 0875-610 343.

CAMPION, PAM (Empl: solo; Est: 1963)
Textile Conservator
Myrtle Cottage, Gretton, Nr Cheltenham, Glos GL54 5EP. 0242-604 227.
5 yrs apprenticeship with H. W. Keil, Cheltenham.

Pc Embroideries commissioned by Ian Hamilton Finlay (The Concrete Poet).

CANE CORNER – BRIGETTE L. STONE (Empl: solo; Est: 1985)
1a Newbridge St, Exeter, Devon EX4 3JW. 0392-218 595.
Working towards Dip given by Basketmakers Assoc; M Devon Rural Skills Trust; M Basketmakers Assoc; has been on several 'refresher' courses at West Dean College.
Pc Specific details of commissions completed given on request. Viewing can be arranged with client's consent.
Before and after photographs available.

CANE & RUSH – HARRIET BISSON (Empl: variable; Est: 1982)
Church House, 7 Church Rd, Butterwick, Nr Boston, Lincs PE22 0HT. 0205-760 762.
Basketmakers Assoc.

THE CANE SMITHS (Empl: 3 self employed; Est: 1978)
10 Windsor Rd, Barnet, Herts EN5 2PR. 081-449 3381.
Brian trained as a chair caner under the late George Pryor (one time chair caner to the present Queen Mother. All the family belong to the Basketmakers Assoc.
Pc General cane repairs to pre-Victorian (inc. a Jacobean settle), Victorian and post-Victorian furniture for very many people and some famous houses.
Will not repair whole cane or ratten furniture.

CANNONS DECORATORS (Empl: 10 + sub-contractors; Est: 1978)
4 Ravenspurn Way, Grimsby, S. Humberside DN31 1XR. 0472-358 552 & 0860-398 135.
BDA; Artex Approved Specialists.
Pc Hospitals, schools, private houses, hotels, factorys, etc.

CANONGATE BUILDING CONSULTANTS
Building Defects & Conservation Consultants
179 Canongate, Edinburgh EH8 8BN. 031-557 2470.
Bill Muir – 25 yrs experience; training in remedial treatment industry   Stewart Brown – worked for Sir Basil Spence, Glover & Ferguson; on RIAS list of Arbiters   James Simpson – trained under Ian Lindsay and Sir Bernard Feilden; M Ancient Monuments Board for Scotland   Mandy Ketchin – co-author of *The Care & Conservation of Georgian Houses.*
Pc New buildings – Queen Margaret College, Magnet plc and Digital plc. Repair and restoration work – Yester House; Arniston House;

FIRMS AND CRAFTSPEOPLE

Hawthornden; Monzie and Rosslyn Castles. Repair and restoration – Alderman Fenwick's house, Newcastle. Work for PSA; Cockburn Conservation Trust.

Independent technical service offered on building failures and disputes; litigation; the technical aspects of historic building conservation; treatment for dampness and timber problems; planned maintenance programmes; stone decay; research on any aspects of building conservation.

CANTABRIAN ANTIQUES
Architectural Antiques
16 Park St, Lynton, N. Devon EX35 6BY. 0598-53282.

Doors; panelling; room dividers; mullion windows; stairways; bannisters; slate floors; pews; counters; bars; railings; etc. Also undertake selected projects/design work – particularly barn conversions, but also restaurant/pub interiors involving the design and supply of suitable materials. Will arrange shipping.

CAPITAL MARBLE LTD (Empl: 15; Est: 1981)
Unit 6, 10 Acklam Rd, London W10 5QZ. 081-968 5340.
Stone Fed; LAMS; UKIC (Stone section); SPAB.
Pc Stone restoration and cleaning – Public Offices Whitehall Blue Sector for PSA. Elevation terracotta works, marble restoration in foodhalls – Harrods. Chiswick House for Eng. Heritage. Cleaning and restoration – Royal Society of Arts.
Brochure.

CAPPS & CAPPS LTD (Empl: 50; Est: 1978)
Repair of Old Buildings
Llowes Court, Llowes, Hay on Wye, Heref HR3 5JA. 04974-602 & 328.
Various qualifications, apprenticeships and memberships in masonry, joinery, bricklaying, plastering.
Pc Masonry – Hereford Cathedral. Stonework – Manorbier Castle. Timber Frame – Luntley Court. Kitts Quarry, Burford, Oxon, etc.
Brochure.

CAPRICORN ARCHITECTURAL IRONWORK LTD (Empl: 8; Est: 1974)
Tasso Forge, 56 Tasso Rd, London W6 8LZ. 081-381 4287.
M BABA; NAFBAE.
Pc Spiral staircase and walkway – Cheyne Walk, Chelsea. Spiral staircase – The Royal Botanical Gardens, Kew. Restoration of Georgian railings and ironwork, Bedford Sq, WC1. Restoration of facade to lecture theatre roof – V & A Museum. Refurbishment of early cast iron railings – Her Majesty's Tower of London.
Specialists in work of any style/period, using historical methods with selected

features in other materials inc. wood; bronze; glass; terrazzo; stone. Stock over 1,000 cast iron patterns. Brochure.

CARDY, E. H. & SON LTD (Empl: 200; Est: 1946)
Builders & Contractors
Broad Oak Rd, Canterbury, Kent CT2 7SN. 0227-763 444.
BEC; ALC; Registered House Builder.
Pc Tylney Hall, Nr Basingstoke, Hants. Canterbury Cathedral. Alms Houses, Canterbury. Stella Maris Convent, Broadstairs. Sittinghurst Castle, National Trust.
Brochure

CARFORD, GEO LTD (Empl: 3; Est: 1969)
Blacksmith
Ingatestone Forge, 3a High St, Ingatestone, Essex CM4 9ED. 0277-353 026.
CoSIRA training course – Principles & Practices of Wrought Ironwork; Agricultural Engineering & Blacksmithing Course; M NAFBAE.

CAROE & MARTIN
Architects
90 Evershott St, London NW1 1BT. 071-387 0477. Penniless Porch, Market Place, Wells, Somerset BA5 2RB. 0749-77561.
RIBA; FSA; ASCHB; SPAB; EASA; Art Workers Guild.
Pc Wells Cathedral. Rochester Cathedral. St David's Cathedral. Parish churches. National Trust – Kingston Lacy; Osterley Park; Dunster Castle; W. Wycombe Park. Landmark Trust – Woodsford Castle; Stogursey Castle; Kingswear Castle. Archaeological investigation – Lodge Farm (1380 house). Medieval wallpaintings – Rochester Cathedral. Plaster conservation – Pembroke College. Various other projects inc. far smaller works.

CARR, MYRNA FABRIC DESIGN (Empl: one; Est: 1984)
Studio 8 & 9, Cleveland Crafts Centre, 57 Gilkes St, Middlesbrough, Cleveland TS14 8JR.
Higher Nat Dip in Art & Design; SIAD in Textile Design.
Pc Several commissions for a variety of companies needing promotional items with own identifying logo, pattern, etc.
Silk fabric, designed to utilize the superb colour and reproductive processes of silk screen printing. Brochure.

CARROLL DECORATORS (Empl: approx 10; Est: 1974)
Unit 23, Lynedoch Ind Estate, Greenock, Renfrewshire PA15 4AX. 0475-29865.

FIRMS AND CRAFTSPEOPLE

5 yrs painting and decoration; C & Gs; Advanced C & Gs; M Master Painters and Scottish Decorators Assoc.
Pc Watt Library and Museum (listed building) – Greenock. Formakin Centre, Bridge of Weir (now Heritage Centre). All types of churches.

CARTER, R. G. LTD (Est: founded 1921, incorporated 1932)
Building Contractors
Drayton, Norwich, Norfolk NR8 6AH. 0603-867 355.
M BEC; Construction Industry Training Board. Approved: Eng. Heritage; City of Norwich; Broadland DC; South Norfolk DC; Norfolk CC.
Pc 'The Old Barge' Public House, King St, Norwich – A. C. Whitwood RIBA, City Architect, City of Norwich. Refurbishment of offices, 26 Tombland, Norwich for Property Partnership. Alterations and refurbishment to 56, 64 King St, Norwich – John Sennitt.

CARTER, R. G. HARLESTON (Empl: 80; Est: 1952)
Building Contractors
37 Station Rd, Harleston, Norfolk IP20 9ES. 0379-852 131.
BEC; NFBTE. Approved: SNDC; MSDC; SCDC; IBC; SCC; various housing associations; Suffolk Preservation; Eng. Heritage.
Pc Pakenham Watermill. Oaksmere. Coldham Hall. Ditchingham Hall. Horham Hall. Works House, Leiston.

CARTER, ROGER PERIOD FURNISHINGS (Empl: 16; Est: 6 yrs)
Kirkby on Bain, Woodhall Spa, Lincs LN10 6YL. 0526-52119 & 53461.
Guild of Craftsmen.
Also large contracts – house projects – carried out. Brochure.

CARTWRIGHT, HARRY (Empl: 30; Est: 1954)
Refinement in Plaster
94 Foxoak St, Cradley Heath, W Midlands B64 5DP. 0384-66657.
FMB; GMC.
Pc Form arches to steel roof trusses – Great Western Arcade, Birmingham. Refurbish and ornamental plaster – Star Hotel, Worcester.

CASE CONSTRUCTION/JOINERY (Empl: 5 (woodwork); Est: 1920)
50 Broad St, Lyme Regis, Dorset DT7 3QF. 02974-3209.
Full Tech Cert – fully trained apprenticeship. Basic course prize winner. M Brit Woodworking Fed.
Pc Complete copy replacement of Georgian entrance poritco – Rock Point Inn, Lyme Regis.

CATHEDRA LTD

CASCIANI, PAUL SAN STAINED GLASS ACTIVITIES (Est: 1971)
11 Dale Close, Thames St, Oxford OX1 1TU. 0865-727 529.
Apprenticeship with James Powell & Son Stained Glass Studio, London; Dip of Merit in Glasspainting, Worshipful Co of Glaziers; A BSMGP; Oxford Craft Guild.
Pc Specialist glasspainting inc. 3 windows – Liverpool Anglican Cathedral (c. 1968-70). Restoration and renewal of shattered Victorian panel – Walgrave Church, Oxon. Appliqué copperfoil table lamps. Pilkington Glass Museums panel based on photomicrograph.
Specialist glass painting. Particular interest in photomicrograph designs. Author Technique of Decorative Stained Glass, (Batsford Craft Series 1985). Runs stained glass courses and gives tours of Oxford's stained glass.

CASEMENTS THE CABINET MAKERS (Empl: one; Est: Jan 1965)
Slack Lane Works, Pendlebury, Swinton, Salford, Lancs M27 2QT. 061-794 1610.
36 yrs experience.

CASSELL, JOSEPH (Empl: one; Est: 1985)
Artist Blacksmith
The Forge, Spennithorne, Nr Leyburn, N. Yorks DL8 5PR. 0969-22865 & 0765-85429.
Metalsmith for 6yrs; 1 yr with Richard Quinnell Ltd (see entry under that name); Royal Electrical; M BABA; registered with Crafts Council.

CASTLE CRAFTS/CASTLE CONSTRUCTION (Empl: 14; Est: 1987)
Specialist Joiners
Unit C3, Rudford Ind Estate, Arundel, W. Sussex BN18 0HY. 0903-730 830.
Apprentice served joiners and boatbuilders; M Fed of Crafts & Commerce.
Pc Keep a photographic record of works carried out from start to completion.

CATHEDRA LTD (Empl: 40; Est: 1974)
Furniture Designers
4 Harrington Way, Warspite Rd, London SE18 5NU. 081-854 2222.
Graduates of London College of Furniture Dip; High Wycombe College of Furniture BA; Thame College Dip; FCSD; MIM Wood Tec.
Pc Nine o'Clock News desk – BBC. Dealer desks – Merrill Lynch. Boardroom furniture inc. Cluttons; Pearson plc; ICI (dining room also). Office suites – AMTM. Dealer room – Salamon Bros. Conference table – British Rail Property Board. Conference suites – Hambros; Shell; BP; etc. Furniture – Mitsubishi. *Brochure.*

FIRMS AND CRAFTSPEOPLE

CATHEDRAL WORKS ORGANISATION (CHICHESTER) LTD (Empl: 30; Est: 1965)
Terminus Rd, Chichester, W. Sussex PO19 2TX. 0243-784 225.
E. F. Bedford, general manager – CGLI Full Tech; LMBA Silver Medal.
All stonemasons have C & Gs.
Pc Restoration at Blenheim Palace; All Souls Church, Langham Place, London W1; Old War Office, Whitehall, London; Oxford colleges.
Brochure.

CATO, LAURA – WOVEN TAPESTRY (Est: 1987)
Warrior Studios, Arch 264, Coldharbour Lane, Loughborough Junction, Camberwell, London SW9 8ST. 071-737 3522.
BA Hons Degree Textiles – Camberwell School of Art & Crafts, 1st Class Degree.
Produces 'rich' tapestries, with an emphasis on colour, texture and dramatic contrast inc. the illusion of depth. Also undertakes teaching and is Artist in Residence, Rufford Craft Centre, Nottingham.

CAUDELL RESTORATIONS (Empl: solo; Est: 1960)
Furniture Restorer
55 Stowe Rd, Orpington, Kent BR6 9HG. 0689-73631.
5 yr apprenticeship served with Saundersons; GMC.
Pc Various Museums inc. Swedish & German. Royal Household work undertaken when with Boswell Restoration of London.

CELTIC STUDIOS LTD (H. P. THOMAS)
Stained Glass Artist/Painter
5 Prospect Place, Swansea, W. Glam SA1 1QP. 0792-654 832.
NDD; FMGP; GMC.
Pc Post Liberation memorial window, Christ Church Cathedral, Falkland Islands. Lady Chapel and Clerestory windows, Market Harborough Parish Church. Burma Star memorial window, Llanbadarn Fawr, St Padarn's Church. Window, St Helen's Church, Stapleford, Nottingham.

CEMENTONE BEAVER LTD
Tingewick Rd, Buckingham MK18 1AN. 0280-823 823.
This company produces the Wykamol range of products. Also injection mortar for dpc formation in random stone walls; additives for re-plastering after dpc insertion; silicone based external water repellent; multi-coat plastering tanking system. All products for chemical dpc are approved by BSI. Company gives a 30 yr work guarantee for insertion of chemical dpc, etc. Details of the company's approved specialist contractors, available on request. Produce an ecologically safe range. Brochure.

CERAMIQUE INTERNATIONALE LIMITED (Empl: 12; Est: 1977)
Hand-painted Ceramic Tiles
386 Kings Rd, Chelsea, London SW3 5UZ. 071-351 3467.
Pc St James Park Hotel, London. SW1. Ladbrooke Hotel, Amsterdam. Grundy Park Leisure Centre. Picadilly Underground Station.
A ceramic tile importer (all material is exclusive in the UK).

'CHAIRPERSON, THE' – MR HILARY B. MELLING (Empl: solo; Est: 1982)
77 Hanney Rd, Steventon, Oxon OX13 6AN. 0235-832 429.
Reseating of stools and chairs in seagrass, twine, cane and rush.

CHAIRPERSONS OF MARSHFIELD (Est: 1980)
Cane & Rush Seating.
40 High St, Marshfield, Chippenham, Wilts SN14 8LP. 0225-891 431 (24hrs).
Pc Mainly antique dealers and furniture restorers, but many 'one-off' private clients inc. British and foreign royalty.
Experienced in close cane; blind cane; double panels; medallion; spiral and fan back chairs. Also oversee frame repairs.

CHAPEL STUDIO (A. FISHER, P. ARCHER, R. J. HOLLOWAY) (Empl: 10; Est: 1973)
Stained Glass Artists/Painters
Chapel Studio, Bridge Rd, Hunton Bridge, King's Langley, Herts WD4 8RE. 09277-66386.
Fellows and Associates BSMGP.
Pc New work inc. windows and rooflights for secular and religious sites; private residences; schools; casino; convent and churches. Conservation work inc. medieval glass – Exeter Cathedral; Lincoln Cathedral; Westminster Abbey. Period glass – Brighton Pavillion (inc. 2 yrs experimental work on enamels and stains); Oxford colleges; National Trust properties and churches.
Will undertake specialist cleaning, protection of fragile glass by double plating, re-leading, re-glazing and general protection from erosion and weather. Brochure.

CHAPEL STUDIO, THE
Stained Glass Artist
Icklingham, Nr Bury St Edmunds, Suffolk.
D A Edin.
Pc Work to be seen in Staffs, Leics, Scotland, Notts, Heref, Cambs, Midlands. Will send information detailing previous commissions to anyone interested.

FIRMS AND CRAFTSPEOPLE

CHAPLIN, GRAHAM STAINED GLASS DESIGNS (Empl: solo; Est: 1986)
45 Muxton Lane, Muxton, Telford, Shropshire TF2 8PD. 0952-604 775.
DATEC Dip Vocational Art & Design (Stained Glass); HND Architectural Stained Glass.
Pc Restoration of 6 heraldic windows inc. 3 new heraldic shields involving acid etching, sand blasting, painting and enamelling – Lutwych Hall, Much Wenlock, Shropshire.

CHAPMAN, ALBERT E. LTD (Empl: 30; Est: 1930)
Traditional & Modern Upholstery
17 Crouch Hill, London N4 4AP. 071-272 2536 & 071-272 8602.
B. E. Chapman MBE, managing director – F AMU; C & Gs 1st Class. Craftspeople trained in house or via colleges.
Pc Upholstery – French furniture, Wallace Collection. Silk wall covering – St James's Palace, Buckingham Palace. Period style curtains and draperies – Bodelwyddan Castle, Clwyd. Restoration of upholstery of royal coaches, Royal Mews, Buckingham Palace.
Only reproduction of chairs to match existing undertaken, not general reproduction work. Will also undertake silk wall coverings. Brochure.

CHAPMAN, PETER
See CHRISTIAN REPRODUCTIONS – PETER CHAPMAN

CHAPMAN, PETER ANTIQUES & RESTORATION (Empl: 2; Est: 1971)
Architectural Antiques & Furniture Restorers
10 Theberton St, Islington, London N1 0QX. 071-226 5565.
Dip Art & Design (Hons) London; LAPADA.
Pc Restoration of the Seddon Desk from the 1851 Exhibition. Restoration of Pugin furniture from Parliament Building. Restoration of Mackintosh/Bugatti.
Also hand-colours leather upholstery.

CHAPPELL, GEOFFREY KEITH (Est: 1960)
Painter – Murals, Graining & Marbling, Stencilling
9 Lower Chapel Rd, Hanham, Bristol, Avon BS15 3DH. 0272-671 255.
C & Gs.
Pc Marbling and graining – The Bristol Museum & Art Gallery; Blair Castle Museum. Graining – The Brunel Board Room, Old Temple Meads Station, Bristol; Lord Mayor's Mansion House, Bristol. Marbling – Guild Hall Bath & Pump Rooms. Marbling, graining – The Close Hotel, Tetbury, Glos; Chew Court, Endon House.

CHARLESWORTH, M. K.
See 'ONE-OFF JOINERY'

CHAUNCEY'S ARCHITECTURAL ANTIQUES

CHARNWOOD FOREST BRICK & TILE WORKS LTD (Empl: approx 50; Est: 1887)
Old Station Close, Shepshed, Nr Loughborough, Leics LE12 9NL. 0509-503 203 & 504 257.
Pc 30 St James Sq, Pall Mall. Linacre College, Oxford.
Brochure.

CHASE DECORATING & ARTEXING (Empl: 5; Est: 1986)
Ceiling and Decorating Contractors
66 Grove Rd, Drayton, Portsmouth, Hants PO6 1PT. 0705-327 890.
3 yrs apprenticeship, Chichester College Tech, W Sussex. Indentured tradesman – C & Gs Craft, Distinction; C & Gs Advanced Craft, Credit; CITB passed; Associated Exam Board O level Decoration & Design passed; Artex licensed texturer.
A small expanding business of specialist decorators.

CHATFIELD, PHILIP – SCULPTOR (Empl: solo; Est: 1982)
Lower Hareslade Farm, Brandy Cove, Bishopston, Gower, Swansea SA3 3DT. 044 128-4129.
BA Hons (1st Class) Fine Arts, Newcastle University; worked with Jonah Jones and Roy Kitchin, architectural sculptors and lettercutters; M Men of Stones; GMC.
Pc Major series of architectural stone carvings – Maritime Quarter, Swansea (winner of architectural awards, and European Marina winner of Blue Flag 88, 89).
Civic architectural stonework inc. carving; figurative keystones; gable stone panels; portraiture; one-off chimney pieces (abstract and figurative); gallery sculpture; memorials.

CHATTERLEY, G. E. (Empl: solo; Est: 1947)
Architectural Woodcarver & Sculptress
Timewell Cottage, South St, Mayfield, E Sussex TN20 6BY. 0435-872 435.
6 yrs tuition with master carver; 5 yrs working on commissions with president of Master Carvers Assoc; 21 yrs teaching carving and sculpture; M BWA; Past M Art Workers Guild.
Pc 3 ft statue – St John Baptist – Old Malden Church, Surrey. Oak font. Pine fire surround. Forestry commission plaque. Red Cross plaque. Lettercutting and carving in many churches. Animal and bird sculptures from life – private collections.
Details of work available on request.

CHAUNCEY'S ARCHITECTURAL ANTIQUES
Unit G, Junction Rd, Arno's Castle Estate, Brislington, Bristol BS4 3JP. 0272-778 284 & 736 106.

FIRMS AND CRAFTSPEOPLE

Doors; knobs and handles; locks and bolts; ceramic tiles; ridge tiles; finials; chimney pots; wrought-iron gates and railings; rainwater goods; signs; fanlights; ornamental windows; baths; basins; taps WCs; mouldings; carvings; stairs.
Advice given on the type and style of fittings appropriate to the period house involved. Also offer paint stripping, sanding, staining and polishing services.

CHELL, A. M. (Empl: solo; Est: 1986)
Tables, Welsh Dressers, Beds, etc.
165 Manor Rd, Verwood, Wimborne BH21 6DX. 0202-822 646.

CHERKAS, DENNIS VENEERS (Est: 1973)
1 Windermere Hall, Stonegrove, Edgware, Middx HA8 7PY. 081-958 6617.
Supplier of highly decorative veneers for use on architectural panels, furniture, etc. Brochure.

CHERRY & SON LTD (Empl: 30; Est: 1880)
Building Contractors
16 Station Rd, Cropredy, Banbury, Oxon OX17 1PR. 0295-750 209 & 758 118.
Apprenticed. Approved: Diocesan; Eng. Heritage; National Trust; Cherwell District Council.
Pc Major project – Canons Ashby Church for Rodney Melville.
Maintenance – Canons Ashby House for Rodney Melville.

CHERRY'S FURNITURE
The Old Sparrow's Works, Bower Hinton, Martock, Nr Yeovil, Somerset TA12 6LG. 0935-823 843.
Pc Carved four poster bed in English oak.

CHESHIRE RECLAIMED BUILDING MATERIALS LTD
The Old Brick Yard, Mosley Road Junction, Westinghouse Rd, Trafford Park, Manchester, M17 1PY. 061-872 1352.
Suppliers of reclaimed bricks; roofing tiles; natural stone flags.

'CHESHIRE WALLHANGINGS' (Empl: solo; Est: 1984)
20 Avon Rd, Hale, Cheshire WA15 0LB. 061-941 1533.

CHESS INTERIORS LTD (Empl: 8; Est: 1978)
24 Market Place, Chalfont St Peter, Bucks SL9 9DU. 0753-888 422.
All fibrous plasterers apprenticeship served, and one is a Certified Registered Plasterer.

CHRISTIAN REPRODUCTIONS – PETER CHAPMAN

Pc Restoration of ornamental plasterwork matched to existing inc. Frogmore House, Windsor Castle; Admiralty Compass Observatory, Berks; Foxhill House, Reading University; 1 & 2 Temple Gardens, Inner Temple, WC1.
Brochure.

CHILSTONE ARCHITECTURAL ORNAMENTS (Empl: 22; Est: 1958)
Handmade Reconstructed Stone
Sprivers, Hoksmonden, Tonbridge, Kent TN12 8OR. 089 272-3266 & 3553.
Pc Stonework for restoration – Swan Hotel, Bedford. Gate pier capitals, balls and bases (finials) – Buckingham Palace. Balustrade – Hever Castle.
Standard range of columns, copings, balustrades, etc. available. Brochure.

CHINKS VERE GRYLLS (Empl: 2; Est: 1977)
Stained Glass Artist/Painter
Smoke Tree Studio, 1 Mill Lane, Cannington, Somerset TA5 2HB. 0278-653 218.
BSMGP; Dip Architectural Stained Glass (Merit); Brit Artists in Glass. Pc Interior wall/screens – Cibageigy Agrochemicals, Duxford, Cambs; Booz Hamilton, 100 Piccadilly, London W1; Cheltenham Museum & Art Gallery, Clarence St, Cheltenham. Floor to ceiling window for new extension designed by Sir Hugh Casson, Arts & Crafts Gallery.

CHISBURY THATCHERS (Empl: 3; Est: 1975)
The Castle, 12 Farm Lane, Gt Bedwyn, Marlborough, Wilts SN8 3LU. 0672-870 225.
NSMT.
Pc The Old Manor, Little Bedwyn. Barn – Dublins Farm, Wherwell, Hants. Castle Main, Aldbourne, Wilts. Mill House, Bishopstone, Wilts. 84 High St, Hungerford, Berks. Well Cottage, Ham, Wilts. Lynch Farm, Shalbourne, Wilts. Orchard Farm House, E Kennet, Wilts. Watermill Cottage, Wherwell, Hants.

CHRISTIAN REPRODUCTIONS – PETER CHAPMAN (Empl: 4; Est: 1983)
Woodturners & Furniture Manufacturers
33–34 Hatherley Mews, Hoe St, Walthamstow, London E17 4QP. 081-520 6441.
'Taught by finest unknown craftsmen (e.g. father-in-law, etc.)'.
Photographs of work available.

FIRMS AND CRAFTSPEOPLE

CHRISTMAS, JACK (Empl: solo; Est: 1980)
Furniture Designer
12 Coombe Gardens, Hughenden Valley, High Wycombe, Bucks HP14 4PD. 024 024 2184.
C & Gs Silver Medal; Nat Dip Design; M CSD; M SD-C.
Pc Ash and rosewood lectern with carved crest – Wycombe Abbey School. A variety of commissions for domestic furniture, tables, chairs, cabinets.
Photographs available.

CHURCH LANE STAINED GLASS (Empl: 11; Est: 1979)
Bridge House, Bridge Rd, Stoke Ferry, Kings Lynn, Norfolk PE33 9TB. 0366-500 945.
M SGA.
Pc Various in all parts of UK, Kenya and Saudi Arabia.
Will give authoritive advice with regard to heraldry.

CINALLI, RICARDO
Mural Artist
6 Puma Court, London E1 6QE
Studied at the Academia Fornells; the Chopin Conservatory; and the University of Rosario (all in Rosario); Harrow School of Art, and Hornsey College of Art, London.
Pc 'The Londesborough Room' – Alexandra Palace, London. 'The Royal Observatory' – staircase, Kew Gardens, London. Dining room – New York City. Music room. Argentinian Embassy, London. 'Venterol' Orangerie, St Etienne de Gress, Provence (tempera on plaster). Work for various private clients in England, France, Sweden and Argentina.

CITY LOCKS
49 Alma Rd, Peterborough, Cambs PE1 3AN. 0733-43476.
M Master Locksmiths Assoc; European Locksmiths Fed; Nat Locksmith USA; Safe & Vault Technology Assoc, USA.

CLADGILD LTD (Empl: 3; Est: 1979)
Cane & Rush Work
Vine House, Fir Green, Reach, Cambridge CB5 0JD. 0638-741 989.
AMU; GMC.
Pc Various trainers in Newmarket. Newmarket Jockey Club. Captain Lemos. Jaguar headquarters. British Bloodstock Agency. National Trust. Mr Robert Holmes à Court.

CLARK, JENNY

CLAGUE (Est: 1937)
Chartered Architects; Town Planners; Interior Designers; Landscape Architects.
c/o *John Clague & Partners*, 62 Burgate, Canterbury, Kent CT1 2HJ. 0227-762 060.
Pc Restoration and conversion of 17th-century town house. Restoration of 15th-century hall house.
Undertakes Quinquennial surveys and repairs, re-ordering, and undertakes the design of new vicarages for many parishes throughout the Canterbury Diocese.
Betts Hanbury Clague, Knockhundred Row, Midhurst, W. Sussex GU29 9DQ. 0730-814 931.
Pc Rebuilding of a dismantled 17th-century barn. Rebuilding of 18th-century coach house and outbuildings
Harrison Clague, 13 North St, Ashford, Kent TN24 8LF. 0233-624 354.

CLARE HOUSE LTD (Est: 1947)
Lighting
35 Elizabeth St, London. SW1. 071-730 8480.
Royal Warrant Holders.
Pc Colefax & Fowler. Malletts. National Trust. Stately homes.

CLARK, COLIN (Empl: 2; Est: 1972)
Hardwood Furniture Maker
The Old Forge, Hampton St, Tetbury, Glos GL8 8LD. 0666-53079.
5 yrs apprenticeship.
Pc Various church work. Art gallery – St James, London. Complete restoration, authentic to the period – 16th-century manor house (view by appointment). Four poster beds, woodturning and carving.

CLARK, JEAN M. (Empl: solo; Est: 1984)
Ceramic Artist
Ely House, Church Walk, Long Melford, Suffolk CO10 9DN. 0787-310 369.
Goldsmiths College Ceramics Teaching Certificate (1 yr course).
Pc Ceramic fountains for clients in London, Sussex and Suffolk. Further details on request.
Fountains, water and plant units for both in and outdoor settings; large pots. Photographs available on request.

CLARK, JENNY (Est: 1985)
Glass Engraver
The Studio, Elmhurst, Dundle Rd, Matfield, Tonbridge, Kent TN12 7HD. 089 282-4562.

FIRMS AND CRAFTSPEOPLE

Pupil of Peter Dreiser; Brit Artists in Glass; GGE; Listed by CCC & Eng. Heritage.
Pcii Burrswood sculpture – Dorothy Kerin Trust. Pieces for presentation – Marconi & Reed International. Sculpture for permanent collection – Pilkington Glass Museum.
Distance prepared to travel depends on current workload.

CLARK, TERENCE (Empl: one; Est: 1966)
Artist Blacksmith
Wildfields Farm, Woodstreet Village, Nr Guildford, Surrey GU3 3DT. 0483-235 244.
BABA; Surrey Guild of Craftsmen.
Pc Several gates and railings – HH Sheik Mohammed Bin Rashid al Maktoum, Newmarket. Votive stand – Guildford Cathedral. Balustrade restoration – National Trust. Gate restoration – Painshill Park, Cobham, Surrey.
Winner of various awards inc. 1983 Addy Taylor Cup given by Worshipful Co of Blacksmiths. In 1986 Mr Clark was the first artsmith to have a gate accepted by the Royal Academy committee under sculpture. Will undertake anything in metal.

CLASSIC RENAISSANCE (Empl: 9; Est: 1985)
Ornamental Plasterwork
9 Kenyon St, Hockley, Birmingham, W. Midlands B18 6AR. 021-233 3837.
Pc Ecton Hall, Ecton, Northampton. Hawthorn House, Birmingham.

CLASSIC UPHOLSTERY (Empl: 4; Est: 1980)
Estate Yard, Upper Harlestowe, Northants NN7 4EH. 0604-584 556.
AMU.

CLEEVE, STEPHEN
Master Thatcher
1 The Ramblers, Forester Rd, Soberton Heath, Nr Southampton, Hants SO3 1QG. 0329-834072.
M NSMT; M NCMTA; Wilts & Hants MTA.
Established for five generations. Estimates given. Surveys.

CLEMENT BROTHERS HASLEMERE LTD (Empl: 55; Est: 1928)
Special Steel Windows & Doors
Clembro House, Haslemere, Surrey GU27 2QE. 0428-3393.
Pc Special steel windows and doors – Wells Cathedral; Southampton University Old Building; Old Manor, Colherne, Wilts. Semi-head steel windows – Kingston U R Church.
No minimum order. Brochure.

COE E.M. (BUILDERS)

CLIFT, NICHOLAS & ASSOCIATES (Est: 1968)
Chartered Architects
4 Morrab Rd, Penzance, Cornwall TR18 4EL. 0736-64327 & 65146.
RIBA.
Pc Engine house conversion to dwelling. Conversion to dwellings – St Erbyn's School. Abbey Hotel renovation. Renovation of Boskenna. St Buryan.

CLOWE, IAN F.
Cabinet Making & Antique Restoration
17 Hermitage Drive, Dumfries DG2 7QF. 0387-64572.
35 yrs experience.
Pc Work for antique dealers and country houses.
Will undertake inlay work, but not marquetry.

CLUBLEY, D. & SONS ROOFING CO (Empl: 4; Est: 30 yrs)
70 South Back Lane, Bridlington, E Yorks YO16 4AJ. 0262-676 169.
BEC; NFRC; FIUR.

CLUCAS, JOY (Empl: solo; Est: 1956)
Machine Embroidered & Appliquéd Wallhangings & Soft Furnishings
49 Guildford Rd, Castle Gardens, Colchester, Essex CO1 2RX. 0206-868 855.
Nat Dip Design; Art Teachers Cert; F SD-C; M Embroiderers Guilds of America & England; Suffolk Craft Soc; Norfolk Contemporary Craft Soc; New Embroidery Group.
Pc Half-centenary hanging – St Mary's, Southampton. Designed and supervised work for Creation centrepiece, Reigate Park Church. Hanging 'Christ' – Church of St Thomas More, London and St William's School, Yorkshire. Banner – Colchester & Colne Masonic Lodge.
Involved in various publications on machine embroidery.

CLUTTERBUCK, PETER
See FORGE, THE – PETER CLUTTERBUCK

COBB, CLIVE & LESLEY (Empl: 2; Est: 1970)
Painted Dial & Lacquer Restoration
Newhouse Farm, Bratton Fleming, Barnstable, Devon EX31 4RT. 05988-465.
5 yr articled apprenticeship in Design; M GMC.

COE, E. M. (BUILDERS) (Empl: 22; Est: 1961)
The Workshop, Hartburn, Morpeth, Northumberland NE61 4JB. 067 072-221.

FIRMS AND CRAFTSPEOPLE

NHBC; FMB. Approved: Eng. Heritage.
Pc New Deanham, Middleton, Morpeth. Old School, Netherwitton, Morpeth. Park Farm, Longwitton, Morpeth. About to commence speculative development – Middleton, Morpeth.
Specialize in restoration of country stone buildings. Also undertakes damp-proofing (Sovereign Chemical).

COFFEY, GRAHAM – STAINED GLASS (Empl: solo; Est: 1986)
8 Walton St, St Albans, Herts AL1 4DQ. 0727-36806.
Art School Training in Fine Art.
Pc Restoration of Victorian leaded lights – St Saviour's Church, St Albans. Restoration of 17th-century leaded lights – Waterend House, Wheathampstead. Numerous domestic stained glass windows in St Albans and locality.

COFFIN, JONES & RODEN (Est: 1874)
Chartered Architects & Surveyors
28 Waterloo St, Weston-Super-Mare, Avon BS23 1LN. 0934-627 531/2.
RIBA; RICS.
Pc Conservation of 25–31 Victoria St, Bristol. Conservation and re-instatement of parapets – St Peter and St Paul, Bleadon. Replacing lead to flat roof – north aisle, Locking Church, Avon. Re-ordering St Martin's Church, Worle with installation of gallery.

COLDREY FURNITURE (Empl: one; Est: 1979)
Mount Zion Mill, Diptford, Nr Totnes, Devon TQ9 7NG.
M Devon Guild of Craftsmen.
Pc Design and manufacture of furniture in various media. Domestic and commercial commissions undertaken from individual items of furniture to whole 'interiors'.

COLE, HECTOR IRONWORK (Empl: solo; Est: 1970)
The Mead, Gt Somerford, Chippenham, Wilts SN15 5JB. 0249-720 485.
Founder M Local Crafts of Wessex; Des Cert to Teach Crafts & Design Technology; M BABA; Cert of Merit of the Worshipful Co of Blacksmiths.
Pc Windows and lanterns – Byebrook Cottage, Castle Coombe. Highgrove House gates for Tetbury Town Council. Gates/sign – Cotswold Perfumery, Bourton-on-Water.
Also restores arms and reproduces swords.

COLEFORD BRICK & TILE CO LTD (Empl: 35; Est: 1925)
Hawkwell Green, Cinderford, Glos GL14 3JJ. 0594-22160.
Pc R H McDougall, Alma Rd, Windsor. Mobil Oil Offices, Mobil

COLLINS, R.G. PARTNERSHIP, THE

Court, Clements Inn, The Strand, London WC2.

COLES, E. (STONEMASONS) (Empl: 4; Est: 1982)
103 Warkton Lane, Kettering, Northants NNI5 5AB.
M CITB.
Brochure.

COLES, ROBERT FURNITURE & ARCHITECTURAL JOINERY
Church House, Broad St, Congresbury, Avon. 0934-833 660.
National Dip Design, Interior Design; C & Gs Cabinet Making; all employees hold C & Gs qualifications; Exhibiting M Somerset Guild of Craftsmen.
Pc Sycamore display tables (joint project with an architectural firm) which gained Exposhop '89 Award. Gold medal for a cabinet at Woodworker show.
Only able to undertake a limited amount of carving work. Brochure.

COLLIER, W. H. LTD (Empl: 26; Est: 1863)
Church Lane, Marks Tey, Colchester, Essex CO6 1LN. 0206-210 301.
Range of handmade bricks (inc. 50 mm and 65 mm), with the characteristic 'folded' texture created by the compression of clay hand-thrown into sanded beech moulds. Also wide range of briquettes and special shapes. Brochure.

COLLINGWOOD, PETER (Empl: solo; Est: 1952)
Weaver
Old School, Nayland, Colchester, Essex CO6 4JH. 0206-262 401.
Trained with Ethel Mairet and Alistair Morton; F SD-C; on Craft Council Index; awarded OBE.
Pc Wallhangings – many architectural commissions inc. Queen Elizabeth Conference Hall, Westminster; W. H. Smith headquarters; several office blocks around Boston, USA; Britannic House (BP headquarters), London; National Grindley's Bank, London. Rugs – mostly for private houses, but inc. Southampton Public Library; New Zealand House, London.

COLLINS, MATTHEW FURNITURE (Empl: 2; Est: 1986)
Arch 403, Lilford Rd, Camberwell, London SE5 9HR. 071-978 8147.
C & Gs Part III Cabinet Making, Chairmaking, Industrial Finishing.
Pc All types of bespoke furniture.

COLLINS, R. G. PARTNERSHIP, THE (Empl: 4; Est: 1938)
Traditional Upholsterers
43 Melton St, Kettering, Northants NN16 9DT. 0536-514 127.
Apprenticeship in Traditonal Upholstery Crafts; M AMU.

FIRMS AND CRAFTSPEOPLE

Pc Reupholstery of chairs – the Great Hall, Rockingham Castle and also the board room, Brownes Hospital, Stamford (medieval almshouses).

COLOUR DECOR (Empl: 75; Est: 1968)
Painter – Murals, Stencilling, Gilding, Marbling & Graining
5–7 Letchmore Rd, Stevenage Old Town, Herts SG1 3JH. 0438-355 414 & 726 072/3.
BDA.

COMA ROOFING LTD (Empl: 126; Est: 1967)
Old Homesdale Rd, Bromley, Kent BR2 9SP. 081-460 3777. FAX 081-313 0415.
NFRC; LCA – Founder Member.
Pc Storm damage repairs – Whitbread Hop Farm and Tourist Complex. Lead and gutter works – Arras Memorial, France. Lead works, re-roofing of East Residence – British Museum. Leadwork renewal – East & West Tower, British Rail.
This firm is able to cope with the most unusual and eccentric specifications, constructing practical solutions to all manner of roofing problems from highly prestigious listed buildings and public works to individual domestic roofs. Brochure.

COMBER & SON
Building Contractors & Specialist Joiners
Sharpthorne, E. Grinstead, W. Sussex RH19 4NS. 0342-810 235.

COMPLETE BATHROOM, THE (Empl: 7; Est: 1983)
61–63 Ber St, Norwich, Norfolk NR1 3AD. 0603-662 716.
Pc Ten bathroom hotel contract – each room containing a genuine jacuzzi (design and installation). Specification and supply of equipment for a large ocean-going yacht.
Brochure.

COMYN CHING LTD (Empl: 240; Est: c. 1723)
Period Hardware
110 Golden Lane, London EC1Y 0SS. 071-253 8414. Showroom: 19 Shelton St WC2H 9JN. 071-379 3026. E. Anglia Office: 77 Dales Rd, Ipswich IP1 4JR. 0473-462 997. Bristol Office: Unit 2 Whitehall Trading Est, Gerrish Av, Redfield, Bristol BS5 9DG. 0272-540 022
M Guild of Architectural Ironmongers.
Stocks a range of antique and modern ironmongery. Brochure.

CONSTRUCTIONAL UNITS LTD

CONNAUGHT SOUTHERN LTD (Empl: 30; Est: 1984)
Head Office: Unit 3 Alexandria Ind. Estate, Sidmouth EX10 9HL. 0395-577 965. London: 127a Tradescant Rd, London SW8 1XD. 071-587 5119.
Concrete Repair Assoc; Concrete Soc.
Pc External restoration – Queens House, Leicester Square, London. Contracts have inc. restoration of churches, manor houses, government and local authority buildings, through to high-rise blocks and concrete bridges.
Specialists in stone restoration, low molecular mortars, concrete repairs, and external insulation. Brochure.

CONNELL, PAUL
Furniture Designer & Maker
18 Montague Rd, Dalston, London E8 2HW. 081-985 0133.
John Makepeace School for Craftsmen in Wood; BA (Hons) Arch, Kingston Polytechnic.
Pc Furniture & lighting – one-off commissions in a variety of materials.
Brochure.

CONROY & BOOTH GROUP (Empl: 150; Est: 1968)
Specialist Joinery
Ryefield Estate, Scholes, Holmfirth, Huddersfield, W Yorks HA7 1UQ. 0484-686 957/8 (joinery) & 0484-684 021/2/3.
M BEC; Stone Fed; BWF; House Builders Fed; Kirkas and also Holme Valley Chamber of Commerce.
Pc Many refurbishment programmes (mainly joinery work on mansion houses, etc). New work and restoration work on churches (mainly supply only). Currently refurbishing a manor house near Salisbury.
Full design consultancy and budgeting available. This firm also constructs houses, using traditional materials and skills, especially natural stone. Brochure.

CONSERVATION BUILDING PRODUCTS LTD
Architectural Salvage
Forge Works, Forge Lane, Cradley Heath, Warley, W Midlands B64 5AL. 0384-64219 & 69551.

CONSTRUCTIONAL UNITS LTD (Empl: 90; Est: 1919)
Quality Architectural & Bespoke Joinery
152–154 Coles Green Rd, Cricklewood, London NW2 7HG. 081-452 3322.

Have an apprenticeship scheme.
Pc 150 dealers desks – Banque Paribas Capital Markets. Design, development and manufacture desks for 'Big Bang'. Joinery, fittings and wall panelling – Marks & Spencer (Uxbridge). The Royal Festival Hall, for the GLC.
Design facilities. Experienced in completing projects to a tight schedule. Brochure.

CONTI, ANNA STAINED GLASS
14 Renness Rd, Walthamstow, London E17 6EX. 081-531 1964.
HND Chelsea School of Art; Dip SIAD; L/SD-C.
Pc Commissions (mainly domestic) made for UK, Europe and USA. Larger work inc. windows for Virgin plc.
Specializing in contempory designs using a strong flowing lead line with mouth-blown 'antique' glass.

CONWAY, JENNIFER (Est: 1972)
Glass Engraver
31 Oxford Rd, Mistley, Manningtree, Essex CO11 1BW. 0206-396 274.
F GGE.
Pc Screens – Barcombe Parish Church, Nr Lewes, Sussex; Little Waltham Parish Church, Nr Chelmsford, Essex. Doors – St Mary's Church, Bramford, Nr Ipswich, Suffolk. Windows – St Peter's Church, Weston Favell, Northampton.
Prefers not to work in situ.

COOK, JENNY (Empl: solo; Est: 1988)
Hand-woven Wallhangings
1 Mill Cottages, Coldharbour Mill, Uffculime, Cullompton, Devon EX1S 3EE. 0884-41289.
West Surrey College of Art & Design; BA (Hons) Woven Textiles; Royal College of Art; M New Fibre Art; M South West Textile Group.
Pc 48 cm × 124 cms tapestry 'Lying Figure' – bedroom, private commission 1987.

COOKS MILLS (BRADFORD) LTD (Empl: 40; Est: 1948)
Fabric Weavers
496 Leeds Rd, Bradford, W. Yorks BD3 9RF. 0274-724 518. FAX 0274-308 710.
Pc Worked with Crown Suppliers supplying fabric to palaces, etc. (both on Dobby and Jacquard looms).
Brochure.

COOKSON'S MASTER LOCKSMITHS & SAFE ENGINEERS (Empl: 5; Est: 1977)
50a Gertrude Rd, W Bridgeford, Nottingham NG2 5BY. 0602-455 404.

CORDAROY, BILL AWCB

Fully apprenticed; Fellow M Master Locksmiths Assoc; M Safe & Vault Technicians Assoc; Tru-centre Manipulation Assoc; M Small Businesses Fed.
Pc Specialist key making and lock rebuilding to country houses, churches and ancient monuments. Specialized refurbishing of all types of safes and strongrooms.

COOMBER, ROY – STAINED GLASS ARTIST (FREELANCE) (Empl: solo; Est: 1944)
39 Vicarage Rd, Bishopsworth, Bristol BS13 8ER. 0272-640 643.
Served apprenticeship; M BSMGP; artist/designer M Stained Glass Assoc of America; winner 1st Scholarship Worshipful Co of Glaziers; accredited teacher of glass painting; SGAA.
Pc Cathedrals of Wells; Gloucester; Hereford; Worcester and many other churches for Solaglas (see their entry further on). Many new commissions in UK and America. Details upon application.

COOPER, HARRY ASSOCIATES (Est: 4 yrs)
Architectural Sculptor
The Studio, 1 Harbour Rd, Seaton, Devon EX12 2LX. 0297-21153.
Pc 4 ft 6 inch copper whale weathervane – Elbow Beach Hotel, Bermuda.

COPPER LAMP CO LTD, THE (Empl; 8; Est; 1985)
Unit D, Nuts Lane, Hinckley, Leics LE10 3EJ. 0455-633 140.
M DLA.
Period style lamps, brackets and posts, made from the highest grade materials, and protected with a baked melamine lacquer. Polished copper or brass, antiqued or black finishes available. Brochure.

CORBETT, ROB (Empl: one; Est: 1964)
Cabinet Maker & Restorer
Corbett Woodwork, Corpusty, Norfolk NR11 6QP. 026 387-268.
Loughborough College; G. T. Ratclyfe Ltd, Kelvedon, Essex.
Pc Font covers for various churches. Pews – New Worship Centre, Walsingham, Norfolk.
Brochure.

CORDAROY, BILL AWCB (Empl: one; Est: 1977)
Metalworker
Old Farm Forge, Back Lane, E Rushton, Norwich, Norfolk NR12 9JE. 0692-650 724.
Apprentice general engineer – D. MacKay, Cambridge; A of The Worshipful Co of Blacksmiths (AWCB); Dip of Merit from AWCB.

Pc Three archway gates – St John's College, Cambridge. A pair of gates – St John's College Chapel, Thorpe Hall, Norwich. Window casements and door furniture.

CORDIN, RONALD ASSOCIATES – ARCHITECTS
Benjamin House, 8 Portland St, Aston, Birmingham, W. Midlands B74 2QH. 021-328 6336.
Dip Arch Nottm; ARIBA.
Pc The Old Farm, 29 Moor Hall Drive, Sutton Coldfield. 68–74 Station Rd, Pelsall, W Midlands. 62 Abbey Foregate, Shrewsbury. Bishops Veseys Grammar School, Sutton Coldfield, W Midlands.

CORNISH STAIRWAYS LTD (Empl: 32; Est: 1976)
3 Jennings Rd, Penryn, Cornwall TR10 9DQ. 0326-74662 & 74362.
M BIM; M C & CA; M ASEE; Cornwall Industrial Design Assoc; Crafts Council.
Pc Buckingham Palace. King Faid & Prince Sulman of Saudi Arabia. Nat West Tower – Bank of Scotland. World Trade Centre – Building Centre.
Established 160 yrs ago, under its parent company's name of Davey & Jordan – one of Britain's best known master blacksmithing businesses, predominantly producing work for the National Trust and London Stately Homes (see entry under that name). Brochure.

CORRIN, ADELLE STAINED GLASS (Est: 1980)
42 Arundel Gardens, London W11 2LB. 071-221 1136.
BA, MA Advanced Dip Stained Glass – Central School of Art and Design (taught by Patrick Reyntiens); A BSMGP.
Pc 4 staircase windows 4 ft × 5 ft (original designs) The City Lit, Keeley House, Keeley St, WC2. Restoration – door panel, Guildford Institute, Ward St, Guildford (both above open to public view). Etched and enamelled panes reproduced (view by appointment only) – 17 St Leonards Terrace, SW3 (featured in *Ala Carte*, Feb '87, p. 109).
When working without a design brief her images are usually abstract, sometimes inspired by natural forms and landscapes. Photographs available.

COSYTHATCH LTD (Empl: 4; Est: 1974)
Brian Draycott, Ken Draycott, Martin Weaver – Master Thatchers
The Oaks, Myddlewood, Shrewsbury, Salop SY4 3RY. 0939-260 449.
M NCMT; M N of Eng MTA; M GMC.
Pc Thatching work carried out for the National Trust, major breweries, Duke of Westminster's Estate, and private property owners.

COURTNEY, ALAN – STAINED GLASS

Cosythatch Ltd also build new houses to accommodate thatching, and design and build authentic English oak-framed thatched country homes – 'The olde worlde charm of a 16th-century house, with all the modern conveniences of a 20th-century home.'

COTSWOLD & CHILTERN MASTER THATCHERS LTD (Empl: 4; Est: 1987)
73 Hughenden Avenue, Downley, High Wycombe. Bucks HP13 5SL. 0494-443 198.
5 yr apprenticeship; director of 'Norfolk Reed Thatchers'; later started own company; joined NSMT; elected on to executive; elected Chairman.
Pc 'Queen Ann's Dolls House' for Queen Mother – Royal Lodge, Windsor. American Ambassador's Summer House – 'Winfield House', Regent's Park. Many listed and historical buildings, too numerous to list.

COTTAGE CRAFT SPIRALS LTD (Empl: solo; Est: 1982)
Pear Tree Farm, Stubbins Lane, Chinley, Derbys SK1L 6AE. 0663-50716.
Numerous jobs in London, York, etc, requiring decorative Victorian spirals.
Brochure.

COULSON & SON LTD (Empl: 64; Est: 1884)
Building Contractors
William James House, Cowley Rd, Cambridge CB4 4WX. 0223-423 800.
BEC; Approved Instafibre Installer; Accredited Wykamol Contractor. Approved: Cambridge City; Huntingdon District; Cambridge CC; Eng. Heritage.
Pc Church repairs – Haverhill U F Church for Cecil Bourn & Woods. New College Building – Downing College for Quinlin Terry. Manor house refurbishment – Denston, Suffolk for Ronald Geary.
Value of work undertaken £20 to £3,000,000.

COUNTRY CHAIRMEN (Empl: 7; Est: 1974)
Home Farm, Ardington, Wantage, Oxon OX12 8PY. 0235-833 614.
Pc Reseating of 1,050 rush seated chairs – Salisbury Cathedral.
Full restoration of frames also undertaken.

COURTNEY, ALAN – STAINED GLASS (Empl: solo; Est: 1936)
The Studio, 9 Stapleton Avenue, Bolton, Lancs BL1 5ES. 0204-42483.
MGP.
Pc Too numerous to mention over a period of 50 yrs.

FIRMS AND CRAFTSPEOPLE

COWIE & ROBERTS (Empl: 3; Est: 1980)
Unit 15, Doole Rd Ind Estate, Llandrindod Wells, Powys LD1 6DF. 0597-4865.
Pc Several conservatories designed and built adjacent to listed buildings (mostly domestic) to match or complement the house or building, whatever the style.
Brochure.

COWPER GRIFFITH ASSOCIATES (Est: 1977)
Chartered Architects
The Barn, College Farm, Whittlesford, Cambridge CB2 4LX. 0223-835 998.
Chris Cowper – Dip Arch; RIBA James Griffith – MA Cantab; RIBA Approved consultant for PSA; M SPAB.
Pc Restoration works inc. 6, 8, & 10 Tower Court, Covent Garden, London; 'La Grange', St Mary, Jersey; Guilden Morden Hall, Guilden Morden, Cambs (the only moated manor house in Cambs); Odsey House. Internal alterations and upgrading – Hockwold Hall. Renovation – 10 Stockwell Park Crescent, London; Clare Farmhouse, Cambs.
Also carries out purpose-made conservatories, and undertakes the design of kitchen units and furniture to individual client's specification. Brochure.

COX & BARNARD (HOVE) LTD (Empl: 16; Est: approx 1919)
Stained Glass Artists/Painters
58 Livingstone Rd, Hove, E Sussex BN3 3WL. 0273-734 906 & 779 157.
Federation of Sussex Industries; GMC; BSMGP.
Pc Restoration work on Winchester Cathedral; Maidstone Museum; London Oratory, Brompton; Windsor Great Park; PSA St Mary's Church, Dockyard, Portsmouth; many churches throughout Sussex, Kent, Surrey, etc.

COX, BOBBIE
Hand-woven Tapestry
Higher Manor, Cudliptown, Petertavy, Tavistock, Devon PL19 9LZ. 082 281-305.
Bath Academy of Art; Devon Guild of Craftsmen. Currently keeper of the ethnographical collection, Dartington College of Arts.
Pc 'Woven Memory' 100 sq ft – IBM Havant. 'Labyrinth' 30 sq ft – Dartington Hall Trust. 'Pieces of Light' a tryptich 84 sq ft – St Stephen's Church, Exeter.
Also undertakes teaching. Brochure.

COX BROTHERS BUILDERS (KENT) LTD (Empl: 70; Est: 1843 (incorporated 1968))
Palmer House, 80/82 Peel St, Maidstone, Kent ME14 2SP. 0622-764 255.
BEC; ECA; CHB; NHBC. Approved: Eng. Heritage; Canterbury & Southwark Dioceses; Maidstone BC; Lewisham London BC; Eng. Estates Ltd; Canterbury CC.
Also undertakes sign writing, perspex illuminated and non-illuminated signs. Details available on request.

COX, GILLIAN (Empl: solo; Est: 1981)
Kestrel Cottage, Spriggs Holly, Chinnor Hill, Radnage, Oxon OX9 4BU. 024026-3374.
BA (Hons) Univ London; A FGE.
Pc Set of Georgian glasses for HM Queen Mother. Sculptures, of which one example is in V & A. Windows in private houses.

COX, NIGEL LTD (Empl: 100; Est: 1981)
128–130 Putney Bridge Rd, London SW15 2NQ. 081-871 2755.
Stone Fed.
Pc Restoration and cleaning – Royal Albert Hall.
Will also supply and fix English and French limestone. Brochure.

COX, PETER PRESERVATION (Est: 1951)
Specialist Contractor
Heritage House, 234 High St, Sutton, Surrey SM1 1NX. 081-642 9444.
BWPA; BCDA.
Eradication of infestation by wood-boring insects and fungal decay; installation of chemical damp-courses; waterproof tanking and plastering; transfusion system. Work ranges from a damp-proof course in a terraced house to the wholesale replacement of timbers in an ancient church. Majority of rising damp work, woodworm and fungal decay treatment is guaranteed for 30 yrs, waterproofing 5 yrs and joinery preservation 10 yrs. Also run an insurance scheme. Brochure.

CRADLEY CASTINGS LTD (Empl: 55; Est: 1927)
Mill St, Cradley, Halesowen, W Midlands B63 2UB. 0384-60601.
Brit Foundry Assoc.
Restoration work normally entails being approached with certain ideas or drawings of the parts required, involving either iron or aluminium castings. If these are within the firm's capacity, they offer a price for the castings and then sell them to the client who is then responsible for assembly. Brochure.

FIRMS AND CRAFTSPEOPLE

CRAFT, ALEXANDER (Empl: solo; Est: 1987)
Drumley, Ladybank, Cupar, Fife KY7 7UZ. 0337-28425.
5 yr apprenticeship as toolmaker; 15 yrs as Production Engineer; C Eng; M I Prod E; 12 yrs as teacher of Technical Education Dip Tech Ed.
Pc Hebridean spinning wheels. All wood (gears, frame, etc.) pendulum clock. Ornate garden gates. Pine furniture and hardwood furniture designed and made to client's specification.

CRAFTY GLASS HOUSE (Empl: 2; Est: 1984)
Stained Glass Artist
5/7 Middlewich Rd, Holmes Chapel, Nr Crewe, Cheshire CW4 7EA. 0477-34372.
Pc Stained glass pictures. Small domestic windows and door panels.

CRAKER, MALCOLM (Empl: solo; Est: 1968)
Thatcher
301 Tring Rd, Aylesbury, Bucks HP20 1PH. 0296-21389.
Trained within an established thatching family; over 20 yrs working as a one-man business.
Pc Details on request.

CRATES, J. & SON LTD (Empl: 60; Est: 1874)
Culverden Yard, Culverden Park Rd, Tunbridge Wells, Kent TN4 9QX. 0892-510 751.
M BEC; registered with Construction Industry Training Board. Approved: Eng. Heritage; Local Authority; Local Health Authority.
A traditional building company whose quality work to listed and historic buildings has been recognized by its receipt of 2 Civic Conservation Awards in recent yrs.

CRAVEN FORGE WROUGHT-IRON (Empl: one; Est: 1964)
Craven Forge, Bradley, Nr Keighley, Yorks BD20 9HF. 0535-33252.
Apprentice in Engineering; M BABA.
Pc Restoration of gates at St Peter's Church, Crosshills, Nr Ketchley. Restoration and replacement of gates at Butterfield Homes, Baildon, Nr Bradford.
Willing to undertake ironmongery, not castings.

CRAWFORD, MATTHEW FURNITURE RESTORATION (Empl: 2; Est: 1983)
Basement, 74–77 White Lion St, London N1 9PF. 071-278 7146 & 837 8175.
Traditional apprenticeship with grandfather.
Pc Regular restoration works for The Iveagh Bequest at Kenwood House, Hampstead, NW3 (National Monuments Trust).

CROCKER, F.H. & CO

Also buys and sells antique writing pieces inc. desks, bureaus, secretaires, etc.

CRAZE, KEN BUILDER LTD (Empl: 2 + 4 training)
'Kosmos', Mawgan Porth, Nr Newquay, Cornwall TR8 4BN. 0637-860 758.
M FMB; M NHBC.
Pc Old Barn conversions, roofs as originally built.

CREATIVE GLASS (Empl: 8; Est: 1980)
140d Redland Rd, Redland, Bristol BS6 6YA. 0272-737 025 & 0600-860 129.

CREWS, ANNE CERAMICS (Est: 1980)
77 Wellington Rd, Edgbaston, Birmingham, W Midlands B15 2ET. 021-440 3459.
Nat Dip in Design.
Pc Kitchen tile mural – private client, Horbury Mews, London. Kitchen tile mural – private client, Ivy Cottage, Tiverton.
Brochure.

CRISS CROSS TEXTILES – JOANNE K. WEBB (Empl: one part time; Est: 1987)
Ilexes, Aston Lane, Aston by Stone, Staffs ST15 0BW. 0785-814 454.
BA Hons Carpet Design & Related Textiles, Kidderminster.
Hand-woven reproduction Kidderminster carpets and rugs, specializing in double cloth carpets.

CRITTALL WINDOWS LTD (Empl: 950; Est: 1889)
Manor Works, Braintree, Essex CM7 6DF. 0376-24106.
M Steel Window Assoc.
Steel windows made to match existing installations. Brochure.

CROCKER, F. H. & CO (Empl: 10; Est: 1880)
Ornamental & Decorative Plasterwork
Crozier Rd, Mutley, Plymouth, Devon PL4 7LN. 0752-661851.
4 yr apprenticeship; indentured through company; 7 yrs apprenticeship.
Pc Guildhall, Plymouth. St Michael's Mount, Penzance. Prideaux Place, Padstow. Shute Gatehouse, Colyton. Barringdon Hall, Plymton. College of Art and Custom House, Exeter.
Also re-render the exterior of buildings and repair decorative mouldings. 'We have been entrusted with numerous complete restorations, from ornate ceilings to decorative facades, many of which are of historical importance.' Brochure.

FIRMS AND CRAFTSPEOPLE

CROMPTON, MICHAEL (Est: 1977)
High-warp Tapestry Weaver
Forge Cottage, Ireshopeburn, Weardale, Durham, DL13 1ER. 0388-537 346.
University lecturer in art/textiles; tapestry studied in France; many one-man exhibitions.
Pc Work is in private and public collections throughout UK and abroad.

CROSS, A. FURNITURE MAKER (OAK) REPRODUCTIONS (Est: 1890)
48 Lychgate Lane, Burbage, Leics LE10 2DS. 0455-633 045.
Mr Cross's grandfather produced Jacobean reproductions, and it is said that pieces of genuine furniture were taken to Burbridge to be copied. These fakes were then sold as originals by certain dealers. Whether this is true or not the grandson seems to have inherited his grandfather's talents, although he marks all his work to ensure that it is not mistaken for a genuine antique. Work is mainly undertaken for period houses and museums, rather than private houses, and output is small.

CROTCH, W. G. LTD (Empl: varies; Est: 1820)
Ornamental Plasterwork
109 Tuddenham Avenue, Ipswich, Suffolk IP4 2HE. 0473-50349 & 520 349.
Pc Weasenham Hall. Royal Villas, Sultanate of Oman. Sennowe Hall. Columbia Hotel, Sri Lanka. Grand Hotel, Sheringham. Guy's Hospital. Sandringham. Sandhurst. Grove Park. Heveningham Hall. Minories, City of London.

CROUCH, SIMON M. F. – MASTER THATCHER (Empl: 5; Est: 1971)
14 Perrywood Close, Holbury, Fawley, Southampton, Hants SO4 1HT. 0703-892 358 & 873 628.
New Forest MTA.

CROWDYS WOOD PRODUCTS LTD (Empl: 4; Est: c. 1961)
Regal Way, Faringdon, Oxon SN7 7BX. 0367-22264.
FIRA; CoSIRA.
Pc Oxford Colleges inc Christ Church; St Cross; Merton; New College; Nuffield. Brewing Research Foundation. Carfax Publishing, Burgess & Son (Abingdon) Ltd. Croner Publications.
Brochure.

CROWNSHAW, PETER (BLACKSMITH) (Empl: 2; Est: 1980)
St Michael's Forge, St Michael's, Tenbury Wells, Worcs WR15 8TG. 0584-811 371.
Almost completely self taught over last 14 yrs.

CRYSTAL LITE CHANDELIERS

CROWTHER OF SYON LODGE
Architectural Antiques
Busch Corner, London Rd, Isleworth, Middx TW7 5BH. 081-560 7978.
Fireplaces – Eng. & Eur from 17th century onwards. 17th-, 18th-, 19th-century wrought-iron gates, wrought/cast iron benches. Period panelling removed from houses, and also designed and made to specification using antique woods. Period garden ornaments and statuary – urns, wellheads, etc.

CRUCIAL TRADING LTD
Specialists in Natural Floorcoverings
PO Box 689, London W2 4BX. 05887-666. FAX 05887 623.
Trade Assoc M IDDA.
Specialist suppliers of natural floorcoverings (inc. seagrass, sisal and coir floorcoverings) and also medieval matting (rush) in various plain and patterned weaves and colourings. A free measuring service is available in most parts of Britain. Details of stockists and samples on request.

CRUMMY, MIKE (Empl: various; Est: 1978)
Creative Blacksmith
Tomatin Smithy, Tomatin, Inverness-shire IV13 7YP. 08082-261 (2442).
Pc Dunbar Hospice, Inverness for National Trust of Scotland. Museum gates, Dunrobin Castle for Sutherland Estates (Countess of Sutherland). Entrance gates – Clan Chisholm Chief's Burial Ground for Clan Chisholm. Historical reproductions – peat spades; Crusie lamps; Cas Chrom; reed lamps; cauldrons; etc.
Able to handle commissions up to a value of approx £25,000 (Nov 1988). Ironmongery, and silver plating only undertaken by arrangement. Brochure.

'CRYSTAL LINES' (Empl: 2; Est: 1983)
Stained Glass Artist
Unit 66, Fox's Factory, Tonedale Mill, Wellington, Somerset TA21 0AW. 082 347-6671.
M Somerset Guild of Craftsmen.
Pc Restoration and commission of country estate and domestic house windows. Stained glass panels and lighting for local wine bars, hotels and restaurants. Numerous local parish church windows restored.
Also has a range of acid etched mirrors and will undertake commissioned glass lighting to suit private, domestic or commercial settings. Salvage panels bought and sold.

CRYSTAL LITE CHANDELIERS (Empl: 3; Est: 1986)
87 The Fairway, Southgate, London N14 4PB. 081-440 0360.
Pc Refurbishment of 17th-century chandelier (gilding, rewiring,

repining) – Museum of St John, Clerkenwell, London.

CTC (Est: 1968)
Woodworkers
6 Banstead Rd, Carshalton Beeches, Surrey SM5 1AX. 081-669 2440.

CULBERT, PIP
Reverse Appliquéd Wallhangings
41 Schubert Rd, London SW15 2QT. 081-874 1275.
ARCA.
Pc Wallhanging 75 cm × 200 cm for private flat in Paris.

CULVERDEN METALWORKS LTD (Empl: 6; Est: 1986)
The Yard, Culverden Park Rd, Tunbridge Wells, Kent TN4 9QX. 0892-510 475.

CUNNINGHAM, JOHN PATRICK DESIGN & CONSTRUCTION LTD (Empl: 12; Est: 1967)
Building Contractor, Sculptors & Architectural Stonemasons, Design Services
Mont-du-Seigneur, Caynham, Ludlow, Shropshire. 0584-2307 & 01-387 9711.
Stonemason to Master Mason C & Gs; Sculptor/Artist Designer; NDD; NHBC; Stone Fed. Approved: Isle of Man and Hereford Dioceses; Eng. Heritage.
Pc Consultancy and restoration work – Chiesa Della Piesa, Venice. Stone facing and dry stone wall (allowing for wildlife) – IMED Pharmaceutical Plant, Donegal. Restoration and new construction – Victorian style terrace, Julian Rd, Ludlow. 2 half-timbered houses – Caynham. Art work – bronze sculptural work, Penn Chemicals. Consultancy services – 19th century building, Four Masters Bookshop, Donegal.
Specialists in stone; frame structures; sculptural detail. Consultancy work undertaken on new classical style buildings, paying attention to the approprate proportions and ordering of the building (all projects researched thoroughly before commencing work). Also experienced in stained glass work. Projects of any size and scope undertaken. Brochure may be available.

CURL, PROFESSOR JAMES STEVENS (Est: 1975)
Consultant Architect
Gibson Hamilton Partnership, Unit 19, Loughborough Technological Centre, Epinal Way, Loughborough, Leics. 0509-610 510 & 0572-755 880.
Ph D(Lond); FSA; Dipl Arch; Dip TP; RIBA; MRTPI; ARIAS; FSA Scot.

CUTHBERTSON, ROBERT H. & PARTNERS

Pc Church restoration, town schemes, mills, houses, etc.

CURADRAFT (GB) LTD
Weatherseals for Listed Buildings
Delmae House, Home Farm, Ardington, Wantage, Oxon OX12 8PN. 0235-833 022.
A unique system of weathersealing which can overcome the need to replace ill-fitting windows and doors in historic houses (inc. leaded lights and stone mullion windows). An air-curing elastomeric rubber is applied to the ill-fitting window or door and left to cure. This forms a gasket to the exact size of the gaps which excludes draughts, noise, water penetration, dust, insects, etc. Available in a variety of colours, it may be applied to timber, metal, stone or brickwork. Work is guaranteed for 5 yrs and is carried out by Curadraft's trained operatives.

CUSTOM DESIGNED PRINTS BY IRENE BROWNING (Est:1975)
60 Wheatlands, Heston, Hounslow, Middx TW5 0SA.
Nat Dip in Design (now BA Art College Degree); Art Teachers Dip; C & Gs Dressmaking; Associate Brit Inst of Interior Design.
Pc Curtains for universities, banks, domestic settings, decorative panels.
Designs can be produced with a certain price range in mind, using batik method, screen printing and embroidery. Fabrics for all interior purposes undertaken.

CUTHBERTSON, JAMES G. ARCHITECTS (Est: 1978)
Cathkin House, 15 Woodside Terrace, Glasgow, Strathclyde G3 7XH. 041 331-2834/5. FAX 041 331 1481.
James G. Cuthbertson – B Arch; RIBA; FRIAS; ACI Arb   Alistair Baird – B Arch Hons; RIBA; ARIAS   Richard Napier – B Sc Arch; Dip Arch.
Pc Renovation works – Pollokshields Church, Glasgow.

CUTHBERTSON, ROBERT H. & PARTNERS (Est: 1952)
Consulting Engineers
13 Eglinton Crescent, Edinburgh EH12 5DF. 031 337-3213.
Staff are Members of Assoc of Consulting Eng; Inst of Civil Eng; Inst of Structural Eng.
Pc 16th-century Tower House, Craig Caffie, Stranraer. 17th-century tenement restoration – Royal Mile, Edinburgh. Restoration of Georgian properties, New Town, Edinburgh. Various historic properties and warehouses – Leith, Edinburgh.

FIRMS AND CRAFTSPEOPLE

CZAJKOWSKI & SON (Empl: 3; Est: 1951)
Cabinet Maker, Restorer & Clockmaker
96 Tor-o-Moor Rd, Woodhall Spa, Lincs LN10 6SB. 0526-52895.
C & Gs; 5 yr apprenticeship; 2 yrs Journeyman; M UKIC.
Pc 5 Griffins carved for staircase in Northampton. 2 carved and gilded side tables – Yorkshire. Turret clock restoration and maintenance – Lincs. Clock case – Scunthorpe Museum. Work in stately homes, private collections and churches. Annual maintainance of St Michael's Church Clock, Coringsly, and other privately held turret clocks. Various restorations and new furniture for London clients.
Brochure.

CZECH & SPEAKE LTD
Edwardian Bathroom Fittings & Fine Aromatics
244-254 Cambridge Heath Rd, London E2 9DA. 081-980 4567.
Brochure.

DALTON, P. (Est: 1981)
Cabinet Maker & Restorer
'Bulges', The Street, Syderstone, Kings Lynn, Norfolk PE31 8SD. 048 523 570.
BA (Hons) 3d (Wood & Metal).
Pc Very varied antique restoration jobs. New work to commission inc. caning, cabinet making and turning, on work varying from the size of a box to a fitted kitchen; from the totally practical to the simply decorative.

DART & FRANCIS (BUILDING CONSERVATION & MANUFACTURING) LTD (Empl: 15; Est: 1800)
Unit 3c, Common Marsh Lane, Marsh End, Lords Meadow Ind Estate, Crediton, Devon EX17 1HJ. 03632-2067.
Approved: Eng. Heritage; National Trust; Exeter Diocese; Devon CC; etc.
Also undertakes ecclesiastical art works, general building and gilding.

DARTFORD METALCRAFTS LTD (Empl: 5; Est: 1947)
Unit 48, Victoria Ind Park, Victoria Rd, Dartford, Kent DA1 5AJ. 0322-23685.
Engineering (Employers London Assoc).
Pc Various contracts for City of Westminster. Renovation of Surrey Docks, etc.

DAVIES KEELING TROWBRIDGE LTD

DARWENT, R. & D. E. FIBROUS PLASTERERS (Empl: 3; Est: 1969)
300 Harrogate Rd, Eccleshill, Bradford, W. Yorks BD2 3TB. 0274-631 365 & 370 386.
FMB.
Brochure.

DAVEY & JORDAN (Empl: 14; Est: 1832)
Artists in Wrought Iron
3/4 Jennings Rd, Penryn, Cornwall TR10 9DQ. 0326-72282.
Associate M, Award winners and medal holders of the Worshipful Co of Blacksmiths.
Pc Royal coat-of-arms – British Embassy, Rome. Wrought-iron gates – Cape Town. Hand forged 5 ft tall flamingos – Bond St, London. Interior screen and railings – Truro Cathedral. Wrought iron screens – Coventry Cathedral. Memorial gates – California, USA. Galleon gates under full sail, with gilded sails – Barclays International.
This family firm are winners of various awards and competitions.

DAVEY, NORMAN (Est: 1964)
Architect
'The Cottage', 2 Heatherley Rd, Camberley, Surrey GU15 3LW. 0276-64615.
Dip Arch (Oxford), 1952; ARIBA, 1953; M ACA.
Pc Conversion of Elmore House, Speen, Newbury, Berks for use as Benedictine Monastery. Proposed repair and restoration – St Paul's Church, Brighton, Sussex.

DAVIES & HADDOCK (Empl: 6; Est: 1958)
Stonemasons
Awel-y-Mor, Mount Gardens, St David's, Haverfordwest, Pembrokeshire SA62 6BS.
BEC.
Pc Restoration – Pembroke Castle.

DAVIES KEELING TROWBRIDGE LTD (Empl: approx 20; Est: 1979)
Specialist Decoration/Design
3 Charterhouse Works, Eltringham St, London SW18 1TD. 081-871 3565/6.
Various qualifications but mostly graduate artists.
Pc 80 interior window shutters – Arabian Roots. Steel shelving end sections – Library, Farnborough College of Technology. Frieze, stylized marbling, ceiling mural – Angel Hotel, Cardiff. Clouded wall finish – refurbishment of Baltic House, City of London. Stencil floor – private client. Landscape mural – private client.

FIRMS AND CRAFTSPEOPLE

A group of professional artists who, although well versed in traditional effects, enjoy developing new techniques, materials and styles. Brochure and portfolio available.

DAVIES, PETER (THATCHER) (Empl: 5; Est: 1975)
Business: Reed Farm, Preston St Mary, Sudbury, Suffolk. Home: 13 York Rd, Sudbury, Suffolk CO10 6NE. 0787-70911.
Full M Suffolk MTA; East Anglian MTA; M NCMTA.
Pc Adams Well Barn – Leavenheath (reed). Delia Smith's roof – Stowmarket (long straw). Several major contracts for BBC TV.
Offer a complete design and build service to thatch owners. New houses also considered. Will undertake chimney rebuilding and associated works.

DAVIES, WILLIAM STAINED GLASS STUDIOS (Empl: 4; Est: 1980)
Millers Hay Studio, 80 Mill Hill Rd, Irby, Wirral L61 4XF. 051-648 3537.
7 yr apprenticeship as stained glass artist; studied at Liverpool College of Art; M BSMGP; GMC; Tutor of stained glass for 20 yrs.
Pc St Aidan's, Billinge, Wigan. St John's, Norley. St John's Hospice, Cheshire. Birkenhead Priory. Wirral Grammar Schools. Work in Liverpool inc. Anglican Cathedral; Metropolitan Cathedral; St Columbas, Anfield; Liver Buildings. Restoration of painted stained glass – numerous churches in the north west.
Also reclaims stained glass from redundant churches, and undertakes teaching and lecturing on the history and subject matter found in stained glass.

DAVIS, PHIL (ARBS) & DAVIS, MIKE (Dip AD RAS Cert) (Empl: 3; Est: 1979)
Architectural Sculptors & Restorers
The Bronze Foundry, St James St, New Bradwell, Milton Keynes, Bucks. 0908-315 841.
Pc Bronze sculpture and door pushes – St Augustine's RC Church, Milton Keynes. Interior atrium, bronze balustrading and structural supports in patinated bronze. 3 life-size bronze sculptures – Queen's Court, Central Milton Keynes. Various repairs and renovations to existing sculpture, etc. Work for films *Alien* and *Little Shop of Horrors* – Animatronics Dept, Pinewood Studios. Work for museums and exhibitions.
Brochure.

DAWES, JOE (Empl: self + one; Est: 1968)
Craftsmen in Wood
The Street, Corpusty, Norwich, Norfolk NR11 6QP. 026 387-512.
Apprenticed; A Inst of Wood Science; F SD-C; A International Inst of

Conservation; Dip Timber Technology; C & Gs 1st Class Cabinet Making; CGLI Advanced Furniture Design; CGLI Advanced Materials.
Pc Restoration of architectural woodwork and furniture – Chorleston House, Sussex. Roof carvings – All Saints', Leighton Buzzard. Various furniture commissions.

DAWSON, BEN FURNITURE (Empl: 20 + 5 staff; Est: 1983)
Eskmills, Musselburgh, Edinburgh, Lothian EH21 7PQ. 031-665 9986 & 653 6316.
Ben Dawson – BA Hons Furniture Design   Craftsmen – BA Hons; City & Guilds.
Pc Various conservation projects for museums and country houses.
Brochure.

DAY, G. W. & CO (Empl: 5; Est: 1950)
Artist Blacksmith
East Shilington Forge, South Chailey, Lewes, E. Sussex BN7 3QY. 0273-890 398.
All employees trained in blacksmithing and wrought-ironwork by CoSIRA; M BABA.
Pc Architectural ironmongery – Battle Abbey. Wrought ironwork – Plumpton Place.

DAY, LUCIENNE
49 Cheyne Walk, London SW3 5LP. 071-352 1455.
ARCA; FCSD; M (and present Master) of Faculty of Royal Designers for Industry.
Pc 'The Window' 6 ft × 5 ft – west foyer, Queen Elizabeth Conference Centre, for Architects Powell Moya & Partners. 'Aspects of the Sun' 15 ft × 8 ft – Kingston building, Architects Ahrends Burton & Koralek.
Abstract, sometimes figurative hand-sewn silk tapestries.

DEANS, TIM (Empl: solo; Est: 1980)
Cabinet Maker
c/o Windmill Furniture, Turnhall Green, Terrace Mews, Chiswick W4 1QU. 081-994 0157 & (home) 081-567 1055.
Tim Deans makes one-off handmade, client orientated, pieces of furniture ranging from game boards to whole bedroom suites, dining tables, and lately abstracts in veneers. Willing to undertake major veneer restoration.

'DEC-ART' (Empl: 10–30; Est: 1983)
Decorating Specialists
50 Rochester Way, Basildon, Essex SS14 3QF. 0268-285 150, 555 082, 0836-282 800 (mobile).

FIRMS AND CRAFTSPEOPLE

C & Gs + 27 yrs experience, and 24 yrs experience respectively.
Pc 8 Chesterfield Gardens, London W1. 16 Charles St, London W1. 6 & 8 Farm St, London W1. 2 The Broadway, Thorpe Bay, Southend-on-Sea, Essex.

DECORATIVE PLASTER CO (NEWCASTLE) LTD
Brunswick Ind. Estate, Brunswick Village, Newcastle-upon-Tyne NE13 7BA. 091-236 4226.
FMB.
Pc Linden Hall. Cragside. Bowes Museum. Shaftoe Hall. Bolam Hall. Beaufont Castle. Lumley Castle. Little Harle Tower. Gibside Banqueting Hall. Walsington Hall. Corby Castle. Bywell Hall. Alnwick Castle.

DECORATIVE TILE WORKS, THE (Empl: 4; Est: 1989)
Jackfield Tile Museum, Ironbridge Gorge, Telford, Shropshire TF8 7AW. 0952-882 840.
Shaun A. Ormrod – BA (Hons)   Adrian R. Bludell – BA (Hons).
Pc Reproduction of 19th-century ceramic tiles and William de Morgan art pottery.
This firm works in partnership with the conservation and restoration team of Jackfiled Tile Museum – the old Craven & Dunhill works, which was the largest producer of decorative tiles in the 19th century, holding over 40,000 original patterns inc. 14,000 original moulds for embossed tiles (these are at this firm's disposal to offer to customers). Guaranteed delivery date. Brochure.

DECORUM DECORATIVE DECORATING (Empl: 3; Est: 1984)
31 Farmfield Court, Thorplands, Northants NN3 1YF. 0604-42935.
Served apprenticeship.
Pc Photographs and samples available to show clients.

DELFTFIELD CO LTD & ONSLOW SERVICES LTD (Empl: 6; Est: 1978, Onslow Services 1987)
Coulsknowe Farm, Dunning Glen, Dollar, Perth FK14 7LB. 025 981-379.
D. M. Williams, director – M Sc Chemical Engineering; Stuttgart Ceramic Engineer, post grad Glaze Technology.
Pc Restoration Mains Street Flat (first marital home of Charles Rennie Mackintosh), now 120 Blythswood St, Glasgow. Original maquette – Our Lady of Gaudeloupe, Villa de Gaudeloupe, Mexico City. 8 million sq ft white porcelain – Gorbals cladding, Glasgow. 485,000 sq m majolica cladding – Benghazi University.
Hand-moulded delft flower bricks; frostproof non-porous terracotta; hand-moulded brick facings; ceramic plaques; slip-resistant finish available.

DENT, ROBERT & SON LTD

Dennis M. Williams (considered an expert in his field) comes from a family whose delft connections span 3 centuries and is able to give technical, historical and aesthetic advice. Onslow Services Ltd undertake cleaning and maintenance, and market cleaning and sealing products. Brochure.

DENNIS, PAUL & SON (Empl: 4; Est: 1980)
Blacksmith
Defynnog, Nr Brecon, Powys LD3 8SB. 087 482-696 & 752.
Full apprenticeship; GMC; M Guild of Wrought Iron Craftsmen in Wales; Prince of Wales Award; Civic Trust Commendation.
Pc Complete rebuild – Edney Gates, Tredegar House, Newport, Gwent. Restoration – White Gates, Leeswood Hall, Clwyd. Complete rebuild – Italian Gates, Bexley London Borough. New entrance gates – Garden Hall, Cheshire.
Brochure.

DENNISON-DRAKE DESIGNS (Empl: 2–3)
Designers, Manufacturers & Restorers of Unusual Lighting & Decorative Objects
Broadrayne Farm, Grasmere, Cumbria LA22 9RU. 09665-733.
Knowledge and experience of antique lighting appliances for over 20 yrs (formerly B. P. Dennison Antiques); M LAPADA; M Portobello Antiques Dealers Assoc.
A business that has evolved from the antique trade into the specialized lighting and design studio of today, having travelled as far as India, Australia and America in the study of lighting and its applications. One-off lighting and contract work for architects, interior designers, museums and individuals.

DENNISON, FREDERICK LTD (Empl: 11; Est: 1937)
Roofing Contractor
26 Crossgate, Durham City DH1 4PU. 091-384 2367.
M LCA; NAPH & MSC.
Pc Renewal of lead roof – The Galilee Chapel and also No 15 The College, for Durham Cathedral.

DENT, ROBERT & SON LTD (Empl: 15; Est: 1874)
Redeness St, Layerthorpe, York YO3 7UU. 0904-622 642.
Brit Woodworking Fed; BEC.
Pc Library – Castle Howard. Peasholm House for York Civic Trust. Coffee yard for York Archaeological Trust. Clifton Methodist Church Refurbishment.
Produce a range of doors. Brochure.

FIRMS AND CRAFTSPEOPLE

DENTON-CARDEW, ANDREW (Est: 3rd generation, grandfather 1887)
Cabinet Maker & Restorer
Street Farmhouse, Thorndon, Eye, Suffolk IP23 7LX. 037 971-413.
Apprenticeship at family workshop; 33 yrs personal experience.
Pc Fitted oak bookcases – Nelson Room, Paston Grammar School, N. Walsham, Norfolk. Grandfather restored Paycocke's House, Essex for National Trust (1909). Family woodcarving (stalls/screenwork) in many Essex/Suffolk churches.

DEREFORD OF BADSEY HALL (Est: 1958)
Art & Mosaic Studio
Badsey, Evesham, Worcs WR11 5EW.
M Inst BE.
Pc Too numerous to mention. Photographs available on request.
Murals, sculpture, reliefs, coats-of-arms in mosaic; ceramic; wood; metals; stained glass; textile hangings and other techniques.

DESIGN IN CANE (Empl: solo; Est: 1988)
2 Church Cottages, West Stafford, Dorchester, Dorset DT2 8AB. 0305-69287.
Self taught over 10 yrs.
Pc Sheet cane radiator covers. Bamboo chair repaired for the film *Out of Africa*. Bed heads and fire screens made to customers own design drawings.
Will undertake new work in cane, rush, ratten, seagrass, etc., but only willow and bamboo repaired.

DESIGN, F. B. (Empl: 5; Est: 1981)
Cabinet Makers & Restorers
14 Hazel Rd, Four Marks, Alton, Hants GU34 5EY. 0420-64470 & 0962-733 432.
Various apprenticed cabinet makers and college leavers; 2 grad furniture designers/makers.
Pc Full refurbishment of period properties (woodworking and design). Work for Winchester Cathedral.
Brochure.

DESIGN GROUP, THE (Est: 1987)
The Old School Room, Long St, Sherborne, Dorset DT9 3BS. 0935-816 481 (3 lines).
Charles Louwerse, partner – BA (Hons); Dip Arch; RIBA Kimberley Jervis, partner – B Ed (Hons)   Roland Rigiani, partner – BA (Hons); M CSD   Staff inc. F G of S.
Pc Restoration and conversion to living accommodation – The Mill House, Marston Magna (incorporating machine room museum, 17th

century); The Malthouse, Halse (retaining original brewing kilns, 18th century). Hunt's Bicycle Shop, Sherborne (Grade II). Conversion – The Friends' Meeting House, Sherborne (Grade II). Refurbishment – Tudor Rose, Sherborne (Grade I). The Red House, Sherborne. Blenstock House, London. Coker Court Cottage. The Priory House, Sherborne.

DESIGN LIGHTS (Empl: one; Est: 1987)
Stained Glass Artist/Painter
Unit 2B, Millbrook Centre, Brock Hill, Wingates Rd, Wigan, Gtr Manchester WN1 2SJ. 0942-824 612.
BA Hons; M BSMGP.
Pc New work inc. Cross window, 'The Loaves & Fishes' – St Peter's, Woolton; family commemorative window, 'The Good Samaritan' – St Peter's, Salisbury; individually designed commissions for private houses. Restoration work inc. Knowsley Parish Church; Colne Parish Church; Barton Friary; St Peter's, Birkdale.

DESIGN SCULPTURE & CRAFTS – JOHN SIDNEY HAYMES HOGG, SCULPTOR (Est: 1952)
'Jota', Dunedin Drive, Ferndown, Wimborne, Dorset BH22 9EB. 0202-893 509.
Graduate B,head and Liverpool Schools of Art; employed by late Herbert Tyson Smith, sculptor, as a stone carver in Liverpool.
Pc Sculpture – New Supreme Law Courts, Lagos, Nigeria. Restoration painting – Senate Committee Room, Parliament Building, Ottawa, Canada. Carving – granite royal coat of arms, British High Commission, Ottawa. Stone carving embellishments – new Littlewoods Building, Liverpool and other works.
Also undertakes mould making for reproduction work in plaster, latex, cylicone rubber; Trajan Roman lettering/inscriptions for foundation stones; modelling for bronze via Morris Singer; industrial patterns; hobby ceramic moulds. Brochure.

DESIGN WORKSHOP (SHELLEY) LTD (Empl: 10; Est: 1967)
Furniture
150 Penistone Rd, Shelley, Huddersfield, W. Yorks HD8 8JQ. 0484-602 996. FAX 0484-603 758.
Principals have degrees in Craft & Design. All craftsmen apprentice trained.
Pc Neuendorf Art Gallery, Frankfurt, Germany. Waddington Galleries, Cork St, London W1. House for Doris and Charles Saatchi, Mayfair, London. Various period house conversions in London.

FIRMS AND CRAFTSPEOPLE

DESIGNER DECORATORS (R. W. A. LEVER) (Empl: 4; Est: 1980)
12 Churchill, Tisbury, Wilts SP3 6HT. 0747-870 032.
GMC.
Ragging; stippling; dragging; trompe-l'œil; French polishing; murals; heraldry.

DESIGNER GLASS
Glass Painter
Unit 7, Glynneath Village Workshops, Glynneath, W. Glam SA11 5HE. Home address: 2 Farm Rd, Trebanos, Swansea, W. Glam SA8 4DE. 0792-842 369.
Dip M CSD; Awarded Dip and Advanced Dip (Dist) by Architectural Stained Glass Dept of WGIHE, Swansea; won Stevens Award with Worshipful Co of Glaziers, London; highly commended for designs for Channel Link Converter Station, Kent.
Pc 2 stained glass windows – Ystradgynlais Community Hospital. Stained glass panels – main entrance, Dwr-y-Felin Comprehensive School, Neath. Numerous private commissions.
The medium of stained glass is associated in the minds of most people with religious buildings. Jeff Evans hopes to change this conception by showing how it can enhance and transform a room or foyer in any home or establishment.

DESIGNER MAKER FURNITURE LTD (Empl: 9; Est: 1984)
Holroyd Mill, Beck Rd, Micklethwaite, Nr Bingley, W Yorks BD16 3JN. 0274-561 209.
Employ graduate designers, HND craftsmen, time served (apprentice trained) craftsmen; M Nat Assoc of Furniture Makers.
Pc Wide range of work making specialist joinery, complete interiors, staircases, furniture, etc. for period homes. Restoration – oak, mahogany and walnut artifacts.
Design and manufacture of period furniture and joinery to fit into specific period style premises, from 17th-century work in native finishes for the National Trust, refractory tables and chairs, through to interiors in Art Deco style. Brochure.

DESIGNERS WORKSHOP, THE (Empl: 2; Est: 1964)
Architectural Sculpture & Artifacts
5–6 Lee St, London, E8 4DY. 071-249 4247.
Dip M CSD.
Pc Life size GRP figures (interpretations of Greek muses) – MEPC. Oak mural of City of London, 5 m × 2.5 m – Rowe & Pitman. Gilded and painted GRP coat-of-arms, 1.25 m × 1.5m – Surrey Heath Council Offices.

Special furniture and fittings; fountains; sculptures and murals; heraldic devices; special signs; screens; ornamental entrance doors; lighting features; etc. Brochure.

DESK SHOP (Empl: 4; Est: 1980)
41 St Clements, Oxford OX4 4AG. 0865-245 524.
All cabinet makers have served full apprenticeships; C & G's Craft Cert; Dip in Fine Woodworking from Rycotewood College.
Pc Furniture for the Chairman of MFI London office.
Traditional office bespoke furniture, particulary reproduction desks of 18th and 19th century design. Also have a standard range of desks. Provide a complete service for director's offices and will carry out schemes using antique furniture if required. Brochure £2.

DEWEY, TIMOTHY H. (Empl: 3; Est: 1966)
Furniture Restorer
The Cottage, Kelston, Bath BA1 9AF. 0225-447 944.
Pc Work for the top end of antique furniture trade and countless private clients.

DGO RESTORATION (Empl: 3; Est: 1969)
Fibrous Plastering & Model Making
Peak Lodge, Peak Lane, Fareham, Hants PO14 2EA. 0329-663 655.
BEC.
Pc Osborne house, Isle of Wight. Broadlands. Hyde Park Hotel, London.
Brochure.

DIXON, J. (JOINERY) LTD (Empl: 50; Est: 1912)
Stevens Rd, Balby, Doncaster, S Yorks DN4 0LT. 0320-852 881.
M Brit Woodworking Fed.
Pc Manufacturers of window and doors to replace/match existing in Regency, Victorian and Edwardian buildings.
Brochure.

DOAK, JAMES (Est: 1973)
Marquetry Restorer
The Saltings, Mill Lane, Marshchapel, Grimsby DN36 5SU. 0472 86-486.
BAFRA.
Pc Total restoration of game table, c. 1770, involving the making of a new leg using old mahogany, re-gluing frame, inlay stringing, replacing missing veneer to top, replacing spats to feet, polishing. Total restoration of 'Caistor' chair, c. 1840, involving splicing new timber to broken sticks, dismantling whole chair, gluing up and polishing.

FIRMS AND CRAFTSPEOPLE

DOBBINS, PHILIP (Est: 1977)
Bespoke Contemporary & Period Furniture
Church Farm, Henshaw, Yeadon, Leeds, W Yorks LS19 7SQ. 0532-502 738.
Unofficial apprenticeship; 11 yrs experience of fine furniture making.
Pc Principally cabinet furniture, chairs and model work. Board room tables – Hill Samuel, Advertising Agencies, etc. Director's desks and prestigious contemporary commercial work.
Maximum commission able to undertake approx 12 ft and 14 ft × 6 ft boardroom tables. Only some small scale ecclesiatical work undertaken. Carving, metalwork, plastic, glass, upholstery undertaken only as part of overall commission. Geometric brass inlay, marquetry/inlay undertaken, but not floral work. Portfolio available.

DOCHERTY, BILL PROPERTY CARE (Empl: 2 + 714 sub contractors; Est: 1983)
28 Friars Lane, Inverness IV1 1RN. 0463-224 411.
Apprenticed since 7 yrs of age by master tradesmen; now 34 and learn new prospective standards all the time.

DODD, P. (Empl: one (blind person); Est: 1979)
Cane & Rush Work
91 Merton Way, E Molesey, Surrey KT8 9PG. 081-979 6635.
RNIB.
Pc Littlewoods Food Store. Many antique dealers. Bentall's. Habit. Perrings Furniture Store. Royal Albert Museum. Many private clients by recommendation.

DODDINGTON HOUSE ANTIQUES (B.A. & L. FRANKLAND) (Empl: 2; Est: 1978)
Cane & Rush Work
2 Benwick Rd, Doddington, Cambs PE15 0TG. 0354-740 755.
Pc Work undertaken for members of BADA, therefore accustomed to working cane and rush on antique furniture.

DODREFN DAFYDD FURNITURE (Empl: solo; Est: 1985)
Old Community Centre, adjacent to Fron-Villa, Llanddewi Brefi, Nr Tregaron, Dyfed SY25 6RS. 09744-219.
C & Gs London Inst, Modular Part 2 Cert in Furniture Craft Subjects and Part 3 Cert in Furniture Advanced Studies; M Mid Wales Development; Welsh Craft Council; Craft Council.
Pc Designed and produced oak furniture – Tretower Court and Castle, a medieval manor house near Abergavenny for CADW. Furniture for clients in Jamaica and Sweden.
Furniture designed (inc standard range) with a Welsh influence inc. Welsh

dressers; bureaux; grandfather clocks; Deuddarn; side boards; chests; dining tables and chairs; Windsor chairs. Brochure and a price list available.

DODSON, CLIVE (Empl: 6; Est: 1979)
Master Thatcher
6 King St, Somersham, Huntingdon, Cambs PE17 3EJ. 0487-840956.
7yr apprenticeship; E Midlands MTA; NSMT.

DONALDSON, JOHN WOODCARVERS (Empl: solo; Est: 1985)
Birchwood House, Livingston Village, W Lothian EH54 7AF. 0506-415 384.
Self taught.
Pc Heraldic crests – Knights of the Thistle, St Giles' Cathedral, Edinburgh. Furniture restoration – Holyrood Palace, Edinburgh. Church statuary and decorative ornament inc. lettering panels in London, Manchester, Liverpool, Middlesbrough and throughout Scotland.
Brochure.

DOROTHEA LTD (Empl: 60; Est: 1972)
Pearl House, Hardwick St, Buxton, Derbyshire SK17 6DU. 0298-79121 & 77115.
Pc Refurbishment and new decorative metalwork (Regency style) – Cadbury Schweppes Headquarters, Connaught Place, London. British Council Shopping Award – Lanes Shopping Centre, Carlisle. Wrought-iron repairs and repolishing of prismatic glass – Bridgewater House, Pall Mall, London. Entrance features inc. clocks, bells, lighting. Staircases – Welbeck College, Worksop. National Trust, PSA, conservation bodies, local authorities.
Also stock a standard range inc. benches, decorative signs, fountains and canopies, colonnades, balustrading, spiral stairs, columns, etc. Brochure.

DOROTHEA RESTORATIONS LTD (Empl: 16; Est: 1974)
Specialists in Museum Architectural & Traditional Mill Work
Riverside Business Park, St Anne's Rd, St Anne's Park, Bristol BS4 4ED. New Rd, Whaley Bridge, Stockport, Cheshire SK12 7JQ. 0272-715 337. FAX 0272-771 677.
Director – Mech Eng apprenticeship; C Eng; MI Mech Eng; BSc. Staff – mostly time served apprenticeships and subsequent training.
Pc Reconstruction – cast iron conservatory, Eng. Heritage; Tudor oak panels, University of Wales. Restoration – wrought-iron Palm House (1825), Bicton Park Trust. Sash windows – Syon Park, London. Replica working cap for high windmill – Wyre Borough Council. Steam and water powered equipment, mills, museum exhibits for

FIRMS AND CRAFTSPEOPLE

Science Museum, National and Landmark Trusts, Local and County Councils – details on request.
Specialist joinery and large scale timberwork; blacksmithing; pattern making; historical research; castings; ; maintenance; project management. Brochure.

DORRIEN, LYNNE (Est: 1985)
Abstract & Bold Geometric Hand-tufted Wallhangings, Rugs & Carpets.
20 North Hill Rd, Leeds, W Yorks LS6 2EN. 0532-780 844.
BA (Hons) Fine Art; MEHB; CSD.
Pc IBM. Swallow Hotel Group. Pentos plc. ASDA. Rugs using company logo – Minale-Tattersfield. Rugs made with client's illustrations – Brian Grimwood.
Also produces a standard range. Brochure.

DOWDING, GRAHAM STAINED GLASS (Empl: 2–3; Est: 1982)
The Studio, Pensile House, Pensile Road, Nailsworth, Glos GL6 0AL. 0453 83-4712.
B Sc (Arch); M SPAB.
Pc Various domestic window commissions. 2 windows – Bisley Methodist Chapel. Major restoration to Victorian glass plus general maintenance – Gloucester Cathedral. Ecclesiastical repairs/restoration.

DRAY, G. R. & SON (Empl: 3; Est: 1962)
Master Thatcher
12 Pethybridge, Lustleigh, Nr Newton Abbot, Devon TQ13 9TQ. 06477-293.
M Devon & Cornwall MTA; M NSMT; MNCMT.
Pc Thatched the tithe barn at Compton Castle, Marldon, Devon for the National Trust.

DREW-EDWARDS KEENE (Est: c. 1900)
Architects, Designers & Technologists
34 Princess Road West, Leicester LE1 6TJ. Other branches in Burnham Market, Norfolk and Woodbridge, Suffolk. 0533-545 015.
Staff inc. Members of RIBA; RICS; EASA; CAA and Society of Antiquities.
Pc Available on request.
Brochure.

DRYDEN & KENNEDY (Empl: 8; Est: 1955)
Roofing Contractors – All Types of Slating & Tiling
Bridge St, Goole, N. Humberside DN14 5ST. 0405-3886.
Pc Bishops Manor, Howden. Lea Bank House, Howden.

DUDGEON, PETER LTD (Empl: 21; Est: 1947)
Upholsterer
Brompton Place, Knightsbridge, London SW3 1QE. 071-589 0322.
Apprenticeships – C & Gs (Upholstery, Soft Furnishing, Frame Making); Trade Associate IDDA; M AMU; M GMC.
Pc Top quality upholstery work for interior designers and individuals over the last 40 yrs. Individual springs and horsehair used throughout.
16 page full colour catalogue available.

DUDMAN, REGINALD W. (Empl: 6; Est: 1962)
Furniture Restorer, Oriental Lacquer & Japanning
45 Windmill Rd, Brentford, Middx TW8 0QQ. 081-568 5249.
Ass IIC.
Pc Restoration and regilding – Throne Canopy, House of Lords and also Iveagh Bequest Adam Furniture, Kenwood House. Conservation of decorated lacquer furniture – Science Museum; V & A; Eng. Heritage; Partridge Fine Arts; Ralee; etc.

DUNN, MARTIN H. (Empl: one; Est: 1980)
Fine Cabinet & Clock Maker
Glebe Farm, Clarkes Rd, N Killingholme, Grimsby, S Humberside DN40 3JQ. 0469-40901.
Family trained; M Guild of Lincolnshire Craftsmen.
Upholstery is sub-contracted.

DUNTHORNE, KEITH REED & STRAW THATCHING SERVICES (Est: 1980)
Green Farm, Burgate Great Green, Diss, Norfolk IP22 1QL. 037 983-457.
CoSIRA Cert's in main materials; M Norfolk, Suffolk and East Anglian MTAs; M NCMTA.

DURANT, CLIFF (GLIMMER GLASS) (Empl: one; Est: 1972)
Stained Glass Artist/Painter
2A New Street, Horsham, Sussex RH13 5DU. 0403-64607.
Apprenticeship at major London studio; GGE; Soc of Glass Technology; BSMGP.
Pc The Manor House, Castle Combe, Wilts. South Lodge, Lower Beeding, Sussex. Horsham District Council, Horsham, Sussex.
Photographs available.

DURLING, W. & O. LTD (Empl: 40; Est: 1874)
Building Contractors
Ightham, Nr Sevenoaks, Kent TN15 9HR. 0732-882 122.

FIRMS AND CRAFTSPEOPLE

BEC. Approved: Eng. Heritage
Pc Johnson Hall Library, Sevenoaks School, Kent for Architect Keith Bennett. St Clare, Kemsing Kent for M. J. R. Wallis. Franks Hall, Kent for Ian Kennard.

DURNAN, NICHOLAS (Empl: solo; Est: 1983)
Architectural Sculptor
84 St Peter's Grove, Canterbury, Kent CT1 2DJ.
3 yrs masonry apprenticeship; Dip Restoration & Conservation of Stone; sculpture conservation training; M UKIC.
Pc Conservation of stone sculpture inc. Wells Cathedral (13th-century figure); Exeter Cathedral (14th-century figure); Canterbury Cathedral (12th-century sculpted capitals).
Also works in alabaster.

DURRANT, JEANETTE (Est: 1980)
Embroidered Wallhanging Artist & Textile Conservator
38 Friars Quay, Norwich, Norfolk NR3 1ES. 0603-613 979.
C & Gs Embroidery – Advanced; Loughborough College Art – Sandwich Course Dip Embroidery; Practical Study Group; Norfolk Contemporary Crafts Soc.
Pc Dorsal panel – Holloway Prison Chapel. 9 banners – Terminal 2, Heathrow Airport. Altar frontal – Hingham Church, Norfolk. St Andrew's hanging – chapel, St Nicholas Church, E Dereham, Norfolk

DURTNELL, R. & SONS LTD (Est: 1591)
Building Contractors
Rectory Lane, Brasted, Westerham, Kent TN16 1JR. 0959-64105.
Bagshot Rd, Bracknell, Berks RG12 3SE. 0344-486 123.
Pc Royal Military Academy, Sandhurst, Surrey. Hendon Manor, Sevenoaks, Kent. The Barons, Reigate, Surrey. Work in London inc. the Eygptian Sculpture Gallery, British Museum; Mayfair Hotel; Institute of Directors, Pall Mall; decorating – Lancaster House, St James's.
Britain's longest established builders, offering a comprehensive restoration and refurbishment service, carried out with the minimum of disturbance. Great emphasis is placed upon the training and development of their workforce.

DYSON, ION (PLUMBING) LTD (Empl: 14+; Est: c. 1804)
Lead Roofing & Cast Iron Rainwater Goods
Buslingthorpe Lane, Leeds, Yorks LS7 2D6. 0532-620031.
LCA; NAPHMSC.
Pc Lead roofing to churches, town halls, etc. in Yorkshire area, i.e.

Halifax Town Hall; Bradford Town Hall.
Only a limited amount of copper roofing work is undertaken.

EAST, GEORGE (Empl: one; Est: 1984)
Master Thatcher
136 Meadow Way, Theale, Reading, Berks RG7 5DG. 0734-302 933.
Apprenticeship; CoSIRA New Entrants Training Scheme; M Oxon, Berks MTA.
Pc Sub-contractor on National Trust properties. Details and photographs of houses and barns given on request.
Willing to undertake sedge ridging.

EATON-GAZE LTD
Decorative Plasterwork
23 Rathbone Place London, W1. 071-636 2617.

EATON, LES BLACKSMITH SERVICES (Empl: solo; Est: 1988)
4 Meadow Walk, Sling, Coleford, Glos GL16 8LR. 0594-34719.
Fully qualified blacksmith; all Army Trade Test passed; GMC.
Pc Duke of Wellington's Death Carriage.

ECKERSLEY, D. STAINED GLASS (Empl: one; Est: 1986)
Stained Glass Artist
No 40 Atlas House, Chorley Old Rd, Bolton, Lancs BL1 4JL. 653 712 & 46880.
Served 5 yr apprenticeship.
Pc Bolton Market Place Complex.

EDELSTEIN, LIVIA (Est: 1976)
Hand-woven & Hand-tufted Wallhangings
9 Church Row, London NW3 6UT. 071-794 1312 & 431 1390.
BA Graphic Design; Cert Art & Design, Textiles; C & Gs Basketry.
Pc 27 wallhangings – British Airports Authority, Terminal 2, Heathrow Airport. 3 m × 4 m tapestry – BP Headquarters (in progress).
Woven tapestries for office reception areas; boardrooms; private houses. 'Using the jewel-like quality of silk ribbon, creating a luscious and curving texture through 3 diminsions is a trademark of this facet of my work'. Portfolio of slides and prints.

EDINBURGH ARCHITECTURAL SALVAGE (Est: 1988)
80 Pitt St, Leith, Edinburgh EH6 4DB. 031-554 7077 & 552 2262.
Also stocks panelling; panelled doors; window shutters; cupboard doors; dados; cast radiators; cast baths; sinks; marble work tops; mouldings.

FIRMS AND CRAFTSPEOPLE

EDINBURGH CERAMICS (Empl: 2 partners only; Est: 1985)
46 Balcarres St, Edinburgh EH10 5JG. 031-452 8145.
Susan Finch and Douglas Dalgleish both have BA (Hons) Art & Design plus post grad Dips Ceramics, Edinburgh College of Art.
Pc 3 large hand-painted tile panels – Waverley Market Shopping Centre, Edinburgh. Reproduction Victorian tiles – Central Bar, Edinburgh (restoration).
Brochure.

THE EDINBURGH TAPESTRY CO LTD (Empl: 9; Est: 1946)
Dovecot Studios, 2 Dovecot Rd, Edinburgh EH12 7LE. 031-334 4118.
Apprenticeship for Master Weaver Degree in Tapestry Weaving.
Commissions carried out to own design, or to the design of artists, textile designers, designers or architects for tufted rugs, hand-woven tapestries and/or decorative kites. Brochure.

EDWARDES, PAUL (Est: 1988)
Stained Glass Artist
11 Sherwell Hill, Chelston, Torquay, Devon TQ2 6LU. 0803-605 742.
Flat Glass Council Certificate.

EDWARDS, JAY – STUDIO WEAVER (Empl: solo; Est: 1984)
Studio: The Handweavers Studio, 29 Haroldstone Rd, London E17. 081-521 2281. 5 Holly Rd, London E11 2PF. 081-989 5110.
Majority of work has to be to commission as the colour and sizing is so critical. Minimum order – 1 yd, maximum – 20 yds.

EICKHOFF, ANGUS (Empl: one; Est: 1980)
Creative Metal
The Forge, Whitehouse, Bridge, Welshpool, Powys SY21 8LX. 0938-3572.
BA (Hons) 3d Design.
Pc Public commissions inc. Processional Cross, St Mary's Church, S. Woodford, London E18. Chandelier light fitting for atrium – Grange School, Rhos, Wrexham, Clwyd and also Lady Chapel, Church of St John-at-Hampstead, London NW3
Although a wide range of jobs are undertaken, inc. reproduction ironwork, the majority of work is contemporary using traditional blacksmithing techniques wherever possible and specializing in lighting. Slides and photographs available.

EIGHT BY FOUR LIMITED (Empl: 5; Est: 1984)
Furniture Designers & Makers
L37 'A' Block, Eastcross Centre, Waterden Rd, London E15 2HN. 081-985 6001.

Both director's have honours degrees in Furniture Design & Making; MCSD.
Undertake a variety of specialist furniture work, always designed to commission, sometimes reproduction. Brochure.

EISL, THOMAS (Est: 1982)
3 Nimrod Passage, Tottenham Rd, London N1 4BU. 071-241 4825.
Crafts Council Index.
Pc Mainly private commissions, but some larger commissions in office developments and refurbishments.
Photographs of recent work available.

EKE, ROGER & SON (Empl: 2; Est: 1969)
Furniture Restorers
Border Villa, Boyton, Launceston, Cornwall PL15 8NW. 056 685 331.
Carving & gilding apprenticeship; C & Gs.
Main work involves restoration of 18th-century carved and water gilded mirror frames and furniture.

ELEGANCE RESTORED BY TONY CHURCHER (Empl: solo; Est: 1986)
Petit Point Reproduced for Furniture
14 The Graylings, Putnoe, Bedford MK41 9BH. 0234-58159.
Self taught; 30 yrs experience; M Embroiderers Guild.
Pc 6 replacement petit point drop in seats for dining chairs, c. 1750. Complete restoration of Victorian lady's chair, c. 1840. Replacement heraldic drop in seat for a dining chair, c. 1880. Family coat-of-arms reproduced in petit point.
Designs and makes canvas work (tapestry) panels for chairs, foot stools, bell pulls, etc. inc. heraldry and ecclesiastical work. Original designs reproduced wherever possible. Will also restore woodwork and undertake re-upholstery where necessary.

ELIFF, P. & SONS LTD (Empl: 14; Est: Ltd Co 1926)
Stained Glass Artist
Mabgate Green, Leeds, Yorks LS9 7DS. 0532-452 751 & 454 512.
M Flat Glass Assoc.
Pc Many local churches.

ELVINS CONSTRUCTION CO LTD
Building Contractors
Reservoir House, Icknield Port Rd, Edgbaston, Birmingham B16 0AA. 021-554 7331.
M BEC; NAPH; MSC; Brit Woodworking Fed; Birmingham Safety Group; Birmingham Construction Training Group. Approved:

FIRMS AND CRAFTSPEOPLE

Health Authority; National Trust; Diocesan (RC & C of E).
Pc St Peter and St Paul's RC Church, Wolverhampton. Biddulph Grange Gardens for National Trust, Architect Anthony Blacklay. St Chad's RC Church, Birmingham, overseen by Weightman & Bullen of Liverpool. Measured term contract – Kenilworth Castle overseen by Eng. Heritage.

EMPRESS STAINED GLASS – ROBERT MULLEN (Empl: one; Est: 1987)
Empress House, Market Square, Llanfair Caereinion, Nr Welshpool, Powys SY21 0RP. 0938-810 743.
Self taught; M Wales Craft Council.
Pc Various domestic commissions fulfilled in the North & Mid Wales, and W. Midlands areas.

ENDERSBY, M. E. BUILDER (Empl: 6; Est: 23 yrs)
21 Chapel Lane, Willington, Bedford MK44 3QG. 023 03 278.
Master carpenter & joiner; experience. Approved: Bedfordshire CC; N Bedfordshire DC; Mid Beds DC.
Pc Many works for Beds CC inc. restoration works – Swiss Garden Old. Restoration of farm building for Whitbread Estate ('to Eng. Heritage standards') for John Manning Partnership, Luton.

ENFIELD FOUNDRY CO LTD (Empl: 30; Est: 1936)
Railway Rd, Waltham Cross, Herts EN8 7JA. 0992-710 224.
Pc Have supplied castings for work on Buckingham Palace; St Paul's Cathedral and St Bartholomew's Hospital.

ENGLEFIELD, ALAN R. (Empl: one; Est: 1981)
Furniture Designer & Maker
Owl Cottage, High St, Netheravon, Nr Salisbury, Wilts SP4 9PJ. 0980-70396.
3 yrs at Rycotewood College, Thame.
Pc 3 yrs as sub-contractor to David Linley Furniture Ltd.

ENGLISH ELM LANDSCAPES (Empl: one; Est: 1982)
Dry Stone Walling
2 Maggs Lane, Whitchurch, Bristol, Avon BS14 0PH. 0272-891 597.
One yr course Dry Stone Walling; 7 yrs experience.
Will also build animal housing with dry stones, i.e. goat shelters; geese houses; sheep shelters.

ERICKSON, GRACE (Empl: one Est: 1980)
Hand-woven Tapestry Designer & Maker
334 Old Laira Rd, Plymouth, Devon PL3 6AQ. 0752-261 788.

BSc Fine Art; Crafts Council Select Index.
Pc 'Earth', 'Sea', 'Sky', tryptych tapestries (each 200 cm × 150 cm) – St Mary's Hospital, London. 'Thames Fantasy' tapestry (100 cm × 375 cm) – Greycoat plc, London. 'Ten Ten Eight Eight', tapestry (69 cm × 56 cm) – private client.
Hand-painting and embroidery are only undertaken occasionally in connection with certain designs.

ERSKINE, ROBERT SIMON (Empl: one; Est: 1983)
Architectural Sculptor
15 Robinson Rd, London E2 9LX. 081-980 3068.
BA (Hons) Degree Fine Art Sculpture; Higher Dip Fine Art Sculpture, Slade School Fine Art, London University; M Art & Architecture.
Pc 16 ft high sculpture – Sun Life Assurance Co of Canada's award winning Headquarters, Basingstoke, Hants. Sculpture – Crown Estate Commissioners, New Shopping Centre, Town Centre, High Wycombe, Bucks.
Site specific sculpture with architecture. Brochure.

ESCOL PANELS (S & G) LTD (Empl: 50; Est: 1964)
Paisley Works, Rixon Rd, Wellingborough, Northants NN8 4BB. 0933-76136.
M – Vitreous Enamel Development Council; Inst of Vitreous Enamellers; BSI (awarded BS5750 Part 2/ISO 9002 Quality Assurance); Northants Chamber of Commerce.
Pc Arabian culture graphics (2 m high × 10 m wide) – Royal Commission of Jubaild and Yanbu, Saudi Arabia. Murals (City Hall) – Metro Station, Singapore. Murals (Raffles City) – Metro Station, Singapore. Murals linked in with Glasgow Garden Festival (Finnieston Station) – Scotrail, Glasgow. Multitude of pub signs.
Photographs available. Brochure might be available.

ESKDALE STONE SUPPLIES – T. H. ATKINSON (Empl: 3; Est: 1988, previously 1970)
6 Whingreen, Sleights, Whitby, N Yorks YO22 5AB. 0947-811 136.
Full apprenticeship to building trade; 24 yrs experience.
Also supplies natural local stone to match existing work.

ESSEX, A. & CO (Empl: 4; Est: 1930)
Furniture Restorers
1 Hope Park Terrace, Edinburgh EH8 9LZ. 031-667 5387.
Cabinet makers/restorers on Edinburgh Conservation list of approved tradesmen.

FIRMS AND CRAFTSPEOPLE

Pc Restoring boardroom furniture for Queen's visit to Scotsman Publications on their centenary. Upholstery works – Merchant Co of Edinburgh. Restoration works – Lord Avonside (High Court Judge), etc.

ETEMADZADEH, DOULAT
Textiles and Interior Designer
7 Hilltop House, 117 Hornsey Lane, London N6 5NW. 071-281 0144.
Graduate MA in Decorative Arts.

E. & T. FURNITURE MAKERS (Empl: partnership; Est: 1985)
Ailies Buildings, Whitesmith Lane, East Hoathly, Nr Lewes, Sussex. 0825-872 527.
Registered professional turner with Worshipful Co of Turners; BA (Hons) 3d Design, Manchester Polytec; M GMC; M Soc of Ornamental Turners.
Pc 7 ft extending table (extends to 10 ft) and a set of 12 chairs in solid mahogany. Design and construction – bedroom in sweet chestnut with four poster bed, period Arts & Crafts house, Surrey. Re-fitting of doctor's surgery in contemporary oak panelling (1900). Conversion of a large piece of oak vestry furniture into several more useful units.
Brochure.

EUROOM INTERNATIONAL (UK) LTD (Empl: 6; Est: 1979)
Furniture Restoration
Vine House, Fair Green, Reach, Cambridge CB5 0JD. 0638-741 989. 13 High St, Newmarket. 0638-662 958. 8–14 Mill St, Mildenhall, Suffolk. 0638-712 502.
AMU; GMC.
Pc Work for National Trust; Mr Robert Holmes à Court; Newmarket Jockey Club; Lord and Lady Fairhaven; British Bloodstock Agency; Jaguar Headquarters; Duchess of Sutherland; Lady Derby; various Arabian Princes; Michael Stoute; Lester Piggott.
Also undertakes restoration of pianos, clocks, barometers, cane and rush.

EVANS, JOYCE CONWY (Empl: solo; Est: 1976)
Embroidery & Needlepoint
4 Cedar Studios, 45 Glebe Place, Chelsea, London SW3 5JE. 071-351 0648.
Des RCA; FCSD; Nat Dip in Design – Embroidery; C & Gs Embroidery.
Pc Altar frontals for both King's College Chapel, Cambridge and Canterbury Cathedral, Kent. Various embroideries – private collections in USA and Australia.

FARLOW, PETER SPECIALIST DECORATORS

EXCLUSIVE DECOR (Empl: 5; Est: 1979)
Specialist Painters
35 Newton Park Rd, Thundersley, Essex SS7 3SD. 0268-774 593.
All employees to C & Gs standards.
Pc Public houses, private dwellings, hotels (inc. Hilton), restaurants.

EXETER MARBLE & SLATE CO (Empl: 4; Est: 1982)
King Edward St, Exeter, Devon EX4 4NY. 0392-221 224.
Undertake orders from within the trade, i.e architects; bathroom companies; interior designers, etc. Offer a complete installation service for marble fireplaces; floors; bathroom items, slate hearths and flooring. Sells reproduction period style mantels in carved pine and plaster. Occasionally stocks original marble fireplaces. Brochure.

FACTORY (Empl: 2; Est: 1985)
Furniture Designers & Makers
The Stableyard, Coleshill, Swindon, Wilts SN6 7PT. 0793-763 829.
Foundation course in Art & Design; B TEC Dip in Furniture Design; Crafts Council setting up grant; Southern Arts grant; attendance at Chelsea Crafts Fair.
Pc Sock display cabinet and till desk – shop in Tottenham St, London for David Clarke Associates (Architects). Garden and conservatory benches – London for Architects' practice. Hat stands – Conference Centres, High Wycombe and London for Honeywell Bull.
Laminates, specialist paint effects to match other decor and lacquering undertaken. Also produce own range of furniture, and accessories. Brochure.

FAIRFAX
Langley Green, Langley Burrell, Chippenham, Wilts. 0249-652030.
London Shop: 568 Kings Rd, London SW6. 071-736 5023.
20 yrs experience in fireplaces and cast iron work.

FALK, GABRIELLA (Empl: solo; Est: 1978)
Weaver
Hare & Hounds, Exton, Dulverton, Somerset TA22 9JT. 064 385 266.
Trained Central School of Art & Design; B Ed (Hons), N London Polytec; M Art & Architecture; M South West Textiles Group.
Brochure.

FARLOW, PETER SPECIALIST DECORATORS (Empl: 8; Est; 1970)
22 Grand Union Centre, Ladbroke Grove, London W10 5AX. 081-969 2847.
7 yr apprenticeship – Woodall & Co Ltd; GMC.
Pc Featured in *Art of Marbling*; *Art of Graining* (Macdonald); *Surfaces*

FIRMS AND CRAFTSPEOPLE

& Finishes; Designers' Guide to Paint Finishes.

'FARM SPINNERS' PENNY WALSH (Empl: 7 members co-operative; Est: 1984)
88 Tynwhitt Rd, London SE4 1QB. Vauxhall City Farm, 24 St Oswalds Place SE11. 081-692 2958.
Penny Walsh MA; RCA; Crafts Council Index; Guild of Weavers, Spinners & Dyers.
Pc Specialized yarns for restoration of ancient and old textiles, handspun and dyed with original recipes. Any quantities.

FARRAR, VICTOR PARTNERSHIP, THE (Est: 1962)
Architects & Surveyors
57 St Peter's St, Bedford MK40 2PR. 0234-53012 & 52602.
Victor Farrar – RIBA; PP FAS; F FAS; F G of S; F RSA   Bruce Deacon – RIBA; Dip Arch   Denis Bettell – M BIAT; AFS

FARRELLY, MARTIN N. STAINED GLASS (Empl: 3; Est: 1986)
Crathes Craft Studios, Milton of Crathes, Banchory, Kincardineshire AB3 3HO. 0339-2327.
C & Gs Dublin; Registered Craftsmen in Conservation, Scottish Conservation Bureau, Edinburgh; Scottish Development Agency, Craftsmen in Stained Glass; Soc of Catholic Artists.
Pc Fully listed in current issue of Scottish Bureau, but inc. Kirkwalls St Magnus Cathedral; Haddon House Chapel; National Trust of Scotland; Dornoch Cathedral; St Machar's Cathedral Church, Aberdeen.
Specialist in heraldry; surveying and reporting on the conservation/ restoration and length of life of existing lead/glass; conservation of destabilized paintwork; graisaille work; restoration of lost paint to flesh (figurative designs).

FEDDEN, BRYANT
Glass Engraver/Lettercutter
Tanyard Bank, Castle St, Winchcombe, Nr Cheltenham, Glos GL54 5JA. 0242 602 782
Crafts Council Index.
Pc Works in Bristol, Gloucester, Manchester, Blackburn, Southwell Cathedrals, churches, hospitals, law courts, businesses, i. e. Chelsea Royal Hospital; Spirax Sarco Ltd; Central Electricity Generating Board.

FEILDEN & MAWSON (Empl: 50 + 8 partners; Est: 1986)
Architects
Ferry Rd, Norwich, Norfolk NR1 1SU. 0603-629 571.

David Mawson – RIBA; FSA. (Architect to Norwich Cathedral)   Simon C. Crosse – AA Dip; RIBA   Geoffrey G. Mitchell – D Arch (Kingston); RIBA.
Pc Conservation to many historic buildings, secular and ecclesiastical inc. Low Pavement, Chesterfield and Ditchingham Hall, Norfolk. Surveys of Osborne House, Isle of Wight and Marlborough House, London.

FELL, ANITA – A. F. DESIGNS (Est: 1980)
Rag Rugs
Secrets, Scout Lane, Whitehill Rd, Crowborough, E. Sussex TN6 1JA. 0892-665 314.
ALA.
Pc Numerous commissions for private homes.
Photographs and slides available on request.

FERRY & MENNIM (Est: 1922)
Chartered Architects & Diocesan Surveyors
12 Minster Yard, York YO1 2HJ. 0904-624 103.
C. S. G. Liversedge – RIBA   R. J. Carr-Archer – RIBA; M York DAC; Cathedral Architect's Assoc; SPAB; ASCHB; Comm Mbr EASA   R. Gardner – MA; RIBA; SPAB; EASA.
Pc Restoration – St Magnus Cathedral, Kirkwell, Orkney. Conversion of country house to hotel – Middlethorpe Hall, York for Historic Houses Assoc (YNSA Award and 2 Commendations, British Tourist Design Award, Jackson-Stops & Staff/Sunday Times Country House Award Commendation). Repairs – King's Manor, Inst of Advanced Architectural Studies, University of York. House and barn conversion – Bryam House, Low Knipe, Cumbria (NE Civic Trust House & Cottage Award Commendation).

FILLARY, TERRY & PAUL (FILLARYS LTD) (Empl: 2; Est: 1968)
Lead Castings
10 Dunbar Avenue, Dagenham. Essex RM10 7JT. 77 Grosvenor Avenue, Islington, London N5 2NN. 081-592 2618.
Both Partners have C & Gs Plumbing; M Inst of Plumbing; MLCA.
Rainwater pipes, hopper heads, cisterns, etc. reproduced in lead inc. match to existing.

FINCH, JOHN A. LTD (Empl: 5; Est: 1934)
Stained Glass Artist
28 Wood Lane, Sheffield, S. Yorks. 0742-336 133.
Learnt by apprenticeship.
Pc National Trust properties. Local churches. Public houses.

FIRMS AND CRAFTSPEOPLE

FINE LINES (Est: 1985)
Stained Glass Artist
Studio 3, 37 City Rd, Cambridge CB1 1DP. 0223-314 321.
BA (Hons).
Traditional stained glass and copper foil techniques used in combination with a new system involving the coating of glass with unstable resins. Highest quality pigments are combined with these resins to produce any colour, and intricate designs are made with a high-grade relief system. This system is considered more versatile in its design potential than traditional methods.

FINEWOOD – ALBERT J. LAIN (Empl: 2; Est: 1985)
T/A Grove House, Rendham, Saxmundham, Suffolk IP17 2AS. 072 878-567.
Specialist teacher training in technical subjects; 21 yrs teaching, Head of Dept; M Assoc of Woodturners of GB.
Four poster beds inc. design with curved canopy. Oak furniture. Copy turning for the trade. Batch designs inc. turned corner and semi-circular shelves, lazy Susans, toilet cabinets.

FIRED EARTH (Empl: 30–40; Est: 1985)
Hand-painted Encaustic & Terracotta Tiles
Twyford Mill, Oxford Rd, Adderbury, Nr Banbury, Oxon OX17 3HP. 0295-812 088.
IDDA.
Brochure.

FIREPLACE (HUNGERFORD) LTD, THE (Est: 1976)
Charnham St, Hungerford, Berks. 0488-83420.
Pc Supplied fenders, fire dogs and irons (all antique) to 7/11 Gloucester Gate, Regent's Park, London.

FIRESTYLE (Empl: 5; Est: 1985)
158 Upminster Rd, Upminster, Essex RM14 2RB. 04024-54136 & 56895.
Marble Mason, C & Gs qualified; M NFC; Solid Fuel Advisory Service.
Pc Various made to measure marble chimneypieces (details available on application).
Specialize in classic and period carved marble chimneypieces, but also undertake other natural stone, and antique brick mantelpieces, with cast iron inserts. A full design and fitting service is available. Brochure.

FISH, THOMAS & SONS LTD (Empl: approx 100; Est: 1811)
Building Contractors
Great Freeman St, Nottingham NG3 5GH. 0602-587000.
BEC; CIB; GMC; BWF; BDA.

FITZGERALD, SEAN

Pc A varied list of new and renovation projects, many of which have attracted craftsmanship awards.
Brochure.

FISH, THOMAS & SONS LTD – SPECIALIST JOINERY
Stapleford Rd, Trowell, Nottingham NG9 3QA. 0602-306 318.

FISH, WILLIAM DESIGN
Interior Design & Renovation
Great Freeman St, Nottingham NG3 5GH. 0602-587000.

FISHER DECORATIONS
See SKIDMORE D.

FISHER, GRAHAM C. (Empl: solo; Est: 1986)
Painter – Marbling & Graining, Stencilling, Broken Colour Work
25 Hunters Crescent, Romsey, Hants SO51 7UG. 0794-523 615.
C & Gs of London Inst in Painting & Decorating (with distinction); M GMC;
All work to date has been of a private nature but hopes to introduce some commercial work in the future.

FISHER, JACK PARTNERSHIP (Est: 1933)
Architects & Surveyors
7 Alexandra Place, St Andrew's, Fife KY16 9XE. 0334-72481.
W. Murray Jack – RIBA; FRIAS   Peter J. Fisher – RIBA; FRIAS   Colin P. M. Fisher – B Arch (Edin); RIBA.
Pc Conservation works throughout Scotland inc. castles, monasteries, churches and stately homes. Consultants to the National Trust.

FISHER, TOM (Est: 1985)
Furniture Designer & Maker
Canalside Works, Back Castleton Close, Armley Rd, Leeds LS12 2DS. 0532-420 848 & 405 962.
BA (Hons), Leeds; Cert of Craftsmanship in Wood, Parnham House.
Domestic furniture, boardroom furniture designed and made to commission. Design work undertaken for industrial manufacturers on a freelance basis.
Brochure.

FITZGERALD, SEAN (Est: 1982)
Furniture
The Studio Workshop, Smithbrook Kilns, Cranleigh, Surrey GU6 8JJ. 0483-275900.
CGLI Furniture; Rycotwood College Cert Fine Craftsmanship &

FIRMS AND CRAFTSPEOPLE

Design; Surrey Guild of Craftsmen (exhibiting M).
Pc 2 low glass top display tables. Walnut and oak. Library bookcases. Set of 8 mahogany dining chairs. Chapel furniture (altar table and stand/lectern).
Brochure and good colour photographs of sample work.

FLEMING, GAIL A. (Empl: solo; Est: 1988)
Textile Designer
10c Waverley Court, Foxbar, Paisley, Renfrewshire PA2 0DR. 041-848 1541.
BA Degree specializing in Embroidered and Printed Textiles and post grad Dip Textiles, Glasgow School of Art; Grad Enterprise & Small Business Course in Business Management.
Pc 'Domestic Fliss'; 'Black Sea'; 'Ziggy' – all machine and hand-embroidered textile panels (framed) in private collections.

FLEMING RANKIN ASSOCIATES (Est: 1984)
Architect
3 Cathcart St, Ayr KA7 1BJ. 0292-262 614.
Architect – RIBA; ARIAS.
Pc Refurbishment/conversion of hotel to ten pin bowling centre.

FLETCHER, GORDON (DRY STONE WALLING & FLAGGING) (Empl: 2; Est: 1984)
12 Selstone Crescent. Sleights, Whitby, N. Yorks YO22 5DJ. 0947-810 732.
Master Craftsman Cert DSWA of GB.
Pc Wall restoration work for North Yorks National Park. Training at Agricultural Colleges and YTS.
Brochure, photographs and testimonials available on request.

FLETCHER, JON (Empl: one; Est: 1987)
Thatcher
31 Beaconsfield Rd, Christchurch, Dorset. 0202-476285.
5 yrs apprenticeship with Master Thatcher.
Pc Portsmouth Council. Southampton Council, Ancient Monuments Soc. McCarthy & Stone, Builders. Whitsbury Estates.
Total renovations and extensions of thatched properties undertaken.

FLEUSS, GERALD (& PATRICIA GIDNEY) (Est: 1974)
Calligraphy & Fine Lettering inc. Gilding
59 Chartfield Rd, Cherryhinton, Cambridge CB1 4JX. 0223-241224.
Gerald Fleuss – Fellow Society of Scribes & Illuminators; M Art Workers Guild.

FORGE STUDIO WORKS

Pc Heraldic design for many clients inc. Cambridge City Council; Chartered Inst of Arbitrators; ANZ Bank; Worshipful Co of Armourers & Braziers; Worshipful Co of Cutlers; Dorchester Brewery. Restoration of lettering and decoration on musical instruments.
Brochure.

FLOWER, NIGEL (Empl: solo; Est: 1980)
Furniture Designer & Maker
Brickfield Barn Woodwork, Gt Ryburgh Rd, Stibbard, Fakenham. Norwich, Norfolk NR21 0EE. 032 878-410.
3 yrs prior to setting up worked in Rob Corbett of Corpusty's Furniture Workshop; now M. Norfolk, Furniture Makers Assoc.

FORBES, DON (Empl: 3; Est: 1979)
Cotterton, Logiealmond, Perth. 0738-88329.
Qualified architectural ironmonger; 30 yrs in trade.
Pc Angel Development, Glasgow. Shopping Centre, Falkirk. Rose Terrace Redevelopment, Perth. New Timeshare Cottages, Kenmore, Perthshire. Various renovation projects throughout GB.
Lead sash window weights and allied products, usually manufactured to client's specifications. Also hold large stocks of cast iron sash weights, and all types of window fittings. Offer complete sash window fittings range to the trade, architects and other specifiers. Brochure.

FORD, THOMAS & PARTNERS (Est: 1926)
Chartered Architects & Surveyors
35 London Rd, Bromley, Kent BR1 1DG. 071-460 8811.
Partners are qualified architects experienced in conservation/ restoration work. M's EASA.
Pc Roof refurbishment/historic survey, interior restoration – The Queen's House, Greenwich (Inigo Jones 1635). Restoration – Eagle House, Mitcham (1705). Restoration and reordering – St Michael, Chester Sq, London. Refurbishment and conversion – 3B Russell Square, London, Burton. Restoration – St John's Church, Hurst Green.
This practice is either currently or has previously worked at all the London National Museums, and hold a consultancy at the British Museum. Architects for over 150 churches and have carried out work at over 200 churches, inc. the rebuilding or restoration of a considerable number badly damaged by fire.

FORGE STUDIO WORKS (Empl: 5 + outworker specialists; Est: 1978)
Stour St, Manningtree, Essex CO11 1BE. 0206-396 22.
BAFRA; only employ high quality craftsmen; one picture restorer

FIRMS AND CRAFTSPEOPLE

MA, ex National Gallery.
Pc Carving – highly decorated doorcase 15 ft × 10 ft, Cabinet Office, 10 Downing St. General restoration of quality furnishings – both trade and private. Ecclesiastical carving and restoration. Museum restoration work inc. British Museum; Wesley Museum; etc. Work for major houses.
Photographs available.

FORGE, THE – PETER CLUTTERBUCK (Empl: 2; Est: 1970)
The Rear of 30 Osborne Rd, Southsea, Portsmouth, Hants PO5 3LT (access via Clifton Rd). 0705-753 562
Apprenticeship blacksmithing; Art School Sculpture; M BABA.
Pc Restoration park gates – Portsmouth City Council. Railings and arch – Gosport Urban Regeneration – Hampshire County Council.

FORREST, DOUGLAS T. ARCHITECTS (Est: 1981)
The Kitchen, Cullen House, Cullen, Banffshire AB5 2XW. 0542-41097 & 40087. FAX 0542 41414.
Douglas T. Forrest and Les F. Hunter – B Arch; Dip Arch; RIBA; ARIAS.
Pc Restoration and conversion – Cullen House, Cullen and also Keith Hall, Inverurie. Restoration and refurbishment – Hatton Castle, Angus. Restoration – Cousins Barm Aberdeen; Tappit Hen, Aberdeen; The Parkway.
Experienced in maintenance, restoration and change of use of historic buildings, as well as involvement in housing, education and theatre projects (both new and refurbishment) in both public and private sectors.

FORSTER, D. L. LTD
Suppliers Upholstery & Other Craft Goods
12 The Ongar Road Trading Est, Gt Dunmow, Essex CM6 1EU. 0371-5201 (5 lines).
AMU.
Brochure.

FOSTER, L. C. & SONS (Empl: 2 partners/apprentice; Est: early 1900s)
Master Thatcher
Spring Cottage, Fyfield, Marlborough, Wilts SN8 3TQ. 0672-810 665.
NSMTA.
Pc Avebury Great Barn.

FOSTER, SUSAN (Est: 1976)
Hand-woven Rugs
9 Windermere Rd, Kendal, Cumbria LA9 4QJ. 0539-26494.

Trained with several weavers in this country and in Scandinavia; belong to several craft organizations.

FORTUNE, TIM BA (Hons) (Empl: unlimited; Est: 1982)
Blacksmith & Ironwork Designer
Filleybrook Forge, Buckhorn Weston, Gillinghan, Dorset SP8 5HE. 0963-70163.
Completed CoSIRA 2 yr training scheme in traditional wrought-ironwork whilst working as trainee blacksmith in Shaftesbury, Dorset (gained award for being most competent student); Salisbury College of Art; 1st Class Honours degree in 3d Design, Manchester Polytechnic.
Commission work carried out all the time on all scales. Portfolio on appointment.

FOULGER & SON – METAL POLISHERS & FINISHERS (Empl: 5; Est: 1967)
Unit 18, Bow Enterprise Park, Cranwell Close, Violet Row, Bow, London E3 EQY. 071-515 5206.
48 years in the trade.
Pc Restoration of bronze door frames, etc. for Savoy Hotel; Claridges; Harrods; B of C.
Specialists in the polishing, tone bronzing, lacquering and maintenance of staircase balustrades; all sorts of frames; shopfronts; doors; sculptures and other components. Also restore and repair antiques inc. French ormulu; chandeliers; brass showcases; fireplaces. Specialized finished surfaces to effluent tanks undertaken.

FOWLER & BRACE (Empl: one; Est: 1986)
Designers & Makers of Furniture
The Workshop, Castle Ditch Lane, Lewes, E. Sussex BN7 1YJ. 0273-479 680.
A. C. Brace, partner – 15 yrs experience cabinet makers and allied trades   B. J. Fowler, partner – M Des RCA; BA (Hons) Dip MCSD; 5 yrs experence   C. Dickson, apprentice – C& Gs Joinery; BA (Hons).
Pc Fitted library in solid English oak – London client. Various fitted wardrobes for architects in London. Handmade burr maple and sycamore standing desk – London. Main entrance doors – AM/EX Bank, Florence, Italy.
Also stock their own range of reception and conference chairs. Brochure.

FOWLER BROS (COWFOLD) LTD (Empl: 55; Est: 1853)
Building Contractors
Henfield Rd, Cowfold, Horsham, W. Sussex, RH13 8BS. 0403-864 373.

FIRMS AND CRAFTSPEOPLE

Directors F CIOB or otherwise professionally qualified in their fields; BEC. Approved: Eng. Heritage; Horsham DC; Brighton BC; West Sussex CC.
Pc Repair works carried out in 3 phases starting in 1985 – Cowdray Ruins, Midhurst for Lord Cowdray (architects: Purcell, Miller, Tritton & Partners).
Also undertakes stone roofing, flint walling, etc.

FOX, A. E. WOODCARVER (Est: 1967)
21 Downham Way, Bromley, Kent BR1 5NY. 081-698 2755.
Evening College; M Guild of Woodworkers; Church of England Listed Craftsman.
Photographs available.

FOX, R. & SONS LTD (Empl: 100+; Est: 1852)
Building Maintenance & Restoration
38–40 St Pancras Way, London NW1 0QP. 071-387 9556. FAX 071-383 4590.
Pc Marble restoration – Lloyds 1958 & 1986 buildings, and also Unilever building. Metal restoration – Britannic House, TSB, Birmingham. Paint and metal restoration – British Telecom and Sandwell MBC. Major stonework restoration – Piccadilly, Manchester. Stone and bronze cleaning – Plantation House, London.
Restoration and maintenance of architectural metalwork; marble; granite; terrazzo; ceramics; wood finishes; facias and signs; high quality cellulose and '2-pack' paint finishes; electrostatic enamelling of metal office furniture; anti-graffiti treatment; chandelier renovation and maintenance; acoustic ceiling tile cleaning. Brochure.

FRANKLAND, B. A. & L.
See DODDINGTON HOUSE ANTIQUES (B. A. & L. FRANKLAND)

FRANKLIN, MICHAEL (Empl: one; Est: 1975)
Master Thatcher
Albion House, 9 Station Rd, Corby Glen, Grantham NG33 4NW. 047 684-375.
Apprenticeship served on Exton Estate, Oakham, Rutland; Secretary and M Rutland & Leics MTA; M NSMTA.
Pc A variety of roofs in the counties of Rutland, Leics, S. Lincs, N. Northants, Norfolk, Herts and Mid-west Wales.

FRANKLIN, W. E. (SHEFFIELD) LTD (Empl: 26; Est: 1883)
Cleaning of Rugs, Tapestries, Curtains & Upholstery
116–120 Onslow Rd, Sheffield, S. Yorks S11 7AH. 0742-686 161.

Nat Carpet Cleaners Assoc; Fabric Care Research Assoc; ASCR of USA; CAMRASO.
Pc Carpets at Chatsworth House and also Harewood House. Upholstery at Nostell Priory.

FRASER, ANSELM ANTIQUE FURNITURE RESTORER (Empl: one Est: 1983)
The Carthouse, Crauchie, E. Linton, E. Lothian EH40 3EB. 0620-860 067.
Trained at the Aruncraft School of Antique Furniture Restoration, in Sussex 1981/82. M Soc of Woodcraftsmen.
'Before and after' restoration photographs available for inspection in workshops.

FRASER, IAN – CERAMICS (Est: 1988)
Clardale, High St, Falkland, Fife KY7 7BU. 0337-57209.
Time served ceramic tiler.
Wall and floor tiling specialist 'highly recommended by Fraser/Gray, builder' in the area.

FREDERICK'S LTD
Architectural Salvage
Frederick's Barn, Rear of 24 London Rd, Southborough, Kent TN4 0QB. 0892-47704.

FREEBORN, E. J. & SON (Empl: 3; Est: 1948)
Furniture Designer & Restorer
2 The Shambles, York YO1 2LZ. 0904-623 153.
All craftsmen receive 4 yrs full apprenticeship.
Pc Too numerous to mention, but have manufactured and restored furniture and woodwork of all types, and in many situations, for 40 yrs.

FREW, JIM RIBA (Est: 1961)
Architect
39 Common Green, Strathaven, Lanarkshire ML10 6AQ. 0357-21076.
A Arch; RIBA; ARIAS; MRSH.
Pc Alterations and extensions to listed buildings within the county.

FRIEND, RODRICK
Stained Glass Artist
Dove Cottage, 40 Summer St, Stroud, Glos GL5 1NT. 04536-70919.
London Certificate of Art & Design; M (Art) RCA (Distinction); AM BMGP.
Pc 5 windows – Roman Catholic Church, Salcombe, Devon.

FIRMS AND CRAFTSPEOPLE

A glass painter who regards the glass as the vehicle, with paint, stain and acid etching the actual artistic medium – light.

FRINTONGATE LTD
Waterproofing & Building Care Specialists
49 Endsleigh Court, Lexden, Colchester, Essex CO3 3QS. 0206-578 760 & 231 337.
Full trade M BEC; FBSC. D. M. Morgan grad (BA), The City Business School (MSc); Dept of Environmental Sciences (University of Lancaster); attended SPAB Autumn repair course.
Pc Re-roofing and renovation – J. Nash's (Architect's) Regent's Park Crescent, London W1. Resin repairs – All Saints' Church, Witham, Essex, RC Diocese of Brentwood.
Undertake all types of waterproofing inc. prevention of dampness, groundwater and rain penetration, and in this connection are consultants to commerce, industry and the building profession. Suppliers of Remmers products.

FRITH, FRANCIS COLLECTION, THE (Empl: 20; Est: 1977)
Charlton Rd, Andover, Hants SP10 3LL. 0264-53113/4.
Brochure.

FRIZZELL, F. G. & PARTNERS (Est: 1951)
133 Aldersgate St, London EC1A 4LE. 071-606 4134. FAX 071 606 2800.
S. Levrant – RIBA; AA Dipl; Dip Cons (AA); Member ASCHB; SPAB; Georgian Group; 30s Soc; Wallpaper History Soc; AM Soc   M. Smith – RIBA   G. McMorrough-Kavanagh – BA; Member AMSOC; Arch Historians of GB; Inst of Project Manager.
Pc Restoration, conversions, etc. of St James's Palace; Kensington Palace; Palace of Westminster; Osborne House; Frogmore House; Burlington House; Royal Hospital, Chelsea; Somerset House; V & A Museum; private listed buildings and commercial refurbishments.
Job values undertaken – £100,000–£6 m.

FRYER, RICHARD (Empl: one; Est: 1974)
Master Thatcher
10 Easthams Rd, Crewkerne, Somerset TA18 7AQ. 0460-74250.
Over 5 yrs training period; M Somerset MTA; Past Chairman; County Rep NCMTA.

FULLER, KATE BADEN
Stained Glass Artist
90 Greenwood Rd, Hackney, London E8 1NE. 071-249 0858.
MA (Royal College of Art) 1969.

Pc 2 windows – Sisters of Christ, Convent Chapel, Wotton under Edge, Glos and St Philip's RC Church, Finchley, London. 2 windows – Whitbread pub outside Winchester. Large mirrored panel for Unilever refurbishment, Blackfriars Bridge.

FURLONG & DAVIES (Empl: 4; Est: 1984)
Roofing Contractors
20 Bryniay Rd, Llandudno, Gwynedd, N. Wales LL30 2EL. 0492-75902 & 82840.
M LCA.
Pc Re-roofing – the nave, Bangor Cathedral, Lady Chapel and north aisle, Llandaff Cathedral. Leadwork contactors, Phrase V – Penrhyn Castle, Bangor.

FURNISHING WORKSHOP, THE (DOROTHY GATES, FAMU) (Empl: solo Est: 1989)
Master Upholsterer
Units 1 & 5 Clyde Road Works, Clyde Road, Wallington, Surrey SM6 8PZ. 081-773 3950.
Served apprenticeship; soft furnishing and upholstery teacher; Vice President AMU.
Lectures and demonstrations at AMU and WEFFA Conferences. 6 books published on soft-furnishing and upholstery. Television programme Better than New *on traditional upholstery. Courses for trade inc. curtains and pelmets; swags and tails; loose covers; upholstery. Brochure.*

GALAXY GLASS GLASGOW (Est: 1980)
Joe Boyle, Berkley Terrace Lane, Charing Cross, Glasgow. 041-221 6765 (24 hrs).
Dip Stained Glass & Mural Design – Glasgow School of Art; they consider their best qualification is 'that we work, design and make to a higher standard than any other company in Britain, and possibly Europe.'
Pc Contract lighting for pubs; discos; hotels; public buildings; etc. Commission windows for domestic, church, public licensed buildings, etc, both in UK and abroad. 'First European retail stained glass shipped by Galaxy'.
Specialize in post modern, deco and Rennie Mackintosh.

GALE, KEITH
Architectural Stained Glass
16 Park St, St James Square, Bath, Avon BA1 2TE. 0225-24826.
B Tech Higher Dip Architectural Stained Glass; M BSMGP.
Pc Toothill Community Centre, Swindon, Wilts.

FIRMS AND CRAFTSPEOPLE

Exhibited throughout England.

GALLIER, PAUL DE (Empl: solo; Est: 15 yrs experience)
Specialist Woodworker
58 Nelson St, Market Harborough, Leics LE16 9AY. 0858-66284
Furniture Design/Making Cert; M SPAB.
Pc 8 handmade windows and doors – listed building in Herts. Work to date inc. furniture restoration/making and designing; various repairs to architectural joinery; purpose made and architectural joinery to specification.
Although will repair staircase and balustrading, does not have sufficient space to manufacture new. Portfolio of work kept for inspection.

GALVIN, C. T. SPECIALIST DECORATOR (Empl: 2; Est: 1973)
25 Eastgate St, Winchester, Hants SO23 8EB. 0962-69763.
Apprenticeship with Frank Devine, decorator, Liverpool; Liverpool College of Art; M GMC.
Pc Restoration and decorative work, inc. antiquing, marbling, dragging, to many parts of Hunton Manor, Hunton, Hampshire (incorporated in *House & Gardens* Dec/Jan/Feb '89).

GARD, NIGEL – MASTER THATCHER (Empl: one; Est: 1970)
1 High Cross, Swimbridge, Barnstaple, N. Devon EX32 0PU. 0271-830 518.
Qualified as a Master Thatcher.
Pc 'I have had over the years the good fortune to be able to help in the restoration of many historic thatched houses, cottages and outbuildings.'

GARMESTON, C. – PAINTING/DECORATING SERVICE
10 Cherry Grove, Frome, Somerset BA11 4AW. 0373-66471.
BDA; GMC.

GARNER, CHARLES F. (Est: 1972)
Wood Carver
The End House, Forster Rd, Salcombe, S. Devon TQ8 8EB. 054 884 2448.
Working in conjunction with joiners & shipwrights in Eng. and France.
Pc Various carved items on furniture, architectural details, ship fittings and figureheads, etc. (the latest on board *The Lord Nelson*).

GARVEY, WILLIAM (Empl: 7; Est: 1971)
Furniture Design & Architectural Joinery
Leyhill, Upton, Pamembury, Honiton, Devon EX14 0JG. 0404-84430.
All employees – combination of apprenticeship and C & Gs, leading to Craft Cert.
Pc Variety of work ranging from individual pieces to complete rooms of architectural joinery. Recent commissions inc. walnut bookcase to house 6 early Victorian bound books; reception desk – Vidal Sasoon Ltd; refurbishment and new furnishing of office – Lincoln's Inn; boardroom furniture – London Law Ltd.

GATES BUILDERS LTD (Empl: 25; Est: 1955)
Green Pastures, Lillingston Lovell, Buckingham MK18 5BD. 02806-444.
BEC; NHBC. Approved: Aylesbury Vale DC; Bucks CC; South Northants DC; Post Office; Anglian Water; Milton Keynes Development Corporation.
Pc Internal refurbishment and external hard landscaping – the Old Goal at Buckingham. Redevelopment of 16th-century cottages into shopping centre – Meadow Row, Buckingham. General repair – Stone Castle, Nr Buckingham. Restoration and refurbishment works inc. brick coach house/barn – Great Harwood, Bucks; brick barn – Great Horwood; – old stables, Buckingham.
A medium-sized company employing approx 30 men, most of whom are craftsmen. Customer satisfaction is high on their list of priorities, and all work receives the personal attention of one of the 3 directors.

GATES, GEOFF – THATCHING (Empl: 1–4; Est: 1967)
'Danebury View', Kents Boro, Middle Wallop, Stockbridge, Hants SO20 8EA. 0264-781 596.
Self taught.
Pc Numerous (approx 6–8 jobs per year)

GAVIN, DAVID FURNISHINGS (Empl: 2; Est: 1982)
Specialist Upholsterers
The Old Coach House, 5 Egerton Crescent, Withington, Manchester M20 9PN. 061-445 4659.
M AMU.
Also willing to undertake linen loose covers, curtains. Some settees and armchairs made to order.

GAYLORDS ANTIQUES (Empl: 5; Est: 1971)
Furniture Restorer & Cabinet Maker
75 West St, Titchfield, Fareham, Hants PO14 4DG. 0329-43402.
All apprenticed.

FIRMS AND CRAFTSPEOPLE

GB GLAZING, STAINED GLASS
109 Clarkston Rd, Glasgow, Strathclyde G44 3BL. 041-637 9739.
Scottish Glass Assoc.
Pc Church of Scotland repair work to various churches and related properties over the last 5 yrs.

GB PROPERTIES
Thatchers
The Manse, 61 Whitsbury Rd, Fordingbridge, Hants, SP6 1LB. 0425-56412 & 55064.
Also undertake the renovation of period cottages.

GEDDING MILL FORGE (E. C. HITCHCOCK) (Empl: 2–3; Est: 1983)
Artist Blacksmith
Mill House, Gedding, Bury St Edmunds, Suffolk IP30 0PZ. 04493-301.
M BABA.
Rebuilding of gates; railings and structural steel items for building repairs; lamps; fireplaces; latches and hinges for gates and doors; locks; ornamental steel brackets; etc. Repairs in wrought/cast iron undertaken, but not new work in this material.

GEERS, PHILIP (Empl: solo; Est: 1973)
Ratten Furniture
Turkey Cottage, Curload, Stoke St Gregory, Taunton, Somerset TA3 6JE. 082 369-571.
M Somerset Guild of Craftsmen; M Basketmakers Assoc.
Pc Extensive – for furniture makers, antique dealers, furniture restorers, hotels and private owners, inc. minor repair to furniture frames.

GEOMETRICAL STAIRBUILDING (Empl: 3; Est: 1984)
22 Taffs Mead Embankment, Cardiff CF1 7RH. 0222-374 960.
A cabinet maker by trade, and a joiner (Stan Thomas, of *Woodworker* magazine).
Mainly the manufacture, installation and restoration of wooden stairs in London and S Glamorgan, but also undertakes circle on circle windows, and very special doors. Carving and turning is only done in connection with stair manufacture.

GIBBS, CHRISTOPHER (Est: 1974)
Incorporated Building Surveyor & Chartered Surveyor
Willow Cottage, 41 School Lane, Tedburn St Mary, Exeter, Devon EX6 6AA. 064 76-440.
FFS; MCSI.

Pc Alterations and extension – Westwood Farm, Hillisleigh, Exeter. Conversion of linhay – Aller Farm, Christow Estate.

GIBBERD, VERNON (Est: 1972)
Architects
45 Glebe Place, Chelsea, London SW3 5JE. 071-351 6728.
Dip Arch; RIBA.
Pc Conversion of 4 listed buildings – St James's Place for J. Rothschild & Co. New aviaries, maze and grotto – Leeds Castle, Maidstone, Kent. Restoration of Old Battersea House, London for Malcolm Forbes. Alterations – Arundel Castle for the Earl of Arundel.

GIBSON & GOOLD LTD (Empl: 50; Est: 1913)
Fireplace Restoration
1/3 Scotland St, Glasgow G5 8LS. 041-429 7997.
SFAS; Nat Fireplace Council; Corgi.
Pc Various restorations in Glasgow area – contracts up to £10,000.
Brochure.

GIDDINGS, CHRISTOPHER JOHN
Master Thatcher
Elm Tree Cottage, 47 Potterne, Devizes, Wilts SN10 5WL. 0380-6160.
Wilts & Hants MTA.

GIDNEY, PATRICIA
See FLEUSS, GERALD (& PATRICIA GIDNEY)

GILBERT, JOAN (Empl: 2 part time: Est: 1965)
Cane & Rush Seating
50 Ashbourne Rd, Derby DE3 3AD. 0332-44363.
Pc Work for London antique restorers and great houses.
All patterns of cane can be reproduced inc. single set; sunset patterns; hanging medallions; blind holes. Only the best materials are used.

GILLETT & JOHNSTON (CROYDON) LTD (Est: 1844)
Designers, Makers, Installers & Servicing Engineers of Tower & Hanging Clocks
Redsan Works, 28 Sanderstead Rd, S Croydon, Surrey CR2 0PA. 081-686 2694 & 081-688 0851.
Pc St James's Palace. Manchester Town Hall. Coventry Cathedral. Tesco Supermarket, Watford. Ottawa Parliament, Canada. Royal Courts of Justice, London. University of Chicago. Shell Mex, South Bank, London. Royal Exchange, London. Toronto City Hall. Mulligar Cathedral, Eire. S'Hertogenbosch, St Jan Cathedral, Holland. Seclin, France. Louvain Library, Belgium.

FIRMS AND CRAFTSPEOPLE

GILLIAM, TONY GLASS ENGRAVING (Empl: solo; Est: 1981)
29 West St, Alresford, Hants SO24 9AV. 0962-734 504.
AF GGE; 1982 Worshipful Co of Glass Sellers Award.
Pc Memorial window (using drill technique) – St Jude's Church, London. Lettering on panel (using sandblast) – Winchester Cathedral. Portrait of founder with views of showroom on goblet (using diamond point) – Electrical Co.

GILSON, DAVID JOINER & TURNER (Empl: solo; Est: 8 yrs self-employed)
Old End Cottage, Zion Hill, Oakhill, Somerset BA3 5AN. 0749-840 675.
C & Gs Intermediate and Final Cert's Carpentry & Joinery.

GLANTAWE STUDIOS (Empl: 4; Est: 1968)
Stained Glass Artists/Painters
118 Glantawe St, Morriston, Swansea, W Glam SA6 8BP. 0792-790 521.
Nat Dip Design; A RCA; Art Teachers Dip; A BSMGP.
Pc New window and restoration – All Saints' Church, Mumbles, Swansea; All Saints' Rhibwana, Cardiff; St Theodore's, Port Talbot; St Joseph's, Umlaneath; St Luke's, Cwmdar, Aberdare; St Paul's, Porth; Berwyn School, Bala; St David's, Morriston; Llansamlet Church, Swansea.
Also works as head of the Stained Glass Dept at Swansea School of Art which 'is the main centre for teaching stained glass, attracting students from far and wide'.

GLASHAUS – ARCHITECTURAL & INTERIOR GLASS (Empl: 3; Est: 1984)
Quay House, Quay Road North, Rutherglen Ind. Estate, Glasgow G73 1LD. 041-613 1414.
Erika Shovelin & Yvonne Smith – BA Hons (CNAA Fine Art) Stained Glass Artist.
Margaret-Anne Jones – 4th yr trainee, Stained Glass Artist.
Pc Guild Hall, Queen St, Glasgow. MacLaurin Art Gallery, Ayr. Leeds Casino. Princes Casino, Sauchiehall St, Glasgow.
Work ranges from standard ranges of moulded glasslight fittings to studio glassware, glass/mixed media sculptural work and complete stained glass schemes.

GLASSLIGHT STUDIOS LTD (Empl: 2; Est: 1982)
1st Floor, The Old Pumphouse, Gloucester Pl, Maritime Quarter, Swansea SA1 1TY. 0792-472 595.
C & Gs Stained Glass I & II. Elizabeth Edmunson – Inst Dip, 4th yr.
Pc Various churches inc. Our Lady of the Rosary, RC Church, Ammanford, Llanbadarn. Fawr Church, Nr Aberystwyth. Also numerous autonomous panels, domestic windows, pub/restuarant

work, restoration, etc.

GLASS MARKET, THE (Empl: 9; Est: 1979)
Stained Glass Artist
Broad Lane, Wooburn Green, High Wycombe, Bucks HP10 0LL. 0494-671 033.
Training and work experience in UK, USA, Canada, Germany and Middle East; Fellowship – Winston Churchill Memorial Trust.
Pc 6 large windows – Bristol University. Numerous church and institution window renovations. Stained glass domes, rooflights and windows in Middle East.

GLASS MOUNTAIN STUDIOS (Empl: one; Est: 1982)
Stained Glass Artist/Painter
Unit 9, 51 Price St, Lancaster Circus, Birmingham, W. Midlands B4 6JZ. 021-359 3124.
Foundation yr and Art & Design Cert, Hammersmith; 6 yr apprenticeship at John Hardman Studios, Birmingham (see entry under that name); AM BSMGP.
Pc 19 ft figurative window – St Mary Magdalene Church, Coventry. 8 panel screen – private home, Maidenhead. Commemorative chapel window – Felixstowe College for Girls. Set of heraldic windows – one of 'Pet Shop Boys'.
Painting; enamelling; etching; staining and gilding. Cleaning, retouching and adjusting undertaken after final installation, ensuring full satisfaction with the final work of art. Conservation work includes the use of specialist adhesives. Glass cleaning will be done using care and specialist solvents. Brochure.

GLASS WORKS, THE (Empl: 2; Est: 1984)
Stained Glass Artist
69 Wellington St, Luton, Beds. 0582-419 902.
Pc Chancel windows – Wester Underwood Church, Olney, Bucks.

GLENWOOD LTD (Empl: 18; Est: 1979)
Construction & Management Services
Glimstock Hill, Lichfield Rd, Coleshill, Birmingham, W. Midlands B46 1LE. 0675-65075.
NHBC; FMB; apprenticed joiner; M CIOB. Approved: Coventry Local Authority; C of E Diocesan.
Pc Restoration of large Elizabethan Manor House. Restoration of Victorian, Georgian and Palladian properties.

GLOVER & STACEY LTD (Empl: 7; Est: 1980)
Archtectural Antiques & Fireplaces
Grange Farm, Grange Rd, Tongham, Nr Farnham, Surrey GU10 1DN.

FIRMS AND CRAFTSPEOPLE

02518-2804. Head Office & Accounts: Oaklands House, Solartron Rd, Farnborough, Hants. 0252-549 334.

Pc Numerous listed buildings on both supply and install basis inc. Hampton Court and York Minster.

GLYNWED FOUNDRIES (Est: 1939)
Building & Construction Products
PO Box 3, Sinclair, Ketley, Telford, Shropshire TF1 4AD. 0952-641 414.
Inst of Plumbers; Brit Foundry Assoc; BSI.

Pc Cast iron rainwater pipes, gutters, etc. for public and historic buildings nationwide inc. Kew Gardens; Wigan Market Redevelopment; Ellen Road Trust Restoration.

Cast iron street furniture, rainwater pipes, gutters and fittings. Brochure.

GMS RESTORATIONS (Empl: 5 Est: 1984, originally 1972)
Furniture Restoration and Reproduction
Office: 38 High St, Wickwar. Workshops: Arnolds Field Estate, Wickwar, Glos GL12 8NP 0454-294251.
GMC; LAPADA; AMU; The Soc of Wood Craftsmen.

Made-to-measure curtains and pelmets; roller and louverite blinds; pianos polished and reconditioned; fabrics and wallpapers by Laura Ashley, Parkertex, Barkers and Pallu & Lake; picture restorations.

GODDEN, J. P. GLASS DESIGN (Empl: 2; Est: 1985)
Stained Glass & Leaded Lights
Teewell Cottage, 8 Gloucester Rd, Staple Hill, Bristol BS16 4SD. 0272-565 804.
Art qualifications.

Pc Bi-centenial window – Winterbourne Methodist Church, Bristol. Numerous interesting commissions in Cotswold area, and restorations of antique windows.

GODFREY, JOAN (Est: 1962)
Hand-painted Ceramic Tiles
The Studio at Kiln Cottage, 38 Boase St, Newlyn, Penzance, Cornwall TR18 5JE.

Pc Ceramic relief hand-modelled panel of Market House, Penzance. Glazing with fused glass decoration, 3 ft × 1 ft 6 inch, Market House Craft Gallery, Penzance.

Also undertakes work with glass-fusing in the kiln; laminated glass panels with fused glass inclusions for small windows, free-standing panels, room dividers, boxes. Brochure.

GOFF, LEONARD (Empl: solo; Est: 1962)
Cabinet Making, Wood Carving, etc
52–54 Carey's Rd, Pury End, Nr Towcester, Northants NN12 7NX.
032-733 666.
Pc Too numerous to detail.

GOLIGHTLY ANTIQUE RESTORATIONS (Empl: 2; Est: 1972)
Furniture Restorer
69 Kent Rd, Glasgow G3 8NG. 041-221 7472.
Employ one cabinet maker and one lassie – a carpenter and trainee cabinet maker.
Pc Repairing antiques for grand house owners and modest house-owners for 30 yrs.

GOLDSWORTHY, ANDREW (Empl: 3; Est: 1972)
Fine Signwriting, Pictorial Inn Signs & Sign Manufacture
Northover Buildings, Beckery, Glastonbury, Somerset BA6 9NY.
0458-34660.
Craft M Somerset Guild of Craftsmen.
Pc Restoration and gilding of ceiling – Sherborne Castle, Dorset. Restoration of fairground architecture (rides/fairground organs) for various clients and collectors. Restoration of unique carved and painted west doors – Norton-sub-Hamdon Church.
A small signwriting business supplying high quality signwriting and pictorial signs to a wide range of businesses and private client's. Painting; gilding; computer cut vinyl lettering; screen printing; illuminated box signs; magnetic signs; perspex.

GOODCHILD DESIGNS (Est: 1987)
1 Great George St, Bristol, Avon BS1 5RR. 0272-291997.
St Martin's School of Art, Foundation yr; C & Gs Carpentry & Joinery, Dist, Credit; Building BSc, 1st yr pass.
Pc References can be supplied.
A designer able to undertake work ranging from special drawings and details of individual period items to complete interior design work. Contract sums from £5,000 to £250,000. Interior design, technical drawings.

GORDON, ALEX PARTNERSHIP (Est: 1948)
Architects & Project Managers
124–130 Tabernacle St, London EC2A 4SD. 01-251 8787.
M RIBA, etc.
Pc Palace of Westminster (over 10 yrs). Morgam Orangery. Historic buildings in Surrey, N. Yorkshire and Humberside.

FIRMS AND CRAFTSPEOPLE

GORDON, ALEX PARTNERSHIP
Architects & Project Managers
Suite 5, York House, 15 Clifford St, York. 0904-627 151.
M RIBA, etc.
Pc Stonework restoration and cleaning – Howden Minster; Hemsley Castle; Scarcroft Lodge. Ceramic tile restoration – York Health Authority.

GOTCH PEARSON – ARCHITECTS & SURVEYORS (Est: earliest constituent 1877)
18 Sheep St, Wellingborough, Northants NN8 1BL. 0933-225 848.
RIBA; FAS; EASA; RSA.

GOULDER, DAVE – DRY STONE WALLS (Empl: solo; Est: 1977)
Rosehall, Lairg, Sutherland IV27 4BD. 054-984 283.
Master Craftsman Cert, DSWA; Instructor with Agricultural Training Board.
Pc Instruction courses in Scotland & USA, resulting in many examples of building, too numerous to detail.
Although no longer able to undertake full time dry stone walling, has extended instruction courses into the private sector.

GOURNEY, DE DESIGNS (Empl: 150; Est: 1987)
Hand-painted Wallpapers
41 Brompton Square, London SW3 2AF. 071-823 7316.
Artists in China and the Phillipines who have received 8 yrs of formal training in art, prior to joining the firm.

GRACE, CAROLE (Est: 1978)
Weaver
Snettisham Studio, 1 Lynn Rd, Snettisham, King's Lynn, Norfolk PE31 7LW. 0485-41167.
Cert Ed FE.
Willing to supply only small quantities of fabric.

GRAFTON/TILLY FINE ANTIQUE RESTORATION (Empl: 3; Est: 1975)
Meadhay House, Dunsford, Exeter, Devon EX6 7HE. 0647-52365.
Ben Grafton – apprenticed to father Francis Grafton, a well known furniture restorer in Bath, for 6 yrs; worked under various people in Italy and France. Petra Tilly – Design Degree; Roger Newton School of Decorative Finishes; 8 yrs experience.
Pc Supplied on request, but unwilling to publish due to respect for clients' privacy.
Specialize in all kinds of gilded, French polished, fumed, limed, lacquered

finishes, inc. museum techniques for the conservation of painted furniture, lacquerwork, gilding and gesso if needed. Will reproduce to match existing and design to specification if work interesting and difficult. Restore and conserve murals and fresco work, but undertake no new work on murals. At present they only undertake site work for short periods, due to the demands of small children, and workshop commitments (5 days in 7 possible for up to a month).

GRAHAMSTON IRON CO LTD (Empl: 300; Est: 1868)
PO Box 5, Gowan Avenue, Falkirk, Stirlingshire FK2 7HH. 0324-22661. FAX 0324 611 463.
Over the yrs apprentices have won many prizes and Certificates of Merit at the National Foundry and Engineering Training Courses.
Pc 12 reproduction cast iron cannons (pattern taken from existing cannon) – Fort George, Inverness.
Founded by William Thomson Mitchell this firm designed and manufactured the 20 ton gateway through which Queen Victoria entered the 1868 International Exhibition in Edinburgh. Today the gateway forms the main entrance to this firm, which still produces Victorian cast iron rainwater, soil and drain goods; dog grates; garden seat ends.

GRANDISON, L. & SON (Est: 1886)
Ornamental Plasterwork
Innerleithen Rd, Peebles, Tweeddale EH45 8BA. 0721-20212.
Prinicpals Leonard S. Grandison – MCIOB and John C. Grandison – B Sc.
Pc Repairs to ornamental ceilings inc. Thirustane Castle, Lauder; Blair Castle, Blair Atholl; Marchmont House, Greenlaw, Berwickshire; Museum of Childhood, High St, Edinburgh.
Also operate 'The Cornice', Scottish Museum of Ornamental Plasterwork, a recreation of a plasterer's casting workshop at the turn of the century, illustrating the main methods of creating ornamental plasterwork at that time. Displayed is one of the largest collections of plaster 'masters' in Scotland which are available for clients' use.

GRANDISSON INTERNATIONAL (Est: 1980)
Craftsmen in Wood
The Old Hall, West Hill Rd, West Hill, Ottery St Mary EX11 1TP. 040 481-2876 & 5400. FAX 040 481-3350.
Hand-carved doors and furniture made to customers' own design and specification. Also produce a standard range inc. doors; four poster beds; head boards; bedroom furniture; fire surrounds and overmantels; wall panelling; office furniture. Brochure.

FIRMS AND CRAFTSPEOPLE

GRANGE 81 LIMITED (Empl: approx 8; Est: 1981)
Design & Construct
Grange House, Steele Rd, Lower Place, London NW10 7AR. 081-950 2915 & 961 4855.
FMB. Approved; St Albans Diocesan; Eng. Heritage; London Boroughs of Barnet and Harrow.
Pc Various, but unable to publish due to respect for clients' privacy. Further information and viewing of properties can be arranged through Peter Blake.
A general contractor covering the whole spectrum from initial design right through to soft furnishings and decorations, specializing particularly in restoration (several such projects are to be submitted for Civic Trust Awards).

GRANGE RESTORATIONS (MICHAEL NICKSON) (Empl: one; Est: 1979)
Fine Furniture Restoration & Conservation
179 Park Avenue, Southall, Middx UB1 3AL. 081-574 8317.
Apprentice served; approx 30 yrs experience; M UKIC; Teacher of Restoration.
Pc Unwilling to give details due to respect for clients' privacy, but inc. museums, major auction houses, and antique dealers.
Willing to consider almost anything in the field of fine furniture conservation and restoration; painted furniture restoration; ivory; tortoiseshell; amber; jade; semi-precious and precious stones inlaid into metal (i.e. swords).

GRATE EXPECTATIONS (Est: 1983)
Period Fireplaces
6 Lee Close, Pattinson North Ind Estate, Washington, Tyne & Wear NE38 8QA. 091-416 0609. 36a Camden Lock, London NW1 8AF. 071-482 2543.
Pc Restoration and supply of original antique fireplaces in cast iron, wood, marble and slate to various large buildings under general refurbishment in the London area.
Brochure.

GRAY, JANE (Est: 1955)
Stained Glass Artist/Painter
Ferry Cottage, Shrawardine, Shrewsbury, Shropshire SY4 1AJ. 0743-850 031.
A RCA; F BSMGP.
Pc Alphabet of flowers (6 panels stained glass) – Marriage Room, Civic Centre, Uxbridge. Arms of the Worshipful Co of Launderers, Glaziers Hall, London Bridge. 15 windows – St Peter's, Martindale, Ullswater, Cumbria.

GREAVES-LORD, SALLY (Est: 1982)
231 Camden Rd, London N7 0HR. 071-609 6068.
1st BA (Hons) Textiles; MA RCA.
Pc Pieces in public collections – V & A 20th century collection. Commissions of banners in silk for Savills, Elementar and many architectural practices.

GREEN, TOBY, DR
Restorer of Rugs
Whitcombe Farm, Beaminster, Dorset. 0308-862 366.
Apprenticeship at Thornborough Gallery, Cirencester and Corpus Christi College, Cambridge University.
As well as restoring Oriental rugs will also save old rugs that have 'become family friends, to make their old age more comfortable and less hazardous to the owner and rug'. Does not work for the trade. May be a long waiting list.

GREENS OF WINCANTON LTD (Empl: 16; Est: 1835)
73 High St, Wincanton, Somerset BA9 9JX. 0963-33215.
BEC; FMB; NHBC. Approved; Diocesan; Somerset CC; Wessex Hospital Authority, etc.
Pc Conversion of barn, Witham Friary for Rodney Goodall RIBA, FRSA, Historic Building Consultant. Renovation – Donhead St Mary for Wm. Bertram & Fell, Bath. Church works for Robert J. Potter & Partners, Salisbury, Wilts.

GREENWOOD, ERIC (Est: 1981)
Professional Dry Stone Walling Craftsman
Ormerod Cottage, Red Lees Rd, Cliviger Burnley, Lancs BB10 4RF. 0282-37704.
Professional Dry Stone Walling Association.

GREEVES, ELEANOR (Empl: solo; Est: 1970)
Hand-screen-printed Ceramic Wall Tiles
12 Newton Grove, Bedford Park, London W14 1LB. 081-994 6523.
Qualified as architect, gaining Architectural Assoc Dip and ARIBA. Studied ceramic screen-printing at Goldsmith's College, London.
Pc Repeated commissions (public buildings for DOE) for Architects Manning Champ & Partners, and also for Green Lloyd Architects (London office buildings). Commissions (restoration work) – Architects Donald Insall & Associates.
Brochure.

GREGSON, DAVID FURNITURE (Empl: 2; Est: 1978)
Bridge Green Farm, Gissing Rd, Burston, Nr Diss, Norfolk IP22 3UD. 0379-740 528.

Norfolk Furniture Makers Assoc; Full M Contempory Applied Artists; Norfolk Contemporary Crafts Society. Suffolk Crafts Society.
Pc Fitted screen and benches (7m × 2m) – Riverside Court, Farnham, Surrey. Credence table – St John The Evangelist Church, Churt, Surrey.
Works using a combination of modern machining methods, traditional hand techniques, depending on the design and function of the piece. Finishing with 'sound designs that are modern, distinctive and functional'. Small batch runs and items suitable for presentation also undertaken. Brochure.

GRICE, ALAN (Empl: 3; Est: 1945)
Furniture Restorer
106 Aughton St, Ormskirk, Lancs L39 3BS. 0696-72007.
Cabinet Maker; ACIOB.
Pc Restoration of antique furniture for private homes.

GRIEVE, THOMAS (Empl: one; Est: 1965)
Dry Stone Dyking & Stone Masonry
Leslie Cottage, Philiphaugh, Selkirk TD7 5LS. 0750-20033.
Served 5 yr apprenticeship; M Dry Stone Walling Assoc.
Pc Dry stone dyking – Buccleuch Estates Ltd; Philipbough Estates; Border Regional Council; Hyndhope Forms Ltd; FBR Kelso; Glasgow Garden Festival.

GRIFFIN, A. E. & SON (Empl: 11; Est: 1853)
Building Contractors
10 North St, Bere Regis, Wareham, Dorset BH20 7LA. 0929-471 253.
R. M. Griffin – MCIOB; firm is M BEC. Approved: Salisbury Diocese; Eng. Heritage; National Trust; Forestry Commission.
Pc Appointed contractor (on permanent basis) for care of Milton Abbey, Dorset under direction of The Sarum Partnership. Numerous contracts for 30 Dorset churches under direction of The Sarum Partnership; Crickhay Partnership; John Stark & Partners; Stephen Hebb. Work closely with Pamela Cunningham, author of numerous books on architectural conservation.
This firm is owned and run by the great grandson and great-great grandson of the founder. The 'average' service of their craftsmen is over 20 yrs. M SPAB.

GRIFFIN & ASHWELL WOODCARVERS (Empl: 3 craftsmen; Est: 1945)
1a Bouverie Rd, Stoke Newington, London N16 0AH. 081-800 4191.
Master Carvers Assoc. Approved; PSA.
Pc House of Lords ceiling. Hampton Court. Oak linenfold – Westminster Palace. Large bracket clock – St James. Garlickhythe, Upper Thames St. Bridgewater House, St James.

GUERNSEY WOODCARVERS

GRIFFITHS, A. D. (VENEERS) LTD (Empl: 3; Est: 1975)
7 Carman St, London E14 6AX. Oak Lodge, Broomhills Chase, Little Burstead, Billericay, Essex CM12 9TG. 071-515 7711.

GRIFFITHS, H. & SON (MELIN TREGWYNT) (Empl: 12; Est: 1912)
Tregwynt Mill, Letterston, Haverfordwest, Dyfed SA62 5UX. 03485-225.
M Brit Design Group; Wales Craft Council; Pembrokeshire Craftsmen's Circle.
Brochure.

GRIFFITHS, M. E. & S. R. GARDEN POTS (Empl: 2; Est: 1975)
The Old School, Culmington, Nr Ludlow, Shropshire SY8 2DF. 058 473-212.
Trained as a repetition thrower.
Pc Have reproduced a number of classic garden pots, floor tiles and edging tiles. Also made a set of plaques, modelled in the last century, for the Ironbridge Gorge Museum.
An established country pottery making traditional items both to own designs and to commission inc. large terracotta garden pots, ornamentation, etc..

GRIFFITHS, T. J. (Empl: 3; Est: 1968)
Master Thatcher
Pixford Lodge, Bishop's Lydeard, Somerset TA4 3HS. 0823-432 662.
5 yrs apprenticeship; Master Thatcher Certificate. M Somerset MTA.

GRUNEWALD, THEO (Empl: solo; Est: 1958)
Artist Blacksmith
2 Cynllan Cottage, Llanharan CF7 9NH. 0443-222 & 229 427.
Journeyman's Cert; Engine Drivers Cert; M BABA; self-employed as artisan blacksmith since 1958.
Pc Fittings – Atlantic College. Church figures made from steel. Candlesticks and crosses for altars. Weather-vanes for London and Swansea Marina. Architects endorsement for Swansea Holiday Inn. Gates, railings etc.

GUBBIN, DAVID (STAINED GLASS) (Empl: 4; Est: 1944)
4 Well St, Exeter, Devon EX4 6QR. 0392-72799.
Pc Stained glass, new and restoration, for approx 50 churches a yr inc. Exeter Cathedral, Exeter City Council, National Trust and public houses, etc.

GUERNSEY WOODCARVERS (Empl: 10; Est: 1978)
Les Issues, St Saviours, Guernsey, Channel Islands. 0481-65373.

FIRMS AND CRAFTSPEOPLE

State's apprentice; Chairman of the Guernsey Guild of Creative Arts. Pc 300 chairs for Peterborough Cathedral.

HADDONSTONE LTD (Empl: 50; Est: 1971)
Reconstructed Limestone
The Forge House, E Haddon, Northants NN6 8DB. 0604-770 711 & 770 365.
BMEG; IDDA.
Pc Replica portico pinnacles replaced – Belvoir Castle, Rutland. Replaced ornamental stonework – Margam orangery, S. Wales. Replacement work to ornate parapet – Waddesdon Manor, Aylesbury.
Brochure.

HALL, ADRIAN WESSEX THATCHERS (Empl: 8; Est: 1984)
7 Poles Lane, Otterbourne, Winchester, Hants SO21 2DS. 0962-713 022 & 0734-328 201.
GMC; applied for membership Assoc of Master Thatchers.
Specializes in restoring tiled/slate roofs that were originally thatched, to their previous state. Free quotations.

HALL, DIANA
See ANGUS DESIGNS

HALL MARQUE DESIGNS (W. B. LEGGETT) (Empl: solo; Est: 1979)
Cabinet Making & Woodturning
The Station House, Digby, Lincs LN4 3NF. 0526-20018.
25 yrs experience cabinet making; on Register of Worshipful Co of Turners.
General repair, repolishing, and manufacturing of domestic furniture. Photographs of previous commissions available to callers.

HALL, PETER & SON (Empl: 9; Est: 1970)
Cabinet Makers & Restorers
Danes Rd, Staveley, Kendal, Cumbria LA8 9PL. 0539-821 633.

HALLAM, PAUL (Empl: one; Est: 1982)
Dry Stone Walling
75 North Rd, Wibsey, Bradford, W Yorks BD6 1RJ. 0274-677 741.
Master Craftsman, Dry Stone Walling Assoc.

HALLIDAYS (Est: 1948)
Designers & Makers of Hand-carved Pine Installations
Head Office & Showrooms: The Old College, Dorchester-on-Thames,

HAMILTON-HILL, MAUREEN

Oxon OX9 8HL. 0865-340 028. London Showrooms: 28 Beauchamp Place, Knightsbridge, London, SW3 1NJ. 071-589 5534.
Master Craftsmen.
Pc Ranges from libraries in universities and panelled penthouse suites to projects for semi-detached houses and country cottages.
Stock antique furniture; reproduction pine mantels; period firegrates, fenders, marble-slips and other fire-side accessories. List of stockists available. Brochure.

HALLWORTH, SIMON
Master Thatcher
7 Raglans, Dawlish Rd, Alphington, Exeter. 0392-431 449.
M Devon and Cornwall MTA.
Pc Work carried out for National Trust.

HAMER, FRANK (Empl: solo, Est: 1978 present studio)
Stoneware Tiles
Llwyn-on, Croes-yn-y-Pant, Mamhilad, Pontypool, Gwent NP4 8RE. 049 528-282.
Craftsmen Potters Assoc of GB; South Wales Potters.

HAMILTON, R. & CO LTD (Empl: 90; Est: 1968)
Period Style Electrical Switches & Lighting Control Systems
Unit G, Quarry Ind Estate, Mere, Wilts BA12 6LA. 0747-860 088.
DLA; Electrical Installation Equipment Manufacturers Assoc.
Pc Lighting control system, with control points on special size plates, finished to blend with wood panelling – Clothworkers Hall, London. Kuwaiti Conference Centre, Heads of States Residences.
Brochure.

HAMILTON, ROSEMARY O. DE C. (Est: 1970)
Interior Designer
44 Moreton St, London SW1V 2PB. 071-828 5018.
IDDA.
Pc Wide selection of domestic and commercial properties inc. Midlands Bank Office, Brussels; 2 chalets in Switzerland; 2 St James's Clubs.

HAMILTON-HILL, MAUREEN (Est: 1986)
Paper & Fabric Screens, Wallhangings & Lampshades
56a King Henry's Rd, London NW3 3RP. 071-586 2344.
M Fibre Art Group; Quilters Guild.
Pc Banner for Masonic Lodge. Ceremonial cloth for British Council of Women.
Photographs available on request.

FIRMS AND CRAFTSPEOPLE

HAMILTON-WESTON WALLPAPERS LTD (Empl: 3; Est: 1981, Ltd Co 1986)
18 St Mary's Grove, Richmond, Surrey TW9 1UY. 081-940 4850.
Trade Associate M IDDA; Wallpaper History Soc. Robert Weston –
BA Arch Hist & Int Design, Univ Oregon (Eugene), USA. An expert
on the history of wallpapers; worked as an architectural historian for
15 yrs; acts as consultant to Eng. Heritage.
Reproduction to authentic scale and colouring of period wallpapers and borders – 2 collections available. Designs can be produced on commission basis. Offer expert advice on period detail and decoration, and have a useful reference library to assist clients with restoration work. Also stock period wallpapers produced by other firms. Brochure.

HAMPSTEAD DECORATIVE ARTS (Empl: associates; Est: 1982)
Painter – Murals, Graining & Marbling, Stencilling, Gilding
35a Dartmouth Park Avenue, London NW5 1JL. 01-284 1830.
Dip London College of Furniture; C & Gs Wood Finishing.
Pc House of Frazer, Oxford St. Barracuda Casino, Baker St. Liberty's
Xmas window. Bonsack Bathrooms, Harrods, Knightsbridge.
Also undertakes teaching at School of Specialist Painting.

HAMPTON, RALPH (Empl: solo; Est: 8 yrs, 4 mths present address)
High Quality Joinery & Furniture
101 Wilmot St, Derby DE1 2JJ. 0332-293 687.
C & Gs Machine Woodworking I & II.
Specializes in traditional design Chinese hardwood furniture and doors and panelling of traditional English type.

HARDGRAVE, JOSEPH LTD (Empl: 20; Est: 1853)
Slate Merchants, Slating & Tiling Contractors
42–44 Church Lane, Bishopthorpe, York YO2 1QG. 0904-704 161/2.
NFRC; BEC.

HARDING, PAULINE
Mural Artist
Flat 3, 18 Nevern Place, London SW5 9PR. 071-370 2141.
Nat Dip in Design (Painting); Art Teachers Cert.
Pc GLC funded mural 'Murals for Peace' project. Various
educational projects (employed as tutor), helping youth groups
design and paint murals.

HARDING RESTORATION (Empl: one; Est: 1987)
Stone, Ivory & Objet d'Art Restoration
Unit 10 Grand Union Centre, Ladbroke Grove, London W10.
081-960 0538.

6½ yr apprenticeship in restoration studio, working on many different pieces inc. scagliola, stone, semi-precious stone, pietra dura, ceramics, enamels and sculpture.
Brochure.

HARDMAN, JOHN STUDIOS (Empl: 10, Est: 1838)
Stained Glass Artist
Lightwoods House, Lightwoods Park, Hagley Road West, Warley, W. Midlands B67 5DP. 021-429 7609.
Pc Rockhampton Cathedral, Australia. St Chad's Cathedral, Birmingham.

HARE, PETER J. SPECIALIST DECORATORS (Empl: 16; Est: 1983)
2 Chestnut Glen, Hornchurch, Essex RM12 4HL. 081-592 0874. HX 54587.
5 yr apprenticeship; City & Guilds with 3 credits; Advanced Craftsmanship Certificate – 2 distinctions and 1 credit.
Pc Restoration of 'Barry' Rooms (5 galleries) – National Gallery. Exterior guilding – Parliament. Livery Halls, Drapers Hall, Saddlers Hall. Major restoration of architecturally significant rooms – Spencer House. Stencilling to 5 galleries – National Portrait Gallery.

HARPER, PAUL (Est: 1986)
Furniture Maker
5a Broad St, Littledean, Nr Cinderford, Glos GL14 3NH. 0594-26255.
2nd Class Dip Hons Furniture Production & Management; 3 yrs making for Peter Milne, designer (see entry under this name).
Pc Large variety of commissions inc. work for churches and private clients.
Works extensively in collaboration with other craftsmen inc. a lettercutter and a blacksmith, mostly to commission.

HARRINGTON, ANTHONY (Empl: 6; Est: 1968)
Wood Carver
Squerries Court Workshops, Squerries Court, Westerham Kent. 0959-64936.
5 yrs apprenticeship, London College of Furniture; M Master Carvers Assoc; Brit Woodcarvers Assoc.
Pc Buckingham Palace. House of Lords. House of Commons. St Paul's Cathedral. V & A Museum. Brighton Pavillion. National Gallery. Ham House. Hampton Court. Clayton House. Clothworkers Hall. Skinners Hall. Spencer House. Shah of Persia. Art and antique dealers. Property in London, New York and Paris.
Brochure.

FIRMS AND CRAFTSPEOPLE

HARRINGTON, CELIA
Rug Designer/Maker
Unit 330, 30 Gt Guildford St, London SE1 0HS. 081-769 6214.
BA (Hons) Textiles; post grad in Textiles.
Pc 2 hand-tufted rugs for Connell May & Stevenson – reception area of William Blake House, London W1. 4 rugs for Pamela Stephenson and Billy Connolly's private residence.
All designs are one-off. Brochure.

HARRIS, JAMES UPHOLSTERY (Empl: 4; Est: 1981)
Unit 67, Abbey Business Centre, 15–17 Ingate Place, London SW8 3NS. 071-627 8232.
M AMU.
Pc Carried out high level of upholstery on Empire suite for antique dealer, subsequently sold at Sotherbys for £22,000 and featured in *Interiors* magazine.
Also manufacture own furniture; traditional and modern settees and sofa beds, and headboards. Undertakes on-site commissions, curtains, caning. Large discounts available on a variety of fabrics.

HARRISON, A. E. & SON (Est: 1865)
Marquetarians
A. C. Harrison, Proprietor, 'Intarsia', 11 Holyrood Close, Trowbridge, Wilts, BA14 0JT. 0225-765 113.
Third generation of marquetarians. A. C. Harrison was indentured to his father, who was in turn indentured to his father (present proprietor's grandfather).
Pc Supplied marquetry for *Queen Mary* liner in 1927 (present owner worked on all of it) and also the Blue Trains of France.
Will produce just one small panel for the restoration of a valuable antique, up to the quantity required to decorate a liner.

HARRISON & PITT CHARTERED ARCHITECTS & SURVEYORS (Est: 1979)
15 Dalton Square, Lancaster LA1 1PL. 0524-32479.
M. A. Harrison – Dip Arch; RIBA   D. W. Pitt – Dip Arch (Dist); RIBA
Architects to Diocese of Blackburn Parsonages Board.
Pc Conversion of Duddon Hall, Broughton-in-Furness. Listed building surveys for PSA, NW Region. Conversion of 3 warehouses, St George's Quay, Lancaster. Various Quinquennial surveys – Blackburn Diocese.

HARVEY, J. T. – PAINTERS & DECORATORS (Empl: 48; Est: 1870)
The Stables, 10 Broughton St Lane, Edinburgh, Lothian. 031-556 1460.
Fed of Master Decorators; time served journeymen.

Pc Marine-Harvest, Craicrook Castle, Edinburgh. Aberuchle Castle, Perthshire. Georgian House, Charlotte Sq, Edinburgh (National Trust). Dining room, George Hotel, Edinburgh.

HARZ, ANTHONY JOHN (Empl: one; Est: 1977)
Master Thatcher
42 Powderham Rd, Newton Abbot, Devon TQ12 1EZ. 6026-68822.
5 yrs apprenticeship; M Devon & Cornwall MTA; NCMT.
Pc New timberwork and recoating in wheat and water reeds. Also consulting with architects regarding roof structure to carry thatch.
Re-timbering without removal of roof only undertaken in certain circumstances.

HATHERNWARE CERAMICS LTD (Empl: 40; Est: 1874)
Station Works, Rempstone Rd, Normanton-on-Soar, Loughborough, Leics LE12 5EW. 0509-842 273.
Pc Red terracotta for new building and renovation – Reading Town Hall. Replacement units to roof area – Savoy Court East, Strand, London. Reconstructed facade – Hallingsworth Building, Calgary, Canada. Replacement balustrades and urns – Cliveden House, Taplow.
Brochure.

HAT INTERIORS – PHILLIPS (Empl: 25; Est: 1897)
Craftsmen in Decorative Plaster
123 Cemetery Rd, Beeston Hill, Leeds, W. Yorks LS11 85Z. 0532-716 605.
M GMC.
Pc Refurbished fibrous plasterwork back to original condition – Belford Hall, Northumberland. Modern GRG/Fibrous Plaster refurbishment – Bond St Shopping Centre, Leeds. Modern fibrous plaster fascias round escalator well – BHS Store, Kensington.
Also offer a comprehensive design service. Produce a standard range inc. corbels; niches; cornices; panel mouldings; ceiling centres. Brochure.

HAT INTERIORS VERONESE (Empl: 34; Est: 1989)
Craftsmen in Decorative Plaster
Interiors House, Lynton Rd, Crouch End, London N8. 081-348 4461.
CITB; LMPA; BEC.
Pc Dorchester Hotel, London. Alexandra Palace refurbishment. Duke of York Theatre.
Offer a complete service that commences with consultancy and design facility, through manufacturing to final installation on site inc. every type of painting, decorating and mirror work. Also stock a large range of standard cornices, models and moulds. Also willing to undertake architectural sculpture in glass re-inforced gypsum. Brochure.

FIRMS AND CRAFTSPEOPLE

HAVERS, HAMILTON (Empl: solo; Est: 1972)
Furniture Restorer
58 Conisboro Avenue, Caversham, Reading, Berks RG4 7JE. 0734-473 379.
Pc Restoration of furniture for Woburn Abbey; Althorp House; Croft Castle; public and private collections, both home and overseas. The top end of trade.
Specialist in English, French and continental period funiture, all forms of marquetry inc. ivory and mother of pearl inlays and tortoiseshell veneers and buhl marquetry.

HAWKINS, NEIL – GENERAL BLACKSMITHS (Empl: 4; Est: c. 1830)
19 Northfield Park, Pilton, Barnstaple, Devon EX31 1QA. 0271-71495.
Apprenticed blacksmith; Nat Cert Blacksmithing; RSS (Hons); etc. Neil Hawkins – Founder M Devon Guild of Craftsmen. David Hawkins – B Sc (Hons) DPS; M Ergs.
Design and make high quality gates, fire-irons, modern and traditional furniture in steel with special finishes and incorporating wooden components. Most work is one-off privately commissioned, but also undertake small batch production (100s, not 1000s). Brochure.

HAYLES & HOWE ORNAMENTAL PLASTERERS (Empl: 45; Est: 1978)
Picton House, 23–25 Picton St, Montpelier, Bristol BS6 5PZ. 46673 & 422 863 (night).
Several degrees and C & Gs indentures; Nat Fed of Building Trade Employees.
Pc Refurbishment/restoration – Hartwell House, Aylesbury. Conservation of Inigo Jones Cube Rooms – Wilton House, Wilts. Replastering of Tudor manor house using 16th century technology and materials – Llanfaiach House, Gwent. Conservation – Jacobean ceilings, Sherborne Castle, Dorset. Scagliola restoration – The Reform Club, Pall Mall, London. GRP ceilings, etc. – Bermuda House, Guernsey (Plasterers Trophy Award South East).
Modelling and moulding scagliola; glass reinforced gypsum. Also experienced in new or unusual work. Standard range inc. ceiling roses; cornices; arches; columns; niches; fire surrounds. Restoration of ancient ceilings.

HAYMAN, G. H.
Master Thatcher
'Pocatello', Hartop Rd, St Mary Church, Torquay, Devon TQ1 4QQ.
Cert Master Thatcher.

HAYMAN, PETER (Empl: solo; Est: 1988)
Stonemason, Carver & lettercutter

Riverside Works, Bathpool, Taunton, Somerset TA1 2DX. 0823-256 028.
C & Gs Advanced Craft 1st Prize; various other technical awards during full indentured apprenticeship; M Somerset Guild of Craftsmen; Somerset Chamber of Commerce.
Pc Carved finials. Tudor fireplaces. Complete mullion windows. Tracery windows. Carved panels. Coats of arms. Lettering. Gargoyles.
Prefers to work on one-off pieces which cannot be mass produced.

HAYNES, NELSON (Est: 1963)
Specialist Joinery
Lawnhill Farm, Eydon, Nr Daventry, Northants NN11 6PE. 029 576-588.
Trade apprenticeship served in joiners workshop, Bosworth & Wakeford, Rugby.
Pc Replacement windows for listed buildings inc. Hinton Manor, Woodford Halse and Greenman, Mollington. Elm table 9 ft × 4 ft, etc. for listed buildings.
All work personally made inc. specialized traditional box sashes.

HAYWARD, JOHN (Empl: one; Est: 1968)
Stained Glass Artist/Painter
Windmill House, Mill Hill, Edenbridge, Kent TN8 5DA. 0732-862 392.
F SMGP.
Pc Stained glass to many churches in UK and abroad – St Mary-le-Bow, Cheapside. Blackburn Cathedral. Dunstable Priory. Walsingham. Stationers Hall, etc. Conservation of a number of important windows (15th to 18th century).
Consultant for stained glass to Dioceses of Southwark and Guilford.

HAYWOOD, THOMAS & SONS LTD (Empl: 6; Est: 1949)
Decorative Lighting
'Falcon Forge', 33 Averyhill Rd, New Eltham, London SE9 2BW. 081-850 5558.
DLA.
Pc RMA Chapel (electroliers). Ideal home exhibition (decorative lighting). Many churches.
Brochure.

HAZLIN OF LUDLOW LTD (Empl: 10; Est: 1974)
Specialists in Fine Woodworking
Old Station Works, Bromfield, Nr Ludlow, Shropshire SY8 2BT. 058-477 439.

FIRMS AND CRAFTSPEOPLE

All apprentice trained.
Pc Many varied contracts inc. Coventry Magistrates Courts; Aberystwith University; Strathallan Hotel, Birmingham.
Brochure.

HEARN-COOPER LTD (Empl: one; Est: 1963)
Restorers of the Antique & Objet d'Art
46 Park Hill Rd, Wallington, Surrey SM6 0SB. 081-647 2715.
'Studied at father's knee'.
Pc Worked on pieces now on show in British Museum; Paul Getty; Bradford and several Museums in Japan. Undertakes work for several London dealers, but for obvious reasons cannot specify individual pieces.

HEDGECOE, MICHAEL (Empl: 11; Est: 1970)
Antique Furniture Restoration
Burrow Hill Green, Chobham, Woking, Surrey GU24 8QS. 09905-8206.
M Brit Antique Furniture Restoration Assoc; LAPADA; GMC.
Pc Work completed in various palaces, DOE.

HEDGEHOG DESIGN (Empl: one; Est: 1985)
Furniture Designer & Maker
2 Turners Green, Wadhurst, E. Sussex TN5 6TU. 089 288-3190.
Bachelor of Fine Arts, Design, University of Michigan, USA; M CSD; M Guild of Woodworkers.
Pc Bench in utile with nautical theme – Bewl Valley Sailing Club. Nautical furniture – M. V. Seamill, Poole Harbour.
Kim Gyr's work has been featured in Design *magazine, and on TVS.*
Brochure.

HEMPSTOCK, J. & CO (BUILDERS) LTD (Empl: 20/40; Est: 1959)
116/118 South St, Openshaw, Manchester, Lancs M11 2FY. 061-223 0638 & 2123.
Pc St Margaret's Church, Altringham. Manchester City Town Hall. Manchester City Fishmarket.

HEMPWAY LTD
See MANOR MORTARS & WEBB & KEMPF LTD

HENDERSON THE BLACKSMITH (Empl: 28; Est: 1890, incorp 1975)
John Henderson Industries Ltd, Inglis Lane, Castleblair Works, Dunfermline, Fife KY12 9DP. 0383-721 123. FAX 0383 723 714.
Pc Restoration and repairs for PSA, Historic Buildings; Edinburgh

HERBERT, STUART

New Town Conservation; Eng. Heritage Trust. Restoration of cast iron balustrade – Princess Street, Edinburgh. New screens – North and South Transcepts, Dunfermline Abbey. Stainless steel reproduction weather-vane – Church of the Holy Rood, Stirling.
Will also make garden furniture, pagodas and gazebos. Brochure.

HENDERSON, MICHAEL (Est: 1976)
Wood Carver
Work: Bristol Craft Centre, 6 Leonard Lane, Bristol, BS1 1EA. 0272-291 234. Home: 10 St Margaret's Place, Bradford-on-Avon, Wilts BA15 1DT. 022 16-3775.
B Architecture.
Pc Many carvings, both freestanding and relief, usually animals and birds. Crosier for Bishop of Bristol. Articulated figures for advertising purposes – Sutcliffe Catering. Also designs and makes chairs, tables, chests, reading stands and other furniture.
Brochure.

HENSHAW, CHARLES & SONS LTD (Empl: 45; Est: 1896)
Specialists in Conservation & Restoration of Statues & Ancient Monuments
Russell Rd, Edinburgh, Mid Lothian EH11 2LS. 031-337 4204.
CCS; METCOM.
Pc Refurbishment and repair of 'Eros' in Piccadilly.
Repair and refurbishment of art metalwork; manufacture of custom designed grilles, gates, and coats-of-arms in wrought iron, steel and bronze in traditional or contemporary design; production of new statues and sculptures cast in aluminium or bronze. Brochure.

HENWOOD DECORATIVE METAL STUDIOS LTD (Empl: 6; Est: 1975)
The Bayle, Folkestone, Kent CT20 1SQ. 0303-50911.
5 yrs apprenticeship, Goldsmith/Silversmith; M Brit Jewellery & Giftware Fed; GMC.
Pc The Compass Rose – Canterbury Cathedral. Restoration of existing metalwork plus custom designs – St Paul's, Dover. A variety of brassware – Brighton Pavillion. All items of metalware – The Guards Chapel, Wellington Barracks.

HERBERT, STUART (Empl: 3; Est: 1987)
Furniture Designer & Restorer
Unit 3, Enterprise Way, Newport, Gwent NP9 4HB. 0633-841 829 & 58571.
Distinction Advanced Furniture Studies in Fine Craftsmanship; previous winner of Livewire Business Awards; awarded 2nd place Welsh National Business Awards.

FIRMS AND CRAFTSPEOPLE

Pc Commemorative bookcase/trophy cabinet – Royal British Legion. Floor to ceiling, 20 ft long, wall unit in solid inlaid mahogany.

HERITAGE FURNITURE LTD (Est: 1985)
Alderflat Drive, Newstead Ind Estate, Trentham, Stoke-on-Trent, Staffs ST4 8HX. 0782-644 144.

HERITAGE PRESERVATION (Empl: 80; Est: 1972)
Painters – Murals, Stencils, Gilding, Graining & Marbling
7 Nuffield Ind Centre, Littlemore, Oxford OX4 5JS. 0865-718 383.
NHBC; BWPA; FME.
Pc Berkhamsted Town Hall. Appleton Manor.

HERITAGE STONE (Empl: 20; Est: 1988)
Reconstructed Stone
Heritage Way, Corby, Northants NN17 1XW. 0536-400 999.
Pc Refurbishment – Bartholomew's Hospital, London. Extension – East Haddon Hall, Northants. 1.8 tonne chimney caps – Royal Mint Court, London. Restoration – Angel Hotel, Northants.
Brochure.

HERITAGE STONE RESTORATION CO LTD (Empl: 18; Est: 1984)
1/7 The Parade, Woodside Crescent, Sidcup, Kent DA15 7JN. 081-300 4127.
Stone Fed; BEC.
Brochure.

HERITAGE TILE CONSERVATION LTD (Empl: 6; Est: 1985)
Unit 1, Stretton Road Ind Est, Much Wenlock, Salop TF13 6AS. 0952-728 157.
UKIC.
Pc Removal and restoration of pictorial tiled panels – various health authorities and museums. Removal and restoration of encaustic tiled floor – the National Railway Museum, York. Restoration and mounting of 4th-century AD Roman Mosaic – Milton Keynes Development Corporation. Removal of Minton tiled interior (butcher's shop) – Sheffield Museum. In situ restoration of washrooms, V & A.

HERON GLASS STUDIOS LTD (Empl: 3 + 2 part time; Est: 1987)
Stained Glass Artist
Unit 8 Aston Rd, Astonfields Ind Estate, Bromsgrove, Worcs B60 3EX. 0527-75466.
BA (Hons) ATC in Glass Design; M GMC.

HICKSON TIMBER PRODUCTS LTD

In house design facility (traditional and modern styles). Decorative glass produced using a new concept of firing permanently coloured, hand-painted, or screen-printed designs into float or obscured glass (up to 2 m × 3 m) which can be toughened, mirrored, laminated or double glazed for use in interior or exterior architectural, public or domestic situations.

HERRIOTT, M. J. (WOODCARVER & FIREPLACE MANUFACTURER) (Est: 1986)
58 Crescent Drive South, Woodingdean, Brighton, Sussex BN2 6RB. 0273-308 454.
Cabinet Making C & Gs; 20 yrs experience of woodcarving.
Pc Fireplace embellishments supplied to Marble Hill Fireplaces, 72 Richmond Rd, Twickenham, Middx (081-892 1488).
Brochure in connection with fireplace side of business.

HETLEY, JAMES & CO LTD (Empl: 35; Est: 1823)
Beresford Avenue, Wembley, Middx HA0 1RP. 081-903 4151.
M Glass & Glazing Fed. Ordinary M BSMGP.
Pc Glass supplied to Coventry; Liverpool; Westminster Cathedrals, etc.
Stock over 500 different types and colours of glass inc. 'antique' (hand-blown glass); a comprehensive range of rolled cathedral and opalescent from the USA and Germany; semi-antique and coloured sheet glass; bullion glass; a full range of accessories – providing the stained glass artist, architect, interior designer, and hobbyist with 'the most comprehensive stock available in the UK and Europe'. Brochure.

HICKS, ANNE & JERRY (RWA)
Painters – Murals
Goldrush, Gt George St, Bristol, Avon BS1 5QT. 0272-260 209.
Both trained at the Slade School of Art and are M's of Royal West of Eng. Academy (Jerry past Chairman); Anne has represented British Woman Painters in Paris; Jerry won the Queen's Silver Jubilee Award for Painting of Great British Achievement.
Pc Relief mural – Bristol Gas showrooms (result of competition). Screen for Bristol Public Health Laboratory. London Dog Training Centre Mural – Bushy. Murals – Indian restaurants in Bristol and London; Bristol Zoo (now demolished with re-building). Ceramic tile design – Bristol University Swimming Baths.

HICKSON TIMBER PRODUCTS LTD (Est: 1946)
Wheldon Rd, Castleford, W. Yorks WF10 2JT. 0977-556 565. FAX 0977-516 513. TELEX 556 303 HTPLTD G.
Pc Recent work using Hickson Treatments inc. the restoration of roofing timbers in the South Transept of York Minster which have

been treated by the Hickson 'vac-vac' process to provide total preservative protection.
Through a nationwide network of treaters and stockest the firm are worldwide specialists in the supply of safe and effective timber pre-treatments and decorative finishes that protect against wood decay, insect attack and the spread of flame. Brochure.

HIDE, W. R. & A., LTD (Empl: 22; Est: 1864)
Specialist Joinery Manufacturers
161 Dalling Rd, Hammersmith, London W6 0ES. 081-743 2589. FAX 081-749 6417.
C & Gs; FMB.
Pc Details available on request.
Brochure.

HIGGINSON, E. A. & CO LTD (Empl: 20; Est: 1931)
Traditional Geometric Staircases & Specialist Joinery Manufacturers
Unit 1, Carlisle Rd, London NW9 0HD. 081-200 4848. FAX 081 200 8249. TELEX 922 444.
NJCBI; BEC; Brit Woodworking Fed.
Pc Windlesham Moor, Surrey.
Also sell a range of staircases with individual components manufactured to individual heights and openings. Ability to undertake design work depends on whether necessary to produce detailed drawings. Brochure.

HILL, JOE
Dry Stone Walling Consultant
90 Holymoor Rd, Chesterfield S42 7DX. 0246-549 433. Game Lea Farm, Eastmoor, Chesterfield, Derbys S42 7DB. 0246-566 557.
Master Craftsman, Dry Stone Walling Assoc.
A consultant, willing to recommend and oversee young craftsmen able to undertake work in all types of stone.

HILL, KEITH & JUDY (Empl: 2; Est: 1977)
Stained Glass Artists
Stained Glass Workshop, Staplehurst, Kent TN12 0NF. 0580-891 692.
Judy Hill – AMGP   Keith Hill – Soc of Heraldic Artists.
Pc Two-light memorial window – St Michael's Church, Beckenham. 10 modern windows – St Peter's Church, Bearsted. 2 windows – St Mary's Church, Chalk, Kent. Memorial window – Staplehurst, Kent.

HILLFIELD STUDIOS LTD (Empl: 14; Est: 1986)
Hand-painted Tiles & Sanitary Ware
Unit 4, Bittern Place, Coberg Rd, Wood Green London N22 6TP. 081-889 5222.
GMC.
Brochure.

HILLHOUSE INTERIORS (Empl: 4; Est: 1984)
Victorian and Edwardian Bathrooms & Kitchens
Rotunda Buildings, Montpellier Circus, Cheltenham, Glos GL50 1SX. 0242-573 787.
Retailers specializing in the supply of traditional reproduction bathrooms (Victorian to Art Deco) inc. period style woodwork to complement the equipment (bath panels, vanity units, wardrobes); tiles; accessories; lights.
Brochure.

HILLIARD, TERENCE (Empl: 4; Est: 1970)
Woodcarver
The Barn, Master Johns, Thorby Lane, Mountnessing, Brentwood, Essex CM15 0SY. 0277-354717.
C & Gs for Carving Modelling Drawing; M GMC.
Pc Various tables and mirrors – National Trust for Scotland.

HILL-NORTON, JENNY (Est: 1976)
Glass Engraver
The Barns, Newton Valence, Alton, Hants GU34 3RB. 042 058-302.
AF GGE.

HINCE, DAVID DECORATORS (Empl: 8; Est: 1982)
33 Dunnisher Rd, Newall Green, Manchester, Lancs M23 8ZL. 061-998 6967.
BDA.
Pc Restoration and reproduction work – Kershawe House, Halifax (Grade I). Full interior decoration to a very high standard – Spanish Consulate, Wilmslow.

HINCHCLIFFE, LAWRENCE & WYNN (Est: 1973)
Architects & Surveyors
Fladbury Mill, Fladbury, Pershore, Worcs WR10 2QA. 0386-860 254.
RIBA; IAAS; NZIA.
Pc Lutwych Hall, Shropshire. Fladbury Church, Worcs. Manor Arms, Abberley. Angel Inn and Posting House, Pershore. The Chequers Inn, Fladbury. Barn conversions.

FIRMS AND CRAFTSPEOPLE

HIND, DON RUGS
38a Main St, Lowick, Berwick-upon-Tweed, Northumberland TD15 2UA. 0289-88301.
Pc Wall murals, hand-carved country scenes (3 m × 1.8 m, 1.8 m × 1.5 m, etc.). Trees, silhouette shaped and mounted (3 m × 3 m, 2.5 m × 2.2 m, etc.).
Specialize in irregular shaped and 3-dimensional work with hand carving, either for floor or for wall.

HINDLE, E. P. (THATCHER) (Empl: one; Est: 1980)
Wayside Cottage, Coker Marsh, E Coker, Nr Yeovil, Somerset BA22 9JZ. 093 586-2658.
4½ yrs apprenticeship; CoSIRA Training Course; Wheat Reed Cert (CoSIRA); M Dorset MTA.
Only undertakes re-timbering if on a small scale.

HINSLEY, T. (TILES) (Est: 1983)
Traditionally Made Kent Peg Tiles & Reclaimed Clay Tiles
Shersby Cottage, Marshside, Chislet, Nr Canterbury, Kent CT3 4EE. 0227-86335 (anytime); 0860-304 314 (days).
Handmade Kent peg tiles; eave tiles; bonnet/hips; ridge; valley; traditional patterned chimney pots. Also stock reclaimed clay tiles; stock bricks; Welsh slates; pantiles; etc.

HINTON PERRY & DAVENHILL LTD (Empl: 75; Est: 1902)
Dreadnought Tiles
Dreadnought Works, Pensnett, Brierley Hill, W. Midlands DY5 4TH. 0384-77405. FAX 0384-74553.
Plain clay roofing tiles and fittings for modern and period roofing.

HIRST CONSERVATION (Empl: 10+)
Conservation of Decorative Wall & Ceiling Finishes
Laughton Hall Farm House, Laughton, Sleaford, Lincs NG34 0HE. 052-97 449.
Inst M of UKIC; M IIC.
Pc Conservation – 19th-century nave ceiling (believed to be largest painted ceiling in Europe), Ely Cathedral. Cleaning and conservation – 14th-century Prior Crauden's Chapel (polychrome), Ely Cathedral. Restoration – library, Newston Abbey, Notts (former home of Lord Byron). Conservation – 14th-century wall painting inc. transfer of paintings on to new lime plaster support, Castor Church, Nr Peterborough.
Also undertakes damp testing and monitoring of historic buildings; advising on plaster and decorative finishes; testing materials suitability and analysis;

analysis of plaster pigments and media; consolidation of decorative timber work; cleaning and conservation of tiles and mosaics; canvas painting; monument conservation.

HISCOTT, AMBER & PEARL, DAVID (Est: 1976)
Stained Glass Artists
Old St Nicholas Chapel, Gloucester Place, Swansea, W. Glam SA1 1TY. 0792-296 458 & 476 128.
A. Hiscott granted The Freedom of The Worshipful Co of Glaziers and The Freedom of The City of London as a result of several awards her work has earned.
Pc Unilever Headquarters, Blackfriars. Entrance canopy – 'Liberty', Regent St. 12 newly designed windows for the reconstruction of Missenden Abbey. European Centre of Folk Studies, Llangollen. The Grand Theatre, Swansea. Hospitals and churches.

H M G OF BRISTOL (Empl: 5; Est: 1987)
Stained Glass Artist
15 Perry Rd, St Michael's, Bristol, Avon BS1 5BG. 0272-298 765 (day) & 429 753 (night).
Apprenticeship; years of experience; GMC; BA Arts.
Pc Re-glazing – Danesfield House. Holly window with artist Richard Boulton. Balcony panels – Eton Square, London. Many other commissions.
This firm feels 'Stained Glass is a media which has been neglected over recent years and has yet to explore its full potential within the modern environment.'
Has a fully equipped mobile workshop. Will advise on specialist glass cleaning and protective measures.

HODGETTS, GRAHAM
Consultant, Technical Advisor & Lecturer on Metalwork
16 Home Park Rd, Saltash, Cornwall PL12 6BH. 0752-846 100.
Technical apprenticeship, Stewarts & Lloyds, Ltd (steelworks); Associate of Welding Inst; Past editor of *British Blacksmith Magazine*; Teaching Cert in Further Education.
Pc Lecturer in Architectural Metalwork to HND, Plymouth College of Art & Design, having run own business for many yrs as a designer/ blacksmith.
Brochure.

HODGSON, JOHN (Empl: solo; Est: 1984)
Fine & Applied Artwork
71 South St, Crewkerne, Somerset TA18 8BD. 0460-76286.
BA (Fine Arts).

FIRMS AND CRAFTSPEOPLE

Pc John Lewis Partnership, Dorchester, Dorset. British Telecom, Southampton. Dean & Dyball Construction, Hythe Marina Village.
Brochure.

HODGSON, SALLY (Est: 1986)
Textile Designer
Higher Plainsteads Farm, Monks Rd, Glossop, Derbys SK13 9JZ. 04574-2547.
BA Textile Design.

HODKIN & JONES LTD (Empl: 90; Est: 1868)
Dunston House, Dunston Rd, Chesterfield, Derbys S41 9QD. 0246-455255.
GMC.
Pc Restoration due to fire damage inc. copying original ornate Victorian interior (over 10,000 individual pieces of plasterwork, ranging from decorative roses under 12 inch in diameter to cornices 10 ft deep and lunette sections weighing 100 kg each) – Albert Hall, Bolton. New Britten Opera House, London. The Victoria Centre, Nottingham. Geometric open work, arches and columns – Middle East Financial Institution.
Restoration work ranging from the repair of a tiny section of a 200 yr old frieze to supplying a special one-off cornice. New work undertaken. Brochure.

HOLDSTOCK, RICKY
Chairseat Weaving
Hillside Cottage, The Forstal, Hernhill, Faversham, Kent ME13 9JQ. 0227-751 204.
Family craft for at least 3 generations; taught by father and grandfather from 1930; writer, lecturer and demonstrator in craft of chair seat weaving. M GMC.
Pc Professional work for many national bodies, local institutions, trade, antique restoration firms, private individuals, and also for journals (see *Living* magazine, Jan 1989). Author of book on chair seat weaving.
Also willing to undertake shaker tape; Scandinavian rush; Danish paper cord and experienced in blind, double, sun-ray, star of David, snowflake, caning methods.

HOLGATE, DAVID (FSDC) (Empl: approx 2; Est: 1970)
Architectural Sculptor
8 Ash Grove, Norwich, Norfolk NR3 4BE. 0603-485 444.
Apprenticed to David Kindersley OBE; FSD-C; M Suffolk Crafts Soc; Norfolk Contemporary Crafts Soc.

Pc Restoration – Suckling tombs, St Andrew's Church, Norwich. Slate rondel for National Inst of Agricultural Botany, Cambridge. Finials – Norwich Cathedral Close.
Brochure.

HOLLAND, GRAHAM D. (Est: 1985)
Architect
15 Tatton St, Knutsford, Cheshire WA16 6AE. 0865-51066.
Dip Arch; Dip Arch Conservation; RIBA; M EASA; Victorian Soc; National Trust.
Pc Restoration works inc. Rode Hall; Gowsish Old Hall; various churches. New period style houses in conservation settings.

HOLLAWAY, ANTONY (Empl: varies; Est: 1959)
Stained Glass Artist
A. H. Associates Ltd, Home Farm House, Bottesford Rd, Allington, Grantham NG32 2DH. Head of Design, Trent Polytechnic Nottingham, Burton St, Nottingham NG1 4BU. 0602-418 248 ext 2443.
ARCA; Art Teachers Dip; FRSA; FCSD.
Pc Replacement of existing glass in Manchester Cathedral with contemporary stained glass. Slab glass and metal compound window – Chemistry Research Laboratory, Boots Co, Nottingham. Bar backs (appliqué glass) – Ranks Ballrooms, Brighton & Watford.
Classical designs are only undertaken for non ecclesiastical sites. Lecturing and teaching undertaken.

HOLLEY & FROST (Empl: 8; Est: 1964)
Specialist Painters & Gilders
44 Hawthorne Avenue, Gillingham, Kent ME8 6TR. 0634-361 595.
Apprenticeship; C & Gs.

HOLMAN, R. W. (Empl: 3; Est: 1969)
Wood Carver
8 Kippington Rd, Sevenoaks, Kent TN14 2LH. 0732-450 408.
Full M Master Carvers Assoc.
Pc Architectural carving – refurbishment works, Grand Hotel, Brighton.
Municipal and school work inc. coats-of-arms, etc. Ecclesiastical carving. Antique repair work inc. clock cases.

HOMECRAFT DYCE (Empl: solo; Est: 1980)
Chair Caning & Sheet Caning
9 Union Row, Dyce, Aberdeenshire AB2 0DQ. 0224-73991.
Basketmakers Association; AMU.

FIRMS AND CRAFTSPEOPLE

HOMEWOOD, JOAN
Cane & Rushwork
Mill Farm House, Arlington, Barnstaple, Devon EX31 4LN. 0271-82306 (nights only).
Pc Re-caned hundreds of chairs over last 15 yrs, inc. a whole double-sided bergere suite.
Rush work only undertaken if good rushes available.

HONEY ALLAWAY (BUILDING RESTORATION) LTD (Empl: 50; Est: 1987)
43 Cranbourne Drive, Otterbourne, Winchester, Hants. 0962-713 976.
2 Webb Rd, Blackheath, London SE3. 081-853 2498.
M Stone Fed.
Also undertakes brickwork and stucco rendering.

HOPLEY & SPEED (Empl: 2 + 20 sub contractors; Est: 1969)
Building Contractors
Thornton House, Guy Lane, Hargreave, Cheshire CH3 7RZ. 0829-40204 & 40425.
Approved: Chester Council.

HOPKINS, JAN (Empl: solo; Est: 1983)
Hand-woven, Hand-tufted Wallhangings & Rugs
27 Benton St, Hadleigh, Ipswich, Suffolk IP7 5AR. 0473-827 172.
LSDC; M Suffolk Craft Soc.

HOPKINS, NOEL LTD
Reclaimed Roofing & Building Materials
48/50 Birch Road East, Wyrley Road Trading Estate, Aston, Birmingham B6 7DD. 021-326 7292 & 705 6000 (night).

HOPSON, JOCK CONSERVATION SERVICE (Est: 1987)
Holes Lane, Olney, Bucks MK46 4BX. 0234-712 306.
University of London & Goldsmiths College; London College of Furniture; C & Gs of London Art School; professional training at Frame Conservation Dept, National Gallery, London.
Pc National Trust (both workshop and in situ). Leicester Museum, Hitchin Museum. Alfred East Gallery, Kettering. Maidstone Museum & Art Gallery. In situ work at various country houses – from fireplaces to frames.

HOREY WOODWORK (ERIC BECKMAN) (Empl: solo; Est: 1986)
Woodturner
48 Sangers Drive, Horley, Surrey RH6 8AL. 0293-782 698.

HOSEGOOD, ALAN (Empl: 2; Est: 1978)
Craftmen in Wood
4 Colston Yard, Colston St, Bristol, Avon BS1 5BD. 0272-268 719.
15 yrs experience, no formal apprenticeship.
Pc Antique restoration, bespoke furniture, fitted and freestanding furniture, interior work such as Japaneses style screens in ash, lined with soshi paper.
On staircases, only able to undertake restoration work. Portfolio available.

HOUGHTON, A. E. & SON LTD (Empl: 16; Est: 1947)
Craftsemn in Architectural & Ecclesiastical Woodwork, Building Contractors
Common Rd, Dunnington, York YO1 5PD. 0904-489 193.
BWF; BEC; York Guild of Building; Fed of Master Craftsmen.
Pc Library and panelling – Sir Tatton Sykes, Sledmore House; Marquis of Normanby, Lythe Hall; Count Bonifazi, Monte Carlo. Restoration work inc. 16th-century roof, Eastington Church; 16th-century panelling – Walburn; Lantern tower and roof towers – Castle Howard; Tower Crossing. Southwark Cathedral.

HOUSTON BOYCE PARTNERSHIP (Est: 1986)
Chartered Architects & Project Managers
21 Carlton Court, Glasgow G5 9JP. 041-429 8808.
Pc Conversion of Victorian stable block to offices – Glasgow. Conversion of Georgian terrace to luxury apartments – Glasgow. Various coach houses to luxury homes.

HOWARD, A. M.
Cob Consultant
'Westleigh', Morchard Rd, Copplestone EX17 5LS. 0363-327.
Full working life as a builder, inc. the restoration of old property, specializing in cob buildings.
'Having had the benefit of knowledge imparted by my grandfather and father, I now advise people on cob buildings as a cob consultant.'

HOWARD CHAIRS (Empl: 8; Est: 1820)
30–31 Lyme St, Camden Town, London NW1 0EE. 071-482 2156.
Handmade easy chairs and sofas using beech frames, horse hair, wadding, etc. Limited stock held as bulk of furniture made to order. Delivery charge outside of London. Brochure.

HUDSON, THOMAS (Est: 1970)
Furniture Maker & Specialist Joinery
The Barn, 117 High St, Odell, Bedford MK43 7AS. 0234-721 133.
Shoreditch College; Goldsmiths College; Camberwell School of Art;

FIRMS AND CRAFTSPEOPLE

M Coll H, Oxford School of Art.
Pc Handmade furniture in many homes and public buildings from Inverness-shire to Cornwall. Panelling and restoration work in many large country houses.
Only relief carving undertaken. Brochure.

HUGHES, HARRIET OWEN (Est: 1962)
Painting Conservator
41 Bluecoat Chambers, School Lane, Liverpool L1 3BX. 051-708 6808.
BA (Hons) History of Art, Courtauld Inst; post grad training in Conservation, Courtauld Inst; M IIC; UKIC; Full M ABPR.
Pc Cleaning and restoration of easel paintings for private clients and institutions (e.g. Merseyside Maritime Museum, Walker Art Gallery). Advice on storage and display, lighting and environmental control.

HUGHES, MARTIN DESIGN (Est: 1984)
Custom-made Ceramic & Painted/polished Wood Lamps
Kimberley House, Kimberley Lane, St Martin's, Oswestry, Salop SY11 3DF. 0691-774 271.
MA Degree in 3d Design (Ceramics), Cardiff.
Also makes cache pots built in wood and painted to any colour; antique style shelf units; mirrors; pot forms. Painted surfaces can be produced in any colour and matched to fabrics, etc. Lampshades to match lamps can be supplied. Photographs and product samples available.

HUGHES, WILLIAM & SONS (Est: 1927)
Building & Restoration Contractors
Churton Rd, Farndon, Chester, CH3 6OP. 0829 270-223 & 588.
2 brothers, time served in father's business; M FMB. Approved: Chester City Council (Conservation Dept).
Pc Part re-building of half-timbered cottage – Lower Peover. Complete refurbishment of Victorian house – Chester. Underpinning and completely restoring Tudor Cottage.

HUNT, DAVID LIGHTING LTD (Empl: 30; Est: 1967)
Tilemans Lane, Shipston-on-Stour, Warwicks CV36 4HP. 0608-61590 & 62836.
M DLA.
Pc Choir stall lighting constructed from early gasolier parts discovered in attic – Beverley Minster. Restoration of fittings – New Swan Theatre, Royal Shakespeare Theatre, Stratford-upon-Avon. 30 ft light fitting – tower with spiral staircase, Stonehouse Hotel, Glos.
Brochures.

HUTTON & ROSTRON ENVIRONMENTAL INVESTIGATIONS LTD

HUNTER & PARTNERS (Est: 1955)
Chartered Surveyors; Incorporated Surveyors; Architects
146–148 Cromwell Rd, London SW7 4EF. 071-373 5193.
Pc Tiffin School (Grade II). National Maritime Museum (Grade I). Grosvenor Estate (Grade II). Carlton House Terrace (Grade I).

HUNTER, LAVINIA (Empl: solo; Est: 1986)
Gilder
4 Seymour Villas, Totnes, Devon TQ9 5QR. 0803-862 153.
M UKIC.
Pc Cleaning and repairs – 'Pyne' frame, Bristol Art Gallery. Regilding – 'Huydon' frame, Exeter Museum. Repair and regild – largest frame in Exeter Costume Museum. Furniture re-gessoed and gilded.

HURD ROLLAND PARTNERSHIP (Est: 1936)
Architects
Rossend Castle, Burntisland, Fife KY3 ODF. 0592-873 535. 32 Fitzroy Square, London W1P 5HH. 071-387 9595. 2–4 Atkinson St, Manchester M3 3HH. 061-832 5322.
MRIBA; MRIAS; M Architectural Heritage Soc of Scotland.
Pc Castle Restorations inc. – Aboyne; Rossend; Beldorney; Tillycairn; Brodie. Tourist facilities – Edinburgh Castle. Re-roofing and fabric repairs – Usher Hall. John Knox Museum, Edinburgh. Scottish National Portrait Gallery. Many restoration projects in the Georgian New Town of Edinburgh.

HUSSEY, ALAN (Empl: solo; Est: 1985)
Contemporary Furniture
Askerwell Workshops, Askerswell, Dorchester, Dorset DT2 9EL. 030 885-544.
BA (Hons) Furniture Design.
Pc Walberswick Silver Jubilee seat.

HUTTON, LEN (Empl: one; Est: 1984)
Hand-forged Wrought-ironwork
The Forge, Bishopsbourne, Canterbury, Kent CT4 5HT. 0227-830 784.
M BABA.

HUTTON & ROSTRON ENVIRONMENTAL INVESTIGATIONS LTD (Est: 1963)
Netley House, Gomshall, Guildford, Surrey. 048-641 3221.
Dr Singh – BSc; MSc; PhD; Full M Brit Mycological Soc; Brit Ecological Soc; TRADA   Huw Lloyd – BSc Wood Science   Geoffrey Hutton – Dip Arch (Dist); ARIBA   M. Rostron – MA; B Arch; ARIBA.

FIRMS AND CRAFTSPEOPLE

Pc Bradstone Brook House. Calke Abbey. Clandon Park. Cullen House. Fort Belvedere. Hampton Court Palace. Mansion House. Mount Stewart. Royal Pavillion, Brighton.
Specialists in building moisture profiles and advice on refurbishment after fire damage; evaluation of health hazards; environmental monitoring; laboratory services; pest management; non-destructive inspection techniques; investigations of building failures; treatment of fungal and insect infestation of buildings.

HYDROTEK (Empl: 12)
Rising Damp Removal, Tanking
Globe House, New St, Chelmsford, Essex CM1 1PP. 0245-358 193 & Freephone 'Osmosis'.
M FMB.
A subsidiary of The Chelmsford Property Preservation Co Ltd, this company is the sole installer for Hydrotek (see Hydrotek Wessex) porous tubes in E. Anglia, Kent and London. They are also approved installers of chemical and 'Lectros' damp proof courses.

HYDROTEK WESSEX (Est: 1989)
Rising Damp Removal
Bleke House, Wessex, Shaftesbury, Dorset SP7 8QA. 0747-54225 & 0800 373 768.
Tony Newell, director – Final C & Gs Brickwork; Master M Guild of Bricklayers; M FMB; holder of Army record for brickwork, Trade Test; Fellow of Faculty of Building.
Pc United Reform Church, Shaftesbury (built in 1666).
Sole installer for Hydrotek (late Doulton Wallguard) porous tubes – the method developed by Royal Doulton from Knapen Tubes used in Continent and UK up to 50s. The system apparently has a long life and is reliable because once installed there is nothing to go wrong. No chemicals or fumes so ecologically harmless. Franchises nationwide, but will also supply.

IBSTOCK BUILDING PRODUCTS LTD (Empl: 1400; Est: 1820)
Leicester Rd, Ibstock, Leics LE6 1HS. 0530-60531.
M GMC.
Pc Replicas of 40 different terracotta bricks – Halsey House, Cromer. Plaque depicting griffin emblem of London Brewers, Fuller Smith & Turner. Emblem of peace and prayer – Mosque, Whitechapel Rd. Co-operation with sculptor, Mary Smith, to create 61 ft × 18½ ft design carved on to green bricks, each brick was numbered before firing.
Specials manufactured in any number, however small; experienced in reproduction for restoration and refurbishment work; create decorative brickwork for both old and new situations, commemorative plaques and logos;

'INNERVISIONS' (D.B. CATSIS)

technical assistance given to sculptors. Brochure.

IFFLAND & ASSOCIATES (Est: 1970)
Land & Engineering Associates
Exchange House, 180–182 St Mary's Lane, Upminster, Essex RM14 3BT. 04022-22623.
M. W. Iffland – FG of S; FRGS; DVW (W Germany)   W. L. Yong – FRICS; FG of S   E. Iffland – FG of S; FRGS   Firm, Founder M UK Land & Hydrographic Survey Assoc.
Pc Monitoring for deformation – church wall, Clerkenwell. Tree conservation site survey. Survey of rear of Wesleyan Chapel, City Rd. 1:50 survey of barn for restoration.
Architectural building engineering and site surveys; building floor plans, sections, elevations; precise monitoring of structures for movement; topographic and photogrammetric control surveys; location of underground services; computerized design and setting out.

ILLUMIN, GLASS STUDIO (Est: 1984)
Stained Glass Artist
82 Bond St, Macclesfield, Cheshire SK11 6QS. 0625-613 600.
10 yrs experience; M GMC.
Pc Many and various.
Brochure.

INCISIVE LETTERWORK (Est: 1986)
3 The Drive, Amersham, Bucks HP7 9AD. 0494-722 386. 54 Gladsmuir Rd, London N19 3J. 071-272 6039.
Annet Stirling and Brenda Berman – Advanced Lettering Dipl; C & Gs of London Art School; M of Letter Exchange; Soc of Scribes & Illuminators.
Pc Commissions from architectural firms inc. 12 inch letters, V-cut into existing Portland fascia and gilded – Garrards of Regent St; 8 inch letters as above – Eastman Dental Hospital, Grays Inn Rd; painted wall inscription, 14 ft × 8 ft – St Luke's, Pinner; opening plaque in slate – Hammersmith Hospital.
Specialists in lettering, in the broadest sense.

INGATESTONE FORGE
See CARFORD, GEO LTD

'INNERVISIONS' (D. B. CATSIS) (Est: 1986)
5 Grange Rd, Clifton, Bristol Avon. 0272-540 576.
BA (Hons) Fine Art.
Pc Broken colour work – Courtroom of Chew Court, Chew Magna.

FIRMS AND CRAFTSPEOPLE

Marbled columns – boardroom, SK Construction, St Anne's, Bristol. Dragging ragging, marbling, etc. – fitted kitchens; bathrooms; fireplaces; etc. Large semi-abstract mural – open air swimming pool project – Eastville Park, Bristol.

INSIDE ART & DESIGN LTD (Empl: 8; Est: 1980)
Stained Glass Artist
84 Herrett St, Aldershot, Hants GU12 4EE. 0252-336 577.
Corporate M GMC.
Pc Design & manufacture of windows for private residences in Britain, Middle & Far East, N Africa.
Willingness to work in situ depends on location.

INVENTIVE DESIGN (Est: 1984)
Cabinet Making
156 Ifield Rd, London SW10 9AF. 071-373 2216.
SIAD; BA Fine Art.
A range or stock designs, which can be produced in special finishes available.
Willing to undertake bronzing; patination; design consultancy. Brochure.

IONA ART GLASS (Empl: 3; Est: 1985)
'Iona', The Woodlands, Warkworth, Northumberland NE65 0SY. 0665-711 533.
Apprentice shopfitter and glazier, John Nilen & Son, Glasgow; M Northumberland Tourist Board; Director Blackfriars Craft Assoc; Founder M Six of the Best Craft Co-operative.
Pc Restorations – Rothbury Council Building (William Morris windows) and also Warkworth St Lawrence Church.
Specialists in English antique glass.

IRONBRIDGE GORGE MUSEUM (Empl: 4; Est: 1983)
The Wharfage, Ironbridge, Telford, Salop TF8 7AW. 0952-583 003.
Time served floor moulders and cupola men.
Pc Work for local and county authorities, architects and private clients inc. street names, plaques, troughs, floor grilles, etc. Iron castings from customers' patterns up to 50 kgs.

IRONCRAFTS LTD (Empl: 4; Est: 1974)
Pattletons, Doleham Lane, Westfield, Hastings, E. Sussex TN35 4ST. 0424-882 840.
5 yr apprenticeship; BABA; GMC.
Pc Restoration of ironwork in many churches. Decorative bridges, balustrading and gates, etc., for major London architects and interior designers.
Brochure.

JACKSON GLASSCRAFT

IRONCRAFTS (STOTFOLD) LTD (Empl: 15; Est: 1949)
Baldock Rd, Stotfold, Hitchin, Herts SG5 4PA. 0462-730 671.
M BABA.
Pc Restoration of north front gates – Hatfield House. Internal balustrading – Business Design Centre, Islington Green, London. West porch gates – All Saints' Church, Leighton Buzzard and also Administrative Centre, Kew Green, Kew Gardens. Railings – Market Cross, Leighton Buzzard. Restoration of gates and railings – Bradenham Manor for National Trust. Brass balustrading, wrought-iron railings – Princess House, Jermyn St, London.
Brochure.

IRWINS
Building Contractors
Low Hall Rd, Horsforth, Leeds, W. Yorks LS18 4EW. 0532-506 811.

ISSAC, HENRY (Empl: 23; Est: 1865)
Engineers & Iron Founders
The Foundry, St Ippollitts, Hitchin, Herts SG4 7NX. 0462-53155.
M of METCON; Engineering Industries Assoc; Brit Cast Iron Research Assoc.
Pc Cast iron windows to customers' sample, originals dated c. 1850. Supply of cast iron replacement parts, fitted by customer for many restoration projects in and around London area, ranging from finials to balustrades.
A village-based family business still on its original site. Brochure may be available.

JACKSON, ADAM (Empl: one; Est: 1983)
Cabinet Maker
Poplars Farm, Beningbrough, York YO6 1BY. 0904–470 842.
Apprenticed to cabinet maker; Musical Instrument Technology Credit Cert; London College of Furniture.
Pc Porter's table and side table – Oakredge Hall, Cambs. Oak church font – Wilberfoss, York. Bishop's chair – Helmsley, Yorks. Dining chairs – St Peter's School, York. Oval mirrors – Duncombe Park. Dining table – Skelton Manor.

JACKSON GLASSCRAFT (Empl: 2; Est: 1969)
Stained Glass Artist
2 Robinson Rd, Loudwater, High Wycombe, Bucks HP13 7BL. 049 481-3220.
Application in progress for the GMC.
Pc Drazin window – Roefield, The Green, Croxley Green, Rick-

mansworth. Autumn Leaves – Mr Nye, Beech Cottage, Deadhearn Lane, Chalfont St Giles', Bucks.

JACKSONS JOINERY (Empl: 60+; Est: 1946)
Plodder Lane, Farnworth, Bolton, Lancs BL4 0LR. 0204-63131.
BEC; Brit Woodworking Fed; TRADA; Joinery Managers Assoc.
Pc Beaumont Private Hospital. Manchester Magistrates Court. Restoration work – Guild Hall, Chester. Heritage Centre, Wigan Pier. Banks and building societies, hotel interiors, office furniture and interiors.
Brochure.

JACKSON, PAT STENCIL INTERIORS (Empl: 2; Est: 1985)
Tal Cottage, Harringworth, Northants NN17 3AD.
M Wallpaper History Soc.
Pc Lady Victoria Leatham, Burghley House, Stamford, Lincs. Poste hotels. Shops, private homes in town and country.
All stencils drawn, cut and executed to the architectural style and period of the surroundings, in close consultation with client. Projects range from a simple motif for a cloakroom, through dados and friezes, to whole room designs. Stencilling undertaken on most mediums. Also runs one-day stencilling workshops. Brochure.

JACQUARD (LONDON) LTD (Empl: 25; Est: 1968)
Traditional Upholsterers
Park House, 140 Battersea Park Rd, London SW11 4NB. 071-627 1228.
AMU; American Soc of Interior Designers.
Pc Many large and prestigious houses in London, the country, France, Austria, Scandinavia, Spain, Switzerland, Bahamas, Middle East, Japan, etc.
Individual furnishings made to specification inc. curtains, draperies, pelmets and blinds made by hand. Also undertakes upholstered walls, tented ceilings with ruched, pleated or stretched fabrics. Brochure.

JAKEWAY, KEVIN (Empl: 3; Est: 1987)
Furniture Designer & Maker
Unit 8, Highfield Ind. Estate, Ferndale Rhondda, Mid Glam CF43 4TA. 0443-756 066 & 684 660 (nights).
BA (Hons) 3d Design.
As well as furniture designed to customer's specification, there is a standard range available in oak, ash, elm and sycamore, but these designs, sizes and woods can be altered to customer's requirements.

JAKIM ARTIFACTS (Empl: 3; Est: 1987)
Studio 4, Ruthin Craft Centre, Ruthin, Clwyd LL15 1BP. 08242-5414 & 0244-679 926 (night).
Foundry technology and 21 yrs foundry experience; BA (Hons) Sculpture, Leeds Art School; HND 3d Design & Technology – Lancashire Polytechnic.
Pc Numerous private commissions inc. bronze busts, sculpture, garden statuary, water fountains, sundials, reproduction cast stone articles, restoration of public monuments, etc.

JEFFREY, ALBERT (Empl: 2; Est: 1966)
Sessay, Thirsk, N. Yorks YO7 3BE. 0845-401 323.
Brochure.

JENNIFER-JANE STAINED GLASS (Empl: 3; Est: 1985)
Abbey Studio, Fintray, Aberdeen AB2 0JB. 0224-791 363.
M BSMGP.
Pc Wide variety of commissions and restorations for ecclesiastical, public, domestic and commercial premises.

JEWELL & COLLACOTT WOODCARVERS (Est: 1980)
51a Northernhay St, Exeter, Devon. 0392-74653 & 67403.
L. Jewell – Master Carvers Assoc   D. Collacott – hardwood joiner and woodcarver; apprentice served.
Pc Woodcarvings – HMS *Warrior* (recently restored); Washington Cathedral and numerous churches worldwide. Individual sculptures of natural themes (birds, fish, etc). Restoration – St John's Cathedral, Jacksonville, USA (Award 1984).
Individually specified decorative doors; bas relief panelling; crested period mouldings and ecclesiastical interior windows. Special carving on staircases and balustrading will be considered. Photographs available.

J. & J. MANUFACTURING
See RYAN, JOHN

JOHNS, PAT (Est: 1973)
Tapestry Designer
12 Hillcrest Park, Pennsylvania, Exeter, Devon, EX4 4SH. 0392-58053.
National Dip Design; M SD-C; M Devon Guild of Craftsmen; trained as painter, lithographer.
Pc Tapestry 'Parish Map', 5 ft × 3½ ft, commissioned by Common Ground. Tapestry, approx 30 ft × 3 ft, commissioned by Teignbridge District Council for the council chamber.
Brochure.

FIRMS AND CRAFTSPEOPLE

JOHNSON, FRANCIS F. & PARTNER (Est: 1938)
Chartered Architects
Craven House, 16 High St, Bridlington, N. Humberside YO16 4PX. 0262-674 143.

JOHNSON, H. & R. TILES LTD (Empl: 2,500; Est: 1979, originally 1901)
Highgate Works, Tunstall, Stoke-on-Trent, Staffs ST2 9PU. 0782-575 575
M Brit Ceramic Tile Council.
Pc Bowater House; Hop & Malt Exchange; Palace of Westminster – all in London. York Railway Museum. The Capitol Building, Washington. The Metropolitan Museum of Arts, New York. The Central Mosque, Lagos. Quebec Parliament Building, Quebec. Summervill House, Kingston, Ontario.
Handmade encaustic floor tiles, and also replacement, restoration and recreation. Also produce tiles cut into geometric shapes, to be tessellated with the encaustics for a 'patchwork' effect. Brochure.

JOHNSON, PHIL (Empl: 15; Est: 1972)
Artist Blacksmith
Ratho Byres Forge, Freelands Rd, Ratho by Edinburgh, EH28 8NW. 031-333 1824 & 1300.
Apprenticeships/qualifications in Blacksmithing and Architectural Metalwork; BABA.
Pc British Rail, Cook St. American Museum, Bath. People's Museum, Royal Mile, Edinburgh. Glasgow Garden Festival exhibit.
Also willing to make garden furniture, fire and hearth accessories. Brochure.

JOHNSTON ERDAL ARCHITECTS
39 Sandport St, Edinburgh EH6 6EP. 031-554 1151. FAX 031-554 8300.
Pc Conversion/restoration – Tyninghame Sawmill. Conservation schemes in Edinburgh inc. London St and Moubray House, High St.

JOHNSTON & WRIGHT, CHARTERED ARCHITECTS (Est: 1885)
15 Castle St, Carlisle, Cumbria CA3 8TD. 0228-25161. FAX 0228-515 559.
Various architectural degrees and diplomas; architects are M RIBA.
Pc Conservation – Cockermouth, Lowther and Whitehaven. Restoration and repairs to buildings of architectural and historic interest.

JONES, ALAN (Empl: solo; Est: 18 yrs)
Dry Stone Walling
1 Parc y Moch, Bryn Bella, Bethesda, Gwynedd LL5Y 3DN. 0248-600 901.

30 yrs experience in dry stone walling. Master Craftsman Cert in Dry Stone Walling.
Pc Instructor for local colleges. National Trust. British Trust Conservation Volunteers. Gwynedd Rural Skills.

JONES, CATRIN (Est: 1982)
Stained Glass Artist
7 Gloucester Place, The Maritime Quarter, Swansea, W. Glam SA1 1TY. 0792-469 256.
College Dip Architectural Glass (Dist); co-director Glasslight Stained Glass Studio 1982-87; SIAD.
Pc Work in Swansea inc. St Mary's Church; St David's Church; St Joseph's Cathedral; private chapel. Private residences in West & South Wales. Work purchased by V & A Museum and private collections, W. Germany.

JONES, CERI LEADLIGHTS (Empl: 2; Est: 1978)
Mole End, Midgham Park, Woolhampton, Reading, Berks RG7 5UG. 0734-712 557.
BA (Hons) 3d Design, LSDC.
Pc Baptistry window – All Saints', Bucklebury, Berks. Repairs and supply of new leaded lights – Framewood Manor, Stoke Poges for Russell Smith Design & Developments. Leaded lights – National Trust renovation for Merry-Croft, Combe End, Whitchurch, and for Grayan Construction, Aldermaston.

JONES, J. H. (Empl: one, self employed; Est: 1977)
Thatcher
12 Mayflower Close, Chittlehampton, Umberleigh, N Devon EX37 9QD. 076 94-305.

JONES ORIGINAL ANTIQUE LIGHTING 1860–1960 (Empl: 3; Est: 1980)
194 Westbourne Grove, London W11. 071-229 6866.
Pc Has provided lighting for many famous people, but unwilling to give details due to respect for clients' privacy.
Original light fittings from 1860–1960 inc. converted Victorian gas fittings, Arts & Crafts, Edwardian, Art Nouveau and Art Deco. Normally hold in stock approx 600 different lights inc. table lamps, wall and ceiling fittings. Through experience this firm has found that home owners are beginning to realize the importance of lighting – 'how it can dictate the total ambience of any area, be it the loo or the drawing room!'

FIRMS AND CRAFTSPEOPLE

JONES, ROBERT (Empl: partnership; Est: 1986)
Mural Artist
20 Waverley Crescent, London SE18 7QS. 081-317 1533.
Robert Jones – BA (Hons) Fine Art, Winchester; MA RCA; Rome Scholarship   Lorraine Jones – BA (Hons) Fine Art, Falmouth; Rome Scholarship; Fellowship (Exeter).
Pc Murals inc. Debenhams, Oxford St for Fitch & Co; Ransome's Restaurant, London; Shell Mex House, London, with GMW Architects; boardroom, Home & County Architects, London; many private commissions. Furniture made from cut out, wooden, figurative shapes painted in a style of illusion, which are then slotted together.

JONES, ROY (Empl: 2; Est: 1950)
Master Thatcher
Engine House Cottage, Onibury, Craven Arms, Salop SY7 9AY. 058 477-350.
Glous, Hereford, Warwicks, Worcs MTA.
Estimates free. Willing to undertake thatching with heather, indoor bars, etc.

JONMAR (Empl: 9; Est: 1959)
Antique Furniture Restorer
The Old Maltings, St Andrew's St, Bury St Edmunds, Suffolk IP33 3PH. 0284-64110.
M AMU.
Pc Still hold main contract for Shrublands Hall Health Clinic (34 yrs on). Repair and regilding – circular mirror, Mayor's Parlour, Clock Museum, Bury St Edmunds.
Also makes handmade curtains, drapes, tails, pelmets and swags.

JOSLIN, J. (CONTRACTORS) LTD (Empl: 40; Est: 1964)
Lower Rd, Long Harborough, Oxon OX7 2LN. 0993-882 153. FAX 0993-882 960.
The Stone Fed; Fed of Building Specialist Contractors; BEC.
Pc Restoration projects in Oxford inc. – All Souls College; Mansfield College; Dorchester Abbey.

JOSLIN, TONY (Empl: 6; Est: 1976)
Black Lane Pots, Hamptworth, Salisbury, Wilts SP5 2DS. 0794-390 796.
Specialize in making replicas for the V & A Museum, the British Museum and other museums. These copies of items in their collections are sold worldwide.

'JUELLE' STAINED GLASS (JUNE STANDING)

JOTCHAM & KENDALL LTD (Empl: 25; Est: 1812)
Building Contractors
4 The Chipping, Wotton-under-Edge, Glos GL12 7AD. 0453-842 391.
BEC.
Pc Conversion/restoration of orangery to drama hall – Westonbirt School, Tetbury, Glos. Civic Trust Award for external restoration of mid 19th-century mill building – New Mills, Kingswood, Wotton-under-Edge, Glos.

JOWETT, H. & CO LTD (Empl: 16; Est: 1949)
Stonemasons
Furlong St, Arnold, Nottingham NG5 7AL. 0602-208 237.
BEC; The Stone Fed.
Pc Restoration work inc. – Clumber Chapel for National Trust; Kedelston Hall for National Trust; Queen St Post Office, Nottingham; St Mary's Church, Derby.

JOWITT, JANET
Textile Restorer
22 Claremont Rd, Twickenham TW1 2QY. 081-892 3818.
Trained 3 yrs at the V & A Museum; worked privately (self-employed) since 1981.
Pc Restored altarpiece – Studley Royal Church, Ripon for DOE. Various curtains repaired and lined, velvet panels cleaned and conserved for period house in Highgate. Painted silk bedcovers cleaned and supported. Work at Ham House.

JOYCE, NICK ARCHITECT (Est: 1989)
44 Friar Street, Worcester, WR1 2NA. 0905-726 307.
BA Dip Arch.
Pc Job architect on 26, 27 Cornmarket, Oxford; Ancient High House, Stafford (phrases II and III); Ankerdine Farmhouse, Knightwick, Worcs; Monkspath Hall, Solihull.

JSR. JOINERY LTD (Empl: 10–12; Est: 1975)
Poole St, Gt Yeldham, Halstead, Essex CO9 4HN. 0787-237 722.
Majority of work is replacement joinery (windows, doors, and stairs), much of it for listed buildings. Brochure.

'JUELLE' STAINED GLASS (JUNE STANDING) (Empl: 3 assistants; Est: 1978)
19 Belsize Park, Hampstead, London NW3 4DO. 071-435 8029.
Tutor at Hampstead Garden Suburb Inst in Stained Glass, Central Sq, NW11. Also Amesteam School in London, London Rd, St John's Wood, NW8.

FIRMS AND CRAFTSPEOPLE

Pc Commissions since 1978 have been primarily for private residences inc. Art Deco, abstract and figurative styles. Screens (5 ft) for religious group. Presently engaged in 7 windows for Franciscan Chapel in Yugoslavia.
Brochure.

KAB TEXTILE DESIGNS (Empl: solo; Est: 1988)
Whitchurch Silk Mill, 28 Winchester Street, Whitchurch, Hants RG28 7AL. 0256-892 030.
1st Class Degree, BA(Hons) West Surrey College of Art; MA (RCA) Textile Design.
Pc Curtains of grading colours for private client's bedroom. Woven fabric for specially commissioned boardroom chairs for company.
Quality silk fabrics produced at the historic Whitchurch Silk Mill (open to the general public, ring 0256-892 065), using the original looms and machinery plus power looms. Production is relatively small scale, but own range of designs can often be altered to accommodate client's needs. Minimum order usually 30 yds, but negotiable.

KANTOROWICZ, NICOLA (Est: 1986)
Stained Glass Artist/Painter
11 Lansdowne Rd, Muswell Hill, London N10 2AX. 081-883 0348.
BA (Hons) Winchester School of Art; Textiles Advanced Dip Stained Glass Design; Hon Sec BSMGP; M BSMGP.
Pc All work in private buildings. Folio available for viewing.

KD CRAFTS (Empl: solo; Est: 1988)
Furniture Maker, Carver & Gilder
Unit B7, Metropolitan Workshops, Enfield Rd, Hackney N1. 081-985 7162.
Apprentice Furniture Maker; C & Gs Advanced in Cabinet Making and also Carving & Gilding; C & Gs in Timber Prep, Finishing, Furniture Making.

KEEVIL, MAURICE E. Est: 1934
Conserves & Restores Murals, Ceiling & Easel Paintings
60 East Hill, Wandsworth, London SW18 2HQ. 081-8745236.
F IIC; Full M ABPR
Pc Restoration of painted ceilings by Antonio Verrio, Hampton Court Palace. Restoration of paintings and murals by William Dyce, Houses of Parliament. Restoration of painted hall ceiling – Royal Naval College, Greenwich by Sir James Thornhill, etc.
Also willing to copy oil paintings.

KEMP, GEORGE STROUD & CO LTD (Empl: approx 50; Est: 1857)
Building Contractors
2–4 Elms Rd, Aldershot, Hants GU11 1LL. 0252-20339. FAX 0252-333 924.
BEC; HBF; active apprenticeship/training programme. Approved: Eng. Heritage; PSA; Hants CC; Surrey CC; Crown Supplies; Rushmoor DC; Surrey Heath DC; Waverley DC; etc.
This firm has had a long association in building, extension, modernization and refurbishment, and have been responsible for many of the existing buildings in Aldershot.

KENDALL, BARRY (Empl: 2; Est: 1978)
Stained Glass Artist
Living Glass Studio, 67 Fulwell Rd, Teddington, Middx TW11 0RH. 081-977 5277.
Self taught.
Pc Various private residences.

KENNEDY, MESSRS GRM, & PARTNERS (Est: 1988)
Chartered Architects, Interior Designers & Structural Engineers
Anchor House, 62 Regent Quay, Aberdeen AB1 2AR. 101 New City Rd, Glasgow G4 9JU. 24 Rutland St, Edinburgh EH1 2AN. 0224-591 272.
Pc Housing restoration projects in Rothes; Elgin and Keith; Sheriff Court House, Aberdeen; Town and County Hall, Aberdeen; 16th-century tollbooth, St Giles' House, Elgin. Project values £60,000–£5 m.

KENNETH-DUNCAN BSc (Est: 12 yrs)
Consulting Engineers
8 Glenhurst Rd, Henley-in-Arden, Warwicks B95 5HZ. 05642-2924. FAX 05642-4980.
BSc (Eng Glasgow); MSE (Civils); BA (Civils, Bristol); FSVA; M Land Inst; Fellow Faculty of Building.
Pc Restoration – Victorian factories, Tyseley, Birmingham. Restoration Victorian trusses – factories, Tipton. Conservation of despoiled sites – Brownhills. Sea walls at San Eglise, Province Maritime, France. Steel framing to Georgian buildings, Central Walsall. Grant conservation.

KENTEL JOINERY LTD (Empl: 10; Est: 1980)
Architectural & Industrial Joinery Manufacturers
Unit 27, Smith's Ind Estate, Humber Avenue, Coventry CV3 1JL. 0203-449 621.
Coventry Chamber of Commerce; FMB.

FIRMS AND CRAFTSPEOPLE

Pc Sliding sash windows – Coombe Abbey.
Reproduction of sliding sash windows, Georgian windows, doors, stairs, etc. Services inc. the grinding of cutters to exact profiles, to carefully reproduce original mouldings. Brochure.

KERLEY, RICHARD (Empl: solo; Est: 1970)
Antique Furniture Restorer & English Water Gilder
6 York Mansions, 84 Chiltern St, London W1M 1PT. 071-486 6483.
Various apprenticeships; London College of Furniture; GMC.
Pc Restoration of Adam fire surround involving carving, missing panel and gilding.

KESTREL JOINERY CO LTD (Empl: 12; Est: 1988, as part of G. Kemp Stroud 1857)
2/4 Elms Rd, Aldershot, Hants, GU11 1LL. 0252-343 959.
Timber Research & Development Assoc; CITB.
Pc Crown Suppliers; hotel groups; banks.
Brochure.

KETTLE, ALICE (Est: 1986)
Embroidered Wall-pieces
6 Clifton Terrace, Winchester, Hants, SO22 5BJ. 0962-64711.
BA (Hons) Fine Art, Reading University; post grad Dip in Textile Art, Goldsmiths College, London University.
Pc Banner – Dance Umbrella Festival, Winchester People's Pageant. Work in collections inc. Embroiderers' Guild (Hampton Court Palace); Springall Collection; W. Sussex College of Higher Education. Private commissions.
Pieces range from very large hangings to smaller pieces, framed and glazed. Information pack available inc. slides and postcards.

THE KEYHOLE (Est: 1984)
'Dragonwyck', Far Back Lane, Farnsfield, Newark, Notts NG222 8JX. 0623-882 590.
G & G's Full Tech; I Eng (CEI); MI Mech IE; SM MLA.
Carry a modest selection of locks for supply to customers, and a large quantity of original keys and blanks.

KEYMER HANDMADE CLAY TILES (Empl: 115; Est: 1880)
Nye Rd, Burgess Hill, Sussex RH15 0LZ. 044 46-2931. FAX 044-871 852.

KIDBY, M. D. BUILDINGS LTD (Empl: 10; Est: 1963)
Conservatories Designed & Manufactured to Customers' Requirements
28 Kennylands Rd, Sonning Common, Reading RG4 9JT. 0734-723 380.

KING, THOS & SONS (BUILDERS) LTD

Pc Can usually make arangements for customers to view completed buildings similar to the kind under consideration.
Free quotations within 25 miles of Reading. Brochure.

KIER MARRIOTT LIMITED (Empl: 135 + apprentices; Est: 1890)
Building Contractors
Mariott House, Rushden, Northants NN10 9EA. 0933-57511.
23 craft apprentices; company inc. on CITB. MNHBC; BEC. Approved: most local authorities within 40 m radius of Rushden; PSA; British Rail; Home Office – Prison Dept.
Pc Refurbishment, repairs and restoration in Northampton inc.Upton Hall; Thornby Hall; Royal Theatre. Alterations – main building, Stowe School. Refurbishment – Ram Jam Inn, Great North Rd, Stretton. St Andrew Church, Great Linford. Masonry repairs and restoration works inc.Castle Ashby; Hinwick Hall; Colworth House and Woburn Abbey.
Restoration projects ranging in value up to c. £500,000.

KIER WALLIS
Building Contractors
2–6 Homesdale Rd, Bromley, Kent BR2 9TN. 081-464 3377.

KILNER, CELIA (Empl: solo; Est: 1986)
Lettercutter
Sheppards Mill, Holmfirth, Huddersfield, W. Yorks HD7 1RW. 0484-685 167.
Advanced Lettering Certificate; C & Gs London Art School.
Pc Architects' plaques. Headstones. Heraldic carving. Lettercutting for interior designer. Heraldic painting (Grand Metropolitan Hotel). Hand lettering for brochures.

KINDLER, ANDREW LTD (Empl: 5; Est: 1985)
Furniture Design & Manufacture
Unit C, 15a Carysfort Rd, Stoke Newington, London, N16 9AF. 071-241 2599.
Graduate of the John Makepeace School for Craftsmen in Wood.
Pc Reception and boardroom areas a speciality.
Will consider any commission from a jewellery box to an entire boardroom.

KING, THOS & SONS (BUILDERS) LTD (Empl: 200; Est: 1933)
Abbotts Ann, Andover, Hants SP11 7BL. 0264-710 404. FAX 0264-710 119.
BEC; LCA. Approved: Eng. Heritage; PSA; Hants CC; Wilts CC; Berks CC; numerous local and health authorities.

FIRMS AND CRAFTSPEOPLE

KINGSWOOD SERVICES LTD (Empl: 12; Est: 1984)
Lighting Manufacturers & Furnishings
Amber Mill, Oakethorpe, Derbys DE5 7LL. 0773-834 684. FAX 0773-520 298.
As well as period and modern purpose built lighting, also hold a standard range of period products inc. furnishings; fountains; pedestals; columns; lanterns; bollards; clocks; railings; bandstand; benches; etc. inc. authentic period designs, dating as far back as the early 19th century. Full design service available. Brochure.

KINLEY, SUSAN (Est: 1981)
Mixed Media Wallhangings
29 Faversham Rd, Catford, London SE6 4XE. 081-690 7505.
BA (Hons) Fine Art/Textiles, Goldsmiths College of Art; MA Royal College of Art & Design; M Craft Council, and on the selected index.
Pc Mixed media wallworks – boardroom, Advertising Standards Office. Back-lit Japanese paper panels – Insurance Building, Sheffield. Large mosaic panel – Royal Angus Hotel, Birmingham. Panels – restaurant/lobby, Sedgewick Centre, Whitechapel. Back lit silk/paper/glass panels – Royal Albert House, Windsor.
Panels and screens made from fine layers of papers and silks, mounted directly on to a surface or suspended between glass or perspex sheets. Postcards of work available.

KIRBY, MICHAEL (Empl: one; Est: 1977)
Master Thatcher
Honeysuckle Cottage, Broadhempston, Totnes, Devon TQ9 6BD. 0803-812 728 & 864 777.
Qualified Master Thatcher; applied for Membership of MTA.
Basic timbering done, but usually employ building contractors for major work and advice. Wheat reed only used for ridging.

KIRKLAND TILES (Empl: solo; Est: 1988)
Kirkland, Kirkpatrick, Durham, Nr Castle Douglas, Kirkcudbright DG7 3EZ. 055 665-371.
Dip in Ceramics, Harrogate College of Art; M Scottish Crafts Association.
Pc Fire surround of 86 hand-painted tiles depicting birds, animals and scenes of places the client knew well. Spanish style wall plaque of peasants plucking chickens 8 ft × 6 ft – private client. Various commissions for kitchens and bathrooms. Hand-painted tiles of fish, geese, flowers, animals and birds.

KNIGHT, ALAN (Est: 1945)
Designer Blacksmith
The Old Chapel, Hanbury, Nr Bromsgrove, Worcs. 021-445 1678.
7 yr apprenticeship; Fellow, and Bronze & Silver Medallist – Worshipful Co of Blacksmiths; F SD-C.
Pc Restoration of ironwork for National Trust – Erddig Park; Powis Castle and others. New work to own design – Worcester, Hereford, Manchester and Chelmsford Cathedrals, and many Parish Churches. Also private homes.

KNIGHT, SIMON (Est: 1982)
Stained Glass Artist/Painter
3 Holmesland Lane, Botley, Southampton, Hants SO3 2EH. 0489-786 281.
Architectural Stained Glass HND (with Merits); 12 yrs experience; M BSMGP; DM CSD.
Pc Mainly secular for public and private buildings.
Mr Knight will refer an enquirer to a specialist if he feels his knowledge in an area is inadequate. Particularly interested in contemporary secular glass, and enjoys working in conjunction with architects and designers.

KNIGHT'S of LONDON (Est: 1984)
Fireplace Consultants
2a Belsize Park Mews, Belsize Village, London NW3 5BL. 071-431 2490.
B Sc.
Pc Restored/installed 8 marble chimneypieces, – 'Lichfield House', St James, London. SW1. 3 fireplaces installed – 'The Holme', Regent's Park, London. Multiple fireplace restoration/installation contracts for Kier Wallis; Costain; Wiltshire.
A non-retail based professional consultancy dealing exclusively with antique and period fireplaces inc. design and planning; search-and-purchase facilities; installation and restoration; full advice and information service. Keep a national register of all available antique and reproduction fireplaces in the UK. The firm negotiates solely on behalf of clients so that the client obtains the best deal.

KNOTT, R. W. & SONS (Empl: 10; Est: 1958)
Church Tower & Spire Restorers, Roofing, Gilding
Midway, Oakhill, Somerset, BA3 5JE 0749-840 496.
FMB; LCA. Approved: Diocesan, Eng. Heritage and Local Authority.
Pc St Mary the Virgin, Bishops Canning. St Mary on the Quay. Kent Temple, Shotover Park, for Sir John Mills/Eng. Heritage. St Peter's, Carmarthen. Cirencester Parish Church. Radley College, Abingdon.

FIRMS AND CRAFTSPEOPLE

Sudeley Castle, Winchcombe. Keble College, Oxford.
An old established firm of church restorers willing to carry out work to historic buildings, monuments, castles, etc. Specialize in towers; roofing (lead and copper); lightning conductors; gilding; woodworm and dry rot treatment.

KNOWLES, B. J. (Empl: solo; Est: 1968)
Joinery
Willoughby Wind, Hindon, Nr Salisbury, Wilts SP3 6EG. 0747-89 382.
4 yr apprenticeship, Craft & Advanced Craft Carpentry & Joinery; O Level Building Practice and Building Construction; M GMC; Inst of Brit Carpenters; Technical M Inst of Building.
Pc Too numerous to detail.

KYME'S STAINED GLASS (Empl: 5; Est: 1982)
69 Gilkes St, Middlesbrough, Cleveland TS1 5EH. 0642-242 612.
Pc Work for Cleveland County Council and District Councils and various breweries. Camerans Visitors Centre. Gift for retiring union president – SOGAT (Printers Union). Hills Interior Design, Middlesbrough. Phoenix Design Consultants, Leeds.

LACEY, AMANDA DAWN (Empl: solo; Est: 1983)
Stained Glass Artist/Painter
14 Woodrolfe Rd, Tollesbury, Essex CM9 85B. 0621-869 412.
M SMGP; Art Qualifications.
Pc Restoration work to Victorian panels – London area and many others. Stained glass panels individually designed doors; interior windows/screens; firescreens; lighting.
Photographs available of work carried out during past 5 yrs.

LAING, CHARLES & SONS LTD (Empl: 3; Est: 1920)
Brass & Iron Founders
28 Beaverbank Place, Edinburgh EH7 4ET. 031-556 3160.
All qualified tradesman; M Inst of Brit Foundrymen.
Pc Bronze armillary – Hunterston Power Station. Various bronze plaques. Various pieces of sculpture exhibited throughout the country. Cast iron railings – Arthur Lodge, and also Playfair House, Edinburgh. Repairs to railings – Holyrood Palace.

LAIRD, MICHAEL & PARTNERS (Est: 1954)
Architects, Landscape Architects, Design Consultants
22 Moray Place & 5 Forres St, Edinburgh, Lothian EH3 6DE. 031-226 6991.

LANGLEY LONDON LTD

Michael Laird OBE, Ian Rogers, Alan Black, Tom Donaldson, C. Hulme Bailey, Roy S. Milne, Brian I. A. Lightbody – FSIA; RIBA; FRIAS; ARIAS; B Arch (Hons).
Pc Restitution – Pilrig House. Restoration works inc. – Easter Elchies House, Morayshire, headquarters of Macallan-Glenlivet plc; Maxwelton House, Dumfries-shire; Blairquhan Castle, Ayrshire; the Manor House, Inveresk. Conservation project for Jenners of Edinburgh.
Awards received from Civic Trust; RSA; Saltire Soc; British Steel Corp; European Architectural Heritage Year; Stone Fed; RICS/ Times Award for Conservation. Consultancy services in interior design, furniture design and selection; will recommend consultancy services for quantity surveying, structural engineering, M & E services and graphic design.

LANE, BREMNER & GARNETT (Est: 1961)
Architects
69 Berkeley St, Glasgow G3 7DX. 041-221 8148.
John Lane – Dip Arch; PPRIAS; FRIBA   Dennis J. Garnett – FRIAS; FRIBA   Duncan Bremner – Dip Arch; FRIAS; FRIBA   Eric S. Waterston – B Arch; ARIAS; RIBA.
Pc Alterations and extensions – Arrochar & Tarbet Hotels. Stone cleaning and repairs – St John's Renfield Church. Conversion works – Luggiebank House, Kirkintillock (to newspaper office and printing works) – Dalzell House, Motherwell; Shieldhill Hotel, Biggar.
Experienced in historic/listed buildings; infill work; project management; dry rot/fungus/beetle; feasibility studies; environmental studies; survey/ valuations.

LANGLEY LONDON LTD
Ceramic Tile & Mosaic Murals
Head Office & Showrooms: Architectural Art Dept, 161-167 Borough High St, London SE1 1HU. 071-407 4444.
M Art & Architecture.
Pc London Transport – Baker Street Station; Tottenham Court Road Station; Oxford Circus Station, etc. Leisure centres inc. Centre Parks, Nottingham; Swansea Leisure Centre. Administration, Jubail, Saudi Arabia. Bus station murals, Nottingham. Pedestrian subways. Private swimming pools. Numerous commercial buildings.
Decorative mural features and finishes for buildings, subways and structures inc. mosaics; ceramic tile murals; overglazed signs. Free design service available inc. computer aided design – sketches and photographs are entered into the computer, which then translates the image into a mosaic of squares. Brochure.

FIRMS AND CRAFTSPEOPLE

LANGLOW PRODUCTS LTD
Specialists in Solvents, Wood Care & Allied Products
PO Box 32, Asheridge Rd, Chesham, Bucks HP5 2QF. 0494-784 866.
In many countries of the world this company supplies a range of products suitable for removing paint from stonework; Roman cement; cast iron; prefabricated metal work; fibrous plasterwork; brickwork; timber; moulded, turned and carved wood. Many of their products have been used on historic buildings inc. Langlow Safer Stripper TM; Langlow Peel Away TM; Patina TM and solvent-based wood preservatives. Brochure.

LANTERN SHOP, THE (Empl: 5; Est: 1973)
415 New St. Sidmouth, Devon EX10 8AP. 0395-513 962.
Pc Work completed for National Trust.
Supply antique lighting goods, brought up-to-date for electricity and fitted with shades (custom-made). Conservation not undertaken, only restoration. Brochure.

LASSEN, MICHAEL G. STAINED GLASS (Empl: 2; Est: 1979)
McArthur Building, Gas Ferry Rd, Bristol BS8 6UN. 12 Ambrose Rd, Clifton Wood, Bristol 8, Avon. 0272-277 191.
Associate BSMGP; Somerset Guild of Craftsmen.
Pc Churches inc. Gt Somerford; Holy Cross, Bedminster; Burnham on Crouch; Merthyr Dyfan, Barry, Wales; Wick, St Lawrence, Avon; Elton Rd, Bishopston.

LAUDER, SYLVIA (Est: 1962)
Rag Hangings & Door Curtains
62 Middle St, Stroud, Glos GL5 1EA. 045 36-5875.
Foundation Course; 3 yrs Specialist Textile Training, Birmingham College of Arts & Crafts; M Gloucestershire Guild of Craftsmen.

LAVAL, IAN (Empl: one; Est: 1971)
Furniture Maker
Meadowbank Farm, Curthwaite, Wigton, Cumbria CA7 8BG. 0228-710 409.
Traditional furniture (mainly made from Cumbrian timber felled and sawn by Ian Laval himself), with clear, simple lines and careful proportions chosen to complement the wood. Visitors welcome at the workshop, which contains a small showroom. Brochure.

LAWRENCE & CO (Empl: 3; Est: 1977)
Stained Glass Artist/Painter
2 Hackington Terrace, Canterbury, Kent CT2 7HE. 0227-452 841.
A BSMGP.

LEATHERLAND, PAMELA

Pc Restoration and new window in churches throughout the country.
Domestic windows are not undertaken.

LAWSON JOHNSTON, PHILIP (Empl: solo; Est: 1971)
Glass Engraver
The Plazzotta Studio, 22 Cathcart Rd, London SW10 9NN. 071-351 0066.
AF GGE.
Pc Lettering, Pentecost scene on church doors/panels – Holy Trinity, Brompton, London. Representation of an exploding champagne bottle – Greens, Champagne Bar, Duke St, London.
Scenes, lettering, coats-of-arms on interior panels, windows, table tops, etc.

LAWTON, ANDREW FURNITURE (Empl: one; Est: 1978)
Goatscliffe Workshops, Grindleford, Derbys, S30 1HG (via Sheffield). 0433-31754.
5 yrs training at the bench; Teachers Cert (Credit); Full M SD-C.
Pc Hall furniture, English oak comprising 3 chairs, lectern and display cabinet – Queen Elizabeth's Grammar School, Ashbourne. Display case – Lincoln County Hospital. Bookcases and room divider inc. site installation for a private client, Nevis, W. Indies.

LAZENBY, ALLAN LEADED LIGHTS (Est: family business 1884)
36a Hampton Rd, Scarborough, N. Yorks YO12 5PU. 0723-365 804.
Years of experience.
Pc Memorial window – St Thomas's Church, Gristhorpe, Filey. Victoria Hotel, Scarborough. Has been entrusted with the restoration and repair of stained glass for many years, by churches and private clients all over the country.
Works with his daughter on the design, manufacture and installation of new windows, canopies, screens, door panels, lighting to complement new or existing decor. See also entry STAINED GLASS DESIGN.

LEAD & LIGHT (Empl: 3; Est: 1973)
Stained Glass Artist
15 Camden Lock, London NW1 8AF. 071-485 4568.

LEATHERLAND, PAMELA
Stained Glass Artist
'Alwyns', Pitton, Nr Salisbury, Wilts SP5 1DU. 072 272-314.
Training as glass painter in stained glass studios; ARCA Stained Glass; M BSMGP.
Pc Many small portable panels for domestic windows. Leaded glass and appliquéd glass landing windows – Stockbridge; Chilbolton;

Southampton. Appliqué glass – internal hatchway, Nr Salisbury. Leaded stained glass – front doors, Shaftesbury, Salisbury.

LECKIE, MONA (Empl: several; Est: 1982)
Cane, Rush, Willow, Ratten, Bamboo
Manor House, Toftrees, Fakenham, Norfolk, NR21 7DZ. 0328-3598.
C & Gs Basketry, Seating. M Basketmakers Assoc.
Pc Antique chair repair for a private client.
Unable to undertake work on whole willow furniture. A variety of baskets available. Brochure.

LEECH, LUCINDA FURNITURE (Empl: 3/4; Est: 1977)
King St, Jericho, Oxford OX2 6DF. 0865-56376.
Cabinet makers hold various qualifications; SD-C.
Pc Memorial chairs – Romsey Abbey. 36 drawer cabinet – collection of Turner engravings, Magdalen College, Oxford. Cabinet bookcase – William Morris Society, Kelmscott House.
Furniture with an emphasis on function, simplicity of outline, the combination of more than one timber, using construction as the decorative element. Showroom open by appointment. Work normally completed within 6 weeks of order. Brochure.

LEGGOTT, W. & R. LTD (Empl: 70; Est: 1881)
Brassfounders & Architectural Metalworkers
Silens Works, East Parade, Bradford, W. Yorks BD1 5HA. 0274-392 716. 21 Bloomsbury Way, London WC1A 2TH.
Guild of Architectural Ironmongers.
Pc Balustrading – Royal Bank of Scotland Headquarters. Pavillions, Birmingham. Alexandra Palace. Brass balustrade – Vanderbilt Hotel, London. Mild steel and cast iron railings, and cast aluminium, decorative grilles – MEPC Buildings, 90 Longacre, London. Wrought-iron decorative gates and railings – Lees Court, London.
Reproduction and refurbishment work inc. architectural ironmongery, metalwork and brassfoundery. Also supply intruder alarms, locks, access and security systems. Brochure.

LEIGHS (EDENBRIDGE) LTD (Empl: 70; Est: 1881)
Building Contractors – Restoration of Timber-framed & Historic Buildings
Shefts Croft, Mill Hill, Edenbridge, Kent TN8 5DB. 0732-862 133 & 862 609.
5th generation of small family firm; M BEC. Approved: Diocese of Rochester; Sevenoaks DC; Kent CC.
Pc Restoration – 96 High St, Edenbridge for The Great Stone Bridge Trust. Restoration and alterations – Truggers Cottage,

Chiddingstone Hoath. Additional workshop – Wolfe Garage. Westorway for P. Johnson Esq. Addition – Hill Hoath House, Chiddingstone. Complete restoration – Paul's Farm, Leigh.
Specialize in the restoration of older buildings in a careful and sympathetic manner, although will carry out extensions and alterations to more modern properties.

LENTON LAMP STUDIOS (Empl: one; Est: 1984)
13 Harrington Drive, Lenton, Nottingham NG7 1JQ. 0602-472 726.
Tiffany reproductions; wall and hanging lamps; Art Deco wall and fan lamps; stained glass windows to specification inc. birds, butterflies, flowers and commemorative window depicting World War II aircraft.

LETCH, STEPHEN J. (Empl: 3; Est: 1979)
Chairman Essex & Herts Master Thatchers Association
Spiggy Holes, Rignals Lane, Galleywood, Chelmsford, Essex CM2 8QU. 0245-72807.
Full M Essex & Herts MTA; Suffolk MTA; E Anglia MTA; Nat Council of MTAs; cups won 1987 for long straw and water reed work.
Pc Thatching work carried out for Moody Properties Ltd and McLaughlin & Harvey plc.

LEVER, R. W. A.
See DESIGNER DECORATIONS (R. W. A. LEVER)

LEWENSTEIN, EILEEN (Empl: solo; Est: 1946)
Architectural Sculptress
11 Western Esplanade, Portslade, Brighton, E. Sussex BN41 1WE. 0273-418 705.
Painting & drawing, West of England College of Art, Bristol & Beckenham School of Art; ATD University of London, Inst of Higher Education. Partner, Donald Mills Pottery. Director, Briglin Pottery Ltd, lecturer in Ceramics, Hornsey College of Art; individual studio potter; F SD-C; Council M Craftsmen Potters Assoc & International Academy of Ceramics.
Pc Screen – facade, Convent of Our Lady of Sion, London, W8.

LEWIS, ELAIN (Est: 1988, formerly working in Beds & Cambs)
Dye-resist Wallhangings
Fossgate Working Gallery, 33B Fossgate, York YO1 2TA. 0904-620 263.
NDD.
Pc Large number of works in the dye-resist method for hotels

throughout the world inc. Hilton, Gatwick; Sheraton, Edinburgh; Shangri La, Singapore; Intercontinental Berlin; Hilton, Ankara; Swallow Hotels; etc.
Presentation prepared where necessary.

LEWIS, JACK (Empl: 2; Est: 1969)
Master Thatcher
Perrins Cottage, Compton Durville, S Petherton, Somerset TA13 5ET. 0460-40027.
Apprenticeship (CoSIRA sponsored) inc. further journeyman experience; M Somerset MTA; M Somerset Guild of Craftsmen.
Pc High Ham Windmill, Somerset (only thatched windmill in England) for National Trust. The Silkhouses, Kilmington, Wilts. Cottage, Blaize Castle Hamlet, Bristol. Work in Massachusetts, USA inc. 9 mths at Plymouth Plantation (reconstructed pilgrim village); Sagamore Bridge Christmas Tree Shop, Cape Cod.

LEWIS, MICHAEL & AMANDA ORIENTAL CARPETS (Empl: 4; Est: 1979)
8 North St, Wellington, Somerset TA21 8LT. 0823 47 7430.
Trained by Persian master restorer; 10 yrs experience.
Pc Clients inc. National Trust, major banks, and private collectors, but they believe the quality of their work is the best recommendation.
Buyers, sellers and restorers of old and antique needlework and/or piled hand-woven rugs and carpets. Will also mount, hang, and/or supply cushions, from fragments of favourite rugs which have 'gone on'. Will locate and supply large carpets if desired.

LEYLAND STAINED GLASS (Empl: 2; Est: 1985)
Worden Park Craft Centre, Worden Park, Leyland, Lancs. 0772-456 673 & 0772-314 771 (Home).
4 yr apprenticeship in design, making up, repair & glazing of leaded lights; 8 yrs experience; 3 yr Stained Glass Course, Swansea College.
Pc Restored leaded light windows at Brindle Parish Church and Burscough Parish Church. Work carried out for Greenall Whittley's & Winstons Pizzas.

LGM LTD (Empl: 6; Est: 1981)
Traditional Upholstery
Coppice Trading Estate, Stourport Rd, Kidderminster, Worcs DY11 7QY. 0562-823 700.
AMU.
Only willing to undertake French polishing on furniture being upholstered.

LGS (Empl: 5; Est: 1980)
Stained Glass Artists
Bothy House, Northop Rd, Halkyn, Clywd CH8 8DF. 0352-781 122.
Pc Many and various; details on application.

LICHTERMAN, HEIDI (Empl: solo; Est: 1981)
Hand-dyed Silk Wallhangings inc. Three-dimensional Designs
The Old Courthouse, Bottisham, Cambridge, CB5 9BA. 0223-811 679.
F SD-C.
Wallhangings from 3 ft × 4 ft to 12 ft × 30 ft, designed for the site. Brochure.

LIEBSCHER, KARL (Est: 1984)
Dry Stone Walling
1 The Row, Easthope, Nr Much Wenlock, Salop TF13 6DW. 074 636-497.
M Dry Stone Walling Assoc.

LIGHTFOOT, CHARLES LTD (Est: 1890)
Stained Glass Artists, Wholesale & Retail Glass Merchants
81 Upper Brook St, Manchester M13 9TB. 061-273 1134/5/6.
Glass & Glazing Fed.
Glass processing and decoration; window and glazing contractors.

LIMELIGHT STUDIOS (Empl: one; Est: 1985)
Artists & Restorers in Glass
Thames St, Leicester LE1 3WN. 0533-531 631. FAX 0533-470 507.
BA (Hons) Degree Stained Glass Design, Edinburgh Art School; Associate BSMGP: M Art & Architecture.
Pc 200 ft fully painted new east window – St Crispin's Church, Leicester. Numerous restorations of valuable church windows throughout the E. Midlands.

LINFORD-BRIDGEMAN LTD (Empl: 100; Est: 1879)
Cathedral Works, Quonians, Lichfield, Staffs WS13 7LB. 0543-414 234.
Craftsmen have passed recognized craft apprenticeships, and are employed direct by the firm. Details available on application.
Brochure.

LINLEY, BEAUFORD D. (SCULPTOR) (Empl: solo; Est: 1969)
Rose Cottage, Boothby Pagnell, Grantham, Lincs NG33 4DG. 047 685-266.
C & Gs Fine Art Cert.

Pc Restoration of carvings in wood and stone. Commemorative plaques – Southwark and Lincoln Cathedrals; York Railway Museum; Southwell Minster. Various bronze portrait heads, animal carvings (wood/stone). Carved stone figures for churches/castles and private houses.
Restoration reproductions and individual designs in wood and resins in various finishes.

LIPPIATT, LIZ (Empl: 3 part-time; Est: 1982)
Textile Workshop
Cirencester Workshops, Brewery Court, Cirencester, Glos GL7 1JH. 0285-656 263 & 650 567. 4 Swan Studios, 69 Deodar Rd, London SW15 2NU. Wanswell Court, Berkeley, Glos GL13 9RT. 0453-810 679.
BA (Hons) 1st Class Fashion Design; Gloucestershire Guild of Craftsmen; Somerset Guild of Craftsmen.
Individual colours and designs for soft furnishings and fabrics. Also special occasion clothes and accessories.

LISI, F. & SON (REED THATCHERS) (Empl: 3; Est: 1958)
Carswell Home Farm, Carswell, Buckland, Oxon SN7 8HQ. 036 787-630.
Pc Historic barn/stable/garage block – Denchworth Manor, Nr Wantage.

LITTLEWOOD, MARGARET
Cane & Rush Seating
18 Main St, Queniborough, Leics LE7 8DA. 0533-600 501.
Attended courses at Denman College and Gt Missenden College.

LIVINGSTON, JUDITH A. (Empl: solo; Est: 1985)
Furniture Design, Restoration & Repair
Willowbrae, 3 Pittenweem Rd, Anstruther, Fife KY10 3DS. 0333-310 425.
BA (Hons) Furniture Design, Newcastle Polytechnic; post grad Dip History of Art, Glasgow University; M Scottish Soc for Conservation & Restoration.
Pc Complete restoration – Victorian Rocking Horse, Museum of Cumbraes. Clavichord stand for Cambridge Fellow. Re-consolidation and replacement veneer work – 18-century furniture, private client, St Andrew's. Various work – Frigate Unicorn Trust, Dundee.

LLOYD OF BEDWYN (Empl: 4; Est: 1790)
Stonemasons
91 Church St, Gt Bedwyn, Marlborough, Wilts SN8 3PF. 0672-870 234.

Seventh generation of family firm.
This firm is fully equipped with a modern plant, and holds extensive stocks of materials – all backed by traditional experience gleaned over hundreds of years.

LLOYD, MATTHEW STAINED GLASS STUDIOS (Empl: 2; Est: 1980)
63 Amberley Rd, Palmers Green, London N13 4BH. 081-886 0213 & 081-449 8878 (answerphone).
Pc Stained glass windows designed specifically for the home environment from the front door to the skylight! Also a range of complementary lighting and mirrors.
Portfolio available by appointment.

LOCKS & HANDLES (ARCHITECTURAL COMPONENTS) LTD (Empl: 14; Est: 1955)
8 Exhibition Rd, London SW7 2HF. 071-584 6800 & 071-581 2401.
Period door furniture. Brochure.

LONDON ARCHITECTURAL SALVAGE & SUPPLY CO LTD, THE
The Vicarage, Mark St, Off Paul St, London EC2A 4ER. 071-739 0448/9.
Peg tiles; pan tiles; slates; plain and fancy chimneypots; beams; wood mouldings; room panelling; marble and stone tiles; tessellated and encaustic pavements; doors; columns; pilasters; 14th- to 20th-century chimneypieces and fire accessories; fencing and gates; door furniture; lighting; ceramics; textiles and papers; pews; benches; bar counters; bathroom furniture and fittings; etc.

LONDON DOOR CO, THE (Empl: 20; Est: 1982)
165 St John's Hill, London SW11 1TQ. 071-223 7243.
Two apprentices; 6 C & Gs Certs; various art colleges.
Internal and external doors inc. period style; room dividers; cupboard doors – all decorated if desired with decorative glass and stained glass. Willing to reinforce the door frame, and provide steel faced doors in 20 styles. A large standard range of doors, door furniture and locks available. All glass may be purchased separately. Brochure.

LONG, MAURICE ARTIST BLACKSMITH (Est: 1986)
The Forge, 10 Pipewell Road Workshops, Desborough, Northants NN14 2SN. 0536-763 050.
BA Degree Silversmithing & Metalwork, Camberwell School of Art & Crafts; M BABA.
Pc Wrought-iron chapel screens – Society of St John the Evangelist, St Edward's House, 22 Great College St, London. Various traditional/ modern shop and public house sign brackets. Commissioned by

FIRMS AND CRAFTSPEOPLE

Jaysigns sign contractors – 305, 307 Upper St, London.
Brochure.

LONG, TIMOTHY RESTORATION (Empl: 4; Est: 1978)
Restoration of English 18th-century Walnut & Mahogany Furniture.
26 Hight St, Seal, Sevenoaks, Kent TN1 5OAP. 0732-62606.
Full apprenticeship with C & Gs; BAFRA.

LONGBOTHAM, JOHN (IRONFOUNDERS) LTD (Empl: 9; Est: 1970)
Broomhill Rd, Bonnybridge, Stirlingshire FK4 2AN. 0324-812 860.
Pc Replaced all cast-iron windows – Kirkcudbright Parish Church, Dumfries. Hopper boxes – Usher Hall, Edinburgh. Railings and lamp post – Fettesrow, Edinburgh.

LONGLEY, JAMES & CO LTD (Empl: 400; Est: 1863)
Building Contractor
East Park, Crawley, W. Sussex RH10 6AP. 0293-561 212. King St, Oldham, Hants RG25 1LW. 0256-704 747. 26 Eccleston Square, London SW1V 1NS. 071-630 7231. Howard Terrace, Brighton BN1 3TR. 0273-202 486.
Annual apprentice/trainee intake (approx 20); BEC; FCEC; Approved: Eng. Heritage; PSA; most Borough and CCs within operational area.
Pc Restoration inc. Temperate House, Kew Gardens; Bushy House, Teddington for NPL; St Nicholas Church, Worth. Completion, inc. rose window – Lancing College Chapel. Richmond Palace Gate House. Gatehouse, Battle Abbey. Fountain Court, Hampton Court Palace.
A long established family run firm.

LONGLEY, JAMES JOINERY (Empl: 150+)
Address as parent company LONGLEY, JAMES & CO LTD (Crawley).
As parent Co, plus TRADA.
Pc House of Commons Library. Joinery for Britiah Embassies worldwide. Restoration work inc. Canterbury Cathedral; Westminster Abbey; Hever Castle. Refurbishment work inc. Ancaster House; Guards Club; St Catherine's Dock.
Brochure.

LONSDALE, STEPHEN LTD (Empl: 120; Est: 1983)
Design, Supply & Fixing of Architectural Carving & Masonry
Building L & M, Northfleet Ind Estate, Lower Rd, Northfleet, Kent DA11 9SN. Edinburgh Masonry Works, Block 1, Wallyford Ind Estate, Musselburgh EH21 8QJ. 0322-847 066.
Stone Fed; London Assoc of Master Stone Masons; BEC.

LOWRY, J. & W. LTD

Pc 63–65 Curzon St, London. Oakhill House, Hildenborough, Kent. Thorndon Hall, Brentwood, Essex. St Paulin's Church, Crayford, Kent. Garden St, Tunbridge Wells. Midland Bank Headquarters, London.
New building and restoration work inc. detailed carving; profile sawing of complex sections and mouldings; full technological backup; constructional details; material selection; performance criteria; etc. Brochure.

LONSDALE & DUTCH (Empl: one; Est: 1921)
Lighting Manufactureres & Restorers
23 B Howe St, Edinburgh, Midlothian. 031-556 3257.
Apprenticeship.
Pc Repair of lanterns and light fittings inc. The Hunterian Art Gallery, Glasgow; Brodie, Fyfie, and Brodick Castles for the National Trust. Fabrication of lanterns for private residences.

LOWCROSS (Empl: 5; Est: 1978)
Traditional Upholsterer
33 High St, Whitchurch, Shropshire SY13 1AZ. 0948-2433 & 4454.
Master upholsterers, master craftsmen; BA (Hons) Textiles & Embroidery.

LOWE, CHARLES (Empl: 7; Est: c. 1845)
Wood Craftsmen
37, 40 Church Gate, Loughborough, Leics LE11 1UE. 0509-212 554 & 217 876.
C & Gs cabinet making plus a 5 yr apprenticeship. All craftsmen have stayed with firm since apprenticeship, except one late arrival, a highly skilled cabinet maker
Pc Four poster replica and half testers – Hanton Old Hall, Derbys. Large internal stair gates to match existing stairs – Quenby Hall, Leics. Supply of antiques and restoration work – Wollaton Hall, Notts County Council.
Work to match existing architectural features, using ancient timber where necessary; early oak style furniture; extensive library of traditional fabrics; cabinet handles cast from original pattern; pictures restored and framed; carpets and rugs to own design; barometers and clocks restored; porcelain restored; cane and rush seating. Brochure.

LOWRY, J. & W. LTD (Empl: 45; Est: 1848)
Building Contractors, Stonemasonry & Joinery Specialists
64 Bath Lane, Newcastle-upon-Tyne NE4 5TT. 091-232 3586.
Indentured apprentices W. E. Lowry – FRICS; MCIOB; ACI Arb Firm – BEC; Stone Fed; Brit Woodworking Fed; NHBC.

Approved: Dioceses of Newcastle & Durham; RC Diocese of Hexham & Newcastle; PSA; Eng. Heritage; 9 Local Authorities; health authorities.

Pc Civic Trust Commendation – All Saints' Church, Newcastle. Civic Trust Award – Black Friars, Friars St, Newcastle. St Oswald's Church, Durham. St Peter's Church, Monkwearmouth, Sunderland. Morpeth Clock Tower. Tynemouth Castle. Newcastle Cathedral extension; Old Berwick Bridge Phase 1, Northumberland CC. Calleston Hall extension.

LUNN, J. S. & SONS (Empl: 3; Est: 1921)
Wrought-ironwork
Old School Works, Red Row, Morpeth, Northumberland NE61 5AU. 0670-760 246.
4 yr apprenticeship in wrought-iron, welding, shoeing and general blacksmithing; gold medallist; AFCL; RSS; DWCF.
Pc Restoration of badly damaged bronze statue of horse and rider (weight 3 tonnes).

LYONS, J. MASTER THATCHER (Empl: 2; Est: 1968)
8 The Paddocks, Little Witcombe, Gloucester. 0452-864 568 & 0452-619 929.
Nat Soc of Master Thatchers.

MABLESON, GUS CERAMICS (Est: 1976)
56 B St Peters Avenue, Kettering, Northants NN16 0HB. 0536-84019.
BA (Hons) 3d Design, Ceramics. Loughborough College of Art & Design.
Pc Low-relief architectural tiles – Warrington & Runcorn District Council; also Manchester City Council (largest tile 62 cm high). Large pots – Swallow Hotel, Peterborough (120 cm high). Replica work, saltglaze beer jugs, flagons, bowls – Nottingham Castle Museum and Fishbourne Roman Palace Museum.
Work inc. architectural tiles and panels; functional domestic pottery (inc. commemorative sprigged ware) sold through shops and galleries. Brochure.

MACC STONE CO (Empl: 20; Est: 1955)
2 Robin Hill, Biddulph Moor, Stoke-on-Trent, Staffs ST8 7N8. 0782-514 353.
BEC; Stone Fed; Nat Fireplace Manufacturers Assoc; Dry Stone Walling Assoc.
Pc Too numerous to detail.
Designers, masons and suppliers of natural stonework. Total design and drawing service available. Undertake setts; paving; interior flooring;

masonry; lintels; mullions; landscaping; monumental work; walling; ashlar; fireplaces inc. stone fire surrounds, slate, wooden and reproduction. The firm takes great pride in the fact that they provide an individual service, and refuse to compromise their standards. Brochure.

MACE INTERIORS
Interior Design
34 Cromer Rd, N. Walsham, Norfolk NR28 0HD. 0692-404 011.
BEC.

MACE, WILLIAM & BROS LTD (Empl: 30; Est: late 1800s)
Building Contractor
34 Cromer Rd, North Walsham, Norfolk NR28 0HD. 0692-403 781.
BEC. Approved: Norfolk CC; N Norfolk DC; Norwich City Council.
Pc Crostwight Hall Development, Nr Honing, North Walsham, Norfolk.
Part of the R. G. Carter group of companies.

MACHAN ENGINEERING LTD (Empl: 8; Est: 1983)
Metalworkers
103 Broad St, Denny, Stirlingshire FK6 6EL. 0324-824 309.
METCON; Fed of Craft & Commerce.
Pc Lighting columns – Axis Centre, London. Railings – TSB, Carlisle. Gates – Peterborough Sports Centre. Canopy – Matlock, Derbys.
Brochure.

MACLEAN & SPEIRS LTD (Empl: 150; Est: c. 1930)
Specialist Painters & Decorators
56 Byron St, Glasgow G11 6LZ. 041-339 8671.
Pc Theatre Royal, Glasgow. Skilled redecoration – HM Theatre, Aberdeen. External painting inc. specialist coatings – Hwange Power Station, Zimbabwe Electricity Supply Authority. Hotels inc. Caledonian; Turnberry; Gleneagles; Peebles Hydro.

MACKENZIE GLASS LTD (Empl: 3; Est: 1955)
Radnor Place, Exeter, Devon EX2 4EJ. 0392-58538 (4 lines).
Glass & Glazing Fed; FMB.

MACKENZIE WHEELER (ARCHITECTS) (Est: 1982)
Embankment Studios, The Embankment, Putney, London SW15 1LB. 081-785 3044.
Robert Wheeler, Ross MacKenzie, Donald MacKenzie – all BA (Hons); Dip Arch; RIBA.
Pc Restoration inc. terrace of listed houses – Deptford, London;

18th-century prison complex, Little Walshingham, Norfolk. Restoration, refurbishment and sensitive alteration, extension and conversion of many historic buildings in urban and rural areas.

MACKIE, RAMSEY & TAYLOR (Est: 1960)
Architects
47 Victoria St, Aberdeen, Grampian AB9 1QA. 0224-639 295.
Chartered Architects.
Pc Restoration of 1850 neo Greek building, Dundee inc. specialist plaster, metal and timber repairs and replacement. Stonework repair – Sheriff House, Dundee. Conversion of redundant ecclesiatical building to flats.

MACMILLAN, CAROL INTERIOR DECORATIONS (Est: 1976)
Altyre House, Gt Horkesley, Colchester, Essex CO6 4AB. 0206-271 225.
M IDDA.

MACPHERSON, DONALD P. (Est: 1961)
Chartered Architect
23 School Wynd, Paisley, Renfrewshire PA1 2DA. 041-889 6727.
B Arch; FRIAS; ARIAS; FSA (Scot).
Pc Restoration works inc. Paisley Abbey; Beith High Church; Dargavel House, Bishopton.

MACRAE, ANTHONY
Stained Glass Artist
1 South St, Lower Weedon, Northants, NN7 4QP. 0327-40313.
Nat Dip in Design, Stained Glass (Special Level).
Pc Restoration – 1890s glass and new designed glass, Lyndhurst Hall, Haverstock Hill, London. New glass designed and executed – new chapel, Cynthia Spencer Ward, Mansfield Hospital, Northampton.

MAIN, MICHAEL LTD
Architectural Antiques
The Old Rectory, Cerrig-y-Drudion, Corwen, Clwyd, N. Wales LL21 ORU. Showrooms: The Coach House, Llanrhaeadr, Denbigh, Clwyd. 049 082-491.
Architectural antiques inc. cast iron columns; doors; pews; panelling; etc.

MAINTRACTS LTD (Empl: 30; Est: 1974)
Plumbing, Heating & Electrical Contractors
3 Boutflower Road, Battersea, London SW11 1RE. 071-228 7034.
Corgi; HVCA; NICEIC; LCA.
Brochure.

MAJELLA, JOSEPHINE (Empl: solo; Est: 1973)
Glass Engraver
The Glass Studio, West Pallant, Chichester. W. Sussex PO19 1TD. 0243-779 289.
Trained Fine Art, Hammersmiths School Arts & Crafts; AFGE; GGE; Guild Sussex Craftsmen.
Pc Stained glass windows – Nutbourne Chapel, Nr Chichester, W. Sussex. Engraved plaque (1 m diameter) for Bank of England, Southampton (now owned by Southampton Council).

MAJOLICA WORKS (Empl: one; Est: 1983)
Handmade, Hand-painted Majolica Floor & Wall Tiles
Studio 1, The Manchester Craft Centre, 17 Oak St, Manchester M4 5JD. 061 835 3581.
Pc Tile panels for walls. Decorative tiles for walls and floors. Murals, tiles for bathrooms, kitchens, terraces, fountains.
As well as tiles of abstract design, often using bright blues and yellows, they produce various forms of decorative and domestic ware .

MAJORFAX LTD (Empl: 4; Est: 1983)
Specialists Ferrous & Non-ferrous Castings
16 Portland St, Walsall, W. Midlands WS2 8AB. 0922-645 815.
Pc Refurbishment of cast-iron work on Leckie House; cast iron street name plaques; bronze statue name plaques – all for the West Midlands Borough Council.

MALDEN JOINERY (Empl: 9; Est: 1934)
The Leggar, Bridgwater, Somerset. 0278-457 371.
Pc Numerous bespoke joinery contracts carried out on behalf of customers and architects. Staircases a speciality in a variety of hard and soft woods.

MALLESON, MICHAEL (Empl: solo; Est: 1976)
Artist Blacksmith Willing to Make Almost Anything in Forged Iron or Steel
Trent Smithy, Rigg Lane, Trent, Sherborne, Dorset DT9 4SS. 0935-850 957.
BABA.
Pc Restoration of 18th-century cast iron gates, Coker Court, Somerset. Restoration of 18th-century railings, Sherborne.

MALVERN STUDIOS (Empl: 4; Est: 1961)
Furniture Maker & Restorer
56 Cowleigh Rd, Malvern, Worcs WR14 1QD. 0684-574 913.
Mr L. M. Hall, proprietor – LAPADA   Mr J. A. Hall – C & Gs

Advanced, Distinction, Antique Restoration; recommended by Museums & Galleries Commission; M BAFRA; Inst of Conservation. Pc Unable to disclose due to respect for clients' privacy.
Handmade furniture; woodworm treatment; woodcarving and hand-polishing; interior design; wallpaper and carpets; upholstery. Retail shop open.

MANGOLD, DEANNE (Empl: solo; Est: 1982)
Stained Glass Artist/Painter
57 Kilvey Terrace, St Thomas, Swansea, Wales SA1 8BA. 0792-460 961.
W. Glamorgan Inst of Higher Education – Higher Dip Architectural Glass; AM BSMGP.
Pc Dare Valley Country Park – Mid Glam. St Lleurwg's Church – Hiwaun, Mid Glam. Numerous private houses.
Work inc. glass painting; acid etching; staining; sandblasting; float glass worked with no limitation of line or division (can be used for shower screens, room dividers, etc).

MANNING, W. J. (Empl: one; Est: 1964)
Specialist Woodwork
83 Milton Crescent, E. Grinstead, Sussex RH19 1TQ. 0342-323 844.
Pc National Trust work inc. Knole; Scotney Castle; Smallhythe Place.

MANOR MORTARS (HEMPWAY LTD) (Empl: 3; Est: 1987)
Denmans Dairy, Barrington, Somerset TA19 0JW. 0460-57017.
Pc Have provided mortars to repair Burstone steps, Sherborne Abbey; numerous churches and statues, and monuments.
Traditional mortars and plasters available in 10 kg and 25 kg bags using slaked lime putty, stone dusts, sands and pozzalanic additives inc. cobs; daubs; hair plasters; roughcasts; various tone repair mortars (e.g. Portland, Bath stone). Also sawn timber laths, riven oak laths, pigments. Mix and match service for lime mortars and washes. Brochure.

MANSELL, TERRY (Empl: one; Est: 1973)
Master Thatcher
The Thatched Cottage, Lower Raydon, Hadleigh, Ipswich, Suffolk IP7 5QS. 0473-822 457.
C & Gs Carpentry & Joinery; Craft Certs, Thatching; M Suffolk MTA; M Nat Council MTA.

MARBLING INC (Est: 1989)
Mandy Llewllyn: 17 High St, Wivenhoe, Colchester, Essex CO7 9BE. 0206-4255 Vicky Jones: 32 New St, Brightlingsea, Essex, CO7 0BZ.

0206-305 331 Zoe Redfearn: 65 Sydney St, Brightlingsea, Essex, CO7 0BE. 0206-304 639.
Partners all have 3 years experience of hand-marbling on fabric for another firm.
Pc have supplied lengths of fabric for curtains; cushion covers; tablecloths; fabrics.
Specialize in the marbling of silks and cottons (although will test print any fabric) for fashion and furnishing using a traditional handmade process. Unlimited colours. Supply 1 m–10 m in one go. Samples available.

MARLEY ROOF TILES (Est: 1924)
1 Suffolk Way, Sevenoaks, Kent TN13 1YL. 0732-741 500.
Re-constituted slate tiles (interlocking single lap); concrete tiles; Victorian ridge and finials (fleur de lys, cock's comb, three hole, ball top, scroll). A range of technical literature is available.

MARSHALL, DAVID (Empl: one; Est: 1968)
Specialist Joinery
Benar, Penmachno, Betws y Coed, Gwynedd LL24 0PS. 06903-312.
Certified Teacher of Woodwork.
Pc References available.

MARSTON & LANGINGER LTD
Conservatory Joinery
George Edwards Rd, Fakenham, Norfolk, NR21 8NL. 0328-4933. 20 Bristol Gardens, Little Venice, London, W9 2JQ. 071-286 7643.
Pc Range from a wall of adjoining glass buildings (spanning over 100 ft) maintained at different temperatures, to a tiny greenhouse for keeping a rare alpine collection. Garden pavilions; glass dining-rooms and restaurants; a grand orangery, America; and even a glass bathroom on a tower, Italy.
Design and manufacture, fitting and furnishing of period style conservatories. Will advise on landscaping, horticultural requirements, heating, lighting, and furnishing the conservatory. A firm which pays great attention to detail. Brochure.

MARTIN, EDWARD & SON LTD (Empl: 2; Est: 1854)
Metalworkers
Mounthope Service Station, Closeburn, Thornhill, Dumfries & Galloway DG3 5HS. 08484-31267.
M NFB & AEA; RSS; AFCL; FWCF.
Pc Wrought-iron screens – American Consulate, Edinburgh. Door furniture – Stirling Castle, Chapel Royal.

FIRMS AND CRAFTSPEOPLE

MARTIN & FROST (Empl: 17; Est: 1896)
Housefurnishing Specialists
83 George St, Edinburgh EH2 3EX. 031-225 2933.
Pc Work in Holyrood Palace, Glamis & Scone Palace, Scotland. Eagle Star Insurance, Green Park, London. Maintenance, repair and supply of old and specially commissioned large carpets.

MARTIN REPRODUCTIONS (Empl: one; Est: 1974)
Furniture Maker & Restorer
Rowden Springs Fishery, Carribber, Linlithgow, W. Lothian EH49 6QE. 0506-847 269.
Pc Desks and light fittings – Glasgow School of Art. Dining table and chairs – Glasgow Garden Festival.
Specializes in reproducing designs by Charles Rennie Mackintosh.

MARTINDALE, C. B. FRIBA (Est: 1890)
Architect Specializing in Care & Development of Historic Buildings.
Bradwell House, Bradwell, Milton Keynes, Bucks MK13 9AE. 0908-221 230.
FRIBA; Past President, EASA.
Pc 16 yrs as Surveyor to Carlisle Cathedral. Consultant to Dept of Environment and National Trust.
Work as a consultant architect extends from Dover to Aberdeen.

MASONRY ASSOCIATES LTD (Empl: one; Est: 1986)
Stonemasons
Wansdyke Workshops, Wellos Lane, Peasedown-St-John, Nr Bath, Avon BA2 9DH. 0761-37481.
Full 'old-fashioned' apprenticeship with Bath & Portland for 7 yrs.
Pc Large amount of restoration work on Brighton Pavillion. Complete renovation of Mews Cottage.

MASTER ARTS PLASTERING CO (Empl: 9; Est: 1983)
Barn Works, Windsor Rd, Worcester Park, Surrey KT4 8EP. 081-330 7723.
BEC; Nat Fed Plastering Contractors.
Pc Harleyford Manor House. Malaysian Embassy, Belgrave Sq. Artillery Barracks, Woolwich.
Brochure.

MASTERSTROKE INTERIORS (ROBERT ALDOUS & VERONICA DUGGIN) (Empl: 2; Est: 1986)
11 Chalmers Rd, Banstead, Surrey SM7. 0737-370 409.
Both partners have degrees in Fine Art; 4 yrs training in marbling and graining.

Pc Marbling – Selfridges Audio and Hi-fi Dept. Decorative finishes – Health Club 'The Peak' and luxury suite – Carlton Towers Hotel. Marbling – Café Royal. Currently working on trompe l'œil murals – Inn on the Park, Park Lane.

MATTHEWS, G. A. (Empl: solo; Est: 1970)
Furniture Designer & Maker
The Cottage Workshop, 174 Christchurch Rd, Ferndown, Nr Bournemouth BH22 8SS. 0202-572 665.
30 yrs experience; CoSIRA trained.
Pc Designed and completed tables and sideboards for clients all over England. Restored many pieces of furniture, and numerous grandfather and long case clocks, of very high value and antiquity. Has undertaken new design work for churches.

MAUND, HEATHER (Empl: solo; Est: 1985)
Hand-woven, Hand-dyed Textiles
32 Abbey Foregate, Shrewsbury, Shropshire SY2 6BT. 0743-245 522.
BA (Hons), 1st Class, Printed/Woven Textiles specializing in woven textiles.
Pc Private commissions for homes and hotels. Work for Seibu Dept Stores in Japan. Work has been displayed in Paul Smith's Contemporary Textile Gallery.
Highly decorative woollen throws, blankets, tapestries or rugs with patterns hand inlaid using traditional techniques. Work has a strong emphasis on pattern and colour, being inspired by African and ethnic sources. Photographs available.

MAYBANK, L. W. & SONS LTD (Empl: 10; Est: 1923)
Painters & French Polishers – Graining & Marbling, Broken Colour Work
9 Greenways, Walton-on-the-Hill, Tadworth, Surrey KT20 7QE. 0737-813 701 & 62295 & 081-394 0053.
All served 10 yr apprenticeships; GMC.
Pc Kensington Palace. Royal Opera House. Theatre Royal. Grove House.

McCALLA, G. B. (Est: 1974, 43 yrs in trade)
Specialist Joinery
10 Raglan Green, Woodside, Bedford MK41 8NB. 0234-50571.
Apprenticeship in carpentry & joinery.
Pc Work on listed buildings making and fitting replacement box frame sashes, doors, casement windows, stairs, etc.

FIRMS AND CRAFTSPEOPLE

McCARTNEY, CREAR
Stained Glass Artist
The Schoolhouse, Wiston, Biggar, Lanarkshire Ml12 6HT. 08995-634.
Dip of Art & Design (Stained Glass), Glasgow School of Art.
Pc 59 stained glass windows made (6 commissions to be completed at present) mostly for Scotland inc. St Magnus Cathedral, Kirkwall, Durnoch Cathedral, but also 18 windows for USA (Walkerton, Indiana). Although the majority of these were for churches, secular commissions also undertaken inc. a large window for offices of Scottish Malt Distillers.

McCAW, NORMA CONSERVATION (Est: 1985)
Wallpaper & Plans Conserved & Restored
The Studio, 107 Shepherd's Bush Rd, London W6 7LP. 071-602 0757.
Camberwell School of Art & Crafts; Paper Conservation, 4 yr course HND BTEC.
Pc Room of Chinese hand-painted wallpaper restored in situ inc. worn edges and discoloration around door handles etc. Restoration of 18th – 20th century architectural prints, plans and drawings inc. transparent paper and photographic plans.
Keen not only to restore works of art, but also to prevent further damage taking place. Will advise on mounting, framing, light, humidity and heat (at levels acceptable in the home). Brochure.

McCLAFFERTY, MARIA DESIGNS LTD
Stained Glass Artist, Glass Etcher
11 Hillside Rd, London SW2 3HL. 081-671 6782.
Pc Design built into original Victorian frame (10 m diameter) using solar-reflective, coloured antique and iridescent glass – rose window, Alexandra Palace, London. Etched glass (300 sq m), Princes Sq, Buchanan St, Glasgow. Rulers Palace, Al-Ain, United Arab Emirates.

McCRONE, PHILIP BUILDERS (Empl: 10; Est: 1972)
Upper Laxton, Nr Corby, Northants NN17 3AZ. 078085-393.
Indentured stonemasons; brick layers and lead workers (CITB and other training course). Approved: Diocesan and local authority bodies; Eng. Heritage.
Pc Blatherwycke Church – Redundant Churches Fund. Boothby Pagnell (Norman) Manor House for Eng. Heritage. Oundle Poor House, Chapel, Ninian Comper. Oundle churchyard table tombs – PCC/Oundle Town Council. Cotterstock Church – DOE. Newton Church Field Centre – LEA/Newton Charity.
Undertakes all types of stonework, natural stone roofing and associated

carpentry, joinery and leadwork, bringing in other specialists (i.e. stained glass workers) as necessary.

McDERMOTT, ALLYSON INTERNATIONAL CONSERVATION CONSULTANTS (Empl: 8; Est: 1980)
Conservation & Reproduction of Historic Wallpapers, Prints, Drawings & Watercolours
Lintl Green House, Rowlands Gill, Co Durham NE39 1NL. 0207-71547.
BA (Hons) History of Art & Design; post grad Dip Conservation, currently studying for Ph D; treasurer of Wallpaper History Society; Committee M Inst of Paper Conservation; Working Party M International Council of Museums, etc.
Pc Unable to specify for reasons of clients' privacy, but inc. country house owners and curators, museums, architects, town planners and associations specializing in the conservation of historic buildings and their contents.
Will also design to specification (stencilling, hand-printing, and hand-painting) using authentic materials and techniques; analyse and identify for reproduction; conservation mount and bespoke framing. Brochure.

McGARRY, M. (Empl: one; Est: 1986)
Painter – Broken Colour Work, Stencilling
53 Lockington Avenue, Plymouth, Devon PL3 5QQ. 0752-783257.
Will not undertake marbling and graining, just sponging, ragging, dragging and other broken colour work.

McKEE, A. (Empl: 12; Est: 1972)
Stained, Painted & Decorative Glass Artists & Craftsmen
34 Old Sneddon St, Paisley, Renfrewshire PA3 2AL. 041-887 6763.
Nat Fed Building Trades; Scottish Glass Merchants Assoc; Glass & Glazing Fed.
Pc Various commissions involving the manufacture and installation of stained glass windows inc. restoration of stained glass windows – Paisley Abbey.
Will also undertake acid etching, sandblasting, glass drilling and glass polishing – either on glass or marble.

McKENZIE, W. J. & SON (Empl: one; Est: 1962)
Specialist Joiner
32 Milner Rd, Dagenham, Essex RM8 2PX. 081-590 4313.
Time served carpenter and joiner (6 yrs); GMC.

FIRMS AND CRAFTSPEOPLE

Mc LAREN GLASS (Empl: solo; Est: 1983)
50 Cross St, Northam, Bideford. N. Devon EX39 1BX. Swansea Stained Glass College, qualifying with SIAD & AMGP; 5yrs self-employed.
Pc Private houses, hotels, pubs, churches. Sandblast emblems on Midland Bank windows.

McLAUGHLIN, JAMES (Empl: solo; Est: 1975, self-employed 14 yrs)
Architectural Sculptor
Studio 49, Bluecoat Chambers, School Lane, Liverpool, Lancs L1 3BX. 051-708 9270.
20 yrs apprenticeship with a well known Liverpool sculptor.

McQUOID, REBECCA (Empl: solo; Est: 1980)
Weaver
The Old Post, 11 Church Hill, Slindon, Nr Arundel, W. Sussex BN18 0RB. 0243-65233.
West Sussex College of Art & Design; various other courses.

MEARS, ROGER ARCHITECTS (Est: 1980)
2 Compton Terrace, London N1 2UN. 071-359 8222.
Roger M. L. Mears, principal – MA Dip Arch (Cantab) RIBA; M SPAB.
Pc Listed building repairs/alterations in 16 Cheyne Walk, London SW1. 12 Lloyd St, London WC1. Church of St Simon & St Jude, Llanddeusant, Dyfed. Repairs, alterations, extensions and conservatories generally.

MEDWAY BRASS RESTORATION (Est: 1986)
1 Lewsome Farm Cottages, Sandway Lenham, Maidstone, Kent ME17 2BE. 0622-859 086.
Pc Restoration of antique brass fixtures and fittings (domestic and nautical), nautical and scientific antiques.

MEECHAM, P. A. CMBHI (Empl: one; Est: 1970)
Clockmaker
The Malt House, Milton-under-Wychwood, Oxford OX7 6JT. 0993-830215.
Professionally trained; Craft M BHI; M BW & CG.
Pc Work spanning from regular maintenance to complete rebuilding and electrification on many church tower clocks and country house clocks in Oxfordshire and near counties.

MELDRUM & MANTELL (Est: 1975)
Architect
30 High St, Banff, Grampian AB4 1AE. 02612-2267.
Henry J. L. Mantell – Dip Arch; ARIAS; RIBA.

MELLING, HILARY B.
See CHAIRPERSON, THE

MERRIMAN, R. T.
Period Fireplaces
11 Constitution Place, Leith Docks, Edinburgh EH6 7DJ. 031-554 6903 & 669 5781.
4 yr apprenticeship in joinery & cabinet making (1968–72); worked within the trade covering all aspects of joinery and related works; C & Gs, Intermediate, Advanced, & FTC.

MERRY-HENRICKSEN, L. CERAMICS (Empl: solo + others as needed; Est: 1979)
Flat 2, 80 Elmbourne Rd, Tooting Bec, London SW17. 081-682 1492.
Ecole des Arts Plastique, France; apprenticeship in South of France; Architectural Assoc.
Pc Relief mural and fountains – Les Almaclies, Dakar, Senegal; housing estate, France. Abstract plant containers – stairwell behind reception, Comet Industry, France.
Ceramic murals and sculptures designed to commission.

METALOCK (BRITAIN) LTD (Empl: 85; Est: 1949)
Metalock House, Crabtree Manorway, Belvedere, Kent DA17 6AB. 081-311 4040.
MOD Approved; Lloyds approved.
Pc Palm House, Kew Gardens involving restoring sills, guttering and floor plates (over 100 yrs old). Repair of 24 inch–48 inch fractures in cast iron architectural columns supporting the roof – Darlington Covered Market. Brighton Pier.
Cold mechanical repair of cast iron and other metals, by peening into prepared apertures layers of multi-dumbbell shaped keys made from a highly ductile alloy. Brochure.

METALCRAFTS, B. C. LTD (Empl: 2; Est: 1946)
Lighting
69 Tewkesbury Gardens, London, NW9 0QU. 081-204 2446.
F. Burnell – 3 yrs apprenticeship in Germany, Art Metal Work; M DLA.
Brochure.

FIRMS AND CRAFTSPEOPLE

MICCOLI, G. & SONS LTD (Empl: 10; Est: 1979)
Stonemasons
99 Tierney Rd, Streatham Place, London SW2 4QH. 081-674 7814.
Pc Restoration – Tower Bridge. Green fibre glass panels fixed around Elephant & Castle Shopping Centre. 12 floor fire escapes, tower block, 2 blocks fixed with Portland stone cladding.
Willing to both restore and fix natural stone and marble, but scagliola fix only.

MICHELMERSH BRICK CO LTD, THE (Empl: 100; Est: 1950)
Hillview Rd, Michelmersh, Romsey, Hants SO51 0NN. 0794-68505.
Pc Restoration work inc. Dublin Castle; Powderham Castle; Lincoln Cathedral; Salisbury Cathedral; various orangeries; gazebos; multiplicity of works to listed buildings.
No minimum order. Brochure.

MIDLAND VENEERS LTD (Empl: 100; Est: 1932)
Hayseech Rd, Halesowen, W. Midlands B63 3PE. 021-550 6441.

MILES, IAN UPHOLSTERY (Empl: 3; Est: 1978)
Unit 10, Oaklands Ind Estate, Braydon, Swindon, Wilts SN5 0A. 0793-854 175.
Time served apprenticeship; M AMU.
This firms feels that their best recommendation is the quality of work done, and pride themselves that they produce everything to the exceptional standard they themselves would expect if they were the client.

MILES, SALLY (Empl: varies up to 4; Est: 1974)
Painter – Murals
37 Englewood Rd, London SW12 9PA. 081-675 4264.
Dip Art & Design, Camberwell School of Art and Crafts; GMC.
Pc Connaught Rooms. Sultan of Brunei. Regines. Colchester Hippodrome. Many private clients. 'She has made a reputation for herself among leading interior designers and architects as being very professional. With her assistants she has accepted and successfully completed the most complicated and demanding of commissions on time.'
Considered one of the foremost trompe l'œil artists in England.

MILLER, JOHN & SONS (Empl: 70; Est: 1875)
Specialist Painters & Decorators
52 Main St, Barrhead, Glasgow G78 1RE. 041-881 1516.
Scottish Decorators Fed.

MIZON, P. & B.

MILNE, B. D. (MASTER THATCHER) (Empl: one; Est: 1977)
15 Fleetwood Crescent, Banks, Southport, W. Lancs PR9 8LP. 0704-231 510.
M North of Eng MTA.
Specializes in restoring previously thatched roofs that are now tiled and slated.

MISSION GLASS (R. & M. BROWNELL) (Empl: 3; Est: 1986)
Stained Glass Artist/Painters
The Old Mission, 89 Bromley Rd, Crockleford Hill, Ardleigh, Essex CO7 7SE. 0206-864 384.
Sheffield and Liverpool Colleges of Art; M BSMGP; PhD History of Art, Essex University.
Pc 'Diana and Actaeon' 4 ft rose window – Royal Derwent Hotel, Castleside, Co Durham. 'Justice' door panel 40 inch × 30 inch – R. Van den Toorn (MEP), Lemmer, Netherlands. 'Four Seasons' internal screen window – lawyers office, Vanden Toorn, Volkers, Zevenbergen, Netherlands. Restoration – Ardleigh Parish Church.
Willing to undertake abstract designs, but not 'modernist' abstract designs.

MITCHELL HARVEY PARTNERSHIP (Est: 1955)
Architects
Broadway House, Peter St, Yeovil, Somerset BA20 1PN. The Redes, Netherbury, Dorset. 0935-76381.
J. C, Mitchell – Dip Arch (Hons); FRIBA   A. J. Harvey – Dip Arch; ARIBA   D. J. Mitchell – BA (Hons); B Arch; RIBA.
Pc Conversion of old farm buildings into craft workshops – Dorset Buildings Preservation Trust, Nethercombe Farm, Sherborne, Dorset. Architects for over 80 local churches to the Diocese of Bath & Wells, and Salisbury.

MITTON, ROLAND (Empl: 2; Est: 1979)
Stained Glass Artist/Painter
14 Mansefield Court, Livingston Village, W. Lothian, EH54 7BJ. 0506-415 702.
DA (Edin); AMGP.
Pc Various commissions both ecclesiastical and domestic; too numerous to detail.

MIZON, P. & B. (Empl: 2 partners; Est: 1978)
Master Thatchers
Whinwillow, High Street, Horseheath, Cambs CB1 6QR. 0223-892 861 & 891 655.
P. E. Mizon – Full apprenticeship; M Midland MTA   B. Mizon – trained by father.

FIRMS AND CRAFTSPEOPLE

Pc White Chimneys, Cardinals Green, Horseheath, Cambs in Norfolk reed. Mrs Stone, Vicarage Cottage, W. Wickham in long straw.

MOCATTA, CHARMAIN
Lettering on Glass
9 Parsons Mead, East Molesey, Surrey, KT8 9DT. 081-979 8877.
Many yrs ago art trained at Kingston upon Thames Polytechnic and the RCA, London. Dip in Calligraphy and Book Binding, Roehampton Institute of Continuing Education; Craft M GGE.
Mrs Mocatta is very keen to pursue her love of lettering into as many fields as possible, and feels that there is great potential in architecture for such work. Using her art training she is also willing to undertake heraldic work.

MODULUS DESIGNS LTD (Empl: 2; Est: 1987)
Furniture Designers & Makers
39–41 North Rd, London N7 9DP. 071-607 9374.
Cert London College of Furniture; registered architect, Dip Arch; M AWG.
Pc Clients inc. DEGW Architects, Lloyds Corporation, Reuters, Woolwich Building Society, Hunt Thompson Architects, BDP Architects, Crompton Strickland Partnership.
We are a small highly skilled workshop specializing in making prototypes and one-off furniture for the design professionals. Brochure.

MOIR, DAVID – ARCHITECT (Est: 1981)
5 Scoonie Place, Leven, Fife KY8 4HB. 0333-23191.
RIBA; RIAS; DA (Dund).
Pc Restoration – Charleton House, Colinsburgh (see *The Field*, 26 Oct 1985). The Grove, Dura Den, by Dairsie. Elie Parish Hall, Elie.

MOLD, PETER (Est: 1986)
Dry Stone Waller
10 Longmead Lynton, N. Devon EX35 6DQ. 0598-52205.
Professional M Dry Stone Walling Assoc.
Pc Traditional reconstruction of dry walling for National Trust, Purbeck, Dorset. Dry walling/landscaping in Australia.

MONCUR, JENNIE (Empl: 3; Est: 1984)
Tapestry, & Designs for Linoleum Flooring
189 Bermondsey St, London SE1 3UW. 071-403 5310. FAX 071-403 5440
BA (Hons), Dept of Textiles, Goldsmith's College, University of London; MA RCA.

MOORE, GORDON

Pc Tapestry – 'Soho Soho' Restaurant, London. Linoleum floor – Inst of Contemporary Arts, London, and also 'Whistles' Clothes shop, Oxford.
Designer and maker of tapestries, tufted rugs, fabrics and linoleum flooring. Work spans from art gallery exhibitions through to design production field; ranging from one-off items to whole interiors, with relating images on wall, furniture and floor. Lecturing and seminars undertaken. Brochure.

MOON, CHRISTOPHER J. (Empl: 8; Est: 1978)
Painters
52 Clare Rd, Kingswood, Bristol, Avon BS15 1PJ. 0272-679 569. FAX 0272-600 528. TELEX 449 897.
M GMC; C & Gs Advanced Decorative Painting; part time lecturer in Decorating, Brunel Technical College.
Pc Palace, villas in Middle East, Morocco. Photographs may be shown to prospective clients.

MOOR, ANDREW ASSOCIATES (Empl: 65; Est: 1984 (UK))
Stained Glass Artists
29 Gloucester Avenue, London NW1 7AU. 071-284 1720.
Pc 65 sq m rose window – Alexandra Palace. 300 sq m barrel vault – Buxton Thermal Baths.

MOORE, A. S. – GRAINER & MARBLER (Empl: solo; Est: 1950)
Majolica/Screen-printed Tile Manufacturer
18 Sedgwick Rd, Leyton, Essex E10 6QR. 081-5581 926.
Pc The Dorchester – Park Lane. Middle East Palaces – Bahrain, Abu Dhabi. Numerous hotels.

MOORE, E. T. (Empl: 6; Est: 1948)
Cane, Rush, Handmade Chairs, Soft Furnishings
Mr M. S. Murchie, proprietor, 141 Battersea Rise, London SW11. 071-228 8997.
AMU; C & Gs Upholstery.
Pc See front cover and centre spread *Traditional Homes Magazine*.
Cane; rushwork; handmade sofas and chairs; wall coverings applied in fabrics; tented ceilings; carpets supplied; curtains made; track fittings; etc.

MOORE, GORDON (Empl: one; Est: 1982)
Furniture Designer & Maker
1 Woodlands, Newton St Cyres, Exeter, Devon EX5 5BP. 0392-851 292.
BA (Hons) Design & Technology; M Devon Guild of Craftsmen; Cert of Education (Woodwork and Metalwork)

FIRMS AND CRAFTSPEOPLE

MOORE, JANE (Est: 1988)
Ceramic Artist
Workshop: 401½ Workshops, 401½ Wandsworth Rd, London SW8 2JP. 071-622 6246 & 071-622 7261. Home: 14 Kildare Terrace, London W2 5LX. 071-229 4631.
Registered architect, AA Dip RIBA; BA & post grad Ceramics, Central School of Art & Design.
Pc Tile mural above double doorway in main entrance corridor – The Central School of Art & Design (raku fired to 1000°C).
Majolica tiles are only produced by screen printing. Brochure.

MORAY STONE CUTTERS (Empl: 10; Est: 1962)
Birnic, Elgin, Morayshire IV30 3SW. 0343-86244.
Grampian Regional Council AAS; GMC.
Pc Stonework – Pluscarden Abbey (Civic Trust Award). Mercat Cross – Aberdeen; Fraserburgh; Forres; Cullen. Plaques – King's College, Aberdeen. Church stonework – Aberdeen; Dufftown; Nairn; etc.
Also supplies sandstone – clashach; spynie; cuttieshillock; newton.

MORE, SARAH (Empl: solo; Est: 1972)
Architectural Lettering
50 Elmdale Rd, Bedminster, Bristol 3, Avon BS3 3JE. 0272-634 389.
Dip AD 3d Design; Cert in Carving; M Art Workers Guild; M SD-C; from Crafts Council Selected Index; recommended by Council for the Care of Churches. winner of Nat Asso of Master Masons lettering prizes.
Pc Recarving inscriptions – Royal Artillery Memorial, Hyde Park Corner. Architectural lettering – Hampshire County Council & London Borough of Lewisham.
Brochure.

MORETON & SONS LTD (Empl: 45; Est: 1826)
Building Contractors
Winnall Valley Rd, Winnall Trading Estate, Winchester, Hants SO23 8UL. 0962-60655.
BEC; NHBC; FMB; BEC Guarantee Scheme. Approved: Hants CC; Winchester City Council; all local health authorities; Basingstoke City Council; Southampton City Council; Test Valley Borough Council; etc.
Also willing to undertake leaded light repairs.

MORGAN FURNITURE LTD (Empl: 120)
Clovelly Rd, Southbourne, Emsworth, Hants PO10 8PG. 0243-371 111. FAX 0243-378 796. TELEX 86140.
Brochure.

MORRISEY, PATRICK (ARTIST BLACKSMITH)

MORGAN, R. V. & CO OF LONDON (Empl: 7; Est: 1983)
Furniture Restorers
5 East Rd, Enfield, Middx EN3 5UU. 081-805 0353.
C & Gs.
Pc Several West End of London antique dealers.

MORLEY UPHOLSTERY LTD (Empl: 20; Est: 1911)
84–86 Troutbeck, Albany St, London NW1 4EJ. 071-387 3846 & 071-388 06511.
AMU; GMC.
Pc 'We are well known in and around London via the most foremost interior designers who carry out projects all over the world.'

MORRIS, HUGH LLOYD (Est: 1987)
Carpentry & Joinery
2 Beech Avenue, Rhos, Nr Wrexham, Clwyd LL14 1AA. 0978-842 595.
4 yr indentured apprenticeship with C & Gs Craft Cert in Carpentry & Joinery.

MORRIS SINGER FOUNDRY, THE (Empl: 40; Est: 1848)
Repair of Sculpture & Architectural Metalwork
Bond Close, Kingsland, Basingstoke, Hants RG24 CPT. 0256-24033.
Formal apprenticeship for sand moulders; wax moulders & chasers.
Pc Bronze gates (18 ft high) by Ulrich Henn – National Cathedral, Washington DC. Aluminium staircase – Hounslow Civic Centre. Sheet bronze clad doors– Hail Airport, Saudi Arabia. 52 ft × 18 ft mural – The Sacre Coeur Chapelle. Sir Charles Wheeler's triton group – Trafalgar Square, London.
Panels; wall cladding; handrails; screens; murals; gates; plaques; fountains; doors and door furniture. Casting range – 2,600 lbs copper-rich alloys; 1,000 lbs lead; 800 lbs light alloys; 25 lbs silver and gold. Have worked with some of the world's greatest sculptors inc. Jacob Epstein, Dora Gordine, Oscar Nemon, Enzo Plazzotta, David Wynne, Henry Moore, Reg Butler, Lynn Chadwick.

MORRISEY, PATRICK (ARTIST BLACKSMITH) (Empl: solo; Est: 1969)
'The Forgery', 1a Ashcombe Rd, Weston-super-Mare, Avon BS23 3DS. 0934-631 449 & 417 510.
C & Gs Welding; Technical Welding qualifications AID & UKAEA; M Welding Inst; M Wessex Guild of Wrought-iron Craftsmen; M BABA; Cert of Merit, Worshipful Co of Blacksmiths, London.
Pc Hand with open bible presented to the Abbaye de Solignac, France by The Worshipful Co of Blacksmiths. Steel/nickel plate iris for British Iris Assoc.
Photographs of specific work available.

FIRMS AND CRAFTSPEOPLE

MOSAIC-ARTS (Empl: 5; Est: 1980)
18 Buckland Crescent, London NW3 5DK. 071-722 1505.
All qualified artists, designers and craftsmen, e.g. Academe des Beaux Arts, Aix-en-Provence.
Pc Flooring designs in shopping arcade with geometric fountain feature – Knights Arcade, Knightsbridge. Swimming pool mosaic – Grand Hotel, Brighton. Mural of logo, Windsor & Newton. 80 sq m mosaic restaurant floor – Kensington Hilton.

THE MOSAIC STUDIO (Empl: solo; Est: 1986)
43 Vallance Rd, London N22 4UD. 081-889 0190.
Fine Art Dip.
Specialize in decorative framing and mirrors, decorative bathroom walls.

MOTTERSHEADS (Empl: 3, not inc. labourers; Est: 1965)
Builders, Joiners, Woodturners & Woodcarvers
Joinery Works, Thomas St, Crewe, Cheshire. 0270-581 659.
Time served apprenticeships. 98% of work approved by the inspecting Architects of Eng. Heritage.
Pc Medieval churches inc. restoration of St Mary's Church, Nantwich; St Oswald's, Malpas, Cheshire. St Boniface, Audlem, Cheshire. 16th-century half-timbered manor house, Highfield Hall. All the above work was carried out in 'phases' over a 5 yr period.
Only prepared to carry out work on medieval churches and other buildings which are Grade I or II listed buildings.

MOULDING, R. & CO (SALISBURY) LTD (Empl: 40; Est: 1908)
Building Contractors
South Newton, Salisbury, Wilts SP2 0QW. 0722-742 228 & 743 613.
FMB; NHBC. Approved: Diocesan; National Trust; many jobs undertaken involving HBC grants.
Pc Re-roofing – Cathedral School, Salisbury (not the close), Wiltshire Architectural Award. Rebuilding and restoration – western end of nave, Sarum St Thomas Church, Salisbury. Re-roofing and structural repairs – No 54 & No 55 The Close, Salisbury. In addition various other simular, but smaller contracts to historic buildings, churches, etc. Structural repairs to oak beams using resin technique – St Thomas Church.

MOUNTS HILL WOODCRAFT (Empl: 4; Est: 1982)
Cranbrook Rd, Benenden, Cranbrook, Kent TN17 4ET. 0580-240 270.
GMC.
Pc Work for English Heritage Trust and Church of England. Battle Abbey.

MUMFORD & WOOD LTD

Small family business producing a wide range of handmade architectural and garden joinery inc. traditional ledged and braced doors; windows; staircase; etc. Also produce furniture inc. refectory style tables; benches; rocking chairs; garden furniture; etc. Brochure.

MRM DESIGNS (Empl: one; Est: 1985)
Furniture Designers
5 Parkfield Avenue, Aldwick, Bognor Regis, W. Sussex PO21 3BW. 0243-263 221.
TEC Dip LCF; CCF Award; BA (Hons) 3d Design, Leeds; CSD.
Commissions and small batches to customers' requirements

MUIR, JANE (Empl: freelance associates; Est: 1968)
Mosaic Artist & Designer
Butcher's Orchard, Weston Turville, Aylesbury, Bucks HP22 5AL. 029 661-2292.
F SCD; M SD-C; Brother of Art Workers Guild.
Pc Mosaic pavement – Princes Square Development, Glasgow. Mosaic murals – Rycote Property Development Co, Open University, Milton Keynes. Mosaic pools – Doha, Arabian Gulf. Mosaic panels commissioned by Oxon County Museum.
Work ranges from drawing and watercolour, through experimental printmaking, to mural commissions in glass mosaic and stone. Particularly interested in relating the materials of the mural to those of the building itself. Also teaches. Brochure.

MUIRHEAD MOFFAT & CO (Empl: part-time staff; Est: 1896)
Furniture Restorer
182 West Regent St, Glasgow G2 4RU. 041 226-3406 & 4683.

MULLEY, PETER (Empl: solo; Est: 1977)
Furniture Maker & Restorer
Oak Tree Design Workshop, Cratfield Rd, Huntingfield, Halesworth, Suffolk IP19 0QB. 098 683 516.
Des RCA.

MUMFORD & WOOD LTD (Empl: 25 Est: 1956)
Purpose-made Sash Windows
Hallsford Bridge Ind Estate, Ongar, Essex CM5 9RB. 0277-362 401.
Brit Woodworking Fed.
Manufacturers of standard and purpose-made double-hung sash windows for single or double glazing, new projects or renovations. Brochure.

FIRMS AND CRAFTSPEOPLE

MUNRO, KENNY (ENVIRONMENTAL ARTIST) (Est: 1982)
Crossroads, Ormiston, E. Lothian EH35 5NL. 0875-33653.
Dip in Sculpture, Edinburgh Art College; Visual Arts Study, Oslo University; Bronze Foundry Practice, Royal College of Art.
Pc Enamel on ceramic tile murals – Ballfield St, Dundee. Metalwork mural – Chapel St, Leith, Edinburgh. Metalwork sign – Advocates Close, Edinburgh. Vitreous enamel mural – Riccarton, Edinburgh. Metal commemorative plaques. Restoration of bronze bells. Collaborations with local authorities and RIAS.
Willing to undertake lost-wax casting in non-ferrous metals; fine art metal working and fabrication; antique reproduction and restoration; casting of artwork into concrete; plaster casting and cornice restoration; portrait heads modelled. Brochure.

MUNRO, THOMAS & CO (Est: 1896, now 3rd generation)
Architects & Surveyors
Mr C. I. Munro, Principal, 62 Academy St, Inverness IV1 1LP. 0463-232 233.
RIBA; RIAS; B Arch (Hons), Heriot Watt, Edinburgh.
Pc Refurbishment works (Grade I) – Dumbars Hospital, Church St, Inverness, and Leadclume Farmhouse, Errogie. Restoration works – Free North Church, Inverness (Grade I) and St Andrew's Cathedral, Inverness.
Engineering only undertaken with assistance of a consultant.

MUNRO, W. I. CHARTERED ARCHITECTS (Est: 1977)
1 Seaford St, Kilmarnock, Strathclyde, Ayrshire KA1 2BZ. 0563-24040.
B Arch (Hons); RIBA; ACI Arb.
Pc Laigh Kirk, Kilmarnock. Trinity Church, Irvine. 78–82 Union St, Glasgow. Fairlie House, by Gatehead, Kilmarnock.

MURASPEC LTD
Specialist Wallcoverings
79/89 Pentonville Rd, London N1 9LW. 071-226 7714. Branch addresses on application.

MW MOULDINGS (LONDON) CO LTD (Empl: 10; Est: 1985)
Decorative and Ornamental Plasterwork
Coppen Rd, Off Selina's Lane, Dagenham, Essex RM8 1HJ. 081-593 5048 & 081-593 5318.
M GMC.
Pc Surrey Quays and Ropemaker St – Docklands. IBM Knolly's House.

NATURE'S WAY (ROB & ANGELA PARKIN)

A full range of components in fibrous plaster, GRP, sand and cement inc. cornices; ceiling mouldings; columns; pilasters; niches; arches; mantels; over-window mouldings; door pediments; canopies; suspended ceilings; etc. From initial site survey to fixing and final decoration, MW Mouldings handle the complete job. Brochure.

MYLNE, DAVID (Est: 1959)
Architect
43 Market Square, Duns, Berwickshire TD11 2AL. 0361-82352.
DA (Edin), Dip Arch; RIBA; FRIAS
Pc Repairs to roof, etc. Dalhousie Castle, Bonnyrigg, Midlothian. Project architect in conversion for Sue Ryder Foundation – Marchmont, Duns, Berwickshire. Restoration of ruin – Hume Castle, Nr Kelso, Roxburghshire. Numerous works to large country houses and listed buildings.

NARRO, DAVID ASSOCIATES (Est: 1986)
Consulting Structural & Civil Engineers
107 Craiglea Drive, Edinburgh EH10 5PQ. 031-447 4860. FAX 031-452 8747.
D. L. Narro – B Sc (Hons); C Eng; MICE; MI Struct E.
Pc Work in Edinburgh inc. Mowbray House, High St; Adam Mausoleum; various 'New Town' properties. Water Tower, Dalkeith. Summerlee Canal Centre, Coatbridge. Bolyton Manse, E Lothian. Conservatory House, Tyninghame. Holy Trinity Episcopal Church, Stirling. Culzean Castle Estate. Tinwals House, Dumfries.

NASH, JOHN R. (Est: 1984)
Architectural Lettercutter
32 Riversdale Rd, London N5 2JT. 071-226 5028.
Fellow Soc of Scribes & Illuminators; Fellow Art Workers Guild; Lettercarving training undertaken with Tom Perkins.
Pc Harry Barnes plaque – cloister, Westminster Abbey. Opening plaque – Qaboos Pavilion, Sandhurst. Foundation plaque – Royal Academy of Music Opera House, etc.

NATURE'S WAY (ROB & ANGELA PARKIN) (Est: 1986)
Landscape & Garden Designers
Rose Cottage, Roman Rd, Burghill, Hereford HR4 7AN. 0432-760 272.
Pc Re-design of UK headquarters landscape – Nature Conservancy Council, Peterborough. Conservation design work – Wildfowl Trust, Slimbridge. Re-creation of wetland habitat in Heref – Wall End Farm Conservation Area. Design, illustrated booklets *Countryside Garden* and *Bird Garden* for Johnsons/RSPB.

FIRMS AND CRAFTSPEOPLE

Specialists in natural and conservation planning inc. detailed layouts and drawings and an advisory and consultation service. This design-based company, sees wildlife and conservation projects through from original conception and on site survey to planning, creation and long term management; and also provides 'in house' complementary interpretation material (i.e. booklet, illustrations, promotional materials, signs).

NATURAL STONE PRODUCTS LTD (Empl: 200; Est: 1987)
Bellmoor, Retford, Notts DN22 8SG. 0777-708 771/2 & 707 178.
Stone Fed; NAMM.
Pc Richmond Terrace, and Lansdowne House, both London (granite). ICI Headquarters, London (hopton wood stone). John Lewis, Edinburgh (sandstone).

NEAL, GEOFF (ROOFING) (Empl: 8; Est: re-established 1979)
The Raylor Centre, James St, York YO1 3DT. 0904-414 181.
Served apprenticeship as slater & tiler; Associate Inst of Roofing; hold Construction Technicians Cert (Parts 1 & 2); M NFRC.
Pc Refurbishment – St William's College, York. Re-roofing – part St John's College, York. Roofing works – Joseph Rowntree Trust, York, and also Dean and Chapter of York.
Experienced in slating and tiling, specializing in traditional roofing and conservation work. A family firm which has been involved in roofing for many yrs, with skills and craftsmanship handed down from generation to generation.

NEAVE, PENELOPE
Stained Glass Artist
58 Hopton Rd, London SW16 2EN. 081-769 2203.
BA Hons (Fine Art) – Central School of Art & Design; apprentice/assistant to Anthony Attenborough, 128 Merton Rd, London.
Pc 2 commissioned memorial windows – Loxwood Parish Church, W. Sussex. Memorial window to Airey Neave DSO OBE – Fryerning Parish Church, Nr Ingatestone, Essex.

NEO DESIGNS (Est: 1986)
Fibrous Plasterwork
21 East St, Wareham, Dorset BH20 4NN. 09295-51163.
Pc Restoration and decoration – ceiling, Creech Grange (17th century)
Stocks a selection of wall plaques (terracotta, varnished) suitable for gardens. Brochure.

NEW, KEITH (Est: 1953)
Stained Glass Artist/Painter
6 Murray Rd, Wimbledon, London, SW19 4PB. 081-9471 740.
A RCA; F BSMGP.

Pc 3 nave windows – Coventry Cathedral. South choir window – Bristol Cathedral. Heraldic windows – Royal College of Physicians, London. East and west windows – All Saints' Church, Isleworth. East window – All Saints', Branston, Lincoln and also St Nicholas Cole Abbey, London. Rose window – Christ Church, Calgary, Canada.

NEW STONE & RESTORATION LTD (Empl: 12; Est: 1957)
1 Pembroke Rd, Ruislip, Middx HA4 8NQ. 0895-676 184.
Pc St Mary's Church and Vicarage, Cadogan St, Chelsea. St Mary's Church, Chesham, Bucks. Restoration of stucco and stonework – Cambridge Terrace, London.
Although founded this century, this firm has a direct line of experience and reliability dating from 1891. Brochure.

NEWCOMBE & SON (Empl: 2; Est: 1980)
Long Case Restoration
89 Maple Rd, Penge, London SE20 8UL. 081-778 0816.
GMC.
Pc English oak veneered with burr walnut bracket clock case made for 1702 movement. Restoration of longcase clocks for Admiralty and Paymaster General.

NEWMAN, A. T. (Empl: varies, 1–2, Est: 1978)
Furniture Restorer
Honeycritch Cottage, Froxfield, Petersfield, Hants GU32 1BQ. 073 084-436.
Dip Fine Antique Furniture, BADA at Credit Level, West Dean College, W. Sussex.
Pc Numerous items of fine furniture restored for Richard Davidson Antiques, Petworth (M BADA) and Roy Barton, Pulborough (M BADA).

NEWMILL CASTINGS LTD (Empl: 6; Est: 1890)
The Foundry, Newmill Rd, Elgin, Morayshire, Grampian IV30 2AE. 0343-45023.
M Inst of British Foundrymen; M of Fed of Small Businesses.
Pc Restoration of cannon on battery – Fort George. Reproduction of gutters – Letham Tower, Huntly. Reproduction of various ornamental items for listed buildings.

NICHOLSON, MADDI (Est: 1986)
Embroiderer
8 Lingey Close, Dalston, Carlisle, Cumbria CA5 7LB. 0228-710 176.
BA (Hons) Textiles – Embroidery; worked in National Theatre

Costume & Prop Dept (Summer '84); M Embroiderers Guild; M 62 Group of Textile Artists; New Fibre Art; Craft North.
Pc Waterproof embroidered fabric banners for building exteriors inc. approx 4 m × 6 m, and flags, 3 m × 2 m, (mining images) – Castleford Civic Centre, W. Yorks; approx 4 m × 2 m – Ruskin Craft Gallery, Sheffield. Large embroidered wall hangings for interiors.
Majority of work is embroidered, using mainly figurative images.

NICHOLSON, PAUL (Empl: solo; Est: 1965)
Restoration Consultant
Grange Farm, Alverton, Notts NE13 9PB. 0949-50053.
MSc; FCIOB; FIBM; MIPM.
Pc St Peter's, Machynlleth. St Asaph Cathedral. St Mary's, Nottingham. St Barnabas Cathedral. Oxford colleges, etc.

NISBET, TIM BA, AFGE (Empl: solo; Est: 1974)
Glass Engraver
Dolphin House, 38 Wodehouse Terrace, Falmouth, Cornwall TR11 3EP. 0326-314 595.
A FGE.
Pc Engraved door panels for home of Trinity House pilot, Falmouth. Engraved glass panel – Porthleven Church.

NIX, ANNETTE (Est: 1987)
Hand-tufted Rugs & Wallhangings
11 Ascham St, Kentish Town, London NW5 2PB 071-267 1597.
BA (Hons) Textile Design.
Pc Commissions for The Royal Academy of Arts, Piccadilly; architects, Wrightman & Bullem; interior designers, Wolff Olins/Hamilton; Paris Ceramics.
Photographs and a portfolio available.

NORBURY, JANE (Empl: solo; Est: 1984)
Architectural Sculpture
Unit 7 Studios, 36/38 Peckham Rd, Camberwell, London SE5 8NG. 071-703 0818 & 071-703 0406.
BA (Hons) Ceramics; M Contemporary Applied Arts; Craft Council Register.
Pc 'Water Maze' fountain – Victoria Park, Bristol. Sundial – Brunel House, Bristol. Window boxes and planter – offices, Eastern Arts, Cambridge. Fountains and sculpture – garden, Dual Paul Design Team.
Garden sculpture (sundials; fountains; decorative planters; etc.) in grogged red terracotta or other clays. Exhibits regularly at the Hannah Peschar Gallery in Eng and Europe. Photographs available.

NORMAN & UNDERWOOD LTD

NORFOLK SHEETLEAD LTD & BKF INDUSTRIAL & DOMESTIC PLUMBING LTD (Empl: 12; Est: 1973)
V. J. Bream, 12 Press Lane, Norwich, Norfolk NR3 2JY. 0606-402 522 & 401 260 (BKF).
Staff apprenticeship served; IOP; C & Gs. Approved: LCA; Norwich Council; Norfolk CC.
Pc 22 tons sheet lead – Melton Constable Hall. Sheet lead – Felbrigg Hall. 14 tons and 12 tons sheet lead – Norwich Union Insurance Buildings. Norwich Law Courts. Sheet copper – Norwich Sorting Office headquarters, and St Felix School, Southwold, Suffolk.

NORGRAVE STUDIOS PARTNERSHIP (Empl: 8 Est: 1975)
Stained Glass Artist
Bentley, Redditch, Worcs B97 5UH. 0527-41545.
Pc Restoration works inc. Lichfield Cathedral; Calke Abbey; St Margaret's, Uxbridge; Brandiston, Norfolk; Bungay St Mary's (inc. reglazing). New stained glass – St Margaret's, Lerwick, Shetland. New heraldry and restoration works – Warwick Castle.
This firm will undertake polycarbonate protection, stainless steel guards, and give attention to ferramenta and casements.

NORMAN JONES SONS & RIGBY (Est: 1913)
Chartered Architects
57–59 Hoghton St, Southport, Merseyside PR9 0PG. 0704-31252. FAX 0704-32833
Degrees and diplomas in Architecture; MRIBA; MMBIAT.
Pc Conservation and reconstruction from Exeter to Scarborough of buildings ranging from cruck framed thatched cottages to stately homes, churches and municipal art galleries; values from £50,000–£500,000.

NORMAN & UNDERWOOD LTD (Empl: 200; Est: 1825)
Stained Glass Artists/Painters, Roofing Contractors
11/27 Freeschool Lane, Leicester LE1 4FX. 0533-532 669. FAX 0533-532669. TELEX 347180 NORMAN G.
Glass & Glazing Fed; Metal Roofing Contractors Assoc; BEC; Nat Assoc of Plumbing, Heating & Mechanical Services Contractors.
Pc Re-glazing and re-laying – main dome and main nave roof, St Paul's Cathedral. Re-laying of milled lead – south transept, York Minster. Stained glass and glazing work, commissions world-wide, particularly the Middle East. Monumental wall of stained glass, toughened glass and stainless steel spanning 100 ft × 50 ft – Data Darbar Mosque, Lahore.
A private family business, who have worked extensively throughout the UK

FIRMS AND CRAFTSPEOPLE

on the restoration of church roofs, county houses and many large public buildings.

NORTH OF ENGLAND CARPET CLEANING CO LTD
86 Aigburth Rd, Liverpool L17 7BN. 051-727 7278.
National Carpet Cleaners Assoc; Fabric Care Research Assoc; NARG; ASCR of USA.
Pc Hawarden Castle, Clwyd, North Wales.

NORTHOVER INTERIORS LTD (Est: 1890s)
Domestic & Commercial Interior Design
82 High St, Reigate, Surrey RH2 9AP. 0737-242 236 & 221 662 (studio). FAX 0737-221 290
M IDDA.
Pc Unwilling to publish information regarding clients due to respect for their privacy, however they have recently been involved in converting a 12th-century building to commercial use, and work inc. both domestic and commercial projects.

NORTH-WEST ARCHITECTURAL ANTIQUES
Old Colliery Buildings, Burtonhead Rd, Ravenhead, St Helens, Merseyside WA9 5DX. 0744-25414.

NORTON, MAGGI JO (Est: 1972)
Fabric Artist
31 Haydon Drive, Joel St, Eastcote, Pinner, Middx HA5 2PL. 081-429 0925.
NDD ATD Cert in Education, University of Bristol.
Pc Sold work in America, Germany and Britain.
Mainly large scale abstract and figurative designs (over 3 ft) with a wide variety of colours using string, ribbon, thick wool worked on canvas and other fabric bases.

NORTON, PETER (Empl: one; Est: 1968)
Fine Individual Furniture & Woodwork
18 Long Lane, Bridlington, E. Yorks YO16 5AZ.
6 yrs apprenticeship in furniture making and general woodwork inc. wood turning.
Pc Heavy oak Jacobean style furniture, four poster beds, chests, etc. High back Windsor chairs. Boardroom tables. Machine carved signs with hand finishing.

NUTTGENS, JOSEPH (Empl: one; Est: 1978)
Stained Glass Artist/Painter
The Stained Glass Studio, Piggotts Hill, North Dean, High Wycombe HP14 4NF. 024 024 3352.

OATES, ROGER DESIGN ASSOCIATES

Central School Dip, ILEA; ARCA; M BSMGP.
Pc Window – Rycote Court, Birmingham St, Aylesbury. Tercentenary window – Royal Welsh Fusiliers, Wrexham. 10 aisle windows – St Martin's Church, Basildon.
Protective measures for glass only undertaken using sub-contractors.

OAK HALL JOINERY (Empl: 4; Est: 1979)
High St, Darsham, Saxmundham, Suffolk IP17 3QQ. 072 877-587.
BA Fine Arts; apprentice served joiner; C & Gs Furniture Design & Restoration.
Pc Joinery at The Priory, Lavenham and other similar properties. Fine joinery in listed grade properties in Convent Garden and also Royal Philatelic Soc. Linenfold door – Ipswich. Gothic sashes for local clients.

OAKHILL FORGE
See MASTERS, D. G. & CO LTD

OAKLEAF REPRODUCTIONS LTD (Empl: 20; Est: 1969)
Simulated Wood Reproductions
Ling Bob Mills, Main St, Wilsden, Bradford, Yorks BD15 0JP. 0535-27878.
Pc Church screen cresting for architect in Manchester. Replacement and skirting moulding – Spencer House, St James, London (working in conjunction with Dick Reid of York, and Ashby & Horner Ltd). 'In both of above cases mouldings were prepared which were indistinguishable from their originals, allowing unlimited, speedy, volume production at a fraction of the price of hand carving.'
Beams; planking; cornices; corbels; linenfold panels; embellishments; cornices; Tudor door arches and posts;mouldings; columns. Standard range inc. linenfold and Jacobean panelling; beams. Offer a commission moulding service reproducing originals. Brochure.

OAKWOOD JOINERY (Empl: 17; Est: 1963)
Orchard Works, Church Lane, Wallington, Surrey SM1 4PD. 081-773 2141.
3 apprentices. Firm MBEC; Joinery Managers Assoc; Brit Woodworking Fed; TRADA; Specialist Contractors Assoc.
Pc Refurbishment – St Mary's School. Restoration – Woldingham.

OATES, ROGER DESIGN ASSOCIATES (Empl: 4; Est: 1975)
Designers & Makers of Woven Textiles
Church Lane, Ledbury, Heref HR8 1DW. 0531-2718. FAX 0531-5570. TELEX 35827 HJP.G.

FIRMS AND CRAFTSPEOPLE

Roger Oates – Dip AD   Fay Morgan – M Des RCA.
Pc Rugs in reception areas of Peat Marwick; Wang; Bryman Airways, London; Harlech Television, Cardiff. Received ROSCOE Award USA for Contemporary Rugs and British Design Award for 2 collections of tufted rugs, abstract and fragments.

OBERON, PEAT – BLACKSMITH (Empl: 2; Est: 1978)
21 Fairfield Avenue, Linthorpe, Middlesbrough, Cleveland TS5 5HB. 0642-816 314.
Originally studied as a craft teacher, so knowledge of woodwork fairly sound, main thesis was on aspects of Heraldry; M BABA, gained a Cert of Merit.
Pc Several restoration projects inc. the repoussé leaves for the balcony – RAC, Pall Mall; water leaves – gates (1720), Eastern Electric Board Training Centre, Essendon, Herts; 18th-century scrollwork and water leaves – new post modern riverside development, Richmond, Surrey.
Work inc. arts & crafts, Art Nouveau, 18th century, 19th century and a small amount of modern work as well as general smithing and fabrication. Experienced in silver, copper and brass using silversmithing techniques.

OCTAGON JOINERY LTD (Empl: 14; Est: 1976)
The Malthouse, The Old Brewery, Norton-Fitzwarren, Taunton, Somerset TA2 6RN. 0823-278 269 & 252 750.
Principal – BSc Eng; ACGI; HNC Bldg; CG Full Tech; etc. 7 time served tradesmen, 2 apprentices, 5 trainees.
Pc St Hugh's Choir roof and stonework restoration – Lincoln Cathedral. Wells Cathedral. Restoration – Orchard Windham, Somerset. Salisbury Cathedral. Various churches.

O'DWYER, MICHAEL (Empl: solo; Est: 1982)
Metalworker
18 Jacques Grove, Silsden, Keighley, Yorks BD20 0HT. 0535-52358.
4 yr apprenticeship; C & Gs, Sheet Metalwork & Fabrication.
Pc Security doors and windows (depicting birds of prey) – Gun Room, Sheik Mohammed's Shooting Lodge. Reproduction items for kitchen door, furniture etc. – Oakwell Hall Museum. Commission for Mallory Park Racing Circuit.
Brochure.

ODYSSEY GLASS LTD (Empl: 25; Est: 1981)
Stained Glass Artists
327 Queens Rd, Halifax, W. Yorks HX1 4PY. 0422 59028 & 58230.
All apprentice trained; GMC. Pc Work on cathedrals and important churches. Many important restoration projects.

OLSON, GARRY & BELL, DAVID

THE OLD BAKERY ANTIQUE RESTORATION CO (Empl: 3; Est: 1974)
23 Lower Fold, Marple Bridge, Cheshire SK6 5DU. 061-427 4699.
3 yr apprenticeship with Mr F. Yewell, restorer, Wooley Bridge, Glossop, Derbys.
Pc Predominantly trade work, particularly for display at antique fairs.

THE OLD BAKERY FURNISHING CO (Empl: 10; Est: 1979)
The Old Bakery, Punnetts Town, Nr Heathfield, E. Sussex TN21 9DS. 0435-830 603.
C & Gs; AMU.
Restored and unrestored antique chairs and sofas sold; curtains; loose covers; carpets; lamps and accessories; fine furnishing fabrics and wallpapers. Also produce and sell new sofas made in the traditional manner using horse hair.

THE OLD CURIOSITY SHOP (Empl: 9; Est: 1972)
27–29 Crown St, Ayr KA8 8AG. 0292-280 222.
C & Gs.
Pc National Trust. Culzean Castle. Cloncaird Castle. Culochan Castle. Carnell House. Skeldon House. Gleddoch House. Blairston. Skelmorlie Castle.

OLD FLAME (Empl: one; Est: 1985)
Antique Fireplaces
Harper's Court, Off High St, Dingwall, Ross-shire. 0349-62096 (shop) & 63446 (night).

OLD OAK BEAMS
Milton Laithe, Gargrave, Skipton, N. Yorks BD23 3NN. 0756-749 268.
Many tons of old oak beams always in stock (redressed by hand, structural and cosmetic). Carved inglenooks a speciality.

OLIVER, STEPHAN (Empl: solo; Est: 1972)
Glass Engraver, & Heraldic Specialist
St Briavels, Wetherden, Stowmarket, Suffolk IP14 3JP. 0359-41248.
Pc Window, 3 ft × 4 ft – St Edmund's Catholic Church, Bury St Edmunds. Window, 12 ft × 8 ft – Stoke Court, Slough, Bucks.

OLSON, GARRY & BELL, DAVID (Est: 1985)
Furniture Designers & Makers
17 Stoney Lane, Wilmslow, Cheshire SK9 6LG. 0625-533 701.
Pc Mostly domestic furniture, but have worked for several churches. Recent commission – 15 ft board room table with chairs, a meeting room table and range of matching office reception furniture.

FIRMS AND CRAFTSPEOPLE

'ONE-OFF JOINERY' – M. K. CHARLESWORTH (Empl: solo; Est: 1978)
Parc-Mawr, Llansadwrn, Anglesey, Gwynedd LL59 5SP. 0248 70- 448.
5 yr carpentry & joinery apprenticeship; C & Gs Advanced Carpentry & Joinery, Advanced Wood-machining, Licentiateship; Ordinary National Cert in Building; HNC Building; Cert Ed/Further Education. Pc Carvings for Nigel Fisher, Rural Conversions Ltd, Oxford. Oak doors and frames, Broxton Old Hall, Nr Chester and also The Carnell-Green Partnership, architectural planners. Rood screen – Llandegai Church, Bangor, Gwynedd.
Secret compartments can be built into furniture. Brochure.

OPTICAL ILLUSION CO (Empl: 3; Est: 1979)
Specialist Painters
51 Preston Drive, Brighton, E. Sussex BN1 6LA. 0273-503 591.
Two hold BA (Hons) Design.
Design; murals; trompe l'œil; graphics; surface details; original art and prints.

OPUS STAINED GLASS (Empl: 4; Est: 1982)
The Old Village Hall, Mill Lane, Poynings, W Sussex BN45 7AG. 0273-500 361 & 857 223.
Produce and restore traditional stained glass windows incorporating painting and etching; sandblasting and etching on glass and mirrors using traditional and modern designs; bending (shaping) glass, e.g. the gasolier lamps, Royal Pavilion, Brighton which were bent, etched and painted as part of the restoration of the Music Room.

O'REILY, M. F. (Empl: 10; Est: 1960)
Restoration & Reinstatement of Ornate Plaster & External Stucco-work
46 Cumbrian Gardens, London NW2 1EF. 081-458 2736.
M Plasterers Craft Guild; Certified Registered Plasterer; M GMC.

ORIGINAL FURNITURE CRAFT LTD (Est: 1946)
Antique Furniture Restoration
105 Boundary Rd, London NW8 0RG. 071-624 7671 & 081-455 8420.
Brochure.

ORNAMENTAL STONE (Empl: 4; Est: 1948)
Sculpture, Carving, Gilding & Fine Art Restoration
Studio Workshop, 39A West Rd, Shoeburyness, Essex. 0702-292 867.
Pc Eagle sculpture – Barclays Bank, Gracechurch St, London. Mill Reef Memorial National Stud, Newmarket.

ORNATE IRONWORKINGS (Empl: one Est: 1986)
Balustrading, Furniture, Ornamental Gates, etc. to Individual Specification
Unit 5, Netley Marsh Workshops, Ringwood Rd, Netley Marsh, Nr Southampton SO4 2GY. 0703-862 229.
C & Gs Craft apprenticeship; Hampshire Blacksmiths & Farriers Assoc.
Pc Double gates – 'Bramshaw Garage', Holdenhurst Rd, Bournemouth.

OSBORNE, A. H. & SON (Empl: 1; Est: over 300 yrs)
Master Thatcher
Potters Farm, Green Lane, Boxted, Colchester, Essex CO4 5TS. 0206-271 861.
Full M Suffolk MTA; Full M NCMTA.
Pc The Yew Tree Public House – Great Horkesley.

OSBORNE, ANGELA (Empl: one + self; Est: 1984)
Textile Restorer
Lockyers Farm, Peak Lane, Compton Dundon, Somerton, Somerset TA11 6PE. 0488-74130.
BA (Hons) Anthropology, Sussex; post grad Dip Creative Embroidery, Brighton Polytech; trained with Clive Rogers Oriental Rugs, Brighton.

OSMINGTON WORKSHOP, THE (Empl: solo; Est: 1968)
Specialist Joinery & Project Management
Brookside, Chapel Lane, Osmington, Dorset DT3 6ET. 0305-832 647.
C & Gs Intermediate and Final Cert; Brit Inst of Management Cert in Foremanship & Works Supervision.
Pc 30 yrs experience of a wide variety of woodworking disciplines, i.e. cabinet making, building, restoration.

OSSOWSKI, A. & M. (Empl: 7; Est: 1961)
83 Pimlico Rd, London SW1W 8PH. 071-730 3256.
M Master Carvers Assoc

OTT, MAX E. LTD
Furniture Restorers and Joiners
1a Southcote Rd, Tufnell Park, London N19 5BJ. 071-607 1384.
M GMC.

OWENS, MR D. R. (Empl: 9; Est: 1932)
Metal Worker
Richard Quinnel Ltd, Oxshott Rd, Leatherhead, Surrey KT22 0EN. 0372-375 148.

4 yr apprenticeship, CoSIRA Blacksmithing Course; 8 yrs experience; C & Gs Sheet Metal Fabrication Parts I, II, III; C & Gs Gas & Arc Welding 216 Course; C & Gs Advanced Gas Shielded Welding; C & Gs Advanced Arc Welding.
Pc Numerous weather-vanes, various gates, railing and firebaskets.

OXFORD ARCHITECTURAL ANTIQUES
The Old Depot, Nelson St, Jericho, Oxford OX2 6BE. 0865-53310.

PALAZZO CERAMICS – NANCY PICKARD (Empl: 2; Est: 1987)
14 Llanbradach St, Grangetown, Cardiff, S. Glam CF1 7AD. 0222-238 644.
BA (Hons) Ceramics, S. Glam Inst of Higher Education.
Pc Creche mural – New S. Glamorgan headquarters. Mosaic and tilework mural – Maindee Baths, Newport.
Will also employ other artists to produce architectural ceramics; murals; commemorative plaques; sculptures; portrait busts; etc. More information available on request.

PALFREY, M. & L. E. (Est: 1975)
Traditional Upholsterer
T/A Brockdish Antiques, Commerce House, Brockdish, Diss, Norfolk IP21 4JY. 037 975-498.

PALMER, A. T. LTD (Empl: 45/50; Est: 1951)
Restoration Specialists
32 Wheeler St, Headcorn, Ashford, Kent TN27 9SL. 0622-890 666. FAX 0622-891 154.
BEC; JIB Plumbing & Electrical; employ; apprentices and other specialists employed as required. Approved: Diocesan, Eng. Heritage; local authorities.
Pc Many local projects for clients who wish to remain anonymous, often without architects, as architectural work can be undertaken in-house. Leeds Castle, Nr Maidstone and National Trust projects.
Work directly with client to achieve the desired intentions, utilizing their own expertise and experience. Strive to employ all their own tradesmen for greater control. Able to tackle almost anything up to approx £500,000. Photographs available.

PALMER, STUART & SHIRLEY (Est: 1975)
Glass Engravers
59 Burwell Rd, Exning, Newmarket, Suffolk CB8 7DU. 0638-77327.
Trained London School of Building; qualified in decoration & design; Nat Dip Design in Signwork; Lecturer at Cambridge College

PARKER, GEO. (JOINERY) LTD

of Arts & Technology. Trained Manchester School of Art; Dip of Associateship in Painting.
Pc Whilst happy to accept commissions for personalized designs and trophies, have expanded into glass doors and windows. New doors – Cherryhinton Church in Cambridge.
Lettering; heraldry; naturalistic and abstract subjects inc. flowers, animals, figures and architecture. Have experimented with a method (believed to be exclusive to them) of applying stained glass on top of clear glass and then engraving over both surfaces.

PANTILES ORIENTAL CARPETS (Empl: 2; Est: 1979)
31a The Pantiles, Tunbridge Wells, Kent TN2 5TD. 0892-30416.
BA (Hons) Woven Textiles, W. Surrey College of Art & Design, followed by 2 yrs working with established restorers.
Pc Work for the National Trust, trade and private clients.
Rugs; carpets; kilims; tapestries; aubussons; needleworks – cleaned, conserved, restored, valued, bought and sold.

PARIS CERAMICS
543 Battersea Park Rd, London SW11 3BL. 071-228 5785 & 071-924 1281.
Terracotta and stone floors reclaimed from period properties all over France, restored and re-laid in traditional way. Floors can be sealed to create a finish that needs no more elaborate maintenance than washing with water. Also stock new terracotta tiles and hand-painted wall tiles, made in Spain using traditional methods. Brochure.

PARIS CONSTRUCTION LTD (Empl: approx 40; Est: 1979)
Paris House, Wilbury Villas, Hove, E. Sussex BN3 6GW. 0273-730 216.
Pool of specialized sub-contractors, plus over 50 employees with a variety of professional/trade qualifications, who are experienced in smaller/refurbishment contracts; BEC. Approved: Brighton BC and Health Authority; BR Board; Crawley BC; E. Sussex CC; S. E. Thames Regional Health Authority; Hastings BC; Horsham DC; Wealdon DC; etc.
Pc Brighthelm Church & Community Centre. Alterations/extensions – Shotters Farm and Turners Hill School. Rosemead School, Littlehampton. West House Dormitory Conversion, Cranleigh School. Contract values up to £4 million undertaken.

PARKER, GEO. (JOINERY) LTD (Empl: approx 50; Est: c.1945)
46 Station Rd, Worthing, W. Sussex BN11 1JP. 0903-37613/4.
Apprentices are trained through CITB; M B & CEHSM; M BWF.
Specialist joinery sub-contractors who undertake work to specification for large contractors, both restoration work to listed buildings and new work.

FIRMS AND CRAFTSPEOPLE

PARKER, KEITH (Empl: one; Est: 1965)
Woodcarver and Sculptor
42 Jeans Way, Dunstable, Beds LU5 4PW. 0582-605 663.
M Milton Keynes Craft Guild; Woodcarving Teacher (Adult Education) for 3 schools.
Pc Matriach panels – Maidenhead Synagogue doors. Crib figures – All Saints' Church, Leighton Buzzard. Carved newel posts – staircase in luxury apartment building, Luton.
Brochure.

PARKER & MOREWOOD LTD (Empl: 7; Est: 27)
Building Contractor
Anchor Hill, Hartshill, Nuneaton, Warwicks CV10 0RT. 0203-392 418.
FMB: NHBC: Construction Industries Training Board. Approved: Warwickshire CC; Coventry City Council; FWB Charles, architects.
Pc Restoration c. 1500 timber-framed building – Northeycote Farm. Reconstruction – 21 Spon St (c. 1600 timber-framed building); Cheylesmore Manor; 9 & 163–165 Spon St, Coventry. All above work overseen by F. W. B. Charles, architect.

PARKER, RON (Empl: solo; Est: 1962)
'Bywood', 211 Avenue Rd, Rushden, Northants NN10 0SN. 0933-312 459.
C & Gs Carpentry & Joinery 1st class F T Cert; C & Gs Woodcutting Machinists; Fellow Inst of Carpenters; Licentiate of CGLI.
Non standard joinery and small furniture, specializing particularly in staircases.

PARKS, E. H. & CO (Empl: 4; Est: 1971)
Master Thatchers
Mead House, 104 Periton Lane, Minehead, Somerset TA24 8DZ. 0643-4939.
5 yr apprenticeship (1959 onward); M Somerset MTA; M NSMT.
Pc Numerous contracts for National Trust Estates inc. Holnicote Estate, Blaise Hamlet, Bristol; Clevedon House. Badminton Estate for Duke of Beaufort.

PARR, JERRY (Empl: 3; Est: 1978)
Master Thatcher
24 Cyril St, Taunton, Somerset TA2 6HP. 0823-274 944.
Served 4 yr apprenticeship; M Somerset MTA.
Carry out a lot of extensions and conversion work (barns, etc.), and fully liase with architects and building surveyors, etc.

PARSONS, JULIE INTERIORS (Est: 1980)
Interior Designer
27 Burnsall St, London SW3 3SR. 071-351 9545.
IDDA.
Pc Luxurious residences – home and abroad.

PAUL, ALISTAIR & CO (Empl: 9; Est: 1974)
Interior Designer & Decorators
107 High St, Honiton, Devon EX14 8PE. 0404-41990.
Pc Mount Edgcumbe House, Cornwall. Powderham Stables, Devon. Cleeve House, Avon.

PAWLEY, DAVID – TURRET CLOCKMAKER (Est: 1965)
8 Enborne Place, Newbury, Berks RG14 6BB. 0635-33519.
M Brit Horological Inst; Brit Watch & Clockmakers Guild.
Pc Numerous clocks and sundials inc. 48 inch external clock and 44 inch vertical south declining sundial finished in solid gold leaf – The Clock House and The Sundial House, Newbury, Berks.
Commercial and industrial clocks; quartz and radio controlled time systems; digital clocks and display systems; sundials designed and manufactured for the precise location required; special feature clocks made. Information and photographs available.

PAYNE, GEOFF & POOLE, ROBERT (Est: 1972)
Rush Seating & Woodturning
The Calf Pens, Cross Tree, Filitins, Nr Lechlade, Glos GL7 3JL. 0367-86522.
Both Members of Craftsmen of Gloucestershire
Pc Seat of Walpole 'Strawberry Hill' chair re-rushed by G. Payne – V & A Museum.

PAYNE, R. D. BUILDING SERVICES LTD (Empl: 8; Est: 1972)
Lawnmead Hardenhuish Lane, Chippenham, Wilts SN14 6HN. 0249-657 133 & 0860-399 200.
Apprenticed Masons & Plasterers; M FMB. Approved: local authorities; N. Wilts District Council.
Pc 37 The Causeway, Chippenham, Wilts.

PEACE, DAVID MBE – GLASS ENGRAVER (Est: 1957)
Abbots End, Hemingford Abbots, Huntingdon, Cambs PE18 9AA. 0480-62472.
ARIBA; Past President & Chairman GGE; FGE; F SD-C; Liveryman Worshipful Co of Glaziers.
Pc Engraved glass in many churches, cathedrals and colleges.

Examples of engraved glass in 10 public collections. Many one-man shows.
Author of Glass Engraving, Lettering and Design, *(Batsford, 1985). Figurative designs are done in association with Sally Scott. Only carborundum engraving undertaken in situ.*

PEARCE, BARBARA (Est: 1985)
Wallhangings & Soft Furnishings
17 Hammer Rd, Simpson, Milton Keynes. Bucks MK6 3NY. 0908-667405.
Cert of Design/Embroidery, Loughborough College of Art & Design; Full M Milton Keynes Craft Guild (juried semi-professional guild).
Pc Handmade paper and embroidery wall pieces. Rag-rug wall hanging. Silk embroidered, patchworked, manipulated cushions). Many woven, embroidered wallhangings.
Brochure.

PEARSON, CAMERON (Empl: 2 + 2 apprentices; Est: 1979)
Specialist Castings
The Ironworks, Sheffield Rd, Chapel-en-le-Frith, via Stockport, Derbys SK12 6PG. 0298-812 740.
Full Tech C & Gs Foundry Tech/Patternmaking; Dip FE; Bradford College of Art.
Architectural castings; heraldry and logos; street signs and plaques; cast signs; opening plaques for buildings; etc. made principally in aluminium, although willing to undertake brass and bronze work. Brochure.

PEARSON, CYNTHIA
Rag Rugs, Needlepoint Embroidery
42 Siviters Lane, Rowley Regis, Warley, W. Midlands B65 8DP. 021-559 3674.
Pc St Aidan's Church. Forest Comprehensive School, Leamore, Walsall. Work sold through galleries and exhibitions. Private and ecclesiastical commissions.
Rag rugs; hooked rugs; canvas work; hand and/or machine embroidery.

PEASE, STEVE, DECORATIVE PAINTER (Empl: 2; Est: 1982)
No 7 Glanmor Crescent, The Uplands, Swansea, W. Glam SA2 0JP. 0792-473817.
Jacob Kramer School of Art & Design, Leeds – Textile Design; Inchbald School of Design, London – specialist finishes.
Pc Trompe l'œil marble panelled showroom door. Interior design commission – Bahrain portfolio. Various interior design commissions – Swansea.

PEMBROKE DESIGN LTD

PEDDIE, DICK & McKAY (Est: 1852)
Architects
44 Constitution St, Edinburgh, Lothian EH6 6RS. 031-555 0077.
Members RIBA.
Pc 16th-century tower house – Black Barony Hotel. Bernard St, and also Seafield Baths, Leith.

PEDLAR, RICHARD CHARTERED ARCHITECTS (Est: 1978)
4 Grove Rd, Blackboy Hill, Redland, Bristol BS6 6UJ. 0272-742 612 & 47318 (night).
RIBA; Dip Arch; Dip in Conservation Studies (York).
Pc Restoration and conversion of 17th-century building into Art Gallery. Restoration of 18th-century Meeting House.

PEDLEY, NICHOLAS G. – FURNITURE MAKER (Empl: 5; Est: 1979)
Unit 5B, Barrowmore Estate, Gt Barrow, Cheshire CH3 7JS. 0829-40554 & 40959.
C & Gs Cert Carpentry & Joinery; 12 yrs full time workshop experience.
Pc Mostly personal commissions.
Mainly works to own designs including church work; shop fittings; furniture and joinery to architect's and client's specifications. Brochure.

PELLY, FRANCES – STONE (Empl: solo; Est: 1986)
Windbreck, Burray, Orkney KW17 2ST. 085-673 310.
Dip Art (Sculpture); practising sculptor for 17 yrs; Associate M Royal Scottish Academy.
Pc Finials – Queen Street Museum, Edinburgh. Wreath in sandstone – RSA Building, Edinburgh. Season stone – private collection, Lord Goold, Glasgow. Naming stone – J. Jolly, Kirkwall.
Willing to undertake work for bronze casting.

PEMBROKE DESIGN LTD (Est: 1969 originally, 1981 Ltd)
Chartered Architects, Construction Managers, Planning Consultants
16 Meyrick St, Pembroke Dock, Pembrokes SA72 6UT. 0646-683 439. 0792-53157. 17 Victoria Place, Haverfordwest, Pembrokes SA61 2JX. 0437-4135. 29 St Helen's Rd, Swansea, W. Glam SA1 4AP. 0792-53157.
Gareth J. Scourfield, director – Dipl Arch; RIBA; AFAS; FFB; ACI Arb W. Keith Williams, director – AMCIOB Colin F. Jones, surveyor – ARICS Julian Mansel-Thomas, architect and interior designer – B Sc; B Arch (Hons).
Pc Restoration – Pembroke Castle; 7 churches and chapels; a Martello Tower and Star Fort. Conservation/conversion of numerous

listed buildings. Consultants to the Pembrokeshire Historic Buildings and W. Wales Maritime Heritage Trusts.
Building and site surveys; advice on building repairs and maintenance; development plans; expert witness on building disputes; arbitration on building contracts; specialist design services; interior design; shopfitting; signs; graphics and colour designs.

'PENDLE STAINED GLASS' (Empl: 2; Est: 1985)
70 Albert Rd, Colne, Lancs BB8 0AG. 0282-869 478 & 866 186.
Self taught & knowledge learnt in visits to Florida & Virginia, USA.
Pc Local listed buildings inc. parish churches, Gawthorpe Hall, and civic buildings.
Stocks a large selection of restored, salvaged town house windows, for sale, for trade, shipping, packing etc. Glass cleaning only undertaken where use of acid applicable.

PENTELOW, GRAHAM ARTIST & CRAFTSMAN IN STAINED GLASS (Est: 1979)
18 Stanley St, Rothwell, Northants NN14 2EB. 0536-710 486.
3 yrs Swansea College of Art, Architectural Glass; A BSMGP.
Pc South aisle window – Chesterfield Parish Church is just one among many new commissions. Has also done a lot of restoration and repair work.
Specialist glass cleaning only undertaken in some cases.

PEPPER, WILLIAM F. R. (Empl: 3; Est: 1973)
Consultant & Advisor on Straw/reed Thatching.
Bridge Rd, Broughton, Huntingdon, Cambs PE17 3AY. 0487-822 505.
M East Midlands MTA.
Pc Council Grant work in Cambs, Herts, Beds, Essex and Suffolk.

PERCHERON, H. A. LTD (Empl: 12; Est: 1898)
Soft Furnishings, Custom-made Trimmings
97–99 Cleveland St, London W1P 5PN. 071-580 1192 & 071-580 5156.
IDDA; BCFA; WEFFA.
Will reproduce trimmings. Will design certain things to client's specification. Brochure.

PERIOD BRASS LIGHTS (Empl: 2; Est: 1966)
9a Thurloe Place, Brompton Rd, London SW7 2RZ. 071-589 8305.
Produce Regency, Adam, Georgian, etc. wall lighting and fittings. Gold plating undertaken but not silver. Brochure.

PERIOD JOINERY (Empl: 5)
3 City Ind Estate, Haven Rd, Exeter, Devon EX2 8DD. 0392-435 237.

C & Gs; all staff have served apprenticeships; GMC; BEC.
Sliding sash windows; casement windows; panel doors; Georgian doors; screens; period mouldings; etc.

PERKINS, TOM (Empl: solo; Est: 1978)
Classical & Modern Lettering in a Variety of Media
40 High St, Sutton, Ely, Cambs CB6 2RB. 0353-778 328.
Assistant to Richard Kindersley; Elected M SD-C; M Craft Council Selected Index; visiting Lecturer, The Calligraphy & Bookbinding Course, Roehampton Inst.
Pc Carved inscriptions – the New War Memorial, Peterborough City Centre. Carved plaques for Mobil Oil Co; British Medical Assoc; Berkshire County Council; Cambridge City Council.
Skills inc. carving; painting; engraving on glass; calligraphy; designs for reproduction, photo-etching, sandblasting, etc. Brochure.

PERMANENT ROOFS LTD (Empl: 28; Est: 1970)
178 Baker St, Enfield, Middx EN1 3JS. 081-363 3600/0036/3062.
FMB; NHIC; Confederation of Roofing Contractors; GMC; Fed of Crafts & Commerce.
Pc Catslide roof with pitched dormers reconstructed to original design – 'Dalmonds', Mangrove Lane, Hoddesdon, Herts. Strip and retile with old tiles, retaining roof sag – 17th-century cottage, 38 Cambridge Rd, Wadesmill, Herts.
This firm is able to reproduce any tile profile from a sample provided. Also undertakes asphalt, bitumin, polymeric and GRP roof coverings.

PETERS, ALAN FURNITURE (Empl: 5; Est: 1962)
Aller Studios, Kentisbeare, Cullompton, Devon EX15 2BU. 088-46251.
7 yrs apprenticeship to Edward Barnsley; interior design training, Central School of Arts, London; Crafts Council Index; F SD-C.
Pc Dining furniture – Farnham Castle. 2 tables – Broughton Castle, Oxon. Chests and benches – Kirkham House, Paignton, Devon for DOE. Complete furnishing of 12th-century Fishermen's Chapel, St Brelade's, Jersey. Altar table – Wolvercote Church, Oxon.
Brochure.

PETTS, JOHN (Empl: 2; Est: 1960)
Stained Glass Artist/Painter
The Old Workhouse Studio, Union Rd, Abergavenny, Gwent NP7 5UW. 0873-7190.
Fellow BSMGP.
Pc Large windows of original design in Britain and the USA inc. 40 ft wide stained glass windows in Brighton and Hove New Synogogue.

FIRMS AND CRAFTSPEOPLE

PHI INTERIORS (Empl: solo; Est: 1960)
Furniture Maker & Restorer
3 Green Lane, Lambley, Nottingham NG4 4QE. 0602-313 477.
1st Class Honours Art, Craft in Wood & Metal, Loughborough University; qualified Teacher and Lecturer in Art & Craftwork; London BA (Hons).
Pc Complete reconstruction of Victorian 'D-end' dining table, also a William & Mary chest on stand. Georgian; Regency; Hepplewhite; Chippendale chairs made to complete sets.
Willing to design interiors to customer's specifications using natural materials such as marble, granite, slate, stone and wood.

PHILLIPPO, ROGER (Empl: solo; Est: 1976)
Glass Engraver
The Bakehouse, Church St, Harston, Cambridge CB2 5NP. 0223-870 277.
Various college qualifications inc. NDD and Des RCA.
Pc Decorative lighting fittings to complement existing decor – No 10 Downing St. Mural for 'Shell' Centre.

PHOENIX FIREPLACES (Est: 1980)
51 Park Lane, Liverpool L17 8UW. 051-727 3578.
Fair Trades Approved.
Pc Maritime Museum, Albert Dock, Liverpool. Ellesmere Port Boat Museum.
Victorian fireplaces inc. cast-iron grates; timber marble and cast-iron original and reproduction fire surrounds; hearths; original and reproduction hand-decorated tiles; copper and brass accessories, fire guards, fenders, fire stools, etc. Brochure.

PICKARD, PERCY LTD (Est: c.100 yrs)
Fagley Quarries, Fagley Lane, Eccleshill, Bradford, W. Yorks BD2 3NT. 0274-637307/8/9.
Suppliers of natural York stone roofing slates. Also suppliers of other forms of natural stone for restoration work and Yorkshire paving slabs.

PICKTREE UPHOLSTERY FABRICS (Empl: one; Est: 1984)
26 Picktree Terrace, Chester-le-Street, Durham DH3 3ST. 091-388 6561.
BA (Hons) Woven & Printed Textile Design, Manchester; Associate M Textile Inst (by examination); one yr experience in industry textile sector.
Pc British Airways Design Selection. Vaux Group. Whitbread.
Wool mark licence holder. Minimum quantity 20 m at trade prices, shorter runs negotiable.

PILKINGTON, SHEELAGH (Est: 1975)
Cane Work
39 Kidmore Rd, Caversham, Reading, Berks RG4 7LR. 0734-478 832.
Yrs of experience; considers the quality of work done is her best recommendation.
Pc Unwilling to give details due to respect for clients' privacy.
Willing to undertake recaning of double or blind caned furniture; spider webs; medallion patterns; close caning; etc. There may be a long waiting list for bergere suites and very large items.

PINCUS, HELEN (Est: 1982)
Art Textiles & Design
Lower Studio, 14 West Lodge Avenue, Acton Hill, London W3 9SF. 081-992 5421.
BA (Hons), Loughborough College of Art & Design (Textile Faculty); M Free Painters & Sculptors.
Pc Numerous private commissions inc. Central London Show Properties, etc.
Hand-worked silk panels designed to enhance any location or size of wall. Can incorporate featured wallpapers, and/or furnishing fabrics if desired. Brochure.

PINFOLD, G. F. – THATCHING & ROOFING (Empl: 2–3; Est: 1954)
20 Marlborough Rd, Chipping Norton, Oxon OX7 5PD. 0608-3548.
Pc Various thatching jobs for Savilles (estate agents) clients. 2 cottages for Viscount Hereford. Re-thatching of The Barley Mow – Clifton Hampden. Also numerous traditional stone (stonesfield slate) roofs, in churches for Eng. Heritage.

PINFOLD, J. H. (Est: 35 yrs)
Master Thatcher
10 Glovers Lane, Middleton Cheney, Banbury, Oxon. 0295-710 699.
M NSMTA; Northants MTA.
Re-timbering only undertaken with assistance.

PINHEY, SALLY (Est: 1984)
Specialist Painter
7 Syward Rd, Dorchester, Dorset DT1 2AJ. 0305-64651.
Pc Bochym Manor, The Lizard, Cornwall. Lea Hall, Lea, Nr Matlock, Derbys. Yuk Chun Restaurant, Clapham Rd, London. Birkin House, Dorchester.
Although willing to take on a variety of work Sally Pinhey specializes in plant-life. She has exhibited with the Art of Living, the Royal Horticultural Society, The Society of Botanical Artists and the Armed Forces Arts Society.

FIRMS AND CRAFTSPEOPLE

PLANNED APPEARANCES LTD (Empl: 4; Est: 1987)
Refurbishment of late Victorian (post 1875) & Edwardian Properties.
28 Elmfield Rd, London SW17 8AL. 7 Holmlea Rd, Chatsworth Rd, Croydon, Surrey CR0 1HA. 081-673 4939 & 081-688 4204.
B. Davey – C Eng   W. Burge – BA.
Pc Refurbishment inc. 2nd floor of Edwardian House, London, SW8 for S. Miller; entire internal structure for S. Hamilton Fairley. Restoration of bannisters and scullery for M. Edwards.

PLANT, TIMOTHY
Artist – Murals
7 Bramham Gardens, London SW5. 071-370 2945.
Pc Trompe l'œil library with clock, vases and a landscape through a window – St John's Wood, London. Panels representing Christ and Virgin Mary – Church, Jundiai, Sao Paulo, Brazil. 12 m × 3 m classical landscape – Pinner, London. 15 m × 6 m fantasia with drapes and figures – restaurant, Waterhouses, Staffs.
The artist offers a wide variety of subject matter to suit different surroundings, is capable of working in most conditions, and is willing to travel extensively for this purpose. Author Painted Illusions *(Ward Lock).*

PLASTER DECORATION CO LTD, THE (Empl: approx 30; Est: 1983)
34 Stannery St, Kennington, London SE11 4AE. 071-735 8161.
Fed of Master Plasterers; BEC.
Pc The Old Vic. Frogmore House. Cheesham Place. National Maritime Museum.

PLASTERITE LTD (Empl: 36; Est: 1976)
Johnsons Yard, School Lane, Seal, Nr Sevenoaks, Kent TN15 0BE. 0732-62671.
BEC; Nat Fed of Plastering Contractors.
Pc Theatre Royal, Portsmouth. 49, 50, 51 Grosvenor St, London W1. 68–73 Cornhill (Heritage Award).
Brochure.

POIRRIER, BILL – BLACKSMITH (Est: 1980)
'Riverden Forge', Roadwater, Watchet, Somerset TA23 0QH. 0984-40648.
CoSIRA courses at Cannington; 5 yr period working part-time with local blacksmith; M BABA.
Pc Mostly small one-off commissions for churches and private individuals – fire-forged using rivets, tenons, clips rather than welding.

POLLOCK CRAFTS (Empl: solo; Est 1987)
Crests, Plaques, Woodcarving & Patternmaking
15 Geils Quadrant, Dumbarton G82 2PR. 0389-67869.
Time served patternmaker. Previous to 1987 several yrs part-time whilst in normal employment.
Pc Various army regiments with plaques. Town Councils. Fabergé clock casing (1 m high) – Smith of Derby, clockmakers. Queens Cross Church, Glasgow. Various carvings and modelmaking – Yarrow Shipbuilders.

PONSFORD, A. J. (Empl: 5; Est: 1962)
Antique Restoration & Cabinet Making
51–53 Dollar St, Cirencester, Glos GL7 2AS. 0285-652 355.
Conservation/restoration of antique furniture; print cleaning and restoration of picture frames and oil paintings.

POOLE, PHIL WOODCARVER (Empl: solo; Est: 1984)
41 Hornsey Rise Gardens, London N19 3PP. 071-281 1328.
Largely self-taught; Brit Woodcarvers Assoc.
Pc Carving inc. mirror and picture frames; pine Victorian corbels; mahogany floor lampstand; oak headboard.
3d figures and animals; relief mouldings; foliage; geometrical designs. Willing to undertake restoration work in relief carving, but mainly interested in original compositions to commission. Brochure.

POPLAR BUILDING (Empl: 5; Est: 1987)
33 Poplar Rd, Warmley, Bristol, Avon BS15 5JX. 0272-605 847.
Apprenticeship with Beazers of Bath; M FMB.
Pc Stone cleaning and restoration – Nos 5 & 7 Rodney Place, and also at Bristol Museum, Clifton, Bristol. Stone walling (stowey stone) – Chew Stoke, Nr Bristol.
Willing to undertake all groundworks preceding stone building, extensions, etc.

PORRITT, DON MCSD (Empl: one; Est: 1964)
Industrial Designer/Silversmith
The Studio, Leathley Rd, Menston, Ilkley, W. Yorks LS29 6DP. 0943-78329 & 74736.
C & Gs Bronze Medal (Diamond Mounting); M CSD.
Pc Silver flagons – Ripon Cathedral (private donor). Crucifixion sculpture (processional cross) – St Michael's Workington. Silver chalice – St Oswald's, Guiseley. Silver plated altar cross and candlesticks – Fulford Church, York.
Photo leaflet available, plus detailed response to enquiry.

FIRMS AND CRAFTSPEOPLE

PORTER, J. H. & SON LTD (Empl: 5; Est: 1935)
Craftsmen in Iron
11 Pembroke Mews, Kensington, London W8 6ER. 071-937 1322.
BABA.
Pc Edwardes Square Railing. Chapel gate and fittings – St Mary Abbots Church.

POSTERITY ARCHITECTURAL ANTIQUES
Baldwins Farm, Newent, Glos GL18 1LS. 053 185-597.
Bi-annual auction sales held in May and October.

POTTER, MARY (Empl: one; Est: 1970)
Batik Wallhangings
Hunters Wood, Laughton, Lewes, Sussex BN8 6DE. 0825-84438.
M Art & Architecture; Crafts Council Selected Index; M Art Workers Guild; M Batik Guild; M Guild of Sussex Craftsmen.
Pc 11 ft long batik on silk, mounted on hardboard – a Home for The Elderly in Hammersmith. Similar hanging for a new hospital in Sussex. Collage on cotton, 90 cms × 110 cms – a concert hall in Sussex.
Brochure.

POULTER, H. W. & SON
279 Fulham Rd, London SW10 9PZ. 071-352 7268 & 081-749 4557.
Also undertake commercial marble work, i.e. tops, vanity units etc., at their workshops – 1a Adelaide Grove, Off Uxbridge Road, London W12

POUNTNEY, JOHN ARCHITECT (Est: 1980)
19 Gainsborough Rd, Bedford Park, London W4 1NJ. 081-995 2253.
Dip Arch (Hammersmith).
Pc Restoration and remodelling of houses, flats and maisonettes in London (mainly Chiswick and Kensington), especially work to listed buildings in conservation areas. Contract value up to £200,000 (1988).

POWELL, HUGH (Est: 1965)
Stable Court, Chalmington, Dorchester, Dorset DT2 0HB. 0300-20721.
Chelsea School of Art; partnership with Carl Edwards for 3 yrs; ran own studio at Farringdon, Hampshire for 20 yrs; F BSGP.
Pc More than 100 windows in this country and Canada (details on application).

PREECE, JAMES STAINED GLASS (Empl: 2; Est: 1984)
Unit 11, Portobello Rd, London W10 5TD. 081-968 8807.
BSMGP.
Pc Many commissions for domestic windows and lamps, conserv-

atories, offices, restaurants and pubs.
Willing to install, but will not do any other work in situ.

PRESERVATION CRAFTSMEN LTD (Empl: 10; Est: 1976)
Timber Preservation & Damp Course Contractors
17 Grand Parade, Forty Avenue, Wembley Park, Middx HA9 9JS. 081-904 09906. 74 Gregories Rd, Beaconsfield, Bucks HP9 1HL. 0494-672 863 & 677 399.
M BWPA; M BEC.
Pc Churches; hospitals; housing; historic buildings.
Preservation of main structural timbers; treatment for wood boring insects and fungal decay; full repairs of dry rot damage inc. any moulding and special features; damp prevention; waterproof tanking.

PRESTBURY POTTERY (Empl: 2; Est: 1967)
Prestbury Pottery, 31 New Barn Lane, Prestbury, Cheltenham, Glos GL52 3LB. 0424-528 156.
M Gloucester Guild of Craftsmen.
Pc Recently reproduced Victorian ridge tiles with 'fretted' designs for private client. Mosaic and tile topped coffee tables have been a standard design for 20 yrs. Reproduction Worcester Roman Pavement undertaken both as framed pictures and as table tops.

PRESTIGE STONEWORK (Empl: self × 4; Est: 1969)
Beech Cottage, Milton Crocketford, Dumfries DG2 8RJ. 055 669-632.
Founder M and Master Craftsman DSWA (no longer a paid up member).
Pc Masonry and dry stone work – Gateway to Scotland Project (pillars and walls), Gretna interchange for SDD. Walking in figure of eight sculpture for Andy Goldsworthy of Pierpont. Many miles of Galloway dry stone walls.
Any masonry or dry stone work undertaken in natural stone, with emphasis now on masonry.

PRESTON, DONALD (Empl: one; Est: 1978)
Antique Restorers
Nidd House Antiques, Nidd House, Bogs Lane, Harrogate, N. Yorks. 0423-884 739.
Personally involved in restoration since 1935; graduated at Rycotewood College, Oxford; AM Inst E; C & Gs London Inst (C Cert F; Cert FC; FCC); M GMC.
Pc References will be supplied on request.
Restoration of furniture, lead sculpture, scientific instruments, long case clocks, mantel clocks, antique fire surrounds; conversions of electric lamps. Brochure.

FIRMS AND CRAFTSPEOPLE

PRESTON, V. (Est: 1987)
Textile Designer
40 Cahir St, London E14 8QR. 071-987 7642.
BA Textile Design.
Pc Tapestries – Mammy Yoko Hotel, Sierra Leone, W. Africa.

PRICE, GRUFFYDD (Est: 1976)
Architect
1 Maes Artro, Llanbedr, Gwynedd LL45 2PZ. 034-123 448.
B Arch (Hons); RIBA.
Pc Work in Gwynedd inc. Portmeirion Italianate Village; Cors y Gedol Hall; Talhenbont Hall.

PRIDE, ERIC ORIENTAL RUGS (Empl: 2; Est: 1979)
44 Suffolk Rd, Cheltenham, Glos GL50 2AQ. 0242-580 822.
GMC.

PRINCE, ALAN – THATCHER (Empl:3; Est: 1975)
Foxhill Hillside, South Brent, Devon TQ10 9AU. 03647-2400.
CoSIRA assisted apprenticeship; M Devon & Cornwall MTA; M Devon Guild of Craftsmen.

PRISMS STAINED GLASS DESIGN (Empl: solo; Est: 1986)
34 Boundary Rd, Swiss Cottage, London NW8 0HG. 071-624 5812.
M Art in Architecture; BSMGP.
Pc Private commissions for domestic interiors.
Windows, screens, lighting, doors, skylights and hanging panels in abstract and stylized linear design, paying special attention to subtlety of colour and type of glass, playing on its diffraction of light and harmonizing with the existing environment.

PRITCHARD, HUGH (STONEMASONS) LTD (Empl: 32; Est: 1984)
100 Kelvinhaugh St, Glasgow G3 8PE. 041-248 2768. FAX 041-221 0693
M Stone Fed.
Pc Conservation of fireplace from Belmont House, Glasgow for Springburn Museum. Restoration of many public and commercial buildings throughout Strathclyde. Reproduction in sandstone of various features and statuary. Stone cleaning by various methods on a variety of materials.

PRITCHARD, I. & P. (Empl: 2; Est: 1981)
Rush & Cane Work
17 Heathcote Grove, Chingford, London E4 6RZ. 081-529 2884.
M Basketmakers Assoc.

Pc Chair caning and rush seating for various well known restorers in the London area.

PROCTOR & LAVENDER LTD (Empl: 200; Est: 1899)
Standard & Special Handmade Bricks using Traditional Techniques
Bridge Estate, Lode Lane, Solihull, W. Midlands B81 2HB. 021-711 1616.
Pc Handmade bricks – Swan Theatre, Stratford-upon-Avon (Civic Trust Award).
A full brick cutting service is available. Brochure.

PROSSER, DEBORAH (Empl: 2; Est: 1981)
Ceramic Artist
Penhalvean Pottery, Redruth, Cornwall TR16 6TQ. 0209-861 224/5.
4 yrs college for BA (Hons) 3d Design, W. Surrey College of Art & Design. Professional and Associate M Cornwall Crafts Assoc; South West Arts; Newlyn Soc of Arts; Penwithick Soc of Arts; Craftsmen Potters Assoc; Brit Crafts Council.
Rawfired earthenware goods using traditional techniques inc. barrel seats; vases; sculptural pieces; ceramic tiles for fireplaces and interiors; domestic ware; hand basins; door handles. Lists of stockists available. Portfolio compiled to suit client.

PROTECTIVE MATERIALS LTD (Empl: approx 50; Est: 1973)
Minster House, Commerce Estate, Kingston Rd, Leatherhead, Surrey KT22 7LA. 0372-376 551.
Repair work using this firm's materials is undertaken by Structoplast Contracts Ltd. Brochure.

PROTOTYPE PRODUCTIONS (Empl: variable; Est: 1952)
Stucco-work & Gypsum
2 Honiton Walk, Longton, Stoke-on-Trent, Staffs ST3 1LS. 0782-325 982.
BA Sculpture & Pottery.
Pc Work commissioned and accepted by Shah of Iran; Prince Charles; Duke of Edinburgh (coats of arms); Harrods; banks and insurance companies.

PRYOR, MICHAEL McKENZIE (Empl: solo; Est: 1984)
Consultant & Specialist in Painting & Decorating Treatments
40 Buckstone Drive, Edinburgh, Lothian EH10 6PQ. 031-445 3216.
Time served painter and decorator, awarded a Full Tech Cert Painting & Decorative work (London C & Gs); M & Past President of Scot Assoc of Painting Craft Teachers.

Pc Marble exhibition stand – Royal Scottish Museum, Edinburgh. Drawn out and painting of Edinburgh City coat of arms – St Giles' Cathedral. Gilding enrichments of ceiling and graining of woodwork – Parliamentary Hall, Edinburgh. Marble front facade – Hong Kong Bank.
Undertakes oil gilding, not water gilding.

PULLAN, PETER (Empl: solo; Est: 1977)
Glass Engraver
Crispian Cottage, Drove Lane, Market Lavington, Devizes, Wilts SN10 4NT. 0380-813 525.
Associate F GGE; M Heraldic Soc; M Soc of Heraldic Arts.
Pc Glass doors – Kennet District Council. Memorial window – RAF Halton Station Church.
Will not install.

PUMFREY, BERNARD (Empl: solo)
Designer & Craftman in Wood
14 Oakleigh Rd, Stratford-upon-Avon, Warwicks CV37 0DW. 0789-67410.
Time served and college trained (Prizeman 1952–54); qualified teacher, Wolverhampton College of Art; LCG; MSD-C; FRSA; Hon LCC ED; F Coll P; AIMWT; Past President Inst & College of Craft Education; Dip Interior Design & Decoration; etc.

PURBECK DECORATIVE TILE CO (Empl: 4; Est: 1951)
Unit 7, 101 Farm Lane, Fulham, London SW6 1QJ. 071-381 6638.
IDDA; GMC.
Pc Motorway service station restaurants. Middle East Ice Rink. Restoration – part of Harrods Food Hall.
Several of this firm's designs have been selected by the Design Council. Will also produce special effects such as rag-rolling on tiles. Brochure.

PUT YOUR FEET UP (Empl: 2; Est: 1983)
Restoration of Upholstery in Traditonal Manner on Antique Furniture
Fulbeck House, Fulbeck, Morpeth, Northumberland NE61 3JT. 0670-518 231.
8 yrs practical experience working on different types of chairs after 4 yrs of college instruction.

PYKE, ANDREW J. (Empl: one; Est: 1978)
Furniture Restorer & Joiner
Grove Farm, Brockweir Lane, Hewelsfield, Lydney, Glos GL15 6UU. 0594-530 924.

QUINNELL, RICHARD LTD

Worked for John Briggs, artist craftsman for 2 yrs; Dip of Loughborough College.
Great emphasis upon involving the customer in the design of the piece, and if possible like to incorporate some feature in the room where it is to be placed.

QUAIL, JANE (Empl: solo)
Architectural Sculptress
Boundary Farm House, Gunthorpe, Norfolk NR24 2NS. 0263-860 826.
Pc 5 ft stone figure (St Margaret of Antioch) over porch of Cley Parish Church, Norfolk. 9 ft × 4 ft oak screen (Christ and saints) – Lady Chapel, St Peter's Church, Plymouth. 3 ft diameter (Assumption) stone relief, carved in situ – Carmel, Presteigne, Wales. 3 ft beech wood crucifix (Risen Christ) – Lady Chapel, Parish Church, Harleston, Norfolk.

QUAIL, PAUL STAINED GLASS
Boundary Farm House, Gunthorpe, Norfolk NR24 2NS. 0263-860 826.
NDD (Painting) ATC; F BSMGP; F SD-C.
Pc Windows in St Paul's Church, West Bridgeford, Notts; St Mary's Cadogan St, Chelsea, SW3; Langham Carmel, Langham, Norfolk; etc.

QUARTLEY, FREDDIE (Est: engraving for 12 yrs)
Glass Engraver Specializing in Lettering & Calligraphy
45 Bainton Rd, Oxford OX2 7AG. 0865-515 691.
AFGE; Dip Lettering, Illumination & Calligraphy.
Pc Window of snowflakes – private commission. Presentation goblets for Princess Margarethe of Sweden. 4 decanters for City of Oxford Magistrates Court (heraldry and lettering). Decanter decorated with Christchurch College arms.

QUIBELL & SON (HULL) LTD (Empl: 30; Est: 1903)
Building, Masonry & Civil Engineering Contractors
Stepney Lane, Hull, N. Humberside HU5 1LJ. 0482-42177.
Apprentice and CITB qualified bricklayers (12); joiners (4); stonemasons (9); others (5).
Pc Restoration work inc. Beverley Minster (stonework); Bishops Manor, Howden; Town Docks Museum, Hull (stonework); Sessions Court, Beverley (roof).
Brochure.

QUINNELL, RICHARD LTD (Empl: 12; Est: 1946)
Master Craftsmen in Iron
Rowhurst Forge, Oxshott Rd, Leatherhead, Surrey KT22 0EN. 0372-37 148. FAX 0372-386 516.

Richard Quinnell, managing director – MA in Natural Sciences; Founder and currently Vice-Chairman of BABA; Hon Life-Member of Artist Blacksmiths Assoc of N. America; FRSA; M UKIC; served on Craft Council Conservation Committee. Other members of firm mostly time served apprentices.
Pc Too numerous to detail but recent projects inc. restoration of bronze statues of Wolfe & Churchill – Westham Green; gates – Ashford Park; complete farriers workshop and tools – USA; door furniture – House of Commons library.
This firm works in a variety of metals and styles, and is able to handle very large projects (both in terms of physical size and value), they collaborate with other specialists when restoring or reproducing mixed-media objects. Brochure.

RABY, JUNE
Architectural Sculptress
92 Dartmouth Park Hill, London N19 5HU. 071-263 7665.
Working as sculptor (mainly ceramics) for past 10 yrs; 1st Class Hons Degree MA.
Bas relief murals; sculptural clocks; variety of exhibition work; research and interest in public art. Photographs and CV available.

RADCLIFFE, LOUIS A. BAUERN KUNS (Est: 1970)
Specialist Joinery
8 Fifth Avenue, Stobhill Gate, Morpeth, Northumberland NE61 2HH. 0670-519 240.
Studied carving and restoration in Wurzburg-am-Main, Germany. Artist-Craftsman.
Numerous works for churches (mostly restoration); iconastic designer for orthodox churches; antique furniture repair and restoration; embellishing existing carvings.

RADFORD & BALL
Glass Engravers, Etchers, Enamellers
144 Russell Mansions (Rear Basement), Southampton Row, London WC2 5AJ. 071-837 5954.
Diane Radford – MA RCA L. Ball – BA/MA RCA.
Pc Unilever House, London. Limestreet Station, Liverpool. NMB Bank, Amsterdam.
Sandblasting, bending and casting. The method and the style of application used will depend on the client's brief. Brochure.

RAFFLE, ANDREW V. MASTER THATCHER (Empl: one; Est: 1984)
Laundry Cottage, Prestwold Hall, Prestwold, Loughborough, Leics LE12 5SQ. 0509-881 426.

RAISON, J.D. & PARTNERS

NSMT; Rutland & Leics MTA; NCMTA.

RAGDON ART (Empl: 2 + 1 part-time; Est: 1988)
Stained Glass Lighting
Ragdon Manor, Ragdon, Church Stretton, Shropshire SY6 7EZ. 06946-389.
Stained glass maker since 1974.
Pc Various commission work undertaken, specializing in the manufacture of luminaires since 1988.

RAILTON, JIM (Empl: 6; Est: 1979)
Architectural Antiques, Cabinet Making, Decorative Finishes
Country Pine Antiques, Nursery House, Chatton, Alnwick, Northumberland. Church House, Chatton, Alnwick, and also 22 Bailiffgate, Alnwick. 06685-323 & 0665-603 616.
B Sc Gt Man.
Pc Worked on several notable country houses and castles in the north inc. Chillingham, Bamburgh and Callaly Castles, and Lorbottle Hall.
Brochure.

RAILWAY FORGE (Empl: one; Est: 1985)
Blacksmith
St Thomas Rd, Newport, Launceston, Cornwall PL15 8DB. 0566-4024.
Apprenticeship and C & Gs.
Pc All work is carried out to commission and has inc. 11 candle lights, 7 ft high. Currently working on contract for a mosque in Saudi Arabia.

RAINBOW GLASS (Empl: 2 + 1 trainee; Est: 1986)
Stained Glass Artists
1 & 2 Great Western Terrace, Yeovil, Somerset BA21 5AA. 0935-23228.
Specialize in combining stained glass with double glazing. The designs are leaded in the traditional way and hand-painted directly on to the glass, then the finished panel is built into a fully finished double glazing unit ready to be installed.

'RAINBOW GLASS' – V. N. VOYSEY (Est: 1987)
Stained Glass Artist
Unit 11, Netley Marsh Workshops, Ringwood Rd, Netley Marsh, Southampton, Hants, SO4 2GY. 703-867 466 & 553 138 (Home).

RAISON, J. D. & PARTNERS (Empl: 6; Est: 1979)
Master Thatchers
1 Deer Park Court, Clopton, Stratford-upon-Avon, Warwicks CV37 0QP. 0789-295 236.

FIRMS AND CRAFTSPEOPLE

All apprentices serve 4 yr training period; M MTA for Oxon, Berks & Bucks.

RANK, NICHOLAS ASSOCIATES (Est: 1983)
Architects, Designers, Historic Buildings Consultants
14 Kennedy St, Manchester M2 4BT. 061-228 7414. FAX 061-228 7423
BA (Hons); B Arch; RIBA; M EASA.
Pc Church reordering – Emmanuel Didsbury, Manchester. Conservation/restoration work to various 16th, 19th, 20th century and medieval churches.

RATFORD BRIDGE, JAMES (Empl: 14 + 8 apprentices; Est: 1948)
Specialist Carpenter & Joiner
Dale Rd, Haverfordwest, Pembs, Dyfed SA62 3SA. 0437-765 814 & 763 623.
All C & Gs Craft and Advanced Craft Carpentry and Joinery; M BEC.

RATTEE & KETT (Empl: 250; Est: 1843)
Building Contractors
Purbeck Rd, Cambridge CB2 2PG. 0223-248 061.
BEC; Stone Fed; London Assoc of Master Stonemasons (Master Builders); Master Carvers Assoc; LDA. Approved: PSA; Eng. Heritage; LDA; local authorities; National Trust.
Pc Ely Cathedral, Architects, Purcell Miller Tritton & Partners. King's College Chapel, Freeland Rttg Roberts. Hatfield House, Herts. Anglesey Abbey, National Trust, PMT – all in Cambridge. House of Lords, Westminster – PSA, D. Insall.
A firm with considerable experience in the restoration and refurbishment of ancient buildings, willing to assist at the design stage and give advice on structural repair techniques. Also undertake modern design and build contracts; commercial and industrial construction; small works; alterations and improvements; architectural sculpture; wood carving; cast stone replicas and garden statuary. Brochure.

RAWLINGS, ERIC DECORATING SPECIALIST (Empl: 6–12; Est: 1968)
Blacksmiths Cottage, 57 High St, Irchester, Northants. 0933-56389.
All apprenticed tradesmen. M BDA.
Pc State room ceiling, Kimbolton Castle. Granville Buildings, Wellingborough.
Photographs available.

RAYMOND, GINNY – POLYCHROME CERAMICS (Empl: solo; Est: 1983)
Garden Flat, 42 Wandsworth Common, Northside, London SW18 2SL. 081-871 3759.

READ, HERBERT LTD

BA (Hons) Degree Ceramics, Bath Academy of Art.
Pc Colour matching plain tiles to complete Dutch tiles around a fireplace. A mural of country folk picking apples, etc., around a kitchen. Large 12 inch × 12 inch tiles plus plain background tiles to match curtain pattern and colours. Mural for bathroom 4 ft × 3 ft of parrot in jungle on 6 inch × 6 inch tiles. New colourways for Victorian designs (chintz and linen); design of an Indian fabric (chintz); choosing and designing colourways for wallpapers and borders – all freelance for Coles of Mortimer St.

RBR CONTRACT SERVICES (Empl: 22; Est: 1980)
Building Contractors
Windsor House, 24 Wycombe Lane, Wooburn Green, High Wycombe, Bucks HP10 0HE. 06285-27794.
Full Membership of TRADA; FERFA; CCS. Approved: various PCC's; Eng. Heritage; DOE/PSA; numerous local authorities.
Pc Kew Palace, Kew, Surrey – DOE/PSA. Hampton Court Palace, Surrey – DOE/PSA. St James's Palace, London. Palace of Westminster. Windsor Castle – Metropolitan Services Ltd. Frogmore House, Windsor Castle. St Agatha's Church, Portsmouth. St George's Church, Thriplow. St Andrew's Church, Chinnor, etc.
A well established organization skilled in a wide range of techniques for the restoration and repair of timber, stone, brick and concrete on commercial, industrial and residential property. Also undertake resin injection; evaluation and assessment of work, inc. statue repair and reinforcement design.

RDS FURNITURE CONTRACTS LTD (Empl: 15; Est: 1984)
1st Floor, Bland House, 1 Upton Rd, Rugby, Warwicks CV21 7DC. 0788-535 580 & 535 589.
Brit Contract Furnishing Assoc; Furniture Industry Research Assoc.
Pc The Burton Group Headquarters, London W1. Manufacturers Hanover Trust, Princes St, London EC4. Citicorp Scrimegour Vickers, Hays Wharf, London SE1.
Specialists in all aspects of English 17th- and 18th- century furniture. Provide consultancy, resource and contracting service covering original and replica pieces.

READ, HERBERT LTD
Specialist Conservators & Restorers
St Sidwells Art Ltd, Tiverton Way, Tiverton, Devon EX16 6TG. 0884-242 102.
Conservators trained at Courtauld Inst, Tate Gallery and C & Gs College, London; staff apprentice trained; M all professional,

FIRMS AND CRAFTSPEOPLE

amenity and associated Societies. Approved: Eng. Heritage; National Trust; National Maritime Museum; V & A Museum; Dioceses and local authorities throughout the country.
Pc Conserving and restoring 19th-century wall paintings – Athington Church. Conservation – panelling, Stokesway Castle. All woodwork since 1955 – National Cathedral, Washington DC. Dismantled and rebuilt 17th-century monument – Colyton Parish Church. Conservation – Queen Anne Walk, Barnstaple; Buckland Church, Worcs and Berkeley Castle. Re-inlay marble and semi-precious stones – Agra Colonnade for V & A Museum.
This firm has a wide range of skills (wood and stone carvers, polychrome and plastic conservators, joiners, gilders and decorators, wood conservators, etc), which means that they rarely sub-contract work, and are able to undertake large complex jobs. Nearly all work is grant aided. They have considerable experience of working in USA. The director lectures on conservation of woodwork at York University and elsewhere.

READ, STEPHEN & CO – CABINET MAKERS (Empl: 3; Est: 1980)
Hales Hall, Loddon, Norwich, Norfolk NR14 6QW. 050 846 356.
Served 4 yr apprenticeship; C & Gs Furniture Trades Cert.

READING, R. J. FURNITURE MAKER & RESTORER (Empl: one; Est: 1983)
'Westwood', Trolliloes, Cowbeech, Nr Hailsham, E. Sussex BN27 4QR. 0435-830 249.
Trained with William Tillman Ltd, Borough Green, Kent.
Unique furniture made to customer's specifications. Photo album available for perusal.

REARDON, MICHAEL & ASSOCIATES (Est: 1970)
Architects, Interior Designers & Historic Building Consultants
Hillborough Barn, Bidford-on-Avon, Nr Alcester, Warwicks B50 4LS. 0789-773 708.
Michael Reardon – MA; Dip Arch; RIBA   John Groom – BA; Dip Arch; RIBA; Lethaby Scholar Members of ASCHB; SPAB; Victorian Society; Sandstone Conservation Group.
Pc Repair and reordering – Birmingham Cathedral. Repair – Hereford Cathedral. Restoration – medieval timber-framed house. Adaption – Victorian building to form theatre.
Architecture undertaken in historically sensitive areas.

RECLAIMED BUILDING SUPPLES (Empl: 8; Est: 1984)
Yard: Wolston Business Park, Wolston, Nr Coventry, W. Midlands CV8 3FU. Office: 15 Spencer Avenue, Coventry CV5 6NQ. 0203-711 090.

REGENT, PETER

Reclaim and sell bricks; tiles; slates; coping stones; granite sets (cobblestones); ridge tiles; doors; sanitary ware; etc. Continually looking for new sources of materials and are able to demolish buildings; so would welcome enquiries of this nature.

RED BANK MANUFACTURING CO LTD (Empl: 450; Est: 1920)
Decorative Terracotta Building Products & Handmade Bricks
Measham, Burton-on-Trent, Staffs DE12 7EL. 0530-70333.
Will match anything that has been made in clay as a building product inc. ridge tiles; finials; sills; lintels; copings; etc. No minimum. Brochure.

REDLAND BRICKS LTD (Empl: 1,000 at 17 works; Est: 1958/59)
Graylands, Horsham, W. Sussex RH12 4QG. 0403-211 222.
Pc Handmade red and grey bricks with 76 different types of special shapes – Reading Town Hall restoration. Handmade Tudor grey-brown bricks – Hampton Court Palace refurbishment.
No minimum order; limitation only on size and shape of special brick. Brochure.

REDMAN, F. & SONS (Empl: 2; Est: 1896)
Furniture Designer & Restorer
J. B. Redman, Proprietor, 9 Hangleton Lane, Hove, E. Sussex BN3 8EB. 0273-415 169.
CGLI Cabinet Making 1st Class Cert, Advanced Design & Construction of Furniture Cert; M GMC.
Pc Restoration of furniture at Buckingham Palace. Design of various pieces of furniture – Franklin Mint Ltd, UK, Japan and Germany. Design work for English Heritage.

REEDWAYS LTD (Empl: 5 thatchers; Est: 1974)
Master Thatcher
Thatcher's Barn, Barrington, Ilminster, Somerset TA19 0JB. 0460 52166.
Somerset MTA; NSMTA; NCMTA.
Pc Commended by Civic Trust for quality and appearance of environment for thatched cottage, 1 Main St, Glamis, Tayside. Many other testimonials available from individual clients.

REGENT, PETER (Est: 1980)
Architectural Sculptor
Windover House, Woodmuir Crescent, Newport-on-Tay, Fife DD6 8HL. 0382-543 192.
Pc Carved oak crests – St John's Church, Perth. Carved sandstone and marble fireplaces – Mount Stuart, Bute. Majority of other work has

been uncommissioned sculpture – see RSA & RGI catalogues.
Although lettering is undertaken it is mainly incidental, plaques are relief carved and basically the only metalwork undertaken is bronze or resin-bronze. No brochure, but specific material could be provided for particular enquiries.

REID, DICK (Empl: 12; Est: 1959)
Wood & Stone Carvers, Cabinet Makers
23 Fishergate, York YO1 4AE. 0904-659 121.
Cabinet makers and woodcarvers apprentice trained; stonecarvers and sculptors art school and apprentice trained; MCA.
Pc Chatelherault – Scotland. Hembury Rotunda. Spencer House, London. York Minster roof. Fairfax House. British Embassys, Tokyo and Oslo. Many stately homes and Cathedrals.

RELIC ANTIQUES
Brillscote Farm, Lea, Malmesbury, Wilts SN16 9PF. 0666-822 332.
Specialist stockists of antique exteriors, interiors and fittings from period shops, bars and hotels in Britain and France, but also stock complete Victorian shop interiors; doorways; pub bar backs; cast- and wrought-iron fittings; Victorian and Edwardian stained and etched panels; garden stone items and other architectural embellishments; doors; etc.

RENNISON, GILL (Empl: solo; Est: 1981)
Stained Glass Artist
Foxhall Studio, Kelshall, Nr Royston, Herts, SG8 9SE. 076 387-209.
Apprenticed to a pupil of John Pipe. Established own studio in 1978.
Pc Commissions inc. all types of stained glass lampshades from wall lights and table lamps through to large theme shades over 1 m diameter for conservatories.
Fact sheets available.

RENOFORS (UK) LTD (Empl: 150+; Est: 1931)
Building Conservation & Restoration Systems
Conservation House, 116 Darwen Rd, Bromley Cross, Bolton BL7 9BQ. 0204-58336. FAX 0204-50070.
BDA. Approved: most local authorities; PSA; DOE; Eng. Heritage.
Pc Barnley, Hastings and Old Whitby Town Halls. Imperial Hotel, Blackpool. Winter Gardens, Blackpool. Milkmaid Fountain, Regent's Park. Tower of London. Westminster Hall.

RENTON, MICHAEL (Empl: solo; Est: 1960)
Designer-Engraver & Lettering Craftsman
Brook Granary, Icklesham, Winchelsea, E. Sussex TN36 4AX. 0424-814 535.

Apprenticeship as commercial wood engraver; studied at Harrow School of Art and C & Gs of London Art School with particular emphasis on lettering and design.
Pc In recent years many commemorative and other inscriptions in stone (sometimes wood and metal), with some heraldic and other carving. Also painted lettering and decoration.

A designer-craftsman interested in original work, rather than reproduction or restoration, who would welcome opportunities to develop lettering as an architectural feature, or in an environmental context. Will design for techniques of which he has no personal experience (i.e. glass engraving). Also works as a wood engraver and illustrator.

RENUBATH SERVICES (LONDON) (Empl: 7; Est: 1965)
248 Lillie Rd, London SW6 7QA. 071-381 8337.
Bath resurfacing; chemical cleaning; repairs to chips and abrasions in pressed steel, cast-iron acrylic and fibreglass baths (both old and new). Brochure.

RESTORATIONS UNLIMITED (Empl: 3; Est: 1982)
Restoration of Furniture, Veneers, Inlays, Seating, Ceramics, Metalwork
Pinkey Park, Malmesbury, Wilts SN16 0NS. 0666-840 888.
Proprietor – a restorer and woodworker all his life. 2 assistants studied under YTS schemes and Chippenham Tech College, and have O & A Levels in Woodwork.
Pc Restoration – Chinese 4 fold screen involving carving in wood, ivory, mother of pearl, etc. Restoration – 16th-century Chinese pottery. Restoration – 16th-century chairs and making a new one to match. Restoration of ivory miniatures.

All types of antique furniture restored inc. lacquer work and gilding; rush, cane and sea-grass re-seating. Also undertakes longcase and bracket clock restoration; ceramic restoration inc. Victorian loo's, cisterns and basins; repair service on brass and copperwork, locks, key cutting etc.

RICE & WALLIS LTD (Empl: 18; Est: 1908)
Specialist Joinery Manufacturere
201 Mina Rd, Bristol, Avon BS2 9YW. 0272-421 088.
Generally all apprentice served tradesmen; M BWF & F of B.
Pc Brunel House, Bristol.
Manufacturers of high class architectural and general joinery, ranging from bank and church work, school, shop fittings, public house bar counters. Brochure.

RICHARD JOINERY LTD (Empl: 26 Est: c. 1964)
Broadwater Trading Estate, Southdownview Way, Worthing, W. Sussex BN14 8NN. 0903-204 206.

Most craftsmen apprenticeship trained to C & Gs. Apprenticeship schemes currently being actively pursued.
Pc Missenden Abbey re-build, Bucks. St Peter's Church, Brighton, Sussex.
Bank, church and office fittings; general joinery; staircases and handrails; hotel and bar fittings. Foreign commissions considered on an individual basis.
Brochure.

RICHARDS, PAUL & PAULE – DECORATIVE PAINTERS (Est: 1985)
Ballroom Workshop, The Mews, Church St, Leominster, Heref. 0544-6320.
Decoration and restoration of antiques that are painted, lacquered and/or decorated; original decoration to match any style with or without aged paint finishes on furniture or objects; specialist paint finishes. Work outside the workshop is undertaken.

RICHARDSON ROOFING CO LTD (Empl: 80; Est: 1980)
49–51 Boston Manor Rd, Brentford, Middx TW8 9JQ. 081-845 4444.
NFRC; Inst of Roofing; LCA; Nat Joint Council for the Building Industry.
Pc Marble Hill House, Richmond Rd, Twickenham. North Kensington Library, Ladbroke Grove, London. British Library, Marylebone High St, London. Great Hall, Tunbridge Wells.
Brochure.

RICHARDSON, SARAH (Empl: solo; Est: 1981)
Stained Glass Artist/Painter
The Doors, Shield Hill, Haltwhistle, Northumberland NE49 9NW. 0498-20911.
Bristol Polytechnic, Foundation Studies; North Staffs Polytech, BA (Hons) specializing in Glass; Newcastle-upon-Tyne Polytech, MA Fine Art; M BSMGP; M BAG.
Pc St Paul's Church, Branxton. Lidean Mill, Selkirk. Theatre in The Forest, Grizedale, Cumbria. 12 small works commissioned by Dan Klein, director, Christies. Woodhorn Church Museum, Northumberland. The Arts & Live Music Association, The Customs House, Mill Dam. S. Shields.
Original design work for windows; internal screens; room dividers and wall panels. Winner of various awards inc. 1988 Sir Arthur Evans Travel Scholarship awarded by Worshipful Co of Glaziers and Painters in Glass. Articles published by British Artists in Glass Newsletter. *Involved in lecturing and teaching both in England and abroad.*

RIDLEY, ANNABEL
Glass Engraver
29 Richmond Hill, Richmond, Surrey TW10 6RE. 081-940 1732.
Craft M GGE.
Pc Yearly Berkshire Environmental Awards. Presentations inc. crests, lettering and logos.

RIDGEWELL, R. B. – RELIABLE SERVICE DECORATORS (Empl: 1; Est: 1974)
11 Woburn Court, Rushden, Northants NN10 9HL. 0933-314 074.
Trade apprenticeship; M BDA.

RIGG, DONAL (Empl: solo; Est: 1981)
Glass Engraver
7 Dalby Close, Ernesford Grange, Coventry, W. Midlands CV3 2GP. 0203-455 352.
Craft M GGE.
Pc Reproduction on flat glass of sculpture of St Michael & the Devil on the wall of Coventry Cathedral.

RING, I. J. (Empl: 3; Est: 1980)
Blacksmith
Newton Forge, Stalbridge Lane, Sturminster Newton, Dorset DT10 2JQ. 0258-72407.
6 yr apprenticeship Cerne Valley Forge; gaining certificates, and winning awards locally and nationally inc. Bath & West Show, Gillingham & Shaftesbury Show, Dorset Arts & Crafts Exhibition, Worshipful Co of Blacksmiths.
Pc Railing – Corfe Castle for National Trust. Gates – Plush Manor; West Hall, Long Burton; Lanchard Farm; etc. Large firebaskets and canopies, spiral staircase, etc.
From small repairs and large restoration work to new pieces made in modern or traditional styles. A variety of work 'at realistic prices' on view at the showroom 6 days a week. Brochure.

RIPLEY, MARK ANTIQUES & FORGE (Est: 1920)
Period Firebacks, Firedogs & Fittings
Robertsbridge, E. Sussex TN32 5NY. 0580-880 324.
M GMC.
A family firm specializing in inglenook fireplaces. Sell a range of reproduction firebacks; firebaskets; canopies; fire-irons; wall lights; etc. Also stock original Victorian firegrates and miscellaneous antique ironwork. Brochure.

FIRMS AND CRAFTSPEOPLE

RITCHIE, DAGEN & ALLAN (Est: 1947)
Chartered Architects, Town Planning Consultants & Arbiters
7 Crichton St, Dundee DD1 3AP. 0382-25209 & 25746.
J. Dagen – DA; Dip TP (Edin); FRIAS; RIBA; MRTPI   F. G. Allan – DA; FRIAS; RIBA; ACI Arb   J. Picken – B Arch; Dip Arch; RIBA; ARIAS.

RIVA DESIGN LTD (Empl: 10; Est: 1983)
Interiors from Concept to Completion
79a Wilmslow Rd, Handforth, Cheshire SK9 3EN. 0625-531 705 & 531 633.
Pc Georgian double doors and semi circular fan lights. Vaulted roof light 9 m × 4 m. Panelled hall with pilasters; Art Nouveau marquetry panels; staircase; doors and portio. Moorish interior with onion domes, barley twist columns, quatrefoil fretwork panels (all in gold-plated ceramic) arabesque carved doors in peach stained sycamore, scagliola floors, lighting system. Kitchen – Grade I listed 19th-century hall.
Corinthian columns and arches; period cornices and friezes; scagliola; trompe l'œil marquetry panels; headed doors; fretwork; turning; gilding; granite; marble; tiles to design; lighting; concept development; perspective visuals. Brochure.

ROBERTS, C. P. SPECIAL WORKS LTD (Empl: 100; Est: 1865)
Building Contractors
Roberts House, Station Close, Potters Bar, Herts EN6 3JW. 0707-51277.
Craftsmen apprentice trained with C & Gs qualifications; all management and surveying qualified and experienced. Approved: Eng. Heritage; PSA; most Greater London local authorities; several Diocesan boards.
Pc Hounslow United Reformed Church. Civic Award for Moreton House (Grade I). Chester Square (Grade II). Sir John Soanes Museum, London. Royal College of Obstetricians and Gynaecologists, Regent's Park. St James's Palace, and Buckingham Palace, London – both for PSA.
Will also undertake electrical and metalwork.

ROBERTS, DAVID & CO (Empl: 3; Est: 1975)
Ornamental & Decorative Cast Leadwork inc. Statuary
Drws-y-Mynydd, Pentre Dwr, Rhos, Wrexham, Clwyd LL14 1DB. 0978-842 070.
LCA.
Pc National Trust. Diocese of St Asaph.

ROBERTS, Dr DAVID & MARION (Empl: 2; Est: 1965)
Specialist Painting
Orbost Gallery, Dunvegan, Skye. 047 022-207 & 463.
D. Roberts – NDD; ATD; MA; Ph D; FSA (Scotland) M. Roberts – NDD; ATD.
Pc Regraining, gilding and retouching panelling (1699) inc. armorials, faux bas, restoring painted panels and views – Marston Hall, Lincs. Marbling fireplaces – Spauby Manor, Lincs. Resprigging fire damaged cornices – Cuidrach House, Skye. Facsimile wallpaper frieze – Talisker House, Skye.

ROBERTS, R. E. & N. M. (Empl: 12; Est: 1981)
Art Tile Distributors & Fireplaces of Yesteryear
Railway Station Platform, Knaresborough, N. Yorks HG 0JB. The Old Granary, Bilton in Ainsty, Nr York YO5 8LG. 0423-863 739 & 0423-358 913.
Pc Tiles specified, supplied and fixed for breweries in the country. Suppliers and fitters of numerous fireplaces to breweries in the north. Various restoration works.
Brochure.

ROBERTSON, CHARLES PARTNERSHIP, THE – ARCHITECTS (Est: 1982)
The Templeton Business Centre, Templeton St, Glasgow G4D 1DW. 041-554 5911.
Professor Charles Robertson – DA; FRIBA; FRIAS; FRAIA; FCIOB James Anderson – DA; RIBA; ARIAS Alan Bayne – B Arch; RIBA; ARIAS.
Pc Regeneration of Scotland Supreme Award – Templeton Business Centre, Glasgow. Historic building restoration – St Mary's Cathedral, Great Western Rd, Glasgow and also former SCWS Headquarters, Leith, Edinburgh. Environmental restoration – New Lanark.

ROBERTSON & COX (Empl: 2; Est: 1980)
Oriental Rug Repair
60 George St, Perth PH1 5JL. 0738-26300.
Apprenticeship and training in Oriental rug repair and restoration.
Pc Numerous repairs for private customers and several for trade clients.
Brochure.

ROBERTSON, GORDON E.
Timber & Wood Repairs to Buildings of Architectural & Historic Interest
Horsepost Lane, Glidden Farm, Hambledon, Portsmouth, Hants PO7 6SD. 070 132-506.

FIRMS AND CRAFTSPEOPLE

Studied Building Construction, Brixton School of Building whilst working with a firm of Consulting Civil and Structural Engineers. Currently reading for a Degree in Technology, Open University, which inc. Technology of House Design and Structural Engineering. GMC.
Pc Too numerous to mention, details on request.
Cabinet making; designer of fine furniture to commission; wood turning; wood carving. Using building knowledge and cabinet making skills he is involved in repair of buildings of architectural and historical interest. Has attended the SPAB Repair Course.

ROBERTSON, IAIN – CARPENTER/DESIGNER (Empl: 2; Est: 1980)
Barn Studios, High St, Farndon, Cheshire CH3 6PT. 0829-270 020.
Pc Furniture for show house, Liverpool Garden Festival. Cheshire County Council. Display pieces for the Army.

ROBINSON, GEOFFREY A. K. (Empl: 3; Est: 1840)
Stained Glass Artist/Painter
T/A Joseph Bell & Son, 68 Park St, Bristol, Avon BS1 5JX. 0272-268 543.
G. A. K. Robinson – Somerset Guild of Craftsmen; BSMGP; SD-C. J. Bell & Son – Corp M GMC.
Pc List available on request.

ROBINSON, J. – CERAMICS (Est: 1972)
Booth House Gallery, 3 Booth House, Holmfirth, Huddersfield, W. Yorks HD7 1QA. 0484-685 270.
BA; MA Art & Design (Sculpture & Ceramics); Chairman and M Northern Potters Assoc; M Yorkshire Mural Artists Group; M Craftsmen Potters Assoc.
Pc Architectural commissions inc. free standing and wall mounted relief sculptures for Grafton Centre, Grosvenor Estates, Cambridge – Architects Fitzroy Robinson; Salter Row, Pontefract – Architects, Landsdown, Twiner, Hott; Riverside Park, Chepstow City Council; Dewsbury Country Park, Kirklees County Council.

ROBUS, CLIVE & ROSEMARY – ACRISE POTTERY (Empl: 6; Est: 1979)
Ladywood Farm, Acrise, Folkestone, Kent. 030 389-3252.
SD-C; M Industrial Artists & Designers.
Pc Extensive coverage of floors and walls in period and listed properties. Kent peg fittings and tiles used extensively throughout Kent and Sussex in the renovation of Kent peg roofs inc. Canterbury Cathedral and many listed properties.
Produce traditional Kent peg tiles, handmade floor and wall tiles; large hand decorated pots decorated with the same delft tin glaze which is used on the hand-painted tiles. Brochure.

RODGER, PAUL (Empl: one; Est: 1980, thatching since 1976)
Master Thatcher
Laurel Cottage, Park Lane, Carhampton, Minehead, Somerset TA24 6NL. 0643-821 293.
Apprenticed to E. H. Parks & Co, Minehead; Hon Secretary Somerset MTA; M Nat Council of Master Thatcher Assoc's; M Somerset Guild of Craftsmen.
Pc Crown Estate Commissioners. National Trust.

RODWELL, DENNIS G – ARCHITECT (Est: 1975)
8 Dundas St, Edinburgh EH3 6HZ. 031-556 6710. Melrose Station Palma Place, Melrose, Roxburghshire TD6 9PR. 089 682-2546.
MA; Dip Arch (Cantab); RIBA; FRIAS; Committee M Edinburgh New Town Conservation Committee; Associate M – SPAB; Architectural Heritage Soc of Scotland; Assoc for the Protection of Rural Scotland; Cockburn Assoc.
Pc Completed restoration schemes inc. 6 – 14 St Mary's St, Edinburgh, received Cert of Merit, NHIC and Commendation Edinburgh Architectural Assoc; The Signal Tower, Shore, Leith; Melrose Station, Melrose, Roxburghshire; 5 Sciennes Place, Edinburgh; Greenside Park, St Boswell's, Roxburghshire, received Commendation, Assoc for the Protection of Rural Scotland; Bowden Old School, Bowden.

ROGER, A. B. & YOUNG – ARCHITECTS (Est: 1950)
2 Market St, Brechin, Angus DD9 6BA. 035 62-2125/6.
Dip Arch; RIBA; RIAS.
Pc Restoration – Ardovie House. Restoration of facade – 121 High St, Montrose. Various works – Brechin Cathedral, Montrose, High Kirk. Surveys of churches, halls and manses for Church of Scotland and local presbyteries.

ROGERS, B. W.
See BEECHWOOD SERVICES

ROGERS, LORIE LAIN (Empl: solo; Est: 1982)
Specialist in the Restoration of Fine Quality Antique Furniture
5 Sunnyside, Bergh Apton, Norwich, Norfolk NR15 1DD. 050 843-613.
Qualified as a woodwork teacher, Alsager College of Education; M Norfolk Furniture Makers Assoc.
Pc Designed and made bookcases of Georgian and Victorian chairs to order.

FIRMS AND CRAFTSPEOPLE

ROGOYSKA, MARTA BA MA (RCA) (Est: 1976/77)
Wallhangings
61B Downs Park Rd, Hackney, London E8 2HY. 071-241 6739.
Pc Castle Howard. BBC. Victoria & Albert Museum. The Whitworth Gallery. The British Medical Association.
Brochure.

ROME, GEORGE (ORNAMENTAL PLASTERWORK) LTD (Empl: 35; Est: 1913)
33 Townsend St, Glasgow G4 0LA. 041-332 8131. FAX 041-331 2546.
Take on and train apprentices annually. Still have people working who served their time with the firm 20–40 yrs ago.
Pc Trinity College conversion. Pump House Conversion to restaurant. Rotunda Conversion to restaurant. Theatre Royal, Glasgow.
A family firm with a very steady reliable workforce. Will also design and build. Have a file of unsolicited thank you letters from satisfied clients.
Brochure.

ROSE OF JERICHO (Empl: 3; Est: 1987)
Traditional Mortars, Plasters & Renders Manufacturers
PO Box 53, Kettering, Northants NN14 3BN. 0536 73439.
This firm is nominated by Eng. Heritage for grant aided work in GB, and Peter Hood has personal experience with Roman and medieval mortars and renders.
Will match any building or decorating material for the repair or conservation of historical houses anywhere in Europe inc. clay, earth, or lime mortars, haired plasters, roughcast, torching, etc. Continually strives to find indigenous raw material and to improve the quality and extent of its products. Coatings inc. limewashes and genuine lead paints which can be matched to old colours using traditionals pigments inc. verdigris, blue verditer and smalt. Minimum quantity 2½ or 15 litres as appropriate.

ROSENGARTEN, BARUCH (Empl: one; Est: 1979)
Wallhangings & Fabric
Bourne Manse, Middleton-in-Teeside, Co Durham DL12 0SN. 0833-40403.
Pc Commission cloth woven for Warner Brothers. Wallhangings – Hallgarth Hall. Woven and embroidered coats-of-arms banners.
Present collection uses wool woven into wallhangings and felted into fibre art pictures.

ROSENTHAL, MARIA – HANDMADE TILES (Est: 1986)
Unit 33, Kingsgate Workshops, 110–116 Kingsgate Rd, London NW6 2JG. 071-249 8425 & 071-328 2051.

Harrow School of Art, Studio Pottery Dip; Teaching Ceramics at Fulham and Chelsea Adult Education Inst, London.
Pc Custom-made tiles for bathrooms (private houses), fireplaces and kitchens.
A range of original wall tiles with raised designs, handmade and dipped in bright colourful glazes developed from traditional Victorian glaze recipes. Brochure.

ROSS, ALAN NDD (Empl: solo; Est: 1974)
Furniture Designer & Restorer
66 Providence Lane, Long Ashton, Bristol, Avon BS18 9DN. 0272-392 440.
Nat Dip in Design, Furniture; Cert Inst of Wood Science; Craft M Somerset Guild of Craftsmen.
Pc Repairing and restoring antique mahogany desk inc. renewing worn out parts and making and fitting missing parts. Antique bookcase inc. all work listed above, plus designing and making new plinth to match. Both pieces were stripped and repolished.

ROUTH, HUGH & HARTLEY, JOHN (Empl: 3; Est: 1977)
Furniture Designer & Restorer
The Tankerdale Workshop, Steep Marsh, Petersfield, Hants GU32 2BH. 0730-893 839.
Ex West Dean students and BADA Dip's; other cabinet making and furniture experience; M BAFRA; M UKIC.
Pc Mostly important furniture for National Trust and similar clients. Also restoration for trade and private clients. Willing to undertake architectural woodwork restoration, panelling and inlaid floors.

ROWAN, COLIN STONEMASONS (Est: 1984)
Keepers Cottage, Guthrie, Nr Forfar, Angus DD8 2TL. 02412-716.
C & Gs Stonemason.
Pc Restoration work – Hatton Castle, Newtyle, Angus and also Claypots Castle, Dundee, Angus.
Detailed stone cutting and carving undertaken.

ROWE, N. DAVID (Est: 1980)
Consulting Engineer
29 Empingham Rd, Stamford, Lincs PE9 2RJ. 0780-52497.
B Sc (Eng); ACGI; C Eng; MICE.
Pc Reconstruction of facade – 10 Red Lion Square, Stamford. Surveys of Oswardby Water Mill and various Georgian buildings in Stamford.

FIRMS AND CRAFTSPEOPLE

ROWNEY, EDDIE (Est: 1955)
Dry Stone Walling
Stonehouse Cottage, Fangdale Beck, Chop Gate, Cleveland.
Master Craftsman, Agricultural Training Board Instructor, M DSWA.
Pc Work carried out for the North Yorkshire Moors.
Instruction, lectures and talks in dry stone walling.

R & R RECLAMATION
Bridge St, Brigg, S Humberside DN20 8LP. 0652-57650.
Reclaimed bricks a speciality, building materials and architectural features inc. paviours; Yorkstone slabs; pantiles; oak timbers; pine doors; quarries; fireplaces; etc.

RUIJTERMAN, JACQUES (Est: 1979)
The Arundel Fine Glass & Engraving Studio, Tarrant St, Arundel, W. Sussex BN18 9DE. 0903-883 597.
F GGE; Tutor West Dean College, Chichester.
Pc Window – St George's Medical School Sports Pavilion. Engraved bowl, Duke of Gloucester.

RUSSELL, BRIAN (Empl: 2; Est: 1976)
All Aspects of Artist Blacksmithing in Various Metals
The Forge, Little Newsham, Winston, Darlington, Co Durham. 0833-65047 & 718 071 (night).
Dip Fine Art; M BABA.
Pc New main gates – Thorp Perrow Hall, Bedale, Yorks and also Wycliffe Hall, Barnard Castle, Co Durham. Decorative metalwork – new organ, Winchester Cathedral. New lighting scheme – Barnard Castle School Chapel.

RUST, MICHAEL (Empl: one; Est: 1969)
Designer Woodcarver
Sycamore Cottage, Hastingleigh, Ashford, Kent TN25 5HW. 023 375-305 & 023 375-363 (night).
M BWA; Lay M Society of Scribes & Illuminators.
Pc Coat of Arms – The Chartered Inst of Bankers. Memorial plaque – Eton College, Windsor. New rood – Hastingleigh Parish Church, Kent. New altar – St Saviour's, Folkestone, Kent.
Architectural and heraldic carving (inc. fire surrounds, panelling, lintels, church furnishings); woodsculpture in the round; lettering; restoration work on period and antique carvings; will make matching pieces; pattern making executed for castings in metal or cold cast resins; mordant and water gilding. Can call on specialist other craftsmen inc. stone carvers and joiners. Brochure.

SAINT BLAISE LTD

RYAN, JOHN (Empl: 10; Est: 1982)
Bespoke Joinery & Woodwork inc. Turning & Copywork
T/A J. & J. Manufacturing, Burrows Lane Farm, Burrows Lane, Eccleston, Prescot, L34 6JQ. 051-426 0534.
A well established firm employing time served tradesmen; operate apprenticeship training allied to local youth training schemes.
Pc Cavern Walks, Liverpool. Portmeiron Hotel, Gwynedd. Liverpool Cathedral (Anglican). Albert Dock Complex, Liverpool.
Brochure.

RYE TILES/RYE POTTERY (Empl: 24 Est: 1946 pottery, 1961 tiles)
Rye, E. Sussex TN31 7DH.
Pc Bond Street Tube Station. Various murals.
Brochure.

RYEDALE THATCHERS (YORK) (Empl: one; Est: 1976)
7 Dewsbury Cottages, Bishophill, York YO1 1HA. 0904-652 516.
CoSIRA apprenticeship; M North of Eng MTA; M NCMTA.
Pc 'Black Bull', Etal, Northumberland. 'Broadway Foot', Bilsdale, N. Yorks. 'Old White Horse', Spalding, Lincs.

SABINE ANTIQUES & RESTORATION SERVICES (Empl: 3; Est: 1974)
38 High St, Stock, Essex CM4 9BW. 0277-840 553.

SADLER, JANE – COLOUR COUNSELLOR (Est: 1988)
Old Manor Farm House, The Square. Long Crendon, Bucks HP18 9AA. 0844-201 692.
Trained in aspects of interior decoration/design by Colour Counsellors Organisation.

SADOLIN (UK) LTD (Empl: 70; Est: 1968)
Decorative Wood Protection Products, Wood Preservatives, Adhesives & Sealants
Tower Close, St Peter's Ind Park, Huntingdon, Cambs PE18 7DR. 0480-50041.

SAINT BLAISE LTD (Empl: 25; Est: 1985)
Conservation & Structural Repairs to Old Buildings
Westhill Barn, Evershot, Dorchester, Dorset DT2 0LD. 0935-83662/3.
C & Gs Stonemasonry; Venice School for Training of Craftsmen in the Conservation of the Architectural Heritage (Dip); MCIOB; M BEC; M LDC; M SPAB. Approved: Eng. Heritage; Bath City Council (Conservation Contracts).
Pc Corfe Castle for National Trust. Lloyds Bank, Cirencester. Cran-

borne Manor, Dorset for The Lord Cranborne. Lyme Regis Church. Frome Church. Bettiscombe Manor. Alfreds Tower, Stourhead. Lulworth Castle.

SAINT GEORGE, AMELIA
Textile Artist & Stenciller
12 Thurloe Place, London SW7 2RZ. 071-584 3863.
M IDDA
Author of The Stencil Book *(Conran Octopus, £14.95). Brochure.*

SALTER, CEDRIC EMRYS (Empl: 2; Est: 1972)
Stonemason
'Ty Cerrig', Idenrhyd Cottage, Tal-y-Cafn, Nr Colwyn Bay, Clwyd LL28 5RW. 0492-650 831.
6 yr apprenticeship with local stonemason; M FMB.
Pc Stonework on bridges at Abergele by-pass and also Albert Docks. Laying granite sets, boundary walls, fireplaces.
Brochure.

SAMBROOK, JOHN – FANLIGHT MAKER (Est: 1986)
Park House, Northiam, E. Sussex TN31 6PA. 079 74-2615.
16 yrs with GLC Historic Buildings Division.
Pc New fanlights – 2 Grade II listed buildings, 6 Bedford Square, London.
Specialist suppliers of fanlights which are careful copies of authentic designs, built in the traditional way from lead, and made individually to order into timber sashes provided by the client. Whilst not affecting the appearance the firm has made some improvements on 18th century practice, eliminating the most usual causes of such decay as occurs in original examples. Brochure.

SANDERSON, ARTHUR & SONS LTD (Est: 1860)
Specialists in Historic Wallpapers
London Showroom: 52 Berners St, London W1. 071-636 7800. Head Office: 100 Acres, Oxford Rd, Middx UB8 1HY. 0895-38244.
Pc Various commissions in both block and screen printing for restoration work in stately homes and royal palaces within the last 12 months.

SANDLEFORD WOODTURNING LTD (Empl: 7; Est: 1982)
Newtown Rd, Sandleford, Newbury, Berks RG15 9BB. 0635-32624. FAX 0635-528 193.
GMC; Rural Development Commission supported.

SAVAGE, DAVID FURNITURE MAKERS

SANDS, WILLIAM & SON (Empl: 4; Est: 1910)
Building Contractors
Punnetts Town, Heathfield, E. Sussex TN21 9DD. 0435-830 211.
GCLI Painting & Decorating; M BEC; M Royal Society of Health.
Approved: Diocesan; Eng. Heritage.
Pc Restoration medieval farm house, architect, John Schwerdt & Partners, Lewes. Hurricane repairs – Heathfield All Saints' Church, architect, John D. Clarke & Son, Eastbourne.
Also undertakes plumbing and heating.

SAPCOTE, WILLIAM & SONS LTD (Empl: 50; Est: 1853)
Building Contractors Specializing in Restoration & Refurbishment
87 Camden St, Birmingham B1 3DE. 021-233 1200.
BEC; Stone Federation. Approved: Eng. Heritage; Diocesan and Local Authorities of Birmingham, Coventry and Worcester, Wolverhampton, Sandwell, Solihull and Dudley.
Pc Oak House, West Bromwich and also Ingestre Hall for Sandwell Architects Dept. Witley Court. Monkspath Hall reconstruction, Solihull Architects Dept. Edmund St reconstruction and new build.

SARUM PARTNERSHIP, THE (Empl: 5 partners; Est: 1930)
Chartered Architects Specializing in the Care of Historic Buildings
De Vaux House, De Vaux Place, Salisbury, Wilts SP1 2SL. 0722-335 306. 62 The Avenue, Southampton, SP1 2TA. 0703-277 672. 38 Bridge St, Andover. SP10 1BW 0264-51431.
K. F. Wiltshire – FRIBA   C. Romans – BA; B Arch   J. Athender – ARIBA   D. Hargreaves – BA; B Arch; FRIBA   A. Mee – Dip Arch; RIBA.
Pc Refurbishment – Worcester Cathedral. Chichester Cathedral. Du Louis Longham Place. St Martin's within Ludgate. Hawtheys.
Particularly interested in stone buildings of historic importance, although the practice has undertaken a variety of new design projects inc. churches and Christian centres; educational buildings; housing; industrial; leisure; libraries; offices.

SAVAGE, DAVID FURNITURE MAKERS (Empl: 4; Est: 1979)
21 Westcombe, Bideford, N. Devon EX39 3JQ. 02372-79202.
M SD-C; M Devon Guild of Craftsmen.
Pc Ebony collector's cabinet. Cherry wood dining table and 12 chairs. Rosewood dressing table and stool.
Brochure.

FIRMS AND CRAFTSPEOPLE

SAVIAC PROTOTYPES – DAVID BALLANTYNE (Empl: varies; Est: 1949)
Craftsman-designer
2 Chewton Farm Rd, Highcliffe, Christchurch, Dorset BH23 5QN. 0425-274 196.
FSD-C; M of Board of Art & Architecture Ltd; Full M Dorset Craft Guild. Represented GB in 'La Ceramique Architecturale', Dossain et Tolra, Paris, 1983.
Pc Ridge and hip – 112 Princes St, Edinburgh. Air bricks – restoration, Fort Newhaven, ex Jennings, Poole 1855. Special chimney pots – Pentlow Towers, Sudbury, Suffolk. 18th-century terrace balustrade – garden at Heckfield, Hants. Fireplace mouldings and tiles – Greystones 1906. Front door – Autistic Soc School, Christchurch.
Will consider almost anything within his capabilities inc replica building elements for restoration and new environmental detailing, mainly in ceramics, but also in wood, metal casting, concrete, etc. Lettering; wall-cladding; mural design in tiles and relief; water display features; bricks; chimney pots; fireplace surrounds; stoneware with enamels.

SCAGLIOLA STUDIO – MICHAEL KOUMBOUZIS (Empl: 3–4, Est: 1986)
7 Newport View, Headingley, Leeds 6, Yorks LS6 3BX. 0532-751 844 & 686 715.
M. Koumbouzis – BA Design   Yvonne Adamson, Consultant – Architectural Conservationist (MA Cons).
Pc 2 large oval scagliola tables – Fountains Hall, Studley Royal and replacement pilasters – Arlington Court, Devon – both for National Trust. Scagliola work inc. Earl Spencer's House; Rothchilds, St James's Place, London. Raby Castle. Restoration of columns – Lord Faversham.
Specialists in all aspects of scagliola work inc. 'inlays', but also undertakes other plaster work, e.g. fibrous plasterwork; stucco-work; stucco-duro; etc. Will undertake chemical and physical analysis to BS; modelling commissions; historic background research; terrazzo and scagliola floors; new scagliola work in any colour or pattern. M. Koumbouzis also lectures on scagliola, its history and application viz conservation, etc.

SCALLYWAG
Antique & Reproduction Pine Fireplaces
187–191 Clapham Rd, Stockwell, London SW9 OQE. 071-274 0300.
Have a comprehensive stripping facility for pine furniture and architectural items.

SCANLAN, ROGER (Empl: 2; Est: 1975)
Master Thatcher
73 Osmund Drive, Goldings, Northampton NN3 4XB. M Northants MTA.

SCARISBRICK & BATE LTD (Est: 1958)
Decorations, Antiques, Contract Furnishing
111 Mount St, London W1Y 5HE. 071-499 2043.
C & Gs of London Institute; Nat Dipl of Design; AIBD; ISID.
Pc Unable to name many clients due to their request for anonymity. Historic restoration of William Kent house (c. 1734), London. Restoration to historic castles and houses and a gondola for National Trust. New main ticket office – Japan Airlines Ltd, London. Boardroom and reception suite, City of London. Various work worldwide.
Small, highly qualified team (inc. an expert with cultural and working knowledge of Islamic art), experienced in historic restoration and all aspects of traditional domestic and contract interior design. They believe the role of an interior decorator is to interpret client's wishes and execute them using their own extensive technical, architectural and furnishing knowledge, but never to force an issue of style.

SCARLETT BURKETT GRIFFITHS (ARCHITECTS) (Est: 1956)
10–14 Macklin St, London WC28 5NF. 071-242 1374.
John Burkett, Partner – AA Dipl; FRIBA; FC Inst Arb   John Griffiths, Partner – MA (Cantab); ARIBA; FC Inst Arb.
Pc Rehabilitation No 38 Grosvenor Square (Grade II). Conservation – Sissinghurst Castle and also Rainham Hall, Essex.

SCHEMES (Est: 1979)
Interior Designer
56 Princedale Rd, London W11 4NL. 071-727 3775 & 1148.
Jenny Ledger, owner – MA (Oxon); M IDDA. Schemes – M Brit Design Group.
Pc Restoration of 17th-century cottage in Wales. Restoration of many 19th-century buildings in London inc. a restaurant. Restoration of Bindon Abbey, Dorset to inc. selection of appropriate furnishings.

SCHOFIELD, JANE ORNAMENTAL PLASTERWORK CONSERVATION (Empl: up to 5; Est: 1979)
50 Fore St, Bradninch, Devon EX5 4NN. 0392-881 174.
BA (Hons) Fine Art; M SPAB.
Pc Palladian Bridge, Wilton. New Parliamentary buildings, Westminster. Numerous smaller private jobs. Work for National Trust; County Councils; HMBC; SPAB; etc.
Specialist in the conservation of early ornamental plasterwork (i.e. pre 1750) lime-based plaster inc. hair plaster and wattle and daub; re-hanging; repairs; cleaning; associated timberwork; renewal of supporting beams where essential. Although works mainly in S. W. England will occasionally work further afield.

FIRMS AND CRAFTSPEOPLE

SCOTT, J. M. I. (Est: 1895)
Consultant to Gotch Pearson, Archtitects & Surveyors
18 Sheep St, Wellingborough, Northants. 0933-76394 & 225 848.
Qualified 1950; registered architect; M EASA; commissioned architect to HMBC (E) since 1978.
Pc New churches – Kettering and Corby. Re-ordering of churches – Harpote and Barton Seagrave. New secondary and primary schools – Diocese of Peterborough. Various works – The High School for Girls, Northampton.

SCOTT, SONIA (Est: 1975)
Original Designs in Traditional or Modern Style Engraved on Glass
Greenhead Cottage, New Galloway, Kirkcudbrightshire DG7 3RN. 06442-349.
Des RCA; Craft M GGE; M Scottish Glass Soc.
Pc Commemorative panel – Lady Boswell's School, Sevenoaks. Memorial plaque – Knockholt Church, Kent.

SELLS, JONATHAN (JONATHAN-LIVING-STONE) (Empl: varies; Est: 1985)
Workshop No 3, Sandy Hill Workshops, Sandyhill Lane, Corfe Castle BH20 5JF. 0929-480 977.
London C & Gs Craft Cert and Advanced Cert in Stonemasonry, C & Gs Cert in Architectural Carving, Heraldry, Monumental Carving, Masonry, Lettercutting, Sculpture; M Nat Assoc of Master Masons; M Nat Assoc of Artists.
Pc Carved Lord on throne – Durlston Castle. Restoration work inc. old headstones dating back to 1700s. War memorial in Wareham; millennium plaque – Corfe Castle. Heavily carved fireplaces commissioned – private client in Dorset.
Specialist in the conservation and restoration of all aspects of stone work from sculpture to building. Photographs and slides available.

SENIOR, RUPERT & WHEELER-CARMICHAEL, CHARLES (Empl: 7; Est: 1984)
Furniture Designers
Whitehouse Workshop, Church St, Betchworth, Surrey RH3 7DN. 073 748-4316.
Trained at John Makepeace School for Craftsmen in Wood.

SERALIAN, H. N. (Empl: solo)
Cane & Rush Seating
79 Mollison Way, Edgware, Middx HA8 5QU. 081-952 6432 (nights and weekends).
A private craftsman working for individuals and antique dealers through personal recommendations. Repairs carried out on part damaged sections of

furniture and stained to match the remainder. Will collect and deliver within a reasonable distance.

SHADES OF LIGHT (Empl: 6; Est: 1982)
Designers & Craftsmen in Stained & Architectural Glass
Unit 40, Wimbledon Stadium Studios, Riverside Rd, Wimbledon, London SW17 0BA. 081-946 9101. FAX 081-947 7311. TELEX 945920 SHADES G.
Associates AMGP.
Pc Christ Church, Shamley Green. St James's Church, Twickenham. Palace Theatre, Cambridge Circus, W1. Numerous palaces, villas and mosques in the Middle East.

SHANNAN, PAUL (Empl: one; Est: 1979)
Master Thatcher
1 Snow Hill, Clare, Nr Sudbury, Suffolk CO10 8QF. 0787-277 014.
Full M Suffolk MTA.
Pc Cavendish Alms Houses.

SHARP E. E. & SON (Empl: 5; Est: 1945)
Master Thatchers
18 Commons Rd, Wokingham. Berks RG11 1JG. Conifers, Church Rd, Farley Hill, Nr Reading, Berks. 0734-781 716 & 732 805.
NSMT.
Pc Worked for Crown Estates Commission.

SHARP & HOWSE LTD (Empl: 30; Est: 1952)
Leadwork, Plumbing, Heating & Ventilating
295–301 London Rd, Oxford OX3 9HL. 0865-60606.
M HVCA; LCA.
Pc Mansard lead roof – Wadham College, Oxford, as illustrated in Lead Development Association's publication *Lead Sheet in Building*.
Experienced in leadwork for modern or traditional buildings inc. repair of existing lead roofs; turrets; gutters; weatherings; etc. Carry out the full range of mechanical and building services inc. air conditioning; refrigeration; water treatment; energy conservation; etc.

SHAW, CHRISTIAN STAINED GLASS (Empl: 2; Est: 1980)
63 Frederick St, Edinburgh EH2 1LH. 031-557 3447 & 556 7710.
Studied Edinburgh College of Art.
Pc St Christopher window – Trannent Parish Church. Restoration – Greyfriars and Bulleuch Church, Edinburgh. Various stained glass lampshades.

FIRMS AND CRAFTSPEOPLE

SHAW, LILIAN STAINED GLASS (Empl: solo, help available; Est: 1986)
Cliftonville, Lincoln St, Llandysul, Dyfed SA44 4BY. 055 932-3577.
1st Class BA (Hons) Fine Art; apprenticeship with Paul Quail, a long established stained glass artist in Norfolk (see entry under that name); M BSMGP.
Pc Abstract design – YMCA, Surbition. 3 panels – restaurant, Wildlife Centre, Neaal. Restoration work carried out for other glaziers. Willy Lott's House, Flatford. Forthcoming work possibly in Pakistan and new church, Norwich.
Slides or photographs available if required.

SHAW HEREFORD CERAMICS GROUP (Empl: 260; Est: 1897)
Waterside, Darwen, Lancs BB3 3NX. 0254-775 111. FAX 0254-873 462. TELEX 63401.
M GMC.
Pc Architectural terracotta – Natural History Museum, London and also Hackney Empire Theatre. Glazed bricks – Templeton Business Centre, Glasgow. Reproduction Victorian Faience tiles – Crown Bar, Belfast.
Brochure.

SHAW, JOHN (Est: 1982)
Architecural Stone & Brush Lettering, Heraldry & Gilding
26 Bridge St, Alnwick, Northumberland NE66 1QY. 0665-510 916.
BA (Hons) Camberwell School of Arts & Crafts; MA, Birmingham Polytechnic; M Art Workers Guild.
Pc Bradford fire disaster commemorative plaque – Bradford Cathedral. Plaque with heraldic carving for visit of Pope John Paul II – Coventry. Numerous plaques for religious and secular buildings throughout UK.
Brochure.

SHELDON H. T. W. (Empl: 2; Est: 1987)
Suppliers of Lead Rainwater Goods for Historic Properties
Lea Hall, Lea, Matlock, Derbys, DE4 5GR. 062 984 265.
Pc Lead rainwater goods for extension to headquarters of Redland Aggregates, Leics and various historic houses.
Patterns faithfully copied. Also stock a small standard range.

SHENTON, JAMES W. LTD (Empl: 40; Est: 1905)
Tinsley St, Great Bridge, Tipton, W. Midlands DY4 7LQ. 021-557 2531/2.
Brit Foundry Assoc.

SHORT, ELAINE F.

SHEPLEY DAWSON ARCHITECTURAL ENGINEERING LTD (Empl: 30; Est: 1972)
Metal Workers
Joseph Noble Rd, Lillyhall, Workington, Cumbria CA14 4JX. 0900-68368/9.
Craftsmanship Certs in Blacksmithing, C & Gs and Engineering Industries Training Board; Dip in Creative Design, Coughsborough Colleges. A. Dawson – Hon Sec BABA.
Pc Restoration – Lorrimer gates and railings, Carlisle Castle. Manufacture and fitting of hot forged gates, railings, screens, etc. all over the UK and Europe. Design, manufacture and installation – interior metalwork, Princes Square, Glasgow.
Brochure.

SHERING BUILDERS LTD (Empl: 63; Est: prior 1800)
53 Church St, Fordingbridge, Hants SP6 1BD. 0425-52276.
BEC; NHBC. Approved: Winchester Diocesan; Eng. Heritage; Hampshire, Dorset and Wiltshire CC's; National Trust; New Forest District Council; Southampton City Council.
Pc Conholt Park, Conholt, Nr Andover. Cruck Cottage, Rockbourne. 10 The Close, Winchester. Marwell Hall, Nr Winchester. Doddington House, Breamore. All Saints' Church, and also St Nicholas Church, Winterslow. All Saints' Church, Milford-on-Sea.

SHERMAN, JACKIE
Cane Seating & Basketwork
9 Turpins Chase, Oaklands, Welwyn, Herts AL6 0QZ. 043 871-6673.
M Basketmakers Assoc.

SHIELD, JOHN – CARVER IN WOOD & STONE (Est: 1988)
Unit 325, Block A, East Cross Centre, Waterden Rd, Stratford, London E15 2HN. 081-986 7706.
Restoration Course, C & Gs Art School, Kensington, London.

SHOLING RE-UPHOLSTERY SERVICES (Empl: 2; Est: 1977)
21 South East Rd, Southampton, Hants, SO2 7PU. 0703-447 823.
5 yr apprenticeship indentures for upholstery and soft furnishings: M AMU (11 yrs).

SHORT, MRS ELAINE F.
Weaver
73 Trowbridge Rd, Bradford-on-Avon, Wilts BA15 1EG. 02216-862 372.
Self-taught weaver/artist; M Wiltshire Guild of Spinners, Weavers & Dyers.

FIRMS AND CRAFTSPEOPLE

Pc Tapestry of wall of Saxon Chapel, Bradford-on-Avon.

SHOUKSMITH, J. H. & SONS LTD (Empl: 150; Est: 1820)
Sheet Lead Work, Plumbing, Heating & Drainage Engineers
Murton Way, Osbaldwick, York YO1 3US. 0904-411 261.
M LCA.
Pc Recovering north transept of York Minster with lead.
Brochure.

SIGNMAKING DEVELOPMENTS (Empl: 27; Est: c. 1850)
T/A The Lettering Centre, 108 Weston St, London SE1 3QB. 071-407 2316.
Long term training; individual qualifications; M GMC.
Pc Sounding board, Thetford. Carving – Australia House. Peers Dining Room ceilings – House of Lords. Small carving details – Westminster Abbey. 120 stone heads – Ashridge Church for DOE. Holocaust Memorial, Hyde Park. Decoration metal – Daiwan at Jeddah. Metal floor plates – Westminster & York Cathedrals.
Undertakes carving and lettercutting in stone, wood, and metalwork. Will provide patterns for specialist castings and ironmongery. Brochure.

SILKROOT (BRIAN LORENTZ) (Empl: one; Est: 1971)
Wallhangings
106A Haverstock Hill, London NW3. 071-482 4576.
Dip HE (Batik); previous M 62 Group (1980–1983, resigned).

SILVERMAN, G. & SON (IMPORTERS) LTD (Empl: 105; Est: 1953)
Importers Division, Stirling Way, Borehamwood, Herts WD6 2BP. 081-953 0553.
Veneered boards particularly for shop and store fitting. Brochure.

SIMANYI CERAMICS (Empl: 2; Est: 1976)
21 Boyn Hill Close, Maidenhead, Berks SL6 4JD. 0628-31091.
M Maidenhead Craft Soc; Henley Art & Craft Guild.
Tile paintings and murals for kitchens and bathrooms. Photographs available.

SIMMONS, ROGER S. – ARCHITECT (Est: 1986)
45 Ferntower Rd, London N5 2JE. 071-354 1786.
Dip Arch; BA (Hons) History of Art; AA Dip Cons; RIBA.
Pc General repairs/conservation to listed buildings inc. domestic, commercial, industrial and ecclesiatical.

SIMMS, J. V. (REIGATE) LTD (Empl: 15; Est: 1962)
Building Contractors
Eagle House, 48 Croydon Rd, Reigate, Surrey RH2 0NH. 0737-249 164.
BEC; NPDC. Approved: Surrey CC; Reigate and Banstead Borough Council.
Pc Idris Jones, 37 Bell St, Reigate, Surrey, architect R. O. Young.

SIMONS CONSTRUCTION GROUP LTD (Empl: 1200)
Outer Circle Rd, Lincoln LN2 4AY. 0522-513 505.
Apprentices in brickwork, plumbing, joinery, painting, electricians, woodwork.
Pc Gate Burton Chateau for English Heritage. Gladstone Buildings, Sheffield. Conversion to shop – Golden Lion Public House, Worcester. Complete restoration of fire damaged Co-op – Lincoln. Shop restoration and extension – Middlegate. National Portrait Gallery, Benningborough Hall. Castle Howard Mausoleum Stowe Pillars.
Various awards from Business & Industry panel, RIBA and Civic Trust. Firm is pursuing BS 5750 (5 companies within the group are accredited to date). Runs courses in building crafts, contact Albert Roberts or David Glasby, National Building Crafts Inst, c/o Simons Construction Group Ltd, 401 Monks Rd, Lincoln, LN3 4NU. Tel: 0522-510 000). Brochure.

SIMPSON, W. B. & SONS LTD (Empl: 60; Est: 1833)
Terrazzo & Mosaics
27–33 Burr Rd, Wandsworth, London SW18 4SG. 081-877 1020.

SINCLAIR, LEE FURNITURE (Empl: 3; Est: 1974)
Endon House, Laneham, Retford, Notts DN22 0NA. 077 785 303.
BA (Hons) 3d Design, Hornsey College of Art; M SD-C.
Pc Conference room furniture – Meritina Ltd and also conference room and reception furniture for Mansfield Knitwear Ltd, both part of the Coats-Viyella Group.

SINCLAIR MELSON DESIGNS LTD (Empl: 60; Est: 1981)
Specialist Upholsterers using Traditional Methods
Unit 5, Hampton Farm Ind Estate, Bolney Way, Hampton Road West, Feltham TW13 6DB. 081-894 1041/2/3.
BCFA; IDDA; LFM; British Design Group.
Brochure.

SINDALL CONSTRUCTION LTD & SINDALL JOINERY (Empl: 76; Est: 1865)
Babraham Rd, Sawston, Cambridge CB2 4LJ. 0223-836 611. 152 Holland Park Avenue, London W11 4UX. Associated joinery works in Portsmouth, Oxford and Banbury.
BEC; NHBC; HBF. Approved: on the lists of 46 public authorities and

FIRMS AND CRAFTSPEOPLE

26 London Boroughs.
Pc Award winners in the field of restoration, recently receiving a commendation for the Ropery Complex, Chatham Dockyard, Civic Trust Awards, the second award of its kind in 2 yrs (previous commendation awarded on the Ancient House, Ipswich). Restoration of Middlesex Guildhall. Currently restoring The Queen's House, Greenwich. Sindall Joinery has undertaken work at Gatwick Airport; Middlesex Guildhall and Alexandra Palace.
Sindall Joinery produce their own range of windows and will make doors other than veneered flush doors. They also provide a design, drawing and planning service, and a structural and engineering service for all architectural joinery. Brochure.

SINKINSON, SIMON (Empl: one; Est: 1982)
Thatcher
Bridge Cottage, Old Romsey Rd, Cadnam, Southampton, Hants. 0703-812 047.
Full 5 yr apprenticeship with Master Thatcher.
Pc Furzey Gardens Estate. Wiggly Manor.
Straw birds and fish.

SITCH, W. & CO LTD (Empl: 12; Est: 1776)
Art Metalworkers, Manufacturers of Electrical Light Fittings
48 Berwick St, London W1V 4JD. 071-4373 776.
Pc English Heritage. Copying of lights for Hampton Court. Candelabras – Osborne House. Renovation of various light fittings for National Trust. Supply lights – Eastnor Castle. Lights for 10 Downing St.
Brochure.

SKEAT, FRANCIS (Empl: 2 freelance)
Stained Glass Artist/Painter
5 Cross Lane, Harpenden, Herts AL5 1BX. 0582-460 747.
Apprenticed Scott Bridgwater Mezzotint Engraving; pupil of late Christopher Webb; F RSA; F, former M of Council and one time editor of *Journal* BSMGP; AWG; M Heraldic Soc.
Pc Over 200 purpose-designed windows inc. Westminster Abbey; Angel Choir, Lincoln Cathedral; Chapel, Selwyn College, Cambridge; Major Hawker Memorial, Long Parish, Andover; Capt Smith Memorial, St Sepulchre's, Holborn; W. window, Bassett, Southampton; cathedral rose window, Harare; Eastwood, Essex; Hubberholme, Yorks; Himeville, Natal; English Church, Antwerp; Helpston, Nr Peterborough; Plemstall, Cheshire; Prestbury, Cheshire.
Will not travel personally if very distant.

SKELTON, MARY HELEN (Est: 1986)
Architectural Lettering
Rose Acre, Malthouse Lane, Hurstpierpoint, W Sussex BN6 9JZ. 0273-832 536.
3 yr apprenticeship in stone carving and masonry with John Skelton. Pc Memorial to Lord Cort in the crypt of St Paul's Cathedral. Stone relief of Lamb and Flag for pub of same name, Easthouse. Recarving of letters on box tomb – Cruckfield Sussex for Mr Clutton.
Stone lettering designed and executed to specification; repainting of old memorials and recarving to make legible.

SKIDMORE, D. (FISHER DECORATIONS) (Empl: 18; Est: 1932)
Specialist Decorators
157 Marston Rd, Stafford ST16 3BS. 0785-51300.
BDA; GMC; C & Gs; FTC; UEI
Pc Work in Staffs inc. Dordfold Hall; Burland Hall, Nantwich; Shugborough Hall; Milford Hall; Blithfield Hall; Chillington Hall; Hatherton Hall. Birmingham Cathedral. St Margaret's, Uxbridge inc. stencilling, heraldry, polishing and gilding. National Westminster Banks in Rugby and Nuneaton. Offices in Birmingham.

SKLOVSKY, ANNA (Est: 1978)
Stained Glass Artist
26 Stockwell Park Crescent, London SW9 0DE. 071-733 4500.
BA Melbourne University; Advanced Stained Glass, Central School, London; M BSMGP.
Pc Numerous domestic stained glass commissions inc. Royal Naval Reserve Memorial window.

SLADDEN, HUMPHREY FINE FURNITURE RESTORATION (Empl: varies 1–2; Est: 1975)
Yard House, South Harting, Petersfield GU31 5NS. 073 085-339.
BADA Dip West Dean College after 2 yrs apprenticeship in cabinet making shop. Currently Senior Tutor in Furniture Restoration, West Dean College.
Pc Conservation and restoration – English and French pieces for Goodwood House, W. Sussex. Specialist work on clock cases (Kribb Tompion, Delander and Graham).
Specializes in the Walnut period.

SLOAN, NICHOLAS (Empl: one; Est: 1977)
Lettercutter
Carey's Mill, Parrett Works, Martock, Somerset TA12 6AE. 0935-823 177 & 0458-252 563. Apprenticed to lettercutter David Holgate, (see

entry under that name); Degree in History of Art from Courtauld Inst, London; M Letter Exchange.
Pc Countless individual commissions, large and small, for a wide variety of clients, inc. much work for poet Ian Hamilton Finlay

SMILES, J. B. (Empl: 18; Est: 1984)
Stonework & Plasterwork Conservation & Restoration
28 Back Rothbury Terrace, Heaton, Newcastle-upon-Tyne NE6 5XH. 091 276-2134 & 6630.
GMC; FMB. 40 yrs experience in the specialized field of restoration and preservation. Periodically engaged as a consultant in instances of careful renovation, etc.
Pc Stonework restoration – Websters Ropery, Sunderland. Traditional replacement of cornices – Jesmond Cemetery. Part restoration of St Cuthbert's Church, Durham City. Stabilizing and re-aligning rose window – Church of Sacred Heart, Blyth Northumberland.

SMITH, D. J. (Empl: solo; Est: 1965)
Wood Carver & Gilder Specializing in 18th-century Carved & Gilt Wood.
34 Silchester Rd, Pamber Heath, Nr Basingstoke, Hants, RG26 6EF 0734-700 595.
Son of a carver and gilder; GMC; Assoc Hampshire Woodcarvers.
Pc Restoration – 19 large cherry wood Queen figures (Greek gods, etc.), Aldermaston Manor. Restoration – carved and giltwood, Earl of Carnarvon, Highclere Castle.

SMITH, GAIL DESIGNS (Est: 1986)
Decorative Glass Design, Restoration or Conservation
Unit 8, Aston Rd, Astonfields Ind Estate, Bromsgrove, Worcs B60 3EX. 0527-75466.
BA (Hons) ATC in Stained Glass; M GMC.
Willing to undertake any design which can be made up into stained glass and/or tiffany panels or permanently fired into glass.

SMITH, H. & E. LTD (Empl: 110; Est: 1926)
Manufacturers of Glazed Tiles & Fireplaces
Britannia Works, Broom St, Off Town Rd, Hanley, Stoke-on-Trent, Staffs ST1 2ER. 0782-281 617 & 260 370.
Brit Ceramic Pottery Manufacturers Fed; Nat Fireplace Manufacturers Assoc.
Pc Restoration work inc. Earls Court Station, London Underground. Wich Library, Vancouver, Canada. Wakefield Opera House, Yorks. Reproduction of Harrods Food Hall at Bruder House, Amsterdam (2 shops). Currently matching embossed tiles made at the turn of the

century for the London Underground.
As well as standard ranges, new ceramic and faïence tiles can be undertaken to customer's own specification. Frost resistant tiles available. Brochure.

SMITH, JOHN & SONS MIDLAND CLOCK WORKS DERBY LTD (Empl: 30; Est: 1856)
27 Queen St, Derby DE1 3DU. 0332-45569. FAX 0332-290 642
Three directors are CMBHI.
Pc Manufacturers of the Great Clock of St Paul's Cathedral. Conversion to electric winding – tower clocks at Westminster Abbey and Windsor Castle, and turret clocks by Tompion and Kribb. Repair and restoration of domestic clocks in the great houses of Derbyshire and Nottinghamshire.
Clocks, new and traditional, individually designed and made (10 yr guarantee). Ancient clocks conserved and restored using many of the traditional craft methods. Over 4,500 public clocks are in the care of this firm's annual maintenance programme. Brochure.

SMITH, JOHN OF ALNWICK LTD (Empl: 6; Est: 1973)
Furniture Design, Production & Restoration
West Cawledge Park, Alnwick, Northumberland NE66 2HJ. 0665-604 363.
Apprenticeship 1967–71.

SMITH, JONATHAN R. H. – GLASS ENGRAVING STUDIO (Empl: one; Est: 1984)
Craftworkshop Unit 8, Tredegar House & Country Park, Coedkernew, Newport NP1 9YW. 0633-810 079.
Served apprenticeship with Stuart Crystal, Stourbridge; C & Gs Glass Manufacture & Processing; Dudley Tech College Cert, Glass Cutting & Decoration; Assessed Craft M GGE.
Pc Presentation punch bowl for HRH The Princess of Wales, commissioned by Welsh Tourist Board. Vase commissioned for ex Indian PM Indira Gandhi. Many more commissions were undertaken when at Stuart Crystal (Stourbridge).

SMITH, PETER E. – THE STONECARVING WORKSHOP (Empl: self-employed assistance; Est: 1983)
20/21 Butleigh Wootton, Glastonbury, Somerset BA6 8TX. 0458-43144.
Foundation Art and 1 yr Sculpture BA, Camberwell Art College; Dip Restoration of Wood, Stone & Allied Materials, C & Gs London Art College; trainee stone carver, Westminster Abbey; assistant to Richard Kindersley (figure conservation) at Wells Cathedral.

FIRMS AND CRAFTSPEOPLE

Pc Designed and carved Paschal candleholder (wood inlaid with Mother of Pearl) – Winchester Cathedral. Carved stone foliage – Brighton Pavilion. Modelled eagles – Barclays Bank. Restoration (copying) of Elizabethan gargoyles at Lacock Abbey.
Modern and restoration work inc. lettering, heraldic carving, sculpture; masonry; conservation; cleaning; historical research; photography; preliminary surveys. Will undertake carving and other such work on marble, but not conservation. Brochure.

SMITH, P. J. I. (Empl: 2; Est: 1979)
Artist Blacksmith
Piggery Ridge, Roddhurst, Presteigne, Powys. 0544-267 810.
Self taught blacksmith; M BABA.
Pc 2 miles of restored railings – Berrington Hall, Leominster for National Trust. Large decorative dome – landscaped garden in Gloucestershire for private client.
Brochure.

SMITH, R. A. – STAINED GLASS DESIGN & REPAIR (Empl: one; Est: 1982)
33 Huddersfield Rd, Elland, W. Yorks HX5 9AH. 0422-77586.

SMITH, ROBERT (Empl: solo; Est: 1975)
Furniture Maker
Gunthorpe Workshops, Melton Constable, Norfolk NR2 2NP. 0263-861 032.
Apprenticed to Rob Corbett of Corbett Woodwork; C & Gs Advanced Craft.
Pc Oak drawbridge – Mannington Hall, North Norfolk. Fitting out aft (main) cabin on luxury yacht 'Sumurun' in Southampton. Oak four-poster bed with solid panelled oak headboard. Work done using recycled timber in oak and pitch pine.
Willing to undertake softwood/hardwood traditional doors and windows, but will not use mahogany, or any tropical forest timbers. Brochure.

SMITH, ROBERT – ARTIST BLACKSMITH (Empl: solo; Est: 1984)
The Forge, Gosport Rd, Farringdon, Alton, Hants GU34 3DL. 1 Gradwell Lane, Four Marks, Alton, Hants GU34 5AD. 042 058-7233.
CoSIRA 2 yr course; BABA.

SMITH, RODNEY – WOODCARVER (Empl: solo; Est: 1981)
Larrick Cottage, Lydford, Okehampton, Devon EX20 4BJ. 082 282-288.
Self taught; winner of 2 silver and 6 gold medals at London & Bristol Woodworker Shows; 4 times Best-in-Show, London Woodworker

Show (now a judge in both competitions); M Soc of Wildlife Art of the Nations; M Brit Woodcarvers Assoc.
Pc Restoration and repair (144 separate pieces of various sizes were carved, fitted and colour matched) – Victorian Chevy Chase Sideboard carved by Gerard Robinson, Grosvenor Hotel, Shaftesbury.
Specialist in wildlife woodcarvings and deep relief pictures, but has completed work in many other styles inc. figure carvings; medieval shallow relief carvings; church figures. Brochure.

SMITH, ROGER E (Empl: solo; Est: 1980)
Furniture Designer & Maker
Barflies, Broadford Bridge, Billingshurst, W. Sussex RH14 9EB. 07983-3695.
Trained as woodwork teacher, taught for 6 yrs.
Pc Church work throughout Sussex, usually in oak. One-off pieces for private clients.
Brochure.

SMITH & CHOYCE LTD (Empl: 18; Est: 1930)
Specialist Joinery
280 Barton St, Gloucester GL1 4JJ. 0452-23531.
BEC.

SMITH WIDDOWSON & EADEM LTD (Empl: 8; Est: 1950)
Architectural Ironmongery
296 Penistone Rd, Sheffield S6 2FT. 0742-852 200.
M Guild of Architectural Ironmongers; Fellow of The Inst. of Craft Education.
Willing to undertake site work if necessary. Brochure.

SMITHBROOK BARN (Empl: 15; Est: c. 1952)
Traditional Wrought-iron Lighting
A281 Main Rd, Smithbrook, Nr Cranleigh, Surrey GU6 8LH. 0483-271 924.
Full M DLA.
Pc Supply a wide variety of end users nationwide as specialist manufacturers of hand-forged traditional wrought-iron lighting.
Brochure.

SMOOR, FRANCE, ARCHITECT, COUNTRY LIFE HOMES LTD (Est: 1973)
Gagie House, Gagie by Dundee, Angus DD4 0PR. 0382 33 207.
M Sc; MRIBA; ARIAS; Dip Arch; Dip TP (Delft).
Pc Easter Ballindean, Steading, Perthshire. Tilquhillie Castle,

FIRMS AND CRAFTSPEOPLE

Banchory. Gagie House and Grange, Esk Cottage, Melville Lasswade, Edinburgh.
Also supply turrets; finials; spires; windvanes; dormers in leadwork, copper and slating; interior furniture to kitchens; libraries; restore and build fireplaces; architectural buildings produced using traditional construction inc. timber trusses.

SOLAGLAS STAINED GLASS (Empl: 11; Est: 1788)
Blaris Ind Estate, Altona Rd, Lisburn BT27 5QB. 0846-275 416. Unit 4, Old No 8 Factory, Upton Rd, Southville, Bristol, Avon BS3 1QZ. 0272-631 257.
All craft employees serve 4 yr apprenticeship; artists are trained in house; design consultant is a M of Stained Glass Assoc of America and BMGP.
Pc Have covered a whole range of work from releading the great west window of Gloucester Cathedral and glazing the cloisters of Wells Cathedral, to private commissions for bathroom windows and the conservation of Victorian door lights.
Visitors are welcome at the studios to see examples of current work and to discuss schemes for new windows or restoration projects. Alternatively their designers will arrange a visit on site or at your home or office. Brochure.

SOLWAY BROWN PARTNERSHIP, THE (Est: 1952 – as Campling & Iliffe)
Chartered Architects
Old Boundary House, London Rd, Sunningdale, Berks SL5 0DJ. 0990-26269.
G. C. Solway, partner – MA (Cantab); Dip Arch; RIBA   A. Brown, partner – Dip Arch; RIBA   S. R. Gillingham, associate – B Arch; RIBA. Pc Cleaning and restoration – St James's Church, Spanish Place, London, and also St Mary's Church & Presbytery, Cadogan St, SW3. Extension to existing stone and flint church – St John the Evangelist, Woodley, Reading. Major reconstruction of fire damaged school building – St Mary's School, Ascot, Berks.

SOLWAY STUDIOS ORNAMENTAL PLASTERERS (Empl: 2; Est: 1984)
76 High St, Kirkcudbright DG6 4JL. 0557-30516.
Dip AD (Hons).
Pc Unwilling to divulge due to respect for clients' privacy, but further details available on request.
As well as undertaking a range of bespoke fibrous and sculpture work this firm stocks a range of fibrous plasterwork. Brochure.

SOUTHWELL STOCKWELL LTD

SOMERSET JOINERY LTD (Empl: 9; Est: 1969)
Parrett Works, Martock, Somerset TA12 6AA. 0935-822 304. 7 The Plains Shopping Centre, Totnes, Devon TQ9 5DR. 0803-865 562.
M GMC; M Brit Woodworking Fed.
Pc Wide range of specialized and security joinery as well as customer designed stairs, extensions, conservatories etc. Reference sites can always be provided on request.
High quality architectural joinery undertaken inc. hardwood conservatories (most styles reproduced) and a standard range of windows and doors. Brochure.

'SOMETHING SPECIAL BY SHARON DOWIE' (Est: 1986)
23 Kingfisher Close, Wheathampstead, St Albans, Herts AL4 8JJ. 058 283-3732.
Trained at Hertfordshire College of Building, specializing in broken colour work; various courses on broken colour work; M NFMP&D; M BDA; M Welwyn Craftworkers Guild.

SOUTH EAST TIME SERVICE (Est: 1979)
12 Stirling Rd, St Leonards on Sea, E. Sussex TN38 9NP. 0424-52309.
Apprenticed to Thwaites & Reed 1947–54; Fellow Brit Horological Inst.
Some leaflets available.

SOUTHWELL, SHEILA STUDIOS (Empl: one; Est: 1975)
Hand-painted Porcelain & China Repairs
7 West St, Burgess Hill, W. Sussex RH15 8NN. 04446-44307.
International Porcelain Art Teachers Assoc; Brit China & Porcelain Artists Assoc Dip; UKCI (Ceramics Section).
Pc Pieces painted to match Egyptian decor; old discontinued tea sets, etc. Restoration of Ming vase. Restoration of CH Meissen figurines.
China and porcelain decoration inc. gilding; lustrework; raised enamels; and gold relief. Produces watercolours and china to specification. Will match old tiles, etc. Author of 2 books on porcelain Painting China & Porcelain *and* China Painting Projects *both published by Blandford Press. Brochure.*

SOUTHWELL STOCKWELL LTD (Empl: 10; Est: 1976)
Founders, Fabricators & Fixers of Georgian & Victorian Cast-ironwork
26a Rye Rd, London SE15 3AY. The Ironworks, Holly Grove, London SE15. 071-635 0950 & 071-639 7864.
70% of employees join from school and are given a 3 yr intensive course at works and on site; a number have C & Gs Dip at various levels.

FIRMS AND CRAFTSPEOPLE

Pc Railings – The Square, Ennismore Gardens SW7. Manufacture of stair balustrades – Old Vic SE1. Iron railings – Georgian Society. £500,000 per annum turnover, mainly with private clients.
This firm has a large range of patterns and original mouldings from which they reproduce railings; balustrades; window guards; bootscrapers; table legs; etc. They also salvage decorative cast ironwork, for re-use or sale through dealers. Brochure.

SPALL, R. J. (Empl: 8; Est: 1962)
Collyweston Stone Slating & Roofing Contractors
Rock House, Collyweston, Nr Stamford, Lincs PE9 3PQ. 078 083-348 653.
M NFRC. Approved: Lincs, Leics, Northants and Cambs Councils.
Pc Extensive roof work to main house and stables – Burghley House, Stamford for English Heritage. Roof work – New Medical Centre, Wharf Rd, Stamford. Roof work – Burton Latimer Hall, Kettering.

SPARROW, ALAN SIGNS (Empl: 3; Est: 1968)
Specialist Painter & Decorator
37 Sunnyside Rd, Barbourne, Worcester WR1 1RL. 0905-28351.
Full Technological Certificate CGLI; Past M Assoc of Painting Craft Teachers; M GMC.
Pc Repainting and gilding – Great Witley Church, Stourport, Worcs. Graining – Cottilion Restaurant, London.

SPEIRS, ARTUR (Empl: solo; Est: 1975)
Artist in Stained Glass
75 Brisbane St, Greenock PA16 8NU. 0475-25649.
Decorative Glass Craftsman; NUFTO; Dip Fine Art, Glasgow School of Art.
Pc Leaded lamp with triumphal banner – Camock Parish Church, Dunfermline. 'Baptism of Christ' (leaded) – Shettleston Parish Church, Glasgow. Cluster of 5 windows in the form of a cross (epoxy resin cast) – Burdiehouse Parish Church, Edinburgh. J. Logie Baird commemorative windows – West Kirk, Helensburgh.

SPENCE & DOWER (Est: 1946)
Architects
1 Osborne Rd, Jesmond, Newcastle-upon-Tyne NE2 2AA. 091-2815 318.
Robin Dower – MA (Cantab); B Arch; Dip LD (N/C); RIBA Tristram Spence – B Arch; RIBA.
Pc Lindisfarne Castle for National Trust. Little Harle Tower, Newcastle-upon-Tyne for Lt Col J. P. P Anderson.

SPENCE, J. F. & SON (Empl: 4; Est: 1896)
Artist Blacksmith
The New Forge, Station Rd, Uppingham, Leics LE15 9TX. 0572-822 758 & 821 348.
All employees and partners have had formal apprenticeships and hold various qualifications; M BABA.
Pc Has manufactured many large sets of gates in the locality. Brass and iron spiral staircase – Goldmark Gallery, Uppington. Windvane and seats – London Dockland Development. Brass windvane – Peterborough Development Corporation.
Will undertake ironmongery, but not castings. Brochure.

SPENCE, ROBERT & CO (Empl: one; Est: 1976)
Cabinet Makers
Hightae, Lockerbie, Dumfries-shire DG11 1JL. 038 781 0449.
5 yr apprenticeship and 20 yrs in cabinet making.
Specializes mainly in the restoration of antiques and the making of the more complex joinery components inc. carvings; turnings; church furniture; etc. Some work can be seen on request.

SPRIGGS, PAUL (Est: 1980)
Woodcraftsman & Rushworker
The Croft, Silver St, South Cerney, Cirencester, Glos GL7 5TR. 0285-860 296.
Trained as an architect; M Gloucestershire Guild of Craftsmen.
Pc Built in display cabinet. Font cover. Various tables. Remembrance Book display case.
Rush seated chairs a speciality.

SPRINGALL, DIANA (Est: 1961)
Designer & Maker of Wallhangings, Embroidered Panels & Vestments
Oast Cottage, Park Lane, Kemsing, Sevenoaks, Kent TN15 6NU. 0732-61501.
NDD Painting ATC, Goldsmiths' College of Art, London; Dip History of Art, University of London; C & Gs Embroidery; Life M The Embroiderers Guild; Chairman and Fellow S D-C; Panel Lecturer V & A Museum.
Pc Embroidered panel – library, University of Sheffield. Panel – Mobil North Sea Ltd. A semi-circular double sided internal window – Church of St Anne & All Saints', Lambeth. Panel – Dahchi Kangyo Bank, Monument, London.
Brochure.

FIRMS AND CRAFTSPEOPLE

SQUIRES IRONDESIGNS (STEEL ERECTIONS) LTD (Empl: 15; Est: 1962)
Burgess Rd, Ivyhouse Lane Ind Estate, Hastings, E. Sussex TN35 4NR. 0424-428 794.
Gates, railings, staircases, balustrading, etc. made to specification. However do not produce door and window furniture to match required period style. Brochure.

STAINED GLASS DESIGN PARTNERSHIP (Empl: 6; Est: 1980)
31 Fenwick Rd, Kilmaurs, Kilmarnock, Ayrshire KA3 2TE. 0563-38189.
Susan Bradbury and Paul Lucky, partners – C & Gs Stained Glass; Dip Architectural Glass, Swansea College of Art; elected Fellows of BSMGP, RSA and Soc of Antiquaries of Scotland.
Pc New stained glass windows and screens – New School of Art, Newcastle. Restoration – great south window (40 sq m), Court of Session, Parliament Hall, Edinburgh. Restoration – Dunfermline Abbey; Cathedral of the Isles and many churches of all denominations. 19 windows designed to depict Jewish festivals – New Gosforth Synagogue.
Will only undertake protective measures on glass which they have made or restored themselves.

STAINED GLASS DESIGN BY VALERIE GREEN (Empl: 2; Est: family business 1884)
Stained Glass Lighting
Killerby Lane, Cayton, Scarborough, N. Yorks YO11 3TR. 0723-581 236.
Teaching Cert; apprenticed to family firm.
Tiffany style lampshades and bent panels of the Art Nouveau period; wall and table lamps in Art Deco style and modern designs. Co-operates with Allan Lazenby (see entry under that name) to produce complete stained glass schemes inc. windows and ceilings. Brochure.

STAINED GLASS OVERLAY (Empl: 6; Est: 1987)
23 Westbourne Avenue, Emsworth, Hants PO10 7QT. 0243-378 121.
Pc Palm Court Café, Palace Pier, Brighton. The Galley, High St, Swanage. Chapel window – St John's College, Southsea.

STAINED GLASS OVERLAY UK LTD (Empl: 45; Est: 1986)
PO Box 65 Norwich, Norfolk NR6 6ES. 0603-485 454.
Pc TUC Museum, Manchester.

STANCLIFFE, MARTIN (Est: 1976)
Architects
Martin Stancliffe Architects, 29 Marygate, York YO3 7BH. 0904-644 001/2/3.

STARLING, R. & R.

MA Dip Arch; RIBA; M ASCHB; M Council for the Care of Churches Executive Committee; M ARCUK; M The Georgian Group; M York Georgian Society; Civic Trust Award Assessor.

Pc Restoration and conversion works inc. 18th- and 19th- century house, Duncombe Park Mansion, Helmsley, Nr York; Beninbrough Hall, York (plus construction of new). Stonework and roof repairs – Lichfield Cathedral. Survey of Monument inc. fitting out of Cell 8 as reconstruction of original – Mount Grace Priory, Osmotherley, N Yorks. Reconstruction of part mid-18th-century country house following fire – Nostell Priory, Nr Wakefield. Restoration – Fountains Hall, Studley Royal, Fountains Abbey Estate, Ripon.

STANTON LEADED LIGHT WINDOWS (Est: 1982)
36a George St, Weston-super-Mare, Avon BS23 3AS. 0934-416 507.
Served apprenticeship.
Pc Bishop's Palace Wells, Churchill Court. Design and manufacture – stained glass windows, Mr Butcher, Trewartha Park Chapel. David Thomas Memorial Church.
Manufacture of leaded light windows, and restoration of stained glass windows. Free quotations – site houses quoted for at special prices.

STANTON, PETER ANTIQUES (Empl: 3; Est: 1982)
Antique Furniture Restoration of 17th, 18th, & 19th Century
The Old Pottery, Chapel Hill, Truro, Cornwall TR1 3BN. 0872-70262.
CMC; 24 yrs experience.
Pc Restoration – 3,200 yrs old decorated Egyptian Mummy Case (outer coffin), The Royal Inst, Truro Museum.

STARK, JOHN & PARTNERS (Est: 1885)
Architects & Consultants
13 & 14 Princes St, Dorchester, Dorset DT1 1TW. 0305-62636. FAX 0305-60960
Ronald Jones – AA Dip; ARIAB; Diocesan Surveyor; Eng. Heritage Commissioned Architect; EASA   Anthony Jaggard – FRSA; Council Royal Archaeological Inst; ASCHB; SPAB; Georgian Group; Victorian Soc   Michael Howarth – Dip Arch; ARIBA; EASA; SPAB.
Pc Consulted on the following works – Callaly Castle, Northumberland; Hoddam Castle, Dumfries; Ince Castle, Cornwall; Lulworth, Dorset; Wardour Castle, Wilts.

STARLING, R. & R. (Empl: 4; Est: 1969)
Furniture Designers & Makers
The Old School, Upton Cheyney, Bitton, Bristol, Avon BS15 6ND. 0272-323 603.

FIRMS AND CRAFTSPEOPLE

Brit Furniture Manufacturers Assoc; Somerset Guild of Craftsmen.
Complete dining room suites and boardroom furniture in mahogany, plus a wide range of pieces for the whole house.

STARLITE CHANDELIERS LTD
127 Harris Way, Windmill Rd, Sunbury-on-Thames, Middx TW16 7EL. 0932-788 686. FAX 0932-780283. TELEX 8811327 STARCO G. DLA.
Will design the smallest wall bracket or the largest chandelier from a rough designer sketch or to precise specifications. Frames are craftsman-made in the UK and gold-plated in some of the most advanced computerized plants in Europe. Starlite's own team of expert installers will, on request, dress complicated crystal structures at the installation site, wherever it may be.

STATION ROOFING SUPPLIES (Empl: 10–12; Est: 1989)
Hoole Bridge, Hoole, Chester CH2 3NQ. 0244-350 820.
An established builders' merchant sited close to the centre of Chester, currently specializing in new and reclaimed roofing materials. The firm also stocks a large selection of unique handmade tiles, bricks, etc for the discerning architect/developer, and sells the full range of materials you would expect to find in any builders' merchants.

STEAD, GEOFFREY
Architectural Antiques
The Old Rectory, Dowdeswill, Cheltenham, Glos GL54 4LX. 0242-820 571.

STEEL ARTS LTD (Empl: 30; Est: 1966)
Elizabeth Ind Estate, Juno Way, New Cross, London SE14 5RW. 081-692 9586.
Pc Work in London inc. stainless steel and glass balustrade – Property Security Investment Trust, Fleet Rd, Fleet, and also Trafalgar House Developments, Plumtree Court; ornamental railings – Land Securities Management Ltd, 5 Old Queen St; painted mild steel balustrade with brass handrail – 71–79 Knightsbridge; ornamental gates – Union Office of Post Office Workers, Crescent Lane. *Brochure.*

STEELES CARPETS (Empl: 40; Est: 1947)
The Carpet Mill, Barford Rd, Bloxham, Banbury, Oxon OX15 4HA. 0295-720 556 & 721 000.
Specializes in bespoke Wilton weaving. Brochure.

STEEN, IAN ARCHITECTS (Est: 1978)
48 Mill Way, Granchester, Cambridge CB3 9NB. 0223-845 131.
Ian Steen – MA; Dip Arch (Cantab); RIBA   Janet Livesley – BA; Dip

Arch George Davidson – B Sc (Hons); Arch Dip Arch; RIBA.
Pc New Surgery, Gold St, Saffron Walden. The Jarman Centre, Duchess Drive, Newmarket Outdoor (Activity Centre). New Surgery, 1 Drings Close, Over.

STEINBUGLER, C. J.
Hooky Mats & Puaddy Mats
Banks House, Brampton, Cumbria CA8 2JH. 069 77-3044.
Will undertake restoration of reproduction rugs, or genuine that are not in too bad a condition. Some photographs available.

STENNING, P. R. MILLWRIGHTS CO (Empl: variable; Est: 1972)
89 Barrington Rd, Goring-by-Sea, W. Sussex BN12 4SB. 0903-503 328.
Apprenticeship as a millwright engineer; engineering qualifications.
Pc Watermill and windpump – Singleton Open Air Museum. Watermill – Bartley, Kent. Restoration for National Trust – Houghton Mill. Renovation – Bromham Mill, Bedford for Bedford Council, and also Lode Mill for National Trust.

STEVENSONS OF NORWICH LTD (Empl: 51; Est: 1982)
Quality Plaster & GRP Mouldings
Roundtree Way, Norwich, Norfolk NR7 8SH. 0603-400 824.
Pc Chillingham Castle. Hitchin Priory. Indian High Commission. Park Court Hotel.
Standard range inc. pilasters and pedestals; corbels and brackets; arches; ceilings; cornices; centrepieces; niches; fireplaces; specialist exterior mouldings in GRP or cement; lead coloured rainwater hoppers; etc. Brochure.

STEWART, ANGUS (Empl: 5, Est: 1978)
Cabinet Maker & Restorer
Sycamore Barn, Industrial Park, Bourton-on-the-Water, Nr Cheltenham, Glos GL54 2HQ. 0451-21611.
BAFRA; UKIC.
Pc Work for both private and trade clients.
Also undertakes lost wax casting and brass reproduction; caning; clock and barometer restoration.

STINSON, DILYS (Empl: one; Est: 1984)
Weaver
2 Craythorne House, Beacon Oak Rd, Tenterden, Kent TN30 6RZ. 05806-5192.
Dip (Tapestry Weaving), West Dean College; 8 yrs experience weaving and dyeing at West Dean Tapestry Studios; M New Fibre Arts; M 62 Group.

FIRMS AND CRAFTSPEOPLE

Pc Three panels in flat-weave tapestry, used as doors to a coat closet in Tudor House.

STOCK FURNITURE RESTORATIONS LTD (Empl: 10; Est: 1979)
The St, Hatfield Peverel, Chelmsford, Essex CM3 2HD. 0245-381 173.
M BAFRA.
Brochure.

STOKE-ON-TRENT WORKSHOPS FOR THE BLIND (Empl: 3 + 4 if required; Est: 1901)
Cane & Rush Seating
211 City Rd, Fenton, Stoke-on-Trent, Staffs ST4 2PN. 0782-48801.
Workshop trained.
Pc New rush seats for Lichfield and Southwark Cathedrals. Renovation of total seating of churches.
Brochure.

STOKES, MICHAEL (Empl: solo; Est: 1985)
Stained Glass Artist/Painter
Longdale Rural Craft Centre, Longdale Lane, Ravenshead, Notts. 0623-794 858.
BA (Hons) Fine Art; M BSMGP.
Pc 2 single windows depicting figures – All Saints' Church, Annesley. One window depicting Joseph and Mary – St Catherine's Church, Cossall, Notts.
Upon receipt of outline requirements and dimensions will provide quotations free of charge and obligation.

STONEGUARD (Empl: 200; Est: 1966)
Head Office: Baynes House, 380 Chester Rd, Old Trafford, Manchester M16 9EA. 061-848 7881. Highgrove Way, Eastcote Rd, Ruislip, Middx HA4 8EA. 0895-675 577. 341 Glasgow Rd, Blantyre, Glasgow G72 9HN. 0698-825 220. 19 Manor Place, Edinburgh EH3 7DK. 031-226 2830.
BEC; Stone Fed; Construction Industry Training Board; Nat Joint Council for the Building Industry.
Pc ICI Millbank London Restoration. Marble cleaning and restoration – Dober Court, Foreign Office.
Repair and replacement of stone, brick, terracotta, granite, marble and concrete; repointing; cleaning; GRP and reinforced concrete replacements; cast stone; resin injection; water repellent systems; painting and decorating.
Brochure.

STUART

STONEWEST COX LTD (Empl: approx 240; Est: 1987)
Lamberts Place, St James's Rd, Croydon, Surrey CR9 2HX. 081-684 6646.
M Stone Federation. Approved: PSA
Pc Restoration and cleaning, supply of precast stone – St James's Court Hotel, Buckingham Gate, London. Restoration and cleaning – Maesteg Town Hall, Mid Glam and also Theatre Royal, Newcastle. Stonework renewal and stone carving, internal cleaning – Scottish National Portrait Gallery, Edinburgh.
Building facade restoration of terracotta/faience, stone, brick, and precast materials inc. specialist consolidation; project management; consultation and design service; defect analysis; masonry production (inc. work for new buildings). Contract range £5,000–1,500,000. Brochure.

STOURBRIDGE STAINED GLASS (Empl: varies; Est: 1980)
63 Hagley Rd, Stourbridge, W. Midlands DY8 1QR. 0384-440 172.
BA (Hons) Glass Design.
Pc Priory College, Stamford, Lincs. Gate House, Tolethorpe, Stamford. Globe Carpets, Lye, W. Midlands.

STRIDE, CHRISTINA (Est: 1978)
Mixed Media Wallhangings & Fabrics Made for Soft Furnishings, Blinds, etc
22 Adisham House, Pembury Rd, London E5 8LH. 081-533 2177.
BA (Hons) Textile Design; post grad Dip Textile Art, Goldsmiths' College, University of London; post grad in Art Therapy.
Only able to supply small quantities.

STRUCTOPLAST CONTRACTS LTD (Empl: 45; Est: 1980)
Specialist Contractor
Minster House, Commerce Estate, Kingston Rd, Leatherhead, Surrey KT22 7LA. 0372-376 551.
M FERFA. Approved: general local authority lists.
Pc Restoration works inc. Nelson's Column, Trafalgar Sq; St Benet's Church.
Specialists in concrete repairs; resin injection; specialized grouting; waterproofing; diamond drilling; dowelling; etc.

STUART (Empl: 25; Est: 1975)
Barrington Court, Barrington, Nr Ilminster, Somerset TA19 0NQ. 0460-40349.
Pc Restoration and new work to match existing inc. Littlecot House, Wilts; Blakesley Hall Museum; Oakwell Hall Museum; North Devon Museum; various National Trust properties and private houses from

early medieval to 18th century. Restoration/reconstruction – Laudian Screen and stalls, The Chapel, Lambeth Palace for Archbishop of Canterbury.
A group of companies specializing in 16th and 17th century originals and reproductions inc. oak furniture; architectural joinery; architectural antiques; slipware and delft-ware pottery; reproduction tapestries; lighting; tiles; paintings; brass; soft furnishings; early woven fabrics (40 authentic designs); garden ornamentation. Brochure.

SUE'S SEWS (Est: 1984)
Mrs Sue Weeks, 7a Institute Rd, Swanage, Dorset BH19 1BT. 0929-424 566.
Teacher of Art, Fabric Painting & Associated Crafts; Dorset Craft Guild.
Pc Hand-painted fabric lengths, wallhangings on silk, place settings to match wallpaper or cutlery, mock windows and views through, for wallhangings, quilted, embroidered and beaded. Hand-painted and quilted cushions.
Will consider any challenge, within her capabilities.

SUGG LIGHTING LTD (Empl: 45; Est: originally 1837)
Sussex Manor Business Park, Gatwick Rd, Crawley, W. Sussex RH10 2GD. 0293-540 111.
Pc Hotels, restaurants, churches, palaces etc – too varied to specify.
Brochure.

SUMMERS, ROYSTON & ASSOCIATES, ARCHITECTS & DESIGNERS (Est: 1964)
3 North Several, Blackheath, London SE3 0QR. 081-852 5346.
MA (Cantab); AA Dip; ARIBA.
Pc Restoration works inc. Bishop's Palace, Winchester; Redlynch Park, Somerset; Chateau la Roche Beaulieu, St Emilion, France.
Definition and development of briefs; technological developments; furniture design. Seeks to be judged by its 'highest standard of design', and to this end has cultivated productive working relationships with Europe's leading specialist consultants. Pride themselves that many of its briefs have been based on apparently intractable problems, and many of its solutions have been highly innovative.

SUNRAYS (GRAHAM SMITH)
Weather-vanes
284 Bournemouth Rd, Charlton Marshall, Blandford, Dorset DT11 9NG. 0258-53374.
Designer and maker of one-off and standard weather-vanes, handmade in steel, inc. an original design for Poole Borough Council Architects Dept. Brochure.

SUNRISE STAINED GLASS (Empl: 4; Est: 1983)
58–60 Middle St, Southsea, Hants PO5 4BP. 0705-750 512.
J. Tarrant (joint proprietor) BA (Hons); M BSMGP; Glass Association.
Pc Private houses, restaurants, public houses and shops, restoration of church windows, new windows in church buildings using contemporary and traditional designs.

SUTTON, HAZEL TRADITONAL UPHOLSTERY & RESTORATION (Est: 1986)
8 London Rd, St Agnes, Bristol, Avon BS2 9QE. 0272-552 763 & 541 895.
G & G's 555 Traditional Upholstery & Restoration (distinctions in both).
Pc Upholstery for Freud's of London. Upholstery and prop making for Welsh National Opera, Cardiff. Upholstery for Plymouth Theatre Royal.

SWAN UPHOLSTERY (Empl: 6; Est: 1984)
5–7 George St, Romford, Essex RM1 2DT. 0708-40569.
35 yrs experience in the trade; BTEC HND in Furniture Studies (son); M AMU.
Pc Contracted to London Hilton, Park Lane. Ambassadors Club, W1. Stafford Hotel, W1. Numerous pubs, clubs, etc.

SWINGLER, E. J. & J. KENNEDY ASSOCIATED (Empl: 3; Est: 1970)
Stained Glass Artists
E. J. Swingler: 25 Daglands Rd, Fowey, Cornwall PL23 1JN. 2132-072 683. J. Kennedy: 17 Western Rd, Grandpont, Oxford OX1 4LF. 0865-249 020.
Apprenticeship. Approved: CCC; National Trust; Dept of Restoration of Antique Glass, V & A Museum.
Pc Canons Ashby Church and Trerice, Cornwall – both for National Trust. Many parish churches.

SYMM & CO LTD (Empl: 150; Est: 1827)
Specialist & General Building Contractors
Osney Mead, Oxford OX2 0EQ. 0865-249 567.
Directors and Management M's Inst of Building. Craftsmen apprentice trained. Company M BEC. Approved: PSA; Eng. Heritage; National Trust; University of Oxford; Oxford Diocesan Board; Oxford colleges; Oxfordshire CC; Oxford City Council.
Pc Conversion and restoration – Bucknell Manor. Conversion to renowned 'Le Manoir aux Quat' Saisons' restaurant and hotel – Great Milton Manor. Thame Park. Britwell House. Restoration of state rooms – Halton House. Bear Hotel, Woodstock. Taplow Court.

FIRMS AND CRAFTSPEOPLE

Heythrop Park. Blenheim. Numerous Oxford colleges.
High-quality joinery inc. hardwood panelling and traditional historic house work both in UK and USA; restoration; fine interior decoration; stone cutting (see associated Co Axtell Perry Symm Masonry); leadwork (see Sharp & Howse Ltd). Brochure.

SYMONDS, D. S. (Empl: 4; Est: 1973)
Master Thatcher
Dormer Cottage, N. Chideock, Bridport, Dorset DT6 6LG. 0297-89644.
M Dorset MTA
Pc Park Farm Barn Conversion – Chideock. Bramley Cider Barn – Axminster.

SYSON, LESLIE BA, DLC (Hons), MCC Ed (Empl: one; Est: 1867)
Furniture Designer
Church House, Congleton Rd, Eaton, Congleton, Cheshire CW12 2NH. 0260-274 331.
C & Gs Cabinet Makers Cert, Leicester College of Art; trained as Teacher of Woodwork (1st Class Honours), Loughborough College; M College of Craft Education; M Assoc of Brit Craftsmen.
Pc Private clients (details on application).
Business founded by present owner's great grandfather. Brochure.

SZELL, MICHAEL LTD (Est: 1967)
Furnishing Fabrics
47 Sloane Avenue, London SW3 3OH. 071-589 2634.
Pc Clients, both home and abroad, inc. Windsor Castle; Trust House Forte.
Minimum quantity willing to supply is 25–50 metres.

TABNER, LEN
High Bowby, Easington, Saltburn by Sea, N. E. Yorks TS13 4UT. 0287-40948.
Master of Arts Degree in Fine Arts.
Pc Work carried out on commission for many private individuals. Industrial and commercial work in collections inc. Science Museum, London and many other public museums.
Also undertakes work on fine art easel paintings and documentation of threatened buildings

TAHLA DESIGNS (Est: 1987)
Onglaze Applied Art inc. Ceramic Tiles
20 Wellington Lane, Montpelier, Bristol, Avon BS6 5PY. 0272-427 318.
Pc Clients inc. London and Bristol architects; BBC Bristol; Institute of

TAYLOR, J.W. LTD

Child Health; Friends of the Earth; Berkeley School of English and private clients.
Brochure.

TALAR CARPET REPAIRS (ORIENTAL) (Empl: 4; Est: 1976)
23 North End Parade, North End Rd, W. Kensington, London W14 0SI. 071-602 0046.
Specialists and experts in the repair and cleaning of Oriental carpets, European tapestries and Aubussons.

TARVER, DAVID
Architectural Sculptor
9 Church St, Belton, Loughborough, Leics LE12 9UG.
ARCA.
Pc Architectural sculpture (capitals) – Richmond Riverside Development and also Regent's Park Development. Heraldic sculpture for architecture in Leics and Derbys. Stone mosaic sculptures – Fisons Ltd. Restoration of bronze, wood and stone sculpture. Portraiture and trophies in bronze. Stone fountain – RNIB Commercial College.
Brochure.

TAYLOR, BRIAN ANTIQUES & FIREPLACES CENTRE (Est: 1977)
24 Molesworth Rd, Stoke Plymouth, Devon PL1 5LZ. 0752-569 061.
BA (Hons).
Sell antique fireplaces, restored where necessary, and arranges for installation.

TAYLOR, FREDERICK (Empl: solo; Est: 1983)
Specialist Painter & Decorator
12 The Banks, Lyneham, Nr Chippenham, Wilts SN15 4NS. 0249-891 248.
Painting & decorating apprenticeship; C & Gs Basic & Advanced Craft Cert's with Credit.
Hand-painted furniture, painted to client's specification to match room decor.

TAYLOR, J. W. LTD (Empl: 70; Est: 1927)
Refurbishment & Joinery Contractors
Ripon Rd, Harrogate, Yorks HG1 2BT. 0423-66751/2.
This firm trains their own apprentices; M BEC; M BWF.
Pc Neacham Hall. Garrowby Hall. South Ollerington Hall. Ledgton Hall. Helperby Hall. Christ Church. St Anne's Cathedral. St Michael's Church.
Will make almost anything of a one-off nature in wood based materials for incorporation into buildings inc. doors; windows; screens; counters; stairs;

balustrades; bank fittings; ecclesiastical joinery; shop fitting. Brochure.

TAYLOR, JOHN (BELLFOUNDERS) LTD (Empl: 20; Est: 1750)
The Bellfoundry, Freehold St, Loughborough, Leics LE11 1AR. 0509-212 241.
Pc Most principal cathedrals in England and USA. Provision of bells for Australia, New Zealand and other parts of the world.
Specialists in the casting and tuning of bells (ranging from a few pounds to 20 tonnes) for churches, town halls and other civic institutions. Purpose designed fittings and frameworks for bell installations is a craft for which this foundry is famous worldwide. Conservation undertaken using traditional materials and methods wherever possible.

TAYLOR, SUTTON CERAMICS (Empl: 2; Est: 1970)
Old House, Lotherton Park – Aberford, Leeds, Yorks LS25 3EB. 0532-812 231.
Craftsmen Potters Assoc; Crafts Council Index.
Although principally known for one-off lustre decorated bowls and chargers, Sutton Taylor does undertake large and small-scale ceramic panels and tiles, and is hoping to develop a range of large scale architectural ceramic panels and screens in collaboration with the painter Michael Sheppard. Brochure.

TEAGLE, ALUN BUILDING CONSERVATION (Empl: 4; Est: 1979)
Ruperra Castle, Lower Machan, Newport, Gwent NP1 8UG. 0633-440 088.
Dip Sculpture; Dip Decorative Building Elements, Royal Soc Industrial Artists & Designers; Associate IIC; M GMC; SPAB.
Pc Conservation of carved corbels – Bishop's Palace, St David's, Dyfed. Floor tile conservation – Neath Abbey. Restoration and consolidation – Eleanor Cross, Herts. Brick repairs and repointing – Ashe House, Hants.
A building contractor specializing in conservation inc. the analysis, specifications and supply of special mortars.

TEILSEN BRIDD (Est: 1988)
Ceramic Artist
Craig yr Iyrchen, Cerrig y Drudion, Corwen, Clwyd LL21 9TE. 049 082-514.
Dip Architectural Glass, Swansea College of Art; C & Gs Architectural Glass; studied 3 Dimensional Design in Glass and Ceramics during 2 yrs at Stourbridge College of Art.
Will consider anything that has to be made to commission in ceramics inc. tiles; handmade bricks; architectural ceramics. Brochure.

THATCHERS

TEMPLE LIGHTING (Est: 1968)
Stockwell House, 1 Stockwell Lane, Wavendon, Milton Keynes, Bucks MK17 8LS. 0908-583 597.
Specialist stockists of 19th- and early 20th-century light fittings, but also deal in other antiques such as 19th-century furniture and decorative items.
Brochure.

TERRACOPIA LTD (Empl: 6; Est: 1980)
Terracotta Planters & Architectural Features
The Castle, Dudleston, Nr Ellesmere, Salop SY12 9EF. 069-175 353.
Pc 100 planters specially created from design features on a restored building.
Reproduction planters designed and reproduced to client's specification.
Brochure.

TEXTILE CONSERVATION STUDIO – KSYNIA MARKO Dip AD (Empl: 6; Est: 1982)
39 The Limehouse Cut, Colmans Court, Morris Rd, London E14 6NQ. 071-538 2727.
3 fully trained conservators with 31 yrs accumulative experience; 3 apprentices; UK Institute for Conservation.
Pc Clients inc. National Trust; National Museum; private collectors, etc.
Brochure.

TEYCHENNE, G. C. (Est: 1969)
Conservation & Restoration of Stonework & Plasterwork
The Manor House, Winfrith Newburgh, Dorset DT2 8JR. 0305-852 988.
Sculptor; C & Gs of London; Lutyens medallist; Course Tutor in Conservation of Architectural Stonework; UKIC (Stone Section).
Pc Restoration of 2 Tudor moulded ceilings, 30 ft × 60 ft, Tomson Manor. Conservation of 16th-century Hamstone Preaching Cross and also Egyptian limestone head.
Early plaster mouldings and carved stonework reproduced to march existing.

THATCHER, THE
Flint Cottage, Poy St, Rattlesden, Nr Bury St Edmunds, Suffolk IP30 0SR. 04493-7751.
Full M Suffolk MTA.

THATCHERS (Empl: 2; Est: 1975)
1 Brandon Green, Rugby Rd, Brandon, Warwicks CV8 3HU. 0203-543 025.

FIRMS AND CRAFTSPEOPLE

Local MTA; NMTA; Cairdean Nan Taighean Tugha (Friends of the Thatched Houses – Tiree).
Pc Hugh Millers House, Cromarty (Scottish National Trust). Muck and briar thatching for Avoncroft. Turf and oat thatching to a Blackhouse – Clackhill, Highland Folk Museum. Water Mill restoration, Isle of Skye. Turf thatched cliet restoration, Isle of St Kilda.
Will undertake any ancient or dis-used thatching medium – oats, barley, turf, sods, heather, etc.

THATCHING ADVISORY SERVICE (Empl: 10; Est: 1974)
Rose Tree Farm, 29 Nine Mile Ride, Finchampstead, Berks RG11 4QD. 0734-734 203, 730 766 & 732 361.
GMC; Brit Franchise Assoc.
Pc Has thatched internationally inc. USA, Germany and France. National Trust Properties throughout UK.
Free quotations. There are 3 free brochures available from the Thatching Advisory Service:- Specification; Insuring Thatch; Patch & Thatch. Managing director, Robert West is author of Thatch *(David & Charles).*

THATCHING SUPPLIES LTD (Est: 1980)
Directors: B. Hummerston & F. Littlejohns, Sandbourne, Down End, Croyd, Nr Braunton EX33 1QE. 0271-890 634. Sunningdale, Halwill Junction, Beaworthy, Devon EX21 5TW. 040 922-272.
Both Directors are M's of Devon & Cornwall MTA.
Pc Work undertaken for Landmark Trust; National Trust; new development work in liaison with architects.
Willing to undertake large jobs, and help with planning thatching details.

THIMBLEBY, E. J. & SON LTD (Empl: 20; Est: 1924)
Specialist Woodworkers, Upholsterers & Polishers
Crofton Drive, Allenby Ind Estate, Lincoln LN3 4NS. 0522-533 311.

THIRTY-EIGHT ANTIQUES LTD
Bespoke Furniture, Panelling, Mantelpieces
Royal Ordnance Depot, Weedon, Northants. 0327-40766.
Bookcases and bespoke furniture made out of old components; panelling to order from adapted 18th century and 19th century pieces. All items can be ordered in a wide range of finishes and painted to match a client's colour scheme. Highly decorative (mostly French) antique items stocked, inc. French mantelpieces; original and reproduction Adam style mantelpieces. Thirty-Eight Antiques Ltd deal with trade only and request that customers make an appointment. They are willing to arrange delivery at customer's expense.

THISTLE JOINERY LTD (Empl: 10; Est: 1980)
Bookcases & Library Joinery
77 Ilderton Rd, Bermondsey, London SE16 3JZ. 071-232 1553.
Specialists in bookcases, libraries, etc, in wood for painting, or in some types of hardwood. Brochure.

THOMAS, MICHAEL – COUNTRY FURNITURE (Empl: 2; Est: 1982)
Southrop Farm, Southrop Rd, Hook Norton, Nr Banbury, Oxon OX15 5PP. 0608-730 015.
Trained in antique restoration with busy workshops in Chipping Norton.
Pc 12 ft refectory table in English oak. Clergy and choir stalls and desks (34 persons) – St Nicolas Parish Church, Newbury, Berks. Complete kitchen in solid oak, plus all furniture in reception rooms of house.
Brochure.

THOMAS & WILSON (PLASTERING) LTD (Empl: 100; Est: 1920)
454 Fulham Rd, London SW6 1BY. 071-381 1161/4.
Indenturer apprenticeships issued; M BEC; LMPA.
Pc A large number of contracts ranging from £300,00–£200,000 + in value.
Fibrous plaster specialist in refurbishment and new work from own large stock range of mouldings. Brochure.

THOMASON, PHILIP STONECARVING & DECORATIVE TERRACOTTA (Empl: 3; Est: 1970)
The Old Vicarage, Cudworth, Nr Ilminster, Somerset TA19 0PR. 0460-57322.
Pc Commissions inc. ornamental and figurative stone carvings for Wells Cathedral; Westminster Abbey; Palace of Westminster; Windsor Castle; RMA; Sandhurst; etc.
As well as ornamental and figurative stonework willing to make urns; planters; statuary; balustrading and such like in terracotta. Brochure.

THOMPSON'S, ROBERT CRAFTSMEN LTD (Empl: 36; Est: 1920)
Specialist Woodwork & Furniture
Kilburn, Yorks YO6 4AH. 03476-218.
Specialists in handmade domestic church and boardroom furniture, made from English oak, and incorporating the world-famous mouse trade mark. Commissions can be undertaken for individual carvings and any special item requiring fitting on site can be delivered and installed by this firm. Also produces a standard range of furniture. Brochure.

FIRMS AND CRAFTSPEOPLE

THORNTON, ANDY ARCHITECTURAL ANTIQUES & REPRODUCTIONS (Est: 1975)
Reproductions: Ainleys Ind Estate, Elland, W. Yorks HX5 9JP.
Antique Showroom: Marshfield Mills, Dewsbury Rd, Elland, W. Yorks. 0422-75595.
Pc Various work for hotels, public houses and restaurants inc. a pitch pine interior – The Seventh Trap (a new public house for The Wolverhampton & Dudley Breweries). Stained glass dome, shades, brassware and balustrading – Macey's, Newcastle. Bars, bookcases, fireplace, etched glass screens and brassware – The Village Inn, Gatwick Airport.
This firm produces a very wide range of reproductions antiques (both standard ranges and to order) inc. bars; bar furniture; tiffany shades; a variety of brass goods; street furniture; decorative glass; cast aluminium goods; fairground goods; wood carvings; statuary; etc. Although the firm specializes in producing goods for the bar and restaurant trade, many of their goods have potential use in other areas. Brochure.

THORPE, LAVINIA
Glass Enameller
Brook Cottage, Wheal Butson, St Agnes, N. Cornwall TR5 0PT. 087-2552 160.
Craft M GGE.
Pc Various houses and churches mostly in Wilts where Lavinia Thorpe lived before moving to Cornwall – all done on goblets, decanters, etc.

THRELFALL, PHILIPPA & COLLINS, KENNEDY (Empl: 2 partners; Est: 1968)
Ceramic & Terracotta Murals
18 Tor St, Wells, Somerset BA5 2VS. 0749-72548.
Phillipa Threlfall – studied illustration/ceramics to NDD, Cardiff College of Art Kennedy Collings – read history at Trinity Hall, Cambridge.
Pc 46 ft long collage of historic building facades in Sussex – Sussex Mutual Building Society Head Offices, Hove. 15 panels (each 1.5 m × 1 m) showing Bristol's history, based on seals, tokens, etc., from the locality – Bwadquay House, Bristol. 8 cartouches, approx 1 m sq, based on East India Co crest – Cutlers Gardens, London, EC3. Over 70 ceramic murals and panels, the majority in public places (many based on historical themes).
Although not specifically involved in conservation, their interest in historical associations, and the intricacy of their terracotta relief often results in commissions from clients who are restoring or developing buildings with a historical identity.

THURTON FOUNDRIES LTD (Empl: 15; Est: 1963)
Metalworkers
Thurton, Norwich, Norfolk NR14 6AN. 050 843 301/3.
BCIRA; ABBF; BFA; IBF.
Pc Sandringham. Gt Yarmouth Haven Bridge. Hadleigh Bridge reconstruction.

TIMBERLAND ART & DESIGN (Empl: 2; Est: 1989)
Tapestry Designer
12 Church Lane, Timberland, Lincoln LN4. 05267-222.
BA Fine Art; post grad Tapestry Weaving.
Pc Public commissions inc. a tapestry commissioned by SEWAA and Welsh Arts Council – Mount St School. Private commissions throughout Britain and America.
Tapestries, cushions and chair covers. Brochure.

TIMINGS, CLARE GILDING (Empl: one; Est: 1988)
17 Fore St, Evershot, Dorchester, Dorset DT2 0JR. 0935-83653.
C & Gs of London Art School; Dip Carving, Gilding & Conservation.
Paul Levs, London, 18 mths working as gilder in workshop.
Pc Repairs to various frames – Dulwich Picture Gallery. New work and restoration inc. National Trust properties.
A small workshop using traditional techniques and gold leaf to restore a range of gilded surfaces.

TIMPERLEY DECORATING CO – INTERIOR DESIGNERS & DECORATORS (Empl: 10; Est: 1958)
275 Washway Rd, Sale, Cheshire M33 4BP. 061-973 5167.
Fully qualified in all aspects.

TIPPER, JOSEPH LTD
Metalworker
Willenhall Rd, Darlaston, Wednesbury, W. Midlands WS10 8UJ. 021-526 5353.

TIRLIN PIN DYKERS – NORMAN HADDOW (Empl: one; Est: 1982)
Dry Stone Dykers
12 Cairns Court, Crieff, Perthshire PH7 3SP. 0764-3874.
Dry Stone Walling Assoc Intermediate Craftsman Cert.
Pc Free standing walls and dry stone terrace work.
Willing to consider work anywhere in the world, except war zones.

TK BUILDERS (Empl: 7; Est: 1986)
Building & Civil Engineering Contractors
The Blackcock, Falstone, Hexham, Northumberland NE48 1AA. 0660-40200.

FIRMS AND CRAFTSPEOPLE

All apprenticed trained; C & Gs Site Management.

TOFT, C. G. (LEADED LIGHTS) LTD (Empl: 7; Est: 1972)
Bernard House, 60 Berward St, Uplands, Swansea, W. Glam SA2 0HS. 0792-460 914 & 456 863.
FMB.
Pc Margam Castle – commissioned by W. Glamorgan County Council. St David's Hospital Church – commissioned by Dyfed Health Authority. St Brynach's Church, Nevern, Cardigan – commissioned Roiser, Whitestone & Bartosch. Brecon Cathedral.

TOMKINSON'S STAINED GLASS (Empl: 2; Est: 1979)
52 Islington Park St, London N1. 071-359 0893 & 071-267 1669.
GMC.
Pc Too many to mention.

TOMORROW'S ANTIQUES (Empl: one; Est: 1982)
Furniture Restorer
18 Spenwood Rd, Littleborough, Lancs OL15 8PF. 0706-73571.
6 yr apprenticeship in cabinet making; C & Gs of London (1st Class pass); Full Technological Cert C & Gs; ONC, HNC Building; Licentiate of The Royal College of Advanced Technology Salford.
Pc Design and manufacture of altar table and communion rail, and other church furniture. Manufacture and restoration of clock cases and musical boxes.
Working in conjunction with other craftsmen, this firm can offer complete restoration service of clocks and musical boxes inc. movement and dial restoration.

TOOLEY & FOSTER PARTNERSHIP, THE (Est: 1892)
Architects, Structural Engineers & Interior Designers
Warwick House, Palmerston Rd, Buckhurst Hill, Essex IG9 5LQ. 081-504 9711.
Pc Fire reinstatement – University College School, London. 2 private houses, London. Springboard Housing Assoc, Old Harlow (conservation area). 41/42 Dover St, London (Grade II).

TOULSON, MARY JANE (Est: 1972)
Woven & Hand Tufted Rugs & Wallhangings
1 Wrenshall Cottage, Walsham-le-Willows, Bury St Edmunds' Suffolk IP31 3AS. 035 98 646.
Dip in Art & Design (Textiles), W. Surrey School of Art; Fellow Digswell House Art Centre, Welwyn Garden City; M Suffolk Craft Soc; M Norfolk Contemporary Art Soc.
Pc Rug commissioned by Director of The Victorian Society. Rug

commissioned by Kevin Crossley Holland. Wallhanging – Ixworth Health Centre. Wallhanging bought by Ruth Rendell. Wallhanging woven for Jonathon Porritt, Director FOE.

TOWER KEY CO, THE & (HOMEGUARD LTD) (Empl: 6; Est: 1948)
80–84 St Mary Rd, Walthamstow, London E17 9RE. 081-520 8331/4 & 4464.
Pc Presentation keys for ceremonial openings by Queen Elizabeth II. Antique reproduction keys/locks overhauled and repaired – Downing St; The Treasury; GLC Historic Buildings; Kenwood House and various other listed buildings.
Will also supply architectural ironmongery.

TOWEY, MICHAEL MASTER THATCHER (Empl: 3; Est: 1980)
11 Albemarle Avenue, Withington, Manchester M20 8HX. 061-445 9224.
Cert of Merit in Thatching; joining NSMTA and North West MTA.
Pc From iron age huts and 15th-century barn to modern two-storey houses covering all features.
Has served separate apprentices in Ireland, W. Germany and England, having worked most of his thatching career in these countries, and also in Denmark. Speaks fluent German.

TOWNSENDS (Est: 1978)
Architectural Antiques/Stained Glass Artists
36 New End Square, London NW3 1LS. 071-724 3746. 1 Church St, London NW3 8EE. 071-724 3746. 81 Abbey Rd, London NW8 0AE. 071-624 4756.
Specialists in original antique architectural fittings, tiles and reconditioned fireplaces. The glass department will reproduce existing glass designs, or work to a client's design, as well as supplying a large selection of original antique stained and painted, acid etched and brilliant cut glass. Brochure.

TOWSEY, P. (Empl: 2; Est: 1969)
Traditional Upholsterer
52 Northernhay St, Exeter, Devon EX4 3ER. 0392-50015.
AMU.
Pc Furniture for Mount Edgcombe, Plymouth. Bishops Throne and tapestry kneeler – Exeter Cathedral. Seats in the Exeter Guild Hall.

TOY, R. J. & ASSOCIATES (Est: 1974)
Chartered Architects
Malins Hall, 37 High St, Falmouth, Cornwall TR11 2AF. 0326-311 714.
B Arch (Hons) L'pool; RIBA; ACI Arb.

FIRMS AND CRAFTSPEOPLE

TOYNBEE-CLARK INTERIORS LTD (Empl: as required; Est: 1953)
Chinese & Japanese Wallpapers
95 Mount St, London W1. 071-499 4472.
IDDA.
Pc Have conserved and reinstalled antique Chinese papers throughout the world (America, Europe, Middle East) to the value of £20,000–£30,000 per room. A room of modern Chinese paper averages £8,000–£10,000.
Specialize in original 18th- and 19th- century hand-painted Chinese wallpapers and French hand-painted wallpapers; panoramic papers; modern hand-painted copies of Chinese papers and Japanese silk papers.

T & P LEAD ROOFING LTD (Empl: 20; Est: 1980)
73 Monks Haven, Stanford-le-Hope, Essex SS17 7EB. 0375-676 908.
LCA; all employees are fully qualified plumbers.

TRAYLER, K. J. (Est: 1967)
Cane & Rush Seating
'Fir Close', Clay Common, Frostenden Wangford, Suffolk WR34 8BQ. 050 278-261.

TRENCHARD, SARA (Empl: solo; Est: 1987)
Stencilling, Gilding & Mural Artist
21 Butleigh Wootton, Glastonbury, Somerset BA6 8TX. 0458-43144.
C & Gs in Decorative Arts.
Pc Shop fronts, gilded ornamental mouldings, etc. Restoring and re-gilding of antique mirror frames and other objects such as grandfather clocks; lacquer cabinets; painted corner cupboards, etc. for antique dealers.

TRESKE LTD (Empl: 20; Est: 1972)
Furniture Designers & Makers
Station Works, Thirsk, N. Yorks YO7 4NY. 0845-22770.
C & Gs Woodworking for most of staff.
Pc Numerous churches, cathedrals and private homes.
Have own sawmill, where they prepare home grown hardwoods. Brochure.

TRETOL LTD (Empl: 150; Est: 1937)
Specialist Coatings for Weather Resistance & Repair Materials
86–88 Bestobell Rd, Slough, Berks SL1 4SE. 0753-24164.
Brochure.

TUDOR ROSE RESTORATION

TREZISE, DAVID (Empl: 3; Est: 1972)
Master Thatcher
Stepps House, Stepps Lane, Axmouth, Seaton, Devon EX12 4AR. 0297-20679.
5 yr COSIRA apprenticeship; Certified Master Thatcher; both apprentices have achieved Student of the Year Awards for C & Gs overseen by COSIRA. M Devon & Cornwall MTA.
Pc Too numerous to mention.

TRIST, WILLIAM & McBAIN, ANDREW (Empl: 5; Est: 1975)
Restoration & Conservation of Antique Furniture
9 Canongate Venture, New St, Edinburgh EH8 8BH. 031-557 3828.
Scottish Soc for Conservation & Restoration.
Pc Restoration works inc. Christopher North's desk (founder of Blackwoods Magazine). Chairs designed by Charles Rennie Mackintosh; drop-front Secretaire by Jean-Francoise Oeben and Jean-Henri Reisener; chair caning and picture moulding – Scottish Gallery; The panelled Green Room, Rosslyn Castle for Landmark Trust; room panelling; walnut casket with silver mounts; mahogany cabinet; large reception desk with stained glass panels.

TRUEWOOD PRODUCTS LTD (Empl: 10; Est: 1975)
All Purpose Joinery
Unit 1, Bailey Gate Ind Est, Sturminster Marshall, Wimborne, Dorset, BH21 4DB
0258-857 877.
Only qualified C & Gs tradesmen employed; committed to training programmes inc. indentured apprenticeships for joinery trainees to Advanced C & G's standard.
Pc Joinery produced throughout the S. and S. W. for established construction and renovation companies. Will supply details of previous customers for reference and inspection purposes. 'Have earned a reputation for high quality and unique versatility'.
Standard range of quality replacement or new windows (incorporating high security espagnolette locking systems), 56 mm thick solid panelled high performance doors, and moulded hardwood surrounds to accept aluminium installations. Brochure.

TUDOR ROSE RESTORATION (Empl: family business; Est: 1973)
Furniture Designer & Restorer
Court Cottage, Porthpean Village, St Austell, Cornwall PL26 6AY. 0726-75653.
Sixth generation Woodworker, fully indentured with C & Gs.

FIRMS AND CRAFTSPEOPLE

TUFNELL, R. N. (Empl: 3; Est: 1978)
Dry Stone Waller
Brae House, Balmaclellan, Castle Douglas, Dumfries DG7 3QW. 06442-352.
Holder of DSWA Master Craftsmans Cert; all employees progressing to same.
Pc Designed and constructed exhibit at Glasgow Garden Festival inc. dry stone arch. Multi-terrace work for garden landscaping. Scottish champion. Has taught for British Council. ATB Instructor.
Writer on the subject of dry stone walling and has also done numerous radio and TV interviews. Will provide photographs and descriptions of work on request.

TURN ON LTD – 1850–1930
Antique Lighting
116/118 Islington High St, Camden Passage, London N1 8EG. 071-359 7616.
M Decorative Arts Society, Brighton.
Pc Hire of various fittings to film companies, theatres and exhibitions.

TURNER, EDWIN (Empl: 10; Est: 1969)
Designer, Manufacturer & Restorer of Fine Furniture
Home Farm, Gislingham, Eye, Suffolk IP23 8JP. 0379 83-280.
Pc Embassies; banks; financial institutions; hotels; general manufacturers and other manufacturers.
Brochure.

TURNER & ROSS LTD (Empl: 20; Est: 1946)
Ironworkers
C5–6 North Way, Bounds Green Ind Estate, Bounds Green Rd, London N11 2UN. 081-368 7656. FAX 081-361 0896.
Pc Staircases/walkways – Kentish Homes, Northampton St, N1. Period ironwork – Kentish Homes, Sutton Square, London E9. Staircases – H. Webb Construction.

TUXFORD-WILLIAMS OF WALES (Empl: 23; Est: 1890)
Roofing Specialists
Rear Marineland, Conwy Rd, Llandudno Junction, Gwynedd LL13 9BA. 0492-572 364.
Nat Fed of Roofing Contractors.
Pc Roof renovations inc. part of Ritz Hotel, London; Keswick Hotel, Cumbria; church roof in Canada; Conwy Castle Visitor Centre; Blaenavon Ironworks, Museum; St Mary's Church, Conwy.
Tuxford-Williams of Wales are part of John Williams & Co, Rotherhithe,

London, and together they have over 200 yrs combined experience in the slate and tile roofing industry.

TWIBILL, GEOFF & SONS (Empl: 4; Est: 1978)
Leaded Window & Stained Glass Specialists
99a Blakiston St, Fleetwood, Lancs. 70706-03917.
Served apprenticeships; M GGF.
Pc Grand Theatre, Blackpool. Blackpool Town Hall. Kendal Parish Church. St Theresa's Church. Birkett Houses, Winster, Cumbria. Penrith Castle. Windermere Motor Boat Club. St Andrew's Church, Ashton, Preston. Manxman Nite Spot, Preston, etc.

TYLER, ROGER (Empl: one; Est: 1972)
Marquetarian
9 Perryfields Rd, Bromsgrove, Worcs B61 8SY. 0527-74559.
Self taught; M The Marquetry Soc; AMIMechE.
Pc Various pictorial works. Inlays for antique restoration and reproduction work. Matching inlays for period reproduction fire surrounds.
Photographs available.

UEDELHOVEN & CAMPION (Empl: 3; Est: 1959)
Furniture Restorers
Post Office, Gretton, Cheltenham, Glos GL54 5EP. 0242-604 227.
Both Partners have completed apprenticeships and attended various restoration courses run by CoSIRA.

UK COATINGS LTD (Empl: variable 10–15; Est: 1977, Ltd Co 1987)
Waterproofing & Concrete Restoration Contractors/Stockists of Specialist Products
Unit 1A, Westbridge Ind Est, Pixon Lane, Tavistock, Devon PL19 8DE. 0822-616748 & 613760. Southern Regional Office: 1 Kinson Avenue, Parkstone, Poole BH15 3PH. 0202-742128.
British Woodpreservers Assoc; Concrete Society.
Pc Re-painted mortar joints – Castle Drogo. Replacement of timbers and reslating – 14th-century cottage, Crapstone, Devon. Waterproofed 18th-century cottages – Holt, Nr Wimborne. Restored hardwood vaulting – Calstock Church. Supplied damp proofing materials – Orleigh Court, Buckland Brewer, N. Devon (reputed to be one of oldest continuously habited dwellings in England).
Stock admixes; bonding agents; concrete repair materials; damproofers; epoxy mortars and screeds; flexible coatings; brush applied membranes; nosing repair mortar; polyester repair materials; patching materials; tanking materials; fungicide; masonry sealers; clear surface treatments; silicone and non-silicone surface waterproofers; etc.

FIRMS AND CRAFTSPEOPLE

UNDERFOOT RUGS (Empl: 2; Est: 1988)
334 Old Laira Rd, Plymouth, Devon PL3 6AQ. 0752-261 788.
Grace Erickson, designer maker – B Sc Fine Art.

UNDERWOOD, DAVID – MASTER THATCHER
31 Parkway, Wavendon, Milton Keynes, Bucks MK17 8UH. 0908-584674.
Three yrs apprenticeship; 2 yrs improver; 12 yrs on his own.

UNICORN GLASS WORKSHOP (Empl: one; Est: 1977)
Stained Glass Artist
Tooses Farm, Stoke St. Michael, Bath, Somerset BA3 5JJ. 0749-840 654.
BA Hons Fine Art.

UNIVERSAL RAILING CO LTD (Est: 1988)
Ironworkers
2 Hume Villas, Claypole Rd, Nottingham NG7 6AB. 0602-781 378.
'Apart from specialist one-offs on some of the most important buildings in England, we produce the only entirely cast-iron standard railing and gate systems.' Brochure.

UNIVERSAL STONE LTD (Empl: approx 25; Est: 1936)
132 Ormside St, Peckham, London SE15 1TF. 071-358 0160.
M Stone Fed.
Pc Extensive restoration to Savoy Hotel facade and adjoining buildings in faience/terracotta; St Mary Abbotts church in Bath stone. Crypt restoration – St Martin-in-the-Fields, etc.
Brochure.

UPTON, PHILLIP (Empl: 2 associates; Est: 1978)
Stained Glass Artist/Painter
Cober Valley Centre, Coverack Bridges, Helston, Cornwall. 0326-572 671.
M BSMGP.
Pc Mainly commissions for domestic clients but some church work.

URCH, COLIN J. (Empl: one; Est: 1974)
Cane & English Freshwater Rush Seating
7 Rosamond Cottages, Kingswood, Nr Aylesbury, Bucks HP18 0RG. 029 677-477.
2 yr course Rycotewood College; 2 yrs working with a cabinet maker producing reproduction furniture; 1 yr course with CoSIRA.
Pc Church furniture; museum bookcases; sets of chairs; antique restoration; wood carving; turning; fitted kitchens; panelled rooms.

URQUHART, ALISTAIR G. (Empl: one; Est: 1974)
Stonemason
North Balnagowan, Coull, Aboyne, Aberdeenshire AB3 5JQ. 0339-2179.
Fully time served stonemason.
Pc Restoration work inc. Aboyne Castle; Mockrach Castle; Becdorney Castle; Terpersie Castle; Doune House; work for the National Trust for Scotland.

'USHA'
Freelance Textile Designer
48 Chelmsford Rd, New Basford, Nottingham NG7 7EP. 0602-785 738 & 587 938.
BA (Hons) Printed Textiles; Stage 1 Teaching Cert.
Pc Printed textile collections designed for firms. Hospital commissions inc. wallhangings in Clacton Hospital, Essex and screens for Lincoln Hospital. Back doors designed with pupils in Leicester for the Haymarket Theatre Dance Festival.
Hangings, blinds, curtains, kimonos and scarves screenprinted using torn or cut paper stencils with an emphasis on colour, produced in own studio. Has also worked for companies, producing collections of commercial printed textiles, and has worked as Artist in Residence in schools and community centres.

USHER, JEAN (Est: 1960)
Painted & Gilded Furniture Restorer
42 Southgate St, Bury St Edmunds, Suffolk IP33 2AZ. 0284-754 838.
Pc Work done for antique dealers and Stately homes. Exhibited at major antique fairs.

VARLEY, JOHN (IRONFOUNDERS) LTD (Empl: 50; Est: 1837)
Atlas St, St Helens, Merseyside WA9 1LJ. 0744-23043. TELEX 628 079 UPAGE G.
Engineering (Employers Fed.
Pc Manchester Air & Space Museum, Albert Dock, Liverpool. Manchester Central Art Gallery. Missenden Abbey, Aylesbury. Battersea Park Bandstand. Restoration schemes at Canning St, Liverpool and Hamilton Square, Birkenhead. Stockport Market Hall, Manchester Town Hall.
A family firm manufacturing quality iron castings from the drawing board to finished painting and fixing on site inc. balconies; balustrades; bollards; lighting columns; roof trusses; etc. Pattern, machining and servicing provided. Information pack available.

FIRMS AND CRAFTSPEOPLE

VEETRAC ENGINEERING LTD
Manufacturers of Steel Flooring, Stairtreads & Handrailing
Gaeddington Rd, Corby, Northants NN18 8AA. 0536-60261.
As well as producing open mesh steel flooring, stairtreads and handrailings this firm is willing to undertake the restoration of antique machinery (inc. water or other historical mills), diesel engine restoration and marine engine restoration. A brochure is available covering their steel work.

VENABLES HENRY LTD (Empl: 200; Est: 1858)
Castletown Sawmills, Doxey Rd, Stafford, Staffs ST16 2EN. 0785-59131.
Apprenticeship and training for joiners and machinists; TTF; BTMA; TRADA.
Pc Oak ceiling ribs and carved boss reconstruction – York Minster. Little Moreton Hall, Cheshire. Ann Hathaway's Cottage, Stratford-upon-Avon. Woodbridge Tide Mill, Suffolk. Hutton Castle, Glasgow. Barnard Castle, County Durham. Lincoln College, Oxford.
Timber supplied for restoration; special machining facilities for cambering beams and moulding large sections to match existing; fabrication service offered involving the preparation and fitting of joints so that timbers can be transported to site ready for erection; cleft tile laths; comprehensive joinery manufacturing service.

VENN, EDWARD ANTIQUE RESTORATIONS (Empl: 2; Est: 1979)
52 Long St, Williton, Taunton, Somerset TA4 4QU. 0984-32631.
4 yr apprenticeship; C & Gs Craft, Advanced Craft; Associated M Incorporated Brit Inst of Certified Carpenters; Construction Technicians Cert.
Furniture restoration; handmade furniture; long case clocks; barometers.

VERDIGRIS (Empl: 2; Est: 1977)
Specialist Metalworkers
Unit B18, 31 Clerkenwell Close, London EC1 0AT. 071-253 7788.
M UKIC; ILEA Panel Teacher Jewellery; 3 yrs J. D. Beardmore & Sons, Percy St, W1.
Pc Restoration of helmets – London Fire Brigade Museum. Reproduction handles – Hughendon, National Trust. Restortion of bronze War Memorial plaques – British Rail. Green bronzing – Soc Industrial Artists & Designers.

VERNON, TONY (Est: 1976)
Furniture Restorer
15 Follett Rd, Topsham, Devon EX3 0JP. 0392-874 635.
BAFRA; UKIC; IIC; TATHS.

VICEROY BUILDINGS LTD (Empl: 21; Est: 1984)
Specialist Designers & Manufacturers of Conservatories
Viceroy House, 53 Wessex Trade Centre, Ringwood Rd, Parkstone, Poole BH12 3PG. 0202-734 149 & 744 330.
GMC.
Pc Pigeon Pair PH – Surrey for Watney Coombe Reid. The Clifton Hotel – St John's Wood for Ind Coope.
Designer-surveyors' available to help work out the most cost effective scheme, with specialist advice on optional features such as double glazing. Also produce the 'Mountbatten Pool Hall', which can extend the limited summer swimming season throughout the year. Brochure.

VICKERMAN, E. W. & SONS (Empl: 3; Est: 1975)
Specialist Woodworkers
10 Plantation Gardens, Wigton Lane, Leeds LS17 8RY. 0532-688 129.
Apprenticeship as a cabinet maker.
Pc Constructed a solid carved oak circular seat (2 m in diameter) for 8, Louis XIIII style for head office of the International Westminster Bank in Paris.

VILLAGE DECORATING SERVICES LTD (Empl: 30; Est: 1929)
227 Wood St, Walthamstow, London E17 3LX. 081-5203 691 & 081-521 7178.
BDA; London Assoc of Master Decorators.
Pc Broken colour work, stippling, brush graining, rag-rolling, faux bois, faux marbre, button and French polishing, sign writing, and gilding.

VINEY, TONY (Empl: one; Est: 1984)
Stone Furniture, Polishing & Engraving
Sandy Hill Workshop, Sandy Hill Lane, Corfe Castle, Dorset BH20 5JF. 0929-480 977.
Stone polishing; stone turning; statuary; fireplaces; plaques; fountains.

VITRAIL STUDIOS – P. M. CROOK (Empl: solo; Est: 1980)
Stained Glass Artist
9 Sidney Grove, Fenham, Newcastle-upon-Tyne, Tyne & Wear NE4 5PD. 091-2733 530.
BA (Hons) Fine Art, Newcastle-upon-Tyne University.
Pc Restoration of William Morris/Burne Jones Stained Glass – Laing Art Gallery, Newcastle-upon-Tyne. Several contracts involving the conservation of medieval and Renaissance glass – The Victoria & Albert Museum, London.

FIRMS AND CRAFTSPEOPLE

VIVIAN, SARAH (Empl: 2; Est: 1977)
Woven, Embroidered Panels & Wallhangings
The Vivian Gallery, 2 Queen St, Dawlish, S. Devon EX7 9HB. 0626-867 254.
B Ed (Hons); Dip AD; Cert Ed; C & Gs Embroidery; M Devon Guild of Craftsmen.
Pc Various commissions for woven or embroidered panels or hangings. Church embroidery commission for matching altar frontal, pulpit fall, veil and burse, stole and vestments. Various floor rugs.

V & M JOINERY LTD (Empl: 7; Est: 1979)
Rushmeadow, Scarning, Dereham, Norfolk NR19 2NW. 0362-696 546 & 104.
Apprentice carpenters/joiners; C & Gs, etc.; M BEC; M BWF; M GMC.
Pc Norwich Cathedral; South Norfolk House (SNDC); listed buildings inc. museums; etc.

VOELCKER, ADAM & FRANCES ARCHITECTS (Est: 1982)
Pant Glas Uchaf, Pant Glas, Garndolbenmaen, Gwynedd LL51 9DQ. 076 675 675.
Both partners hold MA (Cantab); Dip Arch; M's SPAB.
Pc Available on request to prospective clients.

VOWLES, MRS N. (Est: 1968)
Cane Work
Countryside, Brent Knoll, Highbridge, Somerset TA9 4EH. 0278-760 422.
Pc Chair seats, stools, bedheads, cradles, day beds, etc.

VOYSEY, V. N.
See 'RAINBOW GLASS' – V. N. VOYSEY

WAIGHT, DAVID – 'FLETCHWOOD FORGE' (Empl: one; Est: 1987)
Artist Blacksmith
61 Spicers Hill, Hounsdown, Totton, Southampton, Hants SO4 4ED. 0703-860 224.
Apprenticeship served with Mr G. Lund of Brockenhurst in the New Forest, under the guidance of CoSIRA. M BABA; M Hampshire Fellowship of Master Blacksmiths and Farriers.
Pc Restoration of entrance gates to Paultons Park, Southampton. Items of ironwork supplied to Marine Archaeology Dept of Oxford University.

WAKEMAN, D. J. & CO LTD (Empl: 3; Est: 1977)
Dealers in Antiques, Cabinet Makers & Restorers
Grove Farmhouse, Dorrington, Shropshire SY5 7SD. 0743 73-388.
LAPADA
Pc Too numerous to list, but has worked on furniture up to £10,000 in value.

WALCOT RECLAMATION LTD
Architectural Salvage
108 Walcot St, Bath, Avon BA1 5BG. 0225-444 404.
This firm aims to provides a complete range of goods and services for restoration and conservation work, and so provide workshop space for a variety of craftsmen whose skills inc. traditional upholstery; manufacture of traditional fireplace surrounds; painting; ornamental metal work; stained glass; joinery; stonework; wood turning. Walcot's own range of goods inc. paving; cobbles; urns; columns; chimney pots; ridging; roofing tiles; rafters and beams; doors; staircases; pews; rainwater goods; etc. Brochure.

WALKER, S. T. & PARTNERS (Est: c. 1935)
Architects & Consultants
9 Frederick Rd, Edgbaston, Birmingham B15 1JG. 021-455 8511
Paul Burley, partner – Dip Arch; RIBA; RBSA   Robert Tolley – B Sc (Hons); Dip Arch; RIBA   Graham Winteringham, consultant – Dip Arch; FRIBA; RBSA.
Pc Repair and consolidation – Ludlow Castle, Salop (11th to 16th century). Refurbishment – church, St Barnabas, Erdington. Maxstoke Castle, Warwicks (14th to 16th century). 17th-century Sudbury Hall, Derbys. 17th-century mansion, Tower of the Winds, Monuments in the Park, Shugborough Hall. Dunham Massey, Cheshire (16th to 18th century).

WALKER, STUART (Empl: 2; Est: 1981)
Dry Stone Walling
8 Vincent Avenue, Eastburn, Nr Keighley, W. Yorks BD20 8UD. 0535-53666.
Dry Stone Walling Assoc Registered Cert.
Pc Built dry stone wall (20 ft long) – Kilnsey Park, Kilnsey, N. Yorks with all the features of dry stone walls, i.e. stiles; bolt hole; cripple holes; etc.

WALLING, MESSRS L. J. STONE MASONRY CONTRACTORS LTD (Empl: 5; Est: 1972)
Unit 33 Hawarden Ind Park, Manor Lane, Hawarden, Deeside, Clwyd CH5 3PP. 0244-536 132.

FIRMS AND CRAFTSPEOPLE

Stone Fed.
Pc Chester Town Hall. St Dyfnog's Church, Llanrhaeadr, Plas Talhenbont, Llanystumdwy. Trevallyn Court, Wrexham.
Brochure.

WALLIS JOINERY LTD (Empl: 56; Est: 1860, Ltd 1986)
Broadmead Works, Hart St, Maidstone, Kent ME16 8RE. 0622-690 960.
Majority of tradesmen have served apprenticeships, often with the company.
Pc Restoration – House of Lords ceiling. Restoration and refurbishment of Grade I listed buildings inc. Hanover Square; Dean St; Queen Anne's Gate; Belgrave Square; public buildings; Natural History Museum; V & A Museum; Foreign and Commonwealth Offices; etc.
Brochure.

WALSH, PENNY
See 'FARM SPINNERS' – PENNY WALSH

WARD, SASHA (Est: 1985)
Stained Glass Artist
19 Salisbury Rd, Marlborough, Wilts SN8 4AD. 0672-55638.
BA MA (RCA).

WARNER, S. (Empl: 2; Est: 1973)
Master Thatcher
1 Brandon Green, Rugby Rd, Brandon, Warwicks CV8 3HU. Local Master Thatcher Assocs; NSMTA; Friends of the Thatched Houses (TIREE, Scotland).
Pc Lewis Blackhouse and Clackmill – Highland Folk Museum. Glendale Water Mill – Isle of Skye. Storehouses (cleits) – Isle of Hirta, St Kilda. Hugh Millers cottage – Black Isle for Scottish National Trust.
Experienced in ancient and dis-used methods or materials such as heather.

WARREN, JOHN (ARCHITECTURAL & PLANNING PARTNERSHIP) (Est: 1964)
Architect
APP House, 100 Station Rd, Horsham, W. Sussex RH13 5EU. 0403-210 612. FAX 0403-210 617
M Litt; RIBA; FRTPI; FSA; Hon Architect, Weald & Downland Open Air Museum, Singleton; Chairman of Trustees (1988), Chalk Pits Museum; President, Wealden Buildings Study Group; Committee M, International Council on Monuments and Sites.

Pc Conservation works inc. St Mary's College of Further Education, Strawberry Hill, Twickenham; West Dean College, W. Sussex; 42 historic buildings in Baghdad, Iraq; historic churches. Survey and conservation advice on 64 historic buildings for PSA. Restorations for Landmark Trust. Development and design control inc. re-erection of timber-framed buildings – Weald & Downland Open Air Museum.

WASLEY, DAVID (Est: 1978)
Artist in Stained Glass/Painter
Somerset House, 145 London Road, High Wycombe, Bucks HP11 1BT. 0494-23978.
MA (RCA); Art Teachers Cert; Dip Art & Design; Central School of Art & Design Dip; A BSMGP; Advisory Council for Supply & Education of Teachers in Adult Education Stage II.
Pc Venice windows – Woodbridge, Suffolk. Kenneth Thompson Memorial Window, Milton under Wydwood. VIth Viscount Gaze Memorial – Firle, E. Sussex. Sir David Wills Nativity. Restoration, Arab Hall windows, Leighton House. V & A Collection.

WATERSLADE FORGE (Empl: 7; Est: 1976)
Designers & Craftsmen in Steel
Holcombe Rogus, Wellington, Somerset TA21 0NS. 0823-872 860.
Chris Webb, owner – BA Des   Michael Cassells and Nicholas Hewitson – C & Gs (CoSIRA trained) blacksmiths.
Pc Theme items – Tobacco Dock Development, London. 111 linear m of railing in keeping with listed property – Taunton.
Specialists in both restoration and new work from 12th century onwards. Able to offer a design service, as well as working with architect's and client's drawings. All works are one-off commissions.

WATES, ROSALIND (Empl: one helper as needed; Est: 1985)
Mosaic Artist
2 Haymoor Cottages, Coxley Wick, Wells, Somerset BA5 1QY. 0749-77117.
C & Gs of London Art School Cert and Post-Cert Award in Decorative Arts; Vargas Eyre prize for Design.
Pc Jacuzzi for Michael and Shakira Caine. 'Roman' mosaic for Christopher Mann, BBC producer.
Willing to undertake any mosaic project of interest. Brochure.

WATSON, W. L. & SONS (Empl: 14; Est: 1927)
Stone & Monumental Masons
29-31 Argyle St, St Andrews, Fife KY16 9BX. 0334-74391.
Pc Restoration of stonework for National Trust of Scotland inc. Fyvie

Castle, Aberdeenshire and House of Dun, Montrose. Restoration of stonework – Cupar Parish Church and also St John's Church, Perth.

WATTS & CO FURNISHINGS LTD
Hand-blocked & Hand-printed Period & Reproduction Wallpaper
7 Tufton St, Westminster, London SW1P 3QE. 071-222 2893 & 071-233 0424 & 071-233 1329.
IDDA.
Pc Exterior to National Portrait Gallery. Bodlewellyn Castle. The Belfry, West Halkin St. The Randolph, Oxford.
This firm is also known for their soft furnishings and fabrics. Brochure.

WATTS, B. J. (Empl: one)
Master Thatcher
Homeleigh Cottage, Aldwincle, Kettering, Northants NN14 3EP. 080 15-679.
5 yr apprenticeship with Rural Industries; Master Thatcher.

WAUGH, SEP (Est: 1979)
Stained Glass Designer, Painter & Craftsman
Studio, 56 Micklegate, York YO1 1LF. 13 Malton Way, Shipton Rd, York YO3 6SG. 0904-610 826.
A BSMGP; Craftmanship Award Society of York & N. Yorkshire Architects; Freeman of Worshipful Co of Glaziers & Painters on Glass.
Pc 100 commissions in UK churches. Numerous repair and restoration commissions in cathedrals and churches in UK.

WAVENEY APPLE GROWERS LTD (Empl: 6–8 Est: 1947)
Handmade Rush Matting & Carpets
Common Rd, Aldeby, Beccles, Suffolk NR34 0BL. 0502-77345.
Pc Extensive carpeting in many National Trust houses and also in museums inc. the Agecroft Museum in Virginia, USA.
Brochure.

WAYMANS LTD (Empl: 33; Est: 1950)
Specialists in the Restoration & Maintenance of Old Buildings
Coppingford, Sawtry, Huntingdon, Cambs PE17 5XT. 0487-832 111.
FMB. Approved: Ely, St Albans Diocesan; Eng. Heritage; Huntingdon, Peterborough, S.Cambs DC.
Pc Structural repairs – Tower, Balshaw. Reordering church – Barnet. Porch repairs, etc. – Keysoe Church, N. Beds. Reshingling spire – St Stephen's, St Albans. Complete new nave roof – Banwell Church, Oundle.
Only undertakes church or listed building work throughout the region (Ely,

Peterborough, St Albans, East Chelmsford, Norwich and London Dioceses); works on approx 100 churches a year. Brochure.

WAYWOOD (Empl: 2 + 2 partners; Est: 1984)
Furniture Creation
Eynsham Park, Sawmill, Cuckoo Lane, N Leigh, Witney, Oxon OX8 6PS. 0993-882 748.
BA Oxon; 2 Dip's in Furniture Design & Craft, Buckinghamshire College. Licentiate SD-C.
Brochure.

WEALD & DOWNLAND OPEN AIR MUSEUM
Singleton, Chichester, W. Sussex PO18 0EU. 024 363-348.
A museum of Buildings. A specialist research library on building history and conservation. Able to supply riven laths, thatching spars and combed reed.

WEATHERHEAD, MARTIN & NINA (Empl: 2; Est: 1976)
Weavers
Snail Trail Handweavers, Penwenallt Farm, Cilgerran, Cardigan, Dyfed SA43 2TP. 023 974-228.
M Wales Craft Council; M Makers Guild in Wales; Founder M Pembrokeshire Craft Markets.

WEAVES & WAXES (Empl: 2; Est: 1980)
Conservation/restoration of Period Furniture
53 Church St, Bloxham, Banbury, Oxon OX15 4ET. 0295-721 535.
GMC.
This firm retails furniture restoration materials and old woodworking tools.

WEBB, ANDREW (3D FURNITURE DESIGNER/MAKER) (Est: 1989)
3 Hawkhurst Rd, Streatham Vale, London SW16 5EB. 081-767 0336 & 081-679 6670.
Foundation (London College of Printing) Commendation; BA Art & Design (Distinction for 3d work), Bradford College; work experience for 'Effigy' Furniture/Interiors.
Pc Has sold work through 'Combined Harvest' interiors shop in Portobello area.
Commissioned interiors of a contemporary nature, made in most materials. Also skilled in printing and photography.

WEBB & KEMPF LTD (Empl: 12; Est: 1983)
Structural Repair, Design, Reproduction, Conservation, Advice & Consultation
Denmans Dairy, Barrington, Somerset.

FIRMS AND CRAFTSPEOPLE

Michael Kempf – artist-sculptor from artist-sculptor lineage; apprenticeship, 5 yrs at Wells Cathedral; 6 yrs conservation/restoration business Robert Webb – B Sc; C Eng; MICE Firm M BEC.
Approved: local authorities in Taunton and Yeovil.
Pc Maude Tomb, Chichester. Steps – Sherborne Abbey. Railings – Landsdown, Bath and also Lord Nelson St, Westminster. Bishops Hull Manor, Taunton. Court House and Treasures House, Martock. Visits can be arranged for certain items.
Will also undertake ironwork (opening casements, ferramenta, gates, grills, etc.) and sculpture (both conservation and original work). The firms subsidiary Hempway Ltd makes and supplies specialist and general mortars under the brand name Manor Mortars. (See entry under that name.)

THE WEE GLASS WORKS (Empl: 6; Est: 1984)
Stained Glass Artist
176 Main St, Prestwick, Ayrshire KA9 1PQ. 0292-76312.
M GMC.
Pc Shenanigans Restaurants, Glasgow. Lovell Homes. New developments throughout Glasgow and Helensburgh. Specialize in custom building lamps and windows for the licensed trade and domestic market, especially one-off designs.

WEINGART, CHRISTEL ASSOCIATES (Empl: 5; Est: 1978)
Architectural & Sculptural Glass
Westall Trading Centre, Holberrow Green, Nr Redditch, Worcs B96 6JY. 0386-793 214.
Degree in Arts & Crafts (Sculpture), W. Germany; M British Artists in Glass.
Pc Indoor glass sculptures and fountains for hotels, shopping arcades and leisure centres – UK and W. Germany. Stained glass panels, ceilings, and modern and traditional lighting – Whitbreads; Ind Coope; Imperial Inns; Ansells; Anchor Hotels. Modern glass lighting supplied to major retail developments, leisure projects and office furnishers.
Designers and suppliers of glass screens, lighting, windows, indoor sculptures and fountains. Techniques used inc. leading, copperfoil, glass painting and laminating, sandblasting, kilnforming, glass bevelling, 3d glass constructions. Brochure.

WELDON STONE ENTERPRISES LTD (Empl: 11; Est: 1977)
106 Kettering Rd, Weldon, Corby, Northants NN17 1QE. 0536-61545.
All personnel are fully trained.
Pc Castle Ashby House. Boughton House. Nat West Banks at Shirebrook and Bishop's Stortford.

Specialists in high quality restoration of masonry.

WELSH, EWAN FURNITURE (Est: 1987)
Designer-Craftsman in Wood
2 Gawthorpe Avenue, Bingley, W. Yorks. 0422-330 378 (workshop) & 0274-565 256 (home).
Graduate of the School for Craftsmen in Wood, Farnham House, Dorset.
Pc Various dining tables and chairs, cupboards, coffee tables designed to client's requirements. *Brochure.*

WENHAM, MARTIN (Est: 1967)
Architectural Lettercutter
68A Greenhill Rd, Coalville, Leics LE6 3RH. 0530-33644.
M of Letter Exchange; M SD-C.
Pc A wide variety of commemorative, memorial and sculptural work in wood, all involving lettering designed to meet the particular needs of each client.

WESSEX IRONCRAFT (Empl: 3; Est: 1977)
Hawkes Farm, Braishfield, Romsey, Hants. 0794-68151.
Associate of The Worshipful Co of Blacksmiths; M BABA; M NAFBAE; HNC Civil Engineering.
Pc Entrance gates – Dogmersfield Park, Hants; Little Durnford House, Wilts and also Newbury, Berks. Cross and Reredos – Romsey Abbey, Hants. Weather-vane – Royal Bath & West Showground, Somerset.
Brochure.

WESSEX MOSAIC STUDIOS LTD (Empl: 2; Est: 1985)
Bretworth, Woodlands, Portishead, Bristol BS20 9HE. 0272-843 022.
Mosiacs made using a new patented process, which uses marble, glass and resins to produce polished panels which are strong, waterproof and suitable for many applications. The design work can be as varied as client's requirements. Brochure.

WEST, ANTONY (Est: 1978)
Metalworker
Home (Antique Restoration): 7 Guilder Lane, Salisbury, Wilts SP1 1HW. Workshop: The Smithy, Farley St, Nether Wallop, Stockbridge, Hants. 0722-22333.
Apprenticeship with specialist firm of wrought-ironworkers.
Pc Complete restoration of North Porch gates – Salisbury Cathedral and also large copper/gilded weather-vane – Andover Town Hall.

FIRMS AND CRAFTSPEOPLE

General blacksmith whose work inc. restoration of antique metalwork, brass, copper and particularly tôle peinte (painted tinware); manufacture of reproduction light fittings, wall lanterns, large tin and wire chandeliers; a repair and copy service to furniture restorers for special fittings, especially in wrought iron.

WETHERBY STAINED GLASS & GLASS MERCHANTS (Empl: 3; Est: 1979)
Scott Lane, Wetherby, W. Yorks LS22 4LH. 0937-65683.
R. J. Beaumont – 7 yrs apprenticeship; 25 yrs experience   M. D. Beaumont – 7 yrs apprenticeship   J. Swales – 3rd yr apprentice.
Pc Howden Minster and many other projects – Eng. Heritage. St Luke Harrogate (change over from Parish church to approx 100 flats). NYCB – Mickleton Church, Doncaster (subsidence damage). Leaded lights, lamps and fittings for public houses such as Greyhound, Bridlington, N. Yorks.

WHEATLEY ORNAMENTAL PLASTERERS LTD (Empl: 20; Est: 1949)
Avonvale Studio Workshop, Avondale Place, Batheaston, Bath, Avon BA1 7SA. 0225-859 678.
FMB.
Pc Clivedon House, Taplow. SEB, Maidenhead. Beckett House. RMCS, Shriversham, etc.
Brochure.

WHEATLEY, RAY – DRY STONE WALLING CONTRACTOR (Empl: solo; Est: 1985)
39 Rushpool Close, Redcar, Cleveland TS10 4EW. 0642-485 863.
M DSWA, and holder of their Initial and Intermediate Craftsman Certs.
Willing to undertake any regional stonework.

WHISTLER, LAURENCE – C.B.E.
Glass Engraver
Iscoed, Ferryside, Dyfed SA17 5UY. 026-785 256.
Pc Many goblets, bowls, decanters etc. Church windows, etc. at Salisbury Cathedral; Sherborne Abbey; Moreton Church, Nr Dorchester, Dorset; Eastbury, Bucks.
Free designing for church windows or house windows etc, in relation to the occasion and purpose. Photographs available.

WHISTLER, SIMON (Empl: solo; Est: 1962)
Glass Engraver
5 Fullerton Rd, London SW18 1BU. 081-8706 083.
Learnt with father Laurence (see above); F GGE; F SD-C.
Pc Memorial window – Church of St Mary, Funtington, W. Sussex. 4

diamond panes to celebrate 400th anniversary of the Armada, Buckland Abbey, S. Devon. Other work generally on glass in the round.
Figurative designs undertaken are mainly landscape and architecture.

WHITE, ANDREW FURNISHINGS (Empl: 4; Est: 1969)
Furniture
17 The Quadrant, Kilburn Lane, London W10 4AL. 081-960 3452.
M AMU.
Pc Confidential.

WHITE, DAVID (Est: 1972)
Master Thatcher
180 North Home Rd, Cirencester, Glos GL7 1DX. 0285-657 127.
Apprenticed to Rural Industries Bureaux (now Rural Development Commission); M Glos Hereford, Warwicks & Worcs MTA; M NAMT.
Pc Pentile Cottage – Rectory Rd, Hampton Bishop, Heref. The Old Thatch, Bredon, Tewkesbury, Glos. Reeve Cottage, Uckinghall, Upton on Severn, Worcs. All the above were thatched in combed wheat reed.
Although own business started in 1972, thatching has been in the family since the early 1900s. David White only works in wheat reed.

WHITE, THOMAS ASSOCIATES (Est: 1957)
Architects & Interior Design Consultants
18a Great King St, Edinburgh EH3 6QL. 031-557 1117.
RIBA; ARIAS; Dip Arch Edin; FFAS.
Pc Restoration and new offices – Craigcrook Castle, Edinburgh. Restoration and repair – Great King St, Edinburgh.

WHITEHEAD, JOHN (Empl: solo; Est: 1973)
Furniture Designer/Maker & Architectural Carver
84 Denshaw Rd, Delph, Oldham, Gtr Manchester OL3 5EU. 04577-4578.
Pc Sanctuary furniture – St George's, Wigan and also furniture for Queens Hall, Methodist Mission, Wigan, both to designs of Architects, Antony Grimshaw Associates. Restoration of painted and gilded figure and headboards on Gondola steam boat on Lake Coniston for National Trust.
Also undertakes architectural carving, lettering, painting and gilding; cane and rush seating. When skills are required which he does not possess, John Whitehead will work with other craftsmen or women to complete the work. Photographs available.

FIRMS AND CRAFTSPEOPLE

WHITEWAY & WALDRON LTD (Empl: 3; Est: 1977)
Architectural Antiques & Stained Glass Artists
305 Munster Rd, London SW6 6BJ. 071-387 3195.
Normal Art School Training followed by work for other companies; 10 yrs experience.
Pc Too numerous to mention, but welcome interested clients in the workshop to see work for themselves.

WHITTLE, D. & SONS (JOINERS) LTD (Empl: 60; Est: 1919)
15–19 Sedwick St, Preston, Lancs PR1 1TP. 0772-53256.
Brit Woodworking Fed; BAC.
Pc Refurbishment – joinery, Midland Bank, Fishergate, Preston. Refurbishment – Mill at White Cross, Lancaster. Restoration – joinery Scarisbrick Hall School, Nr Southport.
A family firm undertaking high quality joinery and building work, using traditional skills combined with the latest technology. Brochure.

WHITWORTH CO-PARTNERSHIP, THE (Est: 1985, previous partnership 1964)
Chartered Architects & Surveyors
47 Crown St, Bury St Edmunds, Suffolk IP33 1QX. 0284-60421.
Martin Whitworth – MA; Dip Arch (Cantab); RIBA   A. Redman – ARICS   P. Orchard – RIBA (Letharby Scholar).
Pc Gold Medal Conservation Award – Denston Church, Nr Bury St Edmunds. Extension for St Edmundsbury Cathedral.

WHITWORTH, JOHN (Empl: solo; Est: turned professional 1982)
Glass Engraver
'Little Alders', 30 Greenway, Campton, Nr Shefford, Beds SG17 5BN. 0462-812 670.
Self taught.
Pc Beckman Industrial European Nation of the Year Menthon St Bernard Trophy. 5 glass plaques commemorating trading links between Britain and Eastern Bloc countries for Felmet Ltd. Glass plinth depicting Martin Luther King for Baptist Church, USA.

WICKHAM, CHARLES – DESIGNER WOODWORKER (Empl: solo; Est: 1978)
Dairy Cottage One, Manor Farm, Fernham, Faringdon, Oxon SN7 7NZ. 036 782-544.
Attended Architectural Association; apprenticeship with Michael Wickham Furniture.
Pc Chestnut and elm solid wood and veneer kitchen. Inlaid ebonized mahogany coffee/go table. Oak and stained and plain glazing. Pair of beech inlaid walnut and yew tables.

Makes individually designed hardwood furniture to commission; joinery to self prepared or received plans; restores antiques. Brochure.

WIDDINGTON STAINED GLASS (Empl: solo; Est: 1985)
'Brayshot', High St, Widdington, Saffron Waldron, Essex CB11 3SG. 0799-41403.
Makes domestic exterior and internal windows, panels, leaded lights, mirrors, lampshades, light-catchers, etc.

WILBIE-CHALK, D. & ASSOCIATES (CONSULTANT ARCHITECT P. CANNERS) (Est: 1944)
Well Close, Rothbury, Morpeth, Northumberland NE65 7NZ. 0669-20430. FAX 0669-21234
MA Dip Arch (Manc); CTP (Manc); ARIBA; Civic Trust Award winner.
Pc Work in Northumberland inc. Dower House, Eglingham Hall: conversion – Cork Mill, Tosson; conversion – Old Coach House, Chatton. War Memorial, Hyde Chapel, See Cross, Cheshire.
Conservation reports, theatre design, logos, heraldry and special design work undertaken.

WILDE, LINDA (Est: 1978)
Glass Engraver
7 Pytches Close, Woodbridge, Suffolk IP12 1SE. 0394-380228.
HND Visual Communication; M CSD; M Assoc of Illustrators; Craft M GGE.
Pc Projects range from designs for mass produced glassware to hand engraving windows, commemorative glassware, trophies, etc. using flexible drive drill or sandblasting.

WILES, STEVE FURNITURE (Empl: solo; Est: 1982)
Gunthorpe Workshops, Gunthorpe, Melton Constable, Norfolk NR24 2NP. 0263-861 032.
12 yrs experience of furniture and timber trades.
Pc General commissions for occasional free standing furniture.
Also willing to supply English hardwoods. Brochure.

WILGRAN
Manufacturers and Suppliers of Fine Cast-iron Work
No 4 Boar's Head Yard, Darley Abbey Mills, Derby DE3 1DSZ. 0332-366 488.
Pc Market Building for Church of England – St Martin-in-the-Fields ('the project required strong reference to traditional styles and workmanship coupled with modern production methods and materials')

FIRMS AND CRAFTSPEOPLE

Services range from design and foundry methods engineering to full supply inc. non-standard and one-off projects in cast iron. Also have standard ranges. Brochure.

WILKINSON, K. A. (Est: 1968)
Furniture Designer & Restorer
Kilvington Studio, South Kilvington, Thirsk, N. Yorks YO7 2LZ. 0845-22328.
Teacher Cert in Specialist Craft/Art, Wood & Metal & Associated Crafts; C & G's Craft Teacher Cert; HNC Building; Teaching College, Shoreditch Training College, Egham, Surrey.
Pc Very wide range of commissions carried out inc. domestic and contract furnishings; ecclesiastical and architecural hardwood fittings.
Showroom open daily. Nearly all work undertaken is to commission, often involving design work.

WILKINSON, R. & SON (Empl: 24; Est: 1946)
Chandelier Manufactureres & Glass Restorers
5 Catford Hill, London SE6 4NU. 081-314 1080. FAX 081-690 1524.
Holder of Royal Warrant to HM The Queen, Glass Restorers; on the list of PSA Specialist Approved Contractors; M GMC; M BGMC.
Pc Supplied reproduction chandeliers and light fittings – The Clothworkers Hall; Bank of England; DHSS Building, Whitehall; Connaught Hotel; Governors' Mansions, Williamsburg, USA. Restorers for DOE; PSA; National Trust; Eng. Heritage.
Brochure.

WILLARM PROPERTIES LTD (Est: 1971)
Building Contractors
'Nia-Roo', Fox St, Ardleigh, Colchester, Essex CO7 7PS. 0206-866 478.
BEC; NHBC; HBF; was registered with the Crafts Council Conservation Register, when in existence.
Pc Kings Cottage, Saxon Cottage, DYDDA House, SCEOPPA House, Whitmore House, Weavershed House – Brook St, Dedham. The Merchants House (Butchers Shop), High St, Dedham.
This firm prefers to work on small houses, and has not found a period which they could not copy or match, yet. Experienced in design and construction details and methods.

WILLIAMS, HAROLD & SONS (Empl: 2; Est: 1950)
Painter – Marbling & Graining
78 Finsbury Rd, Wood Green, London N22 4PF. 081-888 0367.
Was a Member of Master Craftsman Guild when founded, but

resigned.
Pc Matching old English oak – The Round Tower, Windsor Castle. Mahogany work – Marlborough House. Figured antique oak – St Albans Court House. Marble graining in hotels, public houses, synagogues, town halls and has just completed a swimming pool surround for Wates Construction.

WILLIAMS, W. R. (PC) LTD (Empl: 10; Est: 1958)
Specialist Painters
Elm House, Blakeley Rd, Raby Mere, Wirral, Merseyside L63 0NA. 051-334 2164.
Incorp Inst of Brit Decorators & Interior Designers; CGLI, Intermediate, Full Technological, and Advanced Cert's.
Pc Walker Art Gallery, Liverpool. Stencilling in education rooms of Dover Castle. Reproduction and matching existing marble to ornate friezes and beams.

WILLIAMSON, RUPERT FURNITURE (Empl: 3; Est: 1976)
Unit 5, New Bradwell Workspace, St James St, Milton Keynes MK13 0BW. 0908-221 885.
M (Des) RCA.
Pc Boardroom – The British Insurance Brokers Assoc, City of London. Examples in Museums inc. V & A; Buckinghamshire; Royal Scottish; Montreal (Canada).
Domestic and office furniture designed and made, inc. low-cost designs, where a tight budget is essential. Work is also held in public collections. Brochure.

WILLMOTT M. V. (Empl: 3; Est: 1976)
Master Thatcher
Joel Cottage, 54 High St, Stagsden, Beds MK43 8SQ. 02302-2501.
Full apprenticeship completed; M NSMTA; M Northants MTA.

WILSON, JAMES & SON (AUCHMILLAN) LTD (Empl: 18; Est: 1957)
Specialist Joinery
Auchmillan, Mauchline, Ayrshire KA5 6HD. 0290-50253.
Apprenticeships with CITB Building Course for Carpentry & Joinery; M Scottish Building Employers Fed.
Pc Alterations and refurbishments – Newark Castle, Alloway. New Mansion House, Failford House, Mauchline. Alterations and repairs – Caprington Castle, Kilmarnock. Repairs and refurbishment – Auchinleck House, Auchinleck, Cumnock.

FIRMS AND CRAFTSPEOPLE

WINCILATE LTD (Empl: 14; Est: 1945)
Natural Slate Specialists
Aberllefenni Slate Quarries, Machyllenth, Powys SY20 9RU. 065 473-602/3.
Natural Slate Quarries Assoc; Nat Assoc of Monumental Masons.
Pc Supply of slate to numerous contracts inc. Museum of London; Westminster Theatre; Rotherham Civic Centre.
Brochure.

WINDSOR, D. W. LTD (Empl: 27; Est: 1976)
Lighting Manufacturers
Pindar Rd, Hoddesdon, Herts EN11 0EZ. 0992-445 666.
Internal training; M LIF.
Pc Lanterns in Trafalgar Square; Public Records Office; Sandhurst Military Academy; Imperial War Museum; Inst of Chartered Accountants; Metropolitan Police.
This firm specializes in exterior lighting, inc. extraordinary and individual designs and commissions (both period and modern), and restoration of old lamps and lamp posts to their former glory. They stock a large range of handmade 19th century reproduction lighting, and complementary street furniture. Brochure.

WINFIELD STAINED GLASS (Empl: 3; Est: 1987)
Unit 35, Albion Ind Estate, Cilfynydd, Pontypridd, Mid Glam CF37 4NX. 0443-480231.
N.D. Winfield – BA (Hons) Glass Design   S.A. Carbery – BA (Hons) Fine Art.
Pc Restoration work at Duffryn House, South Glamorgan.

WING & STAPLES (Empl: 2; Est: 1965)
Wrought-iron Specialists
The Forge, Motcombe, Shaftesbury, Dorset SP7 9PE. 0747-3104.
5 yr apprenticeship; CoSIRA Welding and Wrought Iron courses; Engineering Drawing; M NAFB & AE; Registered Farrier with Worshipful Co of Farriers.
Pc Work for historic buildings inc. gates for Portland Castle; ironwork – Wardour Castle, and also Stonehenge; restoration of gates – Sherborne Castle and also National Trust in Stourhead and Wilts; stately homes; wildlife parks; retirement homes; Councils.
Brochure.

WINTER, S. & J. SCULPTURE (Empl: partnership; Est: 1983)
Unit 7, Ruthin Craft Centre, Ruthin, Clwyd, N. Wales. 082 42-5185.
Stone Masonry Apprenticeship; Dip Sculpture; M Soc of Heraldic Artists.

Pc Stone coat-of-arms – Mr J. Taylor, Taylor Chapman Associates, architects. Restoration of Lewis Carroll Monument – Llandudno. Full size stone swan – Michael Heseltine MP. Restoration of carved stone fireplace for Portmeirion, N. Wales.
Also undertakes heraldic commissions.

WINTERINGHAM, TONY – FURNITURE (Empl: one; Est: 1981)
42 Goodwins Rd, King's Lynn, Norfolk PE30 5QX. 0553-761 078.
M Des RCA.
Pc Public seating – King's Lynn Borough Council. Conductors stand – Barbican Centre. Reception furniture – Eastern Arts Assoc.
Brochure.

WITNEY RESTORATIONS LTD (Empl: 5–6; Est: 10 yrs)
Antique Furniture Restorer
96–98 Corn St, Witney OX8 7PU. 0993-703 902 & 883 336.
All employees have formal training, at present 3 were trained at West Dean College (Dip), 1 at Ryecotewood (plus workshop training), and 1 on a previous apprenticeship scheme.
Pc Work has been carried out to the highest standards on the most valuable of antique furniture – both English and continental – using traditional techniques, inc. work for clients abroad (mostly in the USA).
Fine furniture, clocks and works of art conserved and restored using traditional methods. Also willing to undertake brass castings using the lost wax process. Ecclesiastical work mainly entails early woodcarvings.
Brochure.

WOOD, CHARLES H. (SECURITY) LTD (Empl: 9; Est: c. 1800)
Locksmiths
296 Penstone Rd, Sheffield S6 2FT. 0742-852 202.
Master Locksmiths Assoc; Nat Supervisory Council for Intruder Alarms.
Locks and fittings repaired, restored, rekeyed or rebuilt. Also special handmade keys, safes, vaults.

WOOD GOLDSTRAW & YORATH (Est: 1874)
Architects & Quantity Surveyors
Churchill House, Regent Rd, Hanley, Stoke-on-Trent, Staffs ST1 3RH. 0782-208 000. FAX 0782-208 712.
Partners have professional qualifications.
Pc Surveyors to Lichfield Diocese since 1947. Numerous projects on churches and historic buildings involving repair and refurbishment.

FIRMS AND CRAFTSPEOPLE

WOOD, LEO (Empl: 2; Est: 1971)
Master Thatcher Specializing in Design, Interior, Scale & Unusual
Nuthatch, 16 West End, Welford, Northants NN6 7HJ. 085-881 782.
7 yrs apprenticeship; 2 journeyman; ACA for NCMTA; M Rutland & Leics MTA.

WOODPOHL LTD (Empl: 3; Est: 1989)
Furniture Makers
Helmut Pohl, Director, 26 John St, Great Ayton, N. Yorks TS9 6DB. 0642-723 036.
2 trained and time served cabinet makers. *Brochure.*

WOODSCAPE – FRANK TIBBS (Empl: one; Est: 1977)
The Poplars, Gwern-y-Brenin, Oswestry, Shropshire SY10 8AR. 0691-652 166.
BA Sculpture; M Brit Woodcarvers Assoc.
Pc Golden Eagle, 2.5 m wingspan – Stoke on Trent National Garden Festival. Bull – interior of Hereford Herd Book Society Offices. 10 carved bird finials – Broxton Old Hall and also 16th-century timber-framed extensions in same manner. Carved capital tops – Caernarvon County Council Offices.
Will cast metal and arrange for GRP to be produced from his patterns. Brochure.

WOOLSEY, ROY (Empl: solo; Est: 1984)
Furniture Maker & Restorer
Unit 2, Archway Shopping Centre, Stalham, Norfolk NR12 9AZ. 0692-734 837.
Apprenticeship with Arthur Bretts, Norwich; C & Gs 1 2 3 & 4.

WOOSTER-WILLIAMS LTD (Empl: 20)
Decorative Veneers
8 Jubilee Rd, High Wycombe, Bucks HP11 2PG. 0494-25372/3.
Panelling to Leicester Crown Court; House of Lords, Dundee Police Headquarters; etc.

WORLD'S END TILES (Est: 1972)
British Rail Yard, Silverthorne Rd, Battersea, London SW8 3HE. 9 Langton St, World's End, Chelsea, London SW10 0JL. 071-720 8358 & 071-351 0279.
Brochure.

WRAYS, CHRISTOPHER LIGHTING EMPORIUM (Empl: 75; Est: 1964)
600/604 Kings Rd, London SW6 2DX. 071-736 8434 (phone for details of nearest branch). FAX 071-731 3507. TELEX 94016296 WRAYS.
DLA.
Pc Specialist lighting fittings for hotels, pubs, restaurants, discos, clubs, bars, shops, etc. Spare parts for oil/gas lamps.
164 page catalogue available.

WREN LOASBY DESIGNS (Est: 1985)
Stencil Artist
Brennels Mead, Highweek Village, Newton Abbot, Devon TQ12 1QQ. 0626-63096.
M Devon Guild of Craftsmen.
Pc Flat in Royal Crescent, Bath. Elizabethan Manor, Devon. Medieval Restaurant, Devon. Hunting Lodge now converted to a hotel. Holne Chase Hotel, Ashburton. Pitt House Restaurant, Kingskerswell. Canonteign Manor, Canonteign. Painted marriage chests, pine toy boxes, shelves and cupboards.
Fabrics, walls, floors, furniture stencilled. Also undertakes mural work.

WRIGHT, K. G. (BUILDERS) LTD (Empl: 18; Est: 955)
Acorn House, Lowick Rd, Islip, Kettering, Northants NN14 3LR. 08012-2586.
FOMB; SPAB; Men of Stones. Approved: Diocesan; Eng. Heritage; Northamptonshire CC.
Pc Repairs – tower stonework, St Michael's, Haselbech, Northants. Replacement/repair of parapet stonework, and replacement of leaded light windows – St Mary's, Leighton, Bromswold, Cambs. English oak screen – St Bartholomew's, Gt Stukeley, Cambs. Rake out and repoint internal stonework – Lyveden New Bield, Brigstock, Northants. Repair of nave roof beam and replacement of stonework – St Mary the Virgin, Podington, Beds.

WRIGHT, SUSAN – TEXTILE DESIGNER (Est: 1980)
Unit 14, Canal Basin Warehouse, Leicester Row, Coventry, Warwicks CV1 4LH. 0203 33-4960.
Polytechnic Cert in Craft Materials; M SD-C.
Pc 'Sully Island' woven hanging commissioned by Sully Hospital, S Glam Health Authority.
Brochure.

W. W. ROOFING (Empl: 7; Est: 1981)
5 Pentridge Close, Nythe, Swindon, Wilts SN3 3RH. 0793-643 839.
LCA.

FIRMS AND CRAFTSPEOPLE

Pc Harleyford Manor, Harleyford, Marlowe. Tallis House, Tallis St, London

WYCOMBE CANE & RUSH WORKS (Empl: 6; Est: 1880)
Victoria St, High Wycombe, Bucks HP11 2LU. 0494-442 429.
Complete furniture restoration undertaken. New ladderback and spindleback chairs, rush seated.

WYNDHAM, JOHN DESIGNS
Furniture Designer & Maker
Westgates, Muddles Green, Chiddingly, Lewes, E. Sussex BN8 6HW. 0825-872 036 & 872 025.
John Makepeace School for Craftsmen, 1979–81.
Domestic work for house and garden.
Also sells silk fabrics. Brochure.

WYNER, ANNA – MOSAIC ARTIST (Empl: freelance fixers; Est: 1970)
2 Ferry Rd, Barnes, London SW13 9RX. 081-748 3940.
Trained as a painter. Mosaic skills self taught.
Pc Mosaic triptych – a Shrine for the Sick, Bayswater. Floor medallion in the hall of a Chelsea House. 10 Renaissance heads – Shopping Mall, Stirling, Scotland. Islamic Winter Garden.
Designs, supplies and fixes mosaics for interiors, swimming pools, churches, etc. Will work in situ or, alternatively, when large installations are involved will create the mosaics in pre-cast concrete panels in the studio, (this also enables work to be shipped abroad where it can be 'slotted' in place).

WYSOCKA, SOPHIE (Empl: solo; Est: 1950)
Mural Artist
Knight's House Studio, Hortcusie Rd, Chelsea SW10 0QX. 071-352 0547.
Pc Unable to specify recent work for reasons of client's privacy.

YATES, NEIL (Empl: 2; Est: 1981)
Glass Engraving using Sandblast Technique
Kendal Glass Engravers, 177 Highgate, Kendal, Cumbria LA9 4EN. 0539-33800 & 21883.
Pc Private customers are the majority of his work. Company's inc. James Cropper plc and Provincial Insurance plc.

YATES, ROGER (Empl: 2 + self; Est: 1976)
Master Thatcher
Lake Farmhouse, Rougham Green, Bury St Edmunds, Suffolk IP30 9JT. 028 486-365.

Roger Yates – time served; Rural Development Commission Certs; M Suffolk MTA; M NCMTA. Employees – time served; C & Gs; Associate M's Suffolk MTA.

YORK HANDMADE BRICK CO LTD (Empl: 40; Est: 1920s (clay products) 1986 (bricks)
Forest Lane, Alne, N. Yorks YO6 2LU. 03473-8881.
Pc All private, housing, refurbishment and conservatories.
This firm makes up to 100,000 handmade bricks per week, inc. handmade specials to order in both size and shape. Each brick is moulded by hand, hand set and burnt in traditional Newcastle down draught kilns. They are also one of the few British manufacturers of terracotta floor tiles made using old techniques. Also distribute reclaimed bricks and roof tiles.

YORKE, SANDRA
Wallhangings
Lynton, Manchester Rd, Baxenden, Accrington, Lancs BB5 2QE. 0254-383 166.
BA Hons (1st) Art Design, Fashion/Textiles, Leeds University; MA Textiles, Manchester; Associateship of The Textile Institute.
Pc Wallhanging for All Saints' Library, Manchester Polytechnic and also Freudenberg Nonwoven Ltd.
Brochure.

YOUNG, R. J. & SON (Empl: one; Est: 1969)
Specialist Plasterwork
15 Station Road East, Ash Vale, Aldershot, Hants GU12 5LT. 0252-542 789.
5 yr apprenticeship; 1st Class C & Gs (Inter and Final); Full Technological Cert; M Nat Fed of Plastering Contractors; M GMC.

YOUNG, RORY (Est: 1978)
Conservator of Historic Buildings
5/7 Park St, Cirencester, Glos GL7 2BX. 0285-658 826.
M Art Workers Guild; SPAB; SAVE; ASCHB; Georgian Group.
Pc 'New' gazebo – The Old Manor, Norbury, Derbys (now National Trust owned). Architectural features – 17th-century summerhouse, Trusley Old Hall, Derby. Restoration inc. lime plaster and lime wash – Gornal Ground Old House, Nr Millom, Cumbria. Proposed restoration of stucco exterior and creation of classical courtyard – own house.
Designer, builder and conservator of historic and vernacular houses and garden buildings using traditional methods and materials indigenous to the area. Consultant advisor and lecturer on treatment and conservation of old buildings, inc. teaching builders lime techniques (e.g. how to apply roughcast

and lime/hair plaster). Designer and carver of stone ornament and fire surrounds, lettercutter of memorials and architectural tables. Supplier of own slaked lime for high quality restoration work.

YOUNGER, ALAN (Empl: solo; Est: 1966)
Stained Glass Artist/Painter
44 Belvedere Rd, Upper Norwood, London SE19 2HW. 081-653 3376.
F BSMGP; M Art Workers Guild.
Pc Heraldic stained glass work for Post Office headquarters. Conservation of important Possetti window in Bradford Church.
Specialist cleaning only undertaken in connection with conservation work.

YOXFORD CARRIAGE WORKS LTD (Empl: 4; Est: 1988, sole traders 15 yrs +)
Furniture Maker
Cotton Yard, High St, Yoxford, Saxmundham, Suffolk IP17 3EY. 072 877-652 & 654.
Suffolk Craft Society.
Pc Ushers chairs – Snape Maltings Concert Hall Auditorium. Yoxford PO Shop fittings.
Also design and make kitchens, bedrooms, columns, doorways, fireplaces, lift interiors, etc.

ZSCHOCK, KERRY VON (Empl: solo; Est: 1984)
Hand-painted Majolica Tiles
4 Wycliffe Terrace, Bath Rd, Nailsworth, Glos GL6 0QW. 045 383-2809.
BA (Hons) Bath Academy of Art & Design.
Pc Delicatessen and Bakery – Pershore Food Market. Ruskin Mill, Nailsworth, Glos. Various private homes locally, inc. own home. Littleworth House, Amberly, Nr Stroud, Glos.

Associations

ANCIENT MONUMENTS SOCIETY
St Andrew-by-the-Wardrobe, Queen Victoria St, London EC4V 5DE. 071-236 3934.
Founded in 1924 for the study and conservation of ancient monuments, historic buildings, and fine old craftsmanship. Willing to suggest new uses for existing buildings and to advise how such plans may be carried out sympathetically. Publishes *Transactions*, bound and illustrated books containing scholarly papers of interest to architects, architectural historians and archaeologists. All subscribing Fellows receive a copy of the *Transactions* and three newsletters each year informing them of the progress of the Society's work, publications of interest and news about architectural conservation in general. All members automatically become members of the Friends of Friendless Churches, a body that owns 20 disused churches and chapels, with whom the AMS is in partnership.

ARCHITECTURAL HERITAGE FUND, THE
17 Carlton House Terrace, London SW1Y 5AW. 071-925 0199.
Established in 1976 as the UK's national revolving fund, The Architectural Heritage Fund helps preservation trusts acquire and rehabilitate historic buildings which might otherwise be neglected or destroyed. Assistance takes the form of low-interest loans (5%) to organizations with charitable status, for up to half the cost of preservation projects which involve either a change of ownership, or a change in the use of the building being saved. The Fund maintains a register of trusts: has published a model constitution for a building preservation trust; and generally tries to help and advise people

interested in setting up a trust or doing a preservation project. Contact: Barbara Wright.

BRITISH ARTIST BLACKSMITHS ASSOCIATION
All other enquiries other than membership contact Alan Dawson, Honorary Secretary, Shepley Dawson Architectural Engineering, Joseph Noble Rd, Lillyhall, Workington, Cumbria CA14 4JX.
BABA exists to promote the highest standards of craftsmanship and design among Artist Blacksmiths in Great Britain aiming to provide a forum for the exchange of ideas: encourage a greater awareness of the applications of the art of the blacksmith: encourage communication and goodwill among artist blacksmiths of all nations. Membership is open to anybody who supports these aims. Contact: Peter King, Membership Secretary, Rosebank, Plaxtol, Sevenoaks, Kent TN15 0QL.

BRITISH DECORATORS ASSOCIATION
6 Haywra St, Harrogate, N Yorks HG1 5BL. 0423-67292-3.
Regional offices are willing to introduce members of the public and main contractors to suitable member firms (contact The Regional Secretary in your area). Member firms are bound by the Association's Code of Practice. The BDA will also provide arbitration in cases of dispute between clients and member firms.
- London & S E Region BDA, PO Box 111, Aldershot, Hants GU11 1YW. 0252-21302 & 336 318.
- Midlands & SW Region BDA, 12/15 Union House, Union Drive, Boldmere, Sutton Coldfield B73 5TN. 021-355 1068.
- NW Region DBDA, 50 Heaton Moor Rd, Heaton Moor, Stockport, Cheshire SK4 4NZ. 061-432 7612.
- Northern & NE Regions BDA, 6 Haywra St, Harrogate, N Yorks HG1 5BL. 0423-507 473.

THE BRITISH SOCIETY OF MASTER GLASS PAINTERS
c/o Office: 6 Queen Square, London WC1. 081-883 0348.
Members are able to offer all services connected with the conservation, restoration, design and manufacture of stained/painted glass. The Society can recommend specialists in any area (i.e. medieval), deal with enquiries from students, architects, historians, and such like. Produces two magazines, a journal, courses and careers and book lists.
Contact: Hon Secretary, Nicola Kantorowicz.

ASSOCIATIONS

BRITISH WOOD PRESERVING ASSOCIATION
6 The Office Village, 4 Romford Rd, Stratford, London E15 4EA. 081-519 2588.
An impartial body which collects information on the preservation and fireproofing of timber; sponsors scientific research into the use of preservatives and fire retardents. The Association offers a free advisory service on all problems connected with timber preservation; issues leaflets dealing with all practical problems, the latest developments in research and on safety precautions relating to the use and handling of preservatives; holds an annual conference; maintains a panel of lecturers whose services are available on request; arranges visits to the works and laboratories of manufacturers and treaters; issues a news sheet to all members.

CHARLES BROOKING
The Brooking Collection, Woodhay, White Lane, Guildford, Surrey GU4 8PU. 0483-504 555.
Charles Brooking specializes in the history and the development and construction of certain period features, inc. ironmongery; doors; windows; firegrates; staircases and rainwater-heads. The Brooking Collection charts the development of these features from the 17th century to the present, and consists of over 25,000 items. A dating service for buildings post 1700 is also available, with an emphasis on the correct reinstatement of period features.

THE BUILDING CONSERVATION TRUST
Apartment 39, Hampton Court Palace, E Molesey, Surrey KT8 9BS. 081-943 2277.
Care of Buildings is the operating name of the Building Conservation Trust, an independent educational charity which aims to promote good standards of repair, maintenance and improvement of all types of buildings. A permanent exhibition is maintained encouraging the proper repair, maintenance and improvement of property of all types and ages.
Contact: John Griffiths, Director.

BUILDING RESEARCH ESTABLISHMENT
Garston, Watford WD2 7JR 0923-894 040.
The Government's research and development organization. The results of its research are published in *BRE Digests, Defect Action Sheets* and other reports. Advice and consultancy services are available for a fee.

ASSOCIATIONS

CADW – WELSH HISTORIC MONUMENTS
Brunel House, 2 Fitzalen Rd, Cardiff CF2 1UY. 0222-465 511.
A division of the Welsh Office, which deals with ancient monuments in state care, and also – through the Historic Buildings Council for Wales – can offer advice and grants to owners of historic buildings of outstanding architectural or historic interest for repair works. May also be able to assist in the conservation of scheduled ancient monuments in Wales.

CATHEDRAL ADVISORY COMMISSION FOR ENGLAND
83 London Wall, London EC2M 5NA. 071-638 0971.
The CAC advises the Deans and Chapters of cathedrals, and cathedral architects, on a wide variety of conservation matters. In the near future it will become a statutory body.
Contact: Peter Burman, MA FSA, FRSA, Secretary or Dr Richard Gem, Deputy Secretary.

COGNIZANCE (Est: 1986)
An Agency for Heraldic Artwork
St Briavels, Wetherden, Stowmarket, Suffolk IP14 3JP. 0359 41248.
Agency for artists and craftsmen, who are interested in undertaking commissions – in their own media – of a heraldic nature. All are interested in heraldry and consequently are 'sufficiently informed to produce heraldic items of a suitable quality'. Skills covered inc. metal castings; stonework; wood carvers; hand-painted ceramic tiles; screen-painted tiles to special order; hand-painted wallpaper; hand-painted mural work; engraved windows; interior glass screens, table tops, etc.; stained glass windows, lighted murals, etc; muralists; heraldic painters; calligraphers; gilders; sculptors; lettercutters; heraldic design and artwork in different media. Willing to work where required.

THE COMMUNITY ENTERPRISE TRUST LTD
Woodlands, Wooler Rd, Hartlepool, Cleveland TS26 0DR. 0429-273 341.
A registered charity involved in Employment and Enterprise Training, established for 8 years. Community work with voluntary groups extends to substantial renovation and restoration projects. Skills embrace joinery, carpentry, forge work and production of working drawings for construction and replication purposes. The team includes people with a keen interest in local history projects, which extends to basic pre-project research. Previous projects have included The Hart Mill, an 1830 grain mill complete with cruck roofing. Marine replication of deck furniture for HMS *Warrior* (1860s first iron clad

battleship). Period cottage restoration (beamed ceilings, etc.). Inglenook fireplaces.

THE CONSERVATION UNIT
Museums & Galleries Commission, 7 St James's Sq, London SW1Y 4JU. 071-839 9340.
The Conservation Unit maintains a Conservation Register, which provides an authoritive guide to the professional expertise available. For a small fee enquirers are provided with a list of up to five conservators or restorers able to carry out the work needed in a particular part of the country, together with details of their workshops and advice on how to select and deal with them. The Unit also provides information about training in conservation and may assist conservators with grants to enhance professional skills and fund research. The teaching series *Science for Conservators* has been re-issued and other publications are planned.

CONTEMPORARY APPLIED ARTS
43 Earlham St, Covent Garden, London WC2H 9LD. 071-836 6993.
Contemproary Applied Arts run a commissioning service, which will put individuals in touch with artists and craftspeople. They are willing to advise on large-scale projects such as companies refurbishing their offices, or those that are considering an investment in an art collection. At the other end of the scale, they can equally well deal with an order for one special chair, a set of dinner plates or a retirement present. There is a gallery where smaller pieces are displayed and a slide archive. They will liaise between client and maker, organizing matters and will remain involved with every stage of the project.

COUNCIL FOR THE CARE OF CHURCHES
83 London Wall, London EC2M 5NA. 071-638 0971.
The CCC is the central co-ordinating body of the 40 Diocesan Advisory Committees for the Care of Churches (DACs) and advises on all aspects of conservation touching churches and their contents, and acts as a channel for grant aid.
Contact: Peter Burman, MA FSA, FRSA, Secretary or Bill Martin, Conservation Administrator.

CRAFTS COUNCIL
Gallery address: 12 Waterloo Place, London SW1Y 4AU. Administration: 1 Oxendon St, London SW1Y 4AT. 071-930 4811.
The Crafts Council promotes the work of leading craftspeople in a variety of ways, through exhibitions, and education programme and

ASSOCIATIONS

by publishing its own magazine *Crafts*. The Information Centre in the gallery building contains a slide library where visitors can view the work of outstanding craftspeople, and a data-bank on these and other designer makers practising in England and Wales. Information staff welcome enquiries by telephone and letter and can arrange slide loans and commissions for people unable to visit the gallery.
Contact: Anne French, Information Officer.

DEVON RURAL SKILLS TRUST
Cockington Court, Cockington Village, Torquay, Devon TQ2 6XA. 0803-605 377.
Contact for details of craftspeople undertaking all rural skills in Devon inc. basket makers; stone walling; thatchers; hedge builders of various kinds; wood carvers; carriage makers; wheel wrights; blacksmiths; weavers; spinners; coopers, etc.

EDINBURGH NEW TOWN CONSERVATION COMMITTEE
13a Dundas St, Edinburgh EH3 6QG. 031-557 5222.
This committee administer grants for the 18th and 19th century 'New Town', which is one of the largest unspoiled 'Georgian' city developments in the world, and has managed to halt much of the decay on the northern fringe. In partnership with the District Council and the Old Town Committee for Conservation the committee operates and is now expanding an Architectural Salvage scheme, recycling building materials for re-use within the Edinburgh district. A maintenance manual *The Care & Conservation of Georgian Houses* written for proprietors, architects and surveyors, is produced, published by Butterworths. An annual maintenance inspection service is available within the New Town, and walks are organized by the Committee.

ENGLISH HERITAGE
The Historic Buidings & Monuments Commission for England.
25 Savile Row, London W1X 2BT. 071-734 6010.

FRIENDS OF FRIENDLESS CHURCHES
12 Edwardes Square, London W8 6HG. 071-602 6267.
The aims of this charity are the preservation of churches and chapels of architectural or historic interest, which are in danger of collapse or demolition or conversion to unsuitable use, and are outside the scope or policy of other organizations. The Society is not a grant-making body and normally takes over the ownership or a long lease of buildings it adopts.
Contact: Ivor Bulmer-Thomas.

ASSOCIATIONS

THE GEORGIAN GROUP
37 Spital Square, London E1 6DY. 071-377 1722.
This Group exists to save Georgian buildings, monuments, parks and gardens from destruction or disfigurement, and where necessary to encourage their repair or restoration; to stimulate public knowledge of Georgian architecture and town planning, and of Georgian taste as displayed in the decorative arts, design and craftsmanship. To promote the appreciation and enjoyment of all products of the classical tradition from the time of Inigo Jones to the present day. A registered charity, the Group works in close association with other organizations devoted to preserving our heritage.

THE GUILD OF MASTER CRAFTSMEN
166 High St, Lewes, E Sussex BN7 1XU. 0273-478 449.
The Guild is open to all skilled people (and companies who employ them) who practise or support a craft, trade, art, profession or vocation. It strives to recognize craftsmanship, safeguard high standards, foster appreciation and identify, protect, promote and reward craftsmen and women, whether they work alone or with others. Maintains a central register of Members classified by craft, and geographical area. Details are available on request.

LETTER EXCHANGE
See THE SOCIETY OF SCRIBES & ILLUMINATORS

MEN OF STONES
The Rutland Studio, Tinwell, Stamford, Lincs PE9 3UD. 0780-63372.
This Society aims to stimulate public interest in architecture and good buildings of all periods; to encourage the study, practice apprenticeship to, and appreciation of the constructional Arts and Crafts of Architecture, inc. stonemasonry, sculpture, carving, painting, gilding, pargetting, wrought iron, and cast lead work; to save from disfigurement and destruction buildings of good architectural character; to prepare reports and schedules of ancient and historic buildings and sites; to afford service in regard to conservation, repair and use of period buidlings, the re-use of good stone and other materials from demolished or derelict buildings.

NATIONAL SOCIETY OF MASTER THATCHERS
73 Hughenden Avenue, Downley, High Wycombe, Bucks HP13 5SL. 0494-443 198.
This Society aims to protect and support the very highest of standards in craftsmanship within the thatching industry in this country. All thatchers wishing to join the National Society have their

work inspected, and are only able to become members if their work meets with approval. The Society also assists the thatch owning public as much as possible, not only helping them to select a craftsman to maintain their roof, but also by giving advice and help to improve their understanding of the qualities and problems of a thatched house.
Contact: Chairman, Christopher White.

THE SCOTTISH SOCIETY FOR CONSERVATION & RESTORATION
100 Holeburn Rd, Newlands, Glasgow G43 2XN. 041-637 4149.
SSCR exists to promote the conservation and restoration of Scotland's historic and artistic artefacts. The Society seeks to maintain and improve standards of practice in the field of conservation by providing a forum for all those concerned with these objectives. The Society publishes a *Bulletin* and a *Newsletter* which give technical notes, book reviews, reports on other relevant meetings (included when appropriate), details of SSCR meetings, a diary of conservation-related events, information about other groups and societies, information on various aspects of conservation. One or two day meetings are organized on a variety of subjects (e.g. lining methods for paintings, modern metals in museums). Evening lectures, receptions and summer visits also take place. Training courses are organized subject to demand.

SOCIETY FOR THE PROTECTION OF ANCIENT BUILDINGS
37 Spital Square, London E1 6DY. 071-377 1644.
Founded in 1877, the SPAB is a source of information and advice on the conservative repair of historic buildings of all types. Issues technical publications; runs courses for both owners and professionals; offers general technical advice and information; runs scholarship training scheme for architects and fellowship training scheme for craftsmen; sells by post books on repair of buildings; has separate section on windmills and watermills.

THE SOCIETY OF SCRIBES & ILLUMINATORS
54 Boileau Rd, London SW13 9BL. 081-748 9951.
The Society was founded in 1921 with the aim of advancing the crafts of writing and illuminating, and publishes a journal *The Scribe* and also the *Calligraphers Handbook*; organizes a series of one-day workshops on specialist subjects. Over 500 books and periodicals are housed in the library. The Society has established the Letter Exchange, which includes over 60 of the UK's top professionals involved in the whole spectrum of the lettering arts and crafts inc. architectural lettering. The aims of the Letter Exchange include the

ASSOCIATIONS

promotion of fine lettering in all media; mounting exhibitions; publication of a periodical devoted to the lettering arts; and creating a forum of discussion of common interests. It is supportive of specialist lettering courses in art colleges through its members who practice as educators. Membership is by election through an executive committee made up of specialists in all aspects of the lettering arts and crafts and typographic design.
Contact: Mrs Susan Cavendish.

THE VICTORIAN SOCIETY
1 Priory Gardens, Bedford Park, London W4 1TT. 081-994 1019.
This National Amenity Society concerned with the protection of historic buildings of the Victorian and Edwardian periods, campaigns to save 19th and early 20th century buildings and provides advice on conservation issues.